# THOMAS MANN

Here is the best picture
ever made of me!

Thomas Mann

# THOMAS MANN

## Life As a Work of Art

A BIOGRAPHY

### HERMANN KURZKE

*translated by Leslie Willson*

 PRINCETON UNIVERSITY PRESS  PRINCETON AND OXFORD

*Thomas Mann: Das Leben als Kunstwerk* by Hermann Kurzke copyright
© C.H. Beck'sche Verlagsbuchhandlung, München 1999
English translation copyright © 2002 by Princeton University Press
Published by Princeton University Press, 41 William Street,
Princeton, New Jersey 08540
In the United Kingdom: Princeton University Press, 3 Market Place, Woodstock,
Oxfordshire OX20 1SY

*Library of Congress Cataloging-in-Publication Data*

Kurzke, Hermann.
Thomas Mann : life as a work of art : a biography / Hermann Kurzke ;
translated by Leslie Willson.
p.   cm.
Includes index.
ISBN 0-691-07069-5 (alk. paper)
1. Mann, Thomas, 1875–1955.   2. Novelists, German—20th century—
Biography.   I. Title

PT2625.A44 Z73293 2002
833'.914        2002023665
[B]

British Library Cataloging-in-Publication Data is available

This book has been composed in Palatino

Printed on acid-free paper. ∞
www.pupress.princeton.edu

Printed in the United States of America

1   3   5   7   9   10   8   6   4   2

# Contents

HERMANN KURZKE'S singular biography of Thomas Mann became a bestseller in Germany, with several printings, each new one of which gave Kurzke the opportunity to revise his work. Though the revisions amounted in total to only a few pages, Kurzke felt obliged to make them for the sake of accuracy and completeness. The present translation incorporates the revisions of the various printings with the cooperation of Kurzke, who generously furnished the translator with the new and amended texts of each.

Kurzke, a professor in the comparative literature program at Mainz University, had become an authority on Thomas Mann and his voluminous works over a period of more than thirty years. The biography was written, thus, by a scholar of note for an audience of German readers. It contains an extensive supplement that lists hundreds of footnotes by chapter, a list of sources divided into abbreviated references to titles (largely collections of letters except for those by Mann, memoirs, essays, and previous biographies of Mann), Mann's own volumes of correspondence, and other sources, documents, lists, and collections—but not a full bibliography of the works of Mann. The supplements are followed by a list of works by Thomas Mann that are mentioned in the pages of the biography, and finally an index of persons that includes real people as well as fictional and mythological personages, the latter two set in italics. There is no general index to the biography. The present translator has included only the index of persons. The index of works mentioned in the biography is not included because not everything that Thomas Mann wrote has been translated into English. Translators notes are few in number.

Since the works of Mann available in English are often in translations that are out of print as well as somewhat flawed, the translator of the present work translated all the quotations from Mann without consulting extant translations.

Leslie Willson
Austin, Texas
October 2001

# THOMAS MANN

# I. Childhood and School Days

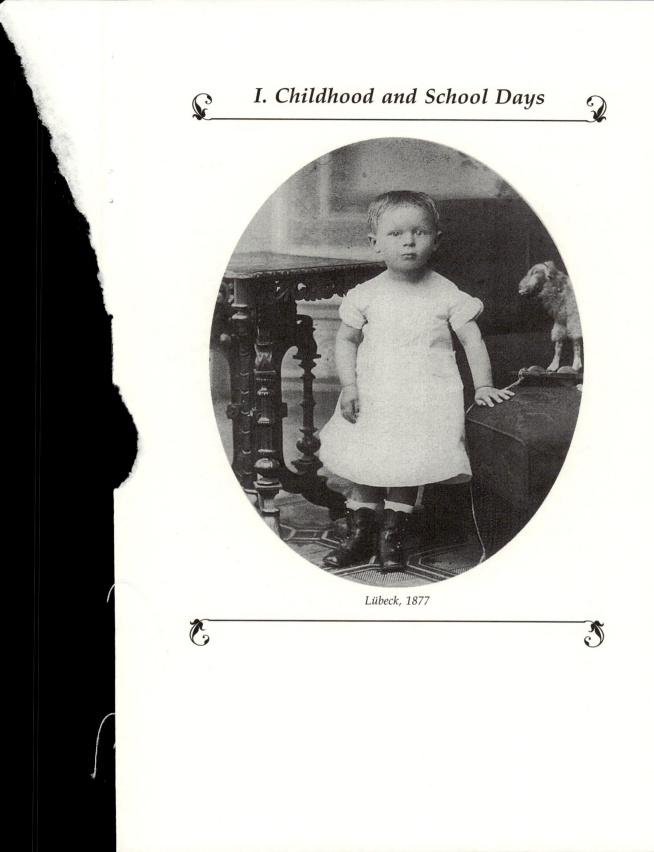

*Lübeck, 1877*

## CHRONICLE 1875–1894

Thomas Mann, or to be precise, Paul Thomas Mann, was born on June 6, 1875, in Lübeck and baptized as a Protestant on June 11 in St. Mary's Church. His parents were very refined people: Thomas Johann Heinrich Mann, born in Lübeck in 1840, and Julia Mann, née da Silva-Bruhns, who had seen the light of day for the first time in 1851 in Brazil. His father was the owner of the Johann Siegmund Mann grain firm, further a consul to the Netherlands, and later the senator overseeing taxes for Lübeck, which joined the German Empire as an independent city-state in 1871. His mother came from a wealthy German-Brazilian merchant family. His older brother Heinrich was born in 1871; the siblings born later were Julia, 1877; Carla, 1881; and Viktor, 1890.

As was customary in his circles, instead of entering the public primary school or elementary school, from Easter 1882 on, Thomas Mann attended a private school, the Progymnasium of Dr. Bussenius, in which there were six grades. In addition to the three primary-school classes, there were the first, second, and third years of the secondary school. He was held back for the first time in the third year and had to repeat it. He transferred at Easter 1889 to the famed Katharineum on Lübeck's Königstrasse. Since he was to become a merchant, he did not attend the humanistic branch but rather the mathematical-scientific branch. In March 1894, after the fourth year (twice), the fifth year, and the sixth year (twice) of secondary school, he left at the age of almost nineteen, with the authorization for one year of volunteer military service but without graduating.

The grain firm had just celebrated its hundredth anniversary (in May 1890) when his father died at the age of only fifty-one on October 13, 1891. His will decreed the dissolution of the firm. His mother left Lübeck a few months later and moved to Munich with her younger children, Julia, Carla, and Viktor. Heinrich, who had also left school without finishing, was at the time already at work as a trainee with the young S. Fischer Publishing Company in Berlin. Thomas boarded for a time with various teachers until he followed his mother to Munich at the end of March 1894.

# HOROSCOPE

My horoscope was propitious; the sun stood in the sign of Virgo and reached its apex on that day; Jupiter and Venus looked at her with a friendly eye, Mercury not adversely, while Saturn and Mars remained indifferent: the moon alone, just full, exerted the power of her reflection all the more, as she had then reached her planetary hour. She opposed herself, therefore, to my birth, which could not be accomplished until this hour had passed.

Smiling, Goethe flirts at the beginning of *Truth and Poetry* with the state of the stars at the time of his birth. Thomas Mann, for his part, gazes up to Goethe when, regarding his hour of birth, he asserts:

The position of the planets was favorable, as adepts of astrology later often assured me—based on my horoscope they predicted a long and happy life and a gentle death for me.

Of course, like his Jacob, he is not sure whether astronomy was to be counted among the true and useful things or more among the abominations. But he had a horoscope made for himself in 1926. It is correct that the position of the planets is described as favorable, since the most influential stars stand in their own or in friendly signs. But the astrological art of prediction was silent about a long life and a gentle death. Here Thomas Mann helped things along somewhat.

When he conjured up the astronomical report in the novel *Joseph and His Brothers*, he also took only what he could use and left out what was a hindrance. The hour hand at Joseph's birth reflects an idealized version of his own horoscope. "I transferred my own to him."

Accordingly, the sun was at its vertex, which was not quite true in reality, and in the Sign of Gemini, while in the east the Sign of Virgo was rising. With Ninurtu (Saturn) it had a trine, which "points a finger to a share in the events in the realms of earth." That was to come true. But above all, Joseph's, that is, Tommy's, birth is in the Sign of Mercury (the Babylonian Nabu, the Greek Hermes, the Egyptian Thot), the familiar mediator and witty scribe who is a reconciler between things and promotes exchange, but who also, fragile and needing contact, is determined more closely by the society in which he happens to be. In our case it is that of the dangerous Nergal (Mars),

the mischief-maker, who lends toughness to the Hermes child, a
that of the seductive Ishtar (Venus), "whose part is moderation a
grace, love and mercy." She peaks at that hour and appears amicabl
with Mercury and the Moon. She also stands in Taurus, "and experience teaches us that, of course, that lends composure and shapes enduring courage and understanding delightfully." Venus, too, receives
a trine from Nergal, but that is not bad at all—it makes her taste not
sweet and pallid but sharp and spicy.

In the final analysis everything takes place between the Sun and the
Moon. The Moon is strong. If Nabu, the smart one, meets it, "then
there is a reaching out into the world." Nabu is the mediator between
the Sun and the Moon, between the world of the father, who stands in
the sign of majestic Jupiter, and the world of the mother, who keeps
with Venus. The father world will become that of duty and responsibility and middle-class society, the mother world that of dream and
temptation, of love and death. Between the two, Thomas Mann will
try to play the role of Hermes.

## SUNDAY BELLS

His birth was easy and happy, like those of his siblings. "I was born
with Sunday bells." The writer does not recall any reluctance to exchange the dark of his mother's womb for the light of day. It was
important for him to have his life appear blessed. "I was born on
Sunday, June 6, 1875, at twelve o'clock noon," he writes in 1936.

Thomas Mann was a Sunday's child, that's true. However, it was
not twelve o'clock when he took his first breath, as can be seen from
the official documentation, but rather a quarter after ten. Goethe was
born at noon (if on his part, he did not give himself a literary helping
hand): "On August 28, 1749, at noon, with the clock striking twelve, I
came into the world in Frankfurt am Main."

The inclination to give his life a "course," a nice and coherent order,
was strong in Thomas Mann. In *A Sketch of My Life* he will announce
for reasons of symmetry that he would die at seventy—later he inter-
prets a serious lung operation in 1949 as the meager fulfillment of
that prophecy. In *My Time*, written in 1950, he reinforces the rhythm
of the quarter centuries. Born in 1875, *Buddenbrooks* finished in 1900,
*The Magic Mountain* in 1925. All of that is only approximately correct,
but it felt good to him to look at it that way. "My time—it was so

changeable, but my life in it is a unity. The order in which my life is related to the times in numbers stirs in me the pleasure I find in all order and coherence." For him it is always a matter of a measure of time. "Childlike pleasure in beginning a new month." All his life he will note down days of commemoration and decisive points of all kinds with special attention. He even sanctified Sunday in his own way—not that he necessarily stopped working, but that he entered the date in red in his diary.

He *wanted* his life to be orderly. It was to be "a well-rounded art work of a life." In truth he conducted a desperate battle against encroaching chaos. Inner chaos threatened through the laziness and dreaminess of his early years, his unrealized homoerotic inclinations, and the desire to let himself go. The chaos of external history brought in 1894 the loss of the world of his origins in Lübeck, and in 1933 that of his chosen home of Munich, followed by change of residence in exile, the renewed homelessness in the United States, and at an advanced age the move to Switzerland. Today Thomas Mann cities interested in tourism carry on the idyllic cultivation of classic writers with traces of his life, but there is not much there. Only late, very late, did the city of Lübeck buy the so-called Buddenbrook House, the house of his grandparents on Mengstrasse. In reality, the architectonic remains of this life exhibit a trace of catastrophy. In May 1942 only the façade of the Buddenbrook House was still standing, and his parents' various other houses in Lübeck have totally disappeared from the face of the earth. Only the foundation of the Munich house on Poschingerstrasse, on which a new postwar construction was erected, remains. The American places of residence are in private hands with no interest in the past. The last place of residence in Kilchberg outside of Zurich was bought by a banker in 1996.

Only in the diaries of his old age did the Sunday's child relax the palliative strictures. "Not *all* of my life was painful. Very likely such a mixture of torment and glory was rare" (September 20, 1953).

Was his birth really so easy and happy?

## IN THE SHADOW OF ST. MARY'S CHURCH

The delivery of a baby is something intimate and private; in the case of Thomas Mann, it took place, as was usual at the time, at home, probably Breite Strasse 36. A baptism, on the other hand, is something public. It signifies not only acceptance into the Church, in this case the Lutheran, but also into middle-class society, with which this church was all-too-intimately connected. To be baptized in St. Mary's: Seen socially, that was the best place. While in the nineteenth century the Lübeckers let their cathedral fall into ruins, stored building rubble in their St. Katharine's Church, and tore down the magnificent Renaissance city gate still situated at the Holsten Gate, they kept faith with St. Mary's Church, located at the market place, and with city hall.

In *The Magic Mountain* old Hans Lorenz Castorp tells his grandson about the baptismal bowl that had for generations received the baptismal water trickling from the heads of the newborn Castorps or, as the case may be, of the Manns, for into this bowl the water from the little head of five-day-old Thomas had flowed. The sexton poured it into the pastor's hollowed hand, "and from there it ran over the crown of your head into the bowl here. But we had warmed it so you would not be startled and not cry, and you didn't either; on the contrary you had been crying before, so that Bugenhagen didn't have it easy with his homily, but when the water came, you fell silent, and showed respect for the holy sacrament, let us hope." It may also have happened like that at the baptism of Thomas—we assume so. Admittedly, the roguish stylization of the scene by the author of *The Magic Mountain* is typical. In the wailing during the sermon he already hints at protest against the bourgeois church and its rhetoric, in the quiet during the flowing application of the baptismal water reverence for an indefinable something more sublime.

St. Mary's Church is not only a place left over from the nineteenth century. Mightier experiences half a millenium older fill its echoing breadth. It belongs among those places "where as you walked, hat in hand, you fell into a certain, reverential, forward-rolling gait, your heels never touching the ground." It conveys two things: the middle-class façade and its opposite, the atmosphere of death. Mann in 1921 calls his hometown a "Dance of Death homeland," with reference to "the humorously macabre thrills that emanated from the Dance of Death frescoes in St. Mary's Church," that late-medieval cycle by Bernt Notke, which burned in the Second World War.

When in California, Thomas Mann heard about the bombing attacks on Lübeck and had to assume that St. Mary's Church could have suffered damage—he did not have much sympathy. "I think of

Coventry," he said in a BBC broadcast, "and have nothing against the idea that everything must be paid for." That takes aim at the guilt of middle-class, National Socialist Lübeck. But after the war, when it is a matter of rescuing and rebuilding St. Mary's Church, he makes a genuine effort to raise the necessary funds. He does not do that for the sake of the citizens of Lübeck but because of the reverential rocking gait. St. Mary's, as middle class as it was mysterious, place of baptism and death, overshadowed besides a childhood dream, the Buddenbrook House in Mengstrasse.

## THUNDER AND LIGHTNING

With "Amen, I know something, Grandfather!" eight-year-old Tony Buddenbrook closes her recitation of the catechism she has learned by heart. What does she know?

> "If it's a warm flash," Tony said, nodding her head at each word, "then lightning is striking. But if there's a cold flash, then thunder is striking."

When old Herr Buddenbrook demands to know who taught the child such idiocy, it turns out that it was Ida Jungmann, the child's recently engaged nanny from Marienwerder in West Prussia. There were nannies not only in the Buddenbrook home but naturally also in Mann's home. They were very influential. Until Tommy's thirteenth or fourteenth year, it was Ida Springer who obviously served as the model for Ida Jungmann. She, too, will have had that fine sense of class and rank that is characterized ironically in *Buddenbrooks*:

> She was a person of aristocratic principles who distinguished exactly between first and second social ranks and between middle class and lower middle class; she was proud as a devoted servant to serve the first social ranks, and she did not like, for instance, to see Toni become friends with a schoolmate who in Mamsell Jungmann's estimation was to be counted only among the upper middle class.

An older brother with three younger siblings experiences his own learning process three more times, that is, when it happens to each of the others. In this way he becomes aware of what the only child or

the last child in the row must remain unaware of because each of
them is too close. Only what is known can become a story. Tommy is
not Tony; it was not he who believed in striking thunder, but he either
observed from a distance how the little story impressed his younger
siblings or he took part early on in the good-natured mockery by
adults about Ida Springer. Incidents of this sort belong at one time or
another to a treasure of family legends whose original kernel of experience disappears more and more behind an anecdotal point that already has something literary about it.

Thomas Mann did not believe in making things up. He is talking
about himself when he writes about Shakespeare: "He much preferred to find ready-made things rather than to make things up." So
we may assume that this small scene, too, is not made up but is experienced, that it comes from the childhood world of Thomas Mann,
and that he had already received it handed on in a half-literary form
as a family anecdote, or had even taken part in its composition. His
older brother, Heinrich, may also have played a role in it. He had an
ear for such funny stories. As the oldest, and also by nature the most
aloof, he had the most unconstrained viewpoint. A satirical point of
view was Heinrich's talent; this rubbed off on his brother. What was
elegiac and idyllic, on the other hand, was Thomas's own and in the
long run more fitting for his basic conservative disposition.

Satire, elegy, and idyll, according to Friedrich Schiller's energetic
insistence on distinction, are forms that are characterized by the
search for something lost and thus by reflective distance. Thomas
Mann does not lose that distance for a moment. As a narrator of his
childhood, he is never childish. Quite a lot can be found in the literary and essayistic work of our author about his own childhood, but it
is as good as always filtered literarily, at the least has passed beyond
first drafts, is made worth telling and acceptable to society. It is revised as a rule satirically, elegiacally, or idyllically.

One can get closest to the unfiltered truth in the diaries. But ordi-
narily children don't keep diaries. It is not clear when Tommy began
keeping one, though probably by the age of thirteen or fourteen. He
had gotten rid of the records of his youth fairly early on. "These days
it has been especially warm for me," he writes on February 17, 1896,
to a friend of his youth, Otto Grautoff. "You see, I'm burning my
collected journals—!" Why? "It was becoming embarrassing and un-
comfortable to have such a mass of secret—*very* secret—writings

lying around." These secrets will certainly have concerned only his youthful and adolescent years, not his childhood, for which reason they will not be discussed until later.

## OTHELLOS

Small chocolate-covered cream cakes, "Moor's heads" were then eruditely called "Othellos," after Shakespeare's drama about the Moor. Thomas's father must have been a most cultured man. At a very hidden place Thomas Mann tells of a daring pedagogical experiment,

> which our father once made with us siblings: He assured us that once in our lives we could eat as many cream puffs, Othellos, and cream rolls at the pastry shop as we wanted. He led us into a sweet-smelling Paradise, let the dream become reality—and we were amazed how quickly we reached the limit of our desire, which we believed to be infinite.

Obviously this father did not want simply to bestow only a few basic principles on his children, but to let them form them from their own experience. Seen superficially, he was successful, at least with his son Thomas, who with all his love for sweets was moderate his whole life in eating as in drinking. In his youth, he says as an old man, "five courses were customary. After the first one I used to go to an adjacent room and lie on a sofa and sleep; the servant had instructions to wake me for the pudding."

But the boy already saw through the great Moor's head feast. "We *had* to be amazed," Thomas Mann writes—amazement was a duty. Apparently the father could not resist prescribing for his children the pedagogically desirable feeling. The boy had noted that. In this middle-class world one could never reveal his *real* feelings. Instead there was always a desirable feeling that should and was allowed to come out. That his children learned to play the expected role was more important to Senator Thomas Johann Heinrich Mann in the final analysis than that they trusted their own experiences and gave them expression. But the personal experience that became evident in the end was not at all amazement, not the aversion to sweets in immoderation (which a bright child knows without such experiments), rather the irony of the comparatively ponderous arrangement of the experiment.

So the father was probably a cultured man, but that culture did not apply to the freedom of the self to learn from its own experience, rather only to the perfection of role playing. The principles of his children should appear as though they came out of their own experience. Their masks should be more believable than the masks of others. They should grow firmly onto their faces. It was not anticipated that ironic skepticism toward the whole educational process would be maintained and that anyone would peer behind the scenery. The masks were supposed to seem natural; that was (and is) the meaning of middle-class education. With Thomas Mann it achieved only partial success in that throughout his life he never escaped this role but instead suffered from it.

## LEAD SOLDIERS AND PLAYING GODS

As a child Tommy owned a blue Hussar uniform, regulation down to the least detail, that had been tailored for him personally. But he did not derive any pleasure from the military masquerade, the twenty-nine year old writes later,

> and I also did not play with lead soldiers with any real passion, although I called as my own very splendid ones, almost as long as my finger, riders that could dismount, whereby I was bothered only by the thick spike that they had between their bow legs.

When he wrote this, he already had his military service behind him, prematurely finished because he was unfit. It had been repulsive— "yelling, wasting time, and iron laurels tormented me beyond measure." He would thus like to have a reason to trace his scorn for the military back to his childhood and to caricature soldiers' games by thick tenons between bow legs. But his parents and relatives gave him the Hussar uniform and lead soldiers with the intention of upholding the state in any case. The young man was supposed to become a brave man.

But Thomas was a dreamy child. He loved his rocking horse tenderly; it had the rough juvenile coat of a Fuchs pony and "the most trusting glass eyes in the world." The puppet theater, which actually belonged to his brother Heinrich, meant even more to him. Most of all he loved playing roles.

For example, I woke up one morning with the resolve today to be an eighteen-year-old prince named Karl. I dressed with a certain charming sovereignty and walked about with the secret of my dignity. You could have lessons, be taken for a stroll, or have fairy tales read to you without interrupting this game for a second; and that was what was practical about it.

Thomas Mann includes this game later, hardly changed, in the life story of the con man Felix Krull. Also the puppet theater is transferred from life into art, first in the tale the "Bajazzo,"* then in the Christmas chapter of *Buddenbrooks*.

"You come from a rich family," says Settembrini to Hans Castorp in *The Magic Mountain*. They were rich in the Mann home as in the Castorp and Buddenbrook homes. Whatever he asked for, "he always got." But the young man hardly needed the stuff, for he invented what he had need of.

The tone of voice of the idyll changes when the writer comes to speak about the children's games. "Playing gods" especially reveals him as the absolute sovereign of a world of fantasy. Such a role naturally feels good. It still comforts the adult shaken by coarse reality, who from a sentimental distance remembers his erstwhile divinity half comically, half wistfully:

As Hermes I hopped through the rooms with paper wingéd shoes, as Helios I balanced a gleaming gold-foil crown on my ambrosial head, as Achilles I dragged my sister, who whether she liked it or not played Hector, mercilessly three times around the walls of Ilion. But as Zeus I stood on a small, red-laquered table, which served as my divine mountain, and in vain did Titans build up Pelion on Ossa, so horribly did my lightning flash from a red horse-lead, that was, in addition, sewn with little bells.

And they had also given him a train. But all his life Tommy was unable to find any interest in technology. That they "crashed most interestingly" is the only information he handed on about his trains. He thought just as little of playing Indian. Probably, seen from the standpoint of his father, he was lacking in masculine courage. That "the constant influence of women to which the boy was subjected

* Translated as "The Dilettante," with Mann's approval, by Helen Lowe-Porter, 1936; again in 1970 by David Luke as "The Joker." (Trans.)

was not likely to stimulate and develop the characteristics of manliness in him" also distresses Senator Buddenbrook in the case of his son Hanno.

## YOUR SAPIENCY AND LÜBECK'S MOST BEAUTIFUL WOMAN

"My childhood was sheltered and happy." Although all the records mentioned to this point bear the stamp of later literary re-formation, we are actually not justified in doubting this statement, for reports about unhappy childhood experiences are not present. Father and mother were loved and respected. The satirical viewpoint, from which the rest of the citizens of Lübeck were inspected, is spared them. To characterize the relationship with his parents, Thomas likes to use the famous verses from Goethe's *Tame Xenias*:

> From Father I have the stature
> for life's most potent gales,
> From Mama the gay nature
> and the desire to tell tales.

Again, a good share of this is style at work and a teasing imitation of Goethe, but there is still something true about it. A retrospect from later days recognizes his father as a lifelong example. "How often in my life have I noticed with a smile, have actually *caught* myself being aware, that as a secret model the personality of my deceased father actually determined everything I did." What was exemplary? Not a little: his father's dignity and sensibility, his ambition and his industry, his personal and intellectual elegance, the bonhomie "with which he was able to accept the plain people who clung to him in a really genuine patriarchal way." Thomas Mann also mentions his father's social gifts and his humor. "He was no longer a simple man, not robust, but nervous and with a great capacity for suffering, but a man of self-control and success, who early on achieved admiration and honor in the world." The social stature of his father must have impressed the young man greatly—at least in retrospect. No wonder, for not every child experiences such scenes:

> I still see him, raising his tophat, walking between the infantry
> sentries presenting arms in front of the City Hall when he left a

*Thomas Johann Heinrich Mann, around 1875*

session of the Senate, see him accepting with elegant irony the respect of his fellow citizens, and have never forgotten the sweeping grief with which, when I was fifteen years old, his city, the whole city, took him to his grave.

As senator he was addressed as "Your Sapiency." Perhaps Thomas Johann Heinrich Mann was even the real regent of the city, "for he administered the taxes."

*Julia Mann, née da Silva-Bruhns, around 1875*

   Ludwig Ewers considered her Lübeck's most beautiful woman:
Julia Mann, née da Silva-Bruhns. His mother had been "extraordinarily beautiful," Thomas Mann confirms in 1930, "with the ivory
complexion of the South, a nobly sculpted nose, and the most attractive mouth I ever encountered." She played the piano, sang like a
bell, and often read aloud with a melodious voice. A German-Brazilian, born in the jungle, raised a Catholic, she stood out in fog-cool
Lübeck. When she told about how she sat with happy Negroes
around a blazing fire and sucked on roast sugarcane, longing ex-
panded the hearts of her children. Faraway places, fairy tales, and

music came from her. She supported the dreamy inclinations of her secondborn, and he thought she loved him especially. "I believe that I, the second one, was closest to her heart." This much from the idyllistic perspective.

Thomas Mann confided a chillier aspect to his American friend Agnes E. Meyer. "Papa" was "a fairly rapt, also feared, enormously busy person of authority." Mama had admittedly been more familiar and more intimate but at the same time also curiously cold. Thomas Mann gave her beauty and her coldness to the mother of the successor to the throne in *Royal Highness*. Prince Klaus Heinrich has a crippled hand that, they say, Mama urged him to conceal in a clever way, "urged him especially when on a tender impulse he was about to wrap both arms around her. Her look was cold, when she cautioned him to pay attention to his hand."

As long as her husband was alive, she conformed to the social norms of the city patricians and also imposed them frequently on her children. Only after the senator's death did it appear that she had never quite fitted in in Lübeck. She also had different interests. "Undercurrents of inclinations toward the 'South,' toward art, yes, toward bohemian things" always had obviously also been present and asserted themselves after the death of her husband and the change in circumstances, which explains her prompt move to Munich. There she even participated in Carnival—"which they would hear about in Lübeck with horror."

The senator's trust in the dependability of his wife seems also not to have been 100 percent. From his last will and testament speaks the fear that Julia could be too weak. "In respect to all the children," he states, "my wife should show herself firm and keep all of them dependent. If she should ever falter, then she should read *King Lear*." King Lear, in Shakespeare's drama, signs over his possessions to his daughters in his lifetime, whereupon they treat him like a beggar.

In his literary portraits of mothers, Thomas Mann strengthens their questionable traits considerably. Frau von Rinnlingen, who charmed men; Gerda Arnoldsen-Buddenbrook with her black-eyed lieutenant; the grand-duchess, who thinks of nothing but her beauty; Senator Rodde's wife with her inexhaustible, never adequately satisfied lust for life, her cooing laugh, and the slightly lascivious half-bohemian traits of her salon—vague doubts are always fostered about the decorousness of the way of life of mother figures. They come from the

intolerant sensitivity of grown-up children in regard to any departure
of a mother from dignity and purity throughout her life, which
Thomas Mann expressed in the late novella *The Black Swan*.

However much Thomas as a child enjoyed what he believed to be
preferential treatment by his mother, the feeling of responsibility
handed down by his father surfaced with equal effect—to such a degree that he even reproached his mother gently because of her leanings toward the South, toward art, and toward bohemian things. He
himself will consciously turn away from the loose artistic life à la
Schwabing. The "South" will later, in the story *Tonio Kröger*, be the
symbol for artistic genius, licentiousness, and irresponsibility, whereas
"North" will stand for fatherhood and a sense of duty.

But we have sufficient grounds to consider that as literature and a
later judgment. An aging mother is in a difficult position compared
with a father who died before his time, one hallowed in memory. In
the real circumstances of his childhood the relationships were more
the opposite. His mother was loved, his father feared. The fifteen year
old was attached to his father "with fearful tenderness." There were
certainly reasons enough for this fear, especially during his school
days, when Tommy's rebelliousness had become open. In *Buddenbrooks*, traumatizing clashes between father and son are depicted.
Hanno is supposed to recite a poem—an emotional catastrophy arises
from it:

"Now, son, let's hear it," the senator said bluntly. He had settled down in an armchair beside the table and was waiting. He
was not smiling at all—today no more than on similar occasions.
Earnestly, raising one eyebrow, he measured little Johann's figure
with scrutinizing, even cold, eyes.

Hanno straightened up. He ran his hand over the smoothly
polished surface of the grand piano, let his gaze glide shyly over
those present, and, encouraged a little by the gentleness gleaming in his grandmother's and Aunt Tony's eyes, he said in a low
but slightly hard-edged voice: " 'The Shepherd's Sunday Song'—
by Uhland."

"Oh, my dear boy, that's not the way," the senator cried. "You
don't hang on to the piano and fold your hands on your belly.
Stand up tall. Speak right out.That's the first thing. Here, stand

between the portieres. And now hold your head up, and let your arms hang quietly at your sides."

Hanno took a position on the threshold to the sitting room and let his arms hang down. Obediently he raised his head, but he lowered his eyelashes until nothing could be seen of his eyes. More than likely, they were already swimming with tears.

"This is the Lord's own day," he said very softly, and his father's voice, which interrupted him, sounded all the louder. "You begin a recitation with a bow, son. And much louder. Now, start again, please—'The Shepherd's Sunday Song.'"

It was cruel, and the senator knew very well that he was robbing the child of his last remnant of composure and self-control. But the youngster shouldn't let himself be robbed. He shouldn't let himself get confused. He should gain steadfastness and manliness. "'Shepherd's Sunday Song!'" he repeated relentlessly and encouragingly.

But it was all over for Hanno. His head sank down on his chest, and his little right hand, which peered pale and with bluish arteries from the tight-fitting, navy-blue sailor's sleeve embroidered with an anchor, was clutching at the brocade of the portiere. "In meadow broad alone I stand," he said, and then it was finally over. The mood of the poem got the better of him. An overwhelming self-pity caused his voice to fail completely and tears to well irresistibly out from under his eyelids.

Thomas Mann was never quite so weak as the figure in his novel. Of course, he did not die at the age of fifteen either. But even if this scene did not occur in real life exactly like this, it nevertheless indicates what was involved. Thomas was not masculine enough for his father. The Hussar uniform and the lead soldiers may have been an attempt to do something about that.

His later development showed that the boy secretly approved. He distances himself from the world of his mother because, like Tonio Kröger, he feels it a bit dissolute. Probably he did his mother a bitter injustice, for the problem was not in her but in him; it was not she who was dissolute, rather he was afraid of his own inner chaos. So the approval of his paternal society could not remove the conflict from the world. The imitation of his father determines his social ap-

pearance, but nothing more. He plays the role his father lived before
him, but he wears it like a mask. His heart is with his mother, while
all his life he dresses properly.

To become a "man" like his father was his life's goal. "Is the artist
even a man at all?" asks Tonio Kröger—not without cleverly making
demands of what is motherly. What is weak and dreamy, what stands
in the way of being a man must be forced into the service of art as a
profession. It is subdued with a balled fist and forced into the cellar of
the soul. There, chained to the rowing benches, sit the nostalgic slaves
where, following the same muffled tempo all their lives, they keep the
galley of work under way.

Just as what is motherly ("the desire to tell tales") corresponds to
the literary work, what is fatherly ("the stature for life's most potent
gales") corresponds to the essayistic work. It was the masculine duty
of his life to defy the telling of tales with something conscientious
offered by the demands of the day. The aggressive anti-Fascist Thomas
Mann, who does not withdraw silent and dreaming into the familiar
home of inner emigration, we owe to his father. So one may talk
about the suppression of what is motherly, but does anything great
ever come into being without suppression?

"My childhood was sheltered and happy." First of all, this means
only that Thomas Mann wanted to see it that way in 1930. It means
that he considered the sufferings of his childhood meaningful from a
later standpoint. Naturally, like all of us, he suffered—he did not
want to abandon the security of the world of wet nurse, nannies, and
mother; he opposed paternal pressure to do well and resisted inclusion in the world of men. Luckily, his father had no talent for tyranny.
His attempts to be succcessful were thwarted by secret melancholy
and his own weakness. At first he wanted to raise Heinrich, then
Thomas, to be the heir of his firm. But then he had insight enough to
arrange the dissolution of the firm in his will. He trusted neither
Heinrich nor Thomas to lead it. In his will he acknowledges Heinrich
had a "dreamy loss of self-control and lack of consideration for
others." He thought more of Thomas: "Tommi will weep for me." But
the one so classified knows that he did not deserve trust at the time.
"I was a foolish young man when I lost my father." The father would
never have imagined that one day his second son, even though on a
totally different path, would become a senator, even if only an honorary one—but he would have been pleased. Even at the age of eighty

Thomas Mann wants to please him, wishes that "he could have followed my path at least somewhat farther along and have seen that, against all expectations, I was able to prove myself in my own way as his son, his real one." At an advanced age he definitely wanted to return to Lübeck one more time. Why? To breathe the spirit of his father. His daughter Erika advised against the trip at that time. Of course, her father knows what such a fine consummation of life costs, senses the tediousness and the awkwardness of encounters to be expected, but sentimental feelings, namely, "the thought of 'Papa,' and a feeling for biographical closure" are the deciding factors. His life should be a work of art, after all! "Papa" should still have been right more than his "dissolute" Mama!

## BED AND SLEEP, ELEGIACAL

As a small child Tommy slept in a crib with a green curtain. He was born in a massive mahogany bed, which then for a number of years stood in his bachelor quarters. One of them (Marktstrasse 5, in Schwabing) he immortalizes in fun in the story "The Wardrobe." "This room was mercilessly stripped, with bare, white walls, against which three bright-red lacquered reed chairs stood like strawberries on whipped cream. A wardrobe, a washstand with mirror . . . The bed, an extraordinarily massive piece of mahogany furniture, stood free in the middle of the room."

The wish and the desire to sleep in the bed in which one was born is revealed in the inclination to return to what is childlike that is described covetously in the essay "Sleep, Sweet Sleep!" Thomas Mann liked to sleep. Sleep is the maternal counterforce to the paternal world of duty and business during the day. Bed is the place of dreams and writing. "Le poète travaille" is said to have stood over the bed of the Symbolist poet Saint-Pol-Roux. Bed is the counter-middle-class place of philosophy, art, and religion. Bed, "that metaphysical piece of furniture in which the mysteries of birth and death occur," is the place of return from desperation into that real and happy state "in which we, warm, unconscious, and with drawn-up knees, as once in the darkness of our mother's womb, again connected at the same time to the umbilical cord of nature, nurture and renew ourselves along mysterious paths."

The aging Thomas Mann slept poorly. He often took sleeping pills. But he claims, as does his Felix Krull, to have been a quiet child as a baby, "not a bawler or troublemaker, but inclined to sleep and doze to a degree most comfortable for my nurses." He had loved sleep and forgetting, even at a time when he had hardly anything to forget. When the duties of the world start to intrude into the splendor of slumber, without hesitation he takes the side of the darkness of the mother. Genuine ardor was to be gained only in sleep, "when the first stage of a life of freedom and inviolability was past and the adversity of life in the form of school began to distort my day."

School is the world of the father, duty, "reality," the first invasion of that horror of expulsion from Paradise that returns again and again in shocks never to be overcome, against which only sleep bestows fleeting respite. "I never sleep deeper, I never enjoy a sweeter homecoming in the womb of night than when I am unhappy, when my work is awry, desperation presses down upon me, human revulsion pursues me into darkness."

## STRETCH, CURTAIL, CORRUPT

Hanno Buddenbrook and his friend Kai picture the "pedagogic body" as a creature really present, "a kind of monster of a repulsive and fantastic shape." The tone of the school chapter is satirical. Following all the rules of art, the novelist makes the teachers look ridiculous:

> He picked up his notebook and leafed through it silently: but since the order in his classroom left much to be desired, he raised his head, stretched an arm out over the surface of the lectern, and while his face slowly swelled and turned dark red, making his beard look bright yellow, waved his feeble white fist up and down a few times, working his lips convulsively and fruitlessly for half a minute long and finally bringing out nothing more than a forced and moaning "Well . . ." Then he struggled a while longer for further expressions of reprimand, at last turned again to his notebook, and his swelling subsided, and he seemed satisfied. This was typical of senior instructor Ballerstedt's way of doing things.

The tone turns into the elegiac with the retrospective of the games of the four-and-a-half-year-old Hanno:

> These games, whose deeper meaning and attraction no adult is able to understand any longer and for which nothing more is needed than three small stones or a piece of wood, perhaps wearing a dandelion bloom as a helmet; but above all the pure, strong, fervent, chaste, still undisturbed and unintimidated fantasy of that happy age when life still hesitates to touch us, when neither duty nor guilt dares lay a hand upon us, when we are allowed to see, hear, laugh, be amazed, and dream without the world's demanding services from us in return . . . when the impatience of those whom we would like to love has not yet begun to torment us for signs and early tokens that we will diligently be able to fulfill these duties— Ah, it will not be long, and with overwhelming, raw power everythng will assail us, violate us, drill us, stretch us, cramp us, corrupt us.

The world lays a hand on him in the shape of the school. Thomas Mann, too, experiences it as assaulting and drilling, as stretching, cramping, and corrupting. "School was actually a rule of fear," he still writes as a seventy-one-year-old. The worst thing was gymnastics— "in spite of Willri, just about the most disastrous thing that I ever encountered so far." We see him before us at the horizontal bar and parallel bars practicing the giant upswing or the shoulder stand, suffering from unmitigated ridicule, probably not as self-assured as it later appears to the glorfying view in the memoir of a fellow student: "In the face of this nonsense he practiced sovereignly passive resistance, gripped horizontal bar and parallel bars almost symbolically with his fingertips as it were, and brushed this to him unworthy apparatus with a scornfully vacant glance." His final report card reveals in gymnastics an "unsatisfactory." To the anger of his father, Hanno Buddenbrook also displays a mute, reserved, and almost arrogant resistance to physical training, and Felix Krull admits that, "in dreamer's fashion" he had "always shunned physical exercise completely." In dreamer's fashion: It is his childhood that infused the youth with the potential of resistance that immunized him early on against the training methods of the Wilhelminian educational establishments. The childhood dreams feed the arrogance that permitted a feeling of vague superiority in spite of bad marks and failing three times. "I despised school, . . . scorned it as a milieu, criticized the manners of its leaders, and early on found myself in a kind of literary opposition to its spirit, its discipline, its methods of obedience training." That is clear. The literary opposition survives from the dream world of childhood that only now, when it is lost, unfolds all its glory. The Prince Karl game and Jupiter's lightning bolts with the horse lead; the fairy-tale hours with his mother; the book of mythology; Andersen; and Fritz Reuter—in his memory they are still much more beautiful than life itself.

His hatred for school torments is reflected in many ways in his works. "I have no sense for facts," writes a disappointed man. School, says Felix Krull, was worse than prison. "The only condition under which I am able to exist is the independence of spirit and imagination, and so it happens that the memory of my long-lasting stay in prison touches me less unpleasantly than that of the bonds of servitude and fear in which the apparently more honorable discipline of the chalk-white, barrackslike house down in the small town struck my sensitive boy's soul." He had never tried in the least to make a secret of his distaste for the despotic stupidity of the institution. "Lazy, obstinate, and full of dissolute scorn about the whole thing" he had sat out the years—again, so says Thomas Mann in person.

The hatred for school is not only fiction—it really existed. The eighteen year old is derisive: "If there is stupidity—then good. That is an indispensably correct principle. That's why I don't like to go to school." The experiences that the pupil was able to have at the venerable Katharineum were scurrilous and ridiculous:

> Herr Gottschalk, the great pedagogue, had the nice habit of asking us, before he whipped us, whether we realized that we had earned the punishment. The fearful Yes that was his answer did not usually come from the heart but from a frightened suspicion that, if we said No, we would receive many more blows.

The final report card of Paul Thomas Mann shows only "satisfactory" and "still satisfactory," in drawing an "only partially satisfactory," in singing "finally satisfactory," and in gym, as already reported, an "unsatisfactory." Anyone who expects at least a good grade in German is disappointed; even in this subject the judgment, verbally as well as written, is "satisfactory." Thomas has the best grade in religion: "very satisfactory." Things were similarly bad for Felix Krull:

> Also at the Easter holidays after my poor father's bankruptcy they refused to give me my graduation certificate by presenting me with the choice of being under the thumb of an authoritarian system not appropriate for my age or leaving the school and losing the social privileges connected with finishing it; and with the happy knowledge that my personal characteristics were more than adequate to make up for the loss of this trifling asset, I chose the latter.

The school, "this hostile institution," responded to opposition with Director Wulicke's grim maxim: "I will destroy the careers of every one of you." Thomas Mann, unruly and more than a match for this, was fairly unaffected by that, anyway:

> By chance a teacher threatened not me but another pupil with the words: "I'll spoil your career for you!" On the same day I read the maxim by Storm: "To become whatever you can, do not shy from work and long hours, but protect your soul from simply getting ahead." Then I knew that the teachers were not my educators but mid-range bureaucrats, and that I had to look elsewhere for my educators, that is, in the sphere of the intellect and literature.

"As a child I wanted to become a pastry cook or a streetcar conductor," the fifty-seven-year-old insists mockingly. "When I saw that nothing would come of that, I just gave it all up." Becoming a writer means not starting out on a career. It means fooling around, remaining undecided, not being subservient to society. School was the arm of that society. It did not produce free men but servants. Thomas Mann found it all right to train born servants as servants, but he himself did not want to be one. He knew well the torments of a youthful existence that is not yet able to identify itself and with an all-too-vulnerable ego feels derision and contempt everywhere—particularly on the part of the fat cats and the solid people, who cast a broad shadow. Nevertheless he had the strength to respond at school, not suffering like Hanno but with that haughty scorn with which he imbued his "Bajazzo":

One thing's for sure, I was an enormously cheerful lad who was able to get respect and popularity from fellow students because of my favorable background, my masterful imitation of the teachers, my thousand actor's tricks, and my superior way of speaking. But it went bad for me in class, for I was too deeply involved in figuring out the comedy in the movements of the teachers to be able to pay attention to anything else, and at home my head was too full of opera themes, lyrics, and colorful non-sense for me to be in a serious condition to work.

"For shame," my father said, and the creases between his eyebrows deepened when after lunch I had brought my report card to him in the living room and he had read the slip, his hand on his lapel.

## FLUNKING

Flunking liberates you. Thomas Mann kept the last two years at school in happiest memory. "The 'institution' expected nothing more of me— I sat through the lessons, but in general lived footloose." What he later thought of as freedom remained marked by that, the good and the bad. Herr Albin, for example, a guest in *The Magic Mountain*, is free: "It's like in high school when it was decided that you would be held back and you weren't asked questions and didn't need to do anything more." Hans Castorp is impressed, "because he himself had been held back in his sophomore year, and he recalled well the somewhat ignominious, but pleasantly untidy state of affairs that he had enjoyed when in the last quarter, he had given up even trying and was able to laugh 'at the whole thing.'" Honor, he ruminates further, has significant advantages, but disgrace has no fewer; indeed, its advantages seem almost boundless.

Herr Albin is tubercular and will die. The freedom of those who are held back reaches its apex when they are claimed by death. No one can demand anything from someone doomed to die. His freedom is honorable but also humiliating, for it avoids society. Thomas Mann, who matured into a republican, denies himself the luxury of death. In *Doctor Faustus* he calls the German enthusiasm for war in 1914 "playing hooky," wild holiday, casting away real duties, and allowing instincts that are not gladly bridled to bolt. The "German revolution" of

1933 appears to him in the same image as a "gigantic impertinence against the will of the world spirit" and a "childish case of playing hooky." Adrian Leverkühn also damns those who run away from school: Instead of intelligently taking care of what was necessary on earth, mankind played hooky and surrendered its soul in doing so. That is aimed at the Nazi years. But already in 1919 Thomas Mann exorted the Germans to remain at a distance from the revelries of chaos and to return to work and duty. His praise of flunking and dissoluteness becomes more and more muffled in the course of his life. The attractive philippic against the graduation certificate that Thomas Mann dared to write in 1917 would no longer have been considered appropriate in the republican years. It is guided by highly personal interests, that is clear:

> Anyone who passed through the nine classes of the secondary school should be permitted with an acknowledging handshake to go through the door to higher education and not be faced with one more perilous impediment. The age of eighteen, nineteen, is absolutely not an age to "test" persons in a somehow solemn and decisive sense. They do not yet understand life, they do not yet love work, perhaps they are temporarily dreamy idlers.

## THE AUTODIDACT

The abundance of education that Mann's later work strews about extravagantly comes only in a very small way from his schooling. Absolutely nothing from mathematics instruction stayed with him. This student of the branch of high school devoted to science and math worked out even the simplest additions and subtractions on paper all his life. He retained a lot of Latin, as numerous phrases sprinkled in his work demonstrate. He did not learn Greek. Because his son was to become a merchant, Senator Buddenbrook believed he was doing him a favor "by sparing him the unnecessary agony of Greek." Tommy's English is said to have been passable. According to his final report card, his French was "satisfactory," but he never liked that language. "My Negro French"—that's how he made fun of himself.

He acquired his education in German literature autodidactically and according to need from case to case. At Christmas in 1889 he was given the works of Schiller. He claims to have spent contented and enthusiastic hours with them "with a plate full of sandwiches." Idealism and sandwiches encroach with irony on one another's territory. Thomas Mann's Schiller is not the man of liberal soapbox speeches. Even the boy treats him in an unusual way. When, disguised as Tonio Kröger, he reads *Don Carlos*, he identifies not with the hero of liberty, Marquis Posa, as would be expected, but in conservative defiance with the king, the lonely and unloved Philip II of Spain, who is deceived by Posa.

> And now the news comes from the king's private quarters to the antechamber: The king has wept. "Wept?" — All the courtiers are frightfully disconcerted, and it is completely overwhelming, because the king is so terribly stiff and stern. But you can easily understand that he cried, and I feel sorrier for him than for the prince and the marquis combined. He is always so completely alone and without love, and now he believes he's found someone, and that man betrays him.

The main reason for the selection of reading material in his youth was the almost breathless imitation of his brother, his elder by four years. Like him, Thomas Mann read Heinrich Heine, then Hermann Bahr and Friedrich Nietzsche; a bit later also Paul Bourget. Perhaps even then the remark of the not-yet eighteen year old that he looked upon the words "good" and "bad" as social billboards with no philosophical meaning, is a trace of Nietzsche, going back to *Beyond Good and Evil*. At the latest the fascination with Nietzsche begins in 1894. His knowledge of Heine is even older, influences his adolescent poems, and probably can be traced back to the songs his mother sang. Thomas Mann was enthusiastic about Hermann Bahr from 1893 on. In its first printing, the prose sketch "Vision" carried the dedication: "To the genial artist Hermann Bahr." The Viennese critic counted as the "man of day after tomorrow," as nineteen-year-old Heinrich Mann informs his friend Ludwig Ewers: "This Bahr perhaps has a great future, all the more since he lives and feels completely in the modern, is aware of its smallest twitches and changes and assimilates them." The ardor of Thomas Mann lasts only until 1895. "The most modern thing today is reaction," he writes on March 5, 1895, to Otto Grautoff. "Do you know that Bahr now swears by the classics? And he is l'homme de tête and always has the right instincts for the latest and coming spirit of the age." Two months later that sounds very different: He had been "stuck on Bahr," but today was a little more mature than at the time "where in the final analysis my diary could just as well have been by the boyishly frivolous and fraudulently sentimental pseudo-Parisian." The French storyteller and cultural philosopher Paul Bourget had been recommended by Bahr and, following him, by Heinrich Mann. The earliest trace of Bourget can be found in the summer of 1894.

Not conveyed by Heinrich, who was by no means as musical as his brother, is the fascination for the musical dramas of Richard Wagner. The introduction to Wagner occurs in 1893, when Emil Gerhäuser was engaged at the Lübeck Municipal Theater. As the precocious reviewer for a student newspaper, "Paul Thomas" reports scornfully that "the mighty Wagner-Gerhäuser evenings of the season" still lay heavy in his stomach and for that reason, as an antidote "Millöcker's carbonic acid music" was of a great help. Nietzsche will speak in a similar way of Bizet's *Carmen*: dry, sunny air after the outbreaks of sweat caused by the siroccos of Wagnerian music. His passion for Wagner will give Thomas Mann numerous fictional figures: Herr Friedemann, Gerda Arnoldsen, Detlev Spinell and Gabriele Klöterjahn, Siegmund and Sieglinde Aarenhold, and others.

## FELLOW STUDENTS

No one endures such opposition without being supported. However cruel, bad, and ridiculous school may have been, as in the famous school chapter at the end of *Buddenbrooks*, it became bearable because of a few fellow students of more than average rank. "On the basis of one or another ability difficult to determine"—to which, for example, belonged a stupendous ability to imitate teachers humorously—Thomas Mann was held "in a certain respect" by the outlaws of the class. He was bound to them by "the pathos of distance" (he took the expression from Nietzsche), "an emotion felt by all those who at fifteen secretly read Heine and in the fifth year of secondary school pass judgment on the world and mankind." His opposition did not bind him to the usual boys who flunked terms. His association was much more exclusive, according to social class, so to speak, neither proletarian nor demimonde like that of his brother Heinrich, who had lived since 1891 as a trainee with the S. Fischer publishing house in Berlin and enjoyed great freedom. His "circle of friends" can be described by "intellect and nobility." Nobility: Among his closest comrades were Hermann Count Vitzthum von Eckstädt, son of a ceremonial master with Emperor Wilhelm II; Detlef Count Reventlow; and Eberhard Count Schwerin, the model for Kai Count Mölln in *Buddenbrooks*. Von Schwerin was a talented funster. When he had to recite Schiller's "The Bell," he included drawing teacher Dräge:

> Muffled its mournful tolling
> accompanies Herr Dräge
> On his last way.

And in addition to nobility, also intellect: First of all was his brother Heinrich, but there were also Otto Grautoff, Korfiz Holm, and Ludwig Ewers, who later were active as writers. Otto Grautoff is that nameless person whom Thomas Mann in his *Summary of My Life* mentions as the son of a bankrupt, deceased book dealer, with whom a friendship had bound him "that proved its worth in fantastic and gallows-humoristic scorn and derision about 'the whole thing,' especially about 'the institution' and its bureaucrats." The correspondence of many years indicates a profound closeness. "We were really intimate," Mann writes Grautoff, looking back, on March 28, 1895, from Munich. "We were shameless in front of one another, spiritual, that was so nice and comfortable." And still Grautoff was for him a dolt. Mann practiced vivisection on him, castigated him for what he hated in himself—for example, a bad style.

We know that Korfiz Holm, who later worked with the August Langen publishing house and smoothed the way for Thomas Mann to *Simplicissimus*, was Mann's gymnastics coach in school. Ludwig Ewers, a few years older, was more the friend of Heinrich than of Thomas but played an important role as a critically observed writer-competitor even during his school days. He was also familiar with Tommy's first love. Erich Mühsam, who later became an important anarchistic writer, also strolled back and forth on the schoolyard of the Katharineum, the high school named for St. Katherine. They probably discussed nothing worth mentioning, but they knew one another; the school was not so large that one could escape a striking figure. They did not meet one another again until 1911. Later, Mann rejected Mühsam decisively, but the hostility remained one-sided.

Next to intellect and nobility must be mentioned as a third group the Jewish fellow students whom Thomas Mann recalls in 1921 in the essay "On the Jewish Question," which remained unpublished at the time. These were the son of a rabbi, Simeon Carlebach; the decidedly ugly Franz Fehér, conversant with the circus, gypsy, and merchant milieus; and the intelligent Willi Gosslar, a kosher butcher's son, who was interested in Tommy's gothic ballads and other lyrical attempts of his boyhood.

It was completely with outsiders that the flunking student surrounded himself. But now the talk will be about ordinary people, especially when first love is involved.

# II. Early Love and First Writings

*Lübeck, 1893*

*Armin Martens, around 1889*

Falling in love with fellow student Armin Martens apparently happened in the winter of 1889–90. The yearning young man wrote a spate of poems to Armin, of which Thomas was later ashamed. During the same winter presumably, the dancing lessons took place that are depicted in *Tonio Kröger*. The original model of "Magdalena Vermehren" fell in love with Thomas Mann at the time. Other experiences with girls from the time in Lübeck can only be assumed but cannot be dated and not fixed by name.

His crush on Williram Timpe, the fellow student from whom Thomas, on the schoolyard of the Katharineum School, borrowed the pencil we know about from *The Magic Mountain*, had a longer duration, probably from the fall of 1890 to the fall of 1892.

During the time of these infatuations Thomas Mann was not an epic but a lyric-dramatic writer. From the documents of that sentimental period only a few blurred traces remain. Printed at the time were only a few poems, sketches, and ecstatic articles that appeared in the two issues of *Spring Storm*, a school magazine, from the first half of 1893.

# FIRST LOVE: ARMIN MARTENS

ON MAY 24, 1931, the *Tagblatt* in Prague published a series of answers to a questionnaire entitled: "My First Love." With a deft hand Thomas Mann wrote:

> Forgive me, I was traveling, in Paris, living in great turmoil, and did not manage to consider your Pentecost questionnaire in time. Anyway, I would only have been able to refer to my youthful story *Tonio Kröger*, which contains all sorts of tales about such sweet pangs.

That sounds insignificant. But the allusion is not to Ingeborg Holm, whom Tonio is wild about in his dance class. There is no biographical model for her. Armin Martens, alias Hans Hansen, is meant, a handsome blond boy, a classmate. The sweet pangs refer to him. At an advanced age, when he began to speak more freely about these things, Thomas Mann unveiled the secret in a letter to Hermann Lange, another comrade in the Katharineum:

> For I loved him—he was really my first love, and one more tender, more blissfully painful was never granted me. Such a thing you never forget, even though seventy richly filled years have passed by. It may sound ridiculous, but I keep the memory of that passion of innocence like a treasure. Only too understandable that he did not know what to do with my rapture, which I once confessed to him on a "big" day. That was partly my fault and partly his. It just died away then—long before he himself, whose charms suffered considerable ravages during puberty, as the first of us all died and decayed somewhere or other. But I set up a memorial for him in *Tonio Kröger*. . . . It's remarkable to think, too, that the entire destiny of that child of man consisted of awakening a feeling that one day was to become an enduring poem.

How hastily he brings in the literary aspect! When he was smitten, he was naturally far removed from the impudent arrogance with which he here diminishes the destiny of his former beloved to a literary figure in *Tonio Kröger*. Should we be upset at that? Let us rather ask what necessity hides behind it. The all-too-brisk chatter conceals something: that he is ashamed of how deeply he was affected. For the experience itself was not yet literary. Only *after* the experience did he vindicate himself with his creation. Still later he develops theories to be able to cope with his embarrassment. According to these, an experience is *justified* by becoming art. A man of letters "experiences in order to express." His life is only material. When it is aimed at enemies, for example at his brother, Thomas Mann has to sharpen it polemically. He then makes the point that artistic genius, is "something *behind which one retires.*" Aestheticism is "the abundantly gesticulating, highly gifted inadequacy for life and love."

The diary obituary for his youthful friend Otto Grautoff (July 15, 1935) will turn out to be as cruel as the look back at Armin Martens:

> Through K[atia]'s mother I learned about the death of O. Grautoff, my school confidant, and the confidant of my passion for W.T., who was elevated into Pribislav Hippe. I have long not bothered about the pompous ass who became so tedious; now the death of the chum of my sorrow- and laughter-filled boyhood years still touches me coldly and sadly. At the same time I cannot but feel that he belonged only to my life and then wanted to be something himself, foolishly.

We will return later to W.T. (Williram Timpe). The Martens experience was previous to that. As Hans Hansen in *Tonio Kröger*, Armin is fourteen. Since the winter sun shines on their strolls, Thomas Mann's first love will have taken place during the winter of 1889–90, in the months in which they also had dancing class together.

From the letter to Hermann Lange we know that Tommy confessed his passion on a "big day," and that Armin did not know what to do with it. The first love ended with a humiliation that Thomas Mann never overcame. The blond, blue-eyed boy laughed at him. We know a little about it because Armin's sister Ilse recalled a lot and passed it on. She is familiar to the reader of the novel *Royal Highness* as the lady of the court, Fräulein von Isenschnibbe, who was so nearsighted that she could not see the stars. At an advanced age Ilse Martens still remembered an emotional poem by Thomas Mann, the refrain of which "What has pale death done to you?" was cooled down by Armin in Low German with the scornful remark: "I don't know, but ask him sometime."

The young man in love had to hide the fact that his sentimental outpourings were made fun of not only by the one he adored but also by his brother Heinrich, who in letters to Ludwig Ewers in November 1889 and on March 27, 1890, butchered them derisively. The first comment is of a general nature, but already bad enough:

> I have always carried on as usual without a word or laughing out loud at the emotional productions of an adolescent, loving soul with which the happy poet also plagued me at times. In the "dramas," along with all the impossibilities that you have brought up in your classic criticism, there are still a few—even if very worn out—thoughts, like oases in the sand. Sand is boring enough. But the water in his lyrics is even more boring. And—so help me God—water everywhere, nothing but water, in which whole flocks of ducks and geese swim around completely unmotivated in the form of "Ah!!!"s and "Oh!!!"s . . . Brrr!

The second comment is even more hurtful, because it takes aim at the homoerotic nature of these poems:

> Since I'm being critical, I'd like to say a few words about the poems by my most promising brother, with which you seem to be so very much in agreement. You can cautiously bring these few words to his attention. In reading his most recent poems (which I enclose), I have not been able to escape the painful feeling that only Platen, the knight of the holy arse, has given me in a similar way. This effeminate, cloyingly sentimental poeticizing of "friendship":
>
> > —as I rested on your breast . . .
> > —as I slung my arm around my friend
> > And rocked myself in sweet desire . . .
>
> If that is true feeling (sad enough, if this is the case!)—then no thanks to fruit, won't even take cheese, rather French leave—

That Ewers was to bring that to Tommy's attention "cautiously" doesn't improve the matter, naturally.

To confess his passion on a big day, to write poems and show them around, to wriggle between happiness and hurt: How well anyone in love can understand that! The early outing ended with deep humiliation. Others put such a thing aside; a highly sensitive poet like Thomas Mann does not. Much in his later behavior is explained by this profound shock, which was deepened more by other humiliations. Feelings are ridiculous; one must not show them, particularly homoerotic ones. Such a love exiles a person from middle-class society. It makes a person impossible even among men of letters in the most intimate circle of friends. You have to hide it, deny it, treat it with irony. Poems in which the heart is alive are inartistic. A creative person must not feel. Only the cold ecstasies of the aesthete are artistic. "If what you have to say is quite important to you, if your heart beats too fervently for it, then you can be sure of a complete fiasco. You will become emotional, you will become sentimental; something unmanageable, unironic, unseasoned, boring, banal will come into being under your hands, and the finality is nothing but indifference among people, nothing but disappointment and misery in you yourself." So speaks Tonio Kröger.

Armin's luster vanished with adolescence. Thomas Mann followed his further life without sympathy, indeed, with aversion. At the end of 1898 he makes notes about him, to use them in one text or another: Armin told everyone openly and cheerfully about his love affairs. After military service he said: "I've forgotten how to treat decent girls." Thomas Mann likes that as little as he does the fact that Armin falls in love with two well-known dancers at the same time. More bitterly it offends him that Armin has instigated a relationship with his sister Julia Mann. Scandals erupt; Martens has to face the consequences and emigrates in 1899 to the then German colony of Southwest Africa. In debt and completely impoverished, he dies on April 1, 1906, in Windhuk.

Previous to that, he had sent a diary from the time of the Herero Rebellion to his sister. She was supposed to ask Tommy, who had just started to become famous, to find him a publisher for it. There is no evidence that the author of *Tonio Kröger* undertook anything. His letter of condolence to Ilse Martens does not mention any such involvement and is half formal, half at a loss:

    *Dear Ilse!*

    *Yes, I received the news today from my wife and then from Lula. I feel the way you do: I can't imagine it, actually can't believe it. Armin, dead, that doesn't make sense, I can't get it into my mind. You know what he was to my first, freshest, tenderest feelings. What can I say? I just can't make up expressive sentences about it. I press your hand most cordially and beg you to convey my sympathy to your mother.*

Your old friend
Thomas Mann

## WILLIRAM TIMPE

"Do *you* happen to have a pencil?" Hans Castorp, deathly pale and with pounding heart, asks Clawdia Chauchat. There then follows the famous conversation in French, at the end of which Clawdia, one of her bare arms raised, her hand on the door hinge, softly says to Hans Castorp over her shoulder, "N'oubliez pas de me rendre mon crayon" (Don't forget to give me back my pencil). Six weeks later in narrative time we discover that he gave back the pencil and received something else in return.

The borrowing of the pencil repeats an event from Hans's school days. Hans Castorp was thirteen years old, in his fourth year of secondary school, a boy in short pants. "In the schoolyard—paved with red brick and separated from the street by a shingled wall with two entrance gates"—thus, for anyone familiar with the locality, unmistakably the schoolyard of the Katharineum—Hans asks a fellow student named Pribislav Hippe, with whom he has fallen in love, son of a secondary school teacher, with bluish-gray Kirghizian eyes and high cheekbones, whether he can lend him a pencil. Glad to, he says. But be sure to give it back to me right after class. "And pulled a pencil from his pocket, a silver-plated *crayon* with a ring that you had to push up to make the red-colored lead emerge from its metal sheath." We find out, too, that Hans took the liberty of sharpening the lead a little, "and in an inner drawer of his desk he kept for almost a full year three or four of the red-colored shavings that fell off." The narrator likewise thinks it essential to inform us that the return of the pencil took place in the most simple way.

The scenes described come from the novel *The Magic Mountain*. There, lending and returning are poetic masks for a sexual act. But the pencil really existed; it is not merely a poetic metaphor. The "pencil shavings of W.T." are recalled in the diary on September 15, 1950. Also as Thomas Mann, on June 3, 1953, strolls through Lübeck,

*Williram Timpe, around 1895*

"Willri Timpe and the pencil" come to mind. Surely, exactly like Hans Castorp in his time, he kept the shavings in his desk.

"W.T." is Williram Timpe, called Willri, the son of the principal Dr. Johann Heinrich Timpe, with whom Thomas Mann after the death of his father and the move of his mother in the fall of 1892 boarded until sometime in 1893. "Thomas, it's past eleven!" the professor used to call out, when his young guest read too long. When Tommy fell in love with Willri cannot be told with absolute certainty. In any event, not at thirteen, as in the case of the literary transmutation into Hans and Pribislav, for "Willri" was later than "Armin." So probably at fifteen, a year after his Armin winter. Then his brother Heinrich's ridiculous suggestion for therapy (in the letter to Ludwig Ewers on November 21, 1890) referred to Willri:

A proper sleep treatment with a passionate not too debauched girl—that will cure him. But don't tell him that. Make the story ironic, that helps. Just don't take it tragically serious! He wants to know "my view" through you. So mention the significant word "idiocy" to him.

If the whole thing, as in *The Magic Mountain*, lasted two years, then the passion would have petered out in the fall of 1892. That would have been at the exact time at which they began living in the same house. This is not necessarily a contradiction. The daily domestic proximity perhaps had a more disillusioning effect than passion from a distance, which shies away from articulation and touch.

But with what feelings may the lazy high school student have moved in with the Timpes! We believe that anxiety grew in him, the trepidation that gripped Hans Castorp when he realizes that he is confined in a small space with Frau Chauchat, confined "with something inevitable or inescapable—inescapable in a pleasurable and tremulous sense. It was full of hope and at the same time also sinister, even ominous." But we also believe that Timpe's charm dissipated quickly with everyday chatter and toothbrushing together, whereas Frau Chauchat was able to remain for many months an unattainable dream.

Unlike Armin, Willri was a model student, but "not that," not what was intellectual, was the reason "why Hans Castorp had borrowed the pencil from him." It was the fascination of his body, it was his grayish-blue Kirghizian eyes, his high cheek bones, and his legs in short pants. That the gym classes were most repellent "in spite of Willri" indicates that it was exciting to watch Willri in gym—while Thomas himself, in the way of dreamers, was averse to physical exercise.

Warned by the case of Armin Martens, this time there was no "big day" on which he admitted his passion to his admired fellow student. If we continue to follow the depiction in *The Magic Mountain*, then Tommy said nothing, rather kept his secret and was content with sublimation. There was no thought that the subject could ever be mentioned. "It wasn't suitable and also not required." A page later it says that Hans Castorp had become accustomed to his quiet and distant relationship to Hippe. He was content with the emotions that were connected with being in love, with whether he would meet him today, pass close by him, perhaps look at him, with the "silent, tender fulfillments which his secret bestowed upon him."

That love is wordless occurs again and again in the works of Thomas Mann. Gustav von Aschenbach (in *Death in Venice*) never speaks a single time to the beautiful boy Tadzio. Hans Castorp doesn't know what to call his relationship to Hippe, for a name means "to classify it as one of life's familiar, commonplace items, whereas Hans Castorp was thoroughly convinced at some subconscious level that anything so personal should always be shielded from definition and classification." Felix Krull, finally, delivers a verbose theory for all that:

> Of tender and hesitant things you should always speak tenderly and hesitantly, and then an additional contemplation will be discreetly added. Only at the two poles of human contact, there where there are no, or no more, words, in a gaze and in an embrace, is happiness really to be found, for only there is completeness, freedom, mystery, and profound ruthlessness. Everything of communication and exchange that lies in between is queasy and half-hearted, is determined, stipulated, and limited by formality and middle-class agreement. Here the word governs—this dull and cool medium, this first evidence of tame, moderate, cultured behavior, so alien to the fervent and mute sphere of nature that one could say that every word in essence and as such was already a phrase. I say that—I who, caught up in the work of giving form to the description of my life, devote the most care imaginable to a belletristic expression. And yet my element is not communication through words. My truest interest is not there. It much more involves the most extreme, discreet regions of human relationships; first where foreignness and middle-class uninvolvement still maintain a free primordial state and glances marry irresponsibly in dreamlike wantonness; but then the other, in which the greatest possible union, trust, and mergence reestablishes that wordless primordial state most perfectly.

The man of words is interested in what is wordless. The millions of words he has generated in the course of his life shroud a primordial muteness. All his talking is the exterior part that conjures up something inexpressible, something holy that is erotic in its essence. To circumscribe the wordless primordial state of dream at least with words, if it has no chance of being realized, is the driving force of ceaseless formulation. The deepest longing of the stream of words is to become silent.

For never does real life satisfy such a longing. It must always remain a dream. That Thomas Mann makes Hippe a thirteen-year-old transports that experience from the apex of puberty into the area of prepuberty and in doing so desexualizes it to some degree—this makes sense in the novel to the extent that fulfilled sexuality is there ascribed to a woman, Clawdia Chauchat, who repeats Hippe typologically. The borrowing of a pencil, seen in this way, is an early presentiment of what is fulfilled sexually only in the relationship with a woman. That the pencil incident in the novel happens not to a sixteen- and seventeen-year-old boy but to a thirteen year old should keep us from the assumption that there were sexual activities between Hans and Hippe as a result. Thomas Mann did not lead a double life. He did not sneak off secretly to young men to perform forbidden acts. He was much too shy for that. "I would never have wanted to go to bed even with the Belvedere Apollo." The reality-free dream world of fulfillments in his fantasy was more important to him than imperfect real touching. "How can you sleep with men?" If one does not, from the start, suspect that these sources are repressing what was "actual," then they are evidence that Thomas Mann, aside from isolated acts of masturbation and unexpected sexual eruptions during the night (incidents that he recorded with comical pedantry in his diaries), had his sexual experiences with women, even if his dreams again and again involved young men.

Is such a thing at all possible? Evidently. Otherwise the long marriage with Katia Pringsheim could not have worked. The practice of sexuality belongs in Mann's world not to the sphere of solitary ecstasy but to raw reality in which one does one's duty. The ecstasies are dreams. Sexuality is not the realm of freedom, of a liberation from limitations, of fulfillment, but a consummated melange composed of duty and rare success plagued by anxieties of impotence, threatened by failure, and therefore under constant examination and self-observation destructive of desire. The familiar *tristitia post coitum* also describes the feeling of Thomas Mann, who considered the resulting "state of remorse and misery" an essential characteristic of the sex act. Everything unrealized in the actual act, in a constantly limited reality also unrealizable, drew the homoerotic dream world to it. He did not want reality; he did not need it.

In *A Sketch of My Life* Mann reports about "late and violently erupting sexuality" and adds he is speaking of the time when he was about twenty. Thomas Mann spent his twentieth year in Munich. The student loves in Lübeck lie so clearly in past time that they cannot have anything to do with it.

In July 1950, at the time of his passion for the waiter Franz Westermeier, Thomas Mann returns to the two earlier love affairs. "He has
been added," he writes about Franz, "to the gallery about which no
'literary history' will report, and which reaches past Klaus H. back to
those in the realm of death, Paul, Willri, and Armin." None of these
experiences can be dated in his twentieth year. Thomas becomes acquainted with Paul Ehrenberg only when he is twenty-four. The people who were the objects of his homoerotic passions contributed no
active part to the eruption of his sexuality.

But maybe women? Servant girls and nursemaids, as with Felix
Krull? Prostitutes? Soapmaker Unschlitt's daughter? Serenus Zeitblom's girl from the lower classes? The Munich girl to whom he did
not act enough like Brackenburg?* The flower girl who made Thomas
Buddenbrook so happy? We know nothing.

## THE SUNKEN TREASURE

"*Fidelity*," thought Tonio Kröger. "I want to be faithful and love you,
Ingeborg, as long as I live." For he was *that* well intentioned. And
nevertheless there was a sad whisper of misgiving in him that he had
also completely forgotten Hans Hansen. That malicious voice turned
out to be right, although Tonio fanned and fed the flames of his love
for a while because he wanted to remain faithful. "And after a while,
imperceptibly, without a commotion or a sound, they still went out."

So much for literature. In life the voice in the end was not right.
Thomas Mann preserved the thought of Armin Marten, that "passion
of innocence," like a treasure. He lets Tony Buddenbrook tend her
unrequited love for Morten Schwarzkopf like a treasure. "She called
to mind everything that she had heard and learned about him in
many conversations, and it gave her a pleasurable satisfaction to
promise herself solemnly that she intended to preserve all of this in
her heart as something holy and inviolable." The secret game of
lovers can make poetry of everything. Comb honey is a natural product—"You know, after all, what you're swallowing"—all her life she
says that, and only she herself knows that it's not a matter of the
comb honey. Her politicizing, too, has an amorous corollary meaning,
no, a principal meaning: "That the King of Prussia had committed a

* Brackenburg—a character in Goethe's play *Egmont.* See below. (Trans.)

great injustice, that the *Municipal Advertiser* was a miserable rag, yes, even that four years ago the federal laws about universities had been renewed, those were honorable and comforting truths for her from now on, a secret treasure that she could look at whenever she wanted."

Her love for Morten, like the boyhood crush of her author, is a "passion of innocence." Perhaps Tommy, too, was once kissed by a friend as Tony was by her Morten (even though it is more probable that he merely dreamed of it): "She didn't even look at him; she simply moved her torso very quietly on the sand dune a bit closer to him, and Morten kissed her on the mouth slowly and awkwardly. Then they looked in different directions at the sand and were immeasurably ashamed." The contents of the sunken treasure are not bedtime stories but comb honey, the king of Prussia, and a halfway, unsuccessful kiss.

"Eternal love for boys" (Diary, June 3, 1953). Again and again there follows one rapture after another, the impossibility of their realization and their memory kept holy. Again and again the fact of being in love is more important than its object. Potiphar's wife, after her attempted seduction of the handsome Joseph was rebuffed, submits again completely to the requirements of her marriage and her rank. Thomas Mann knows her innermost being, for it is his own:

> And still, at the bottom of her soul, lay a treasure of which she was secretly more proud than of all her spiritual and worldly honors and which she, whether she admitted it or not, would not have given away for anything in the world. A deeply sunken treasure that still always quietly shone up into the gloomy day of her renunciation. . . . It was the memory—not even so much of him who, as she heard, had now become lord over the Land of Egypt. He was only a tool as she, Mut-em-enet, had been a tool. Much more and almost independently of him it was the realization of justification, the realization that she had blossomed and glowed, that she had loved and suffered.

## LOST POEMS AND DRAMAS

Thomas Mann is assuredly an epic author. But he did not begin that way. It took a fairly long time, he writes later, "until when I was about twenty, the presumption that I was destined to be a storyteller began to take root in my consciousness." The fourteen-year-old signs: "Th. Mann, lyric-dramatic author."

The early dramas and lyrics were destroyed or lost. There are only a few traces of them. The first poems were addressed to Armin Martens. Heinrich Mann's scornful quotes reveal their style: "—as I rested on your breast . . . / —when I slung my arm around my friend, / And rocked myself in sweet desire." During the time of dancing lessons, love lyrics in the fashion of Heine and Storm came into being. We have a presentiment of more when we remember Tonio Kröger, who likewise possessed "a notebook full of poems written by himself" and, when his heart stirred, during the nocturnal crossing to Denmark, penned a "song to the sea, inspired by love":

> Friend of my youth, ah wild sea weather,
> once more we meet, once more together.

But the poem "was not a finished product, not an experience formed and shaped, recollected in tranquillity and forged into a whole." The early lyrics were obviously histrionic and sentimental. But the mature Thomas Mann will write ironically and artistically.

According to Heinrich Mann, writing to Ludwig Ewers, in the "dramas" of his brother, fourteen at the time, there were nevertheless a few, though worn-out, thoughts. Even the twelve year old as the author of "childish dramas" caused a great stir—"dumb little pieces for the theater that I forced my sisters to perform with me for my mother and my aunts." One of them had the title *You Can't Poison Me*. In it Thomas played a malicious innkeeper who plans to poison and rob a young knight but is prevented from doing so by his beautiful but usually submissive daughter, who loves the knight—"childish, adventurous nonsense, the fabrication of which has not the least thing to do with experience, with emotion." Also *Aischa* could have been a drama; the fourteen-year-old quotes from it the significant words: "Still no news!" The gruesome and pompous was his mode. As a fourth-year student in secondary school he wrote a romance on the heroic death of Arria, the wife of Paetus who, as Pliny the Younger reports, in the year A.D. 42 chose suicide with her husband. Its title was *Paete, non dolet* (Paetus, it doesn't hurt); it opens powerfully with the line: "Deep in Rome's most gloomy dungeon," which suggests a ballad in trochees.

As a sixteen and seventeen year old Thomas Mann was for a time under the influence of Schiller—like his "Bajazzo" he thought and felt in the style of one book until another began to influence him. *The Priests* was the title of an extremely anticlerical drama in blank verse, from which the end of an act stayed in his memory:

> If not done by Satan in the flesh,
> 'Twas done most likely then at least by priests.

His pious grandmother had expressed her deep concern about his liberal fanaticism, "that was certainly nothing more than an empty and adopted attitude."

In the early time in Munich, Mann wrote at least the first act of a fairy-tale play in verse with the title *The Old King*. Fame in the theater must have been on his mind because he described it expressly as written for the stage. He supposedly thought much less of poetry at the time. "Recently I've finished only all kinds of lyrics," he says in an understatement. "Poems require no industry and no endurance, of course. I usually write them evenings when going to sleep." Apparently they reflect that, too. We know only the couplet:

> I create true. With all her dogs
> —draws nigh the huntress Passion.

Thomas Mann divulges it in a late diary note in an obviously crucial connection, for the entry begins with the remark: "Nocturnal visitation." —"Only Mama" could have been a story, as the context of the letter, from which we know this title and nothing else, makes clear.

Mann speaks of all these texts without emotion, in a contemptuous tone. Sentimentality, pathos, pomp, and fad are later repulsive to him, even embarrassing. That he destroyed these works is no accident. The "lyric-dramatic author" had to make way for the epic writer.

## *SPRING STORM* AND OTHER IMMATURE THINGS

*The Spring Storm* was the name of the student newspaper that Thomas Mann edited from May until July 1893 with Otto Grautoff. A double issue (June/July) is preserved, and there is information about another (May). In retrospect Mann writes that he shone there as "a philosophical-subversive lead-article author." This refers to the title article in which the young Paul Thomas—this his scarcely veiled pseudonym—wishes to liberate dusty Lübeck from its smothering shell by way of a spring storm, further to a defense of Heinrich Heine against moraliz-

ing philistines (under the title "Heinrich Heine, The 'Good Man'").
The young editor enjoys being in an adolescent opposition, sentimental and precocious, but naturally also talented.

In *The Spring Storm* there appeared also the poems "Twofold Farewell," "Night," and "The Death of the Poet"; the prose sketch "Vision"; and a few smaller texts. No biographical information can be
gleaned from them, for most of it is third-hand sentimentality and
completely lacks personal expression—thus the following sample
from "The Death of the Poet":

> Let once more you be clasped clinging,
> O life, thou blossoming fay!
> Let be once more, foaming, ringing
> The goblets raised in jubilant hey!

Considering everything we know up to now of our hero, foaming
goblets, wine, women, and song were not his thing. Also the "Twofold Farewell" is awkward. There on an ocean strand a young man
says a tear-drenched farewell forever to a girl in "the evening glow of
a short day on which happiness held us in its arms." The assumptions
should encourage the reader to make all kinds of conclusions but
probably are rather an expression of the fact that the poet has never
experienced the event and therefore is also unable to give a more
exact scenario. The next morning, there follows the official farewell at
the train station with a bouquet of flowers, and parents. "We both
were lying," it reads, when they formally say "Until we meet again!"
for on the evening at the ocean they had already known: "Never—
never again."

In any event, the sentimental setting already expresses the conviction that a great love has no place on earth, that any realization soils
it, and that it cannot be fitted into middle-class life. In *Buddenbrooks*
there will be two couples who give up their love in favor of their
dutiful marriages in order to maintain love as pure dream: Thomas
Buddenbrook, who does not marry his flower girl, but rather the rich
and icy Gerda, and his sister Tony, who has to renounce the student
Morten Schwarzkopf but through the treasure of memory of him also
has the strength to endure the worldly sordidness of two catastrophic
marriages.

The best work from the time of *The Spring Storm* is the sketch "Vision." The situation is crueler than in the poems and for that reason
perhaps a bit truer. It concerns the sadistic conquest of a lover, ba-

sically a rape fantasy. The narrating first person imagines himself in the role of one who coldly observes the budding desire of his female opposite, her throbbing and beseeching convulsive movements, and simultaneously satisfies her and kills her with a look. "But my glance presses heavily upon her and with terrible lust." To love means to destroy, to crush pleading resistance, to humiliate. Now, we must not assume that Thomas Mann did such a thing to a woman. It is much more plausible to see him in the role of the woman. The sketch then becomes an expression of his fear of being raped. The tool is the look. Looks can kill. Anyone who is seen through is done for; Tonio Kröger knows that later. The weapon used in the crime is recognition. To love means being recognized. Thomas Mann is anxious in the role of the lover whose passion is exposed to an impartially dissecting look.

In *On Myself* Thomas Mann mentions that in the narrative attempts of that time he joyfully copied exactly "the singular prose style of the Viennese Symbolist School led by Hermann Bahr." At the time he had sent one of his student products, "a piece of exaggeratedly sensitive and colorist prose," entitled "Color Sketch," to a Lübeck newspaper. At the bottom of the printed rejection slip a rude editor had written the words: "If you have such ideas often, you should really do something about it." Probably "Vision" and "Color Sketch" were identical, for obtrusive color painting is the most important means of structuring the brief text. A crystal goblet, half full of pale gold, in front of it a dull-white girl's hand reaching out, on which a light-blue vein meanders, on a finger a matt-silver ring, bleeding on it, a ruby.

That he copies the Viennese symbolists should not cause us to deny the quality in the text. A not altogether impartial witness remarks on this subject that imitation within certain boundaries is more a sign of talent than a hopeless defect of personality. Next to the flamboyant playfulness with color, there are already traits that point to what is to come. Gerda von Rinnlingen will humiliate Herr Friedemann with a look. Irma Weltner, the lover of the cynic in *Fallen*, also has veins on her hand; there, too, desire turns into vengeance.


## GIRLS IN LÜBECK

The author has not spoiled us with autobiographical remarks on this topic. We hear solely of "dance class eroticism" and a brown-braided dance class partner to whom further love lyrics were devoted. For all else we must rely on the partly overly precise, partly erased traces that actual events left behind in the literary work. But there are reliable witnesses for the dance lessons. François Knaak, whose real name was Rudolf Knoll, was a ballet master in Hamburg and came in the winter to Lübeck to give lessons in the leading circles of the city. In the winter of 1889 the lessons took place in the Mann house on Beckergrube. Thomas is said to have been a good and likable but shy and reserved dancer, as one female participant in the lessons remembers. Also Hans Hansen, excuse me, Armin Martens, was a member of the group. Whether the blonde Inge Holm, Tonio Kröger's adored one from the time of the dance lessons, actually existed is uncertain. The story mentions only a few of her characteristics—only that she "laughing tossed her head to the side in a certain high-spirited way, put her not at all particularly slender, not at all particularly fine little girl's hand to the back of her head, at which the white chiffon sleeve slipped from her elbow," and that she "emphasized a word, an indifferent word in a certain way, at which there was a warm sound in her voice." With a detour to the not particularly fine schoolgirl hand of Clawdia Chauchat, the motif of the hand leads back to Pribislav Hippe, from him to Williram Timpe, so that the crush on Inge could also be the last structuring of a homoerotic experience.

But Magdalena Vermehren "with the soft mouth and the large, dark shining eyes full of seriousness and enthusiasm," who understands Tonio's poems and often falls down while dancing, did exist. In reality she was named Magdalena Brehmer. A daughter of hers lived until recently in Lübeck and at an advanced age told anyone who would listen that her mother never did fall down while dancing. And tears came into her eyes.

In his letter from Berlin of September 16, 1891, Heinrich Mann gave his friend Ludwig Ewers, who apparently had expressed the fear that he was a homosexual, the following advice:

I advise you to avoid any expenditures until you have 10 marks together. Then guide your hurried steps to the street (I've forgotten what it's called) vis-à-vis the Aegidenkirche. The house, upper right in the lane, from outside has shiny brass staircase railings, and inside is the Knoop Guest House, whose one boarder once provided me with my first normal sensuous bliss. Those are sweet memories, things like that.—

We may assume that Thomas Mann, given his close familiarity with Heinrich and Ewers and given a problem of similar proportions, was informed about the Lübeck bordello mentioned. Moreover, the house with the brass railings returns again in *Doctor Faustus*. Heinrich possibly made similar recommendations to his brother. After all, he was not in favor of sublimation. A proper sleep treatment with a not too debauched girl seemed indicated to him at any time. We do not claim that Thomas followed such suggestions and similar ones. We can only say that Hans Castorp owes his sexual initiation to a prostitute. We know furthermore that Felix Krull completed his introduction into higher techniques of love with a prostitute named Rozsa, who in many details resembles the "hetaera Esmeralda" in *Faustus*, in other details those of Clawdia Chauchat from *The Magic Mountain*, and about whom he is able to report with astonishing exactness:

> She had a marvelously foreign appearance: for under a red wool cap cocked to the side of the crown of her head her black hair, cut rather short, hung down in smooth strands and partly covered her cheeks, which seemed softly hollowed out due to the very noticeable bone structure around her eyes. She had a snub nose, her mouth was wide and she wore red lipstick, and her eyes, which were slanted with their outer corners turned upward, gleamed unseeing and uncertain in color, totally her own and not like those of other people. With her red cap she wore a canary-yellow jacket, under which the hardly delineated contours of her upper body were sketched sparingly but lissomly, and I saw well that she was long legged like a foal, which always appealed to my taste. Her hand, when she raised the green liqueur to her mouth, revealed fingers spread and bent upward, and somehow it seemed hot, that hand, I don't know why—perhaps because the veins on its back stood out so much. In addition, the stranger had a habit of pushing her lower lip forward and backward while rubbing it on her upper lip.

He preferred to discover things rather than to invent them: If that is so, Thomas Mann cannot have been entirely without visualization when he wrote these lines. Rozsa was described much more plastically than, for example, Inge Holm. Felix also gives exact information about the inside of the bordello. As far as the sexual acts themselves are concerned, a discreet half-light prevails. In any event, we discover that during intercourse Rozsa emitted short, urgent cries that came from the realm of expression of the circus menagerie, and that she had a way of putting her leg over his, "as though she were simply crossing her own," for "everything she said and did was marvelously unconstrained, bold, and free."

"Rozsa" occurred already during his period as a journeyman. Felix had received his first sexual initiation from the nanny Genovefa, if one disregards the good fortune at the breast of his wet nurse. Felix was sixteen and Genovefa in her early thirties, when he meets the tall, well-nourished blond with her green, provocative eyes and affected movements in the dark hall in front of the door to his small garret room—"a meeting that step by step drifted into the room itself, and there led to complete mutual occupancy." That there might also have been a willing nanny for Thomas Mann can by no means be said with any kind of certainty. Discounting such a thing, the *Summary of My Life* dates the appearance of his sexuality only in his twentieth year, thus about 1895. But in favor of it is solely that Krull's spheres of life correspond entirely to those of Thomas Mann at the time. Frieda Hartenstein was twenty-nine when Thomas, then fourteen and a half, wrote to her: "All of us here wait with *ardent* longing." Of course, only for a letter . . . But he signs as "friend, admirer, and adorer." All of this indicates only a possibility. We don't even know for certain who Frieda Hartenstein was. *Perhaps* a nanny. Knowledge about Thomas Mann's homosexual tendency should not mislead us into failing to consider affection for women at all. "Pretty people are a joy, whether male or female." For the attractive young man from a good home, girls were simply the permitted and easily accessible way. Of course, that must not necessarily have led to "complete mutual possession," as in the case of Felix Krull. Here the artist Thomas Mann will also have given a hint to supplement logically what is missing.

# III. Before Fame

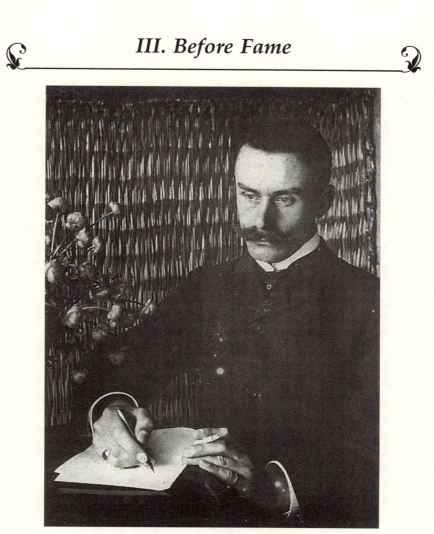

*In the wicker beach chair, around 1900*

At the end of March 1894, Thomas Mann moves to Munich, unenthusias-tically takes an (unpaid) position as a trainee in a fire insurance firm, and quits at the end of August. At this time the story "Fallen," in part written furtively at the sloped desk during office hours, comes into being and ap-pears in October in the naturalistic magazine *Die Gesellschaft,* which opens doors to literary circles in Munich for the nineteen year old. The sphere of his life is the artists' quarter, Schwabing, and the famous Café Central. He becomes a member of an "academic-dramatic club," which stages, for ex-ample, Henrik Ibsen's naturalistic drama *The Wild Duck*: Thomas Mann plays the wholesale merchant Werle. In the winter semester of 1894–95 and in the summer semester of 1895 he attends various lectures in the Technical College on economics, mythology, aesthetics, history, and literary history as an irregular auditor. From August 1895 until November 1896 he contributes short articles to the national-conservative magazine *Das Zwangzigste Jahr-hundert,* edited by Heinrich Mann.

Literarily, Thomas Mann, during the first two years in Munich and after the success of "Fallen," received many setbacks. In any event, "The Will to Happiness" (written in December 1895) appears in *Simplicissimus.* After many lost, frustrated, or never-finished works, "Little Herr Friedemann" (fin-ished in the fall of 1896) brings about his artistic breakthrough.

From July to October 1895, Thomas travels with his brother for the first time to Italy, to Palestrina and Rome. A second, long Italian sojourn lasts from October 1896 to April 1898 and, similar to what Goethe did in his time, leads at first by way of Venice and Rome to Naples (November 1896), then back to Rome (Via del Pantheon 57, until July). The brothers spend high summer and early fall of 1897 together in Palestrina, then the winter of 1897–98 again in Heinrich's apartment, Via Torre Argentina 34. In Italy Thomas first writes a series of small, partly lost works ("Disappointment," "The Dilettante," "Luischen," and with Heinrich the *Picture Book for Good Children*) until in October 1897 he begins work on *Buddenbrooks.*

In the spring of 1898 Thomas becomes an editor and proofreader at *Sim-plicissimus* (until January 1900). He has moved four times by 1899, always within Munich-Schwabing. There in Barerstrasse, in a furnished room rented for sixty marks, he writes in his diary that it is now important to let the Buddenbrook family continue to decline quickly. This was accomplished. The manuscript of the family novel is sent on August 13, 1900, to Samuel

Fischer in Berlin, who at the end of 1900 decides to publish it and brings the novel out in October 1901 in two volumes. During the long waiting period, Thomas writes the story "The Path to the Cemetery" and lays the groundwork for *Tonio Kröger*, "Tristan," and the drama *Fiorenza*.

Now for a while one must imagine the young man of letters in a well-tailored uniform practicing the goose step. From October 1, 1900, to December he fulfills a stint of military service until he is unprejudicially released because of chronic tendinitis.

## DECIDING FOR HIS MOTHER

THOMAS MANN contributed much from his own life to the story "The Dilettante," not only the gabled old city with its Gothic churches and the patrician house, gray with age; not only the clownish talent and the writing of poems; not only the puppet theater, the bad grades, and the comfortable inheritance but above all a stylized image of father and mother. The father in the story is, more than in reality, a vigorous man. The power to bestow favors or to destroy, and to be seen doing so, brings him satisfaction:

> He was a powerful man with great influence on public affairs; I have seen some people leave him breathing fast, eyes sparkling, and others who were broken and in complete despair. For it happened occasionally that I, and also my sisters, were present at such scenes; perhaps because my father wanted to encourage the ambition in me to make it as far up in the world as he had, perhaps also, as I suspect, because he needed a public. Leaning against his chair, clasping his lapel with one hand, he had a way of gazing after the lucky or desolated person that made me feel this suspicion even as a child.

On the other hand, the mother plays the piano in a half light, mostly Chopin, and tells fairy tales "that no one else knew," perhaps the fairy tale about the man who could not sleep, which the passionate dreamer Thomas Mann likes to recall so well:

> ... the story of a man who clung to time and his handling of it with such foolish fervor that he cursed sleep. An angel bestowed upon him a terrible privilege: It took away from him the physical need for sleep; it breathed upon his eyes so that they became like gray stones in their hollows and never closed again. How this man regretted his longing, what he endured as the only sleepless creature among human beings, how he, sadly cursed, dragged through his life until finally death released him, finally night, which stood inaccessible before his stony eyes, accepted him and took him in—I could not describe it in detail, but I know that on the evening of that day I could scarcely wait to be left alone in

my small bed to throw myself on the breast of sleep, that I never slept as deeply as on that night after I listened to this story.

His father was powerful and frank, his mother melancholic, dreamy, and intimate:

> I was sitting in a corner, watching my father and my mother, as though I were choosing between the two and considering whether life were better spent in dreamy thought or in deed and might. And my eyes lingered finally on my mother's still face.

Even during school and also after his entrance into "life" in Munich, Thomas Mann decided first of all for his mother, for his writing and dreams, for loafing about and the bohemian life, for the purity of reality and art. At first he lived with her, in Schwabing at Ramberg-strasse 2, in an apartment that is then described in *Doctor Faustus* as the salon of the wife of Senator Rodde. His later bachelor apartments also were within walking distance; he could comfortably call on his mother for a meal. The artist is a child. "Between child's play and the practice of art there is no breach in my memory, no sharp boundary." Like his Felix Krull he chose an inexact but fundamental freedom "that is utterly incompatible with any kind of use in an obviously real relationship," and for the advantages of a dream, specifically, "complete, unrestrained, and detached irresponsibility."

Yet the decision is not lasting. He had paused for a state of mind to evolve, the young husband will write to his brother on January 17, 1906. He will betray the pure reality of a dream realm and go over to the side of the world of his father.


## FREEDOM

A move would not be anything special in itself. But Thomas Mann's move to Munich is an important prerequisite for him as a writer. Only from a distance does he become conscious of the uniqueness of his Lübeck origins. Only the loss of the world of his childhood and youth makes the memory of it material to play with. Anyone who lives in consonance with his environment does not find it worth passing on. Anyone who wants to be a storyteller must have something special to say. North German, Protestant, Hanseatic Lübeck was something special from the viewpoint of the bohemian life in the southern German,

Catholic metropolis that was so utterly different, a lost world that was re-created at first satirically, later also elegiacally and idyllically. What does a Hanseatic person do in the bratwurst city? Thomas Mann does not look for literature there—"This city is completely unliterary" (but maybe that's more mocking than honest), rather its opposite. He finds that it has a fascination and that it is an advantage "to live in protest and with irony against one's environment: That heightens the feeling for life, one lives more properly and more self-confidently under those conditions."

The sharpening of consciousness had already begun when a rapid social decline had followed the death of his father, the sale of the firm, and the move of his mother. The son of the senator and tax assessor of the city-state, before whom simple people doffed their hats, had within a year become an idle secondary-school student from whom no one expected anything. He was abandoned. The move to Munich was only the consequence of that social shock. In the fact that he dropped out of the world he was destined for lies an essential reason that the novel *Buddenbrooks* could come into being. Because everything in Munich was different; out of the contrast came that gleaming sharpness of memory that distinguishes the novel. It deepened in Italy, where Heinrich and Thomas avoided any contact with their homeland. "If we heard German spoken, we fled." Italy meant the break of any obligation to Lübeck. "When I began writing *Buddenbrooks*, I was sitting in Rome, Via Torre Argentina trentaquatro, three flights up. Lübeck did not have much reality for me, you can believe me; I was not very convinced of its existence. It, along with its inhabitants, was essentially no more than a dream, droll and venerable, dreamed long ago, dreamed by me and my own in a curious way." Because his native town did not want and did not need him, because he in no way felt obligated to it, because almost all the bridges had been burned, he felt free from any kind of consideration. He saw no reason to spare anyone. Had his father been alive, the son, as a member of Lübeck aristocracy, would never have been able to write a novel like *Buddenbrooks*, which betrayed so many private matters from his own and other first families of the city. Only dropping out of the middle-class world made an artist of Thomas Mann.

Thomas Mann had experienced his uprooting subjectively as a liberation. It was made easier for him not only by the consciousness of latent abilities and by the example of his older brother but also because of the simple fact that he was not forced to earn his bread. The nineteen year old angrily defends himself against the insinutation that he was writing for money. But it was easy for him to talk. From the liquidation of the firm, he had at his disposal an annuity in the amount of from 160 to 180 marks a month, which in terms of today's currency would amount to tenfold more. An argument with Otto Grautoff summarizes the level of expenses. In September of 1894 they both speak to the question of whether one could live on 25 marks a month. Thomas Mann makes it clear: "With 100 M. a month you can barely eat modestly, pay rent modestly, and clothe yourself modestly: absolutely *nothing* more than that." On the other hand, 180 marks was comparatively comfortable. The sum remained a nice extra income, even when Thomas Mann was already a well-compensated author. Then, during World War I the value of the mark fell, with it the extra income, and it disappeared entirely in 1923 when the value of the work of his fathers and forefathers shrank to a billionth of its former worth.

That the early Thomas Mann demonstrates such a decisive aware-ness of a pure art that has no obligation to society has these unusually fortunate social circumstances as a prerequisite for his creative work. He knows that, too, and drolly expresses his gratitude to capitalism, that it had permitted him to play a trick on the world. "I don't know hunger," he replies in 1921 to a questionnaire. "In my youth I had those 200 marks a month, which before the war guaranteed social freedom and put me in a position to do what I wanted."

He was free to a rare degree. Thomas Mann is not like you and me. He is highly atypical. He can avoid the usual constraints of life—who else can do that? Aside from the short period as a publisher's editor, Thomas Mann never did have a "real" profession. As his like-minded brother observes, he was "tied to nothing," but just for that reason was a marked man, who bore a relentless obligation. That's not com-fortable. "We needed all the power of resistance of our youth."

Thomas Mann often made dropping out of society a literary theme. The Bajazzo, Tonio Kröger, Felix Krull, Gustav von Aschenbach, Hans Castorp, Joseph, Gregorius: They all lose their homelands and gain an unrooted freedom that obligates them to nothing. Even life as a sol-dier means for Thomas Mann liberation from ordinary society. He does not, of course, for that reason become a consistent adventurer and bohemian. His social conscience keeps gnawing at him. Then his

characters yearn for flower girls and storage workers and blond pig-
tails. Tonio Kröger, Klaus Heinrich, Joseph, and Gregorius look for
contact with "life" and find their way back from cheerful independence to the world of society. Thomas Mann's marriage and his political activities in 1914, 1922, and in exile correspond biographically to
such attempts.

## TALENTED AND CHOSEN

"What a talented person you are!" Ludwig Jacobowski, the editor of
the naturalistic magazine *Die Gesellschaft*, is said to have exclaimed,
when Thomas Mann showed him a novella. Early on, Mann has the
sure feeling of latent abilities, despite his failure in school. All his life
on his brow he will feel the sign of being chosen. "With slight perspi-
cacity you can recognize an artist out of a mass of people, a real one,
not one whose middle-class occupation is art, but one predestined
and damned. The feeling of separation and not belonging, being recognized and being observed, at the same time something regal and
self-conscious in his face. In the features of a prince who, dressed in
plain clothes, walks through a crowd of people, you can observe
something similar." The Prince Karl game of his childhood confirms
the consciousness of being chosen just as the novel *Royal Highness*
does, or the lifelong, often almost comical, imitation of Goethe. Not
by chance is a later novel entitled *Der Erwählte*, The Chosen One,
translated as *The Holy Sinner*. A poem that came into being on January 18, 1899, in Munich and shortly afterward was published in *Die
Gesellschaft*, expresses this exclusive mood with early awareness:

*Monologue*

I am a childish and a fragile boy,
And my spirit erring makes its rounds,
And staggering I grasp at any hand.

And still the hope stirs at bottom
That something that I thought or felt
Will one day famous go from mouth to mouth.

Already sounds my name softly in the land,
Already is it heard in tones of praise:
And those are folk with wit who understand.

Dreaming of a modest wreath of laurel
Often drives my sleep away at night,
That once will decorate my brow, as payment
For this and that I accomplished well.

What is the basis of this? That someone whom others scorn does not exclude the consciousness of being chosen. One can end up as an impoverished refugee child in a Swabian village but, although the native farmers look upon someone who drops in as a worthless vagrant appearing from nowhere, one can feel ennobled because of fate and origin. Social acknowledgment is not everything. Loss produces a feeling of being chosen for such a one much more than an assured rank in society that, having become habitual, has nothing of distinction about it. The quick descent from the first circles of the city-state of Lübeck into the Schwabing demi-Bohemia leaves behind the feeling of being something better in spite of appearances. The lazy secondary-school boy has not concluded from the loss of his social position that it will be marvelous among the outcasts; rather, after short reflection, a brief comparison with his bohemian colleagues, even with such important ones as Frank Wedekind, Stefan George, and his brother Heinrich, he has vowed that he must reach the rank of his father again. Social ambition is one of the reasons for his indefatigable work. He would become a fairly good businessman and earn the money that was necessary to support a large family in difficult times "in accordance with their status" and "maintain a residence" that would be somewhat equal to that of his father.

The feeling of being chosen and his ambition, of course, are of no help at all, if there is no talent. Here, too, his origins were of aid. There is no talk of genetics, but of the stylish atmosphere that surrounded his youth, of housing, clothing, and food. The finely tuned rules of behavior produce quite early a feeling for what is proper that infuses the incorruptible taste of Thomas Mann. We almost never find in him an incongruity of style. Aesthetics is a sublimated theory of conduct. Anyone who knows what is proper learns to place value on the precisely right word, the exactly chosen level of style. Different from Heinrich, who often seeks to provoke and knowingly offends good taste, Thomas finds pleasure in good tone. He does not write with an ax, as Heinrich does at times, but with the stroke of a fine carving knife.

Later, in the *Reflections of a Nonpolitical Man,* Thomas comes into conflict with Heinrich about the formula of Expressionism contra Impressionism. "Expressionism, to speak in general and briefly, is the direction of art that, in strong contrast to the passivity, the humble assimilative and descriptive manner of Impressionism"—in contrast, then, to the manner of Thomas Mann—"despises most profoundly the simulation of reality, decisively dismisses any obligation to reality, and in its stead places the sovereign, explosive, inconsiderate, creative decree of the mind." Obligation in regard to reality leads to a kind of politeness toward it. Life, just as it is, deserves respect. Thomas Mann's definition of Impressionism is undoubtedly conservative in nature. It is no surprise that a polemic against the genre of satire follows, espeically against Heinrich Mann's socially critical novel *The Patrioteer*. Satirical forms, still occasionally found in the early work of Thomas Mann, almost completely vanish in the later works. They are too impolite.

## A METAPHYSICAL MAGIC POTION

The early days in Munich revolved around his ominous twentieth year. The summary of his life dates his reading of Schopenhauer at that time and reports that the essential part of it had been "a metaphysical delirium," which had to do with a "late and strong breakthrough of sexuality," and had been "more passionate-mystical than actually philosophical in nature." The experience had helped him then to take Thomas Buddenbrook to his death. All of this is very strange. What does the reading of the ascetic philosopher have to do with sexuality? What binds passion and mysticism together, and what idea of sexuality did the young man have, when he brings it immediately into contact with death? Even before Freud, Thomas Mann interpreted libido and the death wish psychoanalytically. What libido and the death wish have in common is the dissolving and loosening of bounds, the loss of individuation, and the reunion with the species. He had that from Schopenhauer, above all, and that is what he meant by passionate-mystical nature.

Of course, there are good reasons for the assumption that Thomas's reading of Schopenhauer's chief work, *The World As Will and Idea*, did not occur until the winter of 1899–1900, but that need not play a decisive role, since Thomas Mann knew Schopenhauer previously from Nietzsche, and the "metaphysical magic potion" could also take its ingredients from Nietzsche's essay "What Do Ascetic Ideals Mean?" This process corresponds exactly to the inversion by which Nietzsche turns the philosophy of his predecessor from its ascetic head onto its energized feet, when Mann first of all rejects asceticism as an answer and takes the emotional driving force of the world as the real declaration:

> It was not a matter for me about "wisdom," about the gospel of a reversal of the will through salvation, that Buddhistic-ascetic appendage, that I assessed life purely and polemically in criticism. What affected me in a sensual-supersensual way was the erotic, mystically unified element of that philosophy, which had not in the least determined ascetic Tristan music, and if at the time suicide stood very near to me emotionally, it was just because I had comprehended that it would in no way be an act of "wisdom."

In his essay on Schopenhauer of 1938 Mann heightens it:

> The eroticism of death as a musical-logical system of thought, born out of an enormous tension between spirit and sensuality— a tension whose result and the sparks leaping between them is eroticism—that is the experience of accommodating youth with this philosophy, which youth understands not morally but vitally, but personally—not according to its theory, I mean, not according to its sermon, but according to its nature—and which youth understands correctly.

But what does all of this mean? We look for the foundation of facts and are fogged in verbally between eroticism and metaphysics. But how did he live as a twenty-year-old at the time?

## KLÄRCHEN

While his childhood and youth can be reconstructed almost solely from retrospectives, we are better informed about the early time in Munich because from September 1894 until 1901 about seventy letters to his erstwhile fellow student Otto Grautoff have survived the years. However, some letters are missing, and others are cut to pieces, apparently to protect them from unauthorized curiosity. When in 1949

Thomas Mann learned that these letters still existed, he was startled and asked his informant to buy back the letters. "Since in some instances I instructed that they be destroyed, I cannot have wished that the communications fall into the hands of strangers." Since Otto Grautoff was the confidant of his passion for Williram Timpe, it is naturally possible that, as in the case of the burning of the early diaries, intimacies were the reason for the mutilations of these documents. "I consider them all as completely worthless," Thomas Mann wrote in the same letter, while we are glad that we have at our disposal at least a part of these fertile writings.

Thomas Mann frequently gave his autobiographically tinted writer-heroes a period of lasciviousness on the way to their maturity. "He had become young and crude with time" one finds out about Gustav von Aschenbach, the protagonist of *Death in Venice*. "I often indulged myself excessively, for my flesh was weak," Felix Krull admits. Of Tonio Kröger, who had been drawn to the cities of the south by the blood of his mother, it says that he had fallen "into carnal adventures" and descended far "into lasciviousness and burning guilt."

But Thomas Mann simply made those things up. The letters to his friend transmits not a trace of them. Since the adventures of the flesh and the descent into lasciviousness are also not expressed in any way in concrete terms in his fictional works, we do not have to take the author at his word. For example, prostitutes busy his thoughts, despite Rozsa, only with aversion—"To the servant girls and prostitutes, along with you I say with all my heart—'Disgusting!'" If he was familiar with this sphere, then the Knoop boarding house opposite the Aegidenkirche was probably repulsive to him. The Grautoff correspondence is familiar with the strongly erupting sexuality only from the point of view of a defensive battle.

> I say that you don't have to despise your nether parts, but you may do it gladly; I do it, too, you see. In recent times I have developed almost into an ascetic. In my fair hours I am enthused about pure aesthetic beauty, for the sensuousness of the spirit, for the mind, the soul, feelings in general. I say, let us separate the nether parts from love!

It is clear. We know only very little about love affairs from this period, but still more than nothing. Probably at the end of 1894 the poem "Look here, child, I love you," came into being; it appeared in January 1895 in *Die Gesellschaft*. Here a person wishes to maintain a philosophical superiority in the face of love but fears that it will not work in the long run:

> Look here, child, I love you,
> Nothing can be done;
> Let's just for a little while,
> Laugh at it and run.

> But sometime, unexpectedly,
> Things serious become—
> Look here, child, I love you,
> Nothing can be done!

However, nothing more is known about this "child." Perhaps she existed only in his fantasy. But exactly in his twentieth year, in the early summer of 1895, there was a small love affair. When Otto Grautoff suggests to him that he come to Berlin or Brandenburg, Thomas Mann postpones it. Among the reasons is "Klärchen":

> But in the end, and that's the most dubious point, there is here in Munich somewhere a girl who still has not received enough roses from me, and to whom, degenerate weakling that I am, I have not yet played Brackenburg enough. I have no desire to add to this hint. It depends on how long this foolishness lasts with me; I don't know at all.

We do have the wish to add to this hint. Sending roses lets us deduce a cultured relationship, probably to a middle-class girl. It would not have involved a prostitute or a servant girl. Playing Brackenburg points a finger at Goethe's drama *Egmont*. Pursuing that, something to some extent well founded can be said about this relationship. "Wouldn't you like to hold the skein of yarn for me, Brackenburg?" asks Klärchen at the beginning of the scene "Middle-Class House" in the first act. Brackenburg is a faithful fellow and loves Klärchen; she does find him good-hearted, but to her he is only a kind of brother. If she married Brackenburg, she knows that she would be cared for and would have a quiet life. But Egmont—"This small house is a Heaven, since Egmont's love dwells in it"—will be her death. Klärchen is infatuated with him, not with the holder of the skein of yarn: "Oh, what is a man!" She sings a song with Brackenburg, which ends with the couplet:

> What luck beyond compare,
> To be a real man!

Tears come into Brackenburg's eyes. He knows she does not mean him. He wants domesticity, she wants adventure, even at the cost of her femininity. "Were I just a boy and could always walk with him." Grand, socially impossible love stands in contrast to middle-class, orderly marriage.

The "degenerate weakling" evidently did not feel masculine enough in regard to his Munich girl. Possibly she found him nice, but there was no more than that. In any case, she was probably an individual to whom the young Thomas Mann felt inferior. We will encounter a similar pattern in the courting of Mary Smith and, to a certain degree, also of Katia Pringsheim, who will let him wait a long time before she accepts the engagement. The roses and the Brackenburg comparison lead us to deduce that at the time Thomas Mann was already keeping an eye open for a girl whom he could perhaps marry. He was probably too decadent for that at the time—at any rate he writes to Grautoff of a wave of feeling that seized the modern do-nothing at times, "when suddenly the yearning comes over him for a nice and sound existence among people—when the philistine in him rears up." But such moods went as quickly as they came, "and the good-for-nothing decadent quickly again gives up all claim to becoming something in the world."

The case did not develop as tragically as with Goethe. There was, of course, no Egmont present. The incident came to nothing after Tommy had set off for Italy. The last thing we learn is in the letter of July 10, 1895:

> The farewell from Munich is difficult for me for several reasons; but she wants to write to me.

## QUIET IN ALL THE CELLARS!

Let us remain in the time around his twentieth year and reconstruct a further hidden mini-love affair. "As in Venice at first, in surfeits of dream and rapture," Thomas Mann writes in hexameters in 1919 in "Song of the Child," "so did once more my heart surge in me, ten years later." Ten years later refers to Katia Pringsheim in 1904. "As in Venice at first" must refer to the end of October 1896; there must have been a love affair at the time. It involved a "princess of the East." Perhaps she, like Katia, was black haired with ivory shoulders, "which were shaped childlike and different from our women."

The slender young man found "fat women" repulsive. What appealed to him in women were the girlish and the chaste, the bridelike and the fairylike, the childlike and innocent, slenderness and long legs. There are numerous examples of that in his life and in his literary work, from his infatuation with the actress Agnes Sorma (1899) to Katia Pringsheim, from Gerda von Rinnlingen in *Little Herr Friedemann* to Gabriele Eckhof in "Tristan" and Clawdia Chauchat in *The Magic Mountain* to Rachel and Asnath in the Joseph tetralogy, from Rozsa and Zouzou in *Felix Krull* to Esmeralda in *Faustus*. Albrecht van der Qualen alias Thomas Mann dreams of the archetype as a fantasy in the wardrobe. In a flickering candlelight a young girl appears to him, totally naked, one of her slender, soft arms raised to the top of the wardrobe, with childlike shoulders from which such charm emanates that one can answer only with a sob. Her eyes are black and elongated. Her mouth is, to be sure, a little wide but with an expression as sweet as the lips of sleep when they sink down on our brow after a day of pain. . . . She keeps her heels tight together, and her slender legs are snug against one another.

The young author's first important work, the novella "Fallen," "a young work that makes you grimace because of its immaturity," is no exception. Its hero, Dr. Selten, shares with its creator some circumstances of life, such as the post-secondary-school move from North Germany to South Germany, writing poems, and listening to lectures. He has "touched no woman," he reports, embarrassed and constrained, because he "had not yet had an opportunity." Then he falls in love with Irma Weltner, a pretty actress; her role is that of the naïve lover. Her appearance fulfills the familiar expectations:

Childishly delicate figure, dull blond hair, docile, merry grayish blue eyes, delicate little nose, innocently sweet mouth, and soft, round chin.

Slender white arms and a high girlish voice complete the image. Irma yields to the young student, a romantic love develops. But one day the young man comes to realize that his friend, as was customary in her profession, takes money for the pleasures that she grants older men.

In considering how much in the story is real, let us again begin with what was characteristic according to the already frequently tried motto: He preferred finding to inventing. Characteristic are the kissing of the hand that turns from the formal to the insatiable, the lovesick kissing of the banister that she has touched, and that he wanted to tell his Mama all about it. It also fits the image of the Schopenhauerian theory of desire and the mysticism of unity that Dr. Selten is not aware of his behavior but follows a quietly strong necessity, that the looks become "deep, deep," and that the world falls away at the first kiss. Where the story turns to the sexual, there are small points of reference. He shudders "at how she, who had been a sublime goddess for his shy love, before whom he had felt always weak and clumsy and small, began to sway under his kisses."

We assume disappointment as a basic experience. A sublime ideal image must be besmirched in reality. Such a thing can easily happen when a yearning, but not very audacious, lover must see how with a fresh attack one more experienced takes the supposed fortress before which he has stood for a long time in reverence. It is kitschy but frequently occurs among shy people that no one says a clarifying word, not the woman, because she expects it from the man, not the man, because he wants to be tender and considerate, and that everything shatters against such an obstacle. Thomas Mann was bashful like his caricature Detlev Spinell, who looked aside when he was making love so as not to destroy a nice impression by his greed for reality. Such behavior does not encourage reciprocal love as a rule. "I loved a girl years ago," the unknown man says at the Piazza San Marco in the story "Disappointment," "but she did not love me—no wonder!": a classic situation.

One could easily damage Thomas Mann's claim to purity. "If one is in a condition to fall in love with waitresses and by means of ten-cent pieces inspire their love in return, then that's a matter of a delicacy or an indelicacy of soul," he writes to Grautoff. The *fabula docet* of the story "Fallen" is the yearning for such a delicacy of soul. "If a woman falls out of love today, she will fall for money tomorrow. I wanted to tell you that." Out of love: that's also falling. Love fortifies itself; that's the radical consequence.

"How I hate it, this sexuality." What can you do against it? You can, for example, every morning wash your whole body in cold water. "The latter does me a lot of good." Tommy gives his friend Grautoff the following comically precocious recipe along the way:

> A slow, cautious weakening of the urge and letting it evaporate is necessary, whereby all possible intellectual tricks help that the instinct for self-preservation suggests to one. In the end, one is much too much an homme de lettres and psychologist not to expect to have, in passing, one's superior pleasure in such self-treatment. Some kind of desperation would be senseless at your age. You have time, and the urge for quiet and self-contentedness will get the dogs in the cellar on their chain.

He decorates himself with false feathers for he has the "letting dry up" from Nietzsche. Also, the dogs already are growling in the essay that was basic for Mann's early thought: "What do ascetic ideals signify?"—"Quiet in all the cellars; all the dogs nicely on their chains."

From Naples Thomas Mann writes another revealing letter to the friend of his youth: "What am I suffering from?" he asks. "From sexuality . . ." he answers knowingly, but "will it destroy me? . . . How do I get away from sexuality? By eating rice?" He receives offers, also for catamites. "Here and there, among thousands of other sellers, slyly whispering dealers that ask you to accompany them to supposedly 'very pretty' girls, and not only to girls . . ." But they probably did not reach their target. "They won't quit, they walk along with you and praise their goods until you get rude. They don't know that you've almost decided to eat nothing but rice just to get rid of your sexuality!"

In spite of all the irony, all of this points in the same direction. The breakthrough of sex during the time around his twentieth year was met with a powerful effort toward asceticism. The young man was not happy about this. How could he be? "Deprivation is a tiresome creature, nothing in itself and devouring the little that the day might perhaps contain." The lasting pain of renunciation is turned into the Hell and Paradise of art—"for human privation is assuredly the source of a prophetic intuition, which for the sake of such a wretched origin is by no means less treasured." In the letter of October 25, 1898, again in Munich, Mann quotes August von Platen at length, with the hint that the following lines reproduced his present state with such beauty, clarity, and brevity that, instead of some other explanation he had not shied away from the effort of copying them down:

> So in the end I was quieter and cold,
> And now how much I'd rather like
> To see the world, as out of it, from far away:
> The fraidy heart has suffered
> Desire and fear and dread,
> It has suffered its share of pain,
> And it puts no trust in life;
> For omnipotent nature
> Was only the means
> To build itself a world with its own might.

## KNOWLEDGE IS THE DEEPEST TORMENT IN THE WORLD

In the tone of Platen, Thomas Mann writes a poem a bit later and hides it in a letter:

*Only One Thing*

> We, whom God gave a cheerless mood
> And showed all the depths where shame and dread
> Are always strangers in life to happy people
> Who harmlessly observe the play of existence.
>
> And because to plumb the human soul
> The urge has also captured me scornfully,
> Will I proclaim it to you all with heavy words:
> Knowledge is the deepest torment in the world.
>
> For there is one thing that in all suffering
> Strongly holds us uprightly on and on,
> A comforting game full of the highest, finest joys
> For the most unfortunate: It is the word.

That sounds as though knowledge would hurt. In reality the renunciation of life hurts, for life knows only those who are shut out of it. Only the lively and the vital are happy. "How calm and unperturbed did Herr Knaak's eyes look! They did not look into things to where they become complicated and sad; they knew nothing other than that they were brown and beautiful. But that's why his posture was so proud! Yes, one would have to be stupid to be able to strut about as he did; and then one would be loved."

"Happiness" is always stupid and unconscious. So it cannot be attained through calculation. "Love" is also in Thomas Mann the lovely work of a lack of knowledge. A love that is thoroughly understood is dead. An orgasm that analyzes itself doesn't even happen. "Every first movement, everything involuntary, is beautiful, and awry and altered is everything as soon as it understands itself."

Return to the naïve! is therefore the cry of desperation of the one who is knowing. He loves his dogs—to have something natural about him. But he himself is like Kleist's youth who lost his grace in front of the mirror.

Only a long life will teach him that the supposed destructive power of knowledge is faced by the much greater power of life to constantly bring up something new. There is always enough of the irrational left over. With all the sharpness of his critical comprehension and closures, Thomas Mann himself, seen in a larger perspective, is of a great naïve nature that unwaveringly followed his rules of life, which he was by no means able discerningly to select.

## ELBOW ROOM: LITTLE HERR FRIEDEMANN

During his last year in Lübeck, Thomas Mann was still a "runaway Bahrian." During his first years in Munich he became an artist. What he wrote before 1896 really does not count. There are too many emotional and sentimental passages, for example in "Fallen" or "The Will to Happiness." There is too much that is mediocre, such as the essays for *Das zwanzigste Jahrhundert*. There are too many kitschy poems, as "When evening's light is on the wane." Other stuff, probably also failures, is lost; even a sonnet must have been there, "the first in my life, but nice; Frau Holm was floating in delight." The correspondence with Grautoff mentions numerous unfinished works and work plans, such as the fairy-tale drama "The Old King," the novellas "Out of Pity," "Mama," and "Piété sans la foi," as well as a text, entitled "Antilocho IX," whatever that may have been. In addition, according to the Grautoff letter of January 17, 1896, there are also "In Moonlight" (Palestrina, August 1895), "Encounter" (Porto d'Anzio, September 1895), and "On the Psychology of the Suffering," probably an essay (Munich, December 1895). Further there was "Walter Weiler" as a preliminary stage of the "Bajazzo," and "The Little Professor" as possibly a preliminary stage of "Little Herr Friedemann."

He will have had reasons to destroy everything. Despite that, we would like to have read them, naturally. It is particularly a pity that "Walter Weiler" and "The Little Professor" are not preserved. Otherwise, from the revision, one would have been able to document in detail the artistic process of maturation during those decisive years. But his principal tendencies can also be deduced from the admonitions with which Thomas Mann attended the literary work of poor Grautoff, where he derides everything that he hates in himself. He particularly likes to skewer clichéd and unbelievable phrases:

> No matter how quiet and dignified your writing is kept, you can never prevent me from starting to laugh every time at figures of speech such as "until a swoon embraced my senses," even though you probably will forgive me.

He really laughs mercilessly. A kind of test of ridicule divides what is skilled from failure. It is the aesthetics of *Tonio Kröger* that is prepared unmistakably in those years, the aversion to what is emotional and sentimental, to what is bland and unironic, to what is foolishly serious and banal. A radically artistic viewpoint becomes clear. "I look at the world and myself neither with moral nor with medical but with artistic eyes," the twenty-one-year-old writes resolutely. He calls upon a view essentially different from that of Grautoff, "that is, an aesthetic one in contrast to a political one, and in an unendurable way also a moral one." He cites examples of Grautoff's prose and compares it with his own:

> "Spain, whose population the flood of gold had morally ruined"— that is a slap in the face to me. It goes: "Spain, whose old culture had become overripe with gold, wonderfully sweet and necessarily also rotten and ready to fall" . . . and today at most the president of a pan-German organization is permitted on such occasions to take a mouthful of morality.

But decisive for the awareness of the artistic breakthrough is the following realization:

Since "Little Herr Friedemann" I am suddenly able to find the discrete forms and masks in which with my experiences I can walk among people. Whereas before, if I wanted to confide even just to myself, I required a secret diary.

It seems to him so important that a bit later he repeats it again and clarifies it:

For some time it has seemed to me as though I had gotten my elbows free, as though I had found means and a way to say what is on my mind, to express myself, to realize myself artistically, and whereas I used to require a diary to unburden myself, though privately, I now find novella-like forms suitable for the public and masks to express my love, my hate, my sympathy, my contempt, my pride, my scorn, and my accusations . . . I believe that began with "Little Herr Friedemann."

He writes himself free. He becomes the great storyteller whom we know. He is glad that the time of immaturity is past. "I would not like to be 13 and also not 20 again." The confessional lyric is gone, we hear no more about gothic dramas. Since "Friedemann" his style is essentially ready. Into an advanced age he merely refines himself, extends and deepens himself, but no longer changes himself in principle.

## PRIMAL ODDS AND ENDS

What is Herr Friedemann supposed to mean; what's going on? We know little of "The Little Professor," the putative preliminary stage— only that it was finished in November 1894, and in January 1895 was submitted to *Die Gesellschaft*, in March 1895 to *Moderne Kunst*, both of which did not print it, and that the material and style was no longer Bahrian. The Friedemann story came into being in May 1896 and was finished in September of the same year. That "The Little Professor" is a preliminary stage of "Little Herr Friedemann" is a presumption that is based solely on the similarity of the titles. That Richard Dehmel considers the theme of "The Little Professor" ordinary in comparison with "Fallen" speaks against this presumption. At any rate, one cannot say in regard to the completed story that it has an ordinary theme. On the contrary. According to the writer's own statement, it

concerns the central motif of his entire creative life, about the primal
odds and ends of Thomas Mann that Erika Mann recognizes still in
the work of his old age, *The Black Swan*, when she says to her father
that all his love stories belong to the realm of the forbidden and the
deadly though he was, after all, a happily married man and sixfold
father. "Yes, yes," comments with a smirk the one so recognized.

His son Klaus has also "seen through him." Klaus's diagnosis is
clear as crystal. Thomas writes in his diary

> that the theme of "seduction" is so characteristic for magicians—
> in contrast to me. Motifs of seduction: romance—music—Wag-
> ner—Venice—death—"sympathy with the abyss"—pederasty.
> The suppression of pederasty as the cause of this motif. . . . Dif-
> ferent with me. Primary influence Wedekind—George.—Concept
> of "sin"—not experienced. Cause: realized. Pederasty. Intoxica-
> tion (even intoxication with death) always as an intensification of
> life, gratefully accepted; never as "seduction."

Seduction, sin, repression of pederasty: All his life it will "always be
the same," "primal odds and ends." In *On Myself* we find a passage
that explains everything, which for its part takes over a piece from
the novel *Joseph in Egypt*:

> But only many decades later, in the Egyptian book of my story of
> Joseph, did I once refer to the basic motif that runs through my
> entire work and to an extent holds it together, which the story of
> little Herr Friedemann first began: "How insignificant, compared
> with the depths of time of the world, is the view of our own past
> life! And yet our eye, focused on the individual and the intimate,
> loses itself just as dreamily afloat as did in its early and far-away
> times the eye more magnificently fixed on those of the life of
> mankind—touched by the perception of a unity that is repeated
> in it. As little as humanity itself are we able to penetrate back to
> the beginning of our days, to our birth, or even still farther: It lies
> in the darkness before the first dawn of consciousness and mem-
> ory—in the small view as well as in the large one. But right at
> the beginning of our intellectual activity, when we entered cul-
> tural life, as mankind once did, forming and bestowing our first
> tender contribution to it, we come upon a participation and pre-
> dilection that lets us feel and recognize that unity in happy aston-

ishment—and it is always the same: It is the idea of affliction, the incursion of drunkenly destructive and ruinous powers into a calm life with all its hopes sworn to dignity and a qualified happiness of composure. The song of victorious, apparently assured peace and of laughter-filled life sweeping away the true structure of art—of mastery and subjugation, of the arrival of the alien god—was at the beginning as it was in the middle. And at a late stage of life that indulges sympathetically in mankind's early days, we find ourselves once again held to that old participation as a sign of unity."

In the beginning as in the middle: The arc stretches from "Little Herr Friedemann" to "Death in Venice," the much later story of the coming of the "alien god." And what is the passion of Potiphar's wife for the young stranger, if not once again the collapse of a highly civilized composure tediously gained from insight and denial: the downfall of civilization, the howling triumph of the suppressed world of desire.

Herr Friedemann, hunchbacked and handicapped, has adjusted to a quiet existence without erotic fulfillment when Gerda von Rinnlingen enters his life, turns loose the dogs, and, "a Marshall Niel rose in full bloom" in her radiant hair, destroys his well-tended equilibrium. The celebrated artist Gustav von Aschenbach, accustomed to sublimate all his desires into artistic form, is shattered by his irrational love for the handsome boy Tadzio. The wife of Potiphar has previously led a priestly existence at the side of a castrated man when young Joseph enters her life, causing her immaculate state and her composure to be destroyed, although he does not do as she wishes according to the biblical example.

Thomas Mann's favorite flower was the Marshall Niel rose. He "is" Friedemann, the reading and violin-playing ascetic who has succeeded in chaining up the dogs in the cellar. The basic motif for his life and actions is fear of passion, fear that the carefully tended equilibrium of his life could tip over, fear of the return of what was repressed and the collapse of true construction of art. The psychoanalyst Krokowski in *The Magic Mountain* knows with pleasure how to make it perfectly clear. Only seemingly does the battle between love and chastity end with the victory of chastity. Fear, propriety, aversion born of modesty, a quivering longing for purity—they suppress love, hold it chained in darknesses. But this victory is only Pyrrhic, for the commands of love cannot be fettered, suppressed love continues to strive for fulfillment in darkness and what is deep secrecy; it breaks through the bonds of chastity and reappears, even though in a transformed shape.

In that letter to Grautoff from Naples on November 8, 1896, Thomas Mann gives a few hints about how he himself understands the Friedemann story. The mood that makes up the basic tone of the novella is "yearning for a neutral Nirvana, peace, and sinking into sexuality." Nirvana and peace on the one hand as well as sinking into sexuality on the other seem to be completely opposite things at first glance. But even before the explicit reading of Schopenhauer they combine as evidence of this philosopher and his eroticization of death. Sinking into death as well as sinking into sexuality lifts all separation into a Nirvana that knows no will. When Friedemann surrenders his opposition to love and throws away the structure of art of his previous life, he finds, although he knows that it will be his doom, an understanding with the silent, endlessly indifferent peace of nature. He shuts his eyes, "obedient to the exceedingly strong, painfully sweet power that cannot be escaped." Passion does not separate and differentiate but combines and releases like Death. Something obtuse and lifeless lies in his glance when he is ready to follow Frau von Rinnlingen, "a dull, powerless, and involuntary surrender." And so, since she does not yield to him, death also comes into play as an irresistible dissolving and erasing, as a powerless and involuntary surrender.

> On his belly he pushed himself still farther forward, rasied his torso and let himself fall into the water. He did not raise his head again; not even once did he again move his legs, which lay on the shore.

Thomas Mann survived. He did not surrender the structure of his art, not in the way he lived, but he did again and again in his writing. His lifelong fear of disaster is, however, the central motif that applies this impressive consistency to his life and his works. His great works are always stories of disasters. Personalities everywhere collapse under the assault of what is suppressed. Everywhere, from his early to his latest works, something kept secret is painfully obvious. In "Luischen" it is the corpulence of the fat lawyer Jacoby, which needs to be treated with care, that a lascivious, malicious woman drags into the public eye. Thomas as well as Tony Buddenbrook renounce real love in favor of middle-class order; the happiness in the lives of both is shattered by it. The asceticism of the prior in *Fiorenza* is only a product of the unsuccessful passion for the great courtesan Fiore. Prince Klaus Heinrich in *Royal Highness* experiences disaster as a shameful comedy at the citizens' ball, when after wild dancing with soapmaker Unschlitt's daughter he is caught at the end with the punch bowl lid on his head. In the case of Gustav Aschenbach the seduction is unveiled as homoeroticism and leads to his death. The outbreak of war in 1914 is also a disaster, a wild tossing overboard of civilization for the benefit of primal powers. In *The Magic Mountain* Clawdia Chauchat and Pribislav Hippe depict the temptation of chaos, release, and death. In "Early Sorrow" the world of a child falls apart through love. In the Joseph novel chastity is protected only with effort from the howling triumph of the suppressed world of desires. The tale of Moses, "The Commandment," dictates Jehovah's purity and order in opposition to the cult of Baal, but Moses himself is hot-blooded, slays an Egyptian in fury, and cannot resist the breasts of his Moorish woman. In *Doctor Faustus* the deadly deterioration of the hetaera Esmeralde overpowers the chaste and cool Adrian Leverkühn. In *The Holy Sinner* it is incest; in *The Black Swan* the late love of the already aging resigned Rosalie von Tümmler for young Ken Keaton destroys the artistic construction of life's orderliness. Only in *Felix Krull* does love remain unpunished, but as a fairy tale and wishful dream, by an artist and confidence man facing the dawning of renunciation of a reputable middle-class identity.

In the life of Thomas Mann seduction came principally from boys and young men. It was a matter less of the fear of passion in general than of the fear of homosexuality. That does not mean that the entire attraction of the stories might have lain in the depiction of this special fear. Of course, Thomas Mann was all his life afraid of being outed, afraid of stigmatization, of being recognized and branded. That is by no means everything. The literature of the marked man is, of course, set underway by this fear but does not remain on its fixed course, rather rises, making a virtue of necessity into what is metaphysical and religious. The changed figure of fear is the will to freedom, to a reality-free dream realm of childhood, to the independence from urges, to a redemption of "sin." For the Schopenhauerian there are two ways to liberation from the chains of sex: art and saintliness. Art is liberation from sex insofar as the world, observed purely, offers a

meaningful spectacle. Saintliness consists of disinterested observation
in which there is an end of wanting and the wheel of Ixion comes to a
stop. The artist must be an ascetic. "I don't believe that today someone could be a bon vivant and an artist at the same time."

A great work is more than just a result of its biographical sources.
The fear of disaster may in Mann's personal life have been fear
of homosexuality. But as readers, we may have entirely different
motives. Confused homosexuals are indeed an important group of
readers; we know this, for example, from Kuno Fiedler, who with
significant clarity writes to the novelist: "It is probably so that very,
very many people are grateful to you from their hearts for certain
confirmations—and then even especially grateful that you don't force
them to be clear about *what* has been confirmed for them through
you." But they are obviously not the only group of readers. Ascetics
of *all* stripes can feel at home with Thomas Mann. And not only those
of strict observance but all who abstain. In the final analysis everyone
has experienced the renunciation of urges, and the return of what is
suppressed is not to be found only in psychiatric clinics. No one man-
ages to get by in life without stabilization against infringing chaos;
each one has embarrassments to hide, and the fear of being revealed;
each one knows the fearful anxiety that lies in letting go, in falling out
of character, in the collapse of an identity that these days is more
delicate, more susceptible than it once was when middle-class roles
were more firm and could offer shelter for the chronically rootless
ego. To build a staunch structure of art as Thomas Mann does, to be
loyal all his life to a single publisher and to a single wife, to sacrifice
passion that would go beyond those limits, and to maintain this arrangement with tightly held stubbornness—it is cheap to brand that
as suppression; it is more generous to see the accomplishment of culture in it, the enchantment of suffering, and the passion in a great
body of work. We would not have this work, if Thomas Mann had let
his passion for youthful waiters take its uninhibited course. A neu-
rosis, too, is "a valuable part of the soul." (Use only as directed.)


## THE OPERA GLASS

He was as equally ruthless about the life of others as he was about his
own. He sacrificed himself, but he also sacrificed others. Charlotte

Kestner, born Buff, should from his viewpoint have been glad that Goethe made her into Werther's Lotte. She had to give a lot, but Goethe gave even more. "They sacrificed to the gods, and finally the sacrifice was God." In *The Beloved Returns* Thomas Mann will shape and explicate somewhat more in detail what he had been reproached for all his life: that he was a cold artist who exploited his fellow human beings, abused their trust, and made them mercilessly ridiculous.

Detlev Spinnel's fellow patients call him "the decomposed infant." Detlev Spinell is the name of the writer with a mania for beauty who in the story "Tristan" kills the tubercular woman with the help of art (the murder weapon: Wagner's dramatic opera *Tristan and Isolde*). His round, white, slightly puffy face is beardless, not shaved, "soft, blurry, and boyish, with only here and there a patch of down." In addition, Herr Spinell has an arched, swollen upper lip, large rotting teeth, and feet of a rare size. On his table a book is always lying "printed on a kind of coffee filter paper with letters, each one of which looked like a Gothic cathedral."

In 1900 the writer Arthur Holitscher was on fairly close terms with Thomas Mann; there had been a few confidential conversations. One day when Holitscher was leaving Mann's Schwabing apartment, he stopped for some reason on the street and looked back. "There, up in the window of the apartment that I had just left, I saw Mann, armed with opera glasses, gazing after me. It lasted only an instant; in the next the head disappeared from the window quick as a flash." In a conversation with Arthur Eloesser, Thomas Mann admits without hesitation that he had throughout his life indulged the desire to look down at the street; however, he disputes the opera glasses. He did own a pair, but he never used them. We think he is capable of having used them anyway. Finally, he also observed Katia Pringsheim with opera glasses, as Klaus Heinrich in *Royal Highness* did his Imma.

Then, when "Tristan" appeared, Holitscher at once recognized himself in the decayed infant and suddenly remembered "those opera glasses, which made an eye sharp by nature even sharper." However, he grinned and bore it and not until a few months later did he assert a few moral and artistic reservations toward those actions in a letter.

In *Bilse and I* (1906) Thomas Mann gives his reading of the incident. He does not deny that he had given his character "the mask of a literary man, whom I knew," "a gentleman with an exquisite talent but out of touch with life." But the work did not apply to him: "I was punishing myself in this figure, note that well." The man portrayed then also behaved grandly. "He came to me to shake my hand very heartily," but the gesture was too good for him; there followed what Schopenhauer calls egotistic remorse, remorse that applies not to bad but only to good actions. "He had tried to play the liberated man—he was not liberated. He had tried in vain to deceive himself and me about his true feelings. He fought and was defeated. Not long after, I received from far away a poison letter from him. And now, as I hear, he finds everything that I write is bad."

Who is right here? The figure of Spinell has an artistic necessity and it is of no importance who was involved as a model. Only a very bad (and besides, small, all-too-well-informed) public finds its most important pleasure in gloating over those portrayed. Everyone else sees the Spinell figure as the form of the modern artist par excellence, how he fails when faced with life. The large and general interest in the formation of this theme had to be weighed against the private interest of Arthur Holitscher. Thomas Mann is radical as an artist. "I would like to see a work of art observed as something absolute, out of the question for the middle class." It was extraordinarily difficult for him to forgo a point just to spare private interests. His wife was able to force him to do that sometimes. Hardly ever other people. Today we owe a great number of impressive characters to that radical bent. He looked into things "to the point where they become complicated and sad." That could not have been otherwise. The models were sacrificed to a certain degree, not from personal animosity but for the sake of the work.

Besides, not all of them were angry. Aunt Elisabeth is said to have been flattered when she was addressed as "Tony Buddenbrook." Her private life had, of course, become the property of the world, but she was proud of that.

## GENERAL DR. VON STAAT

"But I have no interest at all in political freedom," writes Thomas to Heinrich on February 27, 1904. "Did not the mighty Russian literature come into being under enormous pressure? Perhaps without that pressure would not have come into being at all?" So he continues, and thereby involuntarily proves that his not having any interest in political freedom means first of all in practice to praise the allure of the lack of freedom.

His Siberia is military service. Among his main memories of it belongs the feeling "of a frightful exterior force of power and, in connection with that, an extraordinarily heightened pleasure of inner freedom, as when I was in the barracks, maybe cleaning my rifle (which I never learned to do), I whistled something from *Tristan*." Nevertheless, he joined up willingly. Military service would be a good antidote for decadence. To Paul Ehrenburg he writes, expectantly:

> At the beginning of this month, and to be specific on the 6th (the matter deserves preciseness), in front of a highly respected high reserve commission to which I had the honor to present myself, I was designated as fit for all branches of the service, from which follows that on the 1st of October, to the horror of all enemies of the Fatherland, I will take up a shotgun. . . . What do you say to that? As for me (you may believe it or not), I am in complete agreement with it and assure you that the gloating and mocking facial expression, which you commenced from the second line of this paragraph on, is simply out of place. First of all, I realize that the German army would not last without me for long. But second, I, arrogantly decadent, imagine it as extremely refreshing for me to be recklessly and vigorously railed at for a year, for which I will give adequate cause. . . . No, joking aside, I am honestly glad that I have not been turned away again.

Who would have thought it! During the first days he looked really good. "He was in the bright blue dress uniform with the red collar, silver guard braids, shiny buttons, and black, gleaming sword belt, a really proper soldier." But that quickly changed. From the garrison hospital on October 24, 1900, Thomas informed his brother Heinrich that he had become an invalid because of his right foot, "which, something I never had an inkling of, is a flat foot and has gotten very bad because of the marching drills." The foot gives him a chance to escape. It ought to be blessed many thousands of times "for as the young doctors tell me, it will probably require Dr. von Staat to discharge me again after about 8 weeks. I just have to get pains in it again and again, they add with confidential cunning. They are two friendly young people who come to visit twice daily in the retinue of the chief doctor, know my works, and are always very polite."

Of course, a little help was necessary. "I hid myself behind Mama's doctor at the time, Court Councillor May, whom I used in the *Confidence Man* as Health Councillor Düsing, an ambitious ass who was a friend of my medical major." The major whispers with the captain, who had previously represented the concept of "Fit for Duty. Next," and "ordered him to see something that isn't there." The captain stands at attention.

The emphatically announced attitude toward state and government is mocking, to be sure, but not contemptuous. The forty-year-old remembers:

> As a boy I liked to personify the State in my imagination, imagined it as a stern, wooden figure in a tuxedo with a black full beard, a star on his chest, and furnished with a military-academic mixture of titles that was suitable to express his power and conformity, as General Dr. von Staat.

With all its irony, a certain respect speaks here. Accordingly, aggressive depictions of high representatives of the state are missing in the entire literary work. To understand the novel *Royal Highness* as a satire of His Serenity completely misses the point, for the book is monarchist, even if not in a stubborn sense, rather in a spirit of reform. It is not a hymn to democracy, and Heinrich is fairly correct when in his epistolary statement of January 5, 1918, he ridicules the characters of this novel as "inconsequential extras to represent the 'Volk.'"

His "I choose the monarchy" from the time of the First World War is therefore not a slip, but rather Mann's political confession from early on. In *My Time* Thomas Mann tells, not without emotion, that as a boy he had seen the old Kaiser Wilhelm—the aged fingers of the hand with which he waved filled up only a part of his white glove—the same thing applies to old Field Marshall von Moltke, who elicited significantly more passionate cheers than young Kaiser Wilhelm II, "the heir to the imperial throne glittering with medals set with diamonds." Felix Krull will have a long audience with the king of Portugal. "A man comes into the world with aristocratic senses," he assures him. He has previously explained to general manager Stürzli: "I find society charming the way it is and am dying to win its favor." Naturally, that is exaggerated and feigned. But it is characteristic of Thomas Mann that he does frequently assign his favorite characters conservative roles but hardly ever revolutionary ones.

Nothing can be established about an interest for liberalism, communism, or social democracy comparable to his monarchical interest in the time up to 1914. In *Buddenbrooks* the Revolution of 1848 is depicted with clear sympathy for the existing city government. The rebellious student Morten Schwarzkopf is a sympathetic young man, but politically a dreamer. It states that he revealed "a defiant expression in his good-natured eyes." The Socialist Party of Germany serves as a pedagogical nightmare. The school director raves: "You have all behaved like Social Democrats!" Everyone laughs, to be sure, but does not for that reason vote social-democratic by a long shot. The Free Thinkers Party "of Eugen Richter, the fat people's tribune," draws ridicule on itself; the phrase "free as Eugen Richter" burlesques the idler who is cobbling together tirades on freedom. That will be revived again later in civilization's literary man in the *Reflections* and in the Settembrini figure in *The Magic Mountain*.

Thomas Mann certainly wrote for *Simplicissimus* and *Die* Gesellschaft, publications that were held to be more or less rebellious. But what he wrote there was by no means oppositional, at any rate not in any kind of specific sense. It is therefore not so out of place that Thomas Mann for a good year (from August 1895 to November 1896) agrees to publish in a national-conservative magazine entitled *Das XX. Jahrhundert*, at the time edited by his brother Heinrich. Thomas wrote eight articles, mostly reviews, for this dubious product. They are by no means blatantly chauvinistic, but they are clearly based on the Wilhelminian power structures. The first defends the conviction for blasphemy that Oskar Panizza received because of his drama *The Council of Love*. The second begins: "A German song that is sung among foreigners—and yet on German soil"; he is praising Gardasee lyrics. The third, "Eastern Province Sounds," to set something against the "bacchantic howling" of Dionysian sentimentalists, lauds a collection of national songs, "that express warm love for the German fatherland and the German language." Apollo contra Dionysus: Nietzsche's foremost place for the twenty-year-old already shows its effect. Even though Mann mostly does not use his more mature level of language, the essay nevertheless contains such statements as: "Now it is quite certain that anyone who does not stand victoriously above his emotions is no artist, no expert, is not able to master them but merely tries to give vent to them with helplessly inarticulate sounds."

The fourth is called "Tirolean Sagas" and reports on superstitious folk stories of the devil and of the "God of the mountain people." The fifth, "A Patriotic Poet," contrasts Gourget's *Cosmopolis* with the dilettantically aestheticizing hedonist, an old Catholic and legitimist; its quintessence reads:

> Patriotic feeling today has again become a literary partiality, and what in Paris has to be nothing more than a decadent joke, a new form of Renan's piété sans la foi, has deeper roots in Germany, for the Germans, as the youngest and healthiest civilized people of Europe, are called upon as no other nation to be and to remain the bearers of love for country, religion, and sense of family.

The sixth contribution praises an author "who once dreamed of the equality of all men as an ideal, and who then learned to be enthusiastic at the appearance of forceful personalities." The seventh, "Criticism and Creation," is of a purely aesthetic nature, with the exception of a small, quickly withdrawn sideswipe at Georg Brandes who, observed as a private personality, "was a completely uninteresting free-thinking Jew." The eighth and last contribution portrays a nobleman with a real sense of honor.

Even if in all of this a course can without doubt be recognized, one must be cautious about all-too-strict judgments. Most of it seems immature, as though it were written as a role that the young author wanted to try out. How loosely the national-conservative mask fit can be recognized by the frivolous tone in which Mann derided the enterprise to Grautoff. The "rather foolish sheet," as he calls it, had showered him with a downpour of books to be reviewed. He always read only the blurb and then wrote, according to his mood, a kindly disposed or a scornful note. Of course, that is more than exaggerated, for first of all, none of his reviews are scornful, and second, after the letter just cited, there is only a single contribution, the eighth one mentioned above. But it does at least show that he did not want *to be thought of* as a chauvinist.

Of course, Mann does also speak to Grautoff in one place about the "very, very uplifting 'national movement,'" but that happens in a completely ironic tone:

> So Schleiermacher and Fichte don't have your approval? Well, that doesn't hurt anyone. But then your patriotic sentiments have probably not sufficiently gained enough strength, for no one can

be offended by a stumbling style; that is very, very unpatriotic. Read competent Reichstags speeches, get some fairly sanctimonious convictions, throw your good taste and your skepticism in the Havel River and embrace our treasured Fatherland with all your heart, as the poet sings with such unusual accuracy.

The patriotic contributor can thus make fun of the saints of the nation, Fichte, Schleiermacher, and Schiller, at the same time. (*For the Fatherland*, the treasured one: that appears in *Wilhelm Tell*.) How he really feels about being German we will take from a remark over beer and wine. For patriotic stuff makes a person tired,

> a dull pressure controls the mind, my eyelids are heavy, my limbs sluggishly fail in their duty, and a liter of marvelous Germanic beer has completely muddied my gaze. Oh, when I think of Chianti, darkly glowing, with which they filled my glass in Italy's *trattoria*!

Neither what was political nor what was patriotic was really urgent for him at the time. He obviously reacted very personally in this area, just as the mood took him, without earnestness, maturity, and deep reflection. His origins had given him a prevailing conservative bent that however was expressed only as vague mistrust of anything revolutionary and had not yet become a faceted crystallization of thought.


## ITALY

The praise of Chianti flows into an eruption of yearning.

> Oh that this summer, which is only now approaching, were already past! If only I could jump on the express train already, to gently sleep through Austria and, like Faust, awaken in "a pleasant region," where beautiful people in abundance called out their "Buon giorno" to me!
>
> For this Munich—have I never admittted it before?—how heartily weary have I grown of it! Isn't it the unliterary city par excellence?

Munich, once a city of artists in comparison with Lübeck, is no longer far enough away—the distance from his homeland must be greater still. Not only the monthly allowance, "which was better in Italian currency," was the cause, rather the will to freedom, the will to art. His main instinct was "to be off and away as far as possible from the German character, German concepts, German 'culture' into the farthest, most foreign South." No, *Das XX. Jahrhundert* must not be taken so seriously. First, Thomas Mann flees from the duties of his father's world into art, into Bohemia, to Italy. Italy is culture. Germany, on the other hand: "—I can't help it: this vague depth . . . this unsocial mediocrity, uncouthness, muteness, seriousness, and solitude of the cultural mode there." Only very gradually will his consciousness of his origins again prevail. "God, leave Italy out of this, Lisaveta," Tonio Kröger will say.

## "AMEN!" MEANS "ENOUGH!"

> When the chief pastor of St. Mary's in Lübeck, kneeling in his pastoral vestments by the deathbed of my father, indulged in loud prayers, after some restless turning of his head the dying man inserted an energetic "Amen!" into the pious nonsense. The clergyman did not let it bother him and actually even mentioned the Amen with praise in his eulogy, while it had at once been clear to me, the adolescent youth, it had meant nothing more than "Enough!"

The early Thomas Mann depicts the Protestant clergy as thoroughly ridiculous, dissembling, estranged from art, without imagination and without understanding; in complete contrast to the Catholic clergy, who are distinguished by style and elegance. The influential experiences come directly from Rome. "If I were to live here, I would probably become a Catholic," he says jokingly. "I was fond of visiting San Pietro, when Cardinal Rampolla, the secretary of state, read the mass in pompous humility. He was an extrordinarily decorative personality, and for reasons of aesthetics I regretted that his elevation to pope would be hindered diplomatically." In Munich also, the Catholic clergy could be carefully studied. That may have become part of *The Confessions of Felix Krull, Confidence Man*. "Spiritual Counselor Chateau was an elegant priest," we read there. The "cheerfully pleasant priest" understands the young man who lost his father, praises his pleasant voice, and predicts correctly that Fortuna will be well disposed toward him. The spiritual counselor, quite the contrary to his

Protestant counterpart, is an aesthete, and not in a profane sense but thoroughly on the basis of his religious dedication: "And anyone consecrated to administer the highest secret of this church, the mystery of Body and Blood—should he not be qualified because of a higher sensibility to distinguish between refined and base human substance?" Logically, Chateau is an aristocrat. Felix Krull emphasizes that affiliation with a venerable hierarchy, which the Catholic clergy represents, develops a perception for the gradations of human worth to a far subtler degree than does life in ordinary society.

The Catholic Church is of help against decadence—that is a further dominant motif. "The old Catholic," reports the twenty-one year old, in agreement with a novel by Paul Bourget, "shows the weary skeptic who strolls with him in the papal garden, the venerable figure of Leo XIII, in whom he sees the physician for the spiritual illness of his friend." The pope fascinates Thomas Mann into an advanced age. "I feel a fraternal sympathy not easy to explain." He writes a papal novel (*The Holy Sinner*) and seeks to have a private audience with Pope Pius XII. "Without the slightest inner resistance the Luther offspring, who by the way really cannot stand Luther, bends his knee before the white figure, deeply moved, and treasures that moment." He reports in his diary (May 1, 1953):

On Wednesday, April 29, a special audience with Pius XII, most moving and most intense experience that curiously continues to have an effect upon me. In the anterooms decorated in red, the meeting with Hutchins and Mortimer Adler, who had to wait until after my private audience. This while standing. The white figure of the pope stepping before me. Emotional genuflection and gratitude for the favor. Held my hand a long time. About the reason for my visit in Rome and my impression of the city, where one wandered through centuries. About Germany, obviously its most fortunate age and the reunification expected in time. Wartburg, his words about it and the unity of the religious world. Did not kneel before a man and a politician but before a spiritually gentle idol who brings to mind the two Western millennia. In leave-taking the presentation of the small commemorative medallion. "I don't know whether in remembrance I may perhaps . . ." Extending his hand. "Is that the ring of the Fisherman? May I kiss i?" I did it. Compliments on my work and dismissal. The

way back shown by the chamberlains in purple silk gowns. Standing through the audience reminiscent of Napoleon with Goethe
in Erfurt.

In reality, the visit, at least from the standpoint of the other side, is
said to have been much more fleeting. It may have lasted only a quarter of an hour. There is even doubt about whether it was a conversation between only the two of them and not, rather, a reception for a
small group. Also "an audience while standing" was naturally not a
distinction, as Thomas Mann movingly leads us to believe in remembering Goethe with Napoleon, rather the opposite. But the need was
so great after the crowning of his life with a reception by the highest
authority in the world (that's how he must have taken it), that he took
refuge in small cosmetic corrections. The rounding out of the structure of a life becomes a strong motif again. On the way back to his
hotel he passes the place where, at the beginning of his life almost
sixty years before, he had asked an arrogant prelate about Cardinal
Rampolla. "How different it is now!" he comments. "O strange life,
led up to now as by no other, suffering and incredibly uplifted."

   Earlier, the note in the diary reports: "Similar behavior toward the
Catholic Church as toward Communism. Not a word against either of
them! Let others be zealous and fear theocracy and censure." Because
Mann was a lover of communism, the curia originally wanted to
block the audience. They were not badly informed in those circles.
They liked neither communists nor Protestants. But they underesti-
mated this Protestant. He should have deserved a long private, seated
audience.

   But the chief pastor of St. Mary's—he was named Paul Emil Leopold Friedrich Ranke—was an enemy. He called the Mann family
"degenerate." That goes into *Buddenbrooks* unchanged. "Recently, after
the confirmation class, Pastor Pringsheim said to somebody that they
should give up on me, that I came from a degenerate family." What
Ranke would do, if Grautoff should give up his bookdealer apprenticeship, Thomas Mann caricatures meanly but probably accurately:

   He pulls a long face, snorts through his nose, and says: "Oh God,
   my son! You want to leave a profession that God put you in?"

Pastor Pringsheim, as Ranke, appears at the deathbed of Senator Buddenbrook. He is castigated in accordance with all the rules of art:

Wearing half his vestments, without his clerical ruff but with his long robe, he appeared, glanced at Nurse Leandra with a cold, fleeting look, and at the bed kneeled down on a stool that was pushed up to him. He asked the sick man to recognize him and to lend him an ear for a time, but when this attempt remained futile, he turned directly to God, talked to Him in his stylized Franconian dialect and spoke to him with a modulating voice in now vague, now abruptly emphasized vowels, while on his face dark fanaticism and mild transfiguration took turns. . . . While he rolled his R in a peculiarly rich and skillful way, little Johann got the distinct impression that he must just have had coffee and buttered rolls.

Young Thomas, as a child and a youth, received the customary religious education. Prayers at table were taken for granted, at least in the house of his grandparents on Mengstrasse. Sundays Thomas had to go to religious services, and in his old age he still remembers that the sermon in the Marienkirche began always with "Grace be with you all!" He was confirmed, even though that experience left hardly any literary traces behind, and we therefore have reason to assume that the incident occurred without leaving an impression. Afterward, he avoided religious services. But he would have been married in church, had his father-in-law not been so decisively opposed to it. His children, naturally, were baptized and confirmed. But the parents left praying with them up to the maids.

## A SCAVENGER

The religious experiences of his childhood left behind numerous traces. "A joyful faith has been a legacy in our family," his father stated in his will. The psalm made into a song by Paul Gerhardt, "Entrust Your Paths to the Lord," is written by the twelve-year-old into the autograph album of a fellow student. The "inner power of Lutheran hymns," which Thomas Mann praises once in 1895, comes across otherwise, principally as farce and parody. In a dreadful voice that sounded like the wind trapped in the chimney, "Though Satan should devour me" (a line of verse from "Now all the woods are quiet") rings out on the "Jerusalem Evening." In the Paul Gerhardt hymn "Now Let Us Go and Tread" one couplet reads: "Give to me and all of those, with longing in their hearts. . . ." "When T.M. learned to pray," his daughter Erika wrote, "nearby Denmark was still an enemy to Lübeckers, and since 'Dänen' [Danes] was pronounced like 'denen' [the word in German for *to those*], the pious wish rubbed patriotic Tommy the wrong way." The novelist allows himself a joke with the devotions in the Buddenbrook house when he forces those present to sing the following words to a solemn, staunchly faithful, and deep-felt melody:

> I am a lowly scavenger
> A crippled, limping sinner,
> Foul, rancid sin I did prefer,
> And gorged it down for dinner.
> Oh Lord, please cast a bone of grace
> Before this dog so lowly;
> This bestial sinner, first abase,
> To rise then clean and holy.

Thomas could not have heard this in his childhood, at least not at devotions, at best in a cabaret, for that's where it belongs. It cannot be found in any hymnal of the time.

Thomas Mann also caricatures the blessing at table satirically. "Hans Castorp folded his freshly washed hands and rubbed them together contentedly and expectantly, as he usually did when he sat down at the table—perhaps because his forefathers had prayed before their soup." That is in *The Magic Moutain*. In *Buddenbrooks* unctuous repleteness, which tries to exculpate itself by means of prayer from the ongoing demands of the poor, is unmasked. What is corporal is in denial, as frequently the spiritual is also:

With heaftfelt expression the senator's wife said the traditional grace:

> Come, Lord Jesus, be our guest,
> what Thou hast given us be blessed.

To which she added, as was likewise customary on this evening, a few admonishing words that in the main demanded that all of them think of those who were not so fortunate as the Buddenbrook family on this Holy Evening. . . . And when this was taken care of, they sat down with a clear conscience to a long meal that began at once with carp in melted butter and with an old Rhine wine.

Also Frau Permaneder (Tony Buddenbrook) prays; the narrator is, however, interested only in her lovely posture. Thomas Buddenbrook, on the other hand, does not pray, though he cites prayers when it goes badly for the family and the firm: "Believe me—believe this one thing: Were Father alive, were he here with us, he would fold his hands and commend us all to the grace of God." Only after his reading of Schopenhauer, who was too much for his middle-class brain, does he fall back into the faith of his childhood. Apparently, the narrator does not find that praiseworthy:

> But it so happened that Thomas Buddenbrook, who had stretched out his hands yearningly for lofty and final truths, sank back weakly to the concepts and images, the faithful use of which they had been drilled in since childhood. He walked around and recalled the only and personal God, the Father of mankind, who had dispatched to Earth a personal part of Himself so that He could suffer and bleed for us, Who on Judgment Day would hold court, and at Whose feet the righteous would be rewarded for the troubles of this vale of tears in the course of eternity just beginning . . . this whole, somewhat unclear, and a bit absurd story, which required however no understanding but only obedient faith and which would be at hand in firm and childish words, when the last agonies came. . . . Really?

## BUT THE LITTLE HUNCHBACK, TOO

At first glance the satirical perspective predominates in the theme of religion. Religion serves as a torment for children, like instruction in the catechism at the beginning of *Buddenbrooks*. But there is another side. In a friendship album for Ilse Martens, Mann answers the question in 1895 about his favorite hero in history surprisingly with: "Christ." How does he mean that? At the time, among his favorite authors was Ernest Renan, who had become famous for a demythologizing *Life of Jesus* (first published in 1863). That fits the Renan-inspired title of a planned novella, about which we know nothing otherwise: "Piéta sans la foi." Piety without faith: that was it, that's what he was about; he found that modern. "Piéta sans la foi is the most fashionable thing in Paris now."

Little Hanno also prays, though typically not from a prayer book, but from *The Youth's Magic Horn*; he recites not what is prescribed by the church and the middle class but "The Little Hunchback." The motif of his praying is the horror of reality, such as it is, of the "mystic, sad, and interesting vileness of the work of seven days." Hanno's "pavor nocturnus" goes back to that horror. He speaks in a dream with a heavy tongue (we supplement what he merely indicated by babbling):

> To my garden I will go,
> Onions and sweet peas to sow;
> There a little hunchback stands,
> Sneezing, waving little hands.
>
> To my kitchen I will go,
> To warm my soup up hot;
> There a little hunchback stands,
> Has broken up my pot.
>
> To my little room I go,
> To eat the porridge in my cup;
> There a little hunchback stands,
> Has eaten it half up.
>
> To my attic I will go,
> For kindling for my fire;
> There a little hunchback stands,
> Has stolen half of it entire.
>
> To my cellar I will go,
> To tap my keg of wine;
> There a little hunchback stands,
> Grabs a glass of mine.
>
> I'll sit down at my little wheel,
> To spin my threads to sew;
> There a little hunchback stands,
> Won't let the wheel go.
>
> To my chamber I will go,
> To make up my little bed;

There a little hunchback stands,
And laughs at me instead.

To my prayer stool I will go,
And there I start to pray;
There a little hunchback stands,
There's something he would say:

Little child, oh, I do beg you,
Pray for the little hunchback, too!

First he ruins everything, and then he wants to be included in the prayer! Hanno says to his nursemaid, "He doesn't do it to misbehave, does he, Ida; not to misbehave. . . . He does it because he's sad and then he's even sadder about it. . . . When we pray, then he won't have to do all that anymore." If Hanno prays for the little hunchback, then it is because he identifies with this behavior, which is destructive from the middle-class viewpoint but in a higher sense desperately honest activity. Pots, onions, spinning wheel, mush, and wine: an orderly household is, in the final analysis, a philistine matter and cannot satisfy the deepest longings aimed at one or another solution. There is a nihilistic religiosity in the early Thomas Mann, a religiosity of desperation. It has nothing to do with the ecclesiastical offices that grovel before society.

"I believe," Walter Benjamin writes, "that that 'whole life' about which it is said that it passes through the mind of the dying, consists of such images as those the little hunchback in us all has." The little hunchback does not judge from the standpoint of middle-class society but from that of death. When passages occur in Thomas Mann that reveal religious perplexity, death is always involved. Pastor Ranke is criticized because he is a hypocrite and cannot summon up such perplexity. "Just what is the religious?" Mann asks in 1931 and answers firmly:

The thought of death. I saw my father die, I know that I will die, and that thought is the most personal to me; it is behind everything that I think and write.

So deaths in life as in fiction are completely shattering, also in regard to religion, in contrast to the failure of the churchly custodians of death. Without mockery Thomas Mann tells about the mystical moment of the death of the consul's wife, Elisabeth Buddenbrook, née Kröger, after long, terrible suffering.

> At five-thirty a moment of peace came. And then, quite suddenly, a twitch passed over her face, aged and torn by suffering, a quick, terrified joy, a deep, shuddering, frightful tenderness, quick as a flash she spread out her arms, and with a tremorous and unexpected quickness that one felt—not a second lay between what she heard and her reply—she cried aloud with the expression of unconditional obedience and a boundless fearful and loving submissiveness and surrender: "Here I am!" . . . and died.
>
> Everone was startled. What had that been? Who had called out, so that she had immediately followed?"

Who had called out? For the pious, the answer is clear: Christ. A Latin prayer of the Middle Ages pleads: "In hora mortis voca me!" Call me at the hour of my death. In the translation by Angelus Silesius it became a death song. The last stanza begins: "Call me in my last affliction / And seat me beside Thee, my God."

True religiosity has nothing to do with Pastor Ranke's zealous ceremonies. It is un-middle-class. It throws things off track, as do love and death and art. Art, too. At the beginning of May 1895 Thomas Mann experiences a religious event at a production of Goethe's *Faust* (the beginning of the letter is missing):

> . . . hundreds of angels. A gold staircase leads upward into the boundlessness, and above, one sees the Holy Child in her arms, the Mater dolorosa; at the foot, the late Faust; in the middle, Gretchen. And from soft choruses one hears the celestial verses:
>
> > All that is transitory
> > is only a symbol;
> > what seems unachievable
> > here is seen done;
> > what's indescribable
> > here becomes fact;
> > Woman, eternally,
> > shows us the way.
>
> Perhaps it is ridiculous; but I became pious and devout in my mind at this electrically illuminated glimpse into the metaphysical.

"Perhaps it is ridiculous"—he's a bit ashamed; religious elements are mentioned. Public piety particularly is embarrassing, as in Tony's prayer at the deathbed of her brother:

> At five o'clock Frau Permaneder was carried away by a thought-less act. Sitting opposite her mother-in-law at the bed, she began suddenly, using her throaty voice, to say the words of a hymn. . . . "Bring now, O Lord," she said—and everyone listened motionless to her—"an ending, to all our pain and woe; Thy strength and mercy sending, the grace of death bestow . . ." But she was praying so deeply from the bottom of her heart that she was occupied only with the words she was then saying and did not consider that she did not at all know the end of the stanza and after the fourth line she had to stop helplessly. She did that, broke off with an elevated voice, and replaced the conclusion with the heightened dignity of her stance. Everyone in the room waited and shrank together with embarrassment.

"Bring Now, O Lord" is the beginning of the twelfth and last stanza of Paul Gerhardt's hymn "Commend Thou All My Griefs." What Tony must replace through the heightened dignity of her demeanor reads in its context:

> Bring now, O Lord, an ending,
> to all our pain and woe!
> Thy strength and mercy sending,
> the grace of death bestow.
> Grant us Thy care in need
> and faithfully commended,
> then all our ways will lead
> most surely into Heaven.

In the course of the novel, from generation to generation, the religious depths increase; what is religious sinks like a stone into the depths of a well. Its expression becomes more and more ashamed, concealed, and suffocated. Old Johann Buddenbrook is cheerful and earthy; the theme does not concern him. Of his son, they already say that "with his enthusiastic love for God and the Crucified Man, he had been the first in his family who had known and practiced uncommon, middle-class, and indiscriminate feelings." Again, concerning his sons (Thomas and Christian) one discovers that they were the first "who shrank back sensitively from the frank and naïve appearance of such feelings." For Thomas, the grand words, mixed with tears, with which Tony loved to speak after the main course and before dessert about the death of her father, are "embarrassing to the highest degree." That does not mean actually that he was unaffected. He responded to such effusions with tactful gravity and composed silence, but "at the very moment when no one had mentioned or thought about the deceased, his eyes would slowly fill with tears without the expression on his face having changed." In the end, Hanno prays for the little hunchback.

# IV. Thomas and Heinrich

*Self-portrait, Christmas 1897, dedicated to his brother Heinrich*

The brothers spent their childhood until 1889 together, when Heinrich at eighteen left school, began a book-dealer apprenticeship in Dresden, and, from April 1891 on, entered service with Samuel Fischer in Berlin as a trainee. Nevertheless they saw one another occasionally. Heinrich frittered away the summer vacation of 1893 with Thomas, and in the early summer of 1894, they were together in Bayreuth.

The death of his father on October 13, 1893, made Heinrich financially independent, so that from 1892 on he could begin an eventful roving life as a freelance writer. His principal places of sojourn were Berlin, Lausanne, Paris, Florence, and Rome, as well as Riva on the Gardasee, where he frequently spent time in a sanitarium because of his weakened lungs. Until 1914 Heinrich had no fixed place of residence. His first novel (*In a Family*) appears in 1894. It is followed by novellas, then the novels *In the Land of Cockaigne* (1900) and with greater success the Renaissance trilogy *The Goddesses* (end of 1902).

The brothers' highest concentration of time together is from 1895 to 1901. From July until October 1895 they for the first time spend several months together in Italy (Palestrina and Rome). In 1895–96 Thomas works on the magazine edited by Heinrich, *Das XX. Jahrhundert*. Thomas's second Italian sojourn from October 1896, until April 1898, brings at times briefer meetings, at other times shared living arrangements for months. On the trip back from Florence in the spring of 1901 Thomas spends a few days with Heinrich in the sanitarium of the alternative physician Dr. von Hartungen in Riva on the Gardasee, which contributes characteristic details for "Haus Einfried" in the story "Tristan" (finished in June or July 1901). Extensive cure sojourns follow in Mitterbad (July–August 1901) and Riva (November and December 1901).

Thomas emerged more and more from the shadow of his brother. The sales success of *Buddenbrooks* (appears, 1901) soon considerably exceeded Heinrich's printings. The younger brother becomes self-confident. At the end of 1903 he criticizes his brother's novel *The Hunt for Love* so fiercely that the discord is patched up only with difficulty. *Professsor Unrat*,* too, (appeared, 1905), one of the best of Heinrich's novels, does not satisfy the demands of his brother. Family matters also come up. Heinrich distances

* Filmed as *The Blue Angel*, with Marlene Dietrich. (Trans.)

himself from the all-too-middle-class marriages, in his opinion, of his sister Julia (1900) and of his brother Thomas (1905). Conversely, his fiancée for a time, Ines Schmied (after 1905), is able to gain the sympathy of the family as little as later the Prague actress Maria Kanová, whom he marries in 1914. The couple settle down in Munich.

Their relationship remains cooperative but always tense. After about 1904 Heinrich moves from his original more apolitical-conservative views toward politics, liberalism, and democracy (*The Small Town*, novel, 1909, *Spirit and Deed*, essays, 1910). Thomas sees this with consternation. Although the suicide of their sister Carla, with whom Heinrich had a very close relationship, again strengthens the solidarity of the rest of the family, the tensions finally erupt when Thomas in the fall of 1914 takes the side of the German nationalistic enthusiasm for war. For years the contact between the brothers is broken.

## PAPA'S DEATH AND GOODWILL

THEIR FATHER had little confidence in his sons when in his will he took the firm away from them, but in doing so he also relieved them of a burden. They owe him this and want to show themselves worthy of their release. What he might well have said about this remains an important motif in decisions throughout their lives. In their memoirs they compete for the goodwill in the hour of their father's death. Both claim to have been especially close to him before the end. Heinrich later writes that the dying man had told the twenty year old "what he had long thought but kept silent: 'I want to help you' become a writer: it was clear to both, each had kissed the other's hand; he kisses it even today." But Thomas remembers "the unforgettable scene in my youth when H. had run away from his fatally ill father, who had come out onto the stair half-landing, while I conversed with him, for which Papa thanked me at his farewell" (Diary, May 25, 1919).

Thomas Johann Heinrich Mann died at the age of fifty-one from cancer of the bladder. "I would so much like to have remained with you," he said on the day he died. Certainly everything would then have turned out quite differently. For his second son, at any rate. Would he then have become a merchant after all, as the poet Jean Jacque Hoffstede suggests for the young Buddenbrook? "Thomas, now, he has a sound and earnest head; he must become a merchant, there's no doubt of that. Christian, on the other hand, seems to me to be a little jack- of-all-trades, don't you think? A bit *incroyable.*"

## IN INIMICOS

"I have become as I am," he said finally, and his voice rang with emotion, "because I didn't want to become like you. If I have avoided you profoundly, then it was because I must guard myself against you, because who and what you are is a danger to me. . . . I am speaking the truth."

These words are said by Thomas Buddenbrook at the end of a bitter quarrel with his brother Christian. They can be applied to Thomas and Heinrich Mann. Of course, Christian Buddenbrook is considered to be a portrait of Uncle Friedel, but that is only a small part of the truth. Beyond that, the figure of Christian has important traits of Heinrich, mirrored in the anxieties of Thomas. When Christian loses face, insecurely concerned about his precious ego, it reflects Heinrich's recalcitrance toward his parents' home but also the fear of his brother of likewise falling out of his role. When Christian runs around with ladies of the demimonde, Heinrich's association with prostitutes and the contempt of the ascetic Thomas for someone who gives his desires free rein are reflected. When Christian Buddenbrook, in spite of his little aches and pains in the novel, outlives his brother Thomas, Thomas Mann's anxious misgivings are haunted by the idea that the frantic impeccability of his way of life is perhaps less healthy than letting himself go.

"The brother problem still appeals to me," Thomas writes to Heinrich on December 5, 1905. His work is full of pairs of brothers, from Thomas and Christian Buddenbrook to Klaus Heinrich and Albrecht in *Royal Highness*, to Grigorss and Flann in *The Holy Sinner*. The great *Joseph* epic is in the final analysis a novel of brothers, even though Heinrich does not directly appear in it.

A brother four years older, who daring and recklessly left school before graduating to begin a book-dealer apprenticeship, who entered S. Fischer, the rising publisher of literary modernity, as a trainee, who visited lectures as an auditor at the Berlin university, who began to write early on and rebelliously, was of course a model for Thomas for a time in regard to independence from the demands of school, his parental home, and society. Thomas admired Heinrich, while his big brother in contrast looked upon him with scorn and disparagement. Gentle, vulnerable, needing love, Thomas was defenseless against the merciless arrogance of his brother. That he was the weaker spurred his literary ambition. In literature he would avenge himself for what he suffered in his life. It is difficult when one is the younger and finds the place at the goal already occupied. The competition is even more subtle when the longed-for place is not that of heritage but that of the opposition. Thomas, too, had fallen out of the role of his forefathers and become a literary man. In a highly uncertain landscape he had to establish himself next to someone already successful. The necessity of differentiating himself literarily was elementary. Before the skill necessary for that was developed, years, of course, passed by.

In those years it was apparent that, as an opponent, Heinrich could not be bested. So only the conservative role remained for Thomas. While by the end of 1904 he went to Lübeck to give a reading and sought a reconciliation with his hometown, Heinrich left the scene of his childhood in 1893 once and for all. But Lübeck was very important for Thomas. "Tommy likes to hear about Lübeck," Heinrich writes to Ludwig Ewers on October 17, 1909.

In addition there was the sexual difference. When Thomas found out how scornfully Heinrich judged his beloved poems, he must have been very hurt. He needed understanding and discretion. The tactless chatter that the letters of young Heinrich to Ludwig Ewers attest to must have offended him. It would have caused him to conceal himself better in the future. The virtuosity of camouflage is also due to the competition with Heinrich.

Only a part of the correspondence has survived the all-too-eventful times. The first piece of writing preserved is dated October 1900. But there must have been letters right after Heinrich's departure for Dresden. When, not yet fourteen, Thomas reports that Heinrich's poems had been read aloud at home "to great applause." Whether these early letters are lost or did not seem worth keeping by Heinrich from the first is not known. Also the replies before 1933 are, with few exceptions, not preserved. Possibly they disappeared with the numerous papers that remained in Munich in 1933.

A correspondence comes into being only when people are separated by distance. As a result they leave out the most intense personal events. The time in Italy, from which we have no letters, was such a time. The brothers planned several works together. Apparently, *Buddenbrooks* also was included at first. They would have had the same secret thoughts, Heinrich recalls in *An Epoch Is Observed*. "We had wanted to write a book together. I was the first to speak, but he was already prepared." Reminiscing from the time of his honeymoon trip, Thomas ruminates that everything was the result of the fact

> that back then in Palestrina we had conceived a kind of "gipper" novel that originally was to have as a leitmotif the beautiful song "The Bus Drives through the City." And in the end it was to be the bus that carries Biermann to prison.

*Buddenbrooks* came out of that. The scandalous Biermann was a con man who had married into the Mann family. In the novel he appears as Hugo Weinschenk, who weds the daughter of Tony Buddenbrook but then has to go to prison for fraud. Obviously, the story of the family was to be told from the perspective of suppressed embarrassments. The expression "gipper" is attested also from the correspondence with Grautoff and means a kind of mockery about everything, an intelligent fooling around full of ironic superiority but without a concrete satirical point. It probably also described the tone of another work, done jointly, which came into existence, but since 1933 has unfortunately been lost, the *Picture Book for Good Children*. The witty little work was written for the younger siblings Julia, Carla, and Viktor and followed the secret goal also of shaking them up in their middle-class security. It made a deeper impression on none of them more than on the youngest brother, Viktor, who even in his old age could recite large parts from memory. A secondary school teacher, Dr. Hugo Giese-Widerlich, with a mischievous expression, the mouth of a fish, thin beard, and a two-row, high-buttoned coat, figures as editor. Drawings, pictures, ballads followed. Thomas at that time also revealed a later neglected talent in drawing. The high point was the Schiller parody, *Robber and Murderer Bittenfeld Overwhelmed by Sunset*. Erika remembers the criminal's name as Bubenhand, not Bittenfeld. Only a few fragments have come down; one of them reads:

> Rogue, the time for you is set,
> Your gaze a nobleness to get,
> With tears your austere cheek is wet
> And grief-torn bones corroded get.
> That tear, from Eden comes that token,
> Rogue, does it mean you're not completely broken?

So the brothers found themselves in satires, grotesques, and parodies. In other words, they found themselves in Heinrich's territory. Gradually a very different style of work developed in Thomas, one that was more ironic, more psychologically realistic and more aesthetic, not aggressive but rather more elegiac, as in the novel of decadence.

The brothers lived together many months in Italy, but nevertheless each of them then wrote his own book. In the case of Thomas, it was *Buddenbrooks*; in the case of Heinrich, it was *In the Land of Cockaigne*. Both novels were begun in Rome in 1897. Heinrich jumped for joy when the talent came upon him. "The rooms in the old Roman houses have a false ceiling of painted paper under the real one: Mice run between the two. It wasn't high; my head truly bumped against the yield of the covering fabric. This small detail impressed on my memory that moment of joy for my whole life."

Certainly they must have talked about a lot of things. Later in his autobiography Heinrich wrote that he had been able to make a contribution to his brother's book. Whether and to what extent they afforded one another a look into their work is another question. Early on it came to jealous reproaches of having stolen one another's motifs. We know something about that from Thomas's letters. "In Riva, in the rowboat," apparently in December 1901, there must have been a scene of that sort because Heinrich had exploited his brother's idea for a novel, "The Lovers," in his own *Goddesses* "in a superficial and grotesque way." We can gather another exchange of words from that time from the *Reflections of a Nonpolitical Man.*

> "You spend too long with the criticism of reality," I heard from nearby. "But you will arrive at art anyway." At art? But criticism of what is real, of plastic morality, is the very thing I felt as art, and I despised the programmatically dastardly gesture of beauty that the virtue of today tried to encourage in me at the time.

But even earlier, in 1897 in Rome, there had been a quarrel. In his draft of a letter of January 5, 1918, Heinrich gives a snapshot of a memorable incident: " 'In inimicos,' you said, at twenty-two, sitting at the piano on the via Argentina trenta quattro, with your back to me. So you haven't changed."

## LORENZO AND THE PRIOR

Their anxiety about competition was not without foundation. Both were busy with the Renaissance at the same time. Heinrich's first great success was the novel trilogy *The Goddesses,* in which the Duchess of Assy, bristling with inner fervor, devotes herself to freedom, art, and love one after the other and counters the cult of the "hysterical Renaissance" inspired by Nietzsche's theory of the superman with a weakly decadent present. But since 1900 Thomas had done research for the Renaissance drama *Fiorenza,* which lets the morality of the ascetic Savonarola triumph over the cult of beauty of the fatally ill

Lorenzo de Medici, called the Magnificent. Lorenzo calls the monk his brother. All the other artists do not count at the hour of death. There is only a single person of equal rank. "You have risen beside me and breathe as high as I . . . You hate me, you reject me, you work against me with all your art—lo, and I, I am not far away from calling you my brother in my heart." Savonarola delivers him a rebuff that could be from Thomas himself: "I don't want to be your brother. I am not your brother." He wants hostility, wants competition. "You should not admire me, you should hate me!" Thomas hated. "You hate where what you despise achieves power," he notes in the seventh *Notebook*. The hate of the ascetic is not ultimately valid to the one who is erotically superior. Savonarola's dark secret is that he once had desired the courtesan Fiore but had been rejected. On the other hand, Lorenzo had possessed her. With that, the prior's asceticism is refuted in its core. It is not freedom from desire but is forced by a sickness, by the impossibility of achieving the sexual goal. He is no angel, but a sinner. "No flesh is pure. One must know the sin, feel it, understand it, in order to hate it. The angels do not hate the sin; they are unknowing." But Thomas Mann hates like one who knows sin.

The courtesan is called Fiore, the city Fiorenza. Since Fiore escaped him, the prior's intent now is to subjugate Fiorenza. He wants to gain power over the mob. The dream of power is a substitute for the dashed dream of love. He wants at least to rip the people away from Lorenzo, who has both Fiore and Fiorenza. Lorenzo for his part could absolutely put up with the prior at his side. He insists once again that they are brothers. But the prior wants hostility. "I am not your brother!" he says again. "I hate this contemptible righteousness, this lecherous understanding, this depraved tolerance of the opposite."

This last remark was certainly not aimed at Heinrich, from whom such "lecherous understanding" did not come after all, rather at the two souls in his own breast. There is something of Thomas not only in the monk but in Lorenzo, too. "Haven't you felt that I contributed at least as much of my own self to Lorenzo as to the prior, that he is at least as subjective and lyrical a figure?" "To understand everything is to forgive everything" was a danger that the aesthete Thomas Mann had studied in himself, not in Heinrich. The clash with "Heinrich" is not in every respect a clash with the real person Heinrich. It has much that is imagined and projected. "Heinrich" was a code word for possibilities and anxieties that were in Thomas himself. "Heinrich" is a role in the structure of art, in which Thomas takes cover from the demands of reality.

Morality contra sensuality: That still sums up the kernel of the problem of the brothers, biographically as well as imagined. When Thomas was barely fifteen, the nineteen-year-old Henry wrote in disillusionment to Ludwig Ewers that whenever there was talk of "love" around him, it was always of sensual love. "'Ideal,' Platonic love simply did not exist." Or, even more coldly:

> For me, "love" is an illusion like everything else. In me at the beginning of the process there are stimulations of the sexual nerves that have no outer causes but only physiological and pathological causes that lie within me. The first female I meet who appeals somewhat to my taste and is available will set off excesses.

The chaste Thomas at a corresponding age tests the drying up of the urge. "I have become as I am because I did not want to be like you."

## CORRESPONDENCE

The letters exchanged with Heinrich are the most important preserved correspondence of all, because Heinrich was the only colleague of equal status. As much as possible, Thomas avoided the great writers of his age, Franz Kafka, Bertolt Brecht, Alfred Döblin, Robert Musil. They would have been too fatiguing for him. What he later exchanged with Hugo von Hofmannsthal and Hermann Hesse were intellectual courtesies that did not reach into the inmost man. He confided really nothing to Gerhart Hauptmann, his competitor for the place of Praeceptor Germanica.

The extant letters are unequally divided. The first group extends from October 24, 1900, to May 7, 1901. Heinrich was in Italy, and Thomas first completed his military service and then set off on his search for money so he could likewise go to Italy. It is a time when the manuscript of *Buddenbrooks* lay unread for months at the S. Fischer publishing house. Literarily, Thomas was quite depressed. "You are blossoming, while right now I have inwardly come to a terrible end." We even learn about plans made for suicide and then canceled. They are in connection with Paul Ehrenberg. He is meant when the letters rhapsodize (February 13, 1901) in code about "an indescribably pure, and unexpected joy of the heart." Thomas shies away from details. "I refrain or postpone the promised confessions" (February 28). "I waive more detailed confessions because writing and sorting out things only heightens and exaggerates" (March 7). He silently indicates the homoerotic occasion: "It doesn't involve a love story, at least not in the usual sense, but a friendship—o surprise!—understood, reciprocated, requited friendship . . . Grautoff even asserts that I am quite simply in love like a sophomore, but that is said as he understands it. . . . But in the main a deeply joyous astonishment prevails over an accommodation no longer expected in this life. Enough of that. Perhaps sometime I'll let more escape me orally" (March 7).

Confidentiality in personal matters does not continue. Most of the letters concern literary topics, exchanges about plans and finished works, about successes and failures, about reviews and publishers, about colleagues and books. In addition, occasionally something concerning the family. But the fundamental motif is literary competition, comparing oneself and asserting oneself, in the course of which Heinrich at first is a nose ahead.

The second group of preserved letters dates from September 15, 1903, to January 8, 1904, and contains in essence a great dispute about Heinrich's novel *The Hunt for Love*. The competitive situation has turned around—*Buddenbrooks* has meanwhile appeared; Thomas has taken the lead. The third group, with great lacunae reaching from February 27, 1904, to June 11, 1906, concerns above all his engagement, marriage, and the first year of wedlock. Thomas conveys thorough information about all that; he evidently feels obliged to account for himself and is in this area far more detailed than earlier about Paul Ehrenberg. His marriage into money should not lead to a separation of the brothers, which he fears: "Neither happiness," says Klaus Heinrich in *Royal Highness*, "nor the love of the people will ever cause me to stop being your brother." Literarily meanwhile Thomas is a man with eighteen printings and is somewhat patronizing. He claims to have cautioned the publisher Albert Langen, "Hold on tight to my brother and never let him fall! *One day* he will have a great success." Of course, he himself, during his engagement and the first year of his marriage, is "tormentingly unproductive." He has learned to praise Heinrich's work in such a way that it is obvious he is lying. "Another

*Heinrich Mann, 1903*

brilliant book," he writes on June 7, 1906, about the volume of novellas entitled *Stormy Mornings*, "that shows all your good qualities, your thrilling tempo, your famous élan, the delightful succinctness of your words, your really astonishing virtuosity to which one surrenders because it undoubtedly comes directly from your passion."

The correspondence then becomes less rewarding, the sentences shorter; birthdays and Christmas are often the occasions for them. Their mother, Julia Mann, writes to Heinrich that Tommy was missing the exchange of letters with him (December 1, 1908). But perhaps that is not true at all. The letters from May 27, 1907, to September 18, 1914, can be considered the fourth group—over seven years only fifty pages. The high points concern family affairs. There is a serious altercation between Heinrich and his sister Julia (married name, Löhr) about the behavior of Ines Schmied, Heinrich's fiancée. Thomas's opinion about that is in the summary: "I always find that brothers and sisters should not ever be able to fall out with one another. They laugh at one another or yell at one another, but they do not part from one another with a shudder. Just think of Beckergrube No. 52! Everything else is secondary!" (April 1, 1909). On the occasion of the suicide of his sister Carla, Thomas issues a further manifesto of that sacred sense of family from their Lübeck childhood. "My feeling of solidarity with my siblings makes it appear to me that our existence has been put in question by Carla's act, our anchoring is loosened. . . . Carla did not give a thought to anybody, and you say: 'That's all we needed!' And yet, I can't help but feel that she should not have allowed herself to part from us. With her act she had no feeling of solidarity, not the feeling of our common destiny. She acted, so to speak, *against a silent agreement*" (August 4, 1910). Heinrich looked at it otherwise. He had loved Carla.

Nevertheless, they helped one another. On April 27, 1912, Thomas Mann supplies details about being mustered into the military and his time there for Heinrich's *Loyal Subject*. Financial help also shows the enduring solidarity with his brother, even though Thomas soon requests that Heinrich repay a loan, since he has taken on the building of a luxurious summer house in Bad Tölz. For his part, Heinrich helps his brother with an intelligent review of *Death in Venice* when he is faced with destructive remarks by the critic Alfred Kerr. Previously he had already defended him against Richard von Schaukal, who had found "sham" everywhere in Thomas Mann.

Meanwhile, Heinrich, with his novel *The Small Town* and his turn to politics and democracy, had intellectually taken the initiative. Contrariwise, Thomas felt rejected. On November 8, 1913, this results in a letter of desperation, of exhaustion; there is talk of scruples and weariness as well as the inability actually to orient himself intellectually and politically. A "growing sympathy with death" was innate in him, "all my interest was always aimed at decadence, and actually that is probably what prevents me from being interested in progress." He was happier about Heinrich's work than about his own. "You do better spiritually, and that is certainly the decisive thing. I am used up, I think, and probably should not have become a writer."

The outbreak of war brings an end for the time being. For Thomas Mann it is a salvation. In his understanding of sibling solidarity he at first cannot at all believe that Heinrich could seriously take a different stand. Entirely guileless, he speaks on September 18, 1914, of the "great, basically decent, even solemn people's war of Germany." With that the correspondence breaks off for years.

## PLEBEIANS AND CHANDALAS, RENAISSANCE MEN AND THE IDEAL OF FEMININE ARTISTIC BEAUTY

"I suffer from feeling hate as from no other feeling," Thomas Mann admits in the seventh *Notebook* (1903). Shortly thereafter: "Most of all I hate those who through the feelings that they awaken in me draw my attention to the weaknesses in my character." The work of his brother puts it to the test. "I am far from despising the 'duchess'; but I *hate* her. That is a confession." The "Duchess" (of Assy) is the chief figure in Heinrich Mann's *Goddesses*. "Nothing in the world is stranger to me," Thomas Mann writes to Richard von Schaukal about Heinrich's novel. "My brother and I have distanced ourselves far from one another; we hardly associate even superficially with one another: a sign, anyway, that we take one another seriously." When Schaukal assumes from that the right for a falling out with Heinrich, it turns out, of course, that such a right belongs to no one but Thomas himself. He complains: "Have I ever given you a reason to believe that I could . . . be pleased with a belittling of the accomplishments of my brother or in any way approve of it?" And he hastens to assure his brother that Schaukal was mistaken to expect any very warm thanks from him for the stupidity. They hate one another on the heights of humanity but stand in common against any attack from farther below. And farther below is everything that does not belong to the family.

Heinrich inflicts deep wounds on Thomas's ego through his very existence and because he is like he is. He awakens feelings in his brother that make the latter aware of weaknesses in his character. Embittered, Thomas notes: "Compared to H., the aristocrat, the glacial one, I am a hardly stalwart plebeian, but equipped with a lot more thirst for power. Savonarola is not my hero for nothing. . . ." A power-hungry plebeian: not a pleasant perception of oneself. So not born for dominance like Heinrich but merely a chandala consumed by it. The self-hatred produced by it is turned outward, becomes hatred of the idea of "Heinrich." In March 1903 Thomas had already once secretly and meanly struck out at *The Goddesses* with the words: "We poor plebeians and chandalas, who honor a feminine ideal of culture and art under the scornful smile of Renaissance men." "What stiff and cold heathens call 'beauty' means nothing." A plebeian is not an aristocratic man of power. He isn't even a "man." His ideal of art is feminine; he believes "in pain, experience, profundity, suffering love." "Chandala" is the term for a low and despised Hindu caste in India. Thomas Mann probably got the word from Nietzsche, who in the *Antichrist* speaks about the "contrast between a *refined* chandala moral sense and one born out of *resentment* and powerless vengeance." From the viewpoint of Nietzsche's Christian, critical superman society, the ascetic person, laden with resentment, is the born Christian. "Savonarola is not my hero for nothing." At another place Nietzsche calls Christianity the "victory of chandala values" and the "collective rebellion of all those downtrodden, miserable persons gone wrong and ending badly." But Heinrich is distinguished. "Popularity is hogwash," says his counterpart in the novel.

The chandala is also helpless and vengeful as a conspirator with the despised sect of homosexuals. The goal to which they are driven is not attainable by them, at least not without their expulsion from society at the same time. Behind talk of the "feminine ideal of art" of the plebeian is also hidden the ideal of the homosexual who abstains while suffering. But Heinrich appears as an aristocrat and a Renaissance *Mann*.

## THE HUNT FOR LOVE

He who was thus attacked, lingering in Italy, had in the meantime taken no notice of the feminine ideal of art and of the mockery of the Renaissance men. He was hastily writing his next novel, *The Hunt for Love*. The chief characters are the decadent heir to millions, Claude Marehn, and the ambitious actress, Ute Ende. A rollicking story unrolls, about money and desires, about acting and sparkle and brutality, as good as without morals, if you don't want to consider a kind of mourning for them. Thomas Mann reacts to the novel with an extraordinarily strong letter (December 5, 1903):

> When I think back ten, eight, five years! How do you seem to me? What were you? An elegant, gallant nature next to whom I seemed all my life to be plebeian, barbarian, and clowning, full of discretion and culture, full of reserve in regard to "modernity," in full measure historically talented, unencumbered by any need for applause, a delicate and arrogant personality for whose literary productions very probably a receptive, choice public was present in Germany now. . . . And today, instead of that? Instead of that now these contorted jokes, these awful, shrill, hectic, convulsive blasphemies of truth and humanity, these undignified grimaces and somersaults, these desperate attacks on the reader's interest!

There follows a literary massacre mowing down everything in its path. It must have felt good to express his hate for once, express it violently, express it with intensity and with exceedingly accomplished expression. The radical split ends up with sexuality and again defends his caution about libertinism. Which is no surprise.

> What is erotic remains, that is to say, what is sexual. For sexuality is not eroticism. Eroticism is poetry, is what speaks to us from the depths, what is unnamed, what gives everything its thrill, its sweet appeal, and its mystery. Sexuality is what is naked, what is not cerebral, what is called by its name. It is often called by its name in *The Hunt for Love*. Wedekind, probably the most impudent sexualist in modern German literature, is likable in comparison with this book. Why? Because he is more demonic. You sense the uncanny, the profundity, the eternal dubiousness of sexuality, you sense a suffering from sexuality, in a word, you feel passion. But the complete moral nonchalance with which your people, if their hands even touch, fall down with one another and make l'amore, can appeal to no better man. This consant listless rutting, this continual odor of flesh makes me tired, makes me disgusted. There is too much, too much "thigh," "breasts," "loins," "calf," "flesh," and it is inconceivable that you would want to start in again every morning, after yesterday a normal, a lesbian, and a pederastic act had taken place. Even in the emotional scene be-

tween Ute and Claude at his deathbed, this scene I would like to have forgotten—even there Ute's "thigh" must unavoidably go into action, and a conclusion was not possible without having Ute walk around in the room naked! I'm not playing Frau Girolamo by writing this. A moralist is the opposite of a preacher of morality: I am completely Nietzschean regarding this point. But only apes and other South Sea islanders can ignore morality completely, and the land of boring vulgarity lies where it hasn't even become a problem, not yet passion. More and more I have understood the identity of morality and spirit and respect the words of Börne that seem to me to contain an immortal truth: "People," he says, "would be more spiritual, if they were more moral."

Notes for a draft of a reply by Heinrich have been preserved. Obviously, he had been affected, for he begins to recognize the fraternal sentiment, acknowledge the equality of rank. "We have the same ideals in us. You long for the wholesomeness of the north, I for that of the south. . . . There are gradations of differences between us. I have so much more of gypsy artistic genius that I cannot resist. I am more Romanic, more alien and unprincipled. And I am so much more abnormal." He defends himself not as something of a Renaissance man but as a decadent. "I am afraid that if I stop, it's all over for me." As for sexuality, he wards off his brother's sublimations as "a bunch of secrets having to do with physical processes." Still valid for him is: "Sexuality is a horribly simple thing."

A long letter of justification by Heinrich, not preserved, follows the attack of December 1903, and for him from Thomas's pen a laborious reconciliation (January 8, 1904):

You do not know how much I hold you in esteem, don't know that when I grumble at you that I do it always with the silent assumption that next to you nothing else easily comes into consideration! It is an old Lübeck senator's son's advantage of mine, an arrogant Hanseatic instinct with which, I believe, I've already made a fool of myself many times, that actually everything else is inferior compared with us.

That's probably how it was, at least for Thomas. Heinrich was considerably more independent of the brotherliness. "My experience of the world is not a fraternal one," he was to emphasize in 1918. His *God-*

*desses*, his *Hunt for Love* come out without allusions to his brother. That was not necessary for him. In *An Epoch Observed* he hands on, retrospectively, an early narcissistic statement by Thomas: "As my brother said—we were both young—in an occasional state of boredom: 'Our friends are not our best side.'" Heinrich had a decisively different opinion even then: "But several were the best of all." He wanted to have nothing to do with the exclusivity of the fraternal relationship.

The clash of ideas does not exclude joint plans for travel. In June 1904 the two plan to meet once again in Mitterbad according to a letter to Heinrich from their mother. Plans are even made for taking an apartment in Munich all together. "For Tommy & I have so nicely figured out how you, T. & I could take an apartment together in Ludwigshöhe, Soll, Gern, or Nymphenb[ad], about 7 rooms, he 2, you 2, I 3 (for Vicco's visits), & could share the expenses." That is obviously only a wishful dream of their then fifty-three-year-old mother and did not come under serious consideration, but it is certainly correct that Thomas, and even though it was only to please his mother, liked to dream up such things. The three brothers again in the childhood symbiosis with their mother: This had its attraction, this was a psychological, even though not a practical, possibility.

## HEINRICH AND KATIA

The most evident argument against such dreams was, of course, Katia. Under the spell of his mother's dream, Thomas felt his marriage to her as a betrayal of the purity of the reality of the siblings' childhood den. "A feeling of the lack of freedom," he writes Heinrich on January 17, 1906, "that I cannot rid myself of up to now, and of course you call me a timid plebeian. But it's easy for you to talk. You are absolute. I, on the other hand, have paused to improve my state of mind."

Heinrich had not appeared at the wedding. His mother, too, was not completely in agreement with Thomas's choice. Heinrich kept her letters on this theme. His mother begs him, first, in spite of all the literary differences and disappointments, not to let the sibling bonds break. "Please, please, dear Heinrich, follow my advice and do not withdraw from T[ommy] and L[öh]s." As far as family solidarity is concerned, she was on Tommy's side. "You are *both* men blessed by God, dear Heinrich—don't let your personal relationship with T. and L. become strained; how could 1 ½ years change things so only because your latest works were not without exception liked. That has absolutely *nothing to do* with your sibling relationship." Katia is too cool for her, the Pringsheim family too rich and too inconsiderate, the wedding not festive enough. She is afraid Thomas could be alienated from her. She has the feeling of having to surrender him, as though he were leaving the family unit. Heinrich, too, was obviously of the opinion that Thomas had changed.

The first thing that the young husband writes is the story "Harsh Hour." In it, Thomas Mann "is" Friedrich Schiller, who is struggling with *Wallenstein*. But there is also a concealed brother. He supposedly has it easier, "the one there in Weimar, whom he loved with an ardent hostility," so, Goethe. "And again, as always, in extreme excitement, with haste and exuberance, he felt the work begin within him that followed this thought: to assert and define his own essence and artistry against the other one."

On the part of the younger brother the state of war remained in the years after the marriage in spite of the continued correspondence. When *Professor Unrat* appears, Thomas confides an "Anti-Heinrich" to his *Notebook*. "I consider it immoral to write one bad book after the other out of fear of suffering from idleness," he lectures sternly, and: "All of that is the most amusing and frivolous stuff that has been written in Germany for a long time." And yet, a little later, Thomas Mann will work up a very similar theme in *Death in Venice*. Besides, *Professor Unrat*, just as *The Hunt for Love*, is a significant book in spite of and just because of the grotesque exaggerations. Thomas could not admit that was true. He obviously would have put into question his own, still all-too-insecure self. What he considered his virtues would appear as weaknesses in this reflection. The state of defense continued.

For the newly married man did not feel at ease. He let his Schiller express what he could not say to Katia:

The years of poverty and emptiness, which he had considered years of suffering and trial—they actually had been rich and fruitful years; and now when a bit of good fortune had settled in, when he had advanced from the exploitation of the spirit into some legitimacy and bourgeois connection, bore an office and

honor, had a wife and children, now he was exhausted and worn
out. Failure and despair—that was what remained.

The young husband's first novel is concerned with the past period of
engagement but at the same time again with his brother. In *Royal
Highness* there is an heir to the throne, Prince Albrecht, and a second
son, Prince Klaus Heinrich. Albrecht plays the Heinrich role, Klaus
Heinrich the Thomas role. He is "tender hearted and prone to tears,"
but the other son "was aristocratic." Albrecht is arrogant. Once he is
supposed to have spoken not a word with Klaus Heinrich for several
years "without a particular argument between the brothers having
been observed." Something similar seems also to have happened in
reality. Klaus Heinrich marries the daughter of a millionaire out of a
sense of duty to the state. Albrecht withers away in genteel solitude.
Here Thomas Mann indulges in a depiction of a wishful dream: that
Prince Albrecht, the lonely and unloved man, will voluntarily abdi-
cate and leave him the throne. From the throne then Thomas Mann
would play the plebeian, as would his Klaus Heinrich:

> "What can I say, Albrecht. You are Father's oldest son, and I have
> always looked up to you because I always felt and knew that you
> are the finer and grander of the two of us, and I'm only a plebe-
> ian compared to you."

# V. The Path to Marriage

*Munich, around 1903*

The path to marriage was, biographically speaking, the path from Paul Ehrenberg to Katia Pringsheim. In the period from 1900 to 1905, which is covered here, Thomas Mann lived in Munich, aside from trips that took him to Florence, Venice, Riga, Mitterbad, Berlin, Polling, Düsseldorf, Königsberg, and Lübeck, among other places. From October until his approaching discharge in December 1900, he served as a one-year volunteer with the Royal Bavarian Infantry Bodyguard Regiment. At the end of 1899 he made the acquaintance of the painter Paul Ehrenberg and his brother Carl, who was a musician. A complicated friendship based on homoeroticism developed with Paul that had its acute phase from 1900 to 1903.

Parallel to the Ehrenberg affair Thomas Mann had also fallen in love with a girl in Florence in May 1901. This supposedly almost resulted in an engagement to Mary Smith. But then the relationship came to naught after letters were exchanged for a while.

In October 1901, the novel *Buddenbrooks* had appeared. Thomas Mann was meanwhile working on *Tonio Kröger* (1900–1903), "Tristan" (1901), *Fiorenza* (1900–1905), and "A Stroke of Luck" (1903). After 1903 his success began to be apparent. "For the first printing of *Tonio Kröger* I have received 400 (four hundred) marks. Please spread this around." After the relationship with Paul Ehrenberg faded away, Thomas Mann looked around methodically for a suitable marriage partner. The first note about Katia Pringsheim is dated August 1903. The year 1904 brings a long period of courtship and waiting until on October 2 the engagement can take place. It was followed on February 11, 1905, by the wedding.

# A STROKE OF LUCK

WHEN THE love for Paul Ehrenberg finally subsided in the late summer of 1903, Thomas Mann writes the short story "A Stroke of Luck" as a commissioned work. It is a discreet vengeance on Paul. The "swallows" have arrived in a small garrison town, a group of girl singers who are accustomed to entertain in the officers' casinos with harmless and silly songs. There is an invitation to a ball, to which the officers bring their ladies. Baron Harry flirts with one of the "swallows" in front of everybody, also in front of his wife, Anna. In a silly scrap with her, he tries to exchange rings, even forces his own wedding ring on her. A painful situation. But the "swallow" begs pardon of Baroness Anna, gives her back the ring, and humbly kisses her hand.

Hardly masked, Thomas Mann himself enters as the narrator. We want, he says, to see into a soul on the wing and only for a few pages, for we are enormously busy. "We come from Florence"—a reference to the work on the Renaissance drama *Fiorenza*. We are on our way "to a royal palace"—the earliest reference to the plan for *Royal Highness*. "Rare, dimly shimmering things are in the process of being put in order." Perhaps he already means his plans for courting a bride.

However Thomas Mann is not recognizable merely as a narrator, but also—disguised—as a literary personage. He "is" Baroness Anna, and the embarrassing flirt is Paul Ehrenberg. In the *Notebooks* the proofs are written down that we will combine into a story. Baroness Anna, so it says in "A Stroke of Luck," loved her husband, "loved him timidly and miserably, although he betrayed her and abused her heart daily." She suffered her love for him "like a female who despises her own tenderness and weakness and knows that power and strong good fortune on this earth are right." Thomas Mann suffered in a similar way. Harry's (Paul's) world is marked by good fellowship, the commonplace, amicability, and activity. But Anna observes the festivities of life from the outside, as does Thomas Mann.

[Anna], tormented by the shrill contrast between the total void and nothingness all around and the prevailing feverish agitation nearby as a result of wine, coffee, sensual music, and dance, sat and watched as Harry bewitched pretty and lively women, not

because that made him particularly happy but because his vanity
demanded that he show himself to the people to be with them as
a happy man who is well provided for, is in no way excluded,
knows no longing. . . . How this vanity hurt her, and how she
nevertheless loved it! How sweet it was to find that he looked
handsome, young, splendid, and beguiling! How the love of others
for him made her own flare up in anguish! . . . And when it was
over, when at the end of a party that she spent in distress and
agony around him, he indulged in ignorant and egoistic praise
about these hours, then those moments came when her hatred
and her contempt equaled her love, when she called him "wretch"
and "kid" in her heart and strove to punish him with silence,
with ridiculous, desperate silence.

All unhappy lovers understand the miserable state in which Baroness
Anna lies sleepless in bed at dawn and reflects about jokes and clever
sayings that she would have had to think of to seem charming, meditates about dreams, how she, weakened by suffering, would weep on
his shoulder and he would try to comfort her with one of his empty,
nice, ordinary expressions. If he would just fall ill! A world of hope
would come into being, in which he would lie helpless and broken
before her as a suffering charge and finally, finally would belong to
her.

## TONIO KRÖGER

We are familiar with that suffering spirit who from the edge of a
party looks longingly at life as it appears in the tale *Tonio Kröger*, that
story of a very clever artist who is in love with blond, naïve life and
its harmless, nice ordinariness, though that life is not in love with
him. Here, too, the Ehrenberg experience was assimilated. On February 8, 1903, Thomas Mann signs a postcard to the Ehrenberg brothers
with "Your Tonio Kröger." Just as Baroness Anna yearns for Harry,
Tonio longs "for the harmless, the simple, and the vivacious, for
a little friendship, devotion, trust, and human happiness." Tonio's
schoolboy love for Hans Hansen, as we have seen, goes back to Mann's
infatuation with Armin Martens. But Paul Ehrenberg also left a significant trace behind in the tale. Again, one has only to transpose the

sexes. No female prototype is known for Hans Hansen's feminine duplicate, "Ingeborg Holm." The heavily veiled biographical knowledge at the time, able to be interpreted at most by those involved, is the affair with Paul. Where do we know this from? We have only to follow the trail that Thomas Mann himself made. For he lends words to his Tonio, in love with Inge, that he himself once sent to Paul. Tonio explains to Lisaweta his longing for the "bliss of the commonplace." He simply would like to have a friend, a human friend. "But up to now I have had friends only among demons, hobgoblins, unfathomable fiends, and cognitively mute ghosts—in other words, literary men." The phrases come directly from life. The seventh *Notebook* preserved them: "P. is my first and only human friend. Up to now all my friends have been demons, hobgoblins, unfathomable fiends, and cognitively mute ghosts—in other words, literary men."

"Back then his heart was alive," namely, when Tonio loved Hans and Inge. At that time he was also writing poetry. What had occurred in all that time in which he had become an artist, he asks, when he sees Hans and Inge in Aalsgaard again. "Paralysis; desolation; ice; and spirit! And art!" But Paul was the cause when Thomas Mann with a fervent heart wrote in his notebook:

> What was so long?—
> Ossification, wasteland, ice. And spirit! And art!
> Here is my heart, and here is my hand.
> I love you! My God . . . I love you!
> Is it so fair, so sweet, so lovely, to be a human being?

The poem is emotional and sentimental, bland and without irony. One sees in it what Thomas Mann means when he has Tonio say to Lisaweta: "If what they have to say matters too much to you, if their heart is too ardent, then you can be certain of a complete fiasco. You will become emotional, you will become sentimental." The warm friendship with Paul is "unliterary." An artist cannot wear his heart on his tongue. He must carefully hide what is confession in his work. From his relationship with Paul, Thomas Mann derived a theory disastrous for the human being in an artist: "Feeling—warm, hearty feeling—is always banal and useless. Artistic are only the irritabilities and cold ecstasies of our spoiled, our artistic nervous system."

At the time his heart was alive. . . . Tonio Kröger's criticism of emotion is connected with the suppression of the experience that lies at the bottom of the tale. Emotion would be feeling, candor, surrender. Irony, on the other hand, is camouflage. Irony means not being surprised by a passion, by a feeling, means to remain superior and be unavailable. "Irony almost always means making superiority out of necessity." Emotion is lyric or dramatic; irony is epic. All that is lyrical is confessional and therefore embarrassing, everything theatrical is too loud and too direct. Lyric and drama are fundamentally emotional. Only narrative can be ironic and discreet.

The renunciation of homoeroticism and turning to marriage is already being prepared secretly at the end of *Tonio Kröger*, where there are allusions to the formal art and the homosexual leanings of August von Platen. Tonio bases his middle-class love for the vivacious and the ordinary biblically on the letter of the Apostle Paul to the Corinthians: "It almost seems to me that it is that love itself of which it is written that one may speak with the tongues of men and of angels and without it yet be a sounding brass and a tinkling cymbal." Thomas Mann found the passage of Goethe, who on December 25, 1825, said to Eckermann that August von Platen lacked love and that therefore one could apply the cited pronouncement of the apostle to him. Tonio Kröger argued with Goethe against Platen; against the (alleged) cold artist, who transformed his unexperienced homosexuality into highly artificial formal art—at the cost of warmth and middle class. But those things exist only in marriage, not in homosexuality, which ejects one from society into the cold. The rejection of Platen by Kröger in favor of middle-class love will be followed by the rejection of Paul Ehrenberg in favor of Katia Pringsheim.

## I LOVE YOU! MY GOD . . . I LOVE YOU!

In the collected works in thirteen volumes, the name Paul Ehrenberg occurs only a single time, in the *Sketch of My Life* of 1930. From that passage one can study how Thomas Mann was able to keep his secrets from the public:

I had a cordial friendship at the time with two young people from my sisters' circle of youthful friends, sons of a Dresden painter and academy professor E. My fondness for the younger, Paul, who was likewise a painter, an academician at the time and

*Paul Ehrenberg, 1902*

student of the famous animal painter Zügel, and besides played the violin superbly, was rather like the resurrection of my feelings for that blond schoolmate [Armin Martens] who had perished, but due to his greater intellectual closeness a lot happier. Karl, the older, a musician by profession and a composer, is today an academy professor in Cologne. While his brother painted my portrait, he played "Tristan" for us in his admirably controlled and melodious manner. Since I also played the violin a bit, together we performed trios, rode bicycles, together visited "the country dance" during Carnival, and often, either at my place or at the brothers' place, had the most pleasant dinners for three. I was grateful to them for the experience of friendship that would otherwise hardly have been my lot. With cultured innocence they overcame my melancholy, shyness, and irritability simply by taking them as positive characteristics and concomitants of talents that they respected. It was a good time.

Painting, music, and country dances—that sounds nice. But it wasn't that simple. Scattered traces that more was involved, to be exact, the "central passionate experience of my 25 years," are preserved here and there, in notebooks, diaries, and in literary works. A summary look back after more than three decades in the diary of May 6, 1934, compares his love for P[aul] E[hrenberg] with that for K[laus] H[euser] and with the schoolboy love for A[rmin] M[artens] and W[illiram] T[impe]:

> . . . looked in old notebooks . . . and engrossed myself in sketches I had made at the time about my relationship with P.E. in connection with my idea for the novel "Lovers." The passion and the melancholy psychologizing feeling of that faded time impressed me intimately with the sadness of life. Thirty years and more have passed since then. Oh yes, I have lived and loved, I have in my way "paid for my humanity." As already at that time, but to a higher degree 20 years later, I have even been happy and was able really to take what I longed for into my arms.
>
> The experience with K.H. was more mature, more superior, happier. But being overwhelmed, as is expressed by certain words of the sketches from the P.E. time, this "I love you—my God—I love you"—an intoxication indicated by the poem fragment "O hark, music!—In my ear a shiver of sound wafts blissfully away—" happened—as is probably proper—just one time in my life. The early A.M. and W.T. experiences retreat far back into the childish, and that with K.H. was a late good fortune with the character of life's benevolent fulfillment, but still without the youthful intensity of feeling, the sky-high jubilation and deep vibrancy of that central heartfelt experience of my 25 years. So it is probably humanly proper and because of this normality I can

perceive my life arranged more strongly in what is canonical than through marriage and children.

Here we are obviously closer to the truth than with the Schwabing country dances. In the following we want to gather everything together that self-censorship failed to see or let slip through. The oldest remnants are a change of address notice in 1899, a New Year's greeting at the end of 1899, an inscription on a photograph dated March 6, 1900, a birthday note of August 8, 1900, and the first extensive evidence, a letter of June 29, 1900, to Paul, who possibly spent the whole summer in Vituchovo near Posen. The letter describes amusingly the muster and Munich cultural life. In any event, there is, by way of an intimation, mention of love in the description of a picture on exhibition of the figure of a young girl who holds a heart in her hand, with which she flirts in an impudent and graceful way, kneeling before her a young man, in his breast a large knife wound, his gaze directed upward, fanatic, blissful, and suffering. "The picture made a strong impression on me, from which without further ado it probably follows that as a painting it is not worth five cents." Thomas Mann may have felt like the one with the wound, thus the strong impression.

The correspondence with Grautoff, which again is preserved from July 11, 1900, on, mentions something about P.E. for the first time on December 19. Even now the characteristic contrast between the ironically arrogant "mind" (Thomas Mann) and naïvely likable "life" (Paul) is clearly recognizable:

> Of course, yesterday evening I was with Paul Ehrenberg, who unnecessarily talked me into going to Gounod's "Margarethe." Those were very nice hours. Next to this honest, cheerful, child-like, a bit conceited but unwaveringly good-hearted comrade I sat on my stuffed chair and listened without all too much excitement and strenuous participation to a soft, sweet, innocent, and peaceful music.

In the winter of 1900–1901 his love must have become deeper, for Thomas writes to Heinrich on February 13, 1901, about "an indescribable, pure, and unexpected joy of the heart" that had shown him "that there is something honorable, warm, and good within me and not merely 'irony,' that within me everything is not yet made deso-

late, overwrought, and wasted by accursed literature." Heinrich must
have inquired further, but Thomas shies back from more precise information. On the other hand, Grautoff probably knew more. Thomas
writes him on February 22, 1901, that he did have the greatest desire
to confess his whole romance to Heinrich but was also afraid of doing
so. "On the other hand, I naturally have again a true longing to roll
the whole thing out broadly and explain myself in detail." We don't
know what there was to explain. The only direct evidence from the
winter of 1900–1901 is a letter to Paul of January 19, which asks pardon for his premature disappearance from a party. "I had contributed
so much repulsively stupid stuff (about Tolstoy, Luther, Christianity,
and the like, I believe) that finally I ran away from myself and hastily
pulled the bedspread over my ears. My feeling of shame has come to
be so painfully strong." That's the harmless version. But there was
something else envisioned in running away: to give a moment of reflection to his beloved.

> He knew it so well, this departure, this silent, proud, and desper-
> ate fleeing from a hall, a garden, from any scene of a happy con-
> vivial group, with the hidden hope of preparing a short moment
> of shade, of perplexed reflection, of sympathy for that bright
> creature for whom one longs.

The time of the country dance and the bicycling probably came afterward. "Do you still remember," writes Thomas Mann on November
22, 1949, to Carl Ehrenberg, "how we bicycled to the Aumeister early
in the morning (your bike was called 'the cow' because it always had
a dirty belly) and after drinking coffee threw stones at empty beer
bottles?" Maybe back then they also rode to Linderhof, maybe at the
time Paul declared King Ludwig II of Bavaria to be "totally mad,"
whereupon Thomas set him straight with a torrent of words and declared his affection for Ludwig. Rudi/Paul seems not to have understood that. "As was his habit in such cases, that is, whenever a point
of view was too new for him, with indignant opened lips he drilled
his blue eyes alternately into my right and left eye while I was
talking."

With the brothers together, something was always happening. Paul
did not know how to loaf, Mann notes in the spring of 1901; he was
somehow always busy "in a nice way." Mockingly the expression is
also used in two letters to Otto Grautoff (January 8 and February 20,

1901). "In a nice way" becomes a leitmotif, planned at first for "The Lovers," used then in *Doctor Faustus*.

When carnival is over, Thomas feels moved to reprimand Otto Grautoff on February 20, 1901. The latter had fallen in love, and lovers usually behave impossibly. "If you want to do me a big favor, then don't talk anymore about the cute little creature who has taken possession of your fine heart as 'your mädel' [*maiden*]." Using that word was not accurate and besides had the effect of being much too narrow. Like his Adrian Leverkühn (in the Faust novel), Thomas Mann does not like the word "mädel." And besides, Grautoff had behaved colossally bad.

> The French say: When a German wants to be graceful, he jumps out of the window. Something similar applies mostly also to "us dead," when we "wake up" [an allusion to Ibsen's drama, *When We Dead Wake Up* ], i.e., when we want to be human beings for once. Mostly! It takes a lot of good taste and feeling for style not to be too outré, not to become distorted. Well, style . . . not just everyone knows what that is. . . . You make me nervous when you play Carnival, and for that very reason I'm glad that Carnival is over. For example, you made me nervous (and apparently not only me) by the stupid shrieking with which yesterday in the Café L. you welcomed Paul Ehrenberg. It's dumb and coarse to believe that this, even during Carnival, is the right way to greet him. It may not matter to you what he thinks of you, you're right there. I'm just afraid that he doesn't know sometimes what really binds us—you and me.

Paul is nice and sociable, frank and talkative; he must have attracted the solitary and melancholy Thomas Mann onto the side of an active life without long shilly-shallying. Exhibitions, excursions, bicycling, concerts, coffee house, opera, balls, visits, playing music formed a colorful roundelay. The already frequently quoted fragment of a love poem that is found in two parts in the seventh *Notebook* can also probably be dated from 1901. In context it reads:

> These are the days of lively emotion!
> You have enriched my life. It blossoms—
> O hark, music! —In my ear
> A shiver of sound wafts blissfully away—
> I thank thee, my happiness! my good fortune! my lucky star!—

What was so long?—
Ossification, wasteland, ice. And spirit! And art!
Here is my heart, and here is my hand.
I love you! My God . . . I love you!
Is it so fair, so sweet, so lovely, to be a human being?

Paul paints a portrait of Thomas Mann—but the man portrayed does not like it. Hans Hansen loves horse books; Paul was a painter of horses. Nicely and sarcastically Thomas writes him in May 1901: "Hooray for your creation! What will become of it? An enormous cow? You did say that you wanted to go from me to the cattle."

The summer of 1901 brings a temporary cooling off. Thomas Mann contacts Paul on July 18, 1901, from Mitterbad near Meran, beginning with a verbose apology for not having written for so long. Also a letter to Grautoff of November 6, 1901, sounds as though they had not seen one another for a rather long time, and as though winter had been the hot season for Thomas Mann at times:

> For me in particular the beginning of the "season" is marked by the reunion with Paul Ehrenberg, which took place recently on the occasion of a luncheon with acquaintances. And last night, at our place, I also heard his violin playing again. He's the same old fellow . . . I, too, am the same old fellow: Still always so weak, so easily seduced, so undependable and little to be taken seriously in my philosophy that I take the hand of life as soon as it is extended to me. Curious! Every year, around the time when Nature turns stiff, life breaks into the summery icing up and desolation of my soul and pours streams of feeling and warmth through my veins! I let it happen.

Disturbing, though, that Paul keeps a weekly wall calendar for his social responsibilities; painful, when one finds oneself as one appointment among others. In January 1902 it reaches a crisis. Thomas Mann feels neglected. He inquires by letter in the hope of reaching Paul's ear "between the two country dances":

> Where is the man who will say Yes to me, to the man, the not very likable, moody, self-tormenting, skeptical, suspicious but sensitive man, quite unusually ravenously hungry for sympathy—? Unwavering? Without letting himself be intimidated and alienated by apparent coldness, apparent rejection. Without, for

example, wanting to explain such coldness and such rejection with indolence and indifference, "that I must first get used to him again," rather keep to myself steadfastly out of inclination and trust? Where is that man? —Deep silence. And when somewhere a cello or a contrabass does a bit of pizzicato, then that would be a mood as in "Lohengrin," Act I, after "Who in the battle of gods . . . ."

The notebook records: "P. came January 30 in the afternoon." He arranges the matter in a nice way. It will have been as in *Doctor Faustus*, where it is Adrian who writes that painfully revealing letter. "At once, urgently, without any tormenting hesitation, at the time there followed a visit of the recipient in Pfeiffering, a discussion, the assurance of the most profound gratitude—a simple, daring, and devotedly tender mode of behavior was revealed, eagerly intended to carefully prevent any embarrassment." Carried out at the end of August 1946, this scene had already been drafted in the notebook of 1902 for the plan for "The Lovers" (where Mann would have masked himself in a female role): "The letter to him, very daring. Followed by his immediate visit, his gratitude, his prevention of any embarrassment on her part. Pact of friendship. Promise of fidelity." But it can be, another note reflects, that the letter, in spite of his decent behavior, impaired more than it was of use. "He is a bit embarrassed. The intimacy, the trusting that he sometimes had, seems missing. His naturalness is a bit disturbed."

A further crisis follows in April 1902. It begins with Mann's irritation caused by the "vivacious family." A "temperamental," "vivacious," and "passionate" family, which has "the Devil in its belly," the notebook reports, fascinates the Ehrenberg brothers, which Thomas finds appalling. "I have heard that now so often, that I'm simply fearful of this frightful family. If I even hear its name, I seem to myself already to be so weak and anemic, that I am suddenly stricken with a hopeless weariness and collapse inside." In the Faust novel Rudi Schwerdtfeger (Paul Ehrenberg), who is loved by Ines Institoris (Thomas Mann), tells constantly about parties where he had to put in an appearance once more. He had also been at the Rollwagen's, "who had those two vivacious daughters." Ines comments: "When I hear the word 'vivacious,' I become alarmed." Rudi indulged everyone with the illusion that he liked best to be with them. "He came at five o'clock for tea and said that he had promised to be somewhere else between five thirty and six o'clock, at the Langewiesch's or Rollwagen's, which wasn't true at all. Then he stayed until six-thirty as a sign that he preferred to be here, was fascinated, that the others could wait—and was so sure of himself in doing so that it had to make anyone happy that it was perhaps possible that someone could really be happy about it."

## THE FLIRTATION SQUABBLE

Out of this there develops the "flirtation squabble," in which Thomas Mann, "although it pierced him to the heart," tries to stand sensibly on Paul's side. "A man so free and chaste," he notes, "how should he not be able to allow himself the harmless narcotic of flirting!" The basic realization follows: "Besides, he is *born* for flirting and *not* for love or friendship. Our friendship is also a flirting, and I am absolutely sure that it would have less attraction for him if it were not." But what about when only one flirts and the other loves?

Baron Harry in "A Stroke of Luck" was also a flirter. Baroness Anna's relationship with him is made fundamental in the Ines-Rudi affair in *Faustus*. The writer carried over some formulations from the Ehrenberg notes literally into the novel—as when he has Ines complain about Rudi's niceness and foppishness, about the frightful social life of artists, about her horror at the intellectual void and nothingness that prevailed at an average invitation,

> in sharp contrast to the feverish arousal connected with it as the result of wine, music, and the undercurrent of relationships between human beings. Sometimes you could watchfully see how one person conversed with another under the perfunctory observance of social formalities and at the same time be quite absent in his own thoughts, that is with another person whom he was watching. . . . And with the decline of the scene, the continuing dérangement, the messed up and dirty image of a salon toward the end of the "invitation." She admitted that sometimes she cried in her bed for an hour after having a party.

The course of the flirting squabble illustrates the climate of that melancholic love story best. We know the details:

And there then followed that long conversation with his brother about association with ladies, flirting, and artistic stimulus through the female, at which in the beginning I took his side so much that he asserted I was speaking to him "from my soul"—and then, made weary by the "classy family" and much else, I fell silent more and more.

Paul excuses himself on the way home. At an advertising kiosk with a poster for a song recital in which Mann was interested, they stop. Paul scornfully: "Religious songs—naw, I'm not goin' there!" With a nervous movement Mann resumes a position before the column. "Won't have time!" Paul corrects himself hastily. Thomas thinks: "How afraid he is of my contempt. The way often, at a switch in my expression, he clumsily, noticeably says what I want to hear!"

Shortly after Thomas had written this, Paul comes, notices that his friend is sad, seeks to reestablish contact. "Later, when with my back to the room I was leaning into the open window, he said loudly: 'Move just a bit to the side, if you will, so I have room, too!' leaned beside me and, after this overture, which was as cordial as possible, began an intimate, quiet, and comradely conversation. Finally he fortunately went so far that he comfortably put an arm on my shoulder. I let it happen. What could I accuse him of? I, too, was already conquered again." But the end is still sad.

We parted as "friends." For a long time I was not so hopelessly distant from him. As I once said to him: "mountains and abysses. . . ." Does he see them? Doesn't he want to see them? I know nothing about him through him. My sad eye saw everything I know.

Thomas wants to torment him a bit. "At our farewell on the street I loosened my hand very quickly from his." He acts as though he does not know whether and when he could visit. With that he wants to force Paul to visit. "But he did not come at all." Detlef will say that about Lilli (in "The Starvelings") and Tonio Kröger about Inge. They do not visit, any more than Paul does. Such a thing does not happen on earth. Nevertheless Thomas had worked out the topics for a discussion. "What I have to confess to him in explanation is, first, that thing with the classy family; second, the impression of the conversation with me about flirting; third his brother's story about his smutty stuff; fourth, the 'religious songs.' It's a bit small, a bit thin, perhaps daring. But I'll know how to arrange it. Will he come?"

The sociable fellow had with amorous friendliness won over the lonely fellow, who now wanted more. He loved Paul's happy naïveté but at the same time suffered from not being understood. On his part, Paul probably had an entirely different opinion. Around February or March 1902, it happened that Thomas wanted to keep the kinship with Hamlet entirely for himself.

> Hamlet—: his enthusiastic weakness, the hyperaesthesia of his conscience, his penchant for pondering, his heated fantasy and denial of reality, his pessimism, his aversion to realization (as far as Ophelia, women, courtiers, all of existence is concerned) (It suffices for him to see through in order to be repulsed)— — — ecce ego!"
>
> P. replied, not without importance:
> "That is true. . . . He holds up a mirror to us!"
> And my soul burst out laughing enormously. . . . My good boy! He was never more distant from me! He resembles Hamlet as I do Hercules!

The following note has a similar scornful tone:

> P.: In Germany, weakness and respect for anything foreign is much too strong.
> I: Your saying that is the best proof that it's no longer the case. If it were still the case, if the feeling were still generally customary, unshaken, & in force, then you would be the last one to change it. Etc.
> P.: Oh. That's very friendly.
> I: O yes, it's absolutely friendly.

From the summer of 1902 there are still a few letters, original, derisive, chatty on cultural matters but without intimacies. Thomas Mann wants to go to Riva on the Gardasee. Once more a renion cannot be expected until November. The announcement does not sound exactly enthusiastic: "At my return, in the middle of November, I will then find you already in Munich again, to which I look forward to a certain extent. Yes, I can be friendly, too."

In 1903 everything goes downhill. "P. is so mean that you can't believe he could ever die. He isn't worth the solemnity and transfiguration of death." The last harmonious evidence is a poem that was enclosed in a letter to Paul of June 19, 1903. With delicate irony Thomas comments: "I hope you will accept the charming little lines that I could not resist saving. If they are bad, they are still well meant. And it does depend on the heart!" The poem reads:

> Here is a man most highly lacking:
> Fully great and small passions packing,
> Ambitious, vain, love hungry, perplexing,
> Vulnerable, jealous, and also vexing,
> Untranquil, extreme, nonstop,
> Now overly proud, a miserable fop,
> Naïve and also fivefold whirled,
> World withdrawn, in love with the world,
> Yearning, weak, a reed in the wind,
> Half visionary, half dumb and blind,
> A child, a fool, and a poet true,
> Painfully caught in folly and will,
> But with the advantage, that to you
> With all his heart he's devoted still.

Different from the ecstatic fragment from the days of vital emotion in 1901, we have here a carefully wrought structure. Its value lies more in self-recognition than in the expression of feeling for Paul, which remains conventional ("with all his heart he's devoted still"). Love has become literature.

Shortly afterward the relationship receives a deep and in the end fatal wound. A letter to Otto Grautoff of August 29, 1903, for the first time indicates the plans aimed at Katia Pringsheim. There must have been wild rows with Paul, as can be deduced from a postcard to him of September 29, 1903. There was an argument, similar to the one in *Doctor Faustus* when Adrian Leverkühn reveals his marriage plans to his friend Rudi Schwerdtfeger. The adjective "human" is inappropriate and even shameful in Adrian's mouth, says Rudi, and Adrian counters: "I am told—by someone who won me over to what is human with amazing patience and converted me to a first-name basis, someone with whom for the first time in my life I found human warmth—that I have nothing to do with humanity, am not allowed to have anything to do with it." From that time on, Ehrenberg is moved into the second rank, the letters become short and unproductive, the meetings more and more rare. He, too, soon marries (the painter, Lilly Teufel).

The whole story should be kept in mind when one speaks of the contradiction between "mind" and "life" in Thomas Mann. The lesson in observation for blond, naïve, blue-eyed "life" happened through Paul. He cannot be used for what is intellectual. He does not understand irony. Even on the occasion of genuine declarations of scorn, he says at most: "That is really very friendly." On the aforementioned postcard of September 1903, Thomas Mann advises him not to read Nietzsche and assigns him the world of *The Magic Flute*. That is not an honor but a humiliation. "Magic Flute" is a code word for the bovine warmth of humanity. "Touching, this spirit of mild and happy humanity," Mann mocks. " 'Virtue,' 'duty,' 'enlightenment,' 'love,' 'humanity'—nice people still believe in that! Today that's all tattered and chewed. . . . Why do you really want to read Nietzsche? Better not to do it!"

He had previously reflected about that with *The Magic Flute* and already written it down. The arrow was sharpened when he shot it from his bow. Years later he turned it over to the hand of Doctor Überbein, who in *Royal Highness* is permitted to once more mock the emotionalism of humanity.


### PAUL'S DEATH

From the time that follows, aside from transfiguring memories of that time ("I loved him, and it was something like a happy love"), there were only sporadic meetings. "Congratulations [on the honorary doctorate] from Paul Ehrenberg, which touches me" (diary, September 13, 1919). "To tea with Paul Ehrenberg in Schwabing," written in the diary of January 2, 1921. "Letter from Paul Ehrenberg out of financial need and thoughtlessness about my own state of affairs. It moved me to see this handwriting again" (March 31, 1933). "New letter from Paul Ehrenberg, to whom I am lending 800 M" (April 10, 1933). After the Second World War he is informed that the Ehrenberg brothers had been involved with National Socialism. Thomas Mann is not convinced of that. "After tea wrote to blind Opitz about the meeting with Carl Ehrenberg and Paul's keeping invisible. . . . which can be explained completely by his bad behavior in regard to the matter of money in 1933 or 34."

Then on November 22, 1949: "News of the death of Paul Ehrenberg
. . . moved by many memories." Delayed greetings still come from
Paul, who in gratitude "for a favor of friendship given many years
before" wishes to send a picture. "Perhaps it will still come" (December 1, 1949). "Letter from Carl Ehrenberg with more details about
Paul's death" (January 1, 1950). That is all.

## CHASTITY

The whole story hardly ever sounds enthusiastic, hardly ever happy.
What did Thomas really find in Paul? One striking trait returns repeatedly: "Purity" is ascribed to Paul, just as to Rudi in *Doctor Faustus*. He was "a chaste person," a human being without vices, "a pure
person," Ines summarizes in *Faustus*, "thus his trusting nature, for
purity is trusting." That was most convincing for Thomas Mann. It
corresponds to the note findings:

> We talked about sexuality, about the precarious situation when
> one doesn't like females but, at most, ladies, and an appetizing
> relationship is too costly; also that both of us were advised, from
> the viewpoint of doctors, to take up a liaison with a married
> woman. Starting from here, I would like to clarify my feelings for
> him, would like to tell him (even though it might not be true)
> that this friendship, also from the standpoint of a psychiatrist, is
> something happier for me, that it has affected me as a pacifier, as
> a medium of purification and release from sexuality.

"Pure" (homoerotic) love seems here to be a release from (heteroerotic) sexuality. That is a highly unusual, even quixotic state of feeling. The good fortune lay in pain. For the very reason that Paul was a
flirt and wanted nothing serious, the purity, which obviously was
among Thomas Mann's strongest impulses, was able to remain
preserved.

In the Faustus novel it is art that purifies. The violin concerto written by Adrian for him serves Rudi for the purification of his sexual
affair with Ines Institoris. Decades later Thomas Mann looks for a
theoretical explanation. Homoeroticism is pure because it remains indifferent to the world of fathering. It is therefore particularly well
disposed and appropriate for sublimation. "Culture separates desires
from their original purposes," it says with particular reference to

same-sex passion in a passage in *Doctor Faustus* that was later excised. Chastity is nothing dismally tormenting—it can be free, cheerful, even high-spirited.

## "DU"—INFORMAL ADDRESS

Thomas Mann used the mode of informal address with almost no one, if the "Du" of innocent childhood with one's own family and Lübeck schoolmates is disregarded. Paul (and his brother Carl) belonged to those few; also Bruno Walter—with whom thirty-four years passed before "Du" was used. Along with the harmless there was a menacing "Du." The Egyptian lady dignitary, who falls in love with her Hebrew servant Joseph, feels she has "become enslaved by 'Du,'" a "slavish 'Du.'" The "Du," says Settembrini in *The Magic Mountain*, is "a repulsive barbarism, a playfulness with primitive origins, a lascivious game that I detest." Since love means the suspension of individualization, removing boundaries, and merging, it is also a slovenly game with the origins of all civilized behavior. Against all propriety Hans Castorp uses "Du" with his Clawdia. "Je t'ai tutoyé du tout temps et je te tutoiere éternellement" (I've used it with you all along and will for all eternity.)

Once, when it was au courant, the perilous "Du" had arisen under the protection of the license of Carnival. From the seventh *Notebook* one can deduce that the Munich Carnival of 1902 played with the origins of all civilized behavior. At the time, after a night of dancing, a woman with a doctorate must have pulled down the arrogant lonely man into the swamp of comingling after a night of dancing. "The 'Du' comes from the Carnival, is a Munich trait! Witness the lady Dr. K. and me on an easy chair at 7 A.M." Both on one chair? Also Clawdia Chauchat is sitting or lying on a chair at the late end of a Carnival party, Hans Castorp at first bending over her, then almost kneeling at her feet. "Je t'aime," he babbles. "Je t'ai aimée de tout temps, car tu es le Toi de ma vie, mon rêve, mon sort, mon envie, mon éternel désir" (I love you. I have always loved you, for you are the 'toi' of my life, my dream, my destiny, my need, my eternal desire).

The formal form of address, the "Sie," creates distance and is protective. The "Du" is revealing and surrendering, thus convulsing to the foundation, thus humiliating when someone unworthy makes use of it deviously. Life wants to make what is refined into something common, wants to pull it down to its flat niveau until it has become a laughingstock with a punch bowl cover on its head. The trauma of abasement goes back to experiences such as happen to Prince Klaus Heinrich with soapmaker Unschlitt's daughter at the citizens' ball. "He saw a desire gleaming in all their eyes and saw that it was their desire to pull him down to them, to have him down there with them. In his happiness, his dream to be with them, down with them, there came from time to time, like a cold, stinging realization that he was deceiving himself, that the warm, wonderful 'we' was deceiving him."

In the Faust novel the daring letter and Rudi's prompt visit of reconciliation lead to a mutual sojourn in a Hungarian castle. When they return from there, they use "Du" with one another. "Fateful 'Du,'" comments the narrator. "It neither befitted the blue-eyed inconsequentiality that it won for itself, nor could the one who submitted to it avoid taking vengeance for the—it may be—pleasurable abasement that happened to him as a result."

The Devil takes care of vengeance. He uses "Du" with Leverkühn, to the latter's indignation. "Our relationship is already such that we can say 'Du.'" He appears in the role of a pimp—"A *strizzi*. A pander." Dragging down is his specialty.

## LITERATURE AND LIFE

The *Notebooks* are not diaries, the letters unproductive as far as intimacies are concerned, the literary work not reliable biographically. We know only stylizations of various degrees concerning what happened, not the events themselves. We have "life," not Life. We are dealing with an author who even instigates experiences for the sake of art. Life becomes literary material. "I am artist enough to let anything happen to me, for I can use everything." From the autumn of the Ehrenberg era there is an arrogant note about it. "Should a famous man and serious artist," with that Thomas Mann means himself, "rather not spend so much time entertaining two eternally nameless children," those are the Ehrenberg brothers (who in a letter from the time are addressed as "Dear children"), "with sparkling letters? I do it anyway; have enough dignity to be permitted to waste a lot. Such letters are a rehearsal of art like any other, and since during afternoons I almost never dare to lay a hand on the real, representative, symbolizing 'work,' then I don't see how better use could be made of the hours." He adds expressly that he is also writing his life. "And by *building beautiful bridges* . . . from my artist's solitude to that little part of the world, I am writing on my own life."

But at the same time he also avoids life for the sake of art. For whoever is alive and happy does not create. The seventh *Notebook* furnishes a plan of a novella (ca. 1903): "A pessimistic writer, in love, gets engaged, marries ('life'). Is so happy that he can no longer work, already completely despairing. Then he observes that his wife is betraying him. Works again." The poet Axel Martini praises roaring life literarily, but personally, out of caution, goes to bed at ten o'clock. Life is the forbidden garden. Every one of us, says Martini, is familiar with the greedy excursions into the festival halls of life. "But we return from there into our isolation humbled and sick at heart." What you have written: You have not really experienced any of it yourself? Prince Klaus Heinrich asks him. The reply could be by Thomas Mann. "Very little, Your Royal Highness. Only very trifling suggestions of it."

Paul Ehrenberg, alias Rudolf Müller, alias Baron Harry, alias Ingeborg Holm, alias Joseph, alias Rudi Schwerdtfeger: Literature offers more than life. Paul's name haunts the whole work cryptically, like Esmeralda does Leverkühn's. The actual kernel of experience is comparatively thin. It has left behind only a few authentic proofs. There are the letters to the Ehrenberg brothers, those to Heinrich Mann, and those to Otto Grautoff. Everything else is already more or less turned into literature: the sparse memoirs of the later years, the *Notebooks*, and above all the literary works. Already in the *Notebooks* the perspective changes between "I" and "they." The "they" notes refer to the relationship of "Adelaide" (Thomas Mann) to "Rudolf Müller" (Paul) in the plan for "The Lovers," and, although it basically involves experiences, it already represents a stylization. The second level of the turn to true literature consists of the works of the early years, thus, "A Stroke of Luck," *Tonio Kröger*, and its sidepiece "The Starvelings"; borderline are *Fiorenza*, "By the Prophet," and "Gladius Dei." The third level contains the later literary works, above all *Joseph in Egypt* and *Doctor Faustus*.

The Joseph novel can use but little from the author's life. "Looking through the notebook from the time of P.E. and Tonio Kröger, I had to confirm with how sparse a choice only the individual and sentimental, modernly observed detail of a passionate sort was appropriate for the stylistics of my book and its mythically primitive world" (diary, January 9, 1935). It is otherwise in *Doctor Faustus*, where many pages go back to the Ehrenberg notes. The P.E. story is told doubly there, once in the relationship of Rudi Schwerdtfeger to Adrian Leverkühn, once in the relationship of Rudi Schwerdtfeger to Ines Institoris. The conclusion turns radical. Because the artist must not love life, Rudi must die. Ines serves as the weapon of the deed, shooting him fatally. In reality it happened not nearly so flagrantly, with the relationship to Paul gently euthanized in favor of Katia Pringsheim. The literary works do make use of the basics of his life story, but Thomas sharpens them in each case toward a different ending, and pursues various possibilities. The P.E. material is fantasized in five different directions:

1. The case of *Tonio Kröger* is closest to reality. This love *should* have no endurance at all, and certainly not be realized physically at all. Love fallen asleep in the heart serves civilized solitude as a motor of production.

2. In the case of "A Stroke of Luck," Thomas Mann's own experience is likewise very close. Suffering loneliness here tests how it can avenge itself literarily by showing Paul his worthlessness.

3. *Joseph in Egypt* concerns a pure man (Joseph, or Paul, as the case may be), who is generally not available for sexuality. In the case of Potiphar's wife, Thomas Mann plays through the nightmare of self-destruction, which would be the result of a physical courtship, a courtship of the unchaste nun for the handsome monk.

4. and 5. In *Doctor Faustus* the catastrophic variations. First, Adrian-Rudi: The loneliness of the artist is here unavoidable and therefore fatal for the life entangled in it. There is fulfillment only in work. The artist kills the life that reaches for him. Then Ines-Rudi: Here the case of sexual realization is played through. When suffering solitude sleeps with "life," there is a kind of rape that ends fatally for the victim.

## MARY SMITH

Interest in the female can also be noted in the middle of the P.E. time. There is no contradiction between homoerotic passions and the gaze at the other sex. Thomas Mann flirted with marriage once already, in May 1901. We know the context of that only from *A Sketch of My Life*:

Once before . . . I had been close to getting married. In a Floren-
tine pension close contact with two table companions, sisters
from England, had developed, of whom I found the older, dark-
haired one likable, the younger, blond one charming. Mary, or
Molly, responded to my affection, and there developed a tender
relationship, about which union through marriage was discussed.
What finally held me back was the feeling that it might be too
early; there were also considerations that concerned the girl's foreign nationality. I believe the small British girl felt the same way,
and in any event the relationship dissolved into nothing.

Thomas Mann was in Florence from approximately April 26 to May
20, 1901. There he met his brother Heinrich. When the latter traveled
for a short time to Naples, Thomas wrote him on May 7:

Miss Mary, whose birthday was day before yesterday and whom
I had given a basket of sweet fruit, gave me a lot of pleasure. But
now, I believe, I'm getting too melancholy for her. She is so *very
clever*, and I am so stupid always to love those who are clever,
although I cannot keep up in the long run.

Perhaps for her birthday this notation was also meant: "Iris-Parfum,
1,25 L[ire] Via Tornabuoni." In the fourth *Notebook* we also have several pages with the results of various games of the brothers or of
Thomas alone with "Miss Edith" and "Miss Mary." But the most important evidence is a letter to Paul Ehrenberg of May 26, 1901, when
Thomas Mann had just returned from Munich:

The thing with the little English girl, who looked as though she
were by Botticelli, only much merrier, was in the beginning a
carefree flirtation, but later took on a remarkably serious character—and indeed (O amazement!) on both sides. Our farewell was
almost stageworthy—although it is actually mean to talk about it
in that tone, but I count on your innate coldness of heart. By the
way, it may well be that the last word has not yet been spoken in
regard to this matter. But if you don't keep your mouth shut, you
lout, you country boy, I'll hire an assassin.

Did Thomas want to make his friend jealous? Did he only talk himself
into being in love? Was the understanding not intimate from the start,
the last word already spoken? The tone of the letter speaks against
such assumptions. If the intention is to make someone jealous, then

being in love is put in the foreground, not intentions of marriage. We must rather proceed from the fact, as has been observed already several times, that homoeroticism and acquaintanceships with girls in the case of Thomas Mann do not travel on a collision track. He felt no contradiction between marrying and being friends with Paul. Rather the opposite. Paul relaxed him for living and thus also opened up the idea of marriage for him. In one letter, Mann finds a formula: "I made him a bit more literary and he made me a bit more human. Both were necessary."

In the fall of 1901, under "send *Buddenbrooks* to," Thomas Mann also listed "Mary Smith." (We know her family name from this list.) A further note proves that also at the end of 1901 letters were being exchanged: "Letter to . . . Mary." The last evidence is the dedication that appears in the late summer of 1902 in the *Notebook* and then in 1903 at the beginning of the story "Gladeus Dei" in the little volume *Tristan* that contains six novellas: "To M.S. in remembrance of our days in Florence." The text is slightly diluted in comparison with the *Notebook* version: "To Miss ———— in friendly remembrance of our happy days in Florence."

The bearer of the common name M.S. has not yet been identified. Anyone who knows an appropriate Mary, who was in Florence with her sister Edith in the spring of 1901, stand up and speak! Perhaps in one English attic or another even today lie the letters of Thomas Mann to her, and no one knows about them. Perhaps Miss Mary also confided in someone at the time? Without further documents the story cannot be judged with certainty. Perhaps it is taken for more important in *A Sketch of My Life* than it really was. The homoerotic inclinations are swept under the table there after all, and Mary Smith might be given more importance as a trial run on the path to marriage, which is then taken with Katia Pringsheim.

## MONEY MATCHES

"We were very rich," said Katia Mann at the age of ninety-four and opened her large, dark, and still expressive eyes very widely. "I had a French governess." She repeated the same two things frequently on the same evening.

"I'm not afraid of wealth." This remarkable admission is made by

Thomas Mann to his brother Heinrich on February 27, 1904. He has married the daughter of a multimillionaire and calculated that in Reichsmarks. He has married as did his Thomas Buddenbrook, who loved a flower girl but took as his wife the rich Gerda Arnoldsen. The flower girl whom Thomas Mann did not marry is Paul Ehrenberg. The turn away from homosexuality is the personal reason for getting married. Its social reason is the reconnection with the world of his fathers. That in spite of all his artist's licentiousness, he had remained a Lübeck middle-class man, Thomas Mann could hardly have said in 1895, but he emphasizes it loudly in the year 1905, shortly after the wedding. When he followed her to Munich, Thomas Mann had decided for the world of his mother, for Schwabing, the Bohème and the dream realm of art free of reality. But "it's not possible always to be interesting. You are ruined from being interesting or you become a master of it." Now comes the time to decide for his father. Marriage and family are the world of the father. In the Joseph novel the leitmotifs are arranged so that to the world of the mother belong incest and promiscuity, homosexuality and, duty forgotten, submersion into sexual chaos, laziness, and regression, while to the world of the father belong marriage, children, work, progress, and duty. In the decisive moments before the seduction, the features of his father will protect Joseph.

Thomas Mann recognized the connections very clearly in his essay "Marriage in Transition." There he says that same-sex love is bound with death because it is unfruitful and unfaithful. "Everything that marriage is—namely, endurance, foundation, procreation, family lines, responsibility—homoeroticism is not." Homoeroticism is connected with aestheticism, which, like it, is part of death. "That all artistic genius inclines in that direction, tends toward the abyss, is only all too certain."

Marriage lacks the tendency toward the abyss, but for that reason, also lacks deep passion. The honest turn to what is personal and private follows:

Hegel said that the most decent path to marriage was the one in which at first the decision for marriage stands and this then finally has the inclination for it as its result, so that at marriage both are joined. I read that with great pleasure, because it was my case.

That was written in 1925. But what really happened during the years between 1900 and 1905? We take a look first at a letter to Paul Ehrenberg from June 29, 1900. Its theme: a money match. Thomas Mann's sister Julia wants to marry the banker Josef Löhr. Paul advises against it. Thomas criticizes him:

> Was that really very reasonable of you? In these things one must not develop too much idealism. Every respect for "love," but one gets along without it. A piece of wisdom, by the way, that is quite repugnant to me myself. But what can you do on this inferior planet?

Money or love? Thomas Mann answers: Money! The marriage became unhappy. Relying on what the successful author later brazenly calls his "instinctual claim to dignity and comfortable abundance of the material things of life" led in Julia's case to a catastrophe. Not in the case of Thomas, we admit unwillingly. He always lived securely in affluence. We would like to have given him a few years of poverty, just so he could get acquainted with it. They would also have produced something literary, would certainly have been something of great use.

## THE COURTSHIP OF KATIA PRINGSHEIM

Kurt Martens, a colleague also in regard to occasional same-sex impulses, became a confidant of his plans for marriage. Martens had married; Thomas Mann wrote him on July 12, 1902:

> You have it very good, my dear fellow; never be ungrateful! I wonder whether possibly for me, a Flying Dutchman, a salvatiom like yours will sometime be afforded?

There follow the lines of music with the notes e, d, c, c, and under that "If he found a woman . . ." from Richard Wagner's opera *The Flying Dutchman*, that fabled figure who, cursed by the devil to sail the seas eternally, may land only every seven years and be released only by a faithful woman. Thomas Mann also felt like a man cursed.

Long before he got acquainted with Katia Pringsheim personally, he saw her in a picture painted by Friedrich August Kalbach entitled *Children's Carnival*. In an address on Katia's seventieth birthday,

Thomas Mann tells how in the seventh grade he saw the picture in a newspaper, clipped it out, and affixed it with thumbtacks over his desk. The five children with black locks and ivory-tinted complexions in Pierrot costumes, "four boys and a big-eyed, sweet girl," were in actuality the children of the Munich professor of mathematics Alfred Pringsheim; so Thomas Mann had his future wife constantly before his eyes even as a schoolboy. Such a good omen fortifies one later in many a vexation. The original of the painting was hanging in the Pringsheim's living room, where Thomas Mann could later admire it.

Before he had exchanged words with her, he already had impressions of her. He used to watch her through his opera glasses in the concert hall. Besides, he saw her often on the streetcar and thus also shared the pretty scene that Katia reports in her memoirs:

> When I was about to get off, the ticket checker came and said:
>     Your ticket!
> I say: I'm just getting off here.
> I gotta have it!
> I say: I just told you, I'm getting off. I just threw it away
>     because I'm getting off here.
> The ticket, I gotta—your ticket, I told you!
> Just leave me alone! I said and jumped down furious.
> Then he yelled after me: Get lost, you hellcat!

That charmed Thomas so much that he decided that, since he had always wanted to get acquainted with her, now he had to. He had consciously contrived the connection by an arrangement with Elsa Bernstein, "who was eager to promote our acquaintanceship and apparently liked to arrange marriages," that Katia and he be invited to a supper. Not entirely by chance, they had sat next to one another. Further invitations followed.

The streetcar and the opera glasses possibly belong in the summer of 1903. The first uncertain evidence of a contact is furnished by the draft of a letter to Otto Grautoff on August 29, 1903: Thomas Mann implores his friend

> not to say anything about the observation I shared with you last night against K——r, not even in the most harmless way. I would not like to appear to him even half as ridiculous as I do to myself. If you knew what kind of marvels and wild tales I have allowed

myself to dream during these days—and nights. . . . What a fool!
a fop, who would do better to sit down on his bottom and work
on something good instead of losing himself in such a fairy tale
of enchantment.

What kind of marvels and tales might those have been? What may he
have observed? Perhaps he and Katia made eyes at each other? At
this point it could not have been much more. K——r is probably Alfred Kerr, the famous literary critic, the Reich-Ranicki* of that time. In
her memoirs Katia mentions that Kerr had wanted to marry her but
she had not wanted to marry him; he held this against his luckier
rival all his life.

From the year 1903 the *Notebooks* also preserve the expression
"eyes, black as pitch"—what he saw was immediately noted down
for later literary use. Katia's eyes are handed on to Imma Spoelmann
in *Royal Highness*, to Rachel in *Joseph and His Brothers*, and to Marie
Godeau in *Doctor Faustus*. They also are found in the "Song of the
Child": "The strange, earnest little face / displayed the paleness of
pearls, and dark, flowing speech / led to a pair of eyes, dominating in
size."

Not until 1904 does Mann put down on paper more and more vivid
things about Katia. The most important is a letter to Heinrich of February 27. It proves irrefutably that there can have been no personal
meeting as yet in the year 1903, also no supper with the Bernsteins.
According to this letter, Thomas did not introduce himself personally
to Katia until February 10, 1904, and in the Pringsheim house, "after
earlier I had only gazed at her, often, long, and insatiably," apparently
with his opera glasses and in the streetcar. As in the case of Hans
Castorp seven months passed, until "after a long, quiet relationship
the first conversation" took place. As with Katia, also Clawdia Chauchat emits enchantment from her eyes, "which at times, with a certain
sideways glance that did not serve to see, could darken in a melting
way completely into the veiled nocturnal."

On the following day there is a large house ball with 150 guests
from literature and the arts, during the course of which the two of
them get better acquainted. A week later there follows a visit for tea
and a conversation for three, with Katia's mother. A meeting at the

---

* Marcel Reich-Ranicki, a brusk, bristly, and probing contemporary critic. (Trans.)

*Katia Pringsheim, 1904*

Bernsteins and an invitation to supper are in prospect for the beginning of March.

The senator's son is impressed by the combination of wealth and
culture. "Pringsheims are an experience that makes me feel complete.
A zoo with genuine culture. The father a university professor with a
gold cigarette case, the mother a Lenbach beauty,* the youngest son a
musician, his twin sister Katja (she is named Katja) a marvel, some-

---

* Franz, Ritter von Lehnbach (1836–1904), famed Munich portrait painter. (Trans.)

thing indescribably rare and precious, a creature who through her mere presence stirs up the cultural activity of 15 writers or 30 painters." Katia is as rare and precious as a piece of jewelry. He calls her "a small miracle of a universal harmonious education, a cultural ideal realized." Money and culture impress him. There is less talk about love.

A letter to Kurt Martens of April 2, 1904, speaks of the "giant progress" in the affair. Perhaps they took a bicycle ride through the English Garden. There cannot yet have been much else. Katia's first opinion turns out to be unfavorable. In the first of the preserved letters written to the streetcar hellcat is the line "because you cannot stand me." Her brothers mock him effectively as a "cavalry captain with an ailing liver." The way to her heart was still far away. On April 9 the *Notebook* comments: "Great discussion with K.P." There exists a letter from the end of April that complains about waiting and reveals jealousy about mathematics and physics. For Katia had taken her high school exam, which was rare for women at the time, and had studied mathematics, which was even more rare. Therefore her feminist grandmother, Hedwig Dohm, was against the connection with Thomas Mann. She did not like to see that marriage and motherhood might alienate her granddaughter from advanced science. "She was a zealous defender of the honor of her sex and its unconditional claim to equality, a passionate fighter for what was called the emancipation of women at the time, yes, an acknowledged leader of that movement." She wrote novels that dealt, in Klaus Mann's short formulation, with misunderstood women "who suffered from their narrow-minded husbands, read Nietzsche, and demanded the right to vote." When Thomas Mann made her acquaintance, she let him know that she "considered him a thief of the free and equal intellectual aspiration of women." There was something true about that. Katia was very talented. She was twenty-one at the time and planned to get a doctorate. And Thomas Mann was in fact no feminist. He had really revealed himself, for example wanted a boy as his first child; there was "no really serious business for a girl." This statement was brought to the attention of the pugnacious grandmother. From then on, Mann was to her a "damned old antifeminist and Strindbergian."

But we're not that far yet. The next thing to follow in the chronology is the note of May 16, 1904: "Second great discussion with K.P. The waiting period began with Thursday, May 19." Katia had left

Munich and remained away almost all summer. What had happened
before her departure we know from a letter to Kurt Martens on July
14:

> Then, on the last afternoon before her departure, her nice little
> twin brother left me alone with her for half an hour. There was
> an unspeakably sweet and tormenting farewell that still abides in
> all my nerves and senses; but that again remained without a pos-
> itive result. Impossible. She cannot, can't "imagine it," can't de-
> cide. As long as the decision is not directly in front of her, then in
> her own words, everything is quite easy, natural, and obvious,
> but when it comes down to it, she looks at me like a hounded
> doe and is beside herself. . . . A psychiatrist and good psycholo-
> gist, Dr. Seif, who like everybody else was certainly informed
> and with whom I talked in detail about the matter, confirmed to
> me (what I had long suspected) that this anxiety about making a
> decision is something notoriously pathological. If I did not pro-
> ceed much more diplomatically and with restraint, nothing would
> come of the engagement, according to his experience. Early Tues-
> day I was on the move, brought her flowers and, since little
> Klaus had taken a touchingly long time to pay the luggage han-
> dler on the side, found an opportunity to tell her how sad my
> mood was. She, too, a little? A little, yes. Very cautiously. But I
> received a long handclasp, and she looked only at me while the
> train was leaving the station. I could die. It is a separation for an
> almost indefinite time.

One can understand her anxiety about making a decision. He must
have pressed her terribly, and that he considers her hesitation something pathological and consults a psychiatrist is evidence of a regret-
able lack of self-criticism and capacity for empathy. Even in the retrospective statement of the ninety year old this seems rather reserved.
"I was twenty and felt good and happy inside, also with my studies,
with my brothers, the tennis club, and with everything, was very satisfied and actually did not know why I should leave it behind so
quickly. But Thomas Mann had the urgent desire to marry me. He
obviously really wanted to and was absolutely reckless." Later he
copied some of the letters from the waiting period to use for the novel
*Royal Highness*. These copies are preserved, but the originals are lost.
So one does not know for sure whether only what was literarily use-

ful was kept but not what was affectionate and spontaneous. For his letters have the effect of being quite stilted, although Katia finds them very passionate "for his situation." Not a hint that he ever lost his composure, although he asserted it: "I know myself, I lose face when I'm in love and must doubt the return of such feelings." His manner of courtship was not exactly alluring. In many respects he was impertinent. He exerted every means, that of radical confession as well as that of painful rhetoric:

—that I am very much aware of not being the man to awaken certain feelings simply and directly. . . . Anyone who never arouses doubt, never consternation, never, sit venia verbo, a little terror, who is simply always merely loved, is a dullard, a shadow shape, an ironic figure. I have no ambition in that direction.

. . . That it is my fault; and thus my constant need to comment to you about myself, to explain, to justify. May be that this need is totally superfluous. You are clever, are discerning out of goodness—and out of a bit of affection. You know that I, personally, humanly have not been able to develop like other young people, that a (talent) as a vampire can have the effect of bloodsucking, absorbing; you know what a cold, impoverished, purely dramatic, purely representative existence I have led for years; know that for years, for important years, I have not respected myself as a human being and wanted to be considered only in regard to being an artist. . . . You understand, too, that that can be no easy, no happy life and even with the strong sympathy of the outside world can lead to no composed and bold self-confidence. A cure of what is representative and artistic that clings to me, of the lack of a harmless trust in my personal, human side, is possible only through one thing: through happiness; through you, my clever, sweet, beneficent, good, beloved little queen! . . . What I beg of you, hope for, long for, is trust, is the unquestionble confidence in me even of a world, even of myself in myself, is something like faith, in short—is love. . . . This plea and yearning . . . . Be my affirmation, my justification, my completion, my salvation, my— wife!

But it still did not proceed. A letter to Martens a few days later (on June 13) complains: "To confront the girl now, with masculine energy, for a decision would mean to wring a No out of her, to the sorrow of both of us." So, for the time being, elaborate letters remain. In general the whole thing probably took place as in *Royal Highness*, where Prince Klaus Heinrich, who like Thomas Mann led only a representative existence, seeks the hand of the prim millionaire's daughter Imma Spoelmann tenaciously and systematically. The writer does not shy away from using his own letters almost word for word in the novel. Notes from the time of his courtship, in part already sketchily made literary, are found in the bundle of material for the novel. Some of them read:

> Dreamed (several times) that I held K's letter in my hand. Once it was very long and so marvelously folded that I could not find the beginning.

> Her naïveté is extraordinary; it is commanding and draws silence. —This strange, good and yet egotistical, unconsciously polite little Jewish girl! I can hardly imagine that she will ever get the word Yes past her lips. (Nervous anxiety before a decision.)

> A letter, perfumed, with her little child's handwriting. Since the window stands open it assumed, through the mixture of its aroma with the fresh air, something curiously vital and physically present. If he holds it to his face, it is something like the aroma of a clean and well-kept human being, who has just come into the room from outside, from wind and cold.

> . . . "Wondrous dream": She dismisses someone menacingly by pointing to me and declaring that she loves me. Painful disappointment upon awakening. But the dream still affects my senses.

> The first love scene in her room, where, with the permission of the baroness, she "shows him her books." —Later in the garden.

Finally, at the end of August, the change seems about to begin. Tonio Kröger had loved "life," but life not him. Now there approaches him "something absolutely and unbelievably new." He even suggests being "dumb" together, as blue-eyed life:

> "To be smart," you see, is something basically common. Anyone who eats two rolls daily, lives cautiously, loves cautiously, and is too cautious to bind his life to his love firmly is "smart." "Dumb"

is everything naïve, noble, and faithful, all brave devotion on earth. Let's be "dumb"—my Katia!

Of course, his calculation remains in spite of all the convulsive emotion shining through the rhetoric. To achieve victory on the emotional front would not suffice. He also had to assert himself socially. The Pringsheim's mixture of culture and money did attract him, but it did not make him meek. Was he not himself an exceptional person? He explained to Katia what made her a princess and him a prince. From his origins and his personal worth he was completely justified in hoping for her. She would "absolutely not step down, absolutely not perform an act of mercy," if one day before the whole world she would take the hand that was held out to her so pleadingly. As it says in "Song of the Child," like a man "I courted my beloved, standing on capable accomplishment." He felt like her equal, even without a gold cigarette case. But did they see it like that from the other side?

## PRINCE AND ALGEBRA

"Imma is a little too saucy," Katia reports in her old age, "I wasn't really like that. At times I liked to let a little superiority shine through, still Imma is too outré in my opinion—but I don't know myself that exactly." That does not have to mean that the essential kernel of the situation did not find expression in the novel. In any event, the novel offers an inside aspect that supplements the otherwise sparse sources with essential points of view.

In the novel Prince Klaus Heinrich gives Imma Spoelmann a gorgeous rose, but it smells of decay. It is a symbol for how what is literary kills life. It has "no soul." Imma then shows the prince her books, as Katia once did Thomas. In doing so, she sees an otherwise carefully concealed, crippled arm—Thomas Mann's artists are always crippled somehow—he loses his composure, sinks down before her, embraces her, stammers "Little sister . . . "—and she kisses his infirmity, his inhibition, his crippled hand. Obviously, she loves his weakness, not his ability to hide it. Sometime later there comes a revealing conversation that, whether it happened in reality or not, is characteristic of Thomas Mann's spiritual state. Klaus Heinrich is struggling, we read, to get Imma to venture out of the clear and frosty realms of algebra and conversational ridicule "into the unfamiliar zone, that warmer, mistier, and more fruitful one, that he showed to her." But she regrets again that both of them lost their composure when they were looking at the books. It gave him pleasure, but she laughingly makes the point that she was not there so he could recover in her presence from his princely existence. It is an empty, only formal, only pretended existence like that of the artist. "You pretended to go to school, you pretended to be at the university, you pretended to serve as a soldier and still pretend to wear the uniform; you pretend to hold audiences, you pretend to be a marksman and Heaven knows what else; you pretended to come into the world, and now I'm supposed suddenly to believe that anything at all is serious about you?" He demands trust from her. She: "No, Prince Klaus Heinrich, that I cannot." Whenever she sees him she feels coldness and fear. "You stand erect and ask questions, but not out of sympathy; the content of the question is of no importance to you, nothing at all is of importance to you, and there's nothing close to your heart. I have often seen it—you speak, you express an opinion, but you could just as well express a different one, for in reality you have no opinion and no belief, and nothing is important to you except your princely composure. . . . How could one trust you? No, it's not trust that you instill but coldness and bias, and if I were to take pains to get closer to you, that kind of bias and clumsiness would prevent me from doing so." He talks to her further, of course, again and again, but what he calls her dread about making a decision remains, "that timidity to leave her cool and mocking realm and to declare herself for him. . . ."

The turnabout happens somewhat differently in the novel than it does in life. Actually, Klaus Heinrich begins to take something seriously—the condition of the state finances—and with a red face begins to study books on economics with Imma. Whenever he raised his head, "he met Imma Spoelmann's eyes, enormous, flaming, and unwavering, which across the table, spoke a darkly eloquent language." Soon an engagement follows. "Little sister," he says to her while dancing, and, "Little bride."


## ENGAGEMENT AND WEDDING

We do not know what finally convinced Katia. September 1904 finally brings her assent, October 4 the engagement. How little "naturally," how strained the whole affair took place can hardly be overlooked. The Hegel quote about particularly moral marriages, in which affection only follows the decision to marry, is affirmed by the biographical findings. The situation also does not improve fundamentally throughout the engagement. The one who had previously demanded trust so convincingly, so articulately, notes in the fall of 1904:

> I must not communicate with her fully. She is not up to my sorrow, my torments. But without this chasm I would probably love her less. I don't love what is like me or merely understands me.

Right after the wedding, in March 1905, the Schiller study "Harsh Hour" comes into being. Schiller observes his sleeping wife. "A black lock curled across her cheek, which shone with the paleness of pearls." He encourages himself, suppressing heavy doubt:

> My wife! Beloved! Did you follow my longing and come to me to be my happiness? You are that, be still! And sleep! Do not now open those sweet, long-shadowing lashes to look at me, so large and dark, when sometimes as though you asked me and sought me! By God, by God, I do love you very much! Only sometimes I cannot find my emotion because I am often tired of suffering and wrestling with the task that I myself set for myself. And I cannot be all too much yours, not be entirely happy in you, for the sake of what is my calling.

No details are known about the engagement itself, but certainly about the trip afterward to Berlin's Tiergarten district to be introduced to Katia's relatives. Again (in a letter to Heinrich of December 23, 1904) there is almost only talk of strain. It is always necessary to be staunch; often "happiness" amounts to gritting your teeth. "The last half of the period of courtship—nothing but a great psychological strain. The engagement—also no fun, you must believe that." Social responsibilities, a hundred new people, displaying yourself, behaving yourself. In between, "day after day the fruitless and enervating ecstasies that are native to this absurd period of engagement"—whatever he may have meant by that.

The meeting of the two families proceeded essentially positively. Except for the feminist grandmother actually everyone was for the wedding, and so it was set then for February 11, 1905. The rich father-in-law set up their home, including telephone. Thomas Mann's furnishings up to that time found no favor in his eyes. "It's rubbish," said Herr Spoelmann disparagingly. Papa Pringsheim did not let his son-in-law take part. Julia, his mother, complains "you scarcely feel like the master in your own home." In a letter to her oldest child she describes the wedding party fairly exactly. There was not much to it. Hairdresser, registry office, at midday a reception at the Pringsheims' Arcisstrasse address, only fifteen persons (Heinrich and Carla were also missing), a few short speeches and toasts—Father Pringsheim would have preferred to dismiss the matter *privatissime*—toward six o'clock the departure of the young couple for Augsburg, from there a continuation of the honeymoon trip to Zurich, where in the Hotel Baur au Lac they lived in grand style. The addresses, it is true, of two Zurich neurologists and a hypnotist are listed in the notebook of the time.

A church wedding did not take place either. If it had, it would have had to be a Catholic one. "A Protestant marriage ceremony has no elegance," says the fictional Herr Aarenhold, like Samuel Spoelmann a portrait of Alfred Pringsheim. Thomas would like to have been married in church, he had written to Heinrich beforehand; after all, he was a Christian and from a good family.

That the proper festive depature was wanting sometimes hurt a bit later. What had remained unfulfilled in life Thomas granted himself in the novel. Klaus Heinrich and Imma marry festively before all the people in the court chapel, and the president of the High Consistory, Dom Wislizenus, preaches on the theme: "He will live, and they will give him gold from the empire of Arabia." But in the dreary reality of February 1905, Julia Mann had reason to complain. She had been invited to nothing but to dine with the young couple. She finds that Thomas should have stepped forward and spoken: "No, as dearly as I love Katia, I want to remain true to tradition and the inclination of my parents and forebears & demand a church wedding." But the sad thing was that the bride herself, in agreement with her father, who was not religious, did not insist on a church wedding. "Oh, Heinrich," Julia sighs, "I was, of course, never in agreement with this choice." She doubts Katia's love a little; she finds her cool.

Happiness—it was work and duty, a "stern happiness," as the formula in *Royal Highness* reads. A defensive letter to Heinrich is of the opinion that happiness had not been given him, he had "submitted to it out of a kind of feeling of duty, a kind of morality, an innate imperative of my own." In other words, life was a *work*: "Had not life and work always been one thing to me?" "Song of the Child" asks, continuing: "Art was not invention to me, only a scrupulous life: / But life and work, too—I never knew how to sever them."

So the prerequisites were not simple, not the most favorable. That affection follows the decision to marry is almost a small miracle. It always remained problematical, but the marriage was not unhappy. More on this in a later chapter.

## KATIA, FICTIONALLY

He makes use of her immediately and over and over. Already in May 1904 in the Schwabing novella "By the Prophet," a short-story writer, hardly disguised, is treated, who attends the reading of the high-flown poet-prophet Daniel, although he has "a certain relationship to life." He has this because he no longer believes he is a Schwabing literary creature from the icy sphere of intellect and art since he has been courting Katia Pringsheim. She appears as "Fräulein Sonja," and here, too, there is something singularly impersonal: "an unbelievable stroke of luck by a creature, a marvel of universal education, a consummate cultural ideal." Her mother, too, appears. In her splendid house she has "door frames made of Giallo antico"; that this was so also at the Pringsheim's we know from a letter. With this small tale, Mann intends to separate himself from the milieu of the Schwabing bohemians in order to appear socially acceptable. In the conversation with "Frau Pringsheim" the story writer reveals his theory about what is lacking in the Schwabingers through Daniel: "Perhaps what is human? A bit of emotion, longing, love?" Evidently, with this he recommends himself. Although, what advantage could he really take of the Schwabingers? "Life" was still only a plan; he was also still nothing but a literary man.

The literary man "experiences in order to express," Mann wrote later in an essay. There has already been mention of how the young husband immediately, in March 1905, put his wife in the Schiller story "Harsh Hour." We have likewise already mentioned that he then used the entire time of his engagement in a novel *Royal Highness* (conceived after 1903, written 1906–1909), although by far not all the details carried over from life into his work could be weighed here extensively, not the "tiger sense" of the father and not his gold cigarette case, not Imma's Indian blood (instead of Katia's Jewishness), as well as the bicycle trip turned into a horseback ride in the novel (of which Katia remained the victor).

It turned out to be more painful when immediately thereafter he revealed further details from his new surroundings and let the wealth, the Berlin Zoo district, a father with a growling voice, a polar-bear skin, and the Jewish twins Siegmund and Sieglinde appear. That happened in the story *The Blood of the Walsungs*, written in the summer of 1905. It ends with sibling incest on the polar-bear skin. It concerned an engagement that was not really desired. Sieglinde is to marry a correct German bureaucrat but is quite content in her sibling den and has no desire for Herr von Beckrath. But "finally, after she had told him often enough that she did not love him, Sieglind had begun to watch him probingly, expectantly, quietly, with a gleaming, earnest look that spoke intangibly, like that of an animal—and had said Yes."

Thomas Mann is otherwise no Beckrath. Only at this one point does the story touch on reality. It may be that here he was shaping his fear of never really being accepted by the strange family, his fear of Katia and her clan being able to cluster together incestuously and deny him entry into the most intimate mystery for all time as a stranger.

But even without that, he had gone too far. When the inaccurate but not surprising rumor spread that he had written a strongly anti-Semitic novella that compromised his wife's family terribly besides, he had to stop the publication of the story. It appeared, then, only many years later. "Of course, I have since then been unable to shake off the feeling of a lack of freedom that becomes very oppressive in hypochondriac hours," Thomas writes to Heinrich, "and, of course, you call me a cowardly bourgeois." But how could he ever believe that he could make use of his new family as material just as uninhibitedly as once when in Italy, on bad terms with his homeland, he had done with his relatives in Lübeck? All his life he lacked an understanding of the pain that he brought to others through real or alleged portraits. Even now he reacted to the insult to his absolute artistic freedom with a radically aestheticized apologia, his first important essay, entitled *Bilse and I*, written in December 1905–January 1906. "The reality that a writer makes useful for his purposes may be his daily world, may as a person be his closest and most beloved; he may show himself to be dependent on the particulars taken from reality, may use its last characteristic eagerly and obediently for his work, still for him—and it should be for everyone!—a bottomless difference will remain intact between reality and his images: the essential difference that forever separates the world of reality from that of art."

Only much later and then much more mediated does Katia appear literarily again, in *Joseph and His Brothers* and *Doctor Faustus*. In the biblical novel, Rachel, Jacob's beloved, has acquired traits of Katia, the touching slenderness and delicacy of her shoulders, her black hair, her lovely face but, above all, again her eyes, "full of sweet darkness," "a deeply, flowing, speaking, melting, friendly night, full of earnestness and mockery." Further, Thomas Mann gives her the difficult delivery of their daughter Erika as the birth of Joseph; with her second delivery (Benjamin) he even lets her die. She has a sister, Lea, who is blurry eyed but efficient in giving birth and bears six sons as well as a daughter. Rachel is the loving one, Lea the physical one. Then, as is well known, two weddings occur. For seven long years Jacob had served for Rachel, but on his wedding night in complete darkness, Lea is substituted. "Lea's was the reality, but the significance was Rachel's."

If the attempt is made to translate it back into what was experienced, then two things result. Rachel is Katia, insofar as she is lovely in the way she is described—that is indisputable. But Lea is Katia too, insofar as she is the mother of six, capable of life. She doesn't resemble her outwardly but from her situation. As her father, Laban, the rich dullard, is also never tired of emphasizing, she is the right one for society because she is the firstborn. We draw conclusions further into the unknown. The two weddings with Rachel and Lea are set by the Bible. But, as always, his own life material could be included in the foreign pattern. Was Lea not Katia, that is, duty? Was Rachel not Paul Ehrenberg, the inclination that forgot duty? The two weddings express the fact that the senses are afflicted by unfruitful and irresponsible homoerotic dreams while reality is fruitful, social, and sexual. In life Katia, in her aura somewhat boylike, probably had the capability of giving both, thus also to satisfy the homoerotic desire a bit. But the conflict continued to smolder. In the Joseph novel Jacob is punished because he has pressed his love for Rachel so exclusively at the cost of his duty in regard to Lea. God takes away his beloved. Only later does Jacob recognize the significance. Rachel, the lovely one, died along the road and was buried with no extravagance. She continues to live in Jacob's memory, even without the Egyptian art of wrapping. When it comes time for Jacob to die, he does not want to be buried in Egypt but in his homeland, however, not next to Rachel, the one loved too much, but in a family vault beside Abraham and Sarah, beside Isaac and Rebecca and, he says expressively, beside Lea, the fruitful one, the mother of the six. That is a decision for duty and against love.

> I loved her; I loved her too much, but not in accordance with feelings and the voluptuous softness of the heart, rather in accordance with greatness and obedience. It is not proper that I lie along the road, but Jacob wants to lie beside his forebears and beside Lea, his first wife, from whom his heirs came.

This is to be translated anew as a duty-conscious renunciation of the luxury of being in love, as a renunciation of homoeroticism in favor of marriage and social duty.

"That she had the most beautiful black eyes in the world, I put foremost—black as jet, as pitch, as ripe blackberries"; that can only be Katia's eyes. In the Faust novel they are given to Marie Godeau, to whom Adrian Leverkühn is thinking of proposing marriage. Decisive for the biographical deciphering is the time sequence of the events. He wants to marry shortly after he has come to use "Du" with Rudi Schwerdtfeger. The narrator is glad that this plan would mean the release "from his elfin bond to Schwerdtfeger" and is inclined to understand the plan for marriage "as a conscious means" to accomplish that. That is very reminiscent of Mann's corresponding plans. Of Rudi it is expected (and perhaps of Paul, too) that the whole effort with which he "won over" the lonely man "with astonishing patience to what is human" and persuaded him to use "Du," should be only a "rehearsal of what is human" and a "prelude" to marriage. What "happened between Adrian and Rudolf Schwerdtfeger, and how it happened—I *know* all about it," says Serenus Zeitblom, "and though the objection might be raised tenfold that I could not know, since I was 'not there.'" He knows about it precisely because he *was* there, personally, in 1903.

The decisive situation of the years 1903 and 1904 was extraordinarily complex. What could he expect, what would the consequences be? Would his artistic structure hold or break? He did not know himself. According to his mood he tried one or another variation of the story as a test. The optimistic possibility, which happily and hopefully strengthens the decision for marriage that was already made, appears first in "By the Prophet." In *Royal Highness* it is stylized and exaggerated in a grandiose fairy-tale manner up to the reconciliation of the artist with life and the people. In both cases one part of what is problematic is left out for the sake of a happy ending. "Harsh Hour" then forms the secret reservation of the artist as a husband and *The Blood of the Walsungs* his fear in the last analysis of having no intrinsic right to press into the bourgeois world. Rachel and Lea depict the division and the bold synthesis that were lived in this life, as far as it was possible. In *Doctor Faustus*, finally, the instance of the catastrophe presents a chance to state again that the isolation of the artist is not resolved, that "life" does not come into it, and that it must always be the murderer of everything alive. It is the old conflict. "Art is hard, but our heart is soft."

# VI. Ambitious Plans

*Munich, 1906*

After the marriage, the first four children come fairly quickly: Erika (born on November 9, 1905), Klaus (November 18, 1906), Golo (March 27, 1909), and Monika (June 7, 1910). A second pair came years later (Elisabeth, April 24, 1918, and Michael, April 21, 1919). On July 30, 1910, Mann's sister Carla killed herself in their mother's apartment in Polling. The years from 1905 to 1914 are a time of relative fame and affluence with reading tours, cures, and vacation sojourns—otherwise, if one disregards a train accident, without striking outer events. A stately summer house is built in 1908 in Bad Tölz. A large family house in Munich-Bogenhausen, Poschingerstrasse 1 (today, Thomas Mann Allee 10) follows, and they move in on January 5, 1914. From 1912 to 1913 Thomas Mann is a member of the Censorship Committee of the Royal Bavarian Police Bureau.

In regard to works, completed are the drama *Fiorenza* (1905), the stories *The Blood of the Walsungs* (1905) and "Harsh Hour" (1905), the novel *Royal Highness* (1909), and the novella *Death In Venice* (1912). Contemplated but never finished are a novel about Frederick the Great, a Munich society novel (entitled "Maya, or The Lovers"), and the story "A Miserable Man." Started are the *Confessions of Felix Krull, Confidence Man* (begun in 1910) and *The Magic Mountain* (begun in 1913). The most important essays of the period are "Bilse and I" (1906), "Essay on the Theater" (1907), "Sleep, Sweet Sleep!" (1909), and "Coming to Terms with Wagner" (1911). The most important plan for an essay is "Intellect and Culture"; an amorphous mass of notes has survived the years, most of them written in 1909.

# FAME!

"AT TIMES my stomach churns with ambition," Thomas Mann had written to Otto Grautoff on November 6, 1901. "Fame seems not to want to fail me completely, *even though* I desire it." Mann was writing *Fiorenza* at the time, one of his most ambitious works. "The suffering must not have been in vain. It must bring me peace!" says Savonarola there. Thomas Mann also claims the formulation for himself: "What? Suffering should have been in vain? Art should be lost . . . it should not be allowed to bring him any fame? Thus ambition speaks. Thus all ambition is *justified*."

The strain is enormous. Every day before noon one "passage"; more is not possible. Not running away at that tempo, also finishing what is begun; for that, Mann affirms in 1907, patience is required, a dogged stubbornness, a self-subjugation of the will under which the nerves are often tense enough to scream. Self-esteem and self-loathing play a game with him. What he has written appears to him "at times so new and beautiful that I chuckle to myself—and at times so silly that I sit on the chaise longue and think I'm dying." Self-love was vitally necessary for the stabilization of an ego strained to the extreme. Concerning "that passion for his ego that burned inextinguishably deep within him," a Schiller very similar to Thomas Mann thinks in "Harsh Hour": "At times he needed only to observe his hand to be filled with an ardent tenderness for himself."

The second life support, after narcissism, was fame, the admiration of the public. "Performing official duties is enjoyable for me," Thomas writes to Heinrich. He dresses well, Erika later reports—"but still has to be corrected at times, since he cannot distinguish green from blue." From appearance to appearance he becomes more confident. "The newspapers printed nice personal descriptions, after I had been so bold and sure at the podium."

Fame alone is not enough for him. He wants to be loved as well. When Kurt Martens predicts to him that he will receive more cool respect than heartfelt love, he argues against it with a reference to *Buddenbrooks* and *Tonio Kröger*. Why should the Germans deny him love? "What fault will they have to find with what makes me human? I was a quiet, courteous person who, through the work of his hands, achieved some affluence, took a wife, sired children, visited premieres, and was such a good German that he couldn't stand being abroad for more than four weeks. Does there have to be bowling and drunkenness, too?"

The greatest enemy of fame is exhaustion. Now, since he had stepped from the exploitation of the intellect into lawfulness and social connection, had wife and children, "now he was exhausted and finished," it is said of Schiller in "Harsh Hour." The already familiar thought is also found here: "Should the suffering have been in vain? I must make myself great!"

Schiller is struggling with his *Wallenstein*. Thomas Mann, too, has the will for what is difficult; he, too, seeks battle-worthy subjects during that time. The years up to his marriage had been years of decisive development. The epochs of life now following had to yield profits. The reunion with the world of his father through his rich marriage made success a duty. But under such strains nothing good comes easily into being. Seen literarily, the decade ending in 1914 is a time of crisis. But from no stage of development do we have so much left lying about, never finished. The "stern happiness" was a strained happiness. The husband wants fame. He wants to become the exemplary national author, like his Gustav von Aschenbach, about whom it is said that the educational authorities adopted texts from his pen for school readers. This wishful dream, too, was eventually to be fulfilled. But the personal title of nobility that was awarded Aschenbach on his fiftieth birthday was dashed in the case of Thomas Mann by the passing of the imperial empire. The first honorary doctorate was offered in 1919 as a substitute, just as proudly used: "In booking, the first use of the doctor title."

## FIORENZA

*Fiorenza*, "a dream of greatness and intellectual power," a case of "the eroticism of fame," a product of "the lust for fame, the anxiety about fame of one caught up at a tender age by success," had been finished amid torments directly before his wedding. That he wrote the last scene in Utting on the Ammersee, alone with his mama, that he was enthused about himself and found the ending so good that he expressly put it in his diary, and with "purple ink," we know from a diary entry of December 6, 1919. We cannot check that, because later in California Mann burned the original diaries of 1904–1905. Anyway, he was very proud of the play and engaged himself again and again in arranging productions, with modest success. His daughter Erika had to play Fiore once, in 1929 in Bielitz near Kattowitz. But that was probably not such a good idea.

The fact that he wrote a drama that made the "attempt at a song in higher tones," is again testimony above all to Mann's ambition, for the dominant late-classicistic taste still held that drama was the highest genre. The fact that in the second chapter of his "Essay on Theater" (1907) he opposes this opinion is likewise ambition, for naturally he would like to create the highest place for the genre he himself controlled best, the novel. The essay is a piece "against theater."

Nonetheless the writer is deeply insulted when Alfred Kerr, the famed critic, viciously derides his drama. "The author is a nice, somewhat vapid little soul, whose roots have their quiet residence in his rump." That was lacking in respect and was coarse and hit only deep within him upon something accurate. All the worse. Kerr also makes snide remarks about being trapped, being sheltered—possibly a well-informed allusion to the writer's marriage to Katia Pringsheim, who once sent Kerr packing. Mann wants to put him in his place. He writes to the critic well disposed to him, Julias Bab: "Do you know why Kerr can know nothing about greatness? Because he has never achieved a great work." That may indeed be true, but even so, what Kerr alludes to is valid, that an actor of greatness is not already great, and that at the time, Thomas Mann wants greatness more than he has it. At any rate, he at least knows how to make a theme of the situation and to draw from it what is best intellectually. "One should not possess," says his Lorenzo de Medici, not riches, fame, or success. "Longing is a giant power; but possession emasculates."

Trapped and sheltered? Kerr has suspected what effort Thomas Mann had to inflict on himself. His Savonarola, the prior of San Marco, is also not a cerebral person voluntarily and supremely but a person forced by his impulses to be cerebral. What is autobiographical in *Fiorenza*, Mann has always suppressed in his interpretations of himself. It is the primal scene of humiliation that appears here again, being ridiculed for desiring, repudiation by life, and the icy constraint to be intellectual. The prior was in love with her, the courtesan Fiore says. She is happy about the power over his drab arrogance that has fallen to her. Out of curiosity she lets it happen that one day, as darkness falls, he is alone in the room with her:

> Then he groaned and was drawn to me and whispered and sobbed and confessed. . . . And when I reproached his actions in pretended astonishment, a madness came upon him, almost inhuman, and gasping he implored me, begging and yearning, to belong to him. Now I, with disgust and horror, pushed him away from me—it may be that I struck at him because he wouldn't loosen his lustful embrace. And when I did that, he rose up with a scream, hoarse and incomprehensible, and took flight, covering his eyes with his fists.

Two dreams propel life: the dream of love and the dream of power. When love is denied, power remains. Fiore humbles Savonarola; instead of her, he conquers Florence.


## HEROISM: FREDERICK THE GREAT

"I am now thirty. It is time to think about a masterpiece." Ambition flames. To write a novel about an important, highly respected Prussian king in the Wilhelminian age means to recommend oneself as a national writer. Even if the reverence for the hero should be reduced by an element of Nietzschean psychology—"depicting a hero human-*all-too*-human, with skepticism, with *spite*, with psychological radicalism, and yet positively, lyrically, out of one's own experience"—gives the impetus to the "greatness" of the figure. "The decisive thing is that a material that I am to endure for a period of years must possess a certain *dignity* in itself as an object. . . . That provides pride in bearing it, offers stability, lets one endure it." The presumptuousness of the venture, of course, lies in the fact "that I, the lyrical writer, undertake to depict *greatness*. Because for that one must have knowledge of greatness, experience and cognizance of greatness. . . . Do I have it?" And looking back, he calls *Fiorenza* and "Harsh Hour" preparatory studies for the theme of greatness. Exalted narcissistically, he continues: "And if I succeed in greatness, which, as I hear, I have managed to do in small measure—making greatness palpable, and depicting it intimately and vitally—then my pride will know no bounds."

He did not succeed. Merely a collection of notes and excerpts is preserved, mainly from the first half of the year 1906. One of these notes indicates a surreptitious personal matter in the choice of subject:

> Frederick's later same-sex propensities. It can be shown very calmly how with age and enormous superiority an erotic relationship with handsome and insignificant young men comes into being, a relationship as for a man with a woman.

It was never completed. In 1914 Mann does write an essay appropriate for wartime, "Frederick and the Grand Coalition," which however for the most part is nurtured from other sources and realizes only very little of the original intention.

That this original intention also had to do with Mann's marriage and, indeed, in a hostile regard, is clear from two letters. Thomas writes Heinrich on January 26, 1910, that anyone who already planned a "Frederick" before *Royal Highness*, had in his heart not really believed in a "stern happiness in marriage" so completely. "Which doesn't prevent being able to believe in it practically." A letter to Ernst Bertram two days later states more precisely that anyone who wanted to write a "Frederick" probably did not believe in a synthesis of Highness and happiness. "Frederick," one can then conclude, is the figure of the *privatim* unhappy ruler excluded from life, who with homoerotic tendencies distances himself as far as possible from wife and family whom he regards as contemptible duties and, towering in solitude, allows himself to be fawned upon by handsome greyhounds. Thomas Mann, too, had a fast dog at the time, the slightly crazy aristocratic collie Motz, who returns as Perceval in *Royal Highness*. The novel of a marriage was workable, but "Frederick" remained untouched, too grand and too daring.

## THE UNSUCCESSFUL BILSE PIECE
## AND OTHER ACTIVITIES

*Bilse and I* is the most important poetic self-reflection of the early period. It defends aestheticism against the objection that in *Buddenbrooks* only the Lübeck middle-class world is portrayed. As a result, important statements are made in this piece. Its tone is somewhat different. It is totally and inappropriately arrogant and offers further proof of the insecurity of Thomas Mann in those years of enormous but at heart aimless ambition. "One day I heard a writer say," he claims— and then quietly cites his own figure, Tonio Kröger. "This writer seemed to me to express that in a melancholy, witty way. . . . But then the writer seemed to me to touch on a second thing." That may be irony, but it is a tormented, an unsuccessful, a bit haughty form of irony.

One may find statements notable as radical aestheticism such as the following: that the true lover of words would sooner make an enemy of the world than sacrifice one nuance. But those are pretty phrases. Biographically speaking, not only nuances but completed tales (*The Blood of the Walsungs*) and great plans for works ("Frederick") are sacrificed at the time. With great effort the Bilse piece takes a position that its author cannot maintain. When his wife Katia later manifests "resistance to the depiction of intimacies" in the harmless "Song of the Child" and compels Tommy to strike two verses "without which the piece is very weak," considerations really became necessary in *Royal Highness*. After the marriage there were again problems of discretion. Thomas Mann could no longer be as ruthlessly honest as in *Buddenbrooks*, had to clarify and keep silent and be diplomatic. The novel was a bit fashionably hypocritical, the author admits in a letter. Indeed. The Bilse essay quotes Friedrich Schlegel emphatically: "The artist who does not sacrifice his whole self is a useless slave." But did Thomas Mann perchance sacrifice his whole self? "I dare not inform her *completely*, of course," he wrote in his *Notebook* in the fall of 1904.

Instead he believed he should spread the suggestion among the public in the fall of 1905 to consider him a person "who will enter the history of literature." Of course, that did come true. But must one brag so? The polemic vein in Thomas Mann is strong, but when it swells, the reasons are not always well chosen. Arthur Holitscher was not entirely so wrong, in the final analysis, when he was annoyed by the portrait that Thomas Mann gave of him in "Tristan." It was not necessary to carry on in public once again about the incident and to call the already victimized man weak and constrained in the Bilse essay. It is unlikely that Thomas Mann himself, had he been portrayed, would have been as sovereign as he claims. He was sensitive. But all the irritability and angry one-sidedness of those years is explained and pardoned by the psychological tension into which he had maneuvered himself.

"I had no wish left to drag such a foolish friend along with me": At that time the literary man Richard von Schaukal also received such a solemn "letter of divorce" dated October 14, 1905. For some years he had praised Thomas Mann. Then he dared to find *Fiorenza* bad, even worse, not even to have read it to the end. In the meanwhile Mann was famous enough; he no longer needed Schaukal and bade him farewell demonstratively. "I declare that our relationship is in dire need of rest and suggest that we forget one another for the moment."

Also, when the psychologically overburdened man got involved with the cultural philosopher Theodor Lessing in 1910, he obviously lacked objects more deserving of his hate. The piece "Doctor Lessing" demolishes a critic who had attacked Thomas Mann in a way that is unseemly. The man who intends to be difficult seeks here a victim who is easy to dispatch. Inwardly discontented, he gets embroiled in base quarreling. That he had gotten involved with Lessing, he admits, had been basically "perplexed thirst for activity." "The secret is that I could not begin the 'Confidence Man'; out of tormented inactivity, I lashed out." Granted, the *Confessions of Felix Krull, Confidence Man*, the first phase of which extended from 1910 to 1913, was also not a dignified object, but still a real one insofar as narcissism, acting, and delight in handsome boys come into their own here. Of course, this novel, too, remained a fragment at the time, but a lucky fragment from which one of the most successful and beloved works of Thomas Mann will later emerge.

The essay "Intellect and Art" should have been able to be compared in rank with Schiller's "On Naïve and Sentimental Poetry," and thus would have fulfilled the criterion of greatness. But "the subject led into the immeasurable, and the essayistic discipline of the author was not sufficient to compose it. So the plan remained an amorphous mass of notes." The notes are preserved and informative but in many regards contradictory. Whether he should consider himself an analytical European literary man or rather a synthetic German writer is completely unclear to the tireless seeker at the time.

Also the plan for the novella "A Wretched Man," which is connected with Lessing and Kerr and was to demonstrate moral decisiveness, remained uncompleted. Perhaps that was good—he may have lacked the greatness, if not also the will for it.

The outbreak of World War I ended the era of indecision and tensions. The "greatness" that he did not succeed in producing by himself now approaches him from history. Mann recognizes it at once as his chance. He immediately makes the war his subject. That, too, was to be revealed later as a mistake, but it did help him out of his creative crisis.

## WORKDAY AND ALCOHOL

Anyway, in the time of ambition he learned how to work. "Every forenoon a step, every afternoon a 'piece'—that's just my way, and it has its necessity." Fewer than thirty lines a day make him discontented. If as a Bohemian he had slept sometimes until noon, even until three o'clock in the afternoon, the married man now sits at work writing as regularly as possible, also on Sunday, also on vacation, from nine to twelve or half past, followed by walks, lunch, rest, writing letters, or researching sources, dinner, conviviality, sometimes reading aloud, otherwise listening to music, reading, and writing in his diary. Too much socializing makes him nervous; theater, wine, and conversation until late in the night are a boost that is punished the next day—"and may be punished in God's name! In the final analysis sin belongs to the moral household." Also nocturnal pollutions, desired and involuntary, bother work, as many diary passages reveal. You wake up angry when a dream has brought the stuff of life gushing, and you afterward do not organize the whole costly forenoon any longer.

Work is necessary for the sake of spiritual welfare; not working is a sin and "a horrible feeling" on top of that, for without work there is no life. "You feel yourself and know something about yourself only when you are doing something. The times in-between are dreadful." Also the times of crisis, when work comes to a standstill, are terrible. Then also sometimes the workday proceeds less precisely, you sleep longer, and go shopping in the light of morning or go get a haircut. When he was not getting ahead with his work, then his profound disgruntlement was shared by everyone who was around him. Whenever something is finished, preparations take place without a pause for the next project, mostly on the next day. What emerged in the course of a lifetime from such tirelessness—with letters and diaries there were certainly five pages daily, eighteen hundred in a year, in sixty years of creation over a hundred thousand written pages—is simply astonishing. Including an enormous number of letters, the av-

erage per day is three to four, written by hand, most of them extensive and loving; only later does he dictate, on many days ten letters.
Letters received are answered at once the next day or the day after, if
they are important. Others lie unanswered longer, but almost every
person who wrote to Thomas Mann received a reply. Letters were his
way of loving people from the distance, breaking out of his solitude,
and yet protecting himself from intrusiveness. "Giving the world its
due and still *protecting oneself* from it reasonably is a trick that must be
learned."

Not stress and pressure or intensity and obsession put him into a
mood to work, rather getting enough sleep and fresh air, "pure air,
few people, good books, peace, peace." Apart from smoking, he lived
fairly conscious of his health and avoided excesses of all kinds. "I was
never a sportsman, but must keep my mobility and have great joy in
driving around in the country." During the early days in Munich,
bicycling plays a large role. There was even horseback riding on the
way to Mitterbad: "I rode a kind of cavalry horse with a fabulous
physique but with the temperament of a sloth and the bad moods of a
jackass without enough sleep." His nervous stomach forces moderation in eating and drinking. Coffee is indigestible, but on the other
hand he likes sweets, liqueur, or cognac. Alcohol is not used for inspiration but for relaxation. A glass of beer with supper creates an easy-
chair comfort and a mood of, "It is finished." It's different with cigars
and cigarettes—they help at work. "While writing, I smoke." An open
sky is good only for dreaming and planning; working something out
requires the protection of a ceiling.

Novels, stories, a drama, essays, speeches, letters, diaries—the
amount of writing accomplished is enormous. He exists not for the
sake of living but for the sake of writing. "He did not work like someone who worked to make a living but like someone who wants nothing more than to work because he has no regard for himself as a
living human being, wishes only to be considered a creator."

## WHY DID I GET MARRIED?

Thomas Mann did not believe that Katia would deceive him, and no
one wanted to suggest it to him. But perhaps he was afraid that sometime it could happen as in the following scene:

Imagine the following fictional character. A man, noble and passionate, but marked in some way and in his mind a dark exception among the proper people, among "the rich, curly-headed
darlings of the people"; genteel now and then, but not genteel as
a sufferer, solitary, shut out from happiness, from the noncha-
lance of happiness and relying entirely on his accomplishments.
Good conditions, everything to outdo the "darlings" who do not
find accomplishment necessary; good conditions for greatness.
And in a harsh, stern, and difficult life he becomes great, carries
out glorious things publicly, is decorated with honors for his services—but in his mind remains a dark exception, very proud as a
man of accomplishment but full of mistrust in his human side
and without faith that he could be loved. Then a young woman
steps into his life, a bright, sweet, genteel creature. She loves him
for what he does and suffers, she spurns all the curly-headed
darlings and chooses him. His incredulous rapture teaches him to
have faith. She becomes his wife, and he is far from jealous in his
marriage. "She had eyes, after all, and chose me." She is his reconciliation with the world, his justification, his perfection; she is
nobility in person. And now, because of some diabolical scan-
dalmongering, this man becomes poisoned slowly with the suspicion that his wife is deceiving him with some smooth and ordinary fellow. Slowly, under torment, doubt gnaws at his pride, at
his new faith in happiness. He is no match for the doubt; he is
not secure; the bitter knowledge arises that the likes of him can
never be sure, that he should never have based his life on happiness and love, and that along with the faith in this love's bliss his
life is also now destroyed. Why did I get married?"

What is Thomas Mann talking about? Always "about me, about me."
The Bilse piece knows that. Every word is aimed at him—although
here he relates the plot of Shakespeare's *Othello*, the master of double
ambiguity.


## MAYA

"Maya" was planned as a social novel. Why did nothing come of it?
At the time, Thomas wrote to Heinrich that his "Frederick" had great-

ness but that he no longer trusted himself to have the patience and the diffidence "to drag the burden *of any kind* of modern novel around for two or three years." The subgenre of social novel did not have his respect at that time, as can be seen; besides, it was Heinrich's specialty. In addition there were probably personal and most intimate private reservations. Munich society would have had to be portrayed. But meanwhile much consideration would certainly have to be taken into account here. The most intimately private matters might have pertained to the content, for basically "Maya" was to treat his relationship with Paul Ehrenberg. The plan was not carried out; the array of notes, however, was carefully preserved. The main part of them came into play only decades later in *Doctor Faustus*. The Munich reservations had meanwhile become invalid; indeed, there even seemed to be the desire to critically allot Munich society a structural lineage: "Prehistory of Fascism." But also in regard to the Ehrenberg reservations Thomas Mann himself, as well as his wife, were more candid than in the early period of their marriage. The background of these matters remained impenetrable to the public anyway, since the biographical sources were not available.

## THE TRAIN WRECK

On the evening of May 1, 1906, Thomas Mann experienced a real train wreck. He had boarded the night express train from Munich to Dresden at 7:00, where after a twelve-hour trip he would have arrived about 6:50. About 9:30, in Regenstauf, a little past Regensburg, there was a terrible crash, for as the result of a defect in a switch the elegant main-line train had knocked a standing freight train off the tracks. There were several persons injured and great damage to property. The author was sitting in a car toward the rear, where there was only a lurch and a heavy jolt to deal with. But the baggage car was directly behind the locomotive and was heavily damaged.

To a literary man, such an incident is a gift from Heaven. It was not Thomas Mann's way to leave it unused; he made notes at once, and two and a half years later enlarged them into a little tale. The accident is only foreground in it. Deeper down it is about ambition and keeping up appearances, about fame and fear. The only thing that really affects the traveler is the fate of his manuscript—"my beehive, my

woven art, my sly fox den, my pride and tribulation." It is said to be
an imposing bundle of pages. It is in the suitcase, and *that* is in the
baggage car.

The hero of the story is on his way to a reading. He likes to do that.
"You put on a show, you make an appearance, you show yourself to
the jubilant crowd." Afterward he wants to take a vacation and write
a bit while doing so. That is why he has taken his manuscript along.
But from the front of the train comes bad news. There is said to be a
wasteland of wreckage there, everything in confusion, torn apart and
crushed. The work of removal is to be undertaken—work of removal
with his manuscript! "I had no copy of what was there, was already
completely formulated and composed, that was already alive and res-
onating—not to mention my notes and sketches, my foraged treasure
of material gathered together, hard earned, overheard, surreptitiously
acquired, suffered through for years."

In May 1906 Thomas Mann had just begun to write his *Royal Highness*. The "beehive" and "fox den" did not exist in reality; there could
be no talk of an "imposing bundle of pages," and whatever he had in
his luggage at the time was not the completely formulated manuscript of a novel. But Thomas Mann obviously wants to present himself as someone who had such a bundle of pages. He imagines himself in the story as a productive writer certain of his goal and
imperturbable. That was his great dream at the time. He creates a
style for himself as a self-assured and successful man who cannot be
thrown off track by something as elementary as a train wreck. He
wants to show himself as a man—contrary to that monocled cavalier
wearing spats who earlier "in view of his rights as a gentleman" denounced the conductor as a horse's ass but in the wreck yells for help
childishly and timorously.

## THE STATE, OUR FATHER, AND
## AN ENLIGHTENED MONARCH

Look at that conductor with the leather bandolier, the imposing
constable's mustache, and the surly vigilant look. Look how he
barks at the old woman in the threadbare black mantilla because
she almost got into the second-class car. That is the state, our
father, authority, and security. No one likes to have anything to

do with him; he is strict, he's probably even coarse, but reliable, he is reliable, and your suitcase is as safe as in Abraham's bosom.

It is not just irony when Thomas Mann characterizes himself in "The Train Wreck" as the "subject of Wilhelm II." He is that not only legally but also from conviction. He is conservative. Because there was seldom a reason to say that expressly, this fact entered public consciousness for the first time in 1914.

He was able to distinguish between the idea and the appearance of a conservative structure of the state. That "gentleman" in spats who shouts at the conductor is caricatured ironically as a negative example of the levels of society that had the say in the Wilhelminian age. Mann has no time for arrogant snobbery, though he does for authority practiced quietly and based on property and person. The manuscript has not been damaged, "the state, our father, again gained stature and good standing." But for a moment, as in Kleist's "Earthquake in Chili," the accident made everyone equal. A special train picks up the passengers. There are no privileges in it. Everyone heads first of all for the first-class car. It doesn't do any good for those who really have a first-class ticket, Thomas Mann and the gentleman in spats, for example. They have to be content with this advice of the common man: "Be glad ya gotta seat!" And the little mother in the dilapidated mantilla, who had been escorted out of second class before, now sits beaming in first class.

It was "as though the common disaster had made everyone who escaped it into *one* family," Kleist writes. People of all social classes mix and share with one another what they have rescued from the catastrophe. There is also talk of "communism" in "The Train Wreck." The gentlemen wearing spats tries "to revolt against communism, against the great leveling in the presence of the majesty of misfortune." The state, our father, does gradually bring about the old order, but at such a moment it is unmistakable that formality and cultured behavior and the separation of classes are only a laborious attempt to bring under scanty control the true essence of things, which is chaotic, disorganized, communistic. Inevitably it happens again and again, in the war for example. Also in 1914 a kind of communism comes about. For Thomas Mann the war is "the unprecedented, the violent and fanciful union of the nation in preparation for a profound test"; the rich will have to give up nine-tenths of their wealth; "there will be a German Commune, voluntary and full of order, so that Germany can exist."

Seen politically, *Royal Highness* is also a conservative book. A decayed monarchy is economically recapitalized. That takes place by means of the injection of capital by an American millionaire. Funds are raised by the marriage of the prince to the millionaire's daughter. There is not a word here in favor of a capitalistic middle-class republic, rather of a physiocratically reformed monarchy. The reform comes from above. The public does not want to share in the reign but wants to see itself represented in the reigning couple, "wants to see something like its soul depicted in its prince—not its purse," wants to see itself depicted "proud and glorious." Although there are reviews that ascribe a democratic tendency to the novel, it is very clear that it concerns a democracy in the sense of the *Reflections of a Nonpolitical Man*: "Democracy . . . comes from above, not from below." Thomas Mann's political dream is the model of a nation of enlightened absolutism. A union of power and intellect must be at the top; then everything can be orderly. That he criticized the existing empire and did not like Wilhelm II, cannot overlook the fact that this state corresponded essentially to his political and economic ideas.

The conservatism of the novel also serves Mann's ambition. The author, who as a result of his marriage belonged and wanted to belong to the leading circles when he writes the first lines of *Royal Highness*, is already talking about the distinction that should be derived one day from it. A man in opposition would have had other desires. Mann then also writes to Martens at the time that further "democratic" works were not to be expected from him. "As far as I can survey my future production, it of course does not have the slightest thing to do with democracy."


## CENSOR ANTI-CENSOR

It fits his image of allegiance to the state that Thomas Mann from April 1912 until May 1913 belonged to the Censorship Board of the Royal Bavarian Police. He resigned when a resolution of the Association for the Protection of German Writers, to which he also belonged, forced him to do so. For membership in the Censorship Board was considered incompatible with membership in the Association, incompatible in general with the dignity of a writer. "That seems too dumb to me," writes Mann to Kurt Martens on May 26, 1913, announces his resignation from the Protection Association, and continues that he naturally is also leaving his position on the Censorship Board "because I don't want to expose myself to the charming insinuation that I had taken a position on the side of the police against intellect, freedom, and collegiality. After all, I am most comfortable as an unofficial and unaffiliated person." At the end of 1918 he does let himself be talked into membership in a "Cinema Censorship Council."

Still, no false impression should arise. Thomas Mann was a liberal in these matters. His activity as a censor took place with the intention "of warning the supervisors of public order against attacks on the works of literary rank." Already in 1907 he had announced that censorship was an inhibiting factor in cultural matters. In 1911 he signed a protest against the police prohibition of the work of Frank Wedekind. His report on Wedekind's *Lulu* recommended the uncut release of the controversial work. Wedekind misunderstood the censorship action, squabbled with Thomas Mann, and came to a reconciliation only upon the latter's resignation as an agent of the police. But the premiere of *Lulu* was nevertheless prohibited; Thomas Mann was in the minority.

The police surveillance of Wedekind was always a matter of sexuality, excuse me, morality. But the ascetic, Thomas Mann, is no hypocrite. At the time, as an expert witness in a pornographic trial, he describes art as a profound and dangerous thing, "which cannot be dealt with through the value judgments of popular pedagogical morality." Sexuality was the root of art. "It has not grown weary of dealing with it—in a sublime and in a graceful or grotesquely obscene way; but if there is an obscene art—there is no immoral, indecent art, for art is essentially decent; it is always a positive moral emancipation of the human spirit; and the most indecent object is absorbed morally by it, if I may express it in that way."

## HOW JAPPE AND DO ESCOBAR HAD A FIGHT

With *Death in Venice*, it is said, homoeroticism returns to the agenda. To be exact, that happens a bit earlier. In November and December 1910 Mann writes the little tale "How Jappe and Do Escobar Got into a Fight" as a commissioned work. It takes place on the beach of his childhood and youth in Travemünde. A first-person narrator appears, who is quite similar to Thomas Mann, as do two friends, one of whom, Johnny Bishop, appeared in real life as his fellow student Johnny Eckhoff.

> Johnny and Brattström lay on their backs completely naked, while it was more comfortable for me to have my beach towel wrapped around my hips. Brattström asked me why I did that, and since I did not know anything suitable to answer to that, Johnny said with his winning, friendly smile: I was probably somewhat too big to lie naked. Actually, I was bigger and more developed than he and Brattström, also probably a little older than they, about thirteen. So I accepted Johnny's explanation silently, although it was a little vexing to me. For in Johnny's company you easily appeared in a rather comical light if you were less small, delicate, and physically childlike than he, who was all of that in such a high degree. Then, with his pretty blue, girl's eyes, at the same time friendly and mockingly smiling, he could look up at you with an expression as though he were about to say: "What a boor you are!" The ideal of masculinity and long pants got lost in his presence, and that at a time, not long after the war, when power, courage, and any kind of rough virtue stood in high regard among us boys and all kinds of things were considered effeminate.

Johnny keeps his childlike and girlish qualities. That must have pleased Tommy. "He looked like a little, thin cupid as he lay there, with raised arms, his handsome blond and curly-haired, long, English head bedded in his slender hands." He dresses elegantly, "namely, in a genuine English sailor suit with blue linen collar, ship's knots, piping, a silver pipe in his chest pocket, and an anchor on the puffy sleeve that narrowed at his wrist."

In a late letter Thomas Mann did indeed write: "By the way, you come up with homosexuality a bit too brusquely. I really didn't think of anything bad with little Johnny Bishop." But we still venture to confirm that the description of Johnny Bishop extensively resembles that of Tadzio in *Death in Venice*. "Softness and tenderness clearly determined his being. No one had dared take scissors to his beautiful hair. . . . The English sailor's suit, the puffed sleeves of which narrowed below and clasped the slender wrists of his still childlike but slender hands, lent with its laces, bows, and embroidery something rich and spoiled to his slight figure."

The fight itself takes place between two somewhat older boys, "both already violent louts." The outcome is not so important, for the real protagonists are two observers, the first-person narrator, whom for the sake of simplicity we will call Tommy, and Johnny Bishop. Neither is a fighter. Tommy feels obliged to watch, in spite of his shyness, "as unwarlike and hardly brave as I was" to venture onto the scene of manly deeds. Johnny is more superior, with all his childlike qualities more manly. On the way to the scene of battle he sings a popular song, "with an indecent variation that had been invented for it by precocious youth. For that's the way he was: With all his childlike qualities he already knew quite a lot and was not too squeamish to put it into words." When the fight then ends harmlessly, Johnny turns away. "He had come there because something real with a bloody outcome was supposed to be offered. When the thing ended in play, he left."

## DEATH IN VENICE

The single successful *and* great work that comes into question here during the years before the war is *Death in Venice*, the story of a popular national poet whose conduct, form, and the artful structure of his life is destroyed by his love for the handsome boy Tadzio. The primal odds and ends come again, the tribulation that drove Herr Friedemann into the water. It is not improbable that the success of *Death in Venice* is indebted to Mann's admission once more of the suppressed theme of homoeroticism. A spasm was released. The early images, those of schooldays in Lübeck, came again. "Former feelings, early, precious distresses of the heart, which had perished in the stern service of his life and now returned changed so curiously—he recognized them with a puzzled, amazed smile." Aschenbach reflects and dreams as Thomas Mann once did on the Lido: "slowly his lips shaped a name," Armin's or Willri's.

It is not a matter of a conscientious novel of marriage but of an irresponsible case of pedophilia on the part of an overwrought Munich writer. It hardly approaches anything close to personal experience. In fact, Thomas Mann had also been in Venice in the year 1911 and there on the Lido, like his Gustav von Aschenbach, who was staying at the Grand Hotel des Bains, had watched a highborn Polish boy on the beach. This Baron Wladyslav Moes has truly almost the same importance as those who belong to his "gallery" (from Armin Martens to Franz Westermeier), but in any case he really existed.

Taken from Mann's own life in detail are also the work and creative psychology of Gustav von Aschenbach. Thomas Mann presents him as the author of his own unwritten works, in fact as the author "of the clear and mighty prose epic of the life of Frederick of Prussia"; as the artist who "wove the character-rich novelistic carpet, 'Maya' by name, which collected so many human destinies in the shadow of an idea"; as the creator of the story "A Wretched Man," which "shows an entire grateful youthful generation the possibility of moral decisiveness beyond the most profound knowledge"; and as the author of the essay on mind and art, "whose organizing power and antithetical eloquence enabled serious critics to set it directly next to Schiller's rationalization about naïve and sentimental poetry." Further, he makes him, surreptitiously but recognizably, the creator of some of Mann's fictional figures. These are Thomas Buddenbrook ("the elegant self-control that to the last second conceals from the eyes of the world an inner subversion, a biological collapse"); Lorenzo de Medici ("the sallow, sensually handicapped ugliness that is able to fan its smoldering passion into pure flame"); Savonarola ("the pale impotence that from the depths of the spirit draws the power to throw a whole exuberant people at the foot of the Cross, at *its* feet"); Prince Klaus Heinrich ("the endearing composure in the vacuous and strict service to formality"); and (probably) Felix Krull ("the false, perilous life, the quickly enervating aspiration and art of the born swindler"). Even more directly taken from his own concerns are the statements on the psychology of artistic effort. That Aschenbach's works did not come into being in one fell swoop, rather "in small daily labors out of hundreds of individual inspirations stacked up into greatness"—that is not only reminiscent of Nietzsche, who ironically calls Wagner a miniaturist, but a truth from the desk of Thomas Mann. The word "greatness" again appears. Gustav von Aschenbach is not great, but like Nietzsche's Wagner he knows how to produce the effect of greatness. He is "the writer of all those who work on the edge of exhaustion, those overburdened, those already worn down, those still standing on their feet, all those moralists of accomplishment who, slight of build and meager of means, at least for a time gain the effects of greatness through rapture of the will and clever management." That could be a precise inner portrait of Thomas Mann in those years.

In addition to the works that he gave him and the psychology of artistic effort, Mann shaped in Gustav von Aschenbach above all his own deepest desires, his deepest fears. Would the alien god sweep away his structure of art? The prospects for rescue seem slight. Truth, "bitter as it might be," in the end demands the admission "that everything in intellect and thought can outmatch the eternally natural in the long run only badly, only with effort, and hardly ever for long." He who sets his eyes on beauty is already risking death. "Aschenbach noted with astonishment that the boy was perfectly beautiful." The details follow. "However it was possibly because the aging man did not want the disillusionment that the rapture was too dear for him." "And leaning back, with arms hanging, overcome and several times seized by tremors, he whispered the standard formula of longing—impossible here, absurd, depraved, ridiculous, and yet sacred, reverent even: 'I love you.'" "His mind and heart were intoxicated, and his footsteps followed the directions of the demon that takes pleasure in stomping the reason and dignity of man underfoot." "What were art and virtue to him in the face of the advantages of chaos?" "And his soul tasted obscenity and the madness of doom."

Thomas Mann did not go as far as his Aschenbach, probably did not lean his brow drunkenly on Moes's door hinge, rather presumably was satisfied with intently observing the limbs of the youthful body on the beach. He asserts: "Seriously, I would not have known what to do with Tadzio." But he recognizes his peril and knows that he plays a role that can at any time shatter under the onslaught of desire. Aschenbach says it: "The master bearing of our style is falsehood and folly, our renown and prestige are a farce, public faith in us is utterly ludicrous, and educating the populace and the younger generation through art is a hazardous enterprise that should be outlawed." A bitter acknowledgment, truth loving, though not entirely true. For the bravery with which the masterful style is played also has its verity: Surrendering senselessly to desire is no more true than refusing it.

## A DEATH IN POLLING

Polling near Walheim was a painters' locale. Rural quiet but also a touch of the bohemian drew Thomas Mann's mother, Julia Mann, after a few years in Augsburg, at first for a short time and after about 1906 entirely to Polling. To this day the locale is marked by a gigantic

*Carla Mann, around 1903*

former monastery park. "Liberalitas Bavarica," it says above the massive tuff stone portal of the monastery church.

Her children often visited her there. In July 1903 Thomas and Heinrich were in Polling together for a while; the last pages of "The Hunt for Love" came into being there. For Viktor, Polling was the transfigured place of memories of numerous vacations and a one-year agricultural practicum. As the boy who rang the bell, he flew up on the bell rope of the monastery church. Julia's daughters also came occasionally. When Carla killed herself in 1910 before the eyes of her mother, Julia returned for a time to Munich but in 1913 moved back to Polling. In 1923, just as the inflation had dissipated her wealth, she died not far away in Wessling. Her sons, all three, were present at her deathbed. Thomas Mann is very moved. "I don't believe I've ever been so sad in my whole life." Julia Mann found her last resting place in the tomb of her daughter Carla in the Munich Wald Cemetery. All three brothers had wept, says Erika, each one at a different moment.

Carla's suicide thirteen years earlier had been a deep emotional shock for the mother and the siblings. We know the events from the mother's letters to Heinrich Mann, from Heinrich Mann's report "Carla," from Viktor Mann's description in *We Were Five*, from Thomas Mann's report in his *A Sketch of My Life*, and most extensively from the transmittal of the events in the novel *Doctor Faustus*, where Polling returns as Pfeffering, the mother as the wife of Senator Rodde, and Carla as Clarissa. Since the story can hardly be told better than there, we will follow portions of chapter 35 of the novel, without indicating in detail the parts transmitted. We add what is necessary to know from the other sources.

Carla was an actress, ambitious, but without sweeping success. Her career stagnated in the provinces. As a woman she loved to do herself up in a worldly and seductive way with makeup, cigarettes, and wheel-sized hats, while at the same time she rejected any male approach scornfully, coolly, and chastely. Only a single time was she vanquished, and that by the advances of a skirt-chaser and provincial roué with fine clothes and a lot of black hairs on his hands, but she refused his cupidities afterward for fear that he would spread it about among people that she had been his lover.

Meanwhile redeeming prospects had opened up to the professionally disappointed woman. The one who offered them to her was Arthur Gibo, a young Alsatian industrialist, who had fallen in love with the scornful blond. He promised to release her from a failed profession and to offer her a secure life as his wife. He hoped to overcome the resistance of his family against the actress, a *boche* in addition to everything else.

Carla was overjoyed. Then the ghost of her past rose up and drove her to her death. That rogue with the hairy hands blackmailed her with his erstwhile triumph. Arthur's relatives, Arthur himself, would find out about his relationship to her if she did not submit to him again. Desperate scenes must have taken place between him and his

victim. He made no secret of the fact that he would never release her.
She would have to live in adultery—that would be righteous punishment for what the lout called her cowardly attempt to find refuge
among the middle class.

An anonymous letter, written by Carla's lover in the third person,
did its work with the Gibo family. Arthur came to Polling to confront
his fiancée. His heart was strait. After a quarrel with him, the unhappy girl hurries with a fleetingly confused and blind smile past her
mother and into her room and locks herself in. The last thing heard
from her is the gurgling of the water with which she tries to cool the
burning that the poison caused in her throat. Afterward she still had
enough time to throw herself on a chaise longue. Dark-blue blotches
on her pretty hands and on her face indicated a rapid death by suf-
focation, the quick crippling of her respiration center by a dose of
cyanide with which a company of soldiers could probably have been
killed. On the table lay a hastily penciled sheet written to her fiancé
with the words: "Je t'aime. Une fois je t'ai trompé, mais je t'aime." (I
love you. I betrayed you once, but I love you.) It was July 30, 1910.

Thomas, who was staying in Bad Tölz, found out about it by telephone on the same evening and set off early the next day for Polling.
Arthur Gibo was inconsolable. I loved her enough to forgive her, he
said. Everything would have been all right, he said. No doubt—says
the Mann clan—if he had not been such an insipid family's boy and
Carla had had a more trustworthy support from him. "Oh, if he had
only been a *man* and had at least *calmed her down*, since he brought on all
the trouble & alone knew everything." He is said not to have honored
her memory. She had not loved him at all, he is said to have asserted
later. Arthur's mother is said to have been even worse. "That hyena
woman Gibo is a tall bony sinister-eyed woman who used to be a
factory worker & milkmaid!!! & wanted to have a young millionairess
as a daughter-in-law; she doesn't consider *family*." Thus Julia Mann
writes Heinrich, offering Frau Gibo for sale to his satirical arsenal.

## SENSE OF FAMILY, A SNAPSHOT

"I cry a lot, my Heinrich, when I am alone: I don't complain that
Carla *did this to me*, but that, without saying a word, *she* bore all the
trouble *alone* &, without being supported, chose such a death." The

mother suffered the most. She is deeply shocked; she would so gladly have helped.

Heinrich loved Carla especially. He experiences her death as a mystery. He had just been in South Tirol. He believed he heard Carla's voice at the hour of her death. "Toward noon I was strolling in an arid garden . . . where I was called: I thought from the house. I was so little prepared that in the first moment it did not occur to me: No one here calls me by my first name. Later in the day the telegram came with the news." Heinrich does not want to dwell on explanations, but he does ask the question about what ways such a message must have taken in an instant in which "the one sending it is engaged in the most intense act of her life, the resolution to die." The question of God follows. "Don't know," he reflects, "I don't know. I've refrained—equally distant from the mysteries and their profanation. As far as I remember, I have never mentioned the name of God in my works. Out of shyness? In order not to be responsible to the Unknown? Perhaps to accommodate a convention of the age? Or, contrarily, as an involuntary protest against its lethargy."

In his description, Viktor Mann is clearly dependent on chapter 35 of *Doctor Faustus*, just as this novel in general gave him what he first needed most in orientation to make his biographical depictions in *We Were Five* at all possible. As a person, he was much too robust to be taken for a literary man. He was a farmer, an army-corps student, an officer and horse lover, blond, blue eyed, and ordinary, inwardly far distant from the subtleties of the other Mann children; only because of this was it possible to survive the Third Reich in Germany unharmed as the brother and uncle of several expatriots. He probably reacts with consternation at Carla's death, but also embarrassingly inappropriately. "You still have four; we're still with you," he stammers, to console his mother.

What moved Lula (Carla's sister, Julia Löhr)? She did not come until the interment. If we follow the depiction in *Faustus*, she accepted the expressions of condolences with tender dignity. In a conversation with her, Tommy had rather the impression that she envied Carla more than she mourned her. Later, she too, in the summer of 1927, will find death by her own hand. She chooses the rope. Tommy is profoundly shaken by her death. He felt it like a bolt of lightning that had struck right next to him. Because what Carla was to Heinrich, Lula was for Thomas: his "feminine alter ego," a kindred spirit in her timidity toward life. She had confessed to him that her leaning to morphine resulted because of her revulsion toward her husband, "what the banker wanted from her all too often she could not offer without the cathartic poison." Now, she had come to grief lamentably, and with her a piece of Tommy's own soul. It was the piece that guarded the structure of art and longed for order and family. "My sister was convention incarnate," Heinrich said in 1927 about Lula. It was more important to her than anything else not to catch anyone's eye, to appear the way you have to. That was what destroyed her."

Heinrich avoided Lula. But Tommy wanted to keep the family together, whatever happened. He beseeched Heinrich: "In my opinion, you are guilty of a lack of self-respect, when you hold *even just one of us* for a common philistine." The danger existed "that the split between you and Lula is something as definitive as Carla's death, even very similar to Carla's death." That's how it happened. In the First World War Tommy's disagreement with Heinrich is added as well and joins the series of outrages to the sense of family. "Pain? It passes. You get hard and numb. Since Carla killed herself and you broke with Lula for life, separation for all time is after all nothing new anymore in our community" (to Heinrich, January 3, 1918).

While Lula's death strikes him in his innermost soul, Thomas reacts to Carla's death with a kind of protest. She shouldn't have dared do that.

> My brotherly feeling of solidarity makes it appear to me that through Carla's act our existence is put into question, our anchoring is loosened. At the beginning I always told myself: "One of us!" Only now do I understand what I meant by that. Carla thought of no one, and you say: "That would be the last straw!" And still I can only feel that she should not have dared separate from us. With her deed she had no feeling of solidarity, no feeling of our common destiny. She acted, so to speak, against a silent agreement.

Thomas writes that to Heinrich on August 4, 1910. Twenty years later Carla's suicide still seems to him "like a betrayal of our brotherly and sisterly community," like the dismissal of a solidarity that he "in the last analysis felt ironically to have precedence before the realities of life and which my sister in my opinion had forgotten by her deed."

Can irony rescue life? Only someone who comes from a strong family knows the feeling of always remaining a special person in the deepest squalor of life. But someone who is proud will not just take but will also give. In order to stand up for oneself, one had to be a match to the demands of this family, and that meant getting something special done. But neither Carla nor Lula succeeded in pulling themselves out of the swamp of mediocrity. They did not die because they lacked family solidarity but because they could not meet the demand.

For that reason Tommy's protest is certainly not appropriate. He has a personal reason at bottom: fear of being threatened, fear of a life-destructive tribulation. Beseechingly he calls upon himself and the other members of his family: Keep the collapsing world upright! You see what will happen otherwise! There is certainly no lack of catastrophes in this family. It is difficult to keep one's composure. Later, with very similar words, he will distance himself from the suicide of his son Klaus much as he did that of his sister Carla.

But he reacted quite differently when no one was looking. Mama sends souvenirs of Carla, also a bit of hair from her as a child. He is touched. "I looked at it afternoons in the garden and thought of my farewell from the deceased girl in Polling, when, alone with her in the room before the coffin was closed, I kissed her on the brow."

## PLANS OF DOING AWAY WITH ONESELF

Heinrich and Thomas fulfilled the claims of the family in their own ways. "It's an old senator's son's prejudice of mine," Thomas writes to Heinrich on January 8, 1904, "that in comparison with us actually everything else is really inferior." That is said half in fun but still helps against the world. You don't do yourself in so easily then. Emotionally the twenty-year-old was very close to suicide. He knew "depressions of a really severe sort with completely seriously meant plans to do away with myself." Longing for death was also not alien to him: "Basically, I wish nothing more for myself than a good typhoid fever with a satisfactory end." Heinrich insists, however, that after the success of *Buddenbrooks* he never saw his brother suffering from life again. But that was, of course, a little bit venomous and, if you consider the depressions of old age, wrong besides. But suicide? There was no question of that anymore. Thomas Mann does not ap-

prove of suicidal acts. They are an irresponsible offense against forbearance, which all of us are in need of. They rip open that abyss,
which it is the task of us all to cross with a disciplined way of life. If
others lose their nerve, whether it be Carla or Julia, Klaus Mann or
Ernst Toller, the fictional Raoul Überbein in *Royal Highness* or Leo
Naphta in *The Magic Mountain*, it is all the more important to pull
oneself together, not to let oneself be infected. "He shouldn't have
dared to do it to them," Thomas Mann writes on May 22, 1949, in his
diary. "He" is his oldest son, Klaus; "them" refers to Katia and Erika,
who cry. Thomas himself stiffens his back instead. It is his way of
coming to terms with the onslaught of the horror of life.

Klaus in his time always praised death. It must be something quite
glorious, the most beautiful moment, the great stepping out of oneself. That goes on into the frivolous. "In Berlin I might be murdered,"
Klaus writes to Erich Ebermayer, "which on the other hand might
appeal to me."

# VII. Jews

*Munich, around 1910*

## THE BLOOD OF THE WALSUNGS
## AND DOCTOR SAMMET

"[O]n the other hand, his wife was simply an ugly little Jew in a tasteless gray dress." There are such people in the work of Thomas Mann. Jewishness is unmistakably an important category. Baroness Ada, the daughter of the ugly little Jewess just mentioned, is introduced as follows:

> Her face, with its full and moist lips, the fleshy nose, and the almond-shaped black eyes over which dark and soft brows arched, in truth did not allow the least doubt about her Semitic descent, at least in part, but was of a very unusual beauty.

The passages come from the story "The Will to Happiness" (written in December 1895). But such a thing is not limited to the early years; Jews are present in almost every larger work by Thomas Mann. As though he wanted to further a cliché, there are Jewish doctors, Jewish bankers, Jewish art dealers, and Jewish music agents. They almost always also bear characteristic physical and intellectual features. The Jewish twins Siegmund and Sieglinde in *The Blood of the Walsungs*, who commit incest quickly before Sieglinde's Christian wedding in revenge because they assume Sieglinde will have to adapt to the Christian boor Beckerath, offer only small resistance to an anti-Semitic interpretation. Especially since the hint is included in Siegmund's answer in the final paragraph to Sieglinde's question about what will happen now, that for an instant "the marks of his race" had stood out "very sharply on his face." The reply was originally to have read: "We've swindled him—the goy." That is how it read in the page proofs. The story was to appear in the *Neue Rundschau* at the beginning of 1906. The *Rundschau* editor, Oscar Bie, objected to the ending so much that the author toned it down into "He will lead a less trivial existence from now on." Thomas Mann then read the story at home to his parents-in-law, where it was found to be excellent. Still the rumor soon raced through Munich that he had written a strongly anti-Semitic novella in which he compromised his wife's family terribly. The incident was considered an act of vengeance, and Thomas Mann was seen to some extent in the role of a Beckerath who took vengeance for the humiliations he had received in the genteel Jewish home. Of course, that was nonsense, but Thomas Mann had the printing stopped at once. "What should I have done? I took a look at my novella in my mind and found that in all its innocence and independence it was not exactly suited to quell the rumor."

Thomas had previously discussed "independence" with Heinrich. Heinrich had believed the original ending was right. Thomas defended his compromise, which was to be only for the publication in the *Rundschau*, not for the book edition:

> Bie is correct insofar as the Jewish expressions fall somewhat out of the style, which certainly does not necessarily prevent their use as a final resource but can also be avoided just as well. You say: To sacrifice what is characteristic to respectability is kitsch. But one can also say: Art means being extremely characteristic without offending any kind of stylistic sensitivity. And "swindled" breaks the style, one has to admit that. Previously such things were avoided, paraphrased, concealed. The term "Jew, Jewish" does not come up. The Jewish tone of voice is alluded to only a few times very discreetly. Of Herr Aarenhold it is said, he was "born in a remote place in the East." "Swindled" does not apply to this kind of ironic discretion, although it is thoroughly founded psychologically. And for me, in an immoral way, style is almost more important than psychology. . . . I say all of this only to justify that I agree with Bie for the *Rundschau*. In the book the version so well endorsed by you will again get its due.

Here the argument is aesthetic, not racist. It is a matter of what is characteristic and what has stylistic integrity. If Thomas Mann withdraws the story, then it is not because he might have considered it anti-Semitic himself but to prevent any kind of debate from arising about it. Out of consideration for his family he does not sacrifice some sort of anti-Semitism but an aesthetic point: "I must recognize that in regard to human beings and society I am no longer free," he writes to Heinrich. At first he had foamed at the mouth a bit, but now he was indifferent. What was good about the story, namely, the depiction of the milieu that he really considered very new, could be used at another time. But then there follow those statements, which in the meantime have become famous, full of a bad conscience because he has sacrificed the freedom of art out of consideration for society:

Since then I cannot rid myself of a feeling of a lack of freedom, which in hypochondriac hours is very depressing, and you, of course, call me a cowardly bourgeois. But it's easy for you to talk. You are absolute. I on the other hand have ceased to fashion a set frame of mind for myself.

This consideration remains in effect all his life. *The Blood of the Walsungs* appeared during Thomas Mann's lifetime only in a limited deluxe edition (1921) and in a French translation. The first thirty copies of the deluxe edition contained a duplicate page with the original ending as an addition.

Another Jewish figure from the early years of his marriage is the physician Dr. Sammet in *Royal Highness*. "His nose, which fell too flatly down on his moustache, indicated his descent." At the birth of Prince Klaus Heinrich he showed himself competent. A conversation with the Grand Duke results:

"You're a Jew?" asked the Grand Duke, throwing back his head and squinting his eyes.

"Yes, Your Royal Highness."

"Ah. —Will you answer another question for me? —Have you ever felt your origin as a hindrance in your business, as a disadvantage in your professional competition? I ask as a sovereign who sets great store on the unconditional and private, not only official, validity of the principle of equality."

"Everyone in the grand duchy," Dr. Sammet answered, "has the right to work." But then he said still more, began with difficulty, let a few hesitant commonplaces be heard, while in an awkwardly passionate way he moved his elbow like a short wing, and added with a muffled but inwardly exuberant and subdued voice: "No principle of equality, if I may permit myself this remark, will ever be able to prevent, in the midst of communal life, exceptions and special forms from being maintained that are distinguished in a noble or disreputable sense from the middle-class norm. The distinguished person will do well not to inquire about the form of his special position, rather to see what is essential in his being distinguished and in any event to derive from it an extraordinary responsibility. One is not at a disadvantage regarding the regular and therefore comfortable majority; rather one is at an advantage when one has an occasion more than they do for unusual accomplishments. Yes. Yes," Dr. Semmet repeated. It was the answer that he strengthened with a double yes.

It is also the answer of Thomas Mann, at least in the time before 1914. It acknowledges the outsider in the Jew but sees an advantage in it. It is in no way opposed to legal equality, but its interest is not aimed at that. It is aimed at the preferential treatment through suffering. The argument is misapplied insofar as one could conclude that if suffering is so fruiful, why ought one to do anything against it? But that is not what it concerns. It concerns actual suffering that is not removed. It concerns discrimination as a fact that is not defended for that reason but, in its indisputable presence, also ennobles, at least in appropriately gifted cases.

The argumentation is extraordinarily typical for the prewar Thomas Mann. He repeats it in 1907 in the small essay "The Solution of the Jewish Question," where—before he expresses himself "seriously" on the subject—he speaks "en artiste." "An artist," he explains, "by his own nature will not be able honestly to wish the general humane equalization of conflicts and distances," for he lives by what is characteristic, what is special, and the aristocratic exception. He will therefore be inclined "to see his brothers in all those about whom people believe they must emphasize that they are people 'too—in the final analysis.' For the sake of this kindredship he will love them and wish for all of them the pride, the love for their destiny that he is aware of for himself."

## ANTI-SEMITISM?

"Mann is unmistakably a great friend of the Jews," observes the National Socialistic petition for the stripping of his German citizenship in a disapproving manner in 1934. Thomas Mann affirmed already in 1913 that he was considered a comrade of the Jews, who had celebrated the mixture of races. In our days, however, Thomas Mann is accused more and more frequently of at least a subliminal anti-Semitism. The argument remains mostly very fragmentary, lists Jewish figures from his literary works, from Naphta to Saul Fitelberg, notices the absence of a description of the Holocaust in the Faustus novel, and cites occasional crude statements in diaries as well as ambiguous expressions in the essays. Throughout, the "passages" draw their offensiveness from a feeling for language that arose only after Auschwitz. Although Thomas Mann writes the essay "The Solution of the Jewish Question" in the summer of 1907, today's reader inevitably associates it with the Final Solution and the Wannsee Conference. But at the time, an existing problem was simply being discussed: How the conflicts with the Jewish minority could be most reasonably solved. Thomas Mann's reply is: Continuation of assimilation, the Europeanization of Jews, cultural support, encouragement of baptism and mixed marriages. To label these suggestions as anti-Semitic requires a great portion of that hypocritical self-righteousness of later generations that were never faced with such decisions.

But Thomas Mann did decide—and in favor of Jews. He married into a Jewish family; during his life his books appeared with a Jewish publishing house; and he trusted the advice of Jewish editors. He had numerous Jewish friends and correspondents, from Samuel Lublinski and Max Brod, Maximilian Harden and Julius Bab, Hermann Broch, Franz Werfel, and Arthur Schnitzler to Bruno Walter, Theodor W. Adorno, and Sigmund Freud. Since he himself was an outsider, he perceived the Jews from early on to be like brothers. Like artists, Jews are superior to established citizens, are more perceptive, have a greater capacity for suffering, and are more expressive.

Besides, the title "The Solution of the Jewish Question" is not by Thomas Mann at all. It is the collective title of a questionnaire sent to a hundred prominent people by Julius Moses, among them numerous Jews. No one took offense at the title at the time. Three suggestions for reply were made: (1) the assimilation of Jews through baptism and mixed marriage, (2) their continued development not as a race but exclusively as a religious faith, and (3) the extensive self-government of Jews in the countries in which they live, or in a Jewish state to be set up in Palestine. None of these suggestions is anti-Semitic. Thomas Mann sticks, theoretically and practically, with the first: assimilation. He was, he says, "a convinced and incontrovertible 'philo-Semite'" and believed that an exodus of Jews would mean the greatest misfortune that could befall our Europe. He continues:

To discuss this indispensable European cultural stimulus that is called Jewry, even today, and especially in Germany—which has such bitter need of it—in any kind of hostile and inimical manner, seems to me so coarse and tasteless that I find myself unfit to lend even a word to such a discussion.

So, a philo-Semite. A subtle counterargument reads that he had repressed his anti-Semitism publicly as he did homosexuality, just to derive all the more pleasure from it. That might be correct, if Thomas Mann lived in our days, at a time and in a society in which anti-Semitism is not welcome in public. But at that time a suppression of anti-Semitic impulses would not have been necessary at all. On the contrary, they would have brought the writer, who had the reputation of being an intellectual and an internationalist, closer to the average German. While the suppressed homoeroticism can be detected everywhere beneath the surface of his work, in the autobiographical subtext, in passages left out, in his diary, in roundabout ways through his sources, such a search in the case of anti-Semitism remains wihout results. What "passages" there are always have a special context and cannot simply be ranked high as universal.

## THE JEWISH GIRL

An exasperated yet yearning note from the summer of 1904 reads: "This strange, kind, and yet egotistical, weak-willed, polite little Jewish girl! I can hardly imagine that she will ever get a Yes past her lips." The young writer was completely aware of Katia's Jewish background, but it was no hindrance, rather an attraction. The family of her father, Alfred Pringsheim, as well as the family of her mother, Hedwig Dohm, were Jewish. But for generations they had also been wealthy and cultivated. What Thomas Mann thought about the solution of the Jewish question were things that had already taken place in Katia's parental home: assimilation, cultural advance, baptism. Why shouldn't then a mixed marriage follow? "No thought of Jewry arises in regard to these people: you sense nothing but culture." Thus Thomas to Heinrich on February 27, 1904. Cultivated Jewishness is distinguished, that's how it is. The newborn daughter Erika promised to be very pretty. "At moments I believe I see a little Jewishness peeking through, which makes me happy every time."

Katia's fictional likeness, Imma Spoelmann, is not of Jewish but of

Indian descent. When Kurt Martens remarks on that disparagingly, it's not funny to Thomas. "You could not possibly call her an impudent, compulsively comical little thing of a lesser race without your lacking personally in the necessary goodwill to understand, and that's too bad, for I could not keep your book away from my wife, and—we could have associated with one another so nicely. But you knew very well what you were doing."

He was angry not only because of Katia. He felt a bit of Indian blood coursing through his own veins from his mother born in the Brazilian jungles, and he was proud of that. The mixture of blood did not bother him. That his first grandson, American by birth, has German, Brazilian, Jewish, and Swiss blood is worth an entry in his diary.


## THOMAS MANN—WASN'T HE A JEW?

Well into the fifties and the sixties you could frequently hear this question. It was not only his expatriation, his internationalism, and his place in the world of letters that brought this author the reputation of being a Jew, but targeted actions from the right. Already in 1907 the anti-Semitic literary historian Adolf Bartels had written that Jews were obviously also represented in decadent literature, whereupon in an enumeration Heinrich and Thomas Mann are mentioned—although with the moderating addition that as the sons of a Lübeck senator they could hardly be pure Jews. He was corrected, but he declares it a lie and (1910) considers the thesis of a "Jewish blood mixture" not finally repudiated. In any case, Bartels concludes insolently that in the case of Thomas Mann, for him it is certain that, independent from the biological evidence, "literarily he belongs to the Jews." Even this subtle differentiation is obliterated again and again in the time following. A list was published in the fairly obscure Berlin *Staatsbürger-Zeitung* on December 1, 1912, that also contained Thomas Mann's name under the headline of JEWISH AUTHORS IN THE S. FISCHER PUBLISHING HOUSE. Thomas Mann repudiates it: "If I were a Jew, I hope I would have enough pluck not to be ashamed of my origin; since I am *not* one—and not with a drop of my blood—I cannot wish for anyone to consider me one." But the newspaper publishes this denial with the added remark that Mann was married to a woman of Jewish descent and deduces cleverly: "such a mixture of races is biologically *recte*, in favor of the *Jewish* side." Thomas Mann denies it anew, particularly since Theodor Lessing, to be characterized below, had carried the thesis of Bartels further.

> My wife is the daughter of Professor Alfred Pringsheim, professor of mathematics at the University of Munich, and on her mother's side the granddaughter of the famous writer Hedwig Dohm. That I had thus entered into a misalliance is not at once clear to my modesty. But just as little have I ever dreamed that through this marriage I had become a Jew and that my person, and especially my work, was now "to be counted biologically on the Jewish side."

That, of course, categories such as blood and descent are not unimportant to Thomas Mann is to be clearly recognized from the closing consideration of the denial:

> If I calmly and deliberately contradict the error regarding my Jewish descent that surfaces here and there, then I do so because I really see a falsification of my nature in it and because, if I were to count as a Jew, my whole work would receive a different, false face. What would the book be that made my name well known, what would the novel *Buddenbrooks* be, if it were to come from a Jew? A snob book . . .
>
> What seems to be alien to a scholar like Professor Bartels about the works by me and my brother will probably, at least partly, be traced back to that Latin (Portuguese) mixture of blood that we actually represent. If he calls Richard Dehmel a "Slavic virtuoso," then let him call us "Latin artists." We are just not Jews.

That naturally was of no avail to those on the right. Adolf Bartels's opinion was that a Portuguese mixture of blood was "fairly dubious," "since the Portuguese people are racially the worst of all the Europeans: note *Meyer's Conversation Lexicon*, where the mixture with Arabs, *Jews*, people from India, and *Negroes* is emphasized." The "Semi-Kürschner," the reference work of the anti-Semites, cites this statement after it reviews the whole debate extensively. There follow further vitriolic statements; for example, the portrait etching by Max Oppenheimer "clearly followed the Jewish traces in the half-breed's face," and that the "pedophilia" in *Death in Venice* was "repugnant, unnatural," in a word: Jewish. The article that follows "Mann, Thomas" in the volume is, in addition, entitled "The Man in the Moon" and contains the observation: "is, according to a Cologne legend, a Jew." Bartels, a terrible man, did not leave the theme alone. "The brothers *Heinrich* and *Thomas Mann* from Lübeck establish a connection with Jewry," it says in 1942 in the eighteenth (!) printing of his *History of German Literature;* the mother of both was Portuguese, "so possibly not without Jewish and Negro blood, and each also married a Jewess." Bartels calls the novel *Royal Highness* an "oratio pro populo iudaico." The quintessence of the portion on Heinrich Mann reads: "Of course, today he is on the Black List." The portion on Thomas Mann ends with the satisfied conclusion: "In December 1936 he was expelled from the community of the German people, as previously his brother Heinrich, his daughter Erika, and his son Klaus were."

## THE HARDEN TRIAL

Famous specifically as Jews, or according to one's standpoint infamous, were the journalists Maximilian Harden, Alfred Kerr, and Theodor Lessing. They did not form a group—on the contary, they hated one another. They share personal and very private connections. Harden, as the editor of *Die Zukunft*—the importance of which during the time of the kaiser resembled that of today's *Der Spiegel* (though with a much smaller circulation)—was a central power in literary life. "My interest in the journalist Maximilian Harden is tantamount to admiration," Thomas Mann stated in 1905. "He was without doubt the most important and interesting journalist Germany has produced," he wrote later to an American doctoral candidate. He sought Harden's recognition, praised him in 1906 in "Bilse and I" as an incorruptibly genuine lover of words who would rather make an enemy of the world than sacrifice a nuance, and occasionally exchanged appreciative letters with him. In January 1916 he wrote an article protesting the banning of *Zukunft*, which however was not published due to considerations of censorship. A short time later, however, Harden, who had at first applauded the war, acknowledged his change from the antidemocratic Saul to the cultural-literary Paul, which was alluded to in a veiled way in *Reflections of a Nonpolitical Man*. With that he became a political oppponent; Thomas Mann replied with a sharp article that, however, remained unpublished.

Between 1907 and 1909 Harden was involved in three sensational court proceedings. From a reliable source, namely, from the deposed Reich's chancellor Bismarck, he had received information about the homosexuality of Philip, duke of Eulenburg, a close confidant of Kaiser Wilhelm II. In *Die Zukunft* he made use of that knowledge at such length and so insistently that he was hauled into court. He won the first trial, since Eulenburg's homosexuality was confirmed by witnesses, lost a second one, since Eulenburg perjured himself; at a third one, which "unmasked" Eulenburg, he won again. The whole thing must be looked at from the viewpoint that at the time homosexuality was considered "an unnatural indecency" and could be punished by imprisonment. But the Germans did not want those around their kaiser to be looked at suspiciously. Harden made himself unpopular, although he won his case. Thomas writes to Heinrich that the number of subscribers to *Die Zukunft* had fallen from eighteen thousand to two thousand as a result of the affair.

Frau Pringsheim, Katia's mother, was a friend of Harden. When the engaged couple had been introduced at the home of her Berlin relatives, Harden is said to have remarked to her that it had been a joy to see both the handsome young people, which had offended Thomas Mann a little bit. Harden's defense attorney was Max Bernstein. The Bernsteins were also closely acquainted with the Pringsheims; Frau Bernstein is said to have invited Katia and Thomas together in 1903 or 1904. As a result, Thomas Mann was informed at firsthand about the Eulenburg trial. He experienced it as a partisan of Harden's. His sentiments seem not to have told him at the time that there were more decent things than the denunciatory polishing off of a homosexual. Add to this, that it did not beseem him in particular to defend such mean branding of a homosexual. We know a little about the "details of the trial that Bernstein told me" from a letter to Heinrich of February 6, 1908, that refers to the second (lost) trial. "Anyway, the intention of the whole thing was shameless. Every other question by Bernstein was rejected by the judge as 'suggestive.'" The witnesses had been intimidated, the state's attorney had threatened the expert witness Magnus Hirschfeld, who himself was homosexual; Harden's excellent closing remarks had been garbled by the press.

It is in any case clear where Thomas Mann stands on the matter: on the side of the Jew Harden. The worst thing was that his opponents had gathered in a "Werdandi Union" protest; "Privy Councillor Thode, Wagner's son-in-law, worse luck, presides, and in a first appeal the Union speaks up with beer-brawling emphasis and in incred-

ible German for health and German heart in art. It was the most re-
volting thing you can imagine."

The open front line is thwarted by a secret one. Thomas Mann
stands on the side of the Jew who persecutes a homosexual, and
against German nationalistic anti-Semites who find Harden un-
German and dirty, without, however, therefore being a defender of
homosexuality. That Thomas Mann did not stand up, as he did later,
against the denunciation of homosexuality probably depends on his
situation at the time. He had just assumed a "stance." With great effort he had subjected himself to his marriage and willfully banned his
homoerotic inclinations to the cellar of his heart, so that he probably
was inclined to demand such an effort also from others. In addition
came the friendship with the Bernsteins, who on their part belonged
to the Pringsheim circle, so that supporting Harden and Bernstein
seemed to be advised out of regard for the families. At any rate,
Thomas Mann was at the time no fighter for the liberalization of association with homosexuality. But he was also no anti-Semite, for it
would nowhere have been easier to put down a Jew than here.

## ALFRED KERR

Alfred Kerr, Thomas Mann writes on April 6, 1943, to Willy Sternfeld,
"is a good hater—I have examples of it. If it were left up to him, I
would long since no longer literarily be alive." That sounds dramatic.
Kerr was the leading critic of the time. He writes like a too-taut string,
hymnic in praise, arrogant and shattering in criticism. He was himself
an artist, a precursor of the Expressionistic style with his precipitous
gestures, thus an opponent of the "Impressionistic" Thomas Mann.
With a light hand the twenty-one-year-old embellishes a small essay
with a mocking attack against Kerr. Kerr had been challenged to a
dual by a writer whom he had criticized. Thomas Mann finds it incomprehensible that a critic could be heated enough to make statements that were meant to insult a writer. After all, a critic was not a
judge but an interpreter; he had the task "of absorbing alien personalities, of disappearing in alien personalities, of seeing the world
through them." Kerr, no doubt, had a different opinion.

In his seventh *Notebook* we find the first trace, dated in the year
1902. "Anyone who is *pure* is trusting," it says there; all restraint rests
on impurity and being besmirched, and then in parentheses the addi-

tion: "Kerr against me." Nothing at the time in writing against Mann by Kerr is known, but there may have been verbal expressions. We conclude, in any case, that Kerr had treated the young author harshly in some way, and Thomas Mann deduced his "impurity" from that. For its part, this could be understood to be antithetical to Paul Ehrenberg, for at the time the trusting and pure one was Paul. Kerr, one may assume, was the reverse side of his friendship with Paul.

Kerr was in the way not only with Paul but also with Katia. There is a draft of a letter in the *Notebook*, dated August 29, 1903, in which Grautoff is requested not to say anythng to "K——r" about an observation not further explained. We know from Katia's *Unwritten Memoirs* that Kerr wanted to marry her, but she did not want to marry him. He resented Thomas Mann dreadfully all his life because of that. So there may have been a very personal motive here for hate and jealousy.

The next contact is dated in September 1905. Thomas Mann announces his positive attitude toward literary criticism and in this connection mentions that he owes so much profound amusement to Doctor Kerr that it would be sheer ingratitude to oppose him publicly. That sounds ironic and probably is, although in the context Thomas Mann defends criticism, even critical lack of respect, and announces that there is no true artist who is not also a critic. When he is annoyed by Kerr, then it is because of all too close proximity, since he is himself a critic; therefore it is a kind of fraternal hate. In fact, many attacks against Kerr resemble those against his brother. In any event, they are not anti-Semitic but are motivated aesthetically or personally.

Through the mediation of Frank Wedekind, Thomas Mann had sent his drama *Fiorenza* to Kerr on October 19, 1905. "It does not have much in its favor, this impossible play; but what it *does* have is perhaps worth being mentioned by name with your discerning art." So now he had demeaned himself, but the man presented with such a gift was silent and did not thank him. Years later he tries it again and signs a postcard that Frank Wedekind had addressed to Kerr:

*Dear Alfred Kerr:*

*Someone you hate would like to greet you. I am pleased to be the mediator.*

*Frank Wedekind.*

*Thomas Mann.*

In "Bilse and I" two months later, the thread is taken up again. Disguised as "Doctor X," Kerr is again reproached with the term "profound amusement." We hear that it deeply insulted him. What the author offers in his defense with now cutting remarks will have given him small comfort:

> I have reason to believe that the critic has mortally taken amiss my term "profound amusement," that he has taken it for mockery, and that he is now my deadly enemy. Why? Due to preciseness. If I had used just any worn-out phrase, had spoken of "true exaltation" or "exquisite pleasure," he would have remained well disposed toward me. But since I tried to strike his effect precisely with a disciplined word, he was infuriated. He does not wish to be an *amuseur*; he wishes to be taken seriously. But an amusement that is "profound" is, I should think, a very serious amusement. In the whole realm of language there seemed to me to be no better combination of words possible than those of "profundity" and "amusement" to describe the effect of his entertaining analysis, his often slightly foolish manner. . . . In vain, the word did damage. Only because it was good and hit the target.

Kerr struck back. The next act is a disparaging review of the novel *Royal Highness*. An innuendo follows without naming names, which Thomas Mann, however, feels is directed at himself. He complains to Heinrich about it in a letter (January 10, 1910), saying that Kerr smuggled the following statement into the *Rundschau*:

> He does not show off sort of like a mediocre novelist boss. Any comically neurasthenic clerk and old sanitorium client who one day writes novels will describe himself in a high social position and cover up his Achilles heel fictionally [Ferse*], etc.

"Neurasthenic" and "sanitorium" let us deduce precise personal information, and the "high social position" probably really refers to the theme of *Royal Highness*. Thomas Mann writes that for days he has not felt good. "I can't use enemies and now even such a horrible kind of enmity inside me; I'm not prepared for that." Still he announces a campaign of vengeance in case Kerr should take a stand and attack him in a way understandable to everyone.

There was no lack of that. Kerr defended himself at the beginning

---

* Kerr's impudent pun on Verse (verses) and Ferse (heel). (Trans.)

of 1913 when *Fiorenza* was staged. Mann called what the famous critic
had contributed to the Berlin newspaper, *Tag*, on January 5, 1913,
"poisonous claptrap" in which the most unsuspecting person would
recognize a personal bloodthirsty intent. "The author is a delicate,
somewhat slender little soul whose roots have their quiet habita-
tion in his rear end" was to be read there, and: "What was to be
gotten by sitting long enough, he has gotten here." The character of Fiore was the work of a philologist. Mann had already demonstrated a certain helplessness in the creation of a feminine person
in a novel about a prince. Something constrained, something servile,
something lacking in lineage, and something flat chested is manifested in him: a "premature back formation"—winter had come before it was summer.

"What a character he has!" writes Mann to Hofmannsthal. "Only a
few people know, of course, how much it is his *character* that speaks
here." What is alluded to here? The subliminal tones of the criticism
turn out to be personal. That Mann had suppressed his impulses with
all too great succcess is its tenor. Kerr was gripped by what was
pathological, Mann writes to the critic Julius Bab. "For radicalism always stops with what is sexual. It doesn't go deeper, he believes."
Kerr had found words of praise only for the early story "The Wardrobe," in which a naked girl appears in the wardrobe and plays cat
and mouse with compulsive desire. Fiore, on the other hand, compels
her lover to be ascetic. How much did Kerr know about Mann's asceticism, how much about his suppressed homoerotic inclinations? Apparently, Mann was afraid of such a thing. If it had concerned something else, he would have expressed himself more clearly in his
relatively numerous statements about these affairs. At the very least,
Kerr had some skepticism about his opponent's masculinity. Perhaps
it was the fact that an "unmanly man" had taken his place in Katia's
affections? The author of the *Fiorenza* criticism harbored against him
"a long-since confessed private animosity," Mann wrote in a letter, "to
reveal the origins of which to you would lead me much too far but
that exhibits the most miserable witness to his character, his humanity." Since he had read those dirty travesties, he had the unbearable
feeling of being besmirched.

He requested that Bab read what Lorenzo says to Fiore: "You—my
sweet, my only one, my fame, my splendor, my love and my power,
the goal of my longing," and then to tell him whether *Fiorenza* was

"philological work" or not. And he should also read the Venetian
story of death. For days after Kerr's critcism, he says, he had considered himself "an industrious little literary worm." But in the next letter to Bab, he confesses that he had himself hardly believed "the feminine allegory," that is, the figure of the great courtesan Fiore. It's true,
too; the little literary worm had no experience with such women,
powerful and sensual. Kerr was not entirely in error. Only someone
who gets something right can do damage.

But Mann probably had experience with Polish boys on the Lido.
Kerr also quickly expressed himself about *Death in Venice*. First he
is amused by the reviews by Mann's relatives, because his grand-
mother-in-law Hedwig Dohm as well as Heinrich Mann had reviewed
*Death in Venice*. Irony was abundantly at his command. "Look how
fine and loving it is when brothers live peaceably with one another."
Then it comes fast and thick. "Grandmama—here I find someone a
little trashy in disguise. Someone who shows an attitude instead of an
ego." Bites hail down: quiet with relish instead of poetic power. Everything squeezed out forcibly. The erotic not experienced: "The feeling of a man for a boy remains uncontured, the realm free of discov-
eries." Everything forbidden toned down. For his handiwork he
gleans things from classical antiquity. "In any event, here pedophilia
is made acceptable for the educated middle class."

Not without good reason does Mann see in that a "poisonous attack." He writes about it to Hans von Hülsen on April 20, 1913, infu-
riated and upset:

> What did you want to reproach the author for? That he is lying,
> dirty, and vile to the point of virtuous misery? But he knows that
> he is all that and wants to be. He is beyond decent and inde-
> cent. . . . You are furious about a bad deed, but he is "demonic."
> What are you trying to do here!

An announcement follows, referring to the planned story "The
Wretched Man," which unfortunately was never realized—otherwise
we would know more.

> But maybe I will say that better to him myself, one day, when I
> decide to tell the story—the story of me and him, which, re-
> ported in comfortable detail, can become fairly entertaining. But
> that is less hasty than may appear to you at the moment. I have
> become a ghostly companion for that man forever.

An enigmatic allusion. What does his lack of haste have to do with the eternal ghostly companion? Actually, just how does Thomas Mann reckon with that "forever"? Did Kerr know something; did he have Thomas Mann in his grip in some respect? Was that why Mann never took vengeance on him publicly? Kerr and Grautoff possibly knew one another, as the note of 1903 shows. Grautoff, on the other hand, knew what Thomas Mann had to hide. Did he perhaps not keep his mouth shut?

During World War I and afterward, Kerr occasionally delivered innuendos at Mann's affirmation of the war. But he dwelt in a glass house, for he too wrote patriotic poems in 1914. The diary notes an attack on the *Reflections* on March 16, 1919. A note on July 6, 1919, presumes that Kerr would thwart his election to the Berlin Academy of Fine Arts. Almost all their meetings are hostile in nature. "Kerr, however weak, is spitting at me once again, it seems to me. What wounds me is actually not the (here fairly dull) insult, but the intention of insulting" (September 4, 1920).

The hate remains; the fear declines a little later on. In 1921, in an article "On the Jewish Question" that is withdrawn before publication, Kerr, who celebrated Gerhart Hauptmann but had torn Carl Sternheim to pieces in a review, is mentioned as a positive example that Jews by no means promote only Jews literarily. Kerr can also play a positive role here as an argument against the nationalistic professor Adolf Bartels. That continues occasionally. In 1926 both travel by chance to Paris and meet one another there. Comically, the unsuspecting German rightists get the idea that they were in the same boat. It is the Jew Kerr of whom Hanns Johst asserts in 1926 that he had slipped away to Paris "with his young man, the credulous Thomas." Thomas Mann finds himself forced to deny that, by calling it a not very fortunate coincidence that his Parisian sojourn took place approximately during the same days as Kerr's. Naturally, an anti-Semitic argument is not to be found in this reply; on the contrary the Munich reactionaries are attacked sharply. In his travelogue "Parisian Account," Mann claims then to appreciate Kerr for his critical talent, but that was probably only diplomacy, for he mentions at the same time as though incidentally that Kerr had "tried to kill him five or six times." Kerr does not deny that without baring his teeth for joy.

Shortly afterward Kerr publishes the satirical poem "Thomas Bodenbruch," which presumably had come into being earlier, probably in 1913. It doesn't amount to much, but again strikes sore spots. The first three (of six) stanzas read:

*I*

Was as a boy already ossified;
    With small talent grumpily bitter.
Then have I literature mystified
    With bourgeois, patrician litter.
        Always boasted with bravour
        That my progenitors were poor.

*II*

I do not write—I jam.
    I do not dream—I cram.
I let words vamp
    That smell of lamp,
    I, leathery scamp.

No fire gives heat,
    I have no wit,
I write with my seat
    On which I sit.

At base not persnickity
    I am merely finicky.

*III*

Full of obstructive apprehension
And hesitating amplitude,
I dress up my ailing tension
And call it "attitude."

A bit later, in 1928, in an article about Bruno Frank, Thomas Mann then places another little innuendo. Alfred Kerr from Breslau, a great magazine writer—he would be the last to deny it, because he'd gotten a taste for it.

> So Kerr, the critic, zestful, sentimental, and impudent, in short, a charming and decisive individuation, has quite simply demolished my books in nimble, murderously cheerful little chapters.

Such ironic digs stopped then, too, at least in public. But in 1933 the diary, again available, offers a rich harvest of unpleasant passages. On April 2, 1933, Mann expresses his repugnance toward a nation that "forces not only the Kerrs and Tucholskis, but also people & intellects like me to leave the country." Only slowly did Mann learn solidarity with the emigrants, and not without inner resistance. One single thing, a private utterance, is really bad: the diary notation of April 10, 1933. It must be said at the outset that the suspicious question at the end, of whether the matter doesn't have two sides, will be clearly denied later. In spite of the following reflection, there can be no doubt of his consistent opposition to National Socialism:

> The Jews . . . That Kerr's spirited and poisonous gibberish about Nietzsche is excluded is no misfortune in the final analysis; nor is the removal of Jews from the judiciary. —Secret, emotional, stressful thoughts. Adversely hostile, base, un-German stuff remains intact in the highest sense in any case. But I'm beginning to suspect that the process could be on the level anyway of those that have their two sides. . . .

Kerr had had to leave Berlin and was already living in exile in Paris. The "misuse of Nietzsche": that has a very personal side, for in the infamous critique of *Fiorenza* Kerr had mocked Thomas Mann as "Little Nietzsche." Also, the term "poisonous" stems here. The old hate does not decrease because of their common fate of exile. On the contrary: Again, Kerr was a ghostly companion, again his hostile brother; Mann couldn't get away from him. The man was "unennobled by misfortune," according to the diary of October 28, 1934. Concerning Kerr's Rathenau book, Mann remarks that the psychological portrait of the unfortunate noble Jewish snob was naturally sharply struck, "but no thanks to the one portraying, who is even more unpleasant." "The old spider," Mann notes on March 19, 1936, again takes up "the old battle of hate." "I know that among emigrants there are many destructive riffraff, and he is one of them." The enmity is still felt in the notations of April 20, 1940 and August 25, 1945. On October 22, 1948, the diary notes Kerr's death without comment.

## THEODOR LESSING

A further enmity, concerning which Thomas Mann does not cut an especially fine figure, can be explained by the pangs and ambition of those years. As in the case of Kerr, the beginnings are shrouded in darkness. One could make an exciting novel out of it; it would be worth it.

Thomas Mann knew the cultural philosopher, mathematician, and physician Theodor Lessing (1872–1933), an all-around talent, a starry-eyed idealist, founder of an Anti-Noise League, assimilated Jew, and at times a Jewish anti-Semite, but also an analyst of that phenomenon (*Jewish Self-Hate*, 1930). Thomas Mann apparently knew this jack-of-all-trades from a Carnival ball in the Löwenbräukeller during his early days in Munich. Lessing lived in Schwabing from 1895 until 1901 and afterward was also very often in Munich. He was able to find out more and, apparently, intimate information about Thomas Mann from two sources. He had known Katia Pringsheim since her early girl-hood and had heard "many confidential things in days when the swaying periphery of young emotions impelled the young woman to talk about disappointments and bitter and unjust things." In a ballad-singer tone Lessing writes the following lines about this: "His little wife Katia gave me many a confession, but here I will keep a strict discretion." The second source was Thomas's sister Carla, whom Lessing saw daily for a while. She was acting in a theater in Göttingen, where from 1906 to 1907 Lessing studied philosophy with Edmund Husserl and wrote theater criticism. "With Tommy's sister, too, in Leinetal, / with Carla I strode once arm in arm. . . . / She's forgotten this. . . . They slandered me / as 'scamp' and 'fool' and 'devil' . . . 'I don't know the guy'." Lessing characterizes her sharply as "a young actress who filled her chaise-longue existence with heroic longing for a millionaire, polishing her nails on very beautiful hands, and reading many novels." There must have been many conversations that, after everything we know, lead to pertinent conclusions: "I believe I grasp Thomas Mann well and sharply. Should it be an illusion, I still know that I know him better than he does me."

Lessing had entry to the Pringsheim house considerably earlier than did Thomas Mann. He was encouraged there; among other things, Father Pringsheim helped him get a position as a university lecturer in Hanover. Before the falling-out, they exchanged letters; Lessing mentions that he has about forty of them from the years 1902 to 1910 from Mann and his relatives. Most of them were probably from Carla. Only one letter is preserved in its original from Thomas Mann to Lessing; a second letter is known from Lessing's copy. The preserved letter (from February 27, 1906) praises a book by Lessing that motivated his possibly correct assumption that in "Bilse and I" Thomas

Mann used terms by him (presumably the term "Erkenntnislyriker"—
cognitive poets).

From the years 1901 to 1904 Lessing was a teacher in the boarding
school Haubinda in Thuringia. His wife Maria Stach von Goltzheim,
noble, blond, beautiful, and not a Jew, had at the time a relationship
with a pupil, Bruno Frank, who later became a writer and was be-
friended by Thomas Mann. In 1904 she ran away with Frank. Lessing
is said to have put up with the relationship, even supported it, according to Thomas Mann, who obtained full information about the
affair, for he planned to use it in a literary piece. Half-lascivious, half-
offended Helmut Institoris in *Doctor Faustus* tolerates the adultery of
his wife with Rudi Schwerdtfeger. For his part, Lessing turns to femi-
nism after this affair and becomes a favorite speaker at societies for
promoting morality.

So an undergrowth of obnoxiousness already lay hidden when the
discord came in 1910. Theodor Lessing had written a fairly shameless
satire against the literary critic Samuel Lublinski, whom among other
things he defamed as a "fat synagogling," a jokester Jew, and a literary babbler. Thomas Mann was supposed to sign a feeble rebuttal but
decided to take the matter in hand himself and "shout the impertinent dwarf down fittingly." Superficially, this engagement had two
causes. First, Mann felt indebted to Lublinski because he had praised
*Buddenbrooks* and had described him as the most important novelist of
modern times. Second, the quarrel served, as Thomas admitted to his
brother Heinrich in a letter of March 20, 1910, to direct his active
disposition onto other paths, since the work on *Felix Krull* was not
proceeding.

Mann admits in the *Reflections of a Nonpolitical Man* that when it
was a matter of the battle of minds and pens, a matter of criticism
and polemics, he did not consider cruelty and even infamy to be at all
prohibited or disgraceful. Poor Lessing was pelted with a hailstone of
words such as "outrageous and without talent," "impudent and brazen," with phrases such as "an abysmal lack of manners" and "rancid
prattle," but worst of all with the following passage that reverses the
skewer that the Jew Lessing had used against the Jew Lublinski:

> Herr Lublinski is not a handsome man, and he is a Jew. But I also
> know Herr Lessing (how can you help who your acquaintances

are!), and I have just this to say: Anyone who may claim to see in him a *shining elf* or the perfect example of Aryan masculinity would have to be indicted for fanaticism.

Although Lessing, if you look at the available photographs, seems quite presentable, Mann continues with an allusion to the Bruno Frank affair:

> Humbling personal experiences, which one would prefer not to use as a weapon against him, should have made him altruistic in reference to physical attraction, and I cannot without grave peril to my well-being recall the horrible anecdote that he once danced totally naked around a fire with other Schwabing ecstatics of both sexes. The saying goes: People who live in glass houses should not throw stones; and anyone who cowers through life as a terrible example of the awful Jewish race betrays more than ignorance, betrays grubby self-scorn, if he lets himself be paid as a lampoon, whose every third word is in a Jewish accent. In the style of the provincial special literary section that has gone wild in satirizing the "esprit-Jewish" type, it is splendidly becoming to him who himself is able everywhere to present himself as nothing more than the weakest and shabbiest example of this type that might in some cases well be worthy of admiration!

The whole disproportionately enormous offering of cudgels for the cause with which Mann lashes out at Lessing can be explained only if there were even deeper reasons. He drops many confidants of the early times, such as Otto Grautoff, after he has success. Perhaps Lessing belonged to those who knew too much, and Mann had to keep at a distance from them because they could be dangerous to his arduously erected façade. That is only a supposition. But in any case one can certainly observe in detail what Lessing thinks of Mann and what he knew about him. A small selection grouped around the theme of "masculinity."

Lessing had halfheartedly challenged his opponent to a duel; the latter had rejected his demand. Lessing finds that unmanly. In his folk-song prologue he makes fun of whether Tom was perhaps hermaphroditic, and rhymes to boot: "If on the street he hears the word man / his legs to tremble then began." He expresses that also in prose. "Tomi, the wifey" would be indignant; that is, "as Katia, his hubby, often assures me," on principle he avoids any opportunity to act heroically.

> What a fine, pallid, little middle-class prince! What a still, late gilt-edged soul, not born of woman; probably bought as an antique by his dear mama at Wertheim's in the "department for arts and craft rarities" cheaply and with taste. . . .
>
> He did not dance along in the great festival of life. Crowned with laurel at a young age, hiding his whinyness under good manners, he gazed with hungry, haunted eyes scornfully at the world that he envied. To me he became the epic reporter on things of the soul that I suffered, unredeemed. But he did not suffer. Neither remorse nor sympathy. He savored his painful petty emotions mirrored in melancholy. I never felt him entwined with strong life. He never was enthusiastic in it but for it. He stood outside, receiving scanty tendernesses and artistic fabrications.

Lessing then reviews "Tobias Mindernickel," that early tale by Mann, in which a cripple kills his dog when the latter is healthy and happy. It is Nietzsche's psychology of the will to power that convinces Lessing, but he then also applies this to the author of this little story.

> To envy other creatures their joy because one feels joyless, oneself to want to see others depressed because one does not have enough strength to give happiness—that is the essence of an ailing will to power. . . . If Friedrich Nietzsche were alive today and needed examples for his heroic psychology of the old moral affects—for the origin of sensitive sympathy from an all-too-human weakness, of moral empathy from poisonous resentment, of squabbling categorical demands from the impotence of tyrannical cravings . . . no other writer of the present in Germany could deliver him such clear proof as this typical dame who constantly reflects a decadent morality under an aesthetic pretext. . . . Thomas Mann is secretly a "moralist," more secretly still, an unethical soul; self-righteous and whiningly altruistic at the same time, egocentric and sentimental at the same time!

That hurt. Mann will counter in 1914 with, "Miserable people boasted ethically." He will have to emphasize that the life of Gustav Aschenbach was manly and brave. He thinks of Lessing in 1918 when Peter Altenberg in a feuilleton article headed "Masculine Letter" attributes feminine tendencies to him. Altenberg was, "like the Jews Kerr and Lessing, my born enemy, a necessary scorner or scorn creator of my existence." But also added is: "I would not feel 'stricken,' if all the presuppositions for such criticism of my nature were not in me."

To be attacked in his sexual honor struck Mann keenly. It is part of the stigma of those who are homosexually inclined to be observed as effeminate. If one considers the style of his attacks, Lessing would not have hesitated to play the homosexual card, too. Presumably, he did not have enough information about it. But, like Kerr, he stomps around in the vestibule of that knowledge among the writer's finest porcelain.

Thomas Mann can't get past it. When Lessing is murdered by Nazi thugs, he writes heartlessly to his son Klaus: "Was always a false martyr." Worse things are in his diary (September 1, 1933): "I shudder at such an end, not because it is the end but because it is so wretched and may be fit for a Lessing, but not for me." A wretched death for a wretched man, that would be all right? But destiny, otherwise strongly mindful of such things, did not take vengeance for this meanness— his own death is gentle and dignified.

## A WRETCHED MAN

The last attempt is to see whether the plans for the story "A Wretched Man" could shed light on the darkness remaining in the matters of Kerr and Lessing. The notations offer very little. There are three, dated 1912 and 1913. One counts "A Wretched Man" under the category of "novellas to be done." Another reads: " 'Wretched Man.' Edhin Krokowski from Lind near Pinne, province of Posen." The place names "Pinne" and "Posen" come from Lessing's Lublinski polemic and thus refer to a relationship with Theodor Lessing and probably also with the theme of Eastern Jewry. The name "Krokowski" is again found in *The Magic Mountain*. There that is the name of a somewhat shady psychoanalyst who lectures about love as a pathogenic power. The third notation reads: "On 'The Wretched Man': S. Kerr about W. Rathenau, 'Pan' II No. 44." But Kerr's aforementioned Rathenau portrait to be read there is not a model for "indecent psychologism," which is discussed in *Death in Venice*, but furnishes characteristics for the figure of the wretched man. Mann thought of making use of Kerr's observations. The "Bucolic Creator of Industry" Rathenau, chief of the the European Common Market, was according to Kerr a tender soul of a vacillating nature, a man of words without deeds. "Anyone who complains in public about the mechanization of the world, should impede it (if he is consistent)—which an industrialist can do only in complete secrecy." Kerr is probably right in that regard. What he reprimands Rathenau for, and what Mann wants to use for his "Wretched Man," is the lack of will, even worse, the striving in vain to come to conclusions. "Someone who wants to slave away—but then still stops being strong too soon." A fine, tender pretender, full of convictions, lacking backbone.

As a second source, mention of the plan is available in correspondence. Most worthwhile here is the letter to Ernst Bertram of January 13, 1913. There it states that "decency as fecklessness" had long been a problem, a theme for him. The story of the "wretched man" will with some certainty one day be written. "Have I done studies!! It could become a really good 'character' novella." The "studies," given the time frame (the appearance of the criticism of *Fiorenza*), refer fairly clearly to Kerr.

The most extensive reference to what Thomas Mann planned is in *Death in Venice*. When the Venetian novella was written, neither Kerr's Rathenau criticism nor his negative review of *Fiorenza* had appeared. In this regard Kerr as a source belongs to a later level than Lessing does, for details that are mentioned in *Death in Venice* refer to Lessing. There Gustav von Aschenbach is named as "the creator of that powerful tale 'A Wretched Man,' which showed an entire generation of grateful youths that ethical resoluteness is still possible beyond the utmost depths of knowledge." So this is the message. A bit later we also learn the content:

How else could the famous story of "A Wretched Man" be interpreted than as an eruption of disgust at the indecent psychologism of the age, embodied in the figure of that soft and silly half-rogue who snatches a destiny for himself by driving his wife—out of omnipotence, out of depravity, out of ethical fecklessness—into the arms of a beardless youth and who believes he can practice base actions out of profundity? The power of the word with which here the castoff is cast off, announced the rejection of all moral sense of doubt, of any sympathy with the abyss,

the rejection of the laxity of the statement of sympathy that to
understand everything means to forgive everything, and what
was prepared here, even completed, was that "miracle of reborn
naïveté," which a bit later in one of the author's dialogues was
spoken of expressly and not without surreptitious emphasis.

Not all of this can be rendered with certainty back into what was
experienced, but there are some reference points. The "soft and silly
half-rogue," that much is certain, was inspired by Theodor Lessing,
whose wife had a relationship with the student Bruno Frank, the
"beardless youth." The motive of the wretched man to put up with,
or even to promote, this relationship is blatant: He wanted to achieve
a fate of sorts surreptitiously, out of "ethical fecklessness" and out of
"profundity." This is based here on Nietzsche's psychology of decadence. Where the tragic passions of the heroic age are lacking, decadent contemporaries of the tragic art help to mimic heroics. It is a
matter of "unmanly" behavior that is loftily stylized.

   Most remarkable are the "profundity" and especially the "ethical
fecklessness," With "fecklessness" only a pretended volition is meant,
the intention to appear as one with volition, the wish to become
someone with volition, while one is just a reed in the wind. Thomas
Mann is most subtle as a psychologist whenever he was able to study
in himself the emotions that are involved. Even when he was not yet
twenty, he embraced *Tout comprendre c'est tout pardonner*. A lax psychologist who cannot judge anything because he "understands" everything, who today sees through this and tomorrow through that
role—whom does this description fit better than the young Thomas
Mann! "Anyone can scold, my friend!" he writes to Otto Grautoff on
January 17, 1896. "It is more becoming for the psychologist to *understand*, to *explain*. Condemning *always* produces lack of understanding
and psychological incapability. Comprendre c'est sourir, Monsieur."

   So let us assume that self-criticism is involved. Let us assume further, that the abasement and unmanliness that he characterizes as the
behavior of the wretched man was known to him also from his own
experience. Perhaps even he himself had once surrendered a beloved
woman, or a male lover, without a struggle, with an understanding
smile, to a rival. All the "fighting," wasn't it ridiculous? The fatalism
of the aesthete sees clearly and understands and suffers, but he doesn't
fight. Anyway, suffering makes him a hero; fighting does not.

Of course, Thomas Mann did fight for Katia. Probably the first time in his life he fought for someone. As we saw, he beleaguered her tenaciously and systematically and in doing so he pushed aside rivals like Kerr. Thomas Mann, the psychologist who understood everything, decided back then to reject the laxness of the homily of sympathy, that to understand everything meant to forgive everything. He turns away decisively from the moral sense of doubt that is unable to believe in itself and its own love. He renounces the "sympathy with the abyss," which one can translate freely as sympathy with homosexuality. He assumes a state of mind. He wants to be a decent citizen. That is his ethical will—but perhaps sometimes it is only a fecklessness.

In the "Wretched Man," he runs into someone who reminds him of the weakness of his own youth, of what he had decided to overcome with his decision to marry. That thereby the "miracle of reborn naturalness" would be his lot is a pious wish. We saw how spasmodic and ambitious, how anxious and strained everything is that Mann does in those years. The miracle mentioned is a quotation from *Fiorenza*, where it is ascribed to the prior. Like Mann's Aschenbach, he previously turns away from aestheticistic laxness. "I hate this contemptible righteousness, this lascivious understanding, this depraved toleration of the opposite!!" he rails at the aesthete Lorenzo. But the latter is acquainted with the psychology of decadence. Since the age is "fine, full of doubt and tolerant, curious, roving, manifold, and boundless," a power "that decisively shuts itself off from the general skepticism" can work unheard of things. One sees that in the case of Gustav von Aschenbach and the intention also of his creator. But to shut oneself off from the skepticism means not to want to know what one does know. "I don't want to know that," says the prior when Lorenzo analyzes him. Can one do that, asks Lorenzo. "Can one not want to know?" The prior insists: "I'm chosen. I am allowed to know and still want to. For I must be strong. God performs miracles. You are witnessing the miracle of reborn naturalness."

That's exactly what is not true. The prior is as prejudiced, as ambitious, tense, and strained as Thomas Mann himself. Gustav von Aschenbach, too, is anything but naïve. The greatness of this story is the fact that the presumed naïveté is unmasked as a tenseness and play-acting that collapses under the onslaught of real passion. *Death in Venice* denies the result of "The Wretched Man." The denial of psychologism did not end with the rebirth of decency but with the return of the suppressed; the termination of sympathy with the abyss ends in the abyss; homosexuality breaks into the tribulation of marriage. "The master attitude of our style is falsehood and foolishness, our fame and position of honor a farce," prattles Gustav von Aschenbach in half-sleep; denial of knowledge leads just as much to the abyss as knowledge that is "knowing, understanding, forgiving." There is no way out here.

As the kernel of Thomas Mann's supposed anti-Semitism, there resides the fear of the threat to life by the intellect. His polemics are so bitter and unjust because he is fighting against himself, against his own better knowledge, because he is afraid for his own composure, form, and dignity. The threat of indecent psychologism is in the final analysis—*Death in Venice* shows this—the threat of the return of suppressed homosexuality. By admitting it again shortly after the Lessing polemic, at least literarily, Thomas Mann took a bit of pressure off himself. He will gradually become freer also regarding psychoanalysis.

World War I brings a relapse. It brings him a chance to feel like a "man" and to reject psychology again. "But psychology is the cheapest and most common thing. There is nothing earthly in which filth cannot be uncovered and isolated by psychoanalysis." Where he gets that is clear: from himself. But in war, other "more manly" laws apply. One should and may now order wretched men behind barriers. "Wretched men swaggered ethically." That referred to Lessing. The theme of the "decency of fecklessness" stimulated him to give it literary form. But it did not after all concern only Lessing, but Savonarola too, Aschenbach too, Thomas Mann himself too. Did he have to denounce such decency? Only again in the twenties will he realize that sympathy with the abyss serves fascism politically. He will destroy decency no more, even desired decency; with a real power of decision and strength of will, he will stand tall.

*Munich, around 1919*

On August 1914 the family was at its summer house in Bad Tölz. Thomas Mann joined in the general enthusiasm for war. Rejected by understanding doctors, he at least wanted to perform service by sharing his thoughts. With this purpose in mind, immediately in August and September 1914, he eagerly wrote "Thoughts in Wartime," then in September or October "Good Military Mail," from September to December *Frederick and the Grand Coalition*, from April to May 1915 the "Letter to the Newspaper *Svenska Dagbladet*" in Stockholm, in the spring of 1916 "To the Army Newspaper A.O.K. 10," but above all in the fall of 1915 until spring 1918 the monumental *Reflections of a Nonpolitical Man*. Meanwhile, work on *The Magic Mountain* came to a halt. The war writings brought him numerous hostilities, foremost from Heinrich Mann, who took up a position in his essay "Zola" (appeared, November 1915) against the German Reich of the time and against his brother. An association with the scholar Ernst Bertram had to provide Mann with a substitute for his lost correspondents.

Customary life—work at his desk, theater, concerts, reading tours, vacations in Bad Tölz—continues during the war, reduced by frequent illness and in the last year also affected by scarcity of foodstuffs. In 1917 the summer house in Tölz is sold and the proceeds placed in war bonds that before their maturity become worthless. In March work on the idyll "A Man and His Dog" (finished middle of October) was begun. The end of the war and the revolution of November 1918 are reflected intensively in his diary. An epoch comes to an end.

## SOLDIER AND MILITARY MAN ASCHENBACH

SO, WHAT reason does a writer like Thomas Mann have," asks Wilhelm Herzog, upset and irritated in December 1914, what reason does the author of *Buddenbrooks* have "to express thoughts in wartime that during peacetime at least he always suppressed?" What reason had a decadent with cultivated manners to describe something so uncivilized as war as something holy, and to be enthused about purification and liberation? In some regards that is the question of all questions. Mann's behavior at the outbreak of war belongs to the great riddles a biography must solve. Generally it appears as a mistake that then is corrected with the change to a republic, as a kind of slip. There is offered only an explanation that at the time, the great majority welcomed the war and Mann joined that majority.

Without doubt Thomas Mann, too, had the frame of mind that inspired that majority to take its stand. But not its reasons, not the appetite for adventure and the national feeling of power, not the boasting about the Sedan and the hundredth anniversary of the 1813 victory over Napoleon in the Battle of Nations are decisive here, rather the special reasons of Thomas Mann should interest us. The intoxication of 1914 must be explained from his life recounted up to this point, not from general history. He does not even want to belong to this general history. "I am solitary," he emphasizes; he does not want to join in the cries for war in the nation. "Thunderous words do not become me." He is no devourer of Frenchmen. Before the war he belonged to a French association "Pour mieux se connaître."

The most important answers at the outset lie in six propositions: (1) The war liberated him from disorientation and gave his life sense and a goal again. (2) The war liberated him from a creative crisis. (3) The war gave him permission for open fraternal hate. (4) The war offered chances to satisfy his ambition for greatness and to become a national poet. (5) The war allowed him to show himself as a "man," in defiance of those who had made him contemptible as a sissy, housemouse, and fine gilt-edged soul. (6) In a subtle way the war even seemed to offer solutions for the conflict between intellect and life, between the world of his father and the world of his mother, between marriage and homoeroticism, between the dream of power and rank

on the one hand and of the dream of love and union on the other—
and not only solutions but intoxicating syntheses!

The "Thoughts in Wartime" have their intellectual prehistory in
*Death in Venice*. Gustav von Aschenbach had already asserted that art
is war; "he too had been a soldier and warrior." The comment by a
colleague, that there was a "military spirit" in the Venetian novella,
Mann notes with satisfaction on August 22. That story about death is
surreptitiously cited in "Thoughts in Wartime." One can read there
about the time before the war, "an ethical reaction had begun," "a
moral solidity again," and "a new will to reject the rejected, to termi-
nate sympathy for the abyss," and further, "a will for rectitude, purity, and composure" had sought to take shape. The most important
(perhaps the only) evidence for these tendencies of the time is the
program of Gustav von Aschenbach, who in "A Wretched Man" had
rejected the rejected, had turned away from the moral sense of doubt,
and from that sympathy with the abyss had gained dignity and sternness as well as masterful classicism.

But the bearer of the warlike vision is the Aschenbach of the second, not the fifth, chapter. The high-minded plan is ruined after all in
the onslaught of passion. Composure and form and mastery collapse,
the virtuous warriors become "like women," the boy Tadzio as Hermes
Psychopompos leads Aschenbach's soul down to Hades; the world of
death is victorious, a world of mingling and without boundaries, of
ethical indifference and pleasure in downfall.

A world that breaks apart in *Death in Venice* was to rise in 1914?
How is such a reversion possible? By the fact that in 1914 something
new is added, namely, real history. In 1912 it was still a matter of pure
fecklessness. Thomas Mann even admits it. He had carried in his
heart the will to deny decadence, "let us say, pessimistically: the fecklessness of that denial." Rectitude and composure were attitudes that
lacked a steadfast *for what reason*? in spite of all fervor. This was now
surprisingly offered by war. Composure, decisiveness, and the power
of will suddenly had an object. Also the wish to become a national
poet was no longer only the ambitious thirst for glory of a man who
wanted to prove himself to his wife; instead real history fawned upon
him. The nation suddenly needed a poet. Thomas Mann could set
himself at the forefront of a great German movement. Now he could
also write his "Frederick," even if only, as the subtitle of the first
edition of *Frederick and the Grand Coalition* reads, as "A Sketch for the

Day and the Hour." While his and Aschenbach's ambitions necessarily were dashed by the war because they were only a strenuous
role that could easily be disparaged by suppressed reality, the year
1914 offered first of all a seductive fulfillment of dreams of synthesis
and utopias of union of his early work. Why is Germany for the war?
"Because it recognized in it the harbinger of its *Third Reich. —*What
then is its Third Reich? —It is the *synthesis of power and mind—*it is its
dream and longing, its highest goal in war—and not Calais or the
'subjugation of peoples' or the Congo." "1914" is the reborn impul-
siveness of *Fiorenza,* the new rectitude of the Venetian novella, the
reconciliation of intellectualism and simplicity, of artist and bourgeois
man, of art and life. That's what it looks like anyway for a moment in
that hour of enthusiastic departure in readiness for death. The Apol-
lonian father's world of duty seems to unite marvelously with the
Dionysian death intoxication of merging and boundlessness.

Thomas Mann realized only much later that reason would have
had to lead him to the side of the war's opponents. In reality the war
was what Tadzio was: the return of what was suppressed, indulgence
in the Dionysian dream of merging and in the death wish. Besides, it
permitted him to turn himself loose in fraternal hate, in relished orgies of abuse with erotically charged words.

Subliminally, the war also had something to do with homoeroticism. To find the evidence, one must think in a roundabout way. The
little war piece "Good Military Mail," written around October 1914,
presents the thesis that the intellect was never closer to life than the
present moment in opposition to the widespread opinion that the raw
reality of war was distant and inimical to everything intellectual. The
proof of that is personal. Thomas Mann quotes letters from military
mail. Soldiers had written to him that *Death in Venice* had never been
closer to them than in the immediacy of trenches. If there really were
such letters (they are not preserved), then the writers may have been
fascinated by the martial morality of Aschenbach as well as by its
opposite, the death wish. Mann calls the love between intellect and
life the profoundest principle. All the happiness of the world was
enclosed in it.

Did not the mind bend down wooing to life and tell it flatteringly
that it is beauty? But how even Nature smiled, when life bowed
in homage to mind—because it recognized itself in it again! A

few wise men and poets have held that here was Eros and nowhere else—in this tender, holy, painful, this divine back-and-
forth between life and mind.

"A few wise men and poets"—this passage is sublimely humorous,
for the one meant is only a single person, Thomas Mann himself. The
quotation comes from *Death in Venice*. Gustav von Aschenbach dreams
of Socrates, how he instructs Phaidros—the elderly-ugly man ("mind")
and the beautiful boy ("life"). Socrates lectures emotionally "that Nature looks on with delight when the Mind bows in homage to beauty."
He speaks "of the holy awe that befalls the noble man when a godlike
face, a perfect body appears to him—how he begins to tremble and is
beside himself and hardly trusts himself to look and honors the one
who has such beauty and would sacrifice to him as to a statue, if he
did not have to fear that he would seem foolish to the people."
  So that is what "Good Military Mail" quotes. In wartime mind and
life come together like Socrates and Phaidros, like Aschenbach and
Tadzio. And they finally come together so that life also approaches
mind; the boy is not only merely rhapsodized but writes letters from
the field. For otherwise than in *Death in Venice*, where it says "that
Nature looks on with delight when the mind bows in homage to
beauty," in "Good Military Mail" it says: "But even Nature now
smiled, when life bowed in homage to Mind."
  Of course, that is abysmally maudlin. "The capability of mankind
to deceive itself is astonishing." The boy—war—remained distant
like all boys in the life of Thomas Mann. "Good Military Mail" is
written shortly after Mann's rejection for service. He does not go to
war but gazes at it adoringly from the distance.


## 1914 IN LETTERS

The report of the mobilization order reached Thomas Mann on July
30. "It has never gotten this far for as long as we've been alive," he
writes to Heinrich. "I'd like to know how you feel about it. I must say
that I feel shaken and ashamed by the awful pressure of reality. Until
today I was optimistic and unbelieving—one has too civilian a frame
of mind to take the monstrous for possible." That was emotional, but
still peaceful. But on August 7, 1914, the emotion of the enthusiasm

for war was fully unfolded. Without having the slightest idea that Heinrich thought otherwise, he confesses:

> I'm still as though in a dream—and yet, after all, one must still be ashamed not to have thought it possible and not to have seen that the catastrophe had to come. What an ordeal! . . . Should one not be grateful for the totally unexpected, allowed to experience such great things? My main feeling is an enormous curiosity— and, I admit it, the deepest sympathy for this hated, fateful, and puzzling Germany.

On August 22 the worried man writes a letter to Samuel Fischer that contains some theses of "Thoughts in Wartime": that he was fed up with the peaceful world; that he had been seized by "a feeling of purification, elevation, liberation"; that nothing greater and more fortunate could happen to the Germans than that the world rose up against them. Besides, the war also solved an artistic problem:

> In the degenercy of my *Magic Mountain*, the war of 1914 must break out as a solution; that was definite from the moment it began.

Heinrich had obviously not yet made himself clear. He had merely hinted that he had hardly any income because his writing at the moment was so useless. Thomas contradicts him vigorously with an argument that shows that on September 18, 1914, Thomas does not yet know where his brother stands:

> Can you really believe that Germany would be so set back in its culture or its civilized behavior by this great, basically respectable, indeed solemn popular war that it could unremittingly reject your offerings?

The popular war leaves Heinrich unbedazzled. Gently and coolly he explains to his brother that Germany will lose the war. Thomas breaks off abruptly. When the "Thoughts in Wartime" appears, it is also obviously clear: The brothers oppose one another.

More reflective tones are discernible in a letter of September 29. Thomas Mann must offer his condolences to his Lübeck colleague Ida Boy-Ed. Her son has fallen in France. Meanwhile the Battle of the Marne, which had stopped the German advance, had ended. It had become clear that there would be no swift victory. Thomas Mann's conscience bothers him because he is not in the field. "The only honorable place is really that in a trench." But he does not really want to be there. He writes to Annette Kolb on October 28 that he cannot at all imagine the longing of the wounded soldier for the trench, where the great frenzy is. Still, from his desk a bit of misfortune seems beneficial to him. "Our victory seems to lie in the consistency of history," he states, but, "seen pedagogically," would it not be good for Germany if it happened as easily as it seemed at the start?

The enthusiast was happy when a postcard from the field from Richard Dehmel arrived for him: "Day before yesterday I read in the trench your thoughts about the war (*Neue Rundschau*). I must say that each word spoke to me from the heart. . . . This quiet pioneer work is perhaps really more fruitful for the future than all the noise of war in the present." That made him feel good. Of course, that his old friend and supporter was in the field, but the much younger Thomas Mann was not, got on his nerves ("My heart and mind wouldn't be able to take it"), but that Dehmel confirmed to him that intellectual war service was important also helped him recover. His reply ends like a hymn:

> One feels that everything will have to be *new* after this profound, violent anguish and that the German soul will emerge stronger, prouder, freer, happier from it. So be it.

A letter of December 15 to his brother-in-law Heinz Pringsheim, who was likewise in the field, speaks about peace negotiations and obscure plans to recompense France with territory gained in Belgium. Kurt Martens receives the last letter of the year 1914 (dated December 30). "The war will definitely last," it says now. The emotion gives way to more basic considerations that lead to *The Magic Mountain*. The love for war, even if the formula does not yet occur, reveals itself as sympathy for death.

> But just as I am, as an artist I will never be able to follow the exhortation to take the side of life against death. I cannot take sides at all—I would feel it an assault on my freedom. Which is more *noble*, life or death? I don't know. Which is more *revolting*, death or life? . . . I find that these questions should be raised— and without obligation—in artistic freedom and made vital without their being settled. In the final analysis, death and life are opposites only aesthetically. In regard to religion, they are one— the same mystery.

## MILITARY SERVICE

That previously, in 1900, Mann did not show himself eager to be a soldier has already been mentioned. At that time he was overwhelmingly tormented by the clamor, waste of time, and iron laurels. He can count on being called up in 1914. His brother Victor is taken immediately as is his brother-in-law Heinz Pringsheim. But he himself belongs to the older age group of the unconscripted reserves, and on August 7 is not yet worried about anything. "Good Military Mail" (September–October 1914) is a justification. "To live like a soldier but not be a soldier" is the motto of the one who remains at his desk. He would like to distinguish himself from those who are "too smart" to sacrifice and look at those in the field mockingly. He writes to Hans von Hülsen on October 21 that he still has not been called up, but he is not comfortable with that. It is only the trench that is honorable. "My military situation is as yours," he writes to Philipp Witkop, full of fear, "only that I am by no means exempt and, if the matter lasts long, which it will surely do (the general staff here figures on 2 years), I will still have my turn somehow." Nevertheless, the letter at year's end to Martens says that he reported for his militia duty promptly. "Where do you have it from, that we'll be called up by April? I also believe our turn is coming. The war will definitely keep on for a long time."

His turn did not come. On October 1, 1915, he writes to Paul Amann how that happened.

As a non-active militiaman par excellence, I always kept only a symbolic relationship with being a soldier. At the beginning of the war the most extreme corruption prevailed about my being mustered up. The staff doctor, an obviously extremely civil man and blindly devoted to belles artes, upon hearing my name proved to be a cheerful official and rejected me "so that I would have my peace." (Literally). A very un-German case of corruption by literature.

Perhaps in reality it was not quite so pleasant. Erich Mühsam writes indignantly in his diary that Thomas Mann had had to stand stark naked in front of some lieutenant or other and provide information in response to his ignorant sniffing around. Where he got his information, we don't know. In any event, the result was release. But Thomas

Mann was still afraid of a remustering of those mustered out. True, people over forty had been excepted for the time being, "but if the war is prolonged, I can still expect some kind of adventure." The remustering came on November 11, 1916; he was rejected for military service because of a weak stomach and nervousness.

Only once, Mann writes in the *Sketch of My Life*, in occupied Brussels, where he was present at a staging of *Fiorenza*, did he come into contact with the military sphere. Then too—it was January 1918—he saw nothing of the front. His war experience consisted of his having breakfast with General Hurt, "in the circle of his officers, trim and friendly people, who all—God knew for the sake of what services—wore the Iron Cross, First Class, on their chests." One of them had later addressed him as "Dear War Comrade," "and really," Thomas Mann thinks, "I let the war approach me as harshly as these gentlemen."

## THOMAS MANN AND THE GRAND COALITION

"The mysteries of sex are deep and will never be completely clarified." One finds remarkable statements in the militarily suitable essay *Frederick and the Grand Coalition*—statements that cause even this text, so clearly involved chiefly with political matters of the day, to be seached thoroughly for clues about his life. Of course, the secrets of sex also have above all to do with politics. France, for example, is a woman, "this nation claims ladies' rights." On the other hand, Germany is a man like Frederick, whom Maria Theresia, she, too, an exemplary woman, never labeled other than "the bad man." "Yes, that he was," adds Thomas Mann, "and, to be sure, just as much a 'man' as he was 'bad.'"

"Wherever I am, Germany is," declares Thomas Mann in 1938, when he steps onto American soil. "Germany today is Frederick the Great," he announces in 1914 in his "Thoughts in Wartime." Frederick is Thomas Mann—the deduction becomes apparent. At least you can experiment with it. In many passages Thomas Mann must have thought: Just like me! Almost like for me! Whereby some narcissistic exaggeration may have been mixed in, for many parallels are indeed real, but others merely wished for, still others half feared.

As the crown prince, Frederick was a feminine and spineless philosopher, certainly demonstrating voluptuousness but secretly threatened by impotence (for the powers of the body, it says in one quotation, had not seconded the inclinations of the will enough). When he comes to the throne, to the general bewilderment he reveals himself as an impassioned soldier. He loves the work so fanatically that average human perception is aware of something arid, inhuman, and inimical to life in it. He has no confidants and lives apart from his wife. He is an ascetic; he is several times called a monk. "He never loved," it is said; an "affliction" had existed in that area, an operation, "and from that point on he was somewhat arrested in his nature" and "the female had played a less creditable role in his life."

"Obviously, Frederick's masculinity was not attracted by the feminine opposite in the usual manner." A dancer who for a time was thought to be the king's lover credited that, in Voltaire's mocking phrase, to the fact that she had the legs of a man. Frederick's marriage was one in name only. He was "antifeminist" and demanded that also from his officers; they were to make their luck with the saber and not with the sheath.

We do not know whether Thomas Mann, too, was hounded by the fear of becoming like Frederick in old age, arid and bad, "cold, bleak, and repulsive." We are again on safer ground when expressions are ascribed to Frederick from the circle of *Death in Venice*, "Thoughts in Wartime," and the postwar essay "Goethe and Tolstoy": "moral radicalism" for example, "resolution" and "radical skepticism," as well as "irony toward both sides" and a nihilistic "fanaticism of accomplishment." What binds Frederick and Thomas Mann is, furthermore, the belief in the "urgency of fate" and the "spirit of history," a suprapersonal, demonic power. Something immense has seized the decadent Thomas Mann in 1914, so that to the astonishment of everyone the fine gilt-edged soul becomes a soldier and warrior. The same power had also seized Frederick as crown prince, when out of the weakling came the monarch.

The propagandistic value of the Frederick essay cannot be overestimated. It consists above all in the fact that for the attack on neutral Belgium, contrary to international law, a stimulating example is found, namely, Frederick's invasion of neutral Saxony in the Seven Years' War. "Absurdly the same, I saw Frederick's history repeated in the genesis of our own war." Germany has a need for ideology; Thomas Mann delivers it expertly. He has no doubt that it involved an infringement of the law. Frederick "had to take on the burden of guilt in order to reveal the guilt of his opponents." As a devotee of Schopenhauer, Mann places no trust in the ability of reasonable men to act. He submits to fatalism. Frederick, too, is not the man of reason but the man of fate.

> His justice was the justice of increasing power, a problematical, still illegitimate, still unsubstantiated justice that had yet to be won, yet to be created. . . . Only when it turned out through success that he was the man commissioned by fate, only then was he just and could he be deemed having always been just. Every deed that earned this appellation is a test of fate, an attempt to create justice, to realize development, and to manage misfortune.

One had to have the "spirit of history" on one's side; that was it. That produced a powerful support. That even permitted what was otherwise forbidden. What was not middle class again came into its right. For being a soldier is not middle class. Thomas had to choose between Frederick and Voltaire. "Voltaire and the king: That is reason and demon, spirit and genius, dry holiness and beclouded fate, bourgeois moralizing and heroic duty; Voltaire and the king: that has been for always and for all time the great civilian and the great soldier." He chose Frederick, chose demon and genius, beclouded fate and heroic duty. And yet ten years before, he had given himself a middle-class constitution, decided for reason and mind, for dry holiness and middle-class moralizing. It was still to take some time before he found his way back to Voltaire.


## THE ORDEAL


"What inspired writers was the war in itself as an ordeal." Again and again Thomas Mann calls the war an ordeal, a deep, powerful ordeal. The word belongs to the primal odds and ends. What holds life together, it says in the Joseph novel, is the idea of ordeal, of "the intrusion of drunkenly destructive and disastrous forces into a composed life sworn to calmness with all its hopes for dignity and a qualified happiness." Thomas Mann goes on to speak of apparently assured peace, of life that swept away the faithful structure of art with a laugh, and of the howling triumph of the suppressed world of desire.

The war, too, is an intrusion of a passion in a life outwardly artistically ordered by middle class, marriage, and family. Applied to the war, the ordeal is finally something permitted. One must not complain about it. "The philanthropist must see to it that he does not put himself into a comical light by poorly directed sympathy." It is good that you can just let yourself go. Finally, even the destruction of middle-class safety is something almost longed for. "If the war lasts long, I will be with fair certainty what they call 'ruined.' For heaven's sake!" This great time provides protection for stepping out of his role, something always secretly wished for. "How the hearts of poets flamed up immediately, now that war came! . . . Now, as though in a competition, they sang the war, jubilantly, with deeply upwelling cries—as though nothing better, more beautiful, happier could happen to them and the people whose voice they are."

## ZOLA

A gush of acid rained down on his beautiful dreams. His brother replied. A great essay by Heinrich, entitled "Zola," bristling with hate, appeared in November 1915. He pretended to be speaking of Emile Zola, the French naturalist, who with his "J'accuse" had enlightened France about truth and justice in the Dreyfus trial. But in a cleverly ambiguous way the essay spoke at the same time about Germany and about the war, about the battle of mind and democracy against demons and enthralled submission. On a further deeper layer of allusion he spoke, in the final analysis, about his battle against his brother. Everything that Thomas related to himself, whether justly or unjustly (probably mostly justly) is learned best with pointed accentuation, with exclamations and emphases from the report that the nonpolitical observer himself gives of the Zola essay:

> These spokesmen and lawyers—they may justify themselves later, if they can—"one thing is for sure from the start: They have it easier. Their way of thinking does not demand that they endure banishment and silence." (Banishment? Silence?) On the contrary, they make the most out of the fact that we others are silent and banished; only they are heard; it is their best moment. No more than human, if they were to realize this and affirm their pretended patriotism even louder than they would perhaps do, if

we others were not to be made oblivious in this way. One would
have to take a look at them to see whether they were not those
who otherwise understood making a profit. Were they perhaps
fighters? . . . What if they were to be told that with their own
hands they had contributed to bringing about the outrageous
thing that is now reality" (the conviction of Dreyfus), "the utmost
falsehood and disgrace" (we're talking here about the conviction
of the Jewish captain) "since they always acted skeptically in
such a fine way against such coarse concepts as truth and justice." . . . "If worse came to worst, no, we did not believe that if
worse came to worst they could become traitors to spirit, to mankind. Now they are that. Rather than turning around and, warding it off, stepping up before their people, they run beside their
people and with its most disgusting seducers and encourage it in
the injustice into which it is being seduced. They, the intellectual
fellow travelers, are more guilty even than the authorities" (of
the Dreyfus trial), "who falsify and break the law. For the authorities the injustice that they do remains injustice; they apply nothing but their own interest, which they establish as that of the
nation's. You false intellectuals turn injustice into justice, and
even into a mission, when it happens through the very people
whose conscience you are supposed to be." . . . "The whole nationalistic catechism, filled with madness and crime—and what
preaches it is your ambition, even more paltry, your vanity. . . .
Through overambitious striving, national writers will definitely
run along for half a generation, if their breath lasts that long,
always inflamed by heightened emotions, avoiding responsibility
for the increasing catastrophe, and, in addition, unaware of it, like
the last man! . . . Now it doesn't matter that you stand against
truth and against righteousness elegantly accoutered; you stand
against them and belong to the low ranks, to what is transitory. You
have chosen between the moment and history and have admitted
that with all your gifts you were only amusing freeloaders."

Thomas Mann sees the Zola essay in January 1916. The shock causes
the general revision essay, which has been in preparation since September 1915, to swell into a thick book. For more than two years
Thomas Mann will work on the refutation of the open and the subliminal reproaches.

## SAYING EVERYTHING

"I want to say everything—that is the significance of this book." In its first printing the *Reflections* has more than six hundred pages. As unrestrained as the opus is considered, as seen unburdening, as much as it contains sparkling formulations and intellectual perception, just as little does it say *everything*. Much more, it keeps out what is private with strict consistency. It is not confessional but rhetorical; it is on stage every moment. It is rhetorical even when it admits its theatricality. "A remnant of role playing, advocacy, performance, artfulness, being above it all, a remnant of a lack of conviction and that poetic sophistry that lets the one who happens to be speaking be right, and who in this case was myself," such a remnant was doubtless left everywhere and had also hardly stopped being half-conscious. That's what it says in the subsequently written preface.

To that extent, "saying everything" does not mean self-revelation but self-defense. Not an inward search of one's conscience, rather an outward assertion is the task of the *Reflections*. When it speaks of intimacy, it means the conflict with his brother Heinrich. But this very thing is not acknowledged when discussed but is staged theatrically. His brother's name is not used, and what really took place between the brothers from autumn of 1914 on must be deduced in any event indirectly. We do not find a real portrait of Heinrich Mann in the *Reflections*. The aggressive letters of December 1903 and at the turn of the year 1917–18 treat the depths of the brotherhood most closely. Here the wounds they inflicted on each other—intentionally and unintentionlly—are palpable. But even these letters do not tell everything by far. The fraternal relationship belongs to the mysteries of this life, to its constantly irritating, constantly goading, and thus productive dark regions.

It should not be irritating that the rhetorical posture of the *Reflections* is that of a confession; it is merely a rhetorical posture. His text has the lack of restraint of a privately written letter, writes Mann. "What is true appears in broad daylight." And he cites August von Platen. "Let the world know me, so that it will forgive me!" The quotation is revealing. Platen's lifelong secret was his homosexuality. Therefore, "Let the world know me" belongs to Thomas Mann's secret quotations. "Let the world know me, but only when everyone is dead," writes the seventy-five-year-old in his diary (October 13, 1950). "Cheerful revelations then, in the name of God." Only the diaries tell "everything." The *Reflections* celebrate only the posture of telling everything.

## EROTICISM AND IRONY

So no unknown intimacies can be expected from the *Reflections*. Like the literary works, they must be back-translated. There are no love affairs, not even in secret allusions, but there is a revealing theory of eroticism. The subject is the self-negation of the mind in favor of life. We will callously translate "mind" with "Thomas Mann" and "life" with "blond boys," knowing that that is not exhaustive. The mind that falls in love with life must negate itself, since the blond boys are appealing only when they are unintellectual.

The thought of power belongs to strong and beautiful life. It is not the writer who has it, rather the naïve-ordinary opposite. Self-negation is characterized as "exuberant, erotically intoxicated submission to 'power.'" This submission is "already not really masculine," but of a feminine nature, to use the word that Mann avoids in this passage.

Thus the psychology of this eroticism is connected to happy submission. Spoken again callously, it is masochistic. The knowledge of the mind about this "unmanly" masochism is the biographical, psychological kernel of Mann's famous irony. The "manly" attitude of ruling, which "knocks off" life, exists in "comprehending." The mercilessness of comprehending is the vengeance of mind for his humiliation. He is humiliated because he loves what has been comprehended and certainly does not want to change it. He is an ironist, not a satirist. The concept of life had become erotic irony in *Tonio Kröger*, "a loving affirmation of all that is not mind and art, that is innocent, wholesome, decently unproblematical, and purely from the mind."

In the chapter "Irony and Radicalism" powerful definitions follow. The ironist is conservative, it states, but only when he does not signify the voice of life, which wants itself, "rather the voice of the mind, which does not want itself, but wants life." Then, for example, the situation of the mind that wants not war but literature is ironic.

"Here Eros comes into play," Mann continues. Eros affirms a person, regardless of his worth. That, too, is a masochistic determination, for the mind should certainly not look away from worth but does so with so many boy waiters. Rapture remains: "so there is between them no union, rather only the brief, intoxicating illusion of union and understanding, an eternal tension without a release."

"The mind that loves is not fanatic; it is ingenious, it is political, it courts, and its courting is erotic irony. There is a political term for that; it is called 'conservatism.' What is conservatism? The erotic irony of the mind."

## FRATRICIDAL WAR

Thomas Mann cites the statement from *Fiorenza*: "Yearning is gigantic power, but possession emasculates." That is aimed at his brother, insinuating that he appeases eroticism. Heinrich is the hedonist, Thomas the ascetic.

But in practical life the "Heinrich" of the *Reflections* is not credited with having sexual pleasure. Civilization's literary man is criticized as an aesthete who celebrates only the role and gesture of the pleasure lover without having the capability for it. Aestheticism, it states, is "the expressive and highly gifted impotence for living and for loving." Aestheticism is the "rhetorically resolute 'love for humankind,'" but this is only peripheral eroticism; "when it is proclaimed, when it is boasted about, then usually something is amiss at the core." Three small points of reference follow:

"Love" as ideology is opposed to love in practice. Heinrich is declared an ideologue, whose core is wanting. But the embarrassing thing is that this aestheticism, the impotence for living and for loving, and peripheral eroticism, all of these are reproaches that at least in equal measure apply to Thomas. Whether they apply to Heinrich at all is not a subject of debate here, although his eroticism in all probability was less peripheral than that of his younger brother. Heinrich certainly had more reason to reproach the latter of being withered and lacking masculinity than did Thomas. At the beginning of "Zola" he had written: "It is a matter for those who are to wither early to step up with self-assurance and in a worldly manner at the beginning of their twenties." But that was going too far for Thomas. He saw himself constrained to emphasize his masculinity.

As a "brother," Thomas Mann does battle with aspirations that he studied in himself. "Civilization's literary man," whom he attacks so spiritedly, is himself, and he knows that; "we are alone," he notes ambiguously. The *Reflections* is artful shadowboxing. Heinrich writes about Zola and his adversaries but means the democratic activists of 1914 and their adversaries, essentially himself and his brother. Thomas writes about the international world of letters and the native Germans, but almost always means Heinrich and himself. He does not mention his brother's name a single time, but continually addresses him directly, concealed in rhetorical phrases: "How do you then face me, man, artist, brother, with your negative chatter?" He even reports conversations; for example, he had wanted to enthuse him, civilization's literary man, for Paul Claudel, but received the answer that there were more important things. That probably was not long before the war. But above all, he quotes maliciously and anonymously almost all the writings by Heinrich from the years 1910 to 1917. The *Reflections* conceals behind the mask of his brother all that was repulsive, hostile, and tormentingly incomprehensible. From "Zola" and the *Reflections* whole conversations can be pieced together, and again it can be shown that they mutually accuse one another of being afraid of being themselves.

One of these accusations reads: Profiteer! Aiming at the spokesmen and advocates of the war, Heinrich had written that they were benefiting from it, "that we others keep silent and are banished; only they are heard; it is their happiest moment." Thomas replies personally, almost falling out of his role: "My happiest moment! Fool, don't you see that it is your happiest moment, much more yours?!" Each believes the other has it easier. Those who had become national poets through excess ambition to "make it," Heinrich taunts, "were they perhaps warriors?" No, they were only entertaining freeloaders. Thomas shoots back with a comedic rhetorical cascade that mocks his brother's warriorhood as operatic posturing:

A freeloader. Because: "Were they perhaps warriors?" O no, I was never a warrior, nothing of the sort! I never stood there, one hand on my heart, the other held up, and recited the *contrat social*. I did not chant that some "gentlemen" or other should be hanged on a lamp post and did not plead to get rid of great men because they lowered standards. I did not maintain that the republic was the ideal of truth, also did not scorn humankind laden eternally with suffering by assuring them tremblingly that their path led "to something very beautiful, completely serene," further did not call each one an idiot or a rascal who could not believe that and did not cry out: "I, who love, should be heard!" I remember that I distanced myself from all of that. And consequently I was no warrior. Consequently I was a freeloader.

"In my view it is the desire for effectiveness that corrupts you," Thomas had written to Heinrich on December 5, 1903. The latter strikes back in the Zola essay: "But you are all there not to serve but to shine and be noticed." Thomas counters:

> The scene in the comedy must be written about how the young idealist comes to the master of the revolutionary tone of voice and warns him that it is time, the moment is there, when he must step forward and do something. The master will refuse. . . . "O no, young man, you ask me to do the wrong thing. . . . Imagine that power might lay its hand on me. . . . No, no, dear friend, farewell! You interrupted me on an eventful page about freedom and happiness that I would like to finish before I travel to the spa. Go, go, and do your duty! *Votre devoir, jeunes hommes de vingt ans, sera le bonheur!*"

The conclusion quotes in French the final statement of Heinrich Mann's essay "The Young Generation": "Your duty, twenty-year-olds, will be happiness!" Thomas criticizes the sentimentality of such statements correctly. The "master of the revolutionary tone of voice" is a theatrical man. Thomas Mann sees through him because he knows the temptations of an operatic gesture, because he knows role-playing, the mania for having an effect, the will to greatness all too well. What he perceives as "brother" is what he learned from Friedrich Nietzsche's unmasking of Wagner. Like Nietzsche's Wagner, Heinrich is (Thomas is) an aesthete with a mania for creating an effect, who knows nothing genuine but as a performer knows how to stage the effect of what is genuine. The work does not live, rather is "made, contrived, artful, an artifact."

In spite of the narcissistic trait that places these projections of his own troubles onto his brother, the quarrel remains typical. One should not make them pathological and thus elude their content. The problem of the inability of the aesthete to act concretely, of the inappropriateness of the writer for serious politics, is real. Even if Thomas Mann has studied all of that in himself, his knowledge remains worth listening to. That he shapes the world according to his needs decreases the content of knowledge of his statements only relatively, not absolutely. Even if he goes so far that he declares all European wars to be fratricidal and thus to be processes in his own inner self, a kernel of truth beyond the narcissistic abandon remains.

## OPINIONS

From the viewpoint of today's customary perspective of the majority, the *Reflections* is a reactionary book, for it expresses the appropriate opinions, confirming the leftist liberal cliché to the point of comedy. One can read, for example, that the most decent form of life worthy of a human being is that of the lord of the manor. The much-maligned authoritarian state is and remains that form of government that is appropriate, comfortable, and desired by the German people. "I want the monarchy," the nonpolitical observer emphasizes, because only it offers a guarantee of political freedom. Life is brutal, horrible, and base in any time. "Happiness" is a mirage; never will the harmony of individual interest bow to that of the community, "and you cannot explain to people why some must always be lords and others servants." In addition, national turbulences arise. He cites with visceral agreement the view that the character of the German people is the most perfect moral apparatus the world has ever seen. He invents the formula "eccentric humanity of the war" and utters the statement that the war, that the years-long daily nearness of death, has spiritual purification, exaltation, profundity, and ennoblement as a consequence. That may be correct in individual cases. Of course, the increasing brutality of war catches the eye of today's observer more forcefully.

The *Reflections* has always been measured by such opinions, and that the same book at numerous places distinguishes between reality and opinion has been ignored. Reality is the deciding factor, but opinions are mere talk as long as they do not agree with reality. That in this case only opinions are conservative, but reality and style are international, intellectual, literary, and democratic—that is the decisive fundamental insight of the *Reflections*. "Conservative? Of course, I'm not; even if I wished to be in regard to opinion, it still would not be in my nature, which, after all, is what works." Even in regard to the enthusiasm for war, it soon becomes just so-so. "The war is passé and rotten, that I know."

Seen as such, even the most glaring "opinions" of the book are: literature! Their rhetorical significance outweighs their factual significance as a rule. Like Heinrich, Thomas is a civilized man of letters—naturally, what else? He is no nationalistic German lazybones—who could think that even for a moment! In fact, with all his work he pressed on with decadent refinement, not with some kind of strong man's national fitness program. He knows that to the point of its being comical. Don't his novels jeopardize the desire for reproduction? With the appearance of *Buddenbrooks* a decline in the birth rate never seen before in Germany set in. He writes about the most German of his books that it was "a monument to the decline of national health." Germany's turn to literature means a decline in vitality. During Mann's creative years "German prose improved; at the same time the approval and knowledge of the means of contraception penetrated into the smallest village."

If Being and not opinions is decisive, then what "is" Thomas Mann? An aesthete and man of letters, an artist without doubt. But artists have no points of view. "What validity do opinions have in the realm of art?" An artist is someone who lets the one who is talking be right, even though it be the Devil himself. The whole excited clamor of the *Reflections* is a role. A weak ego plays it to become firm, to appear to be firm. "And reeling I grip any strong hand." The war had offered a strong hand. Finally it seemed to be possible to find a firm place, to become a personality. "Personality is being, not meaning." But the insecurity of the un-middle-class aesthete and ex-bohemian, who lost his father, whose erotic constitution had no place in this world, who had to find a profile, remains. With the *Reflections* he seeks to give himself a political framework. Unlike his marriage, it does not have a lengthy existence.

## ATTEMPT AT A RECONCILIATION

On December 27, 1917, in an article in the *Berliner Tageblatt* with the headline: *World Peace?* were the sentences:

"Even the grandest feeling becomes small when it is embellished with great concepts; a bit of goodness from person to person is better than all the love for mankind." That's how it is, believe it! Rhetorical, political love for humankind is a fairly peripheral kind of love and is usually announced most warmly where it is lacking in essence. Be better yourself, less hard, less dogmatically obscure, less offensively self-righteous before you play at being a philanthropist. . . . Someone may have great success who knows how to say nicely: "I love God!" But if he meanwhile "hateth his brother," then, according to the Gospel of St. John, his love of God is nothing but belles lettres and a sacrificial smoke that does not rise.

Heinrich relates the words to himself, and rightly so. A letter prepared for his brother, of which a draft has been preserved, is entitled "Attempt at a Reconciliation." In it Heinrich defends himself above all against the accusation of fraternal hate. But the letter was not adroit. Its proud and unctuous formulations were not suited to touch his brother's heart. Certainly, the love for humankind was love for an idea, Heinrich lectures, "but anyone who could lift his heart into such vastness will also often have proved it in a narrow sphere." Heinrich emphasizes that he has always followed his brother's work benevolently, although for all of that he has received almost nothing in return. He acknowledges appropriate things in the structure of his brother's character: "I knew that to stand certain you needed self-restraint, even the resistence of others," but someone who desires reconciliation does not help things along by first seeing so mercilessly through the person addressed. Further, he reminds him of old wounds. The announcement of the birth of his child had not been well received. In his response, Thomas will assert the contrary, that at the time Katia had written to Heinrich's wife tenderly, humanly, and at length and had received impudence in reply. Again Heinrich calls the tenderness arrogance and admits that afterward he had to "dictate" impudences to his wife. The attempt at a reconciliation comes to a close with an offer all too full of reservations. "Perhaps my declarations of today will find a better hearing. That would be possible, if your latest complaint against me is dictated by pain. Then you might find that you do not have to think of me as your enemy."

Taken altogether, that was more a self-assertion than a cordial step.

That made the repudiation easy for Thomas Mann. Probably at this time he had not been ready for a reconciliation anyway. There was, after all, the book with hundreds of pages against Heinrich that would not have been publishable if there were a reconciliation; the war was not yet over either. He needed him as an opponent; Heinrich had recognized that correctly. And so it turned out that Thomas's reply further deepened their opposition to one another. It is preserved, dated January 3, 1918. It is bitter. "You forget or are silent about how often you mercilessly mistreated my simplest and strongest feelings before I reacted with a single sentence in opposition." Not his, but Heinrich's behavior, had been extreme in the war. He had not struggled for two years to write a letter that naturally breathed triumph "in order with this letter, no line of which was dictated by anything other than moral security and self-righteousness, to sink with a sob on your breast." Rhetorically brilliant but deeply insulting and cutting off any access, Thomas makes the central formulations of his brother's letter destructively ridiculous. The conclusion is succinct, brilliantly constructed, and hopeless. "Pain? It happens. You become hardened and dulled. Since Carla killed herself and you chose life with Lula, separation for all eternity is nothing new anymore in our relationship. I did not make this life. I despise it. One has to live it to the end as well as one can."

Heinrich started to reply but did not send off the finished letter. The draft of his reply is self-confident, genteel, farsighted, and forceful. "Dear Tommy, I would have to remain mute at such bitterness and accept the 'separation for all eternity' as it is offered. But I don't want to neglect anything. I want to help you all I can to see things more correctly later, when everything is past." He denies that his experience of the world is fraternal. "You don't bother me." That might not be completely true. "Don't relate my life & actions to yourself anymore; it doesn't involve you & without you would literally be the same." That, too, is not completely honest in consideration of the specific sorties in the Zola essay. But Heinrich went down the path to social matters earlier than Thomas. So against the reproach of being self-righteous he can accurately bring to bear the "raving passion for his own self" of which he accuses his brother:

You owe this passion to a few narrow but concluded creations. You owe it especially to arrant disrespect for things not adequate for you, a "contempt" that is frivolous like no other, in short, the inability ever to understand the real seriousness of an unfamiliar life. All around you are unimportant extras who represent "the Volk" as in your song of praise of *Royal Highness*. Extras might have a destiny, or even ethics? . . . But do I too have the presumption to have a moral will; how does it seem to you? Under the image of a clownish show-off & brilliant wheeler-dealer. You poor fellow!

The inability to take an unfamiliar life seriously produces monsters—& so you find that my letter, which was a gesture of simple amity, breathed triumph! Triumph over what? That matters "stand and lie" in a fair way for me, that is, the world in shambles & 10 million corpses under the earth. That certainly is a vindication! That promises gratification for the ideologue. But I'm not the man to tailor misery & the death of peoples to the favorite diversions of my mind, not me. . . .

The hour is coming, I certainly hope, in which you will see people, not shadows, & then also me.

That is dated January 5, 1918. If it had reached Thomas Mann, would he have known how to reply? The diagnosis was in many ways apt. Science can furnish the technical term: narcissism. It is not enough to extend that as a reproach and to demand post facto that Thomas Mann should at the time have behaved differently. Narcissism is a prerequisite of the creation of his works; "You owe it," Heinrich had determined quite correctly, for "a few narrow but concluded creations." Without narcissism they would not have come into being, or not as they are. Had Thomas Mann been a heartily good fellow human being, he would have merged into society like most, and then he would not have written his works. He simply could not change. He had to take this path as far as it was practical. Only when he had arrived at a dead end was he forced to make a partial turnaround. Only the reconciliation with his brother and the gradual turn to republicanism that followed it forced narcissism back a bit. But in any case, he then found new enemies who helped in the stabilization of his always threatened sense of self, and new friends in the form of a powerful state that finally promised him greatness, declared him finally a popular national writer, which he had not become in the time of the kaiser in spite of all the war cries. "I will help you with all my might to see things more justly later, when everything is past." Heinrich Mann was right this time.


## MYSTICISM

In peace and prosperity material and social satisfactions can to a certain extent compensate for the lack of good sense. Not during wartime. Those satisfactions were not granted at all to Thomas Mann; on the contrary, he even became a bit impoverished and from 1914 to 1918 had neither public honors nor literary successes. They were the most difficult years of his life. Nevertheless, for the first time in his life he had made it clear where he stood, found a place, experienced sense and goal. What had existed previously? In retrospect the author of the prewar novel *The Magic Mountain* had in regard to all his outward activity revealed himself as hopeless, without prospects, covertly perplexed. He meditates that if time confronts with a hollow silence the consciously or unconsciously posed question about a last—more than personal, imperative—significance of all endeavor and activity, then paralysis will be the result, psychologically, morally, in the end even physically. The war that brought an end to this hollow silence did not, as obliging human reason would prefer, offer absurdity, but rather meaningfulness. That had to be taken as a fact, and for that reason we shall remain with this point for a while.

It is easy to unmask great realms having this meaningfulness as mere ideology. An outward struggle logically reconciles an inner one; common need creates solidarity; a strong opponent preserves a strong experience of identity. Lonely people are suddenly embraced, and isolated intellectuals disappear in a throng of people. They feel that as a meaningful gift, although it is only identity psychology. Many like the comfortable possibility in wartime of flight from civil ethical responsibility. It simplifies things, whether it be that one can break out of desperate or even only unbearable situations that have become boring into the great adventure or whether it be that one can project every interior evil outward and establish a purified order of good and evil. So civilization's literary man, now also Thomas Mann, is the inner Frenchman, whom, turned into the figure of his brother, the war now finally gives license, forbidden in peacetime, to strike. Up to this point, "meaningfulness" is easily seen through and the headache is predictable when the building collapses.

But underneath this is a deep layer not so easily denounced. "Everyone feels and knows that a mystic element is contained in war," the nonpolitical observer writes. "It is the same one that characterizes all the basic forces of life, of reproduction and death, of religion and love." One could add those of art, music, and the ocean, too. With that, the war is coordinated with the basic metaphysical experiences of Thomas Mann that accompany him from his earliest days. It cannot be explained anymore by the ideology of the day in 1914.

So, a mystic element. What does that mean? With Schopenhauer, by mystical Mann understood above all the *nunc stans*, the abiding now, the moment of the suspension of time in which the instant opens up to eternity. The war breaks forth out of the leisurely trade-pursuing time continuum of peacetime. It brings shocks, experiences of abruptness that shred the time continuum like a curtain before eternity. This curtain is, seen with Schopenhauer's Indic mysticism, the veil of Maya, who kindles the illusion that we might be individuals divided in space and time, while in reality everything is simultaneous and everywhere. The war has moments that have more weight than a whole long life. It overrides time as in an intoxication. The author of *The Magic Mountain* knows about opium dreams in which the doped person lives through thirty or sixty years or even leaves behind the boundary of all possibilities of human experiences of temporality, dreams in which images come with such speed as though something had been removed from the brain of the drugged person like in a ruined clock.

Is a long life better than a short one? The short one can be crowded, the long one empty. Is a pain-free life the highest goal? Everything evens out in the gaze of the nonpolitical observer. "Any form of life that is possibly human is in the end something acceptable; life fills it out as it is, in its mixture, its relation to pain and pleasure, desire and torment." Is war worse than peace? It sounds like a betrayal of those who suffer, but what Mann says is true: that the individual always dies only his own death, not that of others, and that untold thousands of deaths do not make it more terrible. It is true that all of us are condemned to a bitter death, not only soldiers, and that there are deaths in bed as horrible as any death in the field. It is also true that each heart is capable of terror to only a limited degree,

> beyond which something else begins: stupor, ecstasy, or something else, something not accessible to the imagination of someone inexperienced, namely, *freedom*, a religious freedom and serenity, a release from life, something beyond fear and hope that indubitably means the opposite of spiritual abasement, the conquest of death itself.

No person responsible for war can claim such statements. If they justify war, they are no longer true but ideological. They are permitted only as expressions of emotion of those who face being killed, not of those who kill. But then that religious freedom and serenity in the face of death can be more humanly dignified than the incomprehensible horror before the terrible destroyer who today seems only intellectually admissible.

## CHURCH

"I am a Christian," Thomas had written to Heinrich on February 27, 1904, but that was nothing more than appropriate in regard to his engagement; he had, after all, also added, "from a good family." More honest probably was the "God does not acknowledge me" from the tale "The Wardrobe." In war, too, mysticism does not mean the turn to the religious practice of a Protestant denomination. Thomas Mann was never a churchgoer, at most an involuntary one in childhood and youth. His later religiosity forgoes organized support. "My thing is, rather, to look the sphinx in the eye alone." As a cult and religious service the Catholic sphere interests him more than the Lutheran one of his origins. "Who knows what the Lutheran church sends into one's house, if one leaves it up to it," he mocks in the "Song of the Child" regarding the baptism of his small daughter Elizabeth in the year 1918, "probably even an oily dolt, which would turn everything into a comedy for me." On the other hand, the Catholic orders of nuns in Lübeck impressed him. "These Protestant women, they are not truth," declares Thomas Buddenbrook, when taken to task about why he prefers the Catholic Gray Sisters to the Protestant ones. "They will all get married at the first opportunity. . . . In short, they're earthy, egotistical, ordinary. . . . The Gray ones are disengaged, yes, very definitely, they are nearer Heaven." Wittenberg plays no role in Mann's life, as does St. Peter's in Rome, where once Cardinal State Secretary Rampolla read the mass in pompous humility. Religiously, that does not mean much, of course. However, the early Thomas Mann treats the Christian God with irony. "The good Lord, hurrah, hurrah, hurrah," he writes to Heinrich after his release from military service.

But, of course, the ascetic detached from the world had a relationship to places cloistered from the world, that is, to churches. "As for me, I have always loved stops in churches," he ponders in the *Reflections*, "and indeed," he says, to differentiate himself from the usual educational tourist, "from an aestheticism that had absolutely nothing to do with cultured knowledge and guidebook education, but was directed to what was human." Churches are places of freedom, of freedom from politics and society.

> Two steps to the side from the amusing highway of progress, and a refuge receives you, where earnestness, quiet, the thought of death abide in verity, and the Cross is raised for prayer. What a boon! What *satisfaction*. Here there is no talk of politics or of business; a man is a man here, he has a heart and makes no secret of it; a pure, liberated, unbourgeois solemn humanity prevails here.

He could well have become a clergyman, he asserts in a letter at the time (not very convincingly). The kneeling human being impresses him particularly. What would have the effect under middle-class circumstances of something theatrical and eccentric is made possible by the Church, and it appeals to the nonpolitical man because of its anticivilian, anachronistic, boldly human impact. "This attitude occurs nowhere else anymore"; but religion, however, the abode of worship, "this sphere of what is extraordinary liberates what is human and makes it beautiful." Much later he will kneel before Pope Pius XII and expressly remark how easy and natural this was for him.

He lived in Munich—it was a matter of the Catholic churches. It was a matter of the aesthetic nostalgia of a Protestant who did not know what to do with his own church anymore. "You are to be en-

vied for your Catholic foundation and connection," Thomas Mann
writes to Reinhold Schneider. "I lack this security, for my Protestant-
ism is merely culture, not religion." Romanticism was homesickness
for the Catholic Church, said Eichendorff. Of course, Thomas Mann
does not go that far. Not a churchgoer himself, he nevertheless did
not want to see the downfall of the Church. The lost foundation of
Christianity, he fears with Maurice Barrès, will not be won by something like rationalistic culture but by heathendom in its lowest forms,
as magic, witchcraft, theosophical aberrations, and spiritual fraud. No
new realization: Where there are no gods, ghosts rule, Novalis wrote
in 1799.

   Aesthetic nostalgia is something different from religious faith, and
yet Thomas Mann claims a kind of piety for himself. It applies "to the
eternal, essential, in short, to what is *human*" that one faces in a church,
"escaped from the evil-seething unrest of some metropolis or other,
surrounded suddenly by echoing quiet, colored gloom, breathed on by
the fragrance of centuries."


## FAITH

For civilization's literary men, churches are doubtless fortresses of super-
stition, and kneeling persons traitors to the dignity of mankind. Because
civilization's literary men are informed, paradoxically for Thomas Mann,
they are the "faithful," they are the doctrinaire preachers who marred his
childhood. They do not have the faintest notion about death and fail as
did Pastor Ranke at the death of his father. The concept of "faith" is cast
negatively in the *Reflections*. "It is the pastoral bumptiousness of being
something better through faith, the self-righteous bigotry of the mission-
ary and the Pharisee, united with constant aggressiveness against the
wretched who do not 'believe.'" This Thomas Mann says not about the
clerics of the Christian churches, but about his brother Heinrich. Obviously, he considers religious criticism cheap. He leaves it to the part of the
opposing side and caricatures it in *The Magic Mountain*, where Settembrini says a few things at Christmas

   about the carpenter's son and rabbi of humanity, whose birthday
   they pretend is today. Whether He really lived is uncertain. But

what was born that day and began its uninterrupted triumphant progress to this day is the concept of the value of the individual soul, together with equality—in a word, individualistic democracy.

As he does against democracy, Thomas Mann also polemicizes in the *Reflections* against a social religiosity that seeks to achieve paradise on earth with the help of reforms. It is definite that this goal will not be reached, rather that the masses of humanity by pursuing it will become more and more covetous, more full of malcontent, more stupid, and more irreligious. "No social religion can bring reconciliation to the life of society. Only real, that is, metaphysical religion can do that by making it understood that in the final analysis whatever is social is subordinated." Martin Luther is said to have remarked that "Christ does not bother about politics."

Its relationship to death is vital for religion. "Sympathy for death"— the formulation is developed in the *Reflections*—is lacking in Settembrini as in Heinrich Mann. Frank Wedekind had died in March 1918, and it was said that his last hours had been filled with religious endeavors; finally he had striven toward God and had perhaps passed away with faith in Him. Heinrich had delivered the funeral oration. It was one of the situations where the brothers had to meet by necessity, painful enough after the attempt for a reconciliation that had just failed at the turn of the year 1917–18, probably ignoring one another in stiff silence. How would the civilized man of letters begin to excuse Wedekind's search for God? "The obligation to spirit," he said at the grave, "which we call religion." He removed the dignity of the search of the deceased by substituting for it today's propaganda for literature, democracy, and politics. "When I had heard that, when I had to witness this unctuous counterfeiting of concepts by a 'churchless' Sunday preacher, had to be present at this attempt to reclaim for politics a soul in extremis yearning for its salvation, I put on my top hat and went home."

But what does he actually want? What practice can be formed on his thin manifestation of sympathy, his aesthetic nostalgias, his shy respect? "But if I say: Not politics but religion, then I don't boast of having religion. That would be far from me. No, I have none." That is to be taken seriously. "I cannot say that I believe in God." Even if he did believe, it would be a long time before he would say so. A kind of discretion regarding the name of God is articulated here, a last remnant of mythical awe at a name from ancient Israel, but above all a kind of modesty, a consciousness of not being able to reach what he meant by such words. Religious discretion distinguishes him from most ordained servants of the church whose well-meant interminable talk causes more damage than does silent skepticism.

Not church, not religion, not belief in God—what he does subscribe to is a shy devoutness understood as a seeking of freedom, as candor, as mellowness, willingness for life and for humility, as trying, doubting, and erring. It is doubt as faith. Religious certainty grows fat, doubt does not, "and it might be more courageous, more moral, more truthful to live composed and dignified in a godless world than to escape the deep and empty gaze of the sphinx by a blind faith like that of belief in democracy." Mann calls such an attempt the "betrayal of the Cross." Abashed, he thus avows a religion, not of salvation, but of suffering that will not be pacified by empty phrases.

Contradictions remain. Thomas Mann is far from through with this subject. Very seldom, but still sometimes, the word "God" is found in his writings in a sentimental sense. In 1914 Germany had believed it was called to be victorious. Now it had turned out quite differently, but perhaps defeat also has a significance? "For an age has come to an end," it says in 1919 in "Song of the Child," "it wants the humanely new / not the doubtful triumph: it wants to unburden itself / of dishonorable, uttermost misery. . . . Does a people even well know / to what end it rises up, / as your Germany did, and why it was thus seized? / Only that God had seized it, it feels this with right in its soul." The passage could later have been very embarrassing for Thomas Mann. The other pole is formed by a definition of God that, governed by interest useful for his work, made God into the highest aesthete—God is Goethe. As categorical as it may sound, it still cannot be made the sole measure. It does not convey much more than the sentimental definition.

> But what is God? Is He not the omnipresent, the pliable prinicple, all-knowing righteousness, all-inclusive love? Faith in God is faith in love, in life, and in art.

The war had forced him to make a general revision of his fundamentals and thus also for the first time to develop a more basic reflection about the Christian religion. He recognizes that his whole direction really requires an affirmative relationship to Christianity. He recognizes that he wants to be religious. He just does not know yet how that can proceed without a betrayal of an intelligence gained through Nietzsche's school. He will continue searching, first in *The Magic Mountain*, but then above all in the great biblical novel *Joseph and His Brothers*, and he will finally find a narrow path.

# IX. Attempts at Orientation

*With German shepherd Lux, also called Lukas, Munich 1932*

# CHRONICLE 1918–1921

We are very exactly informed concerning the time from September 1918 to December 1921 because the diaries from that period were excluded from burning; they were used as a rich source for the Faust novel. Thomas Mann is very intensively interested in the events of the times, the November Revolution and Armistice, the decline of the monarchy, the debates about the Treaty of Versailles, the tragedy of the Bavarian soviet republic (April–May 1919), the Kapp putsch (March 1920), and the beginnings of the Weimar Republic.

After the conclusion of the work on the *Reflections of a Nonpolitical Man* (March 1918, appeared October 1918) and on "A Man and His Dog" (October 1918, appeared April 1919) there follows in March the "Song of the Child" (appeared April–May, 1919). In April 1919, after a four-year interruption, Mann again begins work on *The Magic Mountain*, first revises the part already written and then continues. At the end of 1921 about two-thirds of the novel is finished. Worked into this period repeatedly are also essayistic works, such as the introduction to the *Russian Anthology* (January 1921), "Goethe and Tolstoy" (June–September 1921), the article "On the Jewish Question" (September–October 1921), and the essay "The Problem of Franco-German Relations" (December 1921).

On April 24, 1918, Elisabeth Mann is born, a year later, on April 21, 1919, as the youngest of six children, Michael. In August 1919 Bonn University awards an honorary doctorate to the erstwhile failing pupil. At the beginning of 1922, as the result of Heinrich Mann's life-threatening illness, the reconciliation with his brother comes.

# HEINRICH

BECAME AWARE that I lead a lonely, sequestered, quaint, and gloomy existence. On the other hand, H.'s life is now very sunny" (diary, December 29, 1918). Mann was forced to understand Germany's defeat in 1918 as the victory of Heinrich, civilization's literary man. "The memory returns of how after the collapse, Heinrich passed my house on a stroll along the Silberpappel Allee and full of satisfaction smiled to himself. He had 'won.'" Hate for his brother remains a constant for the years 1918 to 1921. It even seems to vouch for his identity. If you do not know where your path leads, then there is a kind of security if you at least are sure of your enemies. So the clichés of the *Reflections of a Nonpolitical Man* are met everywhere in the diary: criticism of the Francophile, of rhetorical democracy, of the social novel (*The Patrioteer* was written "in platitudes," December 23, 1918), of private luxury amid the impoverished literary cult ("the neck nestled in fur," March 14, 1920), generally of political aestheticism. The anti-Heinrich vocabulary is not particularly chosen: "impudent, stupid, frivolous, and insufferable" (December 4, 1918), "blockhead" (January 20, 1919), "appalling" (November 24, 1919), "hate" (April 3, 1920), "feeling of hatred" (April 29, 1920). Accidental meetings at the theater or at other places tear at his nerves. That leads to hallucinations. "Believed on my way home along the river at evening that I recognized Heinrich ahead of me from behind & walked quickly past in excitement. After all, hardly probable that it was him" (April 18, 1921).

His hate is still used; the *Reflections* just could not appear if he reconciled with his brother. His anxiety about this pursues him into his dreams. On September 30, 1918, he writes in his diary:

> I dreamed that I [was] in closest friendship together with Heinrich and out of sociability let . . . him eat all by himself a small à la creme and two pieces of baked tarts, while I gave up my share. Feeling of perplexity about how this friendship could be consistent with the appearance of the *Reflections*. That could not be and was a completely impossible situation. Feeling of relief upon awakening that it had been a dream.

The enmity is fostered but cannot destroy something deeper, the brotherly sentiment. Heinrich's successes exasperate Thomas, but without malice; he even notes his failures with some stir of emotion. He wants Heinrich to be important so that his hate can also be important. "The case of Heinrich is quite remarkable. His hour is once more past, in spite of his Odeon speech on Eisner" (July 6, 1919). "Heinrich's position, no matter how splendid it appears at the moment, is basically already undermined by events and experiences. His orientation toward the West, his worship of the French, his Wilsonism etc. are antiquated and withered" (March 3, 1920).

Beyond that there is evidence of real solidarity. When someone trashes *The Patrioteer*, Thomas Mann prohibits the question of status regarding him (April 19, 1919). The signatures of the two brothers embellish specific appeals, and their replies appear next to one another on many questionnaires. When there is talk of membership in an academy, Thomas considers whether he should accept only with the stipulation of the simultaneous inclusion of Heinrich (July 6, 1919). When there is a rumor that he is being considered for the Nobel Prize, he notes: "The most pleasant thing would be if they divided it between us" (May 21, 1921). Approvingly, he cites from an article by Egon Friedell: "They would have to be glad to have two such fellows" (March 17, 1919). Goethe reacted similarly to the question in regard to his relationship with Schiller: In spite of everything, Friedell had maintained that Thomas loved his brother and would always love him, his great fraternal polar star. There are also still a few mutual friends, for example Ludwig Ewers, to whom Thomas Mann writes that one should honor contention such as theirs and not wish to remove its deadly serious accent. "Perhaps, separated, we are *more* a brother to one another than we would be at the same dinner table" (April 6, 1921).

## POLITICS: THEORY AND PRACTICE

According to hearsay, Thomas declared himself for the Republic in 1922. The reality is more complicated. In the diaries from 1918 to 1921, particularly in the exciting years 1918 and 1919, there is a lot of politicizing. The spectrum of views expressed is broad and variegated. The opinions of the *Reflections* continue to be valid from the first to the last page, from "I regret not a word" (September 16, 1918) to "Proofs of the new printing of the 'Observ.' arrive; I read them without distress, often with acclamation" (December 1, 1921). The capitulation of Germany, which the nonpolitical man feels as humiliation and self-surrender, unleashes indignation and shock. Conservative Germany has lost. "The catastrophe and international defeat of this intellectual direction and sympathy is there. It is also that of mine" (October 5, 1918). The structure of the nation seems to be dissolving into debating groups of abandoned subjects.

Experimentation with numerous positions follows. Monarchy, social democracy, soviet republic, communism, and all sorts of radical-conservative endeavors: We find statements for and against everything. It is a revolution also for what is happening at the time, he writes. He had rather cold and no longer resentful feelings. Revolutions would come only when they met no further resistance—proof that they were justified. "I look upon the events with tolerable cheerfulness and a certain sympathy" (November 9, 1918). "I say welcome to the 'New World'" (November 10, 1918).

His sympathies for people also offer no unified picture. Thomas Mann speaks with ironic sympathy about the German kaiser, who exacted an unspeakable snivel from the Krupp workers ("Each one has his duty and his burden, you at your lathe and I on my throne!"); he notes "preachers' rhetoric" and "Schiller's sentimentality" (September 12, 1918), but also notes agreement. For the German people, talk like that was most probably still the easiest. However, soon afterward he finds that emperorship was a romantic rudiment and a practical leftover (November 10, 1918). Philipp Scheidemann (September 21, 1918) and especially Friedrich Ebert (February 12, 1919) deserve respect, but on the other hand Karl Liebknecht and Rosa Luxemburg (January 6, 1919) contempt. A certain sympathy is awakened by Ernst Toller, ("who once sent us eggs," April 9, 1919), but hate toward his erstwhile fellow student Erich Mühsam, whose "jargonlike politicizing is disgusting" (July 9, 1919). Gustav Landauer is praised for his "Call for Socialism" (February 22–23, 1919), but Kapp on the other hand is displeasing (March 13, 1920); his putsch is politically unwelcome (March 20, 1920) because he possibly compromises the conservative idea (March 15, 1920). Oswald Spengler, whose *Decline of Western Civilization* is being read with great impression in June–July 1919, is praised emphatically. Hermann Count Keyserling (May 18,

1919) finds much agreement. That "truth and life" belonged to the George Circle is noted on August 1, 1921. The "type of Russian Jew, of the leader of the world movement, this explosive mixture of Jewish intellectual radicalism and Slavic enthusiasm for Christ" meets blatant rejection: "A world that still possesses an instinct for self-preservation must proceed with all attainable energy and summary dispatch against this breed of men" (May 2, 1919). Only "Song of the Child" spreads some small hope. All that was humanely new—we heard it already—manifestly did not want victory but to unburden itself of dishonorable, uttermost misery.

Mann's political views at the time could be quoted endlessly. But are they really so important? That is, if you take a look at his practice of politics, quite a different picture emerges. Let us follow Mann's own guidance: "In national matters very little depends on the opinions and statements of a man; more decisive is his being, his actions." The political experiments in thought have absolutely no foundation at all. They remain nonreferential daydreams, comparable to the boundless "Russian" discussions, without consequence in practice like the debates between Naphta and Settembrini in *The Magic Mountain*. As a voter (for the Bavarian National Assembly) Thomas Mann puts his checkmark on January 12, 1919, for the National-Liberal German People's Party, to be sure, but the party cannot count on him; the Reichstag election on June 6, 1920, finds him a decisive nonvoter. Although Katia was of a different opinion: "K. is trying to persuade me to vote at the coming Reichstag election & indeed for the democrats, to support the bourgeoisie. In any event, I would vote for the German People's Party" (May 25, 1920). But he did not do that either. There were rumors that he (and Heinrich) had joined the USPD* (March 12, 1919). Mann denies it (March 18, 1919) but notes on the twenty-second of the same month that the rumor was not meaningless. Of course, that also has no real substantiation. More significant is his distance from right-radical attempts to form a party. Even if today one finds statements that show up later in the reservoir of ideas of National Socialism, Mann's shying away from involvement with such politics is unmistakable and insuperable. In practice he had nothing to do with those people.

To that extent he remained a nonpolitical man in all the politicizing. How do nonpolitical people behave concretely? They are loyal to

---

* Independent Social Democratic Party of Germany, an offshoot of the SPD. (Trans.)

whatever is in existence. Thus Thomas Mann, who intellectually acted so decisively anti-Republican, in practice was immediately put in the service of the Republic. "A Republican office!" he notes proudly, when he is invited to become a member of the Movie Censorship Advisory Council (December 25, 1918). He accepts and in the time following also serves dependably in his post; this lays the foundation for his good knowledge of film history. A little later, on January 11, 1919, the Reich's Office for Heimatdienst (the precursor of today's Federal Central Office for Political Education) calls upon him for a comment "For the New Germany," and again the nonpolitical observer reacts quite willingly: "The social people's state, as it intends to consolidate itself among us now, lay completely on the path of German development." Shortly afterward, the Reich's Bureau of Economic Demobilization asks him, for the prevention of economic collapse, to encourage the German people to be rational in thought and to work in the service of the new state. Obediently, Mann writes an "Exhortation" that appears on February 14, 1919 in the *Frankfurter Zeitung*. He speaks there, to be sure, of all kinds of things in the spirit of the *Reflections*, makes the war opponents and civilization's literary men responsible for the internal condition of Germany, but ends unmistakably with a call for loyal cooperation:

> Let German workers think about it. Days of revolution are holidays, of course. It is understandable that anyone who has stormed the Bastille in the forenoon hours may not want to start anything legitimate in the afternoon. But now, enough of the honeymoon! It is time to show that the German people know how to conduct an honorable marriage with liberty.

In May 1919, after the defeat of the soviet republic in Bavaria, Thomas Mann and Heinrich write a proclamation that invites the middle class "to become aware of its common destiny with the working people." A short time later a further call appeals to the Bavarian government to be more merciful to the leaders of the soviet republic in Bavaria, who generally had been punished in draconian ways.

From the Left there actually came the reproach that he was making it far too easy with his method for reunification (December 1, 1918). Thomas Mann finds that too severe. But he had agreed to a cosmopolitan declaration anyway, as can be gathered from the diary entry of November 16, 1918. While, based on the *Reflections*, he counted after all as a nationalist, he must have expressed himself in a cosmopolitan and conciliatory way toward the intellectuals of other peoples, making him shake his head in self-irony: "I was surprised at myself. . . . Surprised myself again."

Admittedly, his fidelity to the new regime did not reach as far as its fiscal offices—"the tax had to be declared, &, even if we evade a lot, around 20,000 marks will be taken" (May 25, 1920).

## THE BAVARIAN SOVIET REPUBLIC

In *Doctor Faustus* Serenus Zeitblom tells about the distressing impressions he had received after the World War at the gatherings of certain "soviet intellectual workers" in Munich hotel halls:

> If I were a novelist, I would describe for the reader such a meeting, at which perhaps an author of fiction, not without charm, even in a sybaritic and pensive way, spoke on the theme of "Revolution and Philanthropy" and thereby unleashed a free, all-too-free, diffuse, and scatterbrained discussion carried on by the most aggressive types of those who come out into daylight for a moment only on such occasions: clowns, maniacs, ghouls, evil obstructionists, and street-corner philosophers—I would, I say, describe vividly from very painful memory such a helpless and hopeless assembly of councilors. There were speeches for and against philanthropy, for and against officers, for and against the people. A little girl recited a poem; a man dressed in field gray was wearily prevented from continuing his reading of a manuscript that began with the salutation "Dear Burghers and Burghesses" and would without doubt have taken up the whole night; an angry candidate began to criticize all the previous speakers without dignifying the assembly with his own positive expression of an opinion—and so forth. The behavior of the audience that was reduced to rude boos was turbulent, childish, and brutish, the management incapacitated, the atmosphere terrible, and the result less than zero. Looking around, you wondered repeatedly whether you were the only one who was suffering, and at the end you were glad to gain the open street, where for hours the streetcars had already been stopped, and probably senseless shots echoed through the winter night.

We read the original of the scene in the diary of December 10, 1918. It concerned the first public gathering of the Political Council of Intellectual Workers:

> At tea with K. on Arcisstraße, from there later with K.'s mother in the Bayerischer Hof at the meeting of the "Council." Frank's speech not without charm, but sybaritic and pensive. The discussion horrible, tormenting as usual; the best thing was a small, disdainful, smart Jewish student with the ribbon of the Iron Cross. Speeches also by Friedenthal, Michalski, Skanzony, Kaufmann, a Rhenish youth from an unintellectual sphere who defended the officers, the clown Stückgold, a ghoul of an angry candidate who began to criticize all the previous speakers, etc. The atmosphere terrible. The behavior of the assembled people turbulent, childish, brutish. The management incapacitated. The result minus.

Thomas Mann reacts as an aesthete; he continues: "But you do get to know types of people; on no other occasion do they present themselves more vividly than as discussion speakers. I must decidedly make use of the passion of the times and visit meetings more frequently." In this case, which is rare in the diary, only a few days later, on December 13, 1918, a fictional treatment is envisaged that really followed only decades later:

> Today I thought of making something out of the "Council" gathering but will probably not get to it. What is human is tempting: Frank himself, then Kaufmann, Friedenthal, Stückgold, the Rhenish fellow who spoke against the people, the little girl with the poem, the field-gray uniformed fellow who began to read the essay ("Dear Burghers and Burghesses!"), the evil candidate, the Social-Democrat, an academic who was himself once a worker & had the greatest success, of Skanzoni (against philanthropy), Michalski, finally the public.

At the end of 1918 the soviet councils had reached an end for the time being on the level of the Reich; a parliamentary system had been decided on. On February 11, 1919, the National Assembly had convened in Weimar and elected Friedrich Ebert as the Reich's president. Thomas Mann noted with satisfaction: "It seems like the first attempt at walking after a collapse, like the return of dignity and self-assurance" (February 12, 1919).

However, the system of soviet councils had a sequel in Munich, the Bavarian soviet republic, whose short existence ran its course from the beginning of April until its suppression at the beginninng of May 1919 almost in front of Thomas Mann's house door. As concerns his judgment about the events, an astonishingly clear development is shown that within four weeks of lively agreement leads to a brazen rejection. On April 7 the first measures of the soviet government are noted with impressiveness; it is assumed that the Reich will follow the Bavarian example and that, should radical socialism take lasting form in Germany, the proletariats of the Entente countries would have nothing left to do. "It must be recognized that capitalism is condemned." But already on April 13 Mann comments on the false report—that the soviet government had been overthrown—with the interesting statement that he hated "the irresponsible realizers who compromised the spirit as well as the fellows who have ruined things this time by mismanagement." He reacts according to the model: The idea was good, but the people were bad. Unfortunately, he continues: "I would not have anything against it if they were shot like varmints." There are still more utterances of this sort, but to be fair one should add that shortly afterward Mann signs the above-mentioned call for clemency for the supporters of the soviet council. He also stands up for Ernst Toller. On April 17, emphatically denoting the distinction between theory and interest, he writes: "My attitude toward things very uncertain, but my private wishes are for the entry of the 'Whites' and the establishment of middle-class order." And that's how it happens in the end. "The Munich communistic episode is over. . . . I will not deny a feeling of liberation and exhilaration" (May 1, 1919). But in Munich, gunfire goes on for days. "The cannonades & the rat-a-tat of machine guns was fierce and constant. I was fearful about the outcome of the matter. Finally, as things are now, the definitive victory of the troops has become a personal necessity for life; the opposite outcome would be an unthinkable catastrophe" (May 2, 1919). When the "horrible farce" (May 4, 1919) is finished, our writer seems to be far to the right (May 5, 1919):

To my satisfaction the red flags in the city have disappeared from the Residenz, the War Ministry, etc. Military music played "Deutschland, Deutschland über alles" at the Victory Arch. The Epp Corps has marched in to great jubilation in the best of shape. Things are getting too "military" for K.'s mother, but I am in total agreement and find that it is easier to breathe under the military dictatorship than under the regimen of crapule.

The close encounter with actual history forces Thomas Mann, whatever his opinions, in the end to the side of the bourgeoisie, probably also under the influence of Katia, who looked upon her husband's political dream-hopping with mistrust and was concerned about his toleration. The writer knew that the Munich Revolution did not have this toleration, when he judged as an aesthete and not as a politicizing private citizen. "I find Bavaria primitively comical and see hardly anything but mischief," he was able to note (April 5, 1919). Earlier he had already scoffed at an excursion into the countryside by Prime Minister Eisner. The revolution is only a thing for the cosmopolitan cities, Munich, Augsburg, Nuremberg. "Of course, the state of Bavaria is not by nature a republic of workers & also by no means an area of dominance for Jewish literary men. Eisner was in the countryside. He has become so emaciated that he said no power in the world could get him out again" (January 10, 1919).

Sporadically the Manns feared looting and more, above all during the first phase of the Revolution. "Emptying out the pantry by K. & the children & hiding three-quarters of the supplies in various rooms of the house" (November 8, 1918). "If it comes to an extreme, then it's not impossible that I would be shot as a result of my attitude during the war" (November 11, 1918). Thomas Mann decides that if looters were to come, to hand them two hundred marks: "divides them and keeps my books and things from being destroyed" (November 19, 1918). In April 1919 there is concern about his fine linens (April 17), but Thomas Mann had too many friends among the regents of the soviet republic for his house really to have been in danger. When the "Whites" march in, there is fear of arrest because of some denunciation or other, but quite the contrary happens: Three soldiers appear at the door, introduce themselves as members of the Protection Services, and name a place the Manns can turn to in the event of possible attacks (May 2, 1919).

## REVOLUTION IN RUSSIA

A fraternal worldview colors everything personally, even the attitude toward the October Revolution. With the *Reflections of a Nonpolitical Man* Thomas Mann had been successful for the first time in creating order in his system of ideas. It was a friend-enemy order: here Germany, there France, here inwardness, there politics, here Thomas, there Heinrich. An unforeseen event like the revolution in Russia, which began in February–March 1917 first under Prince Lwow and Alexander Kerenski as a bourgeois revolution and in September as social revolutionaries and then in November (according to the Western calender) under Lenin radicalized as a proletariat and communistic one, had to put the effectiveness of this system unmercifully to the test. At the time, Thomas Mann was not in a position to conceive of a historical event objectively from its own postulates. He based everything on himself. Friend or enemy? To understand meant to categorize it in the chain of antitheses of the *Relfections*, meant—in the polemical words of his brother Heinrich—to tailor the misery and death of peoples on the partialities of his intellect. Is the Revolution civilized and literary as in the West or unpolitical as in the East? Does it happen in the spirit of Heinrich Mann or in the spirit of Dostoyevski? Does it offer affirmation or vexation?

At first Thomas Mann reacts to the bourgeois phase of the Revolution with confusion. "The things in Russia put me in a turmoil," he writes to Paul Amann on March 25, 1917. A bourgeois revolution in Russia? How could that happen? "There *is* no bourgeoisie!" And then immediately follows the reference to the author who decisively steered Mann's judgment of revolution: "What would Dostoyevski have thought and said about all this?"

The first trace of the Revolution in the *Reflections* is a remark written in April 1917 in the chapter "Politics." There it states scornfully, "up to 1917, when it was raised to a republic," Russia had been considered a country in special need of political-societal self-criticism. Russian self-criticism—in Gogol, in Gontcharov, in Turgenev—is something of a model for Thomas Mann. Its negative is the self-righteous satire of civilization's literary men who want only to chide others but except themselves from criticism. That Russia, as a "democratic republic," now seems to have gone over to the side of civilization's literary men where self-criticism is unknown disturbs the argumentation considerably. Russian Jacobins do not fit at all in the Russophile system of Thomas Mann. So at first they are ignored or marginalized.

The next trace is found in a passage written about June 1917. Marxism is not Russian, for it is an "amalgamation of French revolutionism and the English national economy" and thus belongs to the side of the enemy. A bit later, in the context of a complicated deliberation, it is assumed that the "Russian Revolution" must be something desired by civilization's literary men. It is also a matter for them "of the generous confusion, the demolition of the state, the permanent rebellion of the masses, the Revolution."

The following passage, written in August 1917, almost approaches a definition that at its end insinuates the proclamation for a republic by Kerensky on September 17:

"Dostoyevski is forgotten in Russia," a Russian said to me before the war. Now, the Revolution proves it—this desperate brawl between democratic-bourgeois Frenchness and anarchistic Tolstoyism. But we know that "forgetting" is a very superficial psychological process, and no one will be able to make us believe that the imminent proclamation of Russia to be a république démocratique et sociale has anything serious to do with the Russian nation.

Civilization's literary man loved France and the West; Thomas Mann loved Russia and the East. Therefore, it says at the same place, "Russia and Germany belong together." Up to this time Thomas Mann identifies revolution and republic as Franco-Western phenomena; they belong to the world of Heinrich and have nothing serious to do with the Russian nation. But Dostoyevski has serious connections with the Russian nation. Thomas Mann derives his image of Russia from Russian literature of the nineteenth century. To enter upon a bourgeois revolution, the Russians had to forget Dostoyevski.

At the end of October 1917 Thomas Mann, in the chapter in the *Reflections* "On Faith," again takes a position regarding the events in Russia. Since the October Revolution took place only at the beginning of November, according to the Western calender, the following passage still refers to the dictatorship of Kerenski, not to the seizure of power by Lenin. Again Mann makes his judgment with Dostoyevski (previously cited) in the background. The Russian had predicted to the West the collapse of capitalism ("all the banks, sciences, and Jews, all of that will in an instant become nothing") and a revolution of the fourth estate: "the proletariat will fall upon Europe and will destroy all the old things forever." But the waves would dash to pieces on Russia; it would be shown to what an extent the Russian organism differed from the European organisms.

Thomas Mann also must concede that Dostoyevski's analysis was basically wrong, but he does not take up this knowledge, rather looks for possibilities to play down that falsity to be able to stay to the utmost with Dostoyevski. He writes:

> In a way different, as Dostoyevski believed, it has been shown that the national organism of Russia is of another sort from the national organisms of Europe, for the revolution broke out in Russia and not yet in the West . . . a genial dictator followed the bourgeois president.

The "bourgeois president" is Minister-President Lwow, the "genial dictator" Kerenski. "In a way different," Dostoyevski is right. But a reassessment of the Revolution is suggested here as a possibility. Is it perhaps something Russian? The characterization of Lenin as a "genial dictator" does not fit into the scheme of civilization's bourgeois-democratic literary man. In the thought of Thomas Mann at the time it can be understood more as a positive than a negative qualification. In the summer of 1917 he was already dreaming of a Caesarean nation with Hindenburg as leader. And Lenin is characterized by Thomas Mann as a czar, a Genghis Khan, and conspicuously inspired by Naphta in *The Magic Mountain*, a "great pope of thought, full of the destructive zealousness of God," he was comparable to Pope Gregorious, "who himself said: 'Cursed be the man who withholds his sword from blood.'"

In 1917 Russia was still allied with France against Germany. At the beginning of December 1917, Thomas Mann concluded the last chapter of the *Reflections*. In spite of the trouble with the book because of the Revolution, the conclusion of the book is again Russophile. He speaks of the beginning of the negotiations for an armistice with Russia and about the long-cherished wish in his heart for "Peace with Russia! Peace first with Russia!" The nonpolitical observer is glad that the fronts again agree, because the unnatural alliance between Russia and France, "the misalliance of democracy of the heart with democracy as a stale academic-bourgeois revolutionary tirade," is ruptured:

> And the war, if it continues, will continue against the West alone, against the "trois pays libres," against "civilization," "literature," politics, the rhetorical bourgeoisie.

The judgment about Russian matters can be followed in the diary from Sepember 1918 on. Made insecure by the November Revolution

in Germany and the Munich soviet republic, it does fluctuate repeatedly, of course, but where the intellect is concerned it remains positive
in its basic tenor. The practical matter is somewhat different. The
diary entry of November 19, 1918, is characterisic:

> I am horrified by the anarchy, the mob domination, the dictator-
> ship of the proletariat along with all its concomitant and resultant
> phenonema à la russe. But my hate for the triumphant bourgeois
> orator makes me wish for the Bolshevization of Germany and its
> annexation to Russia.

Thomas Mann later imparts the pros to his Serenus Zeitblom: "The
Russian Revolution shocked me, and the historical superiority of its
principles above those of powers that set their foot on our necks no
doubt suffered in my eyes." The cons apply almost always to the
cultural tyranny of the Bolshevists, the repudiation of Dmitri Mereshkovski, for example (diary, January 20, 1919), who had to flee
Russia. But the pros prevail by far, considering the number of their
expressions as well as their emotional temperature. "There is no
doubt that the future belongs to the idea of socialism, yes, of communism *as* idea" (November 29, 1918). "I could not help but put the
capitalist Internationale against the socialist one, which has, of course,
many false features of Saviorism at base but is morality and humanity
itself in comparison with its condemned counterpart" (February 2,
1919). "My sympathy grows for what is healthy, human, national,
anti-Ententistic, *antipolitical* in Sparticism, Communism, Bolshevism"
(March 22, 1919). "It must be realized that capitalism is condemned!"
(April 7, 1919). That the pros will defeat the cons is noted by Mann on
April 30, 1919. "How is it possible not to go over to the side of communism with bag and baggage, for it has the enormous advantage of
being the enemy of the Entente? It has the character of mischief and
of cultural Hottentotism, but in Germany would hardly have it for
long."

Afterward, interest in this subject declines considerably in the diary.
The entry for June 11, 1919, notes once more that a document about
Bolshevism has made an impression, "after I for some time took a
position completely on the side of culture." Two years later Mann is
ashamed, in retrospect, of his Bolshevistic sympathies, occasioned by
the bitter experiences of Mereshkovski. The cultural standpoint is victorious: "Family conversation about Bolshevism. Feeling of shame afterward" (June 17, 1921). Exhausted by the strife over opinion, he

prefers to go walking. "You look up at the sky, you look into the depths of the elegant and tender patter of leaves, your nerves are soothed, and solemnity and quiet return to your mind." Also his criticism of capitalism largely vanishes. In "Mind and Money," written on March 21, 1921, Mann tells about his monthly pension, for which he is indebted to his paternal inheritance, and quite calmly reasons: "In any event, I personally am obliged to be grateful to the capitalistic world order of former times, for which reason it will never befit me to spit on it quite so *à la mode*."

Still, the hope for Russia does not cease to exist. Russia and Germany "should go hand in hand into the future." The revolt against Western civilization "began in the East," Mann writes in December 1921; thus the German path into the future begins with the October Revolution. It has, in any event, become clear to him that the Revolution has nothing to do with Heinrich's Western Jacobinism. Through the Revolution, Russia again turns its face to the East:

> Anyone who might want to indulge in the view that poor Czar Nicholas had fallen victim to the idea of European progress would find himself in a fundamental error. Peter the Great was murdered by him, and his fall opened for the Russian people not the way to Europe but the way home to Asia.

In 1922 Thomas Mann reconciles with his brother Heinrich and in the following years approaches more and more the Western republican positions he had hated for so long. Since the Russian Revolution is "Asian," he must repulse it, just as his Hans Castorp had to learn to resist the "Kirghizian eyes" of Pribislav Hippe and Madame Chauchat. To be sure, in his heart he remains a Russian. "Deepest homeland is truly the East," he writes in "Song of the Child."

In the long run Thomas Mann did not perceive communism but fascism as the opponent approaching him. In the further course of his long life his statements regarding Communist Russia are on the whole relatively friendly. The alliance between Russia and America in World War II satisfied his soul, which thirsted for syntheses. Vanya and Uncle Sam seem related to him, by reason of a certain blithe primitivity. Thus implicitly Soviet Communism glides again in the direction of the "West" in the topography of Thomas Mann, while the sixteen-year battle of the Joseph novels applies to the erstwhile spell of Dostoyevski's so revered Asiatic orientation.

## CONSERVATIVE REVOLUTION

"Really, it is the German task 'to invent something new *in politicis*' between Bolshevism and Western plutocracy" (diary, December 3, 1918). The formula derived from Nietzsche, "something new *in politicis*," which is already encountered in the *Reflections*, is made concrete as a synthesis between the Right and the Left. "Basically, I am also for the 'soviets,' as long as they keep the likes of Mühsam at arm's length," Mann confides in his diary on March 3, 1919, but a short time later makes public that the soviets were to be enlarged into a representation of the classes. It was only a small step for him from the revolutionary soviet state to a conservative class-state. "I do not want mere parliamentarianism. It's just a matter of 'inventing something new *in politicis*' and, to be sure, something German" (March 3, 1919). This new thing is the thought of a conservative revolution. Probably as one of the first in Germany, Mann uses this paradoxical construction of words in an introduction, written in January 1921, to a selection of Russian stories. He speaks of a "Third Reich," whose synthetic idea had been rising for decades beyond the horizon, and speaks of the unification of conservatism and revolution. Nietzsche himself had been nothing more than a "conservative revolution."

The exceedingly heterogeneous thoughts of the conservative revolution form, as is well known, shaped the reservoir of ideas from which the National Socialists then helped themselves. It should therefore be no surprise that during those years there are certain areas of agreement. Thomas Mann, too, makes use of phrases such as "German Communism" and "National Socialism," daydreams about a national uprising as in 1914, "in the form of Communism, for all I care" (March 24, 1919), and about the spiritualization of Marxist class-socialism into a popular community; he excitedly greets Oswald Spengler's document *Prussianism and Socialism*, reads regularly and with pleasure the new conservative magazine *Das Gewissen*, wants to combine German conservatism with socialism (January 19, 1920), and urges a union between Hölderlin and Marx (1925).

All of that remained very vague and contradictory but did not prevent the author of the *Reflections of a Nonpolitical Man* from having a large group of friends at the time and praising authors who later followed the NSDAP or related right-radical trends. That applies to

Ernst Bertram and Hans Pfitzner, to Hanns Johst and Ernst Krieck, to Alfred Baeumler and Oswald Spengler. Once he even reads with agreement a magazine of Dietrich Eckart, who was Hitler's inspiration (December 8, 1918).

Is Thomas Mann for that reason a precursor of fascism? In any case, he did keep his distance from any actual association with the politics of the radical right movements that were forming. Very early, in the summer of 1921, he takes notice of the rising Nazi movement and rebuffs it as "swastika mischief." Even in 1925, when Hitler was still imprisoned in Landsberg, he rebuffs "German fascism" explicitly, resolutely, and—visible from afar—because of its cultural barbarity.

## ON THE JEWISH QUESTION

"Katia's protest. Disgruntlement and uproar." Angry but compliant, Thomas Mann withdrew his already typeset article "On the Jewish Question." "It is on the one hand frivolous and on the other has that autobiographical radicalism to which I tend and which sometimes may be my strength but in such an essay is in the wrong place and would have to be offensive."

At once the rumor spread that Thomas Mann had written an anti-Semitic article. Then as today there were those "who spot anti-Semitism already in the fact that someone does not just turn a blind eye on such a prominent circumstance as the Jewish phenomenon and deny it exists." The essay criticizes anti-Semitism in every line. Scornfully, Mann distances himself in this regard even from Richard Wagner. Anti-Semitic expressions from his side would be tatamount to a grotesque ingratitude, "an ingratitude in a colossal manner that possibly befitted Wagner but not me." The autobiographical radicalism consists of his admission that from his childhood on he owed much to the Jews. Already in school there had been the son of a rabbi, Ephraim Carlebach, handsome and smart, who was able to whisper answers to the failing youngster with incredible skill. There was the Jewish girl Katia, whose description in the "Song of the Child" is cited. And finally there was the open confession that in his reading tours throughout the world it was "almost without exception Jews who received me, sheltered me, fed me, and pampered me." If the essay had appeared, the National Socialists would certainly have picked it up with malice. At the time it was the better part of caution to withdraw the article—Katia was right about that. But from today's perspective, it is regrettable.

The *Reflections of a Nonpolitical Man*, although it was held to be "rightist," offered no sustenance for the anti-Semitism snoopers. Although anti-Semites can be found among the sources for this book—Dostoyevski or Richard Wagner, Houston Stewart Chamberlain or Hans Blüher, for example—Thomas Mann does not make use of the arsenal in this regard. On the contrary, he agrees with the opinion that only through the merging of Jewish elements in its body politic did Germany experience that upbringing that had made the character of its people into the most perfect moral apparatus that the world had ever seen.

Naturally, "passages" can again be found in the diary. "Bavaria, governed by Jewish literary men . . . a slobbery literary profiteer such as Herzog who for years was supported by a movie diva, a money broker and businessman in spirit, with the metropolitan sorry elegance of the Jewish urchin, who ate lunch only in the Odeon bar but did not pay Ceconi's [Mann's dentist's] bills for the partial renovation of his rotted teeth. That's the revolution! It involves Jews as good as exclusively" (November 8, 1918). Again, such passages are faced with an abundance of others that read differently. The already familiar image remains. "Jewishness" was without question a category for Thomas Mann. His attitude toward it is almost always positive but, as is only reasonable with respect to a complex phenomenon, is now and then also critical. He thinks somewhat like Fontane, who would gladly have been displeased with Jews occasionally had not "the Christian element stood far lower in its narrow-mindedness."

Much later, in the diary entry of October 27, 1945, Thomas Mann takes up our contemporary questions. After reading a "perhaps all too rational book about the Jewish question," which argues that the Jews could be considered as a "people" or a "race," he notes:

What should they be called? For there is something different about them, and it is not merely Mediterranean. Is this awareness anti-Semitism? Heine, Kerr, Harden, Kraus up to the fascist type Goldberg—there is definitely one blood line. Could Hölderlin or Eichendorff have been Jewish? Not Lessing either, in spite of Mendelsssohn.

Blinders, without doubt, remnants of a German nationalistic deforma-
tion of observation, of a way of thinking in national typologies that
has its dangers. But within this thought—this cannot be debated—
Thomas Mann regarded the Jews highly, more highly than he did the
Germans. When the Nazis come to power, his place is on the side of
the Jews. "Anti-Semitism is the disgrace of any educated and culturally engaged person."

## DOMESTICS

Thomas Mann did not believe in the sovereignty of the "people" in
the *Reflections of a Nonpolitical Man*. "My God, the people! Does it
have honor, pride—not to mention reason? . . . It has nothing but
violence, combined with ignorance, stupidity, and unjustness." The
closest practical contact the nonpolitical observer had with the "people" was with the servant class. As a rule in the Mann household
there appear to have been three employees at the time: a cook, a
nursemaid, and a housemaid. "I command three hardy servant girls
and a Scottish shepherd dog," he notes in 1907 with ironic pride.
Around 1930 there are even five—a second maid and a chauffeur
have been added. But the reality does not accord with this by far.
"The solution of the servant question is completely unclear." The political philanthropy of civilization's literary man ruined the instinct of
genteel subserviency. "While once the servant class, as well as the
class issuing orders, had its honor, dignity, and beauty, more and
more in all the world it is considered degrading to serve. . . . Loyalty,
attachment to house and family no longer exist; these are considered
as exploitation, and the socialistically intimidated administration of
the law sanctions this attitude by its judgment when it comes to a
forensic clash."

It had come to a forensic clash, probably in 1917. The nursemaid
Josepha Kleinsgütl, called Affa, after more than ten years of service in
the family, had finally turned out to be a kleptomaniac. Everything
that had long been looked for and finally considered lost was found
in her room. Klaus Mann tells the dramatic story about how his father, very moved, found three bottles of his beloved Burgundy wine
in Affa's room, how Affa insisted in tears that it was her Burgundy,

and how in the argument about the red wine she even raised her hand against the writer.

> Yes, something scandalous occurred: She struck at him with her balled fist and might have smashed his nose, had he not jumped aside with surprising presence of mind. Anyway, she hit his left shoulder, whereupon, according to the unanimous reports of all the chroniclers, he distinctly said "Ow!" Some historians claim that after short reflection he also added: "Now all of this really has to stop!"

There was a trial, and Affa won. Klaus Mann describes the scene with great satisfaction and, since he probably was not personally present, with some imagination:

> She represented the oppressed class, the proletariat; she lied with verve and great persuasion. The courtroom was spellbound by her earthy wit, her folksy, ready cleverness. She dominated the scene, glittered and triumphed; Mielein [Katia] and the Magician would like to have sunk through the earth when Affa began to speak about the Burgundy. With touching eloquence she described how they had tried to steal the red wine from her: "Just three little bottles—the only memento that I have from my step-brother, the late frigate captain, and there come these Prussians, these exploiters, these highfalutin' persons and want to take the three little bottles away from me too, where they have a whole cellar full of champagne and schnapps and what all they drink. . . ." From the public there came cries of disgust, of protest. The more my poor parents sank down, the more victoriously Affa beamed.

Back to the *Reflections*. In spite of everything, Thomas Mann continues—in the passage cited in the beginning above—to claim that the willingness to serve was something immortal. The people perceived things aristocratically. Lords and servants, Thomas Mann's Goethe says later, were "God's classes, each one dignified in its way, and the lord had respect for what he was not, for God's class of the servant." Thus, as is well known, it fell in line that in the First World War Thomas Mann denoted lords of the manor "as the most decent and dignified of all forms of life." In any event, self-irony must be counted on.

In the same passage, it is clear that conservative views do not necessarily mean approval of existing conditions, that a much sharper criticism of those in control, too, can be significant. The instinct of wishing to serve no longer gets its money's worth if the order of rank is arbitrary and unfounded. "That the steward who in a modern hotel lobby serves tea to the swell loafing in a leather easy chair and does not himself sit in a leather chair and be served by the swell is nothing but the sheerest coincidence." Felix Krull also finds that frequently those serving could just as well be masters, and many of those who, cigarettes in the corner of their mouths, loll in their deep basket chairs could be waiters. The people—again from the nonpolitical observer—are able to distinguish between a real gentleman and just a newly rich fellow with complete undemocratic certainty. "They serve gladly and without feeling that they are compromising their human dignity in the least where a possibility still exists that they can serve with conviction. It is no surprise that Frau industrialist Mayer serves without conviction and thus badly, disloyally, with a manifestation of insubordination and only for the sake of necessity."

If the opposite argument by insubordinate servants about people of rank were permitted, then it must have come up in a business consultation at the Manns'. In the diaries of 1918 to 1921 there is not the slightest reference to staff wanting to serve who might have been clear about aristocratic instinct concerning the order of rank. That the sensitive gentleman whom they served was a real gentleman and not just a newly rich fellow they either did not know or, what is more likely, could not make Thomas Mann realize. For what does he perceive of personnel? He reprimands Katia "because of her weakness regarding the servants, especially the 'girl' bent on pleasure and thievery, whom she [which is understandable after the Affa trial] does not dare fire" (October 12, 1918). "Furious outburst against the maid Josefa, who showed an unwillingness to take the midwife's equipment back to the latter's apartment, when no male servant was available" (April 21, 1919). "Again angrily brought up the terrible state of affairs with the children and the servant women in front of K.'s mother" (May 1, 1919). "Rage about the turpitudes of the servant girls" (July 4, 1919). "K. constantly in servant-girl calamities" (October 31, 1919). "Katja at the agency to get temporary help because she dismissed the crazy, invective-addicted, and violent cook out of the blue" (November 22, 1919). "Bad midday meal by the coarse, thieving temporary cook, who left again today" (March 14, 1921). "Contrariness in the household; dishonest cook, deaf servant girl" (April 6, 1919). "Very tired, nervous, irritated by the informed babble of the children and the rubbish of the nursemaid, who was playing the *esprit fort*" (June 6, 1921). "New firing of all the servants. Disgust and hate for the good-for-nothing bunch" (June 15, 1921).

War's end, revolution, and republic had brought improvements for the lowest-paid classes, while the middle class had to pay the bill. That is the background of the last entry on the theme of servants (June 21, 1921):

> K.'s negotiations with "helpers." A Dresden councilor's wife is being considered. The impoverished middle class applies for such posts almost without criticism and seems in fact more practicable than the common people, whose sense of justice and humanity is not equal to socialistic enlightenment.

That's actually what happened. It is turned into a story, the Hinterhöfer ladies, two erstwhile bourgeois sisters, who take the posts of cook and chambermaid, "keeping their dignity as former members of the third estate." The lord of the manor's theories about the people willing to serve are obviously scrap paper on the horizon of the metropolitan practice of the postwar years. "The relationship with male and female servants similar to house pets," he writes in 1925, "has fallen completely into decay in the cities, torn into the spheres of social criticism of conscience, emancipation, and dissolution. Everyone sees that the servant class, looming through time as a patriarchcal rudiment, has long since become inwardly impossible due to that generous imprudence of people, and no one foresees what will become of it and how it will end."

With all his theoretical sympathy for Bolshevism, Thomas Mann was in practice manifestly no friend of the proletariat. He completely lacks the ironic sympathy that Klaus Mann summons up for Affa. ("I began to admire Affa. So much perfidiousness was impressive.") Nowhere is there understanding for the situation of the domestics in his house. Perhaps he should only have paid them better to increase their readiness to serve? Instead of that he speaks of the "generous imprudence" of explaining their rights to them.

With all of this he conceals his bad conscience. "I am again wearing furs in the evening," he notes on November 21, 1918, "also usually at

midday on streetcar trips, where it is embarrassing for me to let myself be seen in luxury that could easily excite umbrage and cause bad
blood in these 'social times.'" The wish that he declares at the end of
the war is that he not become impoverished (October 21, 1918). Decades later he will deliberate the purchase of a private beach.

In an early story Thomas Mann had once written what can happen
when a sensible fur-wearer meets a proletarian. Detlef, a very perceptive person, like Tonio Kröger unhappily in love with life, leaves a
noisy party disappointed and unfulfilled. Then he encounters an outcast, "a raunchy, hollow, red-bearded face":

> His eyes slid over Detlev's entire figure, over his fur coat, on
> which his opera glass hung, down to his patent-leather shoes,
> then again boring into his glance with this lecherous and greedy
> scrutiny; a single time the man expelled air through his nose
> abruptly and scornfully.

Detlev wants to say to him: But we are brothers, we are both cast out
by life, both starving. A typical artist, he even accuses him of flaunt-
ing his misery a bit to make an impression. Detlev has no sense for
what is social about the matter, only for what is aesthetic and human.
His consciousness of being unhappy himself turns into an accusation
of the poor man that he does not understand him. Detlef wants to
explain this, but he remembers the appearance of luxuriousness with
which he beckoned to the coachman, his silver case that might have
contained cigarettes, and climbs mutely into the coach, "bewildered,
beside himself about the impossibility of creating clarity here." It
might not have happened much differently for Thomas Mann with
his servants. They could not explain themselves to him, and he could
not explain himself to them.

## A COMFORT: DOGS

> As pertains to me, I feel the summons "to see the human being in
> the last beggar" as past all understanding, as presumptuous, ob-
> soletely humanitarian, smooth talking, and silly. I do not know
> the aristocratic attitude of humanity; I "respect" my dog, too, and
> when the good dog greets me by putting his front paws on my
> chest and laying his tiger head on it too, while I pat his lean

shoulder blade, I feel much closer to him than I do to many a member of the "human race."

He felt himself better understood by his dogs than by human beings. He had dogs all his life, at times even three at one time. They respected his lord-of-the-manor inclinations. That was true especially for Bauschan, his house companion from the summer of 1916 to the beginning of 1920. A patriarchal instinct with a long history, as one reads in the autobiographical story "A Man and His Dog," ordained that he "see in the man, in the head of the house and the family, implicitly the master, the protector of the hearth, the commander, and to respect him [and] to find his dignity of life in the special relationship of a devoted-servant friendship." Bauschan has what is missing in real people. His rustic, tough, trustingly naïve, resistant, and natural character represents "people," as Mann loves them.

His predecessor was the Scottish collie Motz, acquired in 1905 and shot in 1915 because of an incurable sickness, who appears in "A Man and His Dog" as previously in *Royal Highness* with the name of Perceval. He, too, is catalogued in the categories of this idyllic sociology but, different from Bauschan, he does not play "people" but "nobility." True, Percy is a little crazy, but he is an aristocrat. With a genteel person one socializes as an equal with an equal, for the artist, too, feels like an aristocrat, more precisely, a crazy aristocrat. Perceval is an alter ego of the writer: "mind," while on the other hand Bauschan is the antipode: "life."

As a result, Bauschan is also no aesthete. "I don't ask for tricks from him, for example; it would be futile. He is not a scholar, not a market marvel, not a silly-poodle attendant; he is a vital hunting lad and not a professor." A good jumper, he could clear any obstacle, but it had to be a real obstacle, something that he could not crawl under. "A wall, a ditch, a trellis, a solid fence, obstacles like that. A crossbar, a stick held out, those are *not* such things, and so no one can jump over them without coming into a silly contradiction between oneself and things. Bauschan refuses to do that. . . . Flatter him, whip him— there a contradiction of reason prevails against a pure work of art, which you will in no way break." He is people, like Xaver Kleinsgütl, the house servant in "Disorder and Early Sorrow," "a sympathetic Bolshevist," who is accommodating only when it suits him but can be won over for other duties just as little "as one can get some dogs to

jump over a stick." Obviously, it would be contrary to his nature, the
Bolshevist sympathizer opines, "and that is disarming and leads to a
dispensation."

Bauschan is, of course, no artist, but he is life that an artist shapes.
What is articulated is finished, says Tonio Kröger. The artist kills what
he gets in the sights of his words. In an ironic application of this
thought, Thomas Mann therefore takes the responsibility for Bauschan's death. "A bad distemper, combined with purulent pneumonia
carried him off, very quickly, after I had told people about him . . .
and sometimes I cannot suppress the thought that a connection could
exist there, and that what I did was perhaps not done well to that
creature but was sinful." Also the diary entry regarding Bauchan's
euthenasia deals with art and death. The artist pays him last respects
with lines from a poem by August von Platen:

> With Fortune's smile he's also dazed,
> For one dies most beauteously whom in life
> An everlasting song has praised.

Bauschan's successor, the German shepherd called Lux or Luchs, later
Lukas, acquired on March 23, 1920, was obviously not suitable for a
place in literature. He did not fit the patterns of "people" and "nobility," "mind" and "life," rather he was a common watchdog. "Luchs
is a hardly gifted, fawning, sentimentally lustful animal, not very
sympathetic; but he does jump over a stick" (April 13, 1920). "Walked
for an hour with Luchs, whose worst trait is a bad smell. He seems to
wallow in something carrionlike, so that you can't touch him" (April
23, 1920). His master even had to grab a rag to wash up. "During the
evening I had the animal in my room, where he was so bad that I had
to clean it up" (April 8, 1920). With the change of name to "Lukas,"
the negative entries disappear; they seem to have gotten used to each
other.

# X. Family, No Fun Either

*Munich, in the twenties*

From the end of the war until his emigration, except for his marriage itself, which is stable, there is little data to record, at most the intermezzo of his infatuation with Klaus Heuser (1927) and his silver anniversary in 1930. What occupied the married couple were the literary events and their children. Family life is handled relatively straightforwardly in "A Man and His Dog" (written in 1918), in "Song of the Child" (1918–19), in "Disorder and Early Sorrow" (1925), and in *Mario and the Magician* (experienced in 1926, written in 1929). Except for numerous essays his time is filled with work on the great novels (*The Magic Mountain* until 1924, *Joseph and His Brothers* after 1926). In the year 1929 comes the Nobel Prize for Literature. Thomas Mann is at the peak of his fame.

The lives of his two oldest children brought a lot of excitement into the house. Erika, born in 1905, graduated in 1924 after many changes of schools, then went to Berlin as an actress, in 1925 to Bremen, soon thereafter to Hamburg. She was fairly successful, and not only in the plays by her brother Klaus (*Anya and Esther* premiered 1925 in Hamburg and Munich), which got bad reviews but made the Mann children well known throughout the republic. In 1926 she married the actor Gustaf Gründgens, who had just become a great star. But the two eccentrics understood one another only in the theater and lived together only for a short period. In 1927–28 Erika took a trip around the world with Klaus, toward the financing of which the fame of their father proved to be useful. In 1929 her marriage with Gründgens ended. Professionally, her focus shifted from the stage to journalism. A journey to Africa in 1930 introduced experiences with drugs. Erika trained as an automobile mechanic and in 1931 participated in a rally, driving ten thousand kilometers in ten days. Shortly before her exile she founded the cabaret The Peppermill, which was to become one of the most successful enterprises of the literary exile.

Klaus, born in 1906, almost died from a ruptured appendix in 1915. He attended even more schools than his sister, in Munich first a private school, then elementary school, a high school, later (with Erika) the Hochwaldhausen boarding school (spring to summer, 1922), then the Odenwald School (1922–23), then again had private tutoring, in which finally in 1924 he refused to take part, not getting his degree. In the public schools he had become acquainted with the spirit of the youth movement and made many important friendships, including homosexual ones, that marked him for life

(Elmar and Uto). Still, he became engaged as an eighteen-year-old to Pamela Wedekind—the son of an author to the daughter of an author. The age of majority at the time was twenty-one; he could not yet get married. He went to Heidelberg, became a theater critic in Berlin, traveled to Hamburg and in every direction, sometimes even went home. The trip around the world in 1927–28 ended the engagement. Pamela married the much older author Carl Sternheim, which Klaus could not understand. He writes constantly; by 1932 he has published a good dozen books, among them already an autobiography (*Child of His Time*). His plays for the theater provoke scandals but appear on the great stages in Hamburg and Berlin, in Vienna and Munich. Like his sister Erika, long in the sights of the Nazis, he must leave Germany in March 1933.

Golo, born in 1909, was a fairly good student, unlike his older siblings. He, too, spent his elementary school years in a small private school, in 1918 transferred to the Munich Wilhelms-Gymnasium and in 1922 to the boarding school Salem Castle near Überlingen on Lake Constance, where he graduated in 1926. From 1927 until 1932 he studied history, sociology (with Alfred Weber), and philosophy (with Karl Jaspers) in Munich, Berlin, and Heidelberg. When only twenty-three years old he received the Ph.D. degree. In the summer of 1933 exile for him also began, first in France, from 1940 on in the United States. Most of the time he was active as a professor of history. Return to Germany in 1958, after 1964 a freelance writer living in the former house of his parents in Kilchberg, death in 1994 in Leverkusen.

Monika, the fourth sibling, came into the world in 1910, became a writer, in 1939 married the Hungarian art historian Jenö Lényi, who drowned before her eyes in 1940, lived at times again with her parents, then from 1953 until 1988 on Capri. She died in 1992. Elisabeth, the fifth child, was born in 1918, in 1939 married the literary scholar Giuseppe Antonio Borgese, after his death in 1952 became a publisher, oceanographer, and professor of political science in Canada. Michael, the youngest child, was born in 1919, became a musician at first (on the viola), after his father's death became a German professor in the United States, in 1939 married Gret Moser from Zurich (three children), and died in 1977.

## POOR LITTLE KATIA

UNLIKE THE period of the engagement, the marriage itself has hardly been treated literarily, for obvious reasons. So the literary works offer little information about their life together. We also learn almost nothing from the essays. At an advanced age Katia Mann revealed a few things in her *Unwritten Memoirs* that, however, does not relish what is problematical and presents only a selective exterior view of this marriage. A little more can be found in the memoirs of the children. For example, we must thank Golo Mann for the statement: "Thomas Mann was not always equal to Mother's alert, logically juristic intelligence." She called him "doe," or also a "doelike figure of great gentleness"—this we know from Erika; Golo also sketched the "author doe" on occasion. "Mielein is practical but disorganized; the Magician is worldly innocent and dreamy, but organized to the point of pedantry"—Klaus hands that on. Monika knows: "Theoretically he is the head, practically he is the child." Katia, not Thomas, gets a driver's license; she drives fast and carelessly.

The most important keyholes by far are the diaries of 1918 to 1921. Anyone seeking information must be grateful that Thomas Mann wrote down his life like no one else, that so much remains preserved, and that the understanding of the heirs of the copyrights allows us the intrusive study of an exemplary soul. For we know hardly more from his best friends than we do from Thomas Mann.

The first years of marriage for Frau Thomas Mann (as she called herself, as stood on her letterhead) were extremely strenuous. The "stern happiness" demanded much discipline. Six births (and two miscarriages) within fourteen years, war, revolution, and inflation, a difficult husband and tense emotional relationships, all of that together was no small thing. No wonder that there is always talk of illnesses and sojourns at health resorts, that in 1912, for example, six months in Davos is considered necessary. The X ray of Katia's lungs at the time has by chance been preserved. Not a sign of tuberculosis, today's experts say. So we owe the impetus for *The Magic Mountain* to a wrong diagnosis, because when Thomas Mann visited his wife at that time, "a visit for three weeks" like his hero Hans Castorp, the idea of a "sanitorium novella" was born. Also in the diaries from 1918 to 1921 there is frequent talk of Katia's overexertion, of illnesses and

*Katia Mann, about 1920*

sojourns necessary for recuperation. Yet her sense of duty kept her mostly at home. "Desperate about K., who now wants to go to Kohlgrub after all," her husband notes on May 13, 1920, after long indecision. "The truth is that she simply does not want to leave." Just as in *The Magic Mountain*, a doctor had determined that he heard something "up on the right" (April 9, 1920) and suggested a stay in the Black Forest. But then she did go to Kohlgrub (May 27, 1920), only an hour and a half by train south of Munich.

In the essay of 1925 on marriage Thomas Mann remarks, not without a touch of truth, that "the indissoluble bond of two people for life," that is possible really "only with a patriarchal simplicity of temper, of sense, of nerves," was extremely aggravated by the equal status of women and the cultural differentiation. A quite different measure of consideration, tact, diplomacy, tenderness, goodness, indulgence, self-control, and art than were part of a happy marriage in more primitive times had become necessary. Of course, fractiousness had grown extraordinarily, even though separate bedrooms and participation in diverging activities decreased the areas of friction. "Still, the tremor of nameless impatience in the voices of married couples existed even in social situations—an expression that let every moment be prepared for a shameful explosion of a dammed-up host of tormented nerves and desperate petulance." Strindbergian memories appeared with only a slight observation of most marriages, "infernal memories." You could easily get the impression that 90 percent of all marriages were unhappy.

With points of irony, or at least ellipses, Mann concludes the diary entry of September 21, 1919: "K. said her brother Peter had explained at home that we had an 'ideal marriage.'" Of course, it was not that easy. The diaries, at any rate, are acquainted with that irritability and those explosions of dammed-up tormented nerves. The provocations are mostly harmless. The everyday life of the family may offer some highlights. "Afternoon at tea, out of enervation I was unfortunately testy with K. because of her weakness toward the servants" (October 12, 1918). "After supper, disgruntlement with K. 'Guilt' on both sides. She disturbed me, after, very weary, I had just found quiet in a chair, and I could not hide my annoyance, unfortunately" (March 30, 1919). "A new annoyance with K. at breakfast because of the use of too much butter. Needless and regrettable. But it is clear that such a thing always happens when I am somehow overly tired, absorbed, and thus irritable" (April 1, 1919). "Eruption of a tension between K. and me" (October 25, 1919). It also happens that Katia "erupted in great fury" (on November 6, 1919) because of the financial frivolousness of her husband, but also "determined by the bad condition of her nerves." "After supper annoyance at K., who carried embers from the hallway stove into my room, let something fall on the floor, and became unpleasantly testy toward me because I tried to stomp out the embers instead of picking them up" (January 18, 1920). "At home, disgruntlement with K. because nothing was fixed for supper" (March 2, 1920).

But the disgruntlements do not last long. "Reconciliation with K. at evening, she very loving" (October 25, 1919). Katia took on her role as housewife or, to be more exact, overseer of a large household, without

opposition. His life had become her life. She writes without a grudge
that she was "now just his accessory." Frequently she serves her husband also as an editor or typist. Also when English is involved, he
pushes her forward: "my wife, who speaks English better than I"
(June 8, 1921). With a grin he recalls the Kleist anecdote about Johann
Sebastian Bach, "who was accustomed to let his wife take care of all
things in life (as I do), and at her burial, when directions were asked
of him, he said with a sob, 'Ask my wife!'" (April 11, 1920). Once,
when Katia had gone on a trip, it is said that he had to borrow money
because he did not know which bank was his.

He is not an authoritarian husband. He does not lack an understanding of her role, "of my poor little K., whom I love" (July 24,
1919). He often speaks of his worry about her and his sympathy.
"Concern about K. these days, who doesn't look good and frequently
feels weak. . . . And should she die, I would waste away with sadness, which she, by the way, knows and mentioned" (October 11,
1918). "Great anxiety and worry about Katia, who is very frail" (November 3, 1918). "But K.'s nerves gave in, she cried and 'could no
longer live,' overcome recently for an hour by housewifely and other
miseries. Was full of compassion" (November 2, 1919). Trips make
him nervous—Katia begins too late with the packing for her cure in
Oberstdorf: "The usual situation. Compassion for her, melancholy
about her leaving, but also hope for renewed strength for her and rest
for me" (September 3, 1920).

In spite of all the tensions, this does not look like an unhappy marriage. That the wedding anniversary is forgotten need not necessarily
be a bad sign, rather it attests to the established matter of course in a
marriage bond. "It is our *15th anniversary*—I was again reminded of
that only at supper when K. prepared a tea punch. . . . Still in Feldaf-
ing I had my eye on the date but then forgot again. A moving tenderness toward K." (February 11, 1920).

As far as eroticism is concerned, the circumstances were admittedly
precarious. Not infrequently do the diaries note "Intercourse with K."
The sensual aspect of the process is expressly noted less often: "After
supper with K., who let me caress her body, ribs, and breast with my
hand, which aroused my sensuality greatly" (March 12, 1920). "My
relationship toward K. very sensual for several weeks" (October 12,
1921). But it cannot be denied that the problematical statements pre-
dominate. That begins with such subtle differentiations as: "Evening

stroll with Katia, who loves me very much and to whom I am eternally grateful" (August 15, 1919). Why grateful? One of the reasons follows: "Embrace with K. My gratitude for the goodness in her attitude toward my sexual problems is deep and warm" (May 13, 1921). And one more: "Gratitude to K., because in her love she is not in the least confused or disgruntled when finally she inspires no desire in me, and when my lying with her does not put me into a state to arouse her desire, e.g., final sexual desire. The peace, love, and indifference with which she accepts that is admirable, and so I do not have to allow myself to be shaken by it either" (October 17, 1920). There seem to have been sojourns again and again at Katia's side during which no intercourse occurred. That his homosexual tendency plays a decisive role in all of that is not only likely but is also reflected in a diary entry (July 14, 1920):

> Not entirely clear about my state of mind in this regard. There can hardly be any talk of actual impotence, rather more of the usual confusion and undependability of my "sex life." Doubtless, nervous weakness as a result of desires that go toward the other side is present. How would it be, if a boy "were present"? It would, in any case, be irrational, if through a failure whose reasons are not new to me, I let myself be depressed. Rashness, mood, indifference, self-assurance are thus the right attitude, because they are the best "remedies."

A few days later Thomas Mann has an animated conversation on the train with a congenial young man wearing white pants, and he notes (even though with a question mark): "Glad about this. It seems that I am finally through with what is feminine?" (July 25, 1920). Of course, that will prove not to be well founded. But that sexuality in this marriage was an emotional high-wire act emerges from the diaries unambiguously. However, the difficulties in this area were balanced out by strengths in others. To accuse Katia of having sacrificed her life to him, that he misused her as camouflage, hits upon only a very small part of the truth. Thomas Mann knew what he was doing to her, at least in his conscience, "there where the soul plays no tricks." In consideration of all the circumstances, the path that both took was probably the best possible one for them. If they went awry, then it was "because for some people there is no right path at all."

## LONELINESS

He had his secrets. No one, as far as we know, was ever allowed at the time to read in his diaries. Not even Katia. He wrote mostly late in the evening. Such diaries presuppose separate bedrooms. The pressure of intimacy must not be so great that time to write and security from unwanted glimpses are not guaranteed.

"Much could be said about loneliness and 'wife and children.'" He was lonely—even in the family, even and especially in society—but did not try to be otherwise. "The longing for solitude and quiet resembles physical thirst." He had ample company with himself and with the creatures of memory and fantasy resident in him. "If one is profound, then the difference between solitude & nonsolitude is not large, merely superficial." Whoever has profundity is always alone. The danger does not exist that he will be absorbed by society. Even though it might look as though he were a craven middle-class male. "The decisive consideration and certainty remains for me that in accordance with my nature I can conceal myself in the middle class without actually becoming middle class."

He could not easily explain himself to others, not the abysses of his soul in any case. He kept people at a distance, of course, and that might make an arrogant impression, as though he did not need them. But is there not a distancing that is a plea for coming nearer? A plea to win the blamelessly frigid person for humanity with astonishing patience, as Paul Ehrenberg once succeeded in doing? With him it even came to the informal address, the use of "Du," also with Kurt Martens, back at the beginning of the century. But as a husband Thomas Mann freezes up again in regard to others. His brother was a danger; he had no real friends.

He did not wear his heart on his sleeve. Almost everyone saw only his middle-class exterior, considered him a bureaucratic philistine, and was only a bit surprised by the books he wrote. If they were spiteful, they also found his books merely forward. Seen from the outside, his life looked so consummate that no one had sympathy with him. And yet he was suffering! How very much, we know from his diaries. Upon reflection it is judged that they had been ridiculous sufferings, and the matter of his underpants is cited. ("Also, I suffer psychologically and physically that all size 32 underwear is too small for me, size 34 is too big for me.") Of course, he had success. But he needed it, too, to endure the torment of soul that was dealt him.

His suffering from loneliness is easily determined. Thomas Mann is a freezing hedgehog who seeks warmth with other hedgehogs but is prevented from moving close by the mutual bristles. The distance to be covered seems longer and longer to the one in flight. He needs more and more space around him not to feel crowded. But when that space becomes more constricted instead, when they all want to speak more hastily themselves, before the slow one, the one far distant, makes his move, then the result is silence. There is bitterness in silence, but also goodness and resignation: In silence there is understanding that the others cannot give so much space, that they want, understandably, to fill up the space with their own and one cannot demand more from one's fellow human beings. With all his public loquacity, privately Thomas Mann was extremely timid, timid from conscientiousness (for will one really hit upon what counts?), and because, at least in melancholic hours, he thought he was asking too much.

## FATHER OF SIX

There are several literary expositions about Thomas Mann as a father, as a rule somewhat embellished. In the *Confessions of Felix Krull, Confidence Man*, it is Professor Kuckuck, who from a "Sirius distance" looks at the urges of youth, the flirting of his daughter with Felix. In the great biblical novel *Joseph and His Brothers* it is Jacob, the father of twelve sons and a daughter, who is the original prefiguration of fatherhood in the full sense of the lord of the manor, of house and home, of wives and children, servants and maids, herds and domestic animals. The prefiguration of the prefiguration finally, from whom all fatherhood is derived, is God the Father himself. With this novel Thomas Mann has given us much that is familiar. The model for Rachel, whom Jacob serves seven long years, is Katia. The birth of her first child, his daughter Erika, which lasted thirty-six hours, is recognized again in the difficult birth of Joseph. Finally, Rachel's second son, Benjamin, Jacob's youngest, is in many details a portrait of Michael Mann, the sixth and last child of Thomas and Katia. The par-

*Katia Mann, 1919, with (from left to right) Monika, Golo, Michael, Klaus, Elisabeth, and Erika*

tiality of the father is also autobiographical. There are beloved children, namely, Klaus, Erika, and Elisabeth, or as the case may be, Joseph, Benjamin, Ruben, and Juda, and less beloved ones, namely, Golo, Monika, and Michael, or in the novel, the other sons of Lea and the sons of the maids. Looked at instructively, this partiality is a weakness. Those excluded feel it as an injustice but have to accept the relationship of exclusiveness and preference. Since Jacob is no warrior but a ponderer and teller of tales, his sons are in awe of his strongly expressive words and commands but nevertheless deceive him because they know that he cannot defend himself. He himself also feels weak, for example, in comparison with Abraham.

Still closer to his own life and experience is the story written in the spring of 1925, "Disorder and Early Sorrow." It happens in the fall of 1923 at the high point of the inflation and "took place exactly so." Germany is morally shattered and psychologically gone to rack and ruin, "the market woman who demanded 'a hundred billion' for an egg in dried clay had at the time forgotten to be surprised." It goes downhill also with the Mann family, in spite of a small influx of dollars. From the story one can fathom their inner condition at the time fairly exactly, for the members are only superficially disguised. Abel

Cornelius, professor of history, lives exactly like Thomas Mann, has an exhausted wife as does Mann ("worn and subdued from the crazy difficulties of housekeeping") and four children, namely, the eighteen-year-old Ingrid who corresponds to Erika, born in 1908; the seventeen-year-old Bert who takes over the role of Klaus, born in 1906; the five-year-old Lorchen (Elisabeth, "the little kid"); and the four-year-old Beisser (Michael). Golo and Monika are not used. Biographically verifiable also is the house servant Xaver Kleinsgütl, in reality the "windbag Ludwig," in the story "a child and small fruit of the lax time, a genuine example of his generation, a servant of the revolution, a likable Bolshevist." It says as good as nothing against the assumption that the other servants also are taken more or less from the reality of the time, namely, the child's nanny Anna and the two Hinterhöfer sisters, fallen from the middle class, who take care of the positions of cook and chambermaid and suffer tragicomically from their social decline.

"My youngest daughter was sitting on her rocking horse and yelling: 'The dollar is climbing!' when the horse's nose was rising." The inflation carnival unavoidably went to the heads of the other children, too, "the cynical joke of the inflation, to which the most respected experts contributed—all of that makes youth arrogant, pleasure-seeking, and skeptical." The young people who come to the party given by Ingrid and Bert are a colorful mixture: actors and speculators, high school girls and artisans, youth-movement people, and some in tails. The traditional social connections dissolve. "It is a sure thing and popular to disdain traditional rules." Generally, they use the familiar form of address, which in *The Magic Mountain* and in Thomas Mann's house, where Katia all her life used the formal form with her brother-in-law Heinrich, was considered undisciplined. In the story of disorder, he had offered a kind of indulgent homage, Mann writes some years later—although he loved order. In fact, the father, like the youth, wavered between the old and the new. The ironic cultural conservatism of the history professor Cornelius is without combative power, for secretly he sympathizes with the new. Nevertheless he compares his son Bert, who is a clown and wants to be a dancer or cabaret comedian or a waiter in Cairo, with Max Hergesell, who wants to become an engineer, or with the bank official Möller, who really is good as a folksinger. "He would like to be fair; he says tentatively that Bert, with all that, is a fine young man, with perhaps more capital than the successful Möller; that possibly he has a poet in him or something like that, and that his plans to be a dancing waiter are simply boyish flitting about caused by the unsettled times. But his envious paternal pessimism is stronger."

As a father, Thomas Mann, like Cornelius, probably had little authority because only regarding a few points could he come up with the required resolution. Too often he ironized his role, as when he recited a poem about Herr von Walff, who raised his sons himsalff, whereupon both drowned. He had too much understanding for debauchery. That is also true in *Mario and the Magician*, where the parents are too weak to leave the degenerate performance of the magician with their children quickly enough. This story, too, he essentially experienced himself. It is based on a vacation stay in Forte dei Marmi near Viareggio in September 1926. The magician actually existed. Both the children, nameless in the story, an eight-year-old girl and a boy, were obviously Elisabeth and Michael. There was also the father, who was compliant with the degeneracy, even long after midnight. "The children were awake at that time. I mention them ashamed. It was not good here, for them least of all, and that we still had not removed them I can explain only with a certain contagion of general negligence by which we, too, were gripped at this hour of the night. Nothing mattered to us anymore."

One can put on a middle-class mask and for an hour or two deceive society. But masks have no power in the daily rearing of children that goes on for years. The children are aware that the one whom all the world knows only in a fine suit wears a worn-out smoking jacket and a shawl in his study, like a bohemian. Only his true nature prevails. That meant, in the case of Thomas Mann, that he could not maintain a classic middle-class upbringing for his children because he himself had too many artistic sympathies for what was not middle class. At Carnival he came in tails and a top hat with the mask of an idiot. His children could tell a thing or two about his being an actor of great skill when they praise his reading aloud.

So it is then that none of the children became middle-class citizens. What their father managed to keep somewhat covered up is manifested openly by them. It is an artistic family in which everything authoritarian melted in the alkahest of irony. Little Elisabeth called her father "Tommy." The beginning of "Disorder and Early Sorrow" portrays a household with only weak parental authority but with respect on all sides for the aesthetic self-presentations of its individual members.

> The big children call their parents "the old people"—not behind their backs but in speaking to them and with complete affection, although Cornelius is only forty-seven and his wife still eight years younger. "Esteemed Old Man!" they say, "Good Old Lady!" and the professor's parents, who in his homeland lead the distraught and intimidated life of old people, are called in their idioms the "Great Old Ones." As far as the "little children" are concerned, Lorchen and Beisser, who eat in the upper hallway with "blue Anna," so called from the blueness of her cheeks, they address their father by his first name after the example of their mother, so says Abel. It sounds indescribably droll when they call and address him so, especially in the sweet tone of voice of five-year-old Eleonore, who looks exactly like Frau Cornelius in pictures of her as a little girl and whom the professor loves more than anything.
>
> "Oldie," says Ingrid pleasantly, laying her large but pretty hand on her father's, who after middle-class and not unnatural tradition sits at the head of the family table, and to whose left she has her place, opposite her mother—"good forefather, let me remind you gently, for you've repressed it surely. It was this afternoon that we were to have our little revelry, our little dance with herring salad—that means for yourself to keep your composure and not give in; at nine o'clock it will all be over."

Also in regard to the main conflict of the story, the father proves helpless. The party begins, a handsome young man named Max Hergesell dances for fun also with the five-year-old Lorchen, but then abandons her, whereupon she cries uncontrollably. It is once more the disastrous incursion of the demon of love into an orderly life. It is not the father, whose paternal heart is torn "by the shameful horrors of unjust and hopeless passion," who rescues Lorchen but the house servant Xaver, who invites Max Hergesell to Lorchen's small bed. A few halfway truthfully nice words, and Lorchen falls asleep, "and only sometimes still in her slow breathing does a tardy sob tremble forth."

## ERIKA

"I was pleased with Erika and Klaus, and I realized again that of the six I prefer three with rare resolution, the two oldest and little Elisabeth." Erika belonged to the ones chosen, was, as the oldest, "crown princess." He also had the nerve to celebrate ironically the injustice that was a part of being chosen. During the time of the food shortage in the First World War, Erika relates, the children had always divided up the food precisely. One day a fig was left over, and it was clear that it had to be divided among the then four children, and their mother was also of that opinion:

> But what did my father do? He gave this fig just to me alone and said: "Here, Eri, eat it." Of course, I started right in to eat it; the other three siblings stared with horror, and my father said sententiously with emphasis: "One should get the children used to injustice early."

In Erika's retrospective writings her father is presented in a transfigured light. He was a bit doddery as far as everyday things were concerned, but humorous and kindhearted. The mustache, more voluminous then than in later years, tickled when he gave her a kiss. He took his children seriously, gave them much freedom, and did not participate in their everyday life, but knew how to do or say something effective on extraordinary occasions. At Christmas he put together the old manger with the charming wax figures by himself. When at the beginning of 1919 the children produced a play in the house under the direction of Erika and Klaus, he wrote a witty review. "As Luise, Herr Klaus demonstrated great middle-class mentality." It was signed "Dr. Sheepshead," where small crosses were substituted for the "e," the "h," and the "a." He liked to read to the children, fairy tales at first, later his own work; he was curious about reactions. "If we laughed, it was often very comical, then he was awfully glad, and if we had tears in our eyes, then he was quite happy." Sometimes they fell right off their chairs with laughter. For readings they were allowed to enter the otherwise strictly barred study. All the children remember the particular aroma of the leather, printer's ink, cigar smoke, and eau de cologne. The tone of the corre-

spondence with the oldest, which begins early, is lovingly droll. "Dear
Eri-child, accept many cordial best wishes for your birthday and also
forgive us very much indeed for bringing you into the world in unbounded giddiness! Such a thing will not happen again, and, after all,
things have not gone so well for us either."

As a child, Erika belonged to the Herzog Park gang, which spread
terror in Bogenhausen. "We were a wicked and ingenious horde at
the time. . . . We mystified, lied, deceived with brilliance and with an
ease that was to be envied. . . . We announced Maximilian Harden for
tea with the president of the university and sent his apologies soon
after with an arm that had been run over by a streetcar; in order to
plot things, we met, to be cheeky, in the lobbies of the large hotels."
At fifteen Erika answered to a survey that her father played the mountain zither with sincere devotion. She (to be exact, her assumed persona, Ingrid) was able "in a high, floating, ordinary twittering voice
to pretend that she is a shop girl who has an illegitimate child, a son
who has a sadistic tendency and in the country recently tortured a
cow so indescribably that it can hardly be looked at by a Christian."
She was foolish, deceitful, imaginative, dreamy, a gambler. Because
her parents were no match for her educationally, in 1922, together
with Klaus, she was entrusted to the mountain school Hochwaldhausen in the Rhone, a reform pedagogical enterprise, but not some
sort of barracks. There, too, they could not cope with the two of them.
After only four months Erika was again in Munich, where she graduated with the greatest difficulty in 1924.

What is to become of the child? "Erika's profession seems to be
domesticity and a daughter of the house" (diary, November 29, 1918).
She is thirteen at the time. "Made pancakes for our supper today.
Simpatico in her housekeeper's apron and often of a rare beauty."
During the birth of her brother Michael she also meets the test: "Erika
as a substi. housewife, good" (April 21, 1919). She becomes more and
more beautiful, and that impresses him. "In love with Erika, who obviously loves me and is glad about my tenderness" (June 9, 1920).

To be sure, she did not become a housewife but an actress, cabaret
performer, passionate motorist, author of children's books, journalist,
and committed opponent of Hitler. Already in 1933 she had to go into
exile. Her private life was difficult. She loved her brother Klaus and
married homosexuals twice. Her first marriage, to Gustaf Gründgens
("Erika was able to produce the 'yes'-word melodiously") was soon at

an end; the second, with W.H. Auden, was a mere passport marriage. Erika Mann wavered between same-sex inclinations and lovers, most of whom were repulsed. Drugs, too, played a role. What remained and gave her support was always her parents' house. During her time in America she returned to it completely and, according to Katia, became her father's most important helper.

## KLAUS

As a father, Thomas Mann was not the monster that many claimed him to be. After all, he had not had it easy, not with any of his children, all of whom took strange paths and even when grown-up repeatedly lived off of him. Even to Klaus—if one considers what was required in such an unusual case—he was very understanding and in no way unapproachable. For example, as Klaus remembers with pleasure, he had at his disposal "a way of spraying us in the yard with the garden hose that made him very simply a master in that line." He just had a light hand. That is affirmed in the father's diary ("did it to oblige them," June 15, 1919). He was not awe inspiring, rather the opposite, warded off fear. "Come home, if you are miserable," he told Klaus. Even evil spirits respected him. For a time Klaus dreamed regularly about a man who came toward him with his head under his arm. His father advised him to say to the man: "See that you get lost right now! My papa has expressly forbidden you to visit me." Klaus did it, and the spook disappeared. When Katia cried convulsively about the coldness, lovelessness, ingratitude, churlishness, and mendacity of Klaus's diary, which she accidentally found lying open, the Magician remained calm, conscious of having a similar nature. "I will never play the blustering father. The boy can't help his nature, which is a product" (diary, May 5, 1920).

The daily journals, though, do report outbursts of anger (September 27, 1919; April 16, 1921)—once Klaus must even be spanked hard (April 12, 1919)—but much more telling is the self-ironic remark that shows the educationally necessary reenforcement obviously to be a pretense. "In the final analysis it is a duty not to rid oneself of the unpleasant emotion of anger out of self-consideration" (April 4, 1921). All the while, Klaus's stunts strained the family name in no small way. That he secretly sneaked into the study and there read Wedekind can be let pass. Worse were his constant failures at school, the lies, the unauthorized trips, the waste of money, contacts with prominent family friends behind the backs of his parents. Still, they were always quick to forgive; "in the nicest and smartest fashion they let us have our own way."

Klaus feels called to be a dancer and for a time is to become a tenor. Naturally, he was born to be a writer. Also, as such, he early on caused difficulties. When Paul Geheeb, the director of the Odenwald School, complained to Thomas Mann that Klaus had portrayed him coarsely and slanderously, the father defends what he calls his son's "artistic naïveté." The dazzling life that the handsome young man led in the twenties he owes not *only* to his talent but also to the fame of his father, which he knows how to make use of. It might be difficult, even impossible, to step out of such a shadow, but Klaus did not seriously try, or only later did. That his father inscribed for him a copy of *The Magic Mountain* with the dedication, "For my esteemed colleague—his hopeful Father," Klaus could not keep to himself; it was in all the papers. But still, his father stuck by him, in public, too. When the newspapers once again asserted that he found his son's work too "immoral," he became blunt: "I'm no convent-school girl. I do not know who has brought up the fairy tale of my dignified, unappreciative attitude toward the young man; in any event, I'd like finally once and for all to characterize it as a fairy tale." He knows, too, from where this political hot air is coming. "I found 'Anya and Esther' by no means so bad for a first try, as a certain critic, who judges recent literature under the viewpoint of national fitness, tried to make the play." Klaus Mann was at the time nineteen. In contemporary German literature one searches in vain for nineteen-year-olds of this caliber.

The Mann children, especially when one adds to them Pamela Wedekind and Gustav Gründgens, were always fodder for malicious headlines in the gossip sheets, which categorized them as bad apples whom one could take it out on when the real target, their father, seemed to be untouchable. They were prime examples of the Golden Twenties and decorated many a front cover of illustrated magazines. The big-city snobs recognized themselves in them, the more middle-class people did not. For the Nazis they were eyesores of decadence. The Nazis had an easy time finding a majority for this standpoint. That there was more to Klaus, to Erika, became evident only when they were driven out of the country in which they had enjoyed a nice youth full of delectable freedoms.

## GOLO

Angelus Gottfried, to whom the boyhood name of Golo stuck, was one of the unloved children. He heard so often that he was ugly that this idea was planted in him, not to his good fortune. Next to his sensationally attractive older siblings, it certainly had to seem believable to him. He hardly had a chance to find a competitive image next to his famous father, his very accomplished mother, and the highly talented Klaus and Erika. That drove him to be grotesque. Even in the child the role of the darkly comical gnome took shape, quickly affirmed by a mercilessly developing environment in the panopticon of which such a thing would fit. Klaus sketches his younger brother aptly: "With a farcical seriousness, he could be spiteful as well as obsequious. He was eager to serve and stealthily aggressive, at the same time as dignified as a gnome king." In his father's diary he is reviled as being "mendacious, unclean, and hysterical" (January 24, 1920). Also not infrequently there was "anger because of Golo" (July 16, 1921), for the accused affirms it in his memoirs. His father exuded silence, sternness, nervousness, or anger. "Only too well do I remember scenes at the table, eruptions of fury and brutality that were directed at my brother Klaus but drew tears from me."

Golo was not a good-for-nothing. That he too was sent to a boarding school may be traced to his parents' realization that the boy would be able to develop there less disturbed than in such a high-strung home. The sojourn in Salem brought about the desired effect, but on the other hand, and logically, alienated the boy completely from his parents' house. Important friendships came along too. Unlike Klaus, Golo handled his same-sex inclinations discreetly. In the climate of shy caution in erotic matters that had produced the precarious balance between Thomas and Katia, he cannot have felt himself fully accepted. In any case, they certainly knew of it. There were also problems in this regard in Salem. In the schoolteacher Kurt Hahn, Golo had become acquainted with a character who resembled his father too much in at least one aspect. "Kurt Hahn had almost no idea about sexuality and sex education. This was due to the fact that he morally disapproved of the homoerotic tendency that was in him and had suppressed it there with an effort of will that I could not imagine."

Golo suspected only as he grew older, after Klaus had "disappeared," that he could be a serious author. The fact that he was destined to be one, he concealed for a long time, "likely unconsciously because I did not want to encroach upon my brother's territory and because I wanted to wait until after my father's death." He was forty when Klaus died, forty-six when his father died. He had to wait a long time. Only late does his production flow in torrents, do *German History of the Nineteenth and Twentieth Centuries* and *Wallenstein* follow, his chief works as a writer of history. His style is sure, fractious and to the point, distinctive from that of his father. He does not dispute Thomas Mann's reputation as a literary author, but finds him naïve as a politician.

In the story of Golo's emancipation there had been severe setbacks for which he was not to blame. In 1933 he had tried to live a few months more in Germany but was forced back into the lap of his family. He would have been a welcome hostage for the Nazis and would certainly soon have been arrested. His memoirs offer a diary entry of June 3, 1933, just as he arrived in southern France. "Now the family is the only thing I have left; that cannot bode well." Right after that there follows a harsh judgment about his papa: "Strolled last night with Heinrich along the sea; I feel really sorry for him; he wears his fate with dignity, yes, even with charm, and is not so ladylike in his pains, offended by the whole world like the old man." Golo never uses the nickname "the Magician." He writes "TM" or "the old man." But he accepts the duties that his exile dictates to him, helps his father with the editing of his magazine *Maß und Wert*, and occasionally writes articles at his request. After his father's and in particular Katia's deaths, he became an excellent trustee of the Thomas Mann copyright, although he grew tired of being asked constantly about his father. His hatred of TM increased as he grew older, so that his sister Elisabeth felt compelled to admonish him, "When you get past the age of thirty, you should stop blaming your parents for what you are."

Should this father be chided? He could not change his nature, and much too much tugged at him. Even if he had stuggled to gain a better understanding, then the state of affairs, which as it stood was fateful for this third-born child, would not have been fundamentally changeable. In the final analysis Golo found a highly respectable path.

Unlike Klaus, he was not constantly measured against his father. He was respected for himself, even though inwardly he suffered much for it.

## MONIKA

The next one not loved was Monika. "Disgraced because I did not know my children's birthdays" (diary, April 23, 1919)—that refers to her and to Golo. The diary has as good as nothing kind to report about Monika. Since she did not enjoy Munich's high school for girls, she too was sent to Salem. She later tried applied arts and music. She plagued her parents thoroughly with constant fancies and frequent love affairs. The vocabulary in her father's diaries regarding her hover between "refractory" (September 13, 1934), "nervous and depressed" (Decenber 24, 1936), "easily insulted" (August 7, 1941), "disagreeable" (March 9, 1937), "tasteless" (January 29, 1939), and "wretched" (February 10, 1942). He is exasperated about her and calls arguments unavoidable "as soon as the child is treated like a fully sensible person" (September 25, 1941). She does not retaliate. In her memoirs there is nothing mean about her father, but much that is skeptical. "A gently fanatical tendency toward uniformity and remaining the same always characterized the paternal nature. So my childish or elfin exuberance may have made him somewhat peevish." She does not know whether life in the spotlight of her father was a curse or a blessing. "He was like an orchestra director who did not have to move his baton and who commanded the orchestra by his mere standing there."

She finally found her psychological balance in marriage. She had to be all the more dejected when a German U-boat torpedoed the ship on which she and her husband were sailing to Canada. The lifeboat sank, "we called to one another, I heard his cry, three times, and then nothing more. And then there were nothing but dead people all around me and totally black night." She held on tight to the side of a leaking boat, until at about four o'clock the next afternoon an English warship picked her up. She spent a few crisis-filled years at various locations and again and again with her parents, until in 1953 she had had enough, moved to Capri, and fallen in love with a fisherman with whom she cultivated a companionship hidden from the world until his death in 1985.

Whenever she was asked about the work of her father, she hid behind a feigned ignorance. "I feel made dumb by such conversations and also attacked 'in my roots.'" Her father gives her his *Faustus* with the dedication "For Monika, she will no doubt understand." Her reaction is ambiguous: "There lies a fleeting contemptuousness in it already shrugged off, in place of which trust immediately appears."

She also wrote short poemlike texts. We would gladly say otherwise, but they are really unimportant. One is entitled *Father* and reads: "It appears touching, even deeply moving, whenever a shadow moves over the bright boyish face—the reminder that he is the head of a family, must support it, and at all times is responsible for it."

### ELISABETH

On November 23, 1997, in Frankfurt at the anniversay of *100 Years of Thomas Mann at S. Fischer* she stated that she finally wanted to confront the rumor passing around in recent years that she had had bad parents. Her father had on the contrary been loving. A pianist, journalist, political scientist, ocean biologist: Elisabeth Mann-Borgese is a highly talented woman. "Dear little child" her father still calls her in his old age, in the few letters to her that are accessible, and signs with "Your Herr Papale." He was very dear to her. "Baked little Elisabeth sand-bucket cakes in the garden" (diary, May 21, 1921). In "Song of the Child" he composed the first literary monument for her, more than in "Disorder and Early Sorrow" and *Mario and the Magician*. His heart belonged to the little girl as soon as she came into the world and caught him with her eyes, "which were sky blue at the time and reflected the bright day." That he "loved her from the first day more than the other four taken together," he wrote to Paul Amann—"I don't know why."

Golo Mann took Elisabeth to Switzerland in 1933. At twenty-one she married the Italian antifascist literary scholar Giuseppe Antonio Borgese, who could have been her own father. He was fifty-seven years old at the time and died at sixty. Two daughters were produced by the marriage. In her numerous books and essays Elisabeth avoids statements about her father. Even when it might have seemed reasonable, in her book *The Ascent of Women* he appears almost never, even though the subject of the book is drawn more than necessary from her own biography. In her vision of the future, which takes up the thoughts of Plato, the men are older and richer in experience than their wives. When they have died or otherwise disappeared, "then the moment has come when the wife matures to masculinity. . . . This woman, now about forty-five years old, has lived her life to the full; she has raised children by the man who loved her, learned what she was given to learn as his pupil. If she is herself now in a position 'to convey wisdom and virtue,' then she quite naturally feels herself drawn to a young woman who 'strives to appropriate these for herself.' She will grow into the role of a man; she will become a man." Elisabeth Mann-Borgese was forty-five when these statements were published. She found more recognition for the protection of oceans than for the continued thought of platonic utopias.*

## MICHAEL

Michael Mann was a remarkable person, uptight and eccentric, brusk and capable of enthusiasm, very talented but dissolute, a little hunchback for whom everything goes wrong, although he wants to make everything good. I met him in 1976 in Zurich. He limped like Quasimodo, in principle never got to the subject, and blustered ringingly on world politics, and in doing so always expressed the opposite opinion just as his brother Golo did. He was one of the first to read his father's diaries, for he was to edit them. He wanted to leave out a lot. "One will have to be very selective: The man knew why he retreated into this form." One colleague asserts that Michael lost himself in the work on the diaries. "These diaries of his father made him insane, killed him." It cannot actually have been as bad as that. Admittedly, he did have to read that his abortion had been considered (September 26, 1918), but the decision of his parents was then nevertheless against it: "I am content, look forward to this new life" (September 30, 1918). There is talk very early on of "alienation, coldness, even aversion" toward the youngest (February 13, 1920); "Mischa wiggled, as usual, a bit idiotically in his chair" (May 3, 1920)—that, too, is not nice. "Bibi's unfortunate way of reacting to any kind of remonstrance. He recognizes no endeavor at quiet and clarifying

---

* Elisabeth died in St. Moritz, Switzerland, on February 8, 2002. (Trans.)

words that could occur cheerfully, rather at once becomes stubborn, impudent, and coarse" (July 10, 1934). But as a musician Michael does impress his father. "I was glad about the perseverance of Bibi's practice, which did not irritate me, since I perceive it as serious work" (June 16, 1933). Accomplishment and composure were demanded, in the Mann house as elsewhere.

The diary entries confirm what already appeared in "Disorder and Early Sorrow" (1925) and what Michael, who had always been annoyed about his portrait as Beisser [Biter], as a consequence clearly had to take at face value. Beisser, it says in the story, emphasizes his four-year-old dignity as a male by his composure and the attempt to give his voice a deep, upright ring. Such masculinity was, however, more aspired to than truly assured in his nature, "for, fostered and born in desolate, disturbed times, he has received a quite unstable and irritable nervous system, suffers severely from the disagreements of life, [321] tends to a violent temper and enraged stamping, to despairing and embittered floods of tears about any trifle. . . . He tends to contrition, thinks he is a great sinner because of his fits of anger, that he will not get to Heaven but into 'Hayell.'" The much more unclear but also much more friendly portrait as Benjamin in the Joseph novels could not comfort Michael. The father, Jacob, has lost Joseph and chooses Benjamin now as a substitute. "He loved the youngest boy by far not as much as Joseph," but nevertheless "he pressed him ardently to himself."

There are also drugs and pills in connection with Michael, not too skimpily. He had a small briefcase with a built-in whiskey bar. He died on New Year's Day in 1977 from an overdose of barbiturates combined with alcohol. "Not everybody knows it was suicide, but it was."* Two days earlier, still in good spirits, he had written me that he wanted to return soon to Germany. His ashes were taken to the Kilchberg family grave.

* Elisabeth in *TLS* in 1994.

# XI. In the Magic Mountain

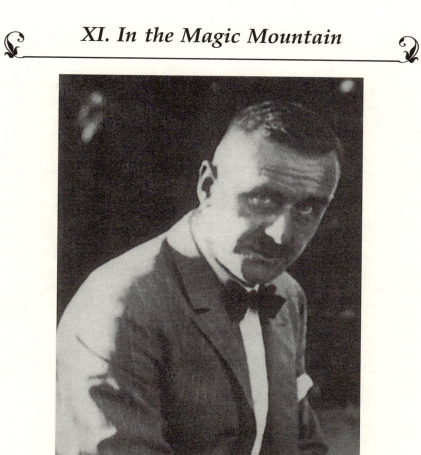

*Munich, around 1925*

*Death in Venice* was not completely finished when Thomas Mann traveled to Davos for a few weeks in 1912 to accompany his wife, who had been prescribed a stay lasting from May to September. The idea of letting a play about a mocking satyr follow Gustav von Aschenbach's tragic story of disgrace soon took shape and led to abandoning the *Confessions of Felix Krull, Confidence Man* again—for decades, as it turned out. The first chapters of *The Magic Mountain* came into being from July 1913 to the start of the war. There is a second brief phase of work in the spring of 1915. At the time, the book developed up to the "Hippe" section. But the problems of the years of war were so urgent for the novelist that he first squeezed in the *Reflections of a Nonpolitical Man*, then "A Man and His Dog" and the "Song of the Child" until finally, on April 9, 1919, he again picked up *The Magic Mountain* material and on April 20 again began to write from the beginning, revising everything that had been written already. Interrupted repeatedly by essays, among them "Goethe and Tolstoy" (first version, 1921) and "An Experience in the Occult" (1923), and by trips, the author worked with practiced doggedness on the weaving of the carpet of his thousand-page novel until the end of September 1924. At the end of November the novel was on the market and at once found an overwhelmingly positive echo.

## WE PHANTOMS ALONG THE PATH

THE TONE, too, reveals something. Until shortly before the conclusion of the novel it is mocking and playful, ironic and supercilious. The narrator is outside. What happens to his hero does not rankle him. But when the war comes, all irony ceases. The tone is now stricken and alarmed, somber to the point of being rhapsodic. "O shame on our phantom safety," the narrator exclaims. Now when it gets serious, he wants to be involved. Like Thomas Mann himself, he is ashamed that he is not a soldier. He had never before cried, not for seven long years, but now when his hero is in the war, he dabs at the corner of his eyes tenderly with his fingertip. He leaves his ironic sofa and makes his way to the arena. The dabbing is a gesture of Settembrini, whose eyes likewise have become moist at the farewell from Hans Castorp.

The sofa is not for us either. We are only timid phantoms along the path. Our perspective is obliquely from below. We look upward to Thomas Mann as the latter does to his Hans Castorp when he must go off to war with a horde of feverish boys. We hold our breath when the dead regain the use of their tongues. They speak freer than when they still lingered in the light and experienced pain. Narrated pain is no longer pain felt. It is bodiless like all that is transparent, like an X ray, and cooled down as art. Even what is tragic now occasionally offers amusement. The dead do not mind.

But storytelling, how much easier that is than living and suffering! O shame on our phantom safety! It is not we who had to endure this life full of torment and brilliance. Safe ourselves, we are know-it-alls and dogmatic like all descendants who associate with the dead. We really do know many things better; we are often right. But we are only tolerated in Hades. We are not permitted to censor the soul whose flight we accompany, remembering. The dead are free. What could we still charge them with? One should not chide and crush others, says the nonpolitical observer, just oneself! Thomas Mann is held to be a Narcissus, but self-criticism was not foreign to him. "Was there ever anyone who had the goblin of creativity breathing down his neck," he wonders with anxious pride, "a joyful fellowman?" He is today mostly considered cold and haughty, using people, masked and repressed—a fascinating monster! From the standpoint of the shades, that is the bickering of opposing parties. Whether every Tom, Dick, and Harry liked you is null and void from the perspective of eternity. In the world of the dead *Tout comprendre c'est tout pardonner* is valid. Or even as Tommy held forth to his school friend in youthful haughtiness: *Comprendre c'est sourire, Monsieur!* In German (in the same passage): "Anyone can scold, my friend. It is truly more fitting for a psychologist to *understand*, to *clarify*. Making a judgment is *always* evidence of the lack of understanding and of psychological inadequacy."

As a human being, Thomas Mann was sealed and let no one look into his heart. With masterly discipline he maintained a façade without which he would have found life unbearable. He was free only in his work; only there did he communicate, also his secrets, protected by the indiscreet discretion of art. The biography of his heart stands spellbound in his writings. Sometimes what he really experienced can be identified beyond doubt in what he writes, sometimes only made plausible without being provable. The boundary between fiction and fact should, of course, remain visible but is occasionally transgressed in the realization that the realms of life that, as is their nature, leave no documents behind, require an interpretation most imperatively.

## THE PYRAMID

*The Magic Mountain* is a degenerate book. It resembles a triangle stood on its head. Every chapter is longer than the one before. The last one is even an extravagance. It could not have ended other than with a thunderclap. It would never have stopped otherwise.

A life form vanishes when it is told to its end. An artist dies when he has used up his stuff of life. When the novel *The Magic Mountain* is finished, Mann is just short of his fiftieth birthday. He has already clearly passed the midpoint of his years. The life drawing to an end is gradually consumed by work. The great late works must get by with ever less life material. Therefore more and more language material is gathered.

Mann made much out of scant experience. The most important impressions occur during his childhood, youth, and the early years of manhood. A description of this life must therefore be broad at the bottom. The foundation of the pyramid is extensive. Every new level is a bit shallower. There is less and less inner material to be told, no matter how much language material the writer can pile up, no matter how many events the great story may shower upon him. Unlike the degenerate *Magic Mountain*, which would like to flow into a stagnant endlessness, toward the end the sand in a biography runs ever faster through the narrows, and the upper layers are erected faster than the lower.

The seed of *The Magic Mountain* is the Williram Timpe story. It was already told in the description of his years in school. Now we miss it. The process is the same with *Joseph and His Brothers* and with *Doctor Faustus*, insofar as they treat the Paul Ehrenberg story. What we report biographically in the following about *The Magic Mountain* are only crumbs of life. The reader knows the primal odds and ends already.

## THE DRIFT NET

The plot is quickly told. The Hamburg merchant's son Hans Castorp wants to take a recuperative vacation before beginning his engineering studies. He therefore travels to his tubercular cousin Joachim Ziemssen in a mountaintop sanatorium in Davos for a three-week visit. The world of the sanatorium catches him in its spell. He falls in love with Clawdia Chauchat, converses with Naphta and Settembrini, and admires Mynheer Peeperkorn. The three weeks turn into seven years. Only the outbreak of war in 1914 abruptly transfers the young man back to the lowlands. Only when he is a soldier, lost in the turmoil of battle, do we lose sight of him.

For this bit of plot Thomas Mann uses a thousand pages. When in 1925 Ida Herz catalogued Thomas Mann's working library, she was amazed at the enormous moraines of material that the work on *The Magic Mountain* had deposited. They remained behind in 1933 on Poschingerstraße, were lost, and can only tediously and incompletely be reconstructed. What can be assembled from the diaries, notebooks, letters, and sources of research gives a fairly fuzzy picture. Medical, biological, psychoanalytical, philosophical, theological, and political material, partly from serious, partly from obscure writings, was used. Sometimes Mann did thorough research, but very often he was satisfied with material he just happened upon. When he had a project in mind, he could use everything. He went through his world like a drift net in which everything useful was caught. Not diligence alone is Mann's secret, but this power of appropriation.

Why did Thomas Mann need this immense mass of material? Up to this point there had already been studies, historical for *Fiorenza*, economic for *Royal Highness*, mythological for *Death in Venice*, but certainly not to this extent. Did he no longer get ideas? To a certain degee that is right. The more one's own life is exhausted as a source, the more important do other sources become. When the self has been told to the end, expansion is required. In great measure it takes up the experience of others. Of course, that has no weight of its own but is subjected to the matrix of world experience that has always already imprinted the perception.

That is how the use of the leitmotif also functions. Because the language material that has been found has no weight of its own, it serves only as a confirmation of a net of references. That Grandfather Castorp wears a stiff collar is not interesting as a fact but as a leitmotif; in the face of death, threatened by a trembling of the chin, one needs such a collar. The less expanse of text each grain of biographical seed lays claim to, the more room is filled by what is acquired by reading; the more space the work with the leitmotif makes use of that assigns the pieces thus acquired their place, the greater as a result does the demand of art also become. Of course, Thomas Mann still speaks of his primal odds and ends, but in a more conciliatory fashion. The art of relating an enormous quantity of material to a tiny kernel of what was experienced becomes greater and greater. Laughter, smoking, the fever thermometer, and the X-ray image: Nothing escapes this gaze that puts the world in order; everything affirms something or other and negates something else.

The kernel of the matter, that a Hamburg patrician's son is exposed to the ordeal of death and Eros is, of course, primal odds and ends. But there is only a little of autobiography in the details. The middle-class heritage has already been utilized in *Buddenbrooks*, the engagement period in *Royal Highness*, the homoeroticism in *Death in Venice*. For *The Magic Mountain* not enough was left over, but not so much was necessary either. That Hans Castorp was held over the same baptismal font as Thomas Mann, that he preferred his butter in the form of small grooved balls, that he had been brought up well, had learned to sit up straight, not chew his fingernails, and not slam doors, all of that he has from his author—also that he is heir to a fortune of 400,000 marks. But he grows up motherless, without the element that creates the artist. He is schooled only about clothing and food, has no artistic power of creation. Unlike his author, he graduates from a high school. He studies engineering—about which Thomas Mann understood nothing—in Danzig, Braunschweig, and Karlsruhe, not Thomas Mann cities. He is not simply another ego of the author's. It is similar with the fellow residents of the enchanted mountain. Heinrich Mann provides a little background for Settembrini, civilization's literary man, but the character in essence is not experienced but constructed and assembled out of a collection of material, as is the Jewish-Communist Jesuit Leo Naphta to a still higher degree. Mynheer Peeperkorn does receive a few traits of Gerhart Hauptmann, but they do not go deep. There was no biographically significant model for Clawdia Chauchat, in spite of a certain dancer with slanting eyes and in spite of a marginal recollection of Katia, who is said not to have been unfamiliar with the vice of chewing fingernails. Only the retrograde connections of the beautiful Russian woman to Williram Timpe are important. The Timpe experience of the high school student Thomas Mann is the most significant autobiographical element in the novel. But it is included with great restraint. It would not have filled a thousand pages.

It was originally conceived as a comical idea that not a highly developed artist as in *Death in Venice* but a mediocre engineering student should be exposed to love and death. Hans Castorp's resistance is slight. "He tried to find out what it would be like if you sat slumped at table, sat there with a slumping back, and he found out that it meant a great relief for the pelvic muscles." Since he is lazy, he is gladly receptive to death, and willingly and adventurously to love. Only war "liberates" him—only then to really beleaguer him. What began as a humorous story of seduction ends as a catastrophe. In the war Eros and the death wish arrive at their actual goal of the prurient and horrible dissolution of the individual in sludge and mud. The novel is a powerful fantasy of the removal of limits, full of delight at the flight from composure and middle-class form but also full of horror at it. In its innermost core the wounds of unresolved homosexuality fester. Like Thomas Mann in the Paul Ehrenberg era, Hans Castorp whispers shaken: "My God," when Clawdia smiles at him without regard, when he dreamily thinks of her mouth and her cheekbones or of "her eyes, whose color, shape, and position cut into his soul, her slumped back, the way she held her head, the vertebra above the neck of her blouse, her arms radiant in thinnest gauze." She is of a type that we know, long legged and not broad in the hips, with a small and maidenly bosom. Peeperkorn then enthuses about the anti-type, calling life "a spread-eagled woman, with breasts swelling close together and a large, soft abdominal surface between inviting hips."

## BONELESS

There is nothing innocuous in this novel. Everything points some-where. Joachim Ziemssen learns Russian. It could not have been Ital-ian, for Russian is a code word—it stands for all kinds of allurements. The sick woman is named Marusya, the lovely Russian woman with the worm-eaten breast who cannot control her laughter. Russian is described as a soft and vague, as though boneless, language. The motif of "boneless" builds a bridge to the boneless coughing of the stuffed shirt, "a coughing entirely without zest and love, that took place not in real bursts but sounded only like a horrible, feeble wal-lowing in the brew of organic dissolution." Regarding it, Hans Cas-torp remarks: "It's just as though you could see inside the person, what it looks like there—everything sludge and mud." It is the truth that Castorp sees there. Inside, the human being is full of sludge. Bones hold the sludge together. Form and beauty are only thin husks and beloved illusion.

Next door lives a Russian married couple. Hans Castorp hears sounds from that room, "a wrestling, giggling, and panting, the shocking es-sence of which could not long remain hidden to the young man, al-though at first, out of his good nature, he tried to interpret it harm-lessly." A "respectable obfuscation" of his expression is the result, "just as though he could and wanted to know nothing about what he was hearing there."

But it is always the same—what cannot be repressed catches up with him. The obfuscation does not stand firm, despite all his respect-ability. It is present again on his countenance when he sits in the X-ray lab where before him Clawdia Chauchat, the Russian lady with the round shoulders whom he loves, is being X-rayed. The X-ray view inside, into the moist web of flesh, against which the bones con-trast sharply, is unseemly, and Hans Castorp at first turns his head aside, again with "a respectable obfuscation of his expression." But only his head. His soft parts are hopelessly lost to the Kirghizian eyes.

The X-ray picture points symbolically at love and death. At death, because it shows the skeleton, but also at love, because the look at sludge and mud is attractive only to the lover who wants to merge, expire, and dissolve at the cost of composure and form. Hans Castorp should thus embrace and press the X-ray machine to his breast as though he associated sensations of happiness with it—thus the advice of the doctor.

## THE MOST SENSUOUS THING I EVER DID

"The MgcMtn is the most sensuous thing that I shall ever write, but in a cool style" (diary, March 12, 1920). The most sensuous? This Hans Castorp has a phallus made of plaster, mocks Robert Musil. Over seven long years he is destined for only one night of love, and we learn about it only from puzzling allusions, such as that he has given back a pencil and gotten something in return. Returning it is supposed to have been carried out in the simplest ways.

In one single passage Thomas Mann has gone a bit farther, in that conversation in French in which Hans Castorp declares his love for Clawdia. "Je t'aime," he babbles, kneeling before her, his head back, continuing to speak with closed eyes. For a whole page Hans Castorp celebrates the human body, not a specific one, not even a specific female or male one, rather the body in itself. French is a hiding place in which Thomas Mann permits details that he has allowed himself nowhere else so bunched up in German. Hymnically Hans praises the backbone, the shoulder blades the way they stand out under the skin of the back, the navel in the soft belly, the blossoming nipples, the blood vessels, the dark sex between the thighs. He enthuses about the armpits, the hollows of the knees, and about the fresh double splendor of the buttocks. "Quelle fête immense de les caresser ces endroits délicieux du corps humain!" What an immeasureable feast, to caress these delectable zones of the human body—"Fête à mourir sans plainte après." Afterward, he wants to die without a complaint.

"But in a cool style." The sentimentality is muffled by the medical, half-scholarly attitude that Hans Castorp has assumed in the conversation with Councilor Behrens and in the chapter "Researches." It

gives the scene a grotesquely comical touch. "Laisse-moi toucher dé-
votement de ma bouche l'arteria femoralis"—Let me kiss the artery in
your leg. Hans also praises the peach fuzz on the skin and the lymph
nodes, which Behrens had told him were located principally "in the
throat, the armpits, the elbow joints, the hollows of the knees, and in
other similar intimate and tender places of the body." The erotic fascination is broken by the abhorrence that the illusionless scientific
look at the body produces. Observed minutely, life is repugnant. For
example, the heart of the matter, procreation: "No contortion and no
ridiculous sham could be imaginable that nature would not seriously
have liked as a variation on this regular process." With purity in
mind, the all-too-close relationship to the bestial offended spiritual
people. The human embryo, thickened fetal slime, insulted humanity;
misshapen it cowered in the womb, "bent over, with a tail not distinguished in any way from that of a pig, with an enormous belly stump
and stubby, formless extremities, the larva of the face bowed over the
swollen belly." Its development seems that of a science whose idea of
truth is unflattering and dismal, as a repetition of the zoological history of the species.

That Mann does not considerately omit the physical is one of the
basic experiences of reading *The Magic Mountain*. Consequently, many
put the book down prematurely. Personally, Mann did not have a
good relationship with blood, flesh, mucus, and secretions, of which a
human being actually consists. As a spiritual man he stood on the
side of the angel who enlightens the fair Joseph in an unmistakable
way about the inner horrors of all flesh:

> I do not say that even just this skin and husk would be most
> appetizing, with its seething pores and sweaty hairs; but scratch
> it only a little, and the salty broth emerges heinously red, and
> farther inside it becomes more and more horrible and is nothing
> but entrails and stench.

Thomas Mann does not want to suppress this knowledge. He is a
Schopenhauerian in this regard. In the section "Snow" he lets his
Hans Castorp dream about the human center, which never can be
only spirit and reason. They exist only "in the quiet gaze at the com-
munion." Only someone who knows the abysses of the flesh can set
foot on the swaying bridge that the spirit builds across them. That is
not a real reconciliation of spirit and body, at the most a difficult armi-

stice. To casually become friends with stench and entrails was not something for our Mann.

## SMOKING

Why does a human being smoke? Out of pleasure and love for death. All his life Thomas Mann smoked cigarettes and cigars. Even as a schoolboy he imagines himself with a Bostanjoglo between his lips, and a few weeks before his death the *Lübecker Nachrichten* reports that he "as always" smokes one cigarette after the other. That was, in the reporter's opinion, "his only lack of restraint." Twelve cigarettes and two mild cigars a day were the rule. Thomas Mann was so well known as a smoker that in 1925 the Hagedorn & Sons firm thought it worthy of consideration to produce a cigar with the name *Thomas Mann*.

Smoking is oppositional. It means doing something irrational against the ingrained rationality of middle-class society. It is the drug of those who are ready to go along with the middle-class game but need permitted compensations to endure it. Thomas Buddenbrook is addicted to small, acrid Russian cigarettes; "he smoked them in slews and had the bad habit of inhaling the smoke deep into his lungs so that he slowly spewed it forth again while talking." He is well aware of the ruinous nature of this activity, but his power of resistance fails him. The doctor prohibits cigarettes for him, but he is far from depriving himself of the numbing pleasure in the desperate realization that things are going downhill for him.

After a meal Hans Castorp smokes a (naturally) Russian cigarette, then a cigar called Maria Mancini. He does not like bourgeois work because it "was something in the way of the unclouded enjoyment of the Maria Mancini." If you have a good cigar, in his opinion, "then you are really secure, literally nothing can happen to you. It's exactly like when you lie on the seashore—then you are just lying on the seashore, aren't you, and you don't need anything more, neither work nor conversation." The ocean is a metaphysical sphere, symbol of infinity, of the dissolution of space and time. Time is an illusion; the true being of things, as it says in the section "Beach Stroll," is an enduring Now. "Had the doctor who first had this thought been walking along the ocean—the weak bitterness of eternity on his lips?" Anyone who lies on the seashore tastes eternity. Smoking is a religious act, a surrender of the self, a dissolution of materiality, self-enchantment, floating into infinity. Smoking is spiritualization. Poetic visions form in smoke. "While writing, I smoke." *Buddenbrooks* came into being "in the fumes of uncounted 3-Centesimi cigarettes." The Mann children smelled the spirit of the Magician in the aroma of cigars in his study.

Opposition, unbourgeois laziness, stupor, religion—the only thing lacking to complete the series of unbourgeois powers is sexuality. Maria Mancini is, so to speak, a woman. A youthful beloved of Ludwig XIV had that name. "What kind of brown beauty is that?" Hans Castorp is asked by Councilor Behrens. The cigar is provided with all kinds of sexual associations. To light up one after another, "that exceeds the power of a man," Behrens chatters and contributes the anecdote about how two small Henry Clays once almost put him in his grave. That had been jolly, although he had been afraid. "But fear and festivity don't rule one another out after all, anyone knows that. The urchin who is about to have a girl for the first time is also afraid, and she is, too, and at the same time they both just melt with pleasure. Well, I would likewise almost melt; I would dance away with heaving chest."

Paul Ehrenberg is a nonsmoker; to be exact, he does smoke sometimes, but actually only for the sake of expressing his well-being; "in reality he resists it somewhat." "Life" does not smoke; only decadence does. Also the storm of vitality that is Mynheer Peeperkorn does not smoke, unlike Frau Chauchat, who lets the smoke bubble from her mouth while she is talking, like Thomas Buddenbrook and, furthermore, also the magician Cipola. "He ejected the deeply inhaled smoke—arrogantly grimacing, both lips drawn back, softly tapping with his foot—as a gray spray between his defectively eroded, pointed teeth." They all live at the abyss, these people, but they have sympathy for the abyss.

## KINGS KNOW NO IRONY

Who is the main man of the Weimar Republic? Thomas Mann or Gerhart Hauptmann (Hauptmann = main man)? Who is the official representative of Goethe on earth? In spite of everything he had to show, Thomas Mann must have had feelings of inferiority. That Hauptmann had nominated him for the Nobel Prize did not improve the matter. Thomas Mann did not want to be grateful to him for anything, him particularly. When Hauptmann wanted to use the familiar term of address with him (as Peeperkorn does with Hans Castorp), it was a matter of somehow getting out of the snare.

Gerhart Hauptmann could feel like a kind of king of the Republic because of his socially committed early works, and Thomas Mann made his obeisance to him in this sense. All the others—Brecht, Musil, Döblin, Hesse, Rilke, George, Hofmannsthal, Tucholsky, Kästner—shrink to dwarfs next to Hauptmann, like Naphta and Settembrini next to Peeperkorn. Of course, the latter is not a man of words but of great gestures; of course, he never speaks a sentence to its end, but he does not have to either; finally, he has a majestic head with a flame of white hair and mighty brow lines. In short, he is a king. And he thus stands outside and above bourgeois society. A king cannot ride in an elevator. He is not an intellectual. "Kings know no irony." An ironist cannot become a king.

Thomas Mann knows that irony is not enough, when it comes down to it. Irony is not the pinnacle. It can undermine greatness, but it itself is not great. Thomas Mann looks for the grand feeling, but at the same time nothing makes him laugh so much. He just longs for opportunities for emotion that are not commonplace. He depicts the death of Rachel in the Joseph novel, the echoes in *Faustus*, and is proud when he can outwit the verdict of sentimentality and the tears flow. Also in *The Magic Mountain*, the most profoundly ironic work by Thomas Mann, the narrator is ashamed of his security at the end, sacrifices irony, and makes way for a gloomy sentimentality. "Will love one day rise even from this world festival of death, even from the evil fervor of fever that ignites the rainy evening sky all around?" But he always had a bad conscience about such sentences.

Peeperkorn is both homage and caricature. Only when Gerhart Hauptmann said yes to Hitler did Thomas Mann lose his anxiety about the competition. He now knew: Where I am, Germany is also. Not where Hauptmann was. Thomas Mann became the emperor of emigration. But Hauptmann had abdicated when he remained in the Reich and hoisted the swastika. Now everything was clear. "I hate this sham whom I helped glorify & who grandiosely rejects martyrdom for himself, for which I know I am not born either, but to which my spiritual dignity perforce calls me" (diary, May 9, 1933).

## THINGS MOST QUESTIONABLE

An embarrassing chapter follows. We do not understand it; we do not
approve of it. It is difficult to imagine, but the elegant, bourgeois
Thomas Mann sneaked off surreptitiously to occult séances, again and
again in the dark tightly gripped the hand of a medium, stared again
and again at a red light where, for example, there hovered an absurd
handkerchief that was led through the room by a clawlike ghostly
hand. His relationships with parapsychology reach much deeper than
might be assumed at first glance. If only they had been related to
usefulness in his work, to get a few atmospheric aids for *The Magic
Mountain*! But he wanted more, looked in all seriousness for the work-
ings of unknown powers. Even the first *Notebook*, written in 1894 in
Munich, contains a remark favoring the occult. Also the tale "The
Wardrobe" (written in 1898) is in many regards an "Essay on Clairvoyance," to quote Schopenhauer, a source who for his part regarded
clairvoyance, somnambulism, telepathy, and similar phenomena as
testimonials of "practical metaphysics," as empirical proof of his philosophy, in which Thomas Mann readily follows him. In November of
1900 Kurt Martens asks him to attend a séance. Martens reports on it
later in his *Unsparing Life Chronicle*: "I had an opportunity to receive a
private demonstration of her spiritualistic phenomena by the much-
discussed 'flower medium' Anna Rothe. Thomas Mann was the first
whom I invited, but he resisted for reasons that probably were only
excuses." To Martens's report, which describes Anna Rothe as a
fraud, Thomas Mann replies in a manner that clearly makes the wish
known that practical metaphyics might be sound: "Your report about
the séance really made me sad! Was the fraud really so blatant? Then
I'm almost glad I was not present." One must resign oneself to the
fact that Mann's relationship to this sphere over the years is almost
that of a believer. But in 1901 Anna Rothe was charged with fraud
and in 1902 convicted.

The address of the best known parapsychologist of his time, Baron
Albert von Schrenck-Notzing (1862–1929), is found already in 1899 in
the third *Notebook*. However, at that time Mann probably had Schrenck
as a "specialist for neuroses" and "sex pathologist" in mind. Tormented by forbidden longings, Mann is interested in a therapeutic

treatment with which he could have reversed his sexual tendencies. Of course, Schrenck at an early time had already conducted parapsychological studies, but he was famous for something else. Several essays by him treat "contrary sexual feelings." His most important book from this time has the title *Therapeutic Suggestion in Psychopathia Sexualis.* He (at times with Sigmund Freud) had conducted hypnosis studies in Nancy and Paris and in the nineties was considered a specialist in homosexuality. His biographer, Josef Peter, reports: "He managed to combat pathological disturbances of sexual desire (especially the contrary sexual feelings) successfully through hypnotic-suggestion therapy and thereby to introduce a new procedure that attracted numerous patients."

Only later was Schrenck talked about as a parapsychologist. In the years 1909 until 1913 he mainly carried out experiments that then were described and documented with photographs in his sensational book *Phenomena of Materialization: A Contribution to the Investigation of Mediumistic Teleplastics.* A loud and derisive discussion erupted. "Protests hail down from the official world of scholars," Thomas Mann writes about it, "against so much confusion, credulity, dilettantism, and fraud. The public . . . held its sides with laughter. And really, the book puts our seriousness to the test, through its text as well as through its accompanying illustrations, which seem grotesque, fantastic, and silly." But the author of *The Magic Mountain* did not belong among the mockers. All his life, in questions of occultism, he had stood "theoretically pretty far to the 'left'"—where by "right" he understands rigidly conservative denial, but by "left" a radical, revolutionary frame of mind that considers the most various things possible. He writes explicitly to Schrenck "that for me there is no longer a shadow of a doubt regarding the reality, the occult genuineness of phenomena."

War came, and with it "undreamed-of upheavals and adventures," so that the second edition of the *Phenomena of Materialization,* which appeared in 1923, found a completely changed atmosphere. "One has had to accept so much that was unimagined, bear such gross things patiently that even now the indignation that one strives to summon up lacks the fitting energy." The war has made people eager to accept the world of the occult. Occult experiences can be had in the tempest of steel. In the *Reflections of a Nonpolitical Man* Thomas Mann describes the condition of a soldier faced with the overwhelming power of death as one free and released, his aspect that of "one intoxicated and in ecstasy." Thus not by chance is it the soldier and warrior Joachim Ziemssen who is conjured up at the séance in *The Magic Mountain.*

A peculiar act is ascribed to Ziemssen at the hour of his death. He moved his right hand repeatedly

> down along the blanket in the region of his hip while raising it a bit on its way back and then with a scraping, raking motion moved it again toward himself, as though he were pulling and gathering something.

The medium Ellen Brand makes the same movement while waking from her trance:

> For a few minutes she moved her hollow hand in the area of her hip back and forth—moved her hand away and with a scooping or raking motion moved it to herself again, just as though she were pulling and gathering something.

The essay "An Experience in the Occult" supplies the explanation that testifies to where Thomas Mann got the gesture, namely, from his experience with the medium Willi Sch.:

> Before turning on the light, they gave the medium time to come to. He took whimsical precautions, consisting of scraping motions of his hand and arm on his flank, movements that, at least in his imagination, serve to pull back the organic powers dispatched but not yet reaching manifestation.

The dying Joachim likewise draws in those powers that in his life did not reach manifestation. Dying is an awakening, the return from a dream. Living is the transmission of ideas that become corporeal forms. The ideoplast retracts his incarnate ideas in dying. In death he will be omnitemporal and omnipresent, free of the limits of space and time. That was actually what Thomas Mann probably expected from the occult.

He knew himself. A diary entry of January 12, 1919, mentions Schrenck's presence at a supper. "I felt and probably expressed the wish to take part in a séance," it says in "An Experience in the Occult," "In the evening at the séance of the Hungarian telepath X" (diary, January 27, 1919). "The experiments, which excited me at first, completely convincing and remarkable." His daughter Monika affirms that he went to such gatherings twice a week. It can be shown that Thomas Mann visited gatherings with Schrenck on December 20, 1922, as well as on January 6 and 23, 1923. He wrote three reports about them, which, with numerous other credulous statements (among them, those by Ludwig Klages and Alfred Schuler), appeared in a collection edited by Schrenck in 1924. For the essay "An Experience in the Occult" he summed up the three sessions in just one. Although the essay is also undeniably the work of a fascinated man, Thomas Mann kept himself somewhat more obscured here, with all kinds of rhetorical displays and with the help of a veil of irony that makes it possible to take the matter seriously or not.

The entire prehistory flows into the chapter "Things Most Questionable" in *The Magic Mountain*. There, at the end, Hans Castorp turns on the light with an energetic hand. The session breaks up with a shock. Mann experienced a similar action with Schrenck but had not done it himself. "In spite of all the host's warnings ahead of time, a skeptical participant suddenly turned the full beam of a flashlight on the medium. He gave a jerk and twisted, froth on his mouth, with convulsive spasms." By turning on the light, Hans Castorp takes on the role of the skeptic, which subsequently Thomas Mann would probably also like to have played. But he had in no way stepped outside this remarkable spell. The conclusion of the essay goes through all kinds of contortions around the question about whether to go to Schrenck again or not. "No, I will not go again to Herr von Schrenck-Notzig. . . . But I will tentatively go to Herr von Schrenck-Notzig, one or two times, two or three times, not more often. . . . I also do not want to go there two or three times, but just one more time, and then never again. . . ." But even that was not the last of it. A letter written on April 21, 1925, to Josef Ponten hints at continuations: "Schrenck was through for this evening, as I had expected from my own latest experiences. The sessions will be resumed again in ca. three months."

The next perceptible trace of interest in the occult is found in the tale *Mario and the Magician* (1930). The hypnotist Cipolla also occupies himself with, among other things, "'magnetic' transference," that is, with long-distance effects in the style of Schrenck, in which "the directive goes out on an unexplored path, from organism to organism." The narrator remarks, somewhat distantly but still self-consciously, that each one had "taken his small, curiously scornful and head-shaking look into the ambiguously unclean and tangled character of the occult, which in the human nature of its bearers is also always inclined annoyingly to mix humbug and a bit of helpful trickery without this having an impact on the authenticity of other parts of the questionable admixture."

So there are ghosts in the literary works again and again: the eerie gondolier in *Death in Venice*, the man on the field in the *Joseph* novels, the apparition of Goethe in the carriage at the end of *The Beloved Returns*, and the Devil in *Doctor Faustus*. This apparition in the twilight refers back to the man dozing on the corner of the sofa whom Thomas Mann once noticed in Palestrina and first gave to his Christian Buddenbrook. Perhaps a writer must be able to see ghosts; perhaps imagination cannot be had without a tendency to hallucination.

In the development of the "Three Reports about Occult Sessions" (written in December 1922–January 1923, each time on the day following each session) through the essay "An Experience in the Occult" (written in January–February 1923) to the section "Things Most Questionable" (written ca. August 1924), what was really experienced fades more and more while what was fictional increases. The reports of the sessions are basically records with only a small addition of interpretation. "An Experience in the Occult" is an essay that makes one session out of the three, that composes, compromises, and typifies the experience as well as provides it with an abundance of theoretical contemplations. "Most Questionable" integrates "An Experience in the Occult" into a forty-page chapter that begins with theory, advances with the appearance of the medium Ellen Brand and a scenic description of her curious abilities, to the conspirative moving of glasses, whereupon a dressing down by Settembrini lets the opposite view have a word: "On the spot he declared little Elly to be a cunning swindler." From then on, Hans Castorp remains obediently at a distance, which is why he has the following spiritualistic experiments only at third hand, and those are the very ones that Thomas Mann personally experienced, the elevation of the handkerchief, for example, and other phenomena of materialization that are elucidated by Schrenckian theories. Only as a last part does the conjuration of the dead Joachim Ziemssen follow, an event that goes far beyond what was personally experienced and also is not reconcilable with Schrenck's theories, insofar as these distinguish carefully between occultism and spiritualism and consider the spritualists charlatans. But the entire preparation for the conjuration is again pure biography—the arrangement of the experiment, the darkness, how the chain is formed, especially how Hans Castorp must constrain and monitor the medium.

The occasion gained something mystical, it states in the first of the three reports, only through the struggling and laboring of the medium, who throws herself back and forth jerkily, whispering, panting quickly and moaning, a condition and activity that is reminiscent "noticeably, unambiguously, and decisively of the act of giving birth." "The sexual impact is so unmistakable that I am not surprised to hear afterward that erections and even ejaculations of sperm, which at times are said to be precipitated, accompany the psychophysical work of the young person." The sperm vanishes in the essay and the novel, probably in conformity with the thought that the procedure can be either an act of giving birth or a sexual act, but not both at the same time. But the motif of giving birth is strengthened and summarized: "A male hour of labor in reddish darkness, with chatter, diddle-dum music, and merry cheers!"

"Things Most Questionable" once more goes farther and in addition underpins the motif of birth to his own life as a father. "We men," he says with a reference to the difficult birth of his daughter Erika,

> if we do not shun what is human, know from one circumstance this unbearable compassion . . . this outraged "Enough!" . . . It is surely clear that we speak about our roles as husbands and fathers, about the act of giving birth that Elly's struggling actually resembled so unambiguously and unmistakably, that even someone who was not yet familiar with it, like young Hans Castorp, who, since even he had not shunned life, thus became acquainted with this act full of organic mysticism in such a shape—in what a shape! . . . It could not be described as anything but scandalous, the characteristics and details of this animated labor room in the red light as well as the virginal person of the one in labor in her flowing nightgown and with her small bare arms, as also concerning the further conditions, the constant easygoing gramophone music, the artificial chatter. . . . And we by no means exclude here the person and position of the "husband"—if we may

observe Hans Castorp, who has after all expressed the wish, as
the proper husband—thus the husband who holds the knees of
the "mother" between his own, her hands in his.

Out of Willi Sch., the medium in labor, and the male labor room in the
essay, there became here a family constellation with father, mother,
and child, in which the "mother" is the medium Ellen Brand, the
"father" Hans Castorp, and the "child" Joachim Ziemssen. Decisively
new, of course, is that in *The Magic Mountain* Mann makes the medium a young woman, while in his time with Schrenck he had
gripped the hands of a young man and held them between his knees
for many hours. "The erotic in 'pedagogical matters,'" he notes upon
rereading the scene in his old age, "finally appearing fairly clearly."

A wedding has to precede a proper birth. Elly is asked whether
she would make a deceased person visible today. In answer to the
question, she whispers, "close to Hans Castorp's ear a hot 'Yes!'" The
result is emotion and shock in Hans Castorp, "born out of confusion,
out of the deceptive circumstances, namely, that a young person
whose hands he was holding had breathed a 'yes' into his ear."

The actually foolish occultism with its moving tables and its elevation of handkerchiefs ran into relationships with the biographical, historical, and philosophical basic problems of his life, with homosexuality, with his marriage to Katia, and with the birth of Erika, with
war, with death, and with a philosophy of life. He acquires a great
burden. From Willi to Elly—that reflects Mann's own path. It reflects
his problems with marriage and fatherhood, his feeling that everything is not quite in order, his horror at propagation, birth, and death.
While as a human being he courageously admits these horrors, his
Hans distances himself from them. He does not want to rely on the
warrior that he propagated and gave birth to with Elly. He turns on
the light.

## FROM LIFE TO HIS WORK

The path from what was experienced in *The Magic Mountain*, from life
to his work, is complicated. In general it involves a double process of
veiling and revealing. Revealing, in that there is talk in the novel
about Timpe and Schrenck although, viewed traditionally, embarrass-

ing, not exactly publicly suitable themes are involved, which is a sign of a deep-seated wish to talk about them for that very reason. The novel offers the possibility of expressing something tabooed that obviously cannot otherwise be talked about. It feels good to break the forced silence, to lose one's self-control, and to reveal oneself.

The revealing is possible only because the novel form permits a veiling. Veiling is the accomplishment of art. Because what was experienced has become a part of a composition, it is no longer imputed by the reader to the individual Thomas Mann. The order of art comes out of the chaos of life. The order of life requires invasions into what has been experienced. Thus the thirteen-year-old Hippe is made out of the fifteen-year-old Timpe, the whole story removed from one reality into the preliminary stage of another one and imbedded into the structure of a leitmotif, in which the reader no longer perceives the "Kirghizian eyes" as a personal experience of the author but as a part of the Russian-Asian motif complex. But there is a kind of double optics involved. We can imagine how Thomas Mann, believing wrongly that his secret is safe, knowingly smiled at the thoughts of the unsuspecting reader of the Hippe episode. But we also see that the reader of today, since he shares this knowledge, does not say, a little disillusioned: Oh, yes, it involves that Timpe of those days, but admires the subtlety with which the unpretentious life is raised to a noble work. "It is surely good," says the narrator of *Death in Venice*, "that the world knows only the beautiful work, not its origins too, not the requirements of its coming into being, for the knowledge of the sources from which inspiration flows to the artist would often alienate the world and in doing so suspend the effects of what is admirable." With regard to the latter, Thomas Mann was wrong. Knowledge of sources does not necessarily alienate, rather also makes it possible for emotion and compassion to intensify. Today Thomas Mann no longer need hide.

*Munich, 1929*

In June 1922 Thomas Mann reconciles with his brother Heinrich. His turn toward the Republic is prepared in the following months and becomes public with the lecture "The German Republic" (October 1922). The echo in the press is lively, postive in the large newspapers, scornful in the sheets on the Left. However, on his reading tours in the following days, along with many readings from his literary works, mostly "Goethe and Tolstoy" and "An Experience in the Occult" are on the program, not the speech about the Republic. In the twenties and early thirties Thomas Mann makes public appearances extraordinarily often, also in other European countries. His world fame grows and with *The Magic Mountain* in 1924 and the award of the Nobel Prize in 1929 reaches its high point. He becomes a member of the P.E.N. Club, later also the Rotary Club. Not only as a writer but also as a journalist, he is constantly present. In 1922 the volume of essays *An Accounting* appears, in 1925 *Efforts*, in 1930 *The Order of the Day*. The great essay "Goethe and Tolstoy" is extensively revised in 1925. Income in dollars from his "German Letters"—eight reports on German intellectual life written for an American magazine—helps him survive the inflation of 1922–23 financially. His fiftieth birthday on June 6, 1925, is celebrated officially in the Munich town hall with the lord mayor and numerous dignitaries.

In January 1926 Thomas Mann travels as a kind of unofficial German cultural ambassador to Paris and documents this sojourn serving international understanding in the report "Parisian Accounting." In June of the same year he gives the keynote address at the celebration of the seven-hundredth anniversary of the city of Lübeck, *Lübeck as a Way of Life and Thought*. The Senate honors him with the title of professor. The pupil who once failed three times had thus become distinguished academically after the College of Liberal Arts at the University of Bonn had already awarded him an honorary doctorate in 1919. As a member of the founding committee Thomas Mann also participates foremost in the establishment of a section for literature in the Prussian Academy of Arts (put into effect in November 1926). His place on this panel represents the leftists. His quarrels with the German nationalists and the National Socialists increase, beginning with "Culture and Socialism" (1927), a rectification in the face of accusations that he had belatedly accommodated the *Reflections of a Nonpolitical Man* to the democratic spirit of the time. More and more all of his journalistic writing is subordinated to the political battle of the day, his "Lessing" (1929), the lecture

"Freud's Position in the History of Modern Thought" (1929), by implication also the Goethe lectures of 1932 ("Goethe As Representative of the Bourgeois Age," "Goethe's Career as a Man of Letters"). His most prominent political appearance is his "German Address," which was read in October 1930 in Berlin, with disturbances by rightist-oriented rioters. His "Speech to Workers in Vienna" (1932) and the "Avowal of Socialism" (January–February 1933) also serve the unmistakable struggle against National Socialism. His involuntary emigration in February 1933 cuts Thomas Mann off abruptly from the organs of publication and possibilities of appearance available to him up to that time, so that his political thought, with few exceptions, must withdraw to the world of the diary for a while.

## THE RECONCILIATION WITH HEINRICH AND
## THE SHIFT TO THE REPUBLIC

WE SAW in an earlier passage that Thomas Mann, in spite of all his Bolshivistic and national-conservative dreams, in practice was a loyal republican right after the end of the war. He loved his Germany also as a republic and also in its misfortune. "Holland is a country worth seeing," he writes to Ernst Bertram on November 4, 1922, "but basically I'm glad to be in Germany again: All the satiety and orderliness gets on my nerves." Besides, as a fatalist of history he clung to the existing power. But now the standing power was the Republic, and so from this viewpoint it is also not entirely surprising that Thomas Mann in 1922 also publicly avows it. "As though the 'Republic' were not still the German Reich," he writes on July 8, 1922, to Bertram. The "shift" in this respect does not go so deep and is not an inexplicable breach in the life of the nonpolitical observer.

But before what was a matter of fact anyway could become public, the relationship with his brother had to be set in order. The threat of death paved the way. Thomas did not want his brother to die unreconciled. Death is a great force; it is more important than opinions. The details can be taken from a letter to Ernst Bertram of February 2, 1922:

My brother (in a higher sense I have, after all, only one; the other [Viktor] is a good fellow, with whom no enmity would be possible) fell seriously ill a few days ago: flu, appendicitis, and peritonitis, operation for bronchial catarrh, which led to fear of lung complications. There was also risk of danger to the heart, and for three or four days the situation was very serious. You can imagine that everyone was agitated. My wife visited his. He was told of my sympathy, my daily inquiries, and I was told about the pleasure that he showed about them. That pleasure is said to have reached its high point when, as soon as such a thing could do no harm, I sent him flowers and a few lines: These had been difficult days, but now we were out of the woods and would walk easier—together, if in his heart he felt as I did. He sent his gratitude and now—whatever our opinions—we wanted "never to lose one another again."

And that is also what happened then. The warlike condition that had lasted between the brothers for almost eight years was ended with a cease fire without there having been a clarification about the controversial points. That was also somewhat painful. Could they be seen together after such a loud and long struggle over principles? Especially in regard to Bertram, his standby during wartime, Thomas Mann had to defend and explain himself. The reconciliation with Heinrich meant a certain embarrassment, which is recognizable in a few exaggerated sentimental phrases in the letter ("how time forged me into a man"). The letter continues:

> Joyfully moved, even adventurously shaken as I am, I have no illusions about the tenderness and difficulty of our newly revived relationship. A modus vivendi of a humanly decent sort will be all that can result. Actual friendship is hardly conceivable. The monuments of our breach continue—besides, I am assured that he never read the "Reflections." That is good—and also not good, for he thus knows nothing of all I have gone through. My heart turns over when I hear that, after reading some sentences in the *Berliner Tageblatt*, in which I talk about people who spread the love of God and hate their brother, he sat down and cried. But I was left no time for tears by the years-long battle for life and property that had to be conducted in a state of physical undernourishment. Concerning this, and how time forged me into a man, how I grew doing that and also became a helper and leader of others—he knows nothing of all that. Maybe he will somehow feel it when we come together again. He is still not allowed to see anyone.
>
> He is said to have become mellower and kinder during these years. Impossible that his views have not undergone any sort of revision. Perhaps there can after all be talk about a certain development toward one another: I feel so good when I remember that my really dominant thought at the time is that of a new, personal fulfillment of the idea of humanity—contrary in any event to the humanitarian world of Rousseau. I will speak about that at the end of the month in the Frankfurt Opera House before "The Magic Flute," on the occasion of "Goethe Week," about which you will have read. It will be official. The president has agreed to participate.

"It will be official": You can see again that even before his expressed avowal to it, Thomas Mann was a figurehead for this republic. President Friedrich Ebert also appeared then as was planned. Thomas Mann, who in the diaries from 1918 to 1921 as a rule gave him positive marks, already knows Ebert personally. At any rate, quite incidentally in a letter of February 19, 1922, he writes that he will see him that evening in the club. Ebert was also present when on February 28 Mann gave a festive speech during the Frankfurt Goethe Week on "Goethe and Tolstoy."

## THE VANQUISHER OF THE ROMANTIC

His reflections continued with some delay. Thomas Mann did not simply jump resolutely into a tradition that was alien to him. He did not simply defect to Heinrich's banners, did not simply quote its authorities—Frenchmen, apostles of culture, democrats. To remain at one with himself, he sought models from his own tradition. Therefore the lecture "On the German Republic" takes its argumentative setting in the armory of the "conservative revolution." There they had celebrated the war enthusiasm of 1914 as the hour of national rebirth. Mann tries to channel this enthusiasm into the republican cause. According to Mann the year 1914, the hour of honor and enthused, self-sacrificial breakup, not 1918, had been the hour of the birth of the Republic. The Republic was to found the "Third Reich" of religious humanitarianism. Mann speaks for the new nation strictly as a conservative. Hans Blüher's idea of a state-building power of homoeroticism is referred to, Nietzsche's "amor fati" is summoned up, Stefan George is bestirred, and repeatedly the Romantic Novalis—none of them democrats.

For the rest of his life Mann was convinced of the moral necessity for his lecture on the Republic, but he harbored with justification only a low opinion of its aesthetic and theoretical quality. He admits frankly in "Culture and Socialism" (1927) that, taken as a literary work, the *Reflections* was far more valid than this paternal encouragement for the Republic. He still does not quite believe in what he says and tries to elude his better judgment with a lot of rhetorical hullaballoo. He is, first of all, only rationally a republican whose deeper sympathies basically continue to belong to the powers of the past.

But in the course of time he finds a more workable model for his conversion than Novalis, Blüher, and George could offer. "No meta-morphosis of the mind," it says already at the end of his acknowledg-ment of the Republic, "is more familiar to us than one whose begin-ning rests in sympathy with death, whose end in a decision for life." He is familiar with this metamorphosis from Friedrich Nietzsche. Per-haps the lecture on the Republic would have been more successful, if it had been planned as a lecture on Nietzsche, for Nietzsche offers Thomas Mann the ideal prefigurative model of the switch. The deter-mining model is Nietzsche's alienation from Richard Wagner. In 1929 Mann asserts that the intellectual-political controversies of the present were no more than journalistic adaptations of the Nietzschean battle against Wagner. The new era that was about to come into existence, the fresh-baked republican Thomas Mann writes, unites "the hero-ically most admirable event and performance of German intellectual history with the self-conquest of the Romantic in Nietzsche and through him." Thomas Mann, too, feels himself to be such a con-queror; in himself he has conquered the love for death, for the past, for the unpolitical authoritarian state. The model of Nietzsche helped him to avoid considering a sudden change of mind or betrayal or self-betrayal to be the correct expressions for the turnaround. "Also Nietz-sche's great, representative self-conquest of the so-called alienation from Wagner, appeared to be betrayal," but in reality he was not Judas but John, who "has become an evangelist of a new union of earth and mankind."

> He was, like Wagner—from whom he parted with his judgment of conscience but whom he loved until his death—from his intel-lectual heritage a late son of Romanticism. But that Wagner was a mighty, successful self-glorifier and self-completer, while Nietz-sche on the contrary was a revolutionary self-conqueror, is the reason that the former remained the last glorifier and infinitely enchanting completer of an epoch, but the latter has become a visionary and leader into a new human future.
>   This he is to us: a friend of life, a visionary of higher humanity, a leader into the future, a teacher of the conquest of all that is in us that opposes life and the future, that is, of what is Romantic. For what is Romantic is the song of homesickness for the past, the song of the enchantment of death; and the Richard Wagner

phenomenon, which Nietzsche loved so infinitely and which his ruling intellect had to conquer, was no more than the paradoxical and eternally riveting phenomenon of the world-conquering intoxication of death.

The conservative revolutionaries also wanted to build the future on Nietzsche, as did the National Socialists. The intellectual republicanism of Thomas Mann has the effect of new wine in old wineskins, not entirely inspiring confidence and easily changeable into its opposite. There are many passages that arouse misgivings. Democracy was in a certain sense after all more of a hindrance, Thomas Mann admitted frivolously in Paris in 1926. "What Europe needs today would be an enlightened dictatorship." Now as before he would prefer not to take sides. He was too free to preach—that he wrote in 1906, and he wrote it still in 1952 when he called the role of an intinerant preacher of democracy comical. Taking sides was unhistoric, only righteousness was historic, as he lets his Professor Cornelius ponder.

## TRILLION-DOLLAR EGGS

The conservative sense of history professor Cornelius is put to a hard test by the inflation, which shatters everyone economically and morally. Of course, for his children it is great fun to go to the store under various assumed names—where five six-thousand-mark eggs are sold per household per week—in order to obtain at least twenty eggs for the family, but morally they suffer damage because very early they learn that in such a world it depends only upon a cleverly staged appearance and not on what is real. "Who in his old days could now deal with trillions and quadrillions, when before he had bargained with thalers and florins and face-value marks, and then with Bismarck's highly stable Reich's marks?" This is the question Thomas Mann asks in 1942 in his "Memories of the German Inflation." He himself had great losses. His father's fortune melted into nothing, his own savings also; the war bonds came back as worthless paper; of the Pringsheim wealth of millions only the art treasures remained (his father-in-law joked that he lived from wall to mouth). Thomas Mann was also cheated beyond that:

During the war I had put 10,000 marks into a friend's country home, where I enjoyed being a guest, and which belonged to me, too, so to speak. . . . In the spring of 1923 it happened that this friend informed me that circumstances had forced him to sell his house, and here were my 10,000 marks back: yes, he added with a smile, they were the same I had helped him with in 1917; they had meanwhile stayed completely untouched in his safe. There I stood, somewhat incredulous, somewhat embarrassed, not yet quite understanding, with the clean, almost new, nicely engraved museum pieces in my hand.

His friend was Georg Martin Richter. He sold his house in December 1923 for two trillion marks.

Thomas Mann was able to cope with that. He owned a house, had a punctually paying publisher, in addition income of foreign currency. Others fared much worse. "I still remember the proud, helpless face with which our old nursemaid assured us one day that she wanted to retire soon and live on her savings." She had a few thousand marks in the bank. For that she couldn't buy even one egg. Those are crimes that brand you. Later Thomas Mann perceives it precisely:

A straight path runs from the insanity of the German inflation to the insanity of the Third Reich. Just as the Germans saw their monetary units swell to millions, billions, and trillions and then burst, they later saw their nation swell to the Reich of all Germans, to lebensraum, to European order, to world dominion, and will also still see it burst. The market woman who in a dull tone asked a "hundred billion" for an egg had at the time forgotten how to be amazed; and nothing since was so insane and horrible that she could be amazed at it. It was during the inflation that the Germans forgot to rely on themselves as individuals and learned to expect everything from "politics," from the "state," from "destiny." They grew accustomed to seeing life as a wild adventure whose end depended not on their own work but on unknown, evil powers. Out of the millions of deceived workers and thrifty savers of that time actually there came the "masses" with which Dr. Goebbels then had to deal. Inflation is a spectacle that makes everyone cynical, hard-hearted, and indifferent. Robbed of everything, the Germans became a nation of robbers.

## THE FIGHT AGAINST FASCISM

But that is wisdom in hindsight. At the time, in the twenties, almost
no one knew in what direction the development was going. If you
consider the nebulous intellectuality of talk about the Republic, then
it is most surprising that serious political consequences grew out of
such a hot-air balloon. The year 1922 means only a relatively small
revision in comparison with what is still to come, the extended,
tough, and merciless battle against political irrationalism and National Socialism. From October 1922 until January 1933 the Mann bibliography by Georg Potempa lists 375 journalistic contributions, some
of them in numerous printings. Hardly one of them is without a political reference; the literary writings as well are almost always in the
service of the great intellectual battles. Whatever his heart might say
about it, Thomas Mann in these years becomes the decisive defendant
of the Weimar democracy.

"Too late and too little" was the opinion of a judgment once put
forward with enormous presumption and frequently repeated concerning Thomas Mann's political talk. Too late: Who else among the
writers in Germany really battled fascism publicly so early, beginning
in 1921, then after 1923 with increasing frequency and stringent consequences? Too little: Who else otherwise really took a position
against the National Socialists so often, so visibly, and so loudly? Perhaps Heinrich Mann or Kurt Tucholsky can be mentioned—in any
case there is enough antifascist honor left over. Before 1933 there is
comparatively little anti-Hitler agitation by the great antipode Bertolt
Brecht. The remaining unpolitical matters in the discussions of Thomas
Mann may be stressed: economics and power politics that was slightly
grounded, the unmistakable conservative bedrock—even then it still
remains that the political path of this writer is completely astonishing
and noteworthy during the twenties. Anyone who represented positions like Thomas Mann did in the First World War and afterward
ended up usually as a National Socialist, as did many of his companions, such as Ernst Bertram, Hans Pfitzner, Josef Ponten, and Alfred
Baeumler.

Not Thomas Mann. If in 1921 he had sought a "third path" between
Rome and Moscow, between Enlightenment and Orientalism, between West and East, then he announced his resolute approach to-

ward the West in the essay "Germany and Democracy" in 1925. Service to life was today service to democracy. German "fascismus" (as Thomas Mann usually wrote it at the time) is an obscurantist relapse, "romantic barbarism." In this text even Nietzsche is counted among the democrats, though not without effort. It was only a superficial implausibility that the spirit of Nietzsche could form the ideological foundation of a German democracy. "Is it not he," asks Mann, "who declared democracy a prerequisite for a new nobility?" and is not he "the prophet of a new union of the earth and humanity?" Those are admittedly eccentric paths.

But such vague pronouncements do not continue. More and more frequently Thomas Mann also involves himself in the wholly concrete day-to-day politics. With the call "Rescue Democracy!" in 1925, after the death of Friedrich Ebert, he turns against the election of Paul von Hindenburg, whom he calls a "warrior from prehistoric times." Still, to say that, he had to take leave of his own earlier sympathies. That Hindenburg, a great man of the German mold, deserved to become the chancellor of the Reich was still to be found in the *Reflections of a Nonpolitical Man*. Mann asserted in a letter to Paul Amann that the exemplary leader Hindenburg, "this great stalwart and provider," was still something exclusively German.

So it was a matter of bidding farewell to all that. Mann, in a letter to Julius Bab of April 23, 1925, construes the candidacy of the erstwhile supreme commander of the German army as a "linden tree," taking up a passage from *The Magic Mountain*, therefore as sympathetic with death. Voters for Hindenburg missed the antecedent self-conquest of Romanticism by Nietzsche and Thomas Mann.

But when in the spring of 1932 Hindenburg ran with the support of the middle-leftist parties during the next election for president, Thomas Mann is said to have publicly supported the reelection of the "warrior from prehistoric times." He was asked whether he wanted to give a campaign speech for Hindenburg. He did decline, but people on the side of the Nazis claimed that he belonged to the circles that had gathered in zealous loud-voiced promotion of the reelection of the hoary field marshal, and they maliciously printed copies of his anti-Hindenburg petition of 1925 and exclaimed scornfully about the reputed "snobbishly cold haughtiness" of the "excessively overrated literary man." The explanation is nevertheless simple. In comparison with Hitler, Hindenburg had seemed the lesser evil at the time.

Regarding further concrete political involvements, there can be mentioned petitions and polemic pamphlets against the death penality, against the conviction of the communist editor Fritz Rau, against the rightist *Berliner Nachtausgabe*, against the conviction of Carl von Ossietsky, and also for "Red Aid," the organization of prisoners, for Ernst Toller and an amnesty of the leaders of the Bavarian soviet republic still in jail, as well as for the founding of a section for literature in the Prussian Academy of Arts. Several times Mann pleaded for the "Reichsbanner Black-Red-Gold," an organization tending to be social-democratic and republican that opposed the nationalistic defense associations of the type of the "Stahlhelm" (a veterans organization). In the final years of the Republic Mann's stance became increasingly social democratic. The "German Address" (Berlin 1930) put it straightforwardly: "That the political stand of German citizens is today on the side of social democracy." He signed a "Call to Vote to the Party of Non-Voters" (September 1930). In October 1932 he gave a prosocialistic speech to workers in Vienna and at the beginning of January 1933 wrote a programmatic "Avowal to Socialism," which on February 19, 1933, when Hitler was already Reich's chancellor, was read aloud by the Prussian minister of culture Adolf Grimme, and, shortly before the elimination of opposition by the press, it had a lively echo in the press in Germany.

At the same time there were always polemical skirmishes aimed directly at the NSDAP, the Nazi Party. "What We Must Demand" (1932) challenges the Papen government to go on the offensive more resolutely against Nazi acts of terror. "Victory of German Prudence" is a call to vote in the election of the Prussian legislature on April 24, 1932, and contains passages that here, representative of many others, may illustrate the unmistakable clarity and severity of Mann's antifascist positions:

> For that reason I despise the dreary amalgamation that calls itself "National Socialism," this falsification of renewal, which, brainless and aimless confusion in itself, will never be able to create anything but confusion and misfortune, this miserable mixture of bad-tempered, old-fashioned minds and the hullabaloo of the masses, prostrating itself before Germanistic school superintendents as though before a "people's movement," while it is incomparably a fraud against the people and a spoiler of youth without equal that covers itself in revolution with a tissue of lies.

That National Socialism allows the petit-bourgeois type of person, who in truth is the prisoner of the past, the possibility of feeling himself a "revolutionary" is in fact one of its chief powers of attraction. Another is its dissolute generosity in making empty promises that gives every, I mean every, kind of dissatisfaction, just and unjust, its due with big words—the most ignoble vote-getting that has ever been attempted. Power at any price, in any way, with any help: that is its "idea"—the power to lead Germany back to the concept that, in dark stupidity, it has of itself. Its love for the German people is hate—green-eyed hate, avidly waiting for its hour, for three quarters of this very people who do not want, as it does, domination by this cudgel-bearing party that is not even a party, rather a mishmash of the most heterogeneous aspirations, needs, desires, and other idealisms.

No free man, no German, who relies on the great intellectual traditions of his people, could breathe even a day in this thralldom—and, furthermore, his breath would be taken away from him, for he would be killed. The lust for murder is written on the brow of this "people's movement," and we must prevent its fairy-tale soul from finding an opportunity to operate. And at the same time we must prevent the furious resistance that its domination would inescapably provoke, a civil war that would almost unfailingly bring about the collapse of the Reich. What is important is to gain time: time for the young German democracy to consolidate, to purify itself, to develop into a truly societal community, time for Europe to emerge from misery into rationality, to decide against the past and, without bloody catastrophes, to find its way from one age into another, into a new way of life. Time, finally, for so-called National Socialism to dissolve into its thousands of fiendish elements and, no longer nourished and favored by misfortune, to return to its native oblivion.

## SEVEN REASONS FOR THE ASTONISHING POLITICIZATION OF THOMAS MANN

How did this massive engagement come about? Would it not have been much more comfortable, after the reconciliation with Heinrich, for him to dedicate himself to his literary work and no longer bother so much about politics?

The narrator of the Joseph novels mentions seven reasons for Joseph's chastity. One of them, the fifth, is his respect for his father Jacob, who loathes the matriarchal mystery. Respect for his father is also the foundation for Thomas Mann's seven reasons. Politics belongs to the world of the father. His father was a senator, a man with public responsibility, and the son wants to be the same.

That corresponds, secondly, as in the Joseph novel, to the resistance to backsliding into matriarchy, that is, into the precivilized stage of animal sacrifice and Baal cultism in place of the developed humanism of monotheism. Fascism seems to Thomas Mann to be such a relapse. The battle that he has had to wage in small details and within himself is repeated in large matters and outside himself. He transfers problematics of his biography to political events. As he had learned to raise the bulwark of the middle class against his own inner perils through bonds with his mother and his incest wish, bohemianism, and homosexuality, so all of Germany should act.

Thirdly, that can also be transferred into what is political inasmuch as his political views, corresponding to the nocturnal realm of the mother, thus his love for the past, for what was nonpolitical, and for the irrational, were only too well known to the author of the *Reflections*. The battle against fascism is the battle against his own fascination through political obscurantism against the political consequences of flirting with death.

The fourth reason may have been company he would have come into contact with without his transformation. He was already fairly bored with Bertram and Ponten and Pfitzner; he had turned away from Spengler; and what otherwise was dashing about on the side of the right horrified him more and more. Cultural barbarity manifestly threatened to come into being through fascism. While in his "Thoughts in Wartime" he had still represented the viewpoint that culture could also "include oracles, magic, pederasty, bugaboos, human sacrifices, orgiastic cults, inquisition, autos-da-fé, Saint Vitus' dance, witch trials, a flourishing of murders by poison, and the most colorful atrocities," whenever such barbarism with a cultural appeal approached him concretely, he reacted simply as a citizen who demanded a state based on law and civilized forms of association. He did not minimize the cultic, cultural foundation of Nazi atrocities.

So much the less when the republican change of 1922 had stirred up the antirepublican dregs and the "chthonic rabble" had badgered him very personally. His opponents quickened the imagination of

Thomas Mann. After all, he was also a great polemicist. His battle against the Left had been sounded in the *Reflections*. Meanwhile, it appeared that the sharp blade could also be used effectively against the Right. Combativeness, polemicism as art, his aggressive joy with words, that struck home—that is the fifth reason.

The sixth: Opponents give one a feeling of identity. They help anyone who does not really know what he is for to know what he is against. The politically unsteady aesthete is stablized by the antifascist battle. Much later Thomas Mann will say that the years of his battle against Hitler had been a morally good period, for it was clear at the time what was good and what was not. In 1921 pure relativism had been dominant. What is good, what is evil? the writer asked at the time. We are just drawing lines in water. "But all things are good as well as bad—God has made them so, and perhaps mankind necessarily goes astray because there is no right way for him at all?" But when it was a matter of going against Hitler, the one who had drawn lines in the water had no doubt about being on the right path.

The Weimar Republic honored his engagement—this is the seventh reason—with high-ranking invitations. It offered him, more than the empire had ever done, the role of cultural representative. This role had to be filled. I was born to be far more a representative than a martyr, said Thomas Mann, when he embraced exile. He was very bitter about being driven from the country and losing the role of Praeceptor Germaniae. In his heart he never gave up that place. Defiantly he will declare in 1938 when stepping upon American soil: Where I am, Germany is.

## JOHST, HÜBSCHER, AND PILOT ROGUES

"I love you very much," Thomas Mann had written to Hanns Johst on September 16, 1920. "You stand for youth, daring, radicalism, the strongest present time." The sentimentality was bound to subside. At first the Expressionist Johst supported the circles of the conservative revolution and then more and more resolutely shifted over to the side of Hitler. His most important forum before 1933 was the "Battle Union for German Culture," a kind of culturally veneered Storm Troopers (SA). In the Nazi period Johst had a rapidly rising career as president of the Reich's Literature Chamber and as an SS major general.

Thomas Mann's shift to the Republic provoked an angry rejection by Johst that defended right-radical youths: "The sword is as sacred to us as your fountain pen is to you and your sort." From then on Johst is usually to be found among the Munich opponents to Mann. When Thomas Mann let the impudent statement slip out that the German people inclined to see the ideal of womanhood in the cow and of manhood in brawlers, Johst defends those ruffians; they had been the people's most vital men, without them neither Potsdam nor Weimar. He repeatedly writes acrimonious articles—"Thomas Mann As Flotsam on the Island of Thirty Coffins" one is called. On October 10, 1933, in a letter to Heinrich Himmler, he finally proposes Mann's incarceration in the Dachau concentration camp.

As can be learned from the diary between September 11 and 20, 1921, thus still before his reconciliation with Heinrich, Thomas Mann had shortened the *Reflections of a Nonpolitical Man* by more than thirty pages for the second edition. The abridgments mainly involved the defusing of the polemics against Heinrich Mann and against Romain Rolland; further, some pages about Germany's conservatism and a few especially flagrant passages about the humanity of war are struck out. The public was made aware of these deletions only much later, so that they had to appear as supplementary alignments of the book with Thomas Mann's new position. The attack came from the young conservative corner, thus from the circle that had been most shocked by Mann's shift; after all he had given them a major work with the *Reflections* that they did not want taken away from them. The Schopenhauer scholar Arthur Hübscher, like Johst at the time still young in years, was nasty in the *Münchener Neueste Nachrichten* on August 23, 1927, saying "that a democratic revision of this most undemocratic book by Thomas Mann should not be foisted off in silence on readers who wished to buy it."

Thomas Mann defended himself and defended the *Reflections*. He defended them in a complicated way. "I renounce your opinions. But your insight remains undeniably correct." Who could understand that? He has turned away from the concept of Volk in the *Reflections* and turned toward socialism—even though "ethically and deliberately, not in accordance with his perhaps romantically death-centered nature." That was far too subtle for a heated-up political atmosphere. Hübscher's view works more plausibly. In the public consciousness he remains the victor. The supposed adaptation of the *Reflections* to the spirit of the age will be charged against Thomas Mann again and again in the following years. It plays a role also in the dossier that the Munich political police had kept on him from the second half of the decade of the twenties on and that later furnished the ammunition for his expatriation and denial of a passport. In this respect it is not merely quarreling in the newspaper features. Johst and Hübscher have something to answer for in the Thomas Mann matter.

Hübscher was at the time the editor of the *Münchener Neuesten Nachrichten,* which was also read daily in the Mann household. In spite of the attacks mentioned, the newspaper had at the same time tried to obtain the collaboration of the famous author. However, he was not to be won over and had written to Hübscher:

> My intelligence and my character resist certain narrow-minded-nesses and malignities. I make no secret of the fact that I want to have nothing to do with people (Munich Univesity professors!) who at Rathenau's murder said: "Bravo, one less!" and that I find the Munich bourgeois press terrible. And since I am writing to you on the very day where our good but misguided city stands on its nationalistic head to honor the two pilot rogues, I also want immediately to admit that this conduct appears to be worse than "Johnny hams it up."

The sentences allude to the two German pilots, Günther von Hühne-feld and Hermann Kohl, who together with the Irishmann Fitzmaur-ice on April 12, 1928, were the first to fly over the Atlantic Ocean from east to west. *Johnny Hams It Up* is a jazz opera by Ernst Krenek, who was not pleased by the response. The fliers were celebrated as national heroes.

Hübscher and his editor colleague Paul Nikolaus Cossmann pub-lished the quotation without authorization in connection with a small documentation of the unfortunate attempt at collaboration. Thomas Mann replied with the polemic "The Pilots, Cossmann, I," which probably correctly decided against Cossmann's assertion that he had to wash himself clean:

> For any child sees, of course, that he published my letters not to wash himself clean (O my God!) but because his well-trained baseness spied a facile expression in one of them that, when it got out, had to set all the German nationalistic press furies after me.

This involved the expression "pilot rogues." For the rightist press it was indeed a welcome opportunity for attacks on Thomas Mann. The resonance of the affair was considerable. The *Völkische Beobachter*, a Nazi newspaper in Berlin, in its edition of August 3, 1928, roundly reviled the "villa owner," "spawner of Klaus Mann," and "friend of the convict Max Hölz" and accused him of pathological vanity. Hanns Johst, too, was again one of the gang. One errs, he wrote, if one assumes humanity, worldly wisdom, and human kindness in regard to Thomas Mann. He existed only "for his own sweet self." Also, in a motion by the National Socialist authorities to revoke the citizenship of Thomas Mann, the "pilot rogues" are cited as proof that Mann lacked any respect for the moral value of a real accomplishment.

Johst, Hübscher, and Cossmann were in themselves only a mosquito bite. However, the texts cited belong to a whole viper's nest of venom that revolved around the reactionary development in Munich. As early as 1923 Thomas Mann had called Munich "the city of Hitler, of the German fascist leader, the city of the swastika." The swastika retaliated in its well- known, hardly squeamish way.

It need not be kept secret, however, that the other side also had its tragedy. The course of the political front does not always follow the antifascist orthodoxy of today. Cossmann, the head of the political editorial staff of the *Münchener Neuesten Nachrichten*, was a Jew. He was oriented to the right, demanded severe judgments in the trials against the Bavarian soviet republic politicians, and in the twenties emphatically championed German nationalistic tendencies. That did not help him. In 1933 he was taken captive by the National Socialists and in 1943 killed in Theresienstadt.

## STORM TROOPERS IN TUXEDOS

Paths lead far to the left and far to the right of Expressionism. Arnolt Bronnen, a talented writer, took both. He began as a successful Expressionistic playwright and was a friend of Bertolt Brecht. A few years later he is found at the side of Joseph Goebbels. Because he was considered a national Bolshevist, Nazi leading lights soon lost interest in him after the seizure of power. Many also thought he was a Jew. Bronnen took the path of a kind of inner emigration. Still later he made a further about-face and spent the last years of his life in the

German Democratic Republic of Ulbricht. His autobiography *Arnolt Bronnen on the Record* appeared in 1954 in the Rowohlt publishing house.

In 1930 Bronnen had written a scornful, murderous review of a play that supported Christian clemency in the infliction of punishment. Thomas Mann felt compelled to engage in a chivalric act. "Christianity," he affirmed, "was and remains a splendid manifestation of the intellectual rebellion of conscience against what is nothing but fatal." He saw the fatal embodied in Bronnen, the "voice of the iron lark," which attacks the "mania of righteousness," because it is nothing but hate of German power in general. "This animal is so impudent and mistrustful," Mann finds relentlessly, speaks about the militarism of scaffold and tomb and about counterfeit bigwigs who with a monocle on their eye flatter power and rasp insults against human decency.

The monocle wearers soon found an opportunity to strike back. We follow his record. On October 17, 1930, Thomas Mann gave his "German Speech" in the Berlin Beethoven Hall to warn the middle class about the National Socialist German Workers Party and win them over to the Socialist Party of Germany. Bronnen found out about it and arranged with a few like-minded comrades, among them Ernst and Friedrich Georg Jünger, to attend the event and right there, as he called it, "to stir up a discussion."

> A few hours before the speech I found out from a telephone call that Goebbels would send twenty SA men to the Beethoven Hall for my support. I was perplexed; I had said nothing to Goebbels about the matter because I gave him no credit for interest in literary celebrities, and I asked the adjutant of the district administrator— he himself was not available—to cancel this unfortunate step. But Count Schimmelmann explained to me that this was a Party order and, besides, the tickets had already been purchased, and tuxedos had already been rented (with deposits) for the twenty SA men.

The Bronnen troop first heats up the atmosphere in the hall with short boos. A mighty "Oho!" causes a brawl, the police intervene, fists and rubber truncheons are swung. "In the expectation of a lot of roughness, I quietly and publicly exchanged my monocle for ordinary, scarcely visible bluish-colored snow goggles—from which later then

came the tale of my disguise with large blue glasses." Bronnen is first
escorted out but then let back into the hall. The affray there had
meanwhile multiplied:

> Everyone was screaming at everyone else, and only twenty-one
> people were quite still: the speaker, Thomas Mann, who stood as
> though lost in the surging waves, and the twenty SA men, who
> were sitting in their rented tuxedos and were afraid of getting
> them messed up, since they had been enjoined with frightful
> threats to take part only intellectually.

But, led by Bruno Walter, who knew his way around, Thomas Mann
left the hall by secret passages and a side exit. "Made halfway unrec-
ognizable with large black glasses," as the incident was depicted in
Walter's memoir, Bronnen had directed the demonstrations. Although
the press reported it differently in part, the SA at the time really protected their tuxedos, and the brawls involved only Bronnen and his
friends.

### ERNST JÜNGER

Among them was also Ernst Jünger. "How could he stand it?" Thomas
Mann asked later. The question makes sense only if he thought Jünger was a cultured man who did not really fit in with his buddies
who surrounded him at the time.

   Also, there is no known word of any significance in print against
Thomas Mann by Ernst Jünger. He did not participate in the riot of
the Bronnen troop, though he quietly approved of it, as Alexander
Mitscherlich, who was also a part of the group, remembers. It almost
seems as though Jünger were giving wide berth to this author, whose
*Death in Venice*, *Reflections of a Nonpolitical Man*, and *Doctor Faustus*
could not have been intellectually far from him, who like him had
gone through the school of Nietzsche and of European decadence,
who like him had tried out nationalism and the conservative revolution. Also in his national revolutionary period, when it went against
Thomas Mann, he pushed others forward. His brother, Friedrich Georg
Jünger, had in 1928 disgorged a few bold statements. "We would be
completely indifferent to Thomas Mann, the exact portrayer of a few
processes of corruption in the human stock, if he had not dared to

come out of his hermetically sealed magic mountain to poke his pen at German nationalism." (Thomas Mann had done that in a polemic "Against the *Berliner 'Nachtausgabe.'*") Like his brother, the young nationalist was proud of the primal experience of his generation: the war. He called it "a fanfare of deep forces that tolerate nothing fragile, nothing dubious, that tidy up with worn-down moralism and open up to humankind a cosmic entrance through all the debris." One would have to have a "club chair in his brain to still rest up today on the phrases of an expired age." With that, impudently and blindly, he means Thomas Mann.

Ernst Jünger's silence is all the more noticeable. In view of the visibility of Thomas Mann and in view of a literary production that lasted eighty years, to which several thousand pages of diaries also belong, when Jünger could have expressed himself irregardless, this requires an explanation. Was it a matter of arrogance, as in the George circle, where one could quote Augustine, Goethe, Kant, or Nietzsche, but—please—not Thomas Mann? Was it a matter of perplexity? Or of the deeper realization that here one stood indeed on the other side as far as opinion was concerned but in essence was yet somehow related? Only at an advanced age does he give a few scattered and hardly productive statements in interviews. During World War II Jünger must occasionally have heard Thomas Mann's radio messages over the BBC. His reaction was negative. He had always been angered whenever yet another German city went up in flames, "and Thomas Mann gives speeches about it." However, Jünger added that he admired Thomas Mann as an extraordinary stylist. "He is one of the few who demonstrated stewardship for the German language." As for the rest, Jünger, unlike most Germans, did not regard emigration as something that separated him from Thomas Mann, rather as something that bound him: "Since he [Thomas Mann] got caught up in this tragic entanglement, I have grown to like him again."

Carl Schmitt saw both of them in the same boat. "Ernst Jünger . . . flotsam of Wilhelminianism; Thomas Mann, too." This statement is taken to the centenarian; he quotes it, discusses it, but, faced with the provocation, does not say a word about Thomas Mann.

Mann, for his part, mostly standing under the influence of Klaus and Erika, let himself be drawn into making sharply acid remarks in letters and diaries—he once calls Jünger "a voluptuary of barbarism"—but restrained himself publicly, probably also because he had not really read anything by Jünger. Occasionally he became aware of secondary literature, as an article about the worker in 1933, when he was reflecting for a while on his Faust project. Could he not have used Jünger magnificently in *Faustus*, among the intellectual precursors of barbarism? Since the Jünger type does not appear, it has the effect again of an omission. When Thomas Mann in the postwar period then for the first time deals with Jünger in a more comprehensive way, although again only because of secondary literature and only in his diary, the result is not hate but inquisitive reflection.

"The two gentlemen probably always kept a distance from one another." Both avoided facing each other. They had a kind of shyness toward one another. Perhaps at times each one found danger exuded by the other. Maybe they were fearful of being called into question. At any rate, neither one ever spoke a conclusive word about the other.

*Kampen on Sylt, 1927*

## A HESITANT COMING OUT

THERE IS, of course, no reason to overestimate the diary entry: "It seems that I'm finally through with females?" (July 25, 1920), since often enough later entries follow it, such as "My relationship with K. very sensual for a few weeks" (October 12, 1921). In the addendum to *Metaphysics and Sexual Love*, Schopenhauer asserts that a pederastic tendency increases at the age at which the ability to sire strong and healthy children declines. "So Nature has arranged it." In order to prevent frail offspring, beyond fifty it allows indifference, even antipathy, toward women to increase so that "the more the power of procreation declines in the man, all the more decisive does his unnatural direction become. —In accord with this, we find pederasty prevailing as a vice of old men."

As a general phenomenon let that be addressed in the usual way. But in reference to Thomas Mann, there are clear hints that his homoerotic interest increased in the 1920s. In reference to the number and clarity of public statements, there is almost a cautious outing. The *Reflections of a Nonpolitical Man* had, of course, loudly proclaimed that to tell *everything* was its purpose, but in all its "Know thyself!" it did not speak of homosexuality. Only in the postwar diary was it clear to Thomas Mann that the *Reflections* were "also" an expression of his sexual inversion (September 17, 1919). The interesting determination had been suggested by his reading of the second volume of Hans Blüher's work *The Role of Eroticism in a Masculine Society*. The first volume, which appeared in 1917 and discussed the "typus inversus," that is, the homosexual type of man, had cited the *Reflections* without naming the author. Eros had been defined as "the affirmation of a human being, regardless of his worth." From Blüher can be gleaned why the passage applied to Thomas Mann, namely, it is no pleasure to have to approve a human being, "irrespective of his worth." Eros is a serious and awesome, a fateful god, not a boy like Amor. To have to single out a human being without regard to worth, "to have to approve a human being unconditionally who perhaps means nothing except for what he is to the other," that is not a game and pastime. Blüher's diagnosis describes the case of Thomas Mann exactly: feeling the object of his love, some handsome young waiter or other, as being unworthy, but nevertheless to be at his mercy. "A man who loves, that is, who is smitten by Eros," Blüher proclaims with grandiose sentimentality, "stands in a hallowed connection that can no longer be turned aside and the idea of which arises from the abysses of human nature. He often stands there, fulfilling his destiny with a bleeding heart." That applies above all to male-male Eros. "The question of worth here almost always destroys the peace of Eros, which is related deeply to the nature of the man."

In a letter of 1920 Mann again comments *ironice* on the Blüher passage from the standpoint of a moralist: "That's a nice affirmation, which 'disregards worth.' Thanks a lot!" That is not comprehensible, if nothing but this text is known. That it in fact made accessible from the sources, in this case from Blüher, what was going on in this life, is one of the most important realizations about the covert way of writing that Thomas Mann uses in regard to homoeroticism. When he avows his use of "double optics," thus a style that is supposed to be comprehensible to the coarsest and the finest, then that also serves as camouflage. There is a sufficiently comprehensible exterior for the coarsest. For the fine and finest, in an extreme case only for himself (for there are certainly enough passages whose covert sense will always remain insoluble), there is a layer of profundity that is meant only for the initiated.

The self-censorship eases in the 1920s. In 1922 in "On the German Republic," Mann writes that society is beginning "to relax the ban of disrepute and calumny that lay on the phenomenon, to regard it more calmly and to talk about its ambiguity in a humane way." Whether inner development of our author plays the main role or general cultural liberalization and sexual emancipation do, in any event, there are from those years, from 1920 until 1933, considerably more public statements on this theme from his pen than in any other period of his life. His reading of Blüher may have helped to ease the stress of suppression, to bring the tabooed area into his consciousness, and to give him a language. Before we consider Mann's public statements, we want first, however, to take a look at the diaries of the years 1918–21 to let what he experienced have a word before we consider what he thought.

## BOYS, 1918–21

If we leave out of consideration casual remarks, such as "Student Trummler, handsome boy" (December 4, 1918) or "On a painting of the Madonna by Ghirlandajo, an extremely charming young saint

captivated me" (December 22, 1918), we come across three relationships worth reporting about. The first, a mini-story, began on December 20, 1918. "I was occupied by an elegant young man with a charmingly silly boyish face, blond, a nice German type, rather delicate,
somewhat reminiscent of Requadt, the sight of whom without question made an impression on me of a sort that I for a long time had not
encountered. . . . I confess readily that an experience could come of
this." "In an adventurous way, I would like to meet the young man
of yesterday again" (December 21, 1918). "Slept excitably as a result
of erotic images in the evening." "Out of weariness, forgot yesterday
to note that the Hermes-like elegant young man who made an impression on me several weeks ago was present at the speech. His face,
along with his slight youthful figure, has from its handsomeness and
foolishness something antique, something 'divine' about it. I don't
know what his name is, & it doesn't matter" (March 30, 1919).

The second case made a deeper impression—young Oswald Kirsten,
a ship-owner's son, who fascinated Mann during a vacation in Glücksburg from July 15 to August 6, 1919. The mood is familiar: the air of
the Baltic, the colors, the smells, the language, the type of person,
everything as back then. "Tonio Kröger, Tonio Kröger. It's always the
same and the stimulation deep. The Kirsten ship-owner's family from
Hamburg, with the two bell-bottomed sons, of whom the one has an
Armin Martens's skull" (July 24, 1919). The memory of Armin Martens, the friend of his youth, who came to life again as Hans Hansen
in *Tonio Kröger*, is immediately extended into a line that leads into the
novel *The Magic Mountain*: "Kirsten = Hans Castorp," it says on the
same day. "I continually watch the Kirstens, who have large proper-
ties here, with affection. Today saw the young people playing ball in
the park" (July 31). On August 1 Thomas Mann becomes more detailed. The passage shows us what Hans Castorp looked like in the
imagination of his creator at the time.

> In the evening we saw the two young Kirsten men helping to get
> a boat into the water. The one who with his blond type reminds
> me of A.M. was afterward with us on the bridge. . . . His legs are
> somewhat bowed, his figure, although slender, tends to square-
> ness, his gait to marinerlike swaying. His blue eyes lie deep and
> close to one another. . . . his nose is turned up without really
> being a snub nose, his complexion somewhat flawed. The color

of his hair and the form of his head are like with A.M., also his physical build reminds me of him. This memory seizes me. Youthful mood and youthful pain.

Like Tonio Kröger, Thomas Mann watches the admired boy dancing. "Among those youths of 'mine,' more delicate and finer than the other, completely the mariner type. While dancing he places his left hand on her waist, not flat but on its side" (August 3). The last entry (August 5) is the most important:

> Several times yesterday I had direct impressions of young Kirsten. He was showing pictures at a neighboring table, where I heard him speak with a fairly deep voice & a strong Hamburg accent, and I could see his hand. Except for his misformed nose, his face is handsome and fine. He seems to have an inclination for isolation and sitting quietly (at the tennis court). If I'm not mistaken, I heard him mention Oswald. He has never looked at me, not even in passing. It appears to me that he avoids it out of discretion. So here then would be the "never growing old" that is to become "closely entwined" with Glücksburg, the obligatory "springtime" that only half—(half?)—unfolds.

So much sentiment for someone whom he obviously has seen from close up for the first time! With its classification as never becoming obsolete, the experience is given a high dignity. It is the dignity of a predecessor, August von Platen, who in Venice experiences a similar suffocated love and immortalized it in a sonnet, to the beginning of which Thomas Mann's diary entry alludes:

> Since where beauty prevails, love prevails
> No one could ever be amazed,
> That I cannot quite be silent, dazed
> At how your love my soul assails.

> I know, for me this feeling never will be old,
> For with Venice it is closely ramified:
> Always from my breast a sigh will glide
> For springtime that will only half unfold.

Glücksburg was Mann's Venice, at least for a few days. The Platen imitator, however, having left and being much occupied, notes self-ironically a short time later: "And, Doctor, don't you even think of

Oswald Kirsten anymore?" (August 12). He had received the honorary doctorate from Bonn University, experienced much excitement,
also "had intercourse with K. (frivolously, with impunity, I hope)"—
anxiety about a new pregnancy lasts quite a while. Oswald Kirsten is
never mentioned again. But shortly after Glücksburg the Hippe episode in *The Magic Mountain* is written (August 15); the O.K. experience probably indirectly benefited it.

The third erotic blunder involves his own son Klaus. He is twelve
when his father for the first time has a suspicion that there was something unusual about the boy. There is still a light in the children's
room:

> It became evident that Eissi lay fantastically exposed on his bed
> in the lighted room. He had no answer to my questions. Adoles-
> cent games or the inclination toward sleep-walking episodes that
> we noticed already in Tegernsee? Perhaps both together. How
> will the boy's life turn out? Someone like me "should" obviously
> not bring children into the world. But this "should" deserves its
> quotation marks. What is alive not only wants itself because it is
> alive but also has wanted itself because it is alive (September 20,
> 1918).

The diary attentively notes the physical signs of growing up (September 19, 1918). "Klaus very charming" (April 20, 1919), it notes occasionally, and "I am glad to have such a handsome boy as a son"
(December 24, 1918). From May to July 1920 primarily, the relationship with his adolescent son had a fond tone. "I was tender with
Erika, whom I found strong, brown, and pretty, and let Klaus note my
affection by petting him and cajoling him into being in good spirits,
even though life 'was not always so easy.' I assume his masculinity
gets to him" (May 25, 1920). From May 27 on, Katia is away for a
treatment in Bad Kohlgrub. "After supper, tender with Eissi" (June
14). "Klaus, to whom recently I feel very drawn. . . ." (June 22). In the
background "conversations about man-to-man eroticism" take place;
a long letter is written to Carl Maria Weber on this topic, while the
diary reveals: "In love with Klaus during these days" (July 5). "Eissi,
who enchants me right now" (July 11). "Delight over Eissi, who in his
bath is terribly handsome. Find it very natural that I am in love with
my son. . . . Eissi lay reading in bed with his brown torso naked,
which disconcerted me" (July 25). "Last night read a world-weary

disjointed novella by Eissi and critiqued it at his bed with endearments, which I believe he enjoyed" (July 27). "I heard noise in the boys' room and surprised Eissi completely naked in front of Golo's bed acting foolish. Strong impression of his premasculine, gleaming body. Disquiet" (October 17, 1920). Of course, the father allowed himself no more than this mute disquiet, and this, too, he finally again forbade himself. The later notations return to paternal virtue and daily routine.

## WEBER, WYNEKEN, WICKERSDORF

On July 4, 1920, during the time he was in love with Klaus, Thomas Mann wrote the long and detailed letter about homoeroticism to Carl Maria Weber. Why him, of all people? Who is Carl Maria Weber anyway? In the diary of July 5, 1920, Thomas Mann calls him by his nom de plume, "Olaf." Even before the First World War, as a student in Bonn, Weber was interested in the author and invited him for readings. In a high school newspaper he writes a laudatory review of *Death in Venice*. All his life he maintains a loose contact in letters with Thomas Mann. The letters preserved, however, are all so unimportant that the single important one stands out all the more. That Weber was a pacifist and an Expressionistic writer puts him politically on the side of the opponents of Thomas Mann at the time. Weber was the friend of one of those opponents, the Expressionistic activist Kurt Hiller. But this opposition obviously concerned only their opinions. "The special erotic disposition," Mann writes to Weber in that great letter, "is in an ideological regard obviously just as indifferent as in an aesthetic and cultural one." In other words: You can be politically and aesthetically inimical but friendly on the basis of a common erotic tendency.

Reform pedagogy builds a further bridge. Weber was a teacher and in 1921 joined the Free School Community of Wickersdorf, founded and directed by Gustav Wyneken. Thomas Mann had also gotten personally acquainted with Wyneken. In general he had good contacts with the state school movement and the school reform movement, but still his children had frequented the boarding schools Hochwaldhausen, Odenwaldschule, and Schloss Salem. Why not the fourth famous address that there was, why not Wickersdorf? For the sake of artistic structure. The children were to be brought up middle class; their tendencies in other directions were to be disciplined as his father had disciplined him. From the confessions of Klaus and Golo we know that in Salem and in the Odenwaldschule things took place in an excessively proper way. In Wickersdorf, on the other hand, the educational values of boy-love of ancient Greece were decidedly preached and carried out in practice. "It is a rare irony," writes the founder roguishly, that our institutions of youth education are still called "Gymnasiums." "Gymnos" means naked, and "gymnasion" are places where they are devoted to the development of the body while naked." Among the pedagogical directors Hermann Lietz, Paul Geheeb, and Gustav Wyneken, the last was the most persistent in this regard. He kept nothing to himself. A boy *ought* to experience the difference regarding the ancient appreciation of youth. He should himself "feel so surrounded, so carried away, so enthusiastic about the love of his beloved director that nothing else in his soul should remember the old arrangement in which the young person is the object and material of the teacher." The physical belongs to that concept. Wyneken admits to having embraced naked boys; however he denies any actions that went beyond that.

As a result, he twice lost his position as director of the school inspired and founded by him, the first time in 1910, the second time at the end of 1920. He replied to the allegations that charge him with indecencies with minors and dependents with the spirited defensive statement "Eros." "Perhaps," he writes self-confidently, "anyone who never loved a fine boy passionately cannot relate to the happiness that 'opened the hearts of the Greeks.' Then may he with modesty and respect stop before one of the sanctuaries closed to him and not consider as degenerates and cripples just those who are equal to *both* wings of Eros."

By way of Willy Seidel, a writer who was a friend of both, Carl Maria Weber had sent to Thomas Mann a small volume of poetry that became the immediate reason for the great letter. The poems—*The Garlanded Silenus, Verses from a Comforting Corner*, the collection was called (Hanover: Steegemann, 1919)—had appeared under the pseudonym "Olaf," which Thomas Mann himself translates into C.M. Weber in his diary of July 5, 1920. They clearly afforded to the trained glance the inference of the homosexual tendencies of its author and thereby may have given the impulse for Mann to confide so openly to a rather more distant than close acquaintance. "I wish," he wrote to him to begin with, "that you had taken part in the conversation that I had recently on a long, extended evening with Willy Seidel and a third artist companion, Kurt Martens, about these things"—a conversation that, according to his diary, took place on July 1, 1920 ("From his autobiography M. read boarding school adventures. Conversations about man-to-man eroticism, during which it got very late")—"for it would be highly undesirable for me if to you—and to others— the impression would remain that I would deny a way of feeling that I respect because almost necessarily—with much more necessity anyway than the 'normal'—it has *spirit*—or, as far as it is amenable to me—and I can say it is that in a hardly tentative way—I would want to repudiate it." That is very convoluted, but in essence clear, "a hardly tentative way" one could translate as "imperative"—that way of feeling is imperatively amenable to him. As a precaution Weber inquired once more, and the reply, still convoluted, but in the final analysis unmistakable, reads:

> "Hardly tentative," that is: almost imperative. You did not understand that and praised me for my empathetic ability. But that's not the way things are: and without a personal emotional adventure, Death in V. would not have come out of the Goethe novella.

The present letter had, somewhat more cryptically but for the expert still clearly enough, explained by *Death in Venice* that the story had a "hymnal origin" and that "a personally lyrical travel experience" was at its base that had made him turn things topsy-turvy through the introduction of the motif of "forbidden love." Then Mann had quoted a passage from the irony chapter of the *Reflections* and concluded: "Tell me whether one can 'betray' oneself better." As traitorous in this way, he classifies the following analysis of the relationship between life and mind: "Therefore there is no union between them, rather only the brief, intoxicating illusion of union and understanding, an eternal tension without ease. . . ." Thomas Mann considers that a typical homoerotic situation. In the continuation of the thought, too, the homoerotic sense of its source is disclosed. The cautious writer says that in the passage quoted from the *Reflections* his experience of the erotic was expressed perfectly. It dealt with the translation of a love poem into something prosaic, the poem whose concluding stanza begins: "Whoever has thought most *profoundly* loves what is most *alive*." The

line comes from the poem "Socrates and Alcibiades" by Friedrich
Hölderlin, which defends a relationship between two men:

"Why do you always, sacred Socrates,
  Court him, this youth? Know you no one greater?
    Why do you turn with love,
      As on gods, your eye on him?"

He who has thought most profoundly, loves what is most alive,
  Understands high youth, he who has experienced the world,
    And the wise men nod
      Often in the end at the beautiful.

This marvelous poem, Mann comments further, contains "the entire
justification of the emotional direction spoken of and the entire explanation for it, which is also mine."

They communicated in a kind of cryptic language that requires
close reading. It was sufficiently accessible to the intiate and like-
disposed. These stuck together by the pressure of taboo, so that during their lives it never came to a public debate about Thomas Mann's
sexual constitution. The secret was preserved, in spite of such confidants as Carl Maria Weber, Kurt Hiller, Kurt Martens, and Willy
Seidel.

## MONSTROUS INDECENCIES

"Yesterday read with disquiet poems by Verlaine, 'Women' and 'Men,'
that the publisher Steegemann sent. Monstrous sexual offences" (diary,
August 11, 1920). *Women* appeared in 1919, *Men* in 1920 in German and
French in a private printing for subscribers published by Paul Steegemann in Hanover. The publisher asked Thomas Mann for a short comment. Astonishingly, the latter assented. But in fact the small faddist
magazine where the comment was to appear folded.

With an effectively neutral title "Letter to an Editor," Thomas Mann,
it is true, speaks about indecencies and salaciousness but avoids any
word that might point to the homosexual nature of these poems, so
that later the text, without exciting any attention, could be printed in
the collection of essays *Speech and Reply*. Anyone could read there that
the indecency of these poems had shocked him, but no one knew the
poems themselves. The word "shock" always comes into play in

Thomas Mann whenever a homoerotic experience threatens to un-
hinge his middle-class security. In this case it involves poems of dras-
tic physicality that at the time appeared entirely hidden and to this
day are almost inaccessible. Paul Verlaine was not prudish. Three (of
nine) stanzas of the initial poem of the volume *Men* may serve as an
example of what Thomas Mann read as "indecent":

> O do not slander, poet; but take thought!
> To lie with woman is both sweet and fresh
> As is to cuddle up to her soft flesh;
> So many times this joy I, too, have sought.

> A splendid nest of love is her behind!
> Kneeling there I put my tongue in play,
> My fingers in another slot essay,
> Like piglets root in, just their food to find.

> Although who would compare you to the male behind,
> Which had by far proved ever more salacious
> Than joyous blooms and beautiousness vivacious
> As the vanquished and enslaved may find.

Hymnically Hans Castorp also lauds the human body, as many years
later Madame Houpflé does the body of handsome Felix. "Hymnically" is, as we know from the letter to Weber, likewise a secret word
for homoerotic emotion, as is "deeply moved," as is the exclamation
"My God!"

## IMPOTENCE

"The Women at the Well," the review written in December 1921 of a
novel by Knut Hamsun, actually does not deal, of course, directly
with homosexuality but still with a related theme, with the unrealized, here not realizable male sexuality.

The irrevocable prohibition of allowing his homoerotic tendency to
be put into sexual pratice was related for Mann to the problem of
impotence. Not being allowed to do something, understood radically,
meant as much as not being able to do something. Hamsun's protagonist Oliver had had to sacrifice his masculinity with the amputation of
a leg. His wife stays with him, but miraculously brings child after

child into the world. He is still able to preserve his secret. "Perhaps he found his modest happiness doing that—in any event he had no other. Was it thus pure art? Nothing but art." These sentences by Hamsun are the painful background of Thomas Mann's restrained conclusion that the novel dealt "with art as a life-sustaining power, with life as art, art as a substitute"—anyway, that was his "benignly ironic idea."

The eunuch, tragicomical because of his damaged masculinity, who in spite of his ridiculousness bears up in front of a large audience, is an identity figure. Thomas Mann's artists are always somehow damaged in their masculinity. The impotent artist is loved pityingly by his wife; that means worshiped and betrayed at the same time. That Thomas Mann was also betrayed by a woman—the autobiographical comparison does not go that far but does go so far as to say that the theme of impotence was a threatening one for him. Tonio Kröger asks whether the artist is a man at all, or does he not resemble far more those papal castrati whose song is touchingly beautiful, however."

## EROS AS A STATESMAN

A homoerotic sanction is also bestowed upon the Republic. The war had strengthened man-to-man eroticism, it says in "On the German Republic"; it formed the secret cement of monarchistic unions, and even the terror from the right alluded to love affairs between friends in antiquity. "Eros as a statesman," he continues, was one of the concepts current in antiquity that even in our days—an allusion to Hans Blüher's *The Role of Eroticism in a Masculine Society*—had been intellectually publicized. Unlike Blüher, however, Mann wants to channel the waters of homoeroticism into the riverbed of democracy. To want to make the monarchistic restoration a matter of Eros was basically nonsense. While in the *Reflections* democracy was held to be feminine, even as effeminate, in the American poet and homosexual Walt Whitman Mann had now found an author who teaches him to understand democracy as a confederation of men. That he thereby excludes women does not occur to him; in this respect he is exposed to contemporary distortions. An "erotically all-embracing democratic ideology" can be found in Whitman, who "through the love for comrades, through the masculine love of comrades" wanted to make the continent indivisible.

## ON MARRIAGE

The essay "Marriage in Transition," later defused with the title "On Marriage," brings all these series of thoughts together. As Thomas Mann writes to his daughter Erika with a wink, it contains "a dispute on principle with homoeroticism, oy oy." The traditional patriarchal structure of the family is caught up in disintegration. An equilibrium between the sexes is being initiated that feminizes the man and masculinizes the woman. The original and natural bisexuality of human beings is coming to light. Again, Mann knew about it from Blüher. Himself with bisexual tendencies, he has a positive attitude toward this process, as a cultural conservative does not judge it to be decadence but a wished-for liberation of a basic situation. In the following he then extends this bisexuality into a theory of marriage and homoeroticism. He is able to adjust it admirably into his well-known antithetical scheme:

| homoeroticism | marriage |
|---|---|
| art | life |
| death | life |
| artistry | bourgeoisie |
| aesthetics | ethics, morality |
| barren, childless | fertile, procreative |
| vagabond, licentious | bourgeois life, fidelity |
| individualistic | social |
| irresponsibility | life obedient |
| pessimism | life willing, conformist |
| orgiastic liberty | commitment, duty |

Death-linked artistry thus grows out of the world of homoeroticism, life-linked civic duty out of the world of marriage. Boy-love, as the writer lets it be explained from the mouth of Madame Houpflé, is *"un amour tragique, irraisonable,* not recognized, not practical, useless for life, and useless for marrige." The grand, Dionysian passion of love that bursts all middle-class bonds is homoerotic. Marriage, on the other hand, is not defined by eroticism but by duty to family. Marriage comes into being therefore from a decision, while homosexual passion bursts in as a sublime event.

## AGAINST PARAGRAPH 175

Concrete political actions actually accrue out of the cautious outing of the decade of the twenties. Already in 1922 Thomas Mann signs a petition originated by the sexual scholar Magnus Hirschfeld for the abolition of paragraph 175 of the Criminal Code that since 1871 had established the culpability for punishment for the practice of homosexuality, that in 1935 was tightened, and that remained in force until 1969. Until recently it remained unknown that Thomas Mann also wrote an appeal that appeared in 1930 in the journal of the homosexual movement, "Community of Our Own." There was nothing personal in it, after all, because Mann, as far as he was concerned, was not disposed to practice the "unnatural indecency." But he unequivocably supports its being permitted:

> To spy out in an ignorant and tactless manner sexual . . . caresses that two grown people exchange with one another, based on an emotional tendency that is as old as the human race . . . and to threaten such "acts" that don't concern anyone in the least, with imprisonment, and thus to set up good days for extortion . . . is a somewhat awkward way of showing sensibility for morality.

The paragraph must go.

## KLAUS HEUSER AND AMPHITRYON

"As far as anyone can judge, that was my last passion—and it was the happiest." That can be read in the diary of September 22, 1933. What is meant is the infatuation then six years past for Klaus Heuser, whom Thomas Mann got acquainted with in August 1927 in Kampen on Sylt when Heuser was a seventeen-year-old. At their farewell Mann gave him a copy of *Buddenbrooks*, "In memory of the weeks we spent together on the ocean." He almost gives himself away in the hotel guestbook. "On this tremulous ocean I lived intensely." After the weeks of vacation, there followed in October 1927 a two-week visit by the young man in the author's house in Munich and there followed some further visits by the infatuated fellow in Dusseldorf. On October 19, 1927, Thomas Mann writes Klaus and Erika, "I call him 'Du,' and at parting pressed him to my heart with his express consent." Mischievously and cryptically he continues: "Eissi [Klaus] is requested to step back and not disturb my circles. I'm already old and famous, and why should the two of you alone sin as a consequence?"' When the youth had departed, Thomas Mann inquired of Golo: "Now are you happy that this young fool is gone?" "The young fool! Is he gone?" Mephisto asks in Goethe's *Faust*. Klaus Heuser plays Gretchen; Thomas Mann plays Faust and Mephisto simultaneously.

The diaries of 1927 have not been preserved. They could have been productive: "Last night read for a long time in my diary of 1927, the time of my passion for the boy Klaus H." (March 21, 1937). Later notations, however, preserve numerous traces of that experience. K.H. belonged to his "gallery" (July 11, 1950), thus to the series of "great" experiences that reach him from Armin Martens and Willri Timpe via Paul Ehrenberg and in 1950 will still take in Franz Westermeier. Correspondingly, the sentimentality and the deep emotion, correspondingly the long aftereffect. On January 24, 1934, the diary records these sentences:

> Last night it got late because of reading the old diary volume of 1927–28, kept at the time of the sojourn of K.H. in our house and my visits to Dusseldorf. I was deeply excited, stirred, and moved by the retrospection of that experience, which seems today to belong to a different, stronger epoch of my life, and that I keep with pride and gratitude because it was the unexpected fulfillment of a longing for life, "happiness" as it says in the Book of Man, even though not customary, and because the memory of it means "Me, too." Generally, it made an impression to see how I thought back in possession of this fulfillment of the earliest one, of A.M. and those who followed him, and felt all of these cases as though included in the late and astonishing fulfillment, reconciled and made good through them.

For the work on the Joseph novel, Mann engrossed himself in sketches from the Paul Ehrenberg time and compared them with the Klaus Heuser time. "I was actualy happy, already at that time, too," he says about P.E., "but twenty years later to a higher degree," and that refers to K.H., "and could really put my arms around what I longed for" (May 6, 1934). Then the following statements:

> The K.H. experience was more mature, more superior, happier. But a feeling of being overwhelmed as certain words declare in the journals from the P.E. time, this "I love you—my God,—I love you!"—an intoxication, as implied in the poem fragment: "O hark, music! —In my ear a tremor of sound wafts blissfully away—" existed only once—as is probably proper—in my life. The early A.M. and W.T. experiences retreat, in contrast, far back to what was childish, and the thing with K.H. was a late happiness with the character of life-friendly fulfillment, but still without the youthful intensity of emotion, the sky-high jubilation, and profound disquiet by that central experience of my heart in my 25 years. So it is probably humanly proper, and because of this normality I feel my life more strongly integrated into the canonical than through marriage and children.

At the time, letters were still being exchanged with K.H.: "Wrote a letter to Klaus Heuser, from whom I received a card in New York" (June 12, 1934). The letters are lost. A year later there is even a reunion (September 21, 1935).

> Then interrupted by the visit of Klaus Heuser, who traveled via Zurich to see me again for 10 minutes. Unchanged or little changed, delicate, still boyish at 24, his eyes the same. Saw a lot in his face and said, "My God!" Remarkably enough that here recently I thought of him, with the gratitude that I also felt again for that time in his presence. He expected that I would kiss him, but I didn't, rather said something affectionate to him before our parting. It went very fast; he had to leave shortly.

Many years later, on February 20, 1942, Thomas Mann again reread what he had experienced:

> Read for a long time in old diaries from the Klaus Heuser time, when I was a happy lover. The nicest and most touching farewell in Munich, when for the first time I took a "leap into a dream" and his temple leaned on mine. Oh well—lived and loved. Black eyes, the tears shed for me, beloved lips that I kissed—it was there, I had it too, I'll be able to tell myself when I die.

*Klaus Heuser, Sumatra, 1938*

September 1954 brought a last reunion, when after an eighteen-year absence Klaus Heuser returned from China. Thomas Mann notes: "Remained unmarried." Erika scoffs: "Since he couldn't have the M. [Magician = Thomas Mann], he preferred to just let it go." How relaxed the tone has become.

In 1986 Karl Werner Böhm had a conversation with Klaus Heuser from which it emerges that the latter as a young man hardly sensed anything of the significance that the writer gave him. He decisively denies kisses or anything at all that went further. "I was certainly, in the most innocent way, friendly and nice to him, but no more than that. That was all I 'granted.'" The two weeks in Munich in October 1927, Thomas Mann wrote to Klaus and Erika in the letter already mentioned, had belonged to the most wonderful times in the life of the seventeen-year-old; he had it in writing from him. Klaus Heuser sees it quite differently, at least in his advanced years. "Sometimes in the afternoon he called me—it can be that I was in the garden with the children—into his study to read aloud to me from what he had just written. And then asked my opinion about it. —Oh, well, it didn't interest me very much. I probably didn't listen properly either. I sat there, on my chair, and had only one thought: just quickly get back out into the garden, to the children." It apparently did not occur to Mann to talk about anything but literature, and so this experience, too, could have confirmed the old, painful dichotomy of mind and life: Mind is wistfully in love with life, but the latter does not need the former. "The secret and almost soundless adventures of life are the greatest," it states in the same letter. In fact, Klaus Heuser was not supposed to have known anything about what he meant to the writer, also nothing about what the writer actually depicted, though it certainly took place within him: "I call him 'Du'"—which Klaus Heuser disputes—"and at parting pressed him to my heart with his express consent."

But perhaps Klaus Heuser, too, had one thing or another to repress. Is it really pleasant to have been loved by Thomas Mann? To belong among his blond and blue-eyed boys?

The K.H. experience also took literary form. "The introduction to the Amphitryon essay belongs to Klaus H., who granted me the most." In the fall of 1927 Mann wrote a small study for the 150th anniversary of the birth of Heinrich von Kleist with the title "Kleist's *Amphitryon*. A Reconquest," which was read on October 10 in Munich, with Klaus Heuser in attendance. Mann confided in a letter to his grown children Klaus and Erika that he had presented the passages best where "he" had not been without influence. What passages were they? The text of the speech has been preserved as a newspaper article. Kleist's *Amphitryon* has as its subject the piquant tale of the gods in which Jupiter in love visits Alkmene in the shape of her husband, the general Amphitryon. But the real Amphitryon also comes home. Alkmene stands bewildered between man and god, yet sends Jupiter back to his godliness as soon as she has realized what the situation is. It is fairly clear how the lines of identification run. Thomas Mann recognizes himself in the role of Jupiter, who is barred from being really loved by humans. He wants not only to be respected by mankind, to be recognized as a famous artist, but to be accepted as a human being himself and released from his inner loneliness. He understands Jupiter in this sense as "the lonely spirit of the artist," who woos life, is rejected, and, "a triumphant renouncer," learns to be satisfied with his divinity. Alkmene, then, "is" Klaus Heuser, who shows the god appropriate respect but prefers to be with humankind, that is play with the children.

Jupiter had one night with Alkmene; Thomas Mann did not with K.H. That is the difference. Love restricted to earth can never be equal to great, divine love. Amphitryon (Katia) will (would) after Jupiter's night with Alkmene never be capable of rivalry. On the one hand, Thomas Mann saw himself in the role of the renouncing victim. On the other hand, as the enthusiast in love he had been happy enough for his circumstances and believed he had "lived and loved" in the little that had happened to him.

The abovementioned diary entry of July 16, 1950, confirms that the "Introduction" to the Amphitryon essay belonged especially to Klaus Heuser. A passage is alluded to that was not delivered but can be found only in the more detailed printed version of the essay. It speaks ambiguously and deeply of happiness and misery of an always old and always new desire:

> What is fidelity? It is love without seeing, victory over a hated forgetting. We meet a face that we love, and after gazing at it for a while, during which our feeling is reinforced, we are parted from it again. Forgetting is sure, the pain of separation is only the pain about sure forgetting. Our sensual imagination, our power of remembering, is weaker than we would like to believe. We will no longer see and stop loving. What remains for us is nothing but the certainty that each new meeting of our being with this phenomenon of life will certainly renew our passion, will let us again, or actually still let us, love it. Knowledge of the law of our nature and our clinging to it is fidelity. It is love that must forget why; faithful love that may speak as though it were alive because it is sure it will again win love immediately and legitimately when it sees.

## A CANDID CONFESSOR

Mann writes expressly in the essay on marriage that homoeroticism meanwhile enjoys a certain favor in the climate of the times. He continues that it is not coincidental that in France a leading writer of that country has stepped foward with a passionate apologia of that sphere of sentiment. He refers to André Gide with his *Corydon*, which appeared in 1924. A personal relationship ensued, when Gide had read *The Magic Mountain* and had corresponded with Mann about it. In 1925 Klaus Mann became acquainted with André Gide: "Once we ate together at my parents' table in Munich." His father was not at home. A personal meeting with him did not occur until May 11, 1931. A further meeting took place in July of the same year.

At the beginning of October 1929 Thomas Mann reviewed Gide's autobiography, *Si le grain ne meurt*, which in 1930 had appeared in German under the title *Stirb und werde* (Die and Become). The French title alludes to the words of Jesus: "Except a corn of wheat fall into the ground and die, it abideth alone: but if it die, it bringeth forth much fruit" (John 12:24). The German title changes that into an allusion to Goethe's poem "Blissful Longing": "And as long as you have that not, that Death and Rebirth! / You are merely a cheerless guest / on this dark earth." In both cases it is a matter of dying and being reborn, a kind of resurrection. It stands as a cipher for the coming out of a homosexual. Deeply shaken by hours of love with brown boys in Algeria, Gide writes deeply moved (and Mann quotes him compassionately): "I brought along the secret of my resurrection and at the same time an inner disquietude as once Lazarus, the man torn from death, may have known. Everything that had absorbed me previously now seemed to me to be dreary amd unsubstantial. . . . I felt radically transformed."

Half envious, half shuddering, Mann tells about someone who dared exposure. He reports about the social isolation that had been the result of the radical coming out. On the other hand there was the fact that Gide had also married, and he praised Gide's confessional act as a necessity. He cannot come to terms with this man. Like Gide himself, he considers it impossible to write an entirely honest autobiography. "In spite of best intentions to be truthful"—thus he cites Gide—"anyone who describes his own life will attain only a halfway honesty; everything is much more complicated than can be expressed." Yet he maintains: "Your autobiography made a deep impression upon me." The stylized confessional clad in symbol would not suffice for a certain type of writer in the long run, "and since reading your book I dream more definitely of my own life story than I did before." In reality he disapproves of Gide's directness. "Annoyed at him because of his much too direct sexually aggressive behavior toward youth, without respect, deference toward it, without being ashamed of his age, spiritless, actually loveless" (diary, October 6, 1951).

*A Sketch of My Life*, written in 1930, does not have the radicality of Gide in the least. In accord with Nietzsche, he offers a "smart" autobiography, not a true one. The theme of homosexuality does not appear there with a single word. Thomas Mann never wrote a real biography of his life. He keeps hoping that the question at the end of the first part of *Die and Become* can be affirmed: "Could it be imaginable that one could come closer to the truth in a *novel* than in an autobiography?"

## A DON QUIXOTE OF LOVE

With others Thomas Mann was always completely in favor of clear words—but not with himself. According to him, out of ignorance and outdated discretion, literary history had "tried to beat about the bush in a rather silly way about the basic fact of Platen's existence: the fact of his exclusive homoerotic dispostion that was crucial in his life." That is stated in the essay on Platen, which Mann wrote in September 1930. The essay seeks to end the repression. Platen had known and also yet not known this impulse, his deepest one. He interpreted it as the poet's dedication to a higher cause and a holy enthrallment by beauty but was mistaken about the fact that his love was by no means a higher one but a love like any other, even though, at least in his time, with more rare possibilities of happiness. Mann traces the entire cult of Platen back to his homoerotic disposition. "'The degree and form of a person's sexuality,' says Nietzsche, 'extend to the highest peak of his intellectuality.'" Poems are secularized prayers in which inner chaos is subdued by beautiful order. Just as with Platen there are the rigorous lyric forms, the ghazel, the sonnet, the ode, with Mann there are the epic forms, about which it can be said that their character possesses "an artistic psychological affinity to his Eros."

Platen is a Don Quixote who swears "that Dulcinea of Toboso is the most beautiful lady under the sun, although she is a farm girl, or better put, some foolish male student or other named Schmidtlein or German." Venerable and ridiculous at the same time, Thomas Mann

felt the same way. "A Don Quixote of love" like Platen, he too transformed "the nothing but grown-up-straight stature of a few mediocre
youths" into ingenious literature. He too knew "the shuddering, re-
morseless humor of situations into which his quixotic love took him,"
whenever he became infatuated with some fellow or other. But he
also knew the defiant resistance against the humiliation through such
addiction, "the superiority of loving relinquishment of self in regard
to the object of his love, the platonic irony that is the god in the lover
and not in the beloved." He makes the above-mentioned statement
about Platen, but that he is describing himself follows not lastly from
the fact that the statement that the lover is more divine than the beloved is a direct quotation from *Death in Venice*. Also, when in his old
age he again reads Platen's letters and diaries, he thinks constantly of
himself. "In Naples 'love between men is so prevalent that even with
the boldest demands one runs no danger of being rejected.' But he
makes none." Like Platen he abbreviates the names of the beloved so
that once it could also be said about him: "Philology has identified all
of them in accordance with their beginning initials."

So the essays about Verlaine, Kleist, Gide, and Platen are a kind of
masquerade, a possibility of speaking about himself and his own
needs and nevertheless keeping silent at the same time. Double optics, bold items of confession for insiders, venerable propriety for
outsiders.

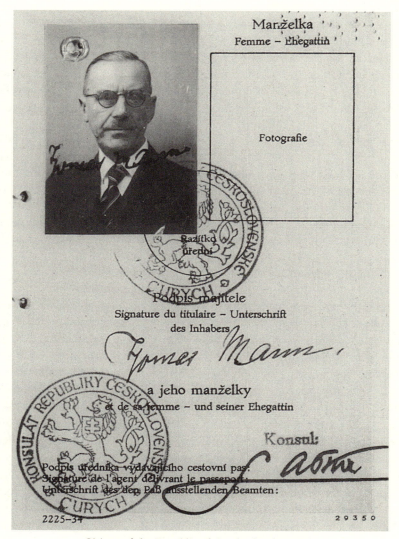

*Citizen of the Republic of Czechoslovakia, 1936*

The appointment of Adolf Hitler to be chancellor on January 30, 1933, had not yet made Thomas Mann think of exile. Life went on. For the fiftieth anniversary of the death of Richard Wagner on February 10 he gave a speech in the Auditorium Maximum of the University of Munich entitled "Suffering and Grandeur of Richard Wagner." On February 11 he traveled with this speech to Amsterdam, Brussels, and Paris. A vacation in Arosa was added, compulsorily continued in Lenzerheide and Lugano (until the end of April). In Arosa, Mann found out about arrests and other infringements in Munich that caused him not to return home for a time. In March he had already resigned from some associations, above all from the conformist Literary Section of the Academy of Fine Arts, and a little later he was expelled from others, from the Rotary Club, for example.

A Munich denunciation turns the attention of the Munich police to him. On April 16 there appears a "Protest of the Richard Wagner City of Munich" against the Wagner speech, signed by numerous Munich dignitaries. A house search and an illegal confiscation of his car follow. A letter of complaint by Thomas Mann to the plenipotentiary of the national government in Bavaria, Franz Ritter von Epp, leads to the intervention of Reinhard Heydrich, who eliminates Epp and at the end of May obtains the confiscation of assets and in June an order of protective custody. Thus Thomas Mann would actually have been arrested upon a return to Munich. He had meanwhile moved to southern France and, after further weeks in a hotel in Bandol, had rented a house in Sanary-sur-Mer, where the family lived from June to September 1933. The next residence was then Küsnacht on Lake Zurich (until 1938).

In August 1933 the family house on Poschingerstrasse in Munich was confiscated without any basis in law and rented out. Although a national flight tax in the amount of 97,000 marks was paid, the legal battle for the house and assets makes no headway. The expatriation of Thomas Mann by the Munich political police is pursued, while for the time being no one in Berlin wants to get involved. In January 1934, therefore, the ill-treated author turns to the interior minister Wilhelm Frick with a detailed letter. After hesitating for a long time, in May 1935 he tries for the release of house and assets, but fails again because of Heydrich, who insists on expatriation and renews the confiscations. In November 1936 Thomas Mann becomes a Czechoslovakian citizen so that the stripping of his German citizenship, which follows at the beginning of December 1936, cannot make him a stateless person.

The years from 1933 to 1936 are filled with work on *Joseph in Egypt*, the third volume of the Joseph tetralogy, published in 1936 in Vienna, the first volume of which (*The Tales of Jacob*) and the second (*Young Joseph*) had appeared in Berlin in 1933 and 1934. The fourth and last followed in 1943, when the S. Fischer publishing house had its headquarters in Stockholm. The first three volumes still sold very well in Germany, while the fourth was able to reach only a small German-language public abroad. That his voice remained audible at all in Germany was an important argument from 1933 to 1936 for Thomas Mann not to irritate the National Socialist authorities by making political statements. He did not remain completely silent during the first three years of his exile, of course, but was still very cautious. He kept postponing a planned "Politicum." Because of this, there arose many conflicts with emigré writers. His own children Erika and Klaus urged him to make a resolute renunciation. Finally, at the beginning of February 1936, this resulted in an open letter "To Eduard Korodi." From then on Thomas Mann again appeared frequently and resolutely with antifascist statements.

# HITLER AND FRIEDEMANN

THERE HAVE been many good and accurate reports about the political and historical events of those years. Therefore they will appear here only very briefly. We want to concentrate on the emotional
impact. The loss of homeland, house, and possessions was an enormous shock. The truly industrious artistic construction of his life had
really collapsed, but not from the inside, rather from the outside. Of
course, that was comparatively less bad, for external things can be
replaced. The first year of exile is then also filled by the effort to
rebuild the ruins of good fortune, to keep the family together, find a
house, buy a car, and get as much money, furniture, and books out of
Munich as possible.

But on the level of its significance, 1933 is a repetition of the ancient
Friedemann shock. The thread of life was torn loose (diary, February
13, 1934), his identity destroyed, his reputation in Germany lost, his
prestige that of a leper. What was lowest was now on top; what was
repressed returned. The ancient fears had been right. The senator was
sitting in the dirt, like the dying Thomas Buddenbrook, like Herr
Friedemann at the river, like the drunken Gustav von Aschenbach
shortly before his death, like Prince Klaus Heinich at the citizen's ball.
The cry "Down with him!" which soap maker Unschlitt's daughter
and her companions in *Royal Highness* had murmured to themselves,
suppressed and incoherent, sounded wild and shamelessly from many
throats. Matriarchal chaos had been victorious over patriarchal order,
the vulgar howling of the suppressed world of desire over middle-
class rationality. The rational republican, which Thomas Mann had
been for ten years, had to recognize that he had lost. For a second
time the powers for which Thomas Mann had burnt incense in 1914
and which had seemed to him at that time vital and historically
mighty had been victorious. "Was all of that not already present in
1914?" the shaken man asks in his diary (March 18, 1934). The year
"1933" had arisen from the longing for "1914." "The moment back
then, afterward so bitterly atoned for, was too enjoyable. The whole
'revolution' served the purpose of restoring it." In actuality the Re-
clam publishing company wants to reprint *Thoughts in War* (diary,
March 17, 1934).

But 1914, with all its sentimentality, had been a writing-desk experience for Thomas Mann. He did not, after all, even have to go to war. But this time he was outside, and the others, the enthusiasts, were inside. From his desk in his day, he could be inexpensively enthusiastic about chaos. But now the horror had intruded on him personally. He did not want it that close. So his answer was not a pleasurable plunge into chaos, rather the strengthening of middle-class option, reason, and dignity, tenacious assertion of the artistic structure against life that wanted to sweep it away.

Mann integrates the experience of 1933 beyond all more precise theories of fascism in his old matrix. His descriptions are shot through with disgust, portray what is mendacious, brutal, stupid, again and again what is base, those who surrender without resistance to cheap impulses. Nazi informers are "gangsters of the worst sort." Hitler, "the brute with his hysterical paws," is the representative "of the lower middle class that was tormented by resentment," a helplessly endeavoring school dropout and poor fellow who confused his hysteria with artistry, his dilettantish stimulation with deep thinking, a "representative of the petty middle class with elementary education who happened to get involved with philosophizing," an immodest and shameless parvenu. German fascism is a "reversion," "a return to earlier conditions," a rebarbarism and forcible simplification, aimed at that refinement and lack of vitality that Thomas Mann had already described in the "Decline of a Family." It is the crude answer to decadence, "the hate of the simplified toward refinement." It is weakness masquerading as strength. "Substitute for the . . . guillotine with 'the ax.' Those are accomplishments!" The decadent man loves what is brutal—Nietzsche had already asserted that.

Overcoming decadence was also always a concern of Thomas Mann himself. A return to the simple, naïve, and wholesome had always piqued his interest, but almost always he had unmasked it as a relapse. "How strong and beautiful is life!"—that is the cry of the weak. The miracle of reborn impartiality of the prior of San Marco was as little convincing as Gustav von Aschenbach's elegant proportions. Artificial naïvité is always doomed to fail—that is the lesson of Thomas Mann. It also turned out to be correct in the case of National Socialism. Contrarily, genuine simplicity survives—the case of Tony Buddenbrook, who all her life did not understand what happened to her but, together with Sesemi Weichbrodt, has the last word in the novel.

But the derivation of fascism from the analysis of decadence also explains why Thomas Mann tries at a few places in his diary to sympathize with the despised phenomenon. "I begin to suspect that the process nevertheless could be in the rank of those that have their two sides. . . ." (April 10, 1933). "The revolt against Jewish things might have my understanding to a certain extent. . . ." (April 20, 1933). "But one must be clear about the fact that, seen nationally and historically, the German reactions are to be weighed positively" (May 12, 1933). In 1938 he will write an essay with the title "Brother Hitler." Of course, we cannot read that as sympathy. On the contrary: No hate is as deep as fraternal hate.

## THE SUITCASE

"Terrible things, yes, deadly things can happen" (April 30, 1933). A heavy, black suitcase turned over in Munich on April 10, 1933, did not arrive in Switzerland. "The chauffeur Hans, gradually recognized as a Judas" (April 28, 1933). Golo Mann remembers:

> In a letter, Thomas Mann had requested me to send him a few stacks of notes as well as a number of oilcloth notebooks that were located here and there in his study, in a suitcase as freight to Lugano. "I count on your discretion that you will read none of these things." An admonition that I took so seriously that I locked myself in his room while I packed the papers. When I came out with the suitcase, to take it to the train station, there stood the loyal Hans: He would gladly relieve me of this burdensome task. All the better—why not? But the suitcase did not arrive and three weeks later still had not arrived, at which my father fell into growing impatience, finally even into desperation.

Whether Hans notified the political police or not, in any case the Lindau border official—he was named Neeb—considered it advisable to open the suitcase. Inside, on the top, he found Thomas Mann's publisher's contracts, sent them surreptiously to Munich to call them to the attention of the police and the fiscal office because of the high sums mentioned in them, waited for their return, repacked them and weeks later sent the piece of luggage to Lugano. He considered what else was in the suitcase, which weighed eighty-three pounds, to be manuscripts of literary works. Actually, the typescript of the Joseph novel was also there. Such a thing was of no interest to the officials. May they be praised for their ignorance! Notwithstanding—we do not know in reality whether border commissar Neeb was actually ignorant. Perhaps he was also a sober man who decided after looking at the papers that such things did not concern the political police and sent only the publisher's contracts to Munich instead of the entire contents. No matter. In any event, the suitcase arrived on May 19 in Bandol. It seemed to be untouched and yet gave the impression of having been rummaged through (diary, May 20, 1933). Thomas Mann was hugely relieved.

Now we do know why the German fiscal authorities during the following months and years are so scrupulously after Thomas Mann. But the nervous states of agitation that plagued the writer frequently in those weeks did not come from that. The secrets of his life were not the publisher's contracts.

Katia, too, did not know precisely what worried her husband so profoundly; at most she suspected something of the kind. "She halfway understands my anxiety about the contents of the suitcase" (April 30, 1933). But just halfway. She, too, was never permitted to read what made the suitcase so explosive: the diaries, probably half a hundred, partly bound, partly black oilcloth notebooks, kept from 1896 until the beginning of 1933. In the hands of Heydrich, who kept like a bloodhound on Thomas Mann's trail, they would have given enough pretext to damage the public esteem of the Nobel Prize recipient heavily, at the time anyway. "Terrible things, yes, deadly things" could have happened. Today we would gladly read those documents. We would better understand over what abysses the persecuted man had to erect his life.

## LET THE WORLD KNOW ME

The anxiety quivers long afterward. Erika Mann reports that at the first opportunity her father burned a lot of papers. In reality it must have happened much later and with much more hesitation. The journals still existed on February 8, 1942. "Took the old diaries and was horrified at them." Not until June 20, 1944 is there the notation: "Began with the destruction of old diaries." But the plan was canceled. Again, almost a year passes. "Aferward, destroyed old diaries, carrying out a long-planned intention. Burning in a stove outside" (May 21, 1945). For twelve more years, frequently perilous years of exile, Thomas Mann carried around the compromising notebooks. What did he need them for? Why did he keep diaries anyway?

> I like holding fast the fleeting day according to its sensual and suggestive, also its intellectual, life and content, less for memory and for rereading than in the sense of accountability, recapitulation, conscious retention, and consolidating control. (February 11, 1934)

The daily journals made him secure. In times of threat, as in the year 1933, they are kept with particular intensity. They even take the place of his literary work when the anxieties of life permit no further work. He writes then not before going to bed but in the bright forenoon.

But accountability, recapitulation, and consolidating control: That is only the morally correct answer, Goethean in tone, Protestant in form. Things did not always go according to rules. There is certainly also what is "false, destructive, and compromising in writing a diary" (February 8, 1942). The "prayerlike communication in the diary" should offer protection against sexual attacks (July 31, 1919). "Why do I write all this?" Thomas Mann asks in his diary at the time with Franzl. "To destroy it in good time before my death? Or do I wish the world to know me?" (August 25, 1950). Platen's "Let the world know me"—that was probably it. He wanted to be understood, not in his lifetime, that was too dangerous, but at some time after his death. Then finally they should love him. The world should know why he had had to disguise himself so perfectly formed. Those who had thought him rich, spoiled, and cold should get to know him as a sufferer. For suffering ennobles. Friedrich Nietzsche explained it to us—it is as though he had known Thomas Mann:

> The spiritual arrogance and disgust of every person who has suffered deeply—it is definitely almost a ranking of merit how deeply people can suffer—the awed certainty by which he is totally imbued and stained because of the ability of his suffering to know more than the smartest and wisest can know, to have been known in many distant, horrible worlds and once "at home," about which "none of you know!"—this spiritual, silent arro-

gance of the sufferer, this pride of the chosen of knowledge, of the "initiated one," of the almost sacrificed one finds all forms of disguise necessary to protect himself from touch by intrusive and sympathetic hands and just in general by everything that is not his equal in pain. Deep suffering ennobles; it divides.

Exactly what was burned in 1944 and 1945, how much and why—we know none of that. Anyway, Thomas Mann went on keeping his diary, and there is no sign of any kind that after the burning he might have written differently or more cautiously. That he spared the journals from 1918 to 1921 from the burning because he needed them still for *Doctor Faustus* shows that a motive for writing and safekeeping, even though subordinate, was also the usefulness for his work. Repeatedly he reads in his diary when something was to be put into shape—mostly the love affairs. It may be that he burned what he thought was dealt with completely and used up in his work. But it may also be that he gave differing answers to the question of burning or saving because his mood vacillated between fear of his contemporaries and courting the love of posterity.

## HOUSE, HEINS, HEYDRICH

Had the Nazis in the spring of 1933 at once expatriated Thomas Mann, confiscated his house, and banned his books, everything would have been much easier. But everything remained in abeyance: the expatriation, the restitution of his possessions, the sale of his books in Germany. It was exasperating. On the one hand, made a fool by the hope for legitimation of his situation, Thomas Mann saw himself forced politically to be cautious. But on the other hand, a resolute declaration of war against him would have helped him out of his ticklish situation. He was actually waiting for such a thing to be able to protest effectively. When it then finally came in the form of the expatriation of December 1936, he immediately reacted clearly and decisively. To have tosssed the gauntlet into the ring at an earlier time, when the Nazis had not yet begun so conclusively to put themselves in the wrong, would possibly have had a lesser effect. It is easy to say today that he should have publicly distanced himself earlier and more courageously. But the situation was not favorable for that. He was stum-

bling around through a matted root system, whereas we who were
born later recognize the entire jinxed forest.

The root system—that was the tough battle about expatriation or
passport extension, about the house and cars and money and publisher. How Erika and Golo Mann, Ida Herz, Marie Kurz, and other
friends little by little on long and winding ways directly or by cover
addresses manage to get manuscripts, books, furniture, the grama-
phone, the silverware, the chandelier, and the writing desk out of
Munich—that occupies the writer of the diary for more than a year. "I
understand less and less," he wrote on April 2, 1934, to René Schik-
kele, "how it is happening that I am to be shut out of Germany for the
sake of these idiots or else just turn over my possessions, house, and
inventory to them. I will not stand aside from the attempt to take
them out of their hands, this Munich rabble." There were valuable
and beloved family heirlooms among them, for example, the baptismal chalice. Should he relinquish all of that for the sake of making a
political point?

Nevertheless, far from all his possessions could be rescued. Most of
the furniture and all kinds of small things remained in the house,
were sold at a forced auction, and are lost or destroyed; other things,
foremost the old manuscripts, came into the hands of the lawyer Valen-
tin Heins, where apparently they were burned in a nighttime bombing—
if they had not already been handed over to the Gestapo. Other things
(valuable books) were preserved by his friend Hans Feist, from whom
they were confiscated and, after an official simply wrote in his own
name, dispersed in every direction. Again, the political police turned
over other books to the municipal library in Munich, which returned
them in 1949. And the two automobiles, "a Horch limousine and a
Buick Phaeton," and also Golo's Auto-Union car, were picked up
from the garage without any legal basis—"not to be secured but simply from then on to be driven and worn out by the Munich SA"—and
that is the way it remained, despite lengthy complaints to the interior
minister.

With the Reich's flight tax, with confiscations of his bank accounts,
and with other expenses of his exile, Thomas Mann certainly forfeited
half of his fortune. In the particulars, that, too, was a process with
loopholes without number. The gray-headed German officials labored
with tenacious perfection. The Munich political police demanded five
thousand Reichsmarks for their "administrative activity."

In spite of everything, it did not go badly for the family even in exile. The fear of becoming déclassé assails Thomas Mann on May 3, 1933, in the Basel Hotel Drei Könige, the most expensive hotel in the city, where a beer costs as much as a glass of champagne around the corner. He had deposited some money in Switzerland—for example, half the Nobel Prize money, which had amounted to 200,000 Reichsmarks. Golo Mann had been able to withdraw 60,000 Reichsmarks just in time, which was sent out of Germany by way of the French embassy. Gottfried Bermann Fischer kept paying well and punctually, and also the income from abroad kept flowing. There could be no talk of a material threat. Quite soon everything came together: a villa, even though rented, an automobile (a Fiat, "since I trust this make, which was our first," further Mouch and Bill, two dogs. The second, however, was no good. "'Bill' has bitten children, is gotten rid of" (August 29, 1935).

Again and again it looked like the property on Poschingerstrasse could be rescued. Katia does advise on April 28, 1933, that the house and assets be abandoned. But why, anyway? During the first months the villa was accessible without any problem, neither watched nor shut up nor under seal. The Manns could even rent it out on June 24, 1933, to an American family for 600 marks a month. Admittedly, "the dangerous fury of the renter" is attested to, when the housekeeper Maria Kurz packs up numerous boxes with books and porcelain (August 11, 1933).

The house is not confiscated finally and effectively until August 25, 1933. Heins, the lawyer, is occupied with the case, enters petition after petition, nourishes hopes for almost two years, although the house meanwhile is rented out further by the political police. The matter drags on. Thomas Mann had long since given it up when, on May 27, 1935, the decision to release it actually comes. The interior minister Wilhelm Frick writes to the Bavarian Interior Ministry:

> I therefore desist from declaring the loss of German citizenship for Thomas Mann. I respectfully request that the declared confiscation of Mann's assets by the Bavarian political police be revoked and a report be received within two weeks concerning this order.

That looks like a victory, but it remains without the anticipated results. For, again, weeks pass. Heins at first writes about the delay of the matter. But on September 4, when a celebration would already be desirable, the truth comes out:

> At home, before supper, dramatically explosive telephone call from Heins's partner Bumann: The confiscation of the property renewed on instructions from Berlin, the expatriotization motion will be examined again. Heins very dejected by the news that corresponds to my expectation and what I had pictured of the situation for myself over the past weeks. I, too, am disappointed, for the rescue of the property would have pleased me. It has now become unlikely (the forfeiture can take place simply on the part of the State of Bavaria, even without expatriation), and my chief wish is that Bermann may finally leave the country, so that I can win independence—which, of course, would not be complete as my books still should find access into Germany.

On instructions from Berlin? But Berlin had until now tried to protect Thomas Mann from the Munich plunderers. Frick had not figured on Heydrich's stubbornness. Where the latter's persistent hate came from remains unexplained. Evidently he considered Thomas Mann's case a highly personal matter. He had meanwhile been transferred to Berlin and become the right-hand man of the deputy chief of the Prussian Gestapo, Heinrich Himmler. In his name he signed the renewed petition for expatriation on July 19, 1935. He repeated and strengthened his request on March 25, 1936, and finally, after Adolf Hitler himself approved, was successful in December 1936. In 1937 the house on Poschingerstrasse was put at the disposal of the Lebensborn foundation, which had made as its goal the breeding of racially pure Arians. Himmler himself is said once to have been resident there; heathen baptisms are said to have taken place. The famous previous owner would likely have been considered a Jew by those who were racially pure. In 1940 the house was divided into rental apartment units, in 1944 struck by the bombs of Allied airmen. A new building was erected on the old foundations in 1957.

A procedure of indemnity for damages (loss of house and assets) ended in the same year (1957) with a payment of 2,399 German marks to Katia Mann as the heir. "The German people are a decent people who love justice and cleanliness. 'Righteous' is the word that its writers favor regarding their views."

## WHERE DID THE HATE COME FROM?

His *Buddenbrooks* was considered a national book; in 1914 he had rejoiced with the Germans, during the war written the *Reflections of a Nonpolitical Man*, and afterward thought and said so much that would have pleased the National Socialists. Could he not have remained in the Reich like Gerhart Hauptmann, could not his books have been honored there further like those by Hermann Hesse? Many in Hitler's Germany thought so, but not enough. The feelings of hate for Thomas Mann have many sources. He is called Jewish, Marxist, intellectualistic, decadent, a snob, a cold wheeler-dealer. The collective word for all of that is un-German. In Thomas Mann, the Germans persecuted everything that they were themselves and yet still believed they should not be. He was the scapegoat who was sent as a substitute into the desert. They believed they cleansed themselves with this "sacrifice." They banned a part of themselves, even the decadence, which was their most human part.

Richard Wagner, the prototype of the decadent artist, stands not by chance at the beginning of the expulsion. The "Protest of the Richard Wagner City of Munich" (April 1933) brings the un-German snob Thomas Mann into conflict with the "right to criticize enduring German intellectual giants." Those who signed the "Protest," half a hundred Munich Cultural Honorees, among them Hans Knappertsbusch, Hans Pfitzner, Richard Strauss, Siegmund von Hausegger, and Olaf Gulbransson, had been considered until then in part colleagues, at times even almost friends. They apparently did not suspect or only half suspected that their "Protest" would call the political police onto the field, that the order for protective custody, the confiscations, the denial of passport extension would be its immediate effect. They had brought a crime down on their heads. Knappertsbusch and Gulbransson soon regretted this, at any rate the diary notes information of this kind. However, Pfitzner persisted, as did Hausegger. The latter complained about "leading artistic creation back to base instincts." As an example, he quoted Mann's statements: "Psychoanalysis claims to know that love is composed of pure perversities. Therefore love still remains the most divine phenomenon in the world. Well then, the genius Richard Wagner is composed of pure dilettantism." Hausegger wishes, instead of this, that art were not the product of pathological overexcitation but "the creative primeval power of the human mind . . . that raises us from an animalistic, emotional condition into freedom in the Kantian sense." He wants art to be clean and intellectual, not animalistic and emotional. That sounds good but is naturally not true. Thomas Mann is embattled because he demonstrates their repressions to the apostles of cleanliness. What is repressed in one's own ego reappears as a crime in others. So it happened that Thomas Mann, since he was cast out, had to bear the sins of the German people.

The enthusiasm of 1933 had given Germans the nice feeling that they were the faithful. Their lives seemed to make sense. Now here came someone, a literary man, an "impotent aesthete," whose *Magic Mountain* was "written, conceived, and constructed with ice-cold intellect but in no phase felt, experienced, and fought for," one of those faithless and aimless, those "elements incapable of renewal and rejuvenation," that had withdrawn to Switzerland where a decadent Europe had at its disposal a final place to stay. "Never have you been able to show us a path, to set an example for wanting to believe in people and God!" complained Karl Justus Obenauer, a Germanist and high SS officer. But belief is something different from wanting to believe. National Socialist belief had to repress what opposed it. Blind mania for belief arose from the deep anxiety over nihilism that Hitler knew how to manipulate. But before Thomas Mann's ironic eye no emotion could stand, and above all no false emotion. He had, after all, experienced all of that. Hate of him is fraternal hate. It applies to the apostates of his own faith.

## TOWERING ALONE

Why send him to the galley, while others go untouched? Why could Gerhart Hauptmann, "this sham," remain and hoist the swastika while the intellectual dignity of the author of *The Magic Mountain* was called to martyrdom? For which he was certainly not born! Inside he was filled with resistance, even with repugnance against exile. After all, he was a Goethe, and *he* had never had to leave his homeland! Had not his Munich house been like the one on the Frauenplan? "That I have been forced out of this existence is a heavy stylistic lapse and error of destiny in my life with which, as it seems, I try to deal in vain." A stylistic lapse: Life as a beautiful composition was threatened. An error of destiny: He was a Sunday's child, not a gypsy in a green wagon. "The inner rejection of martyrdom, the perception of his personal inappropriateness returns again and again."

The grand word "martyr"—one can always say that it was surely not so bad. Certainly not outwardly. When his house and home and hound were reasonably together again, there arose even in him a malicious pleasure that people in Munich had not been able to prevent, "that we live in freedom in a nice house, that we travel to America, even without a passport, etc." (April 27, 1934). But inwardly everything was unstable. States of nervousness, loss of composure, fits of weeping, anxiety, and depression repeatedly afflict this man who has been thrown off track. "Tormenting, deeply depressed, and hopeless conditions, difficult to bear, a kind of psychological periodontitis, come repeatedly, after bright spots" (November 4, 1933). High consumption of pills is the result. He cannot decide between defiance and surrender. He does not know where to go. Nice, Zurich, Basel, Vienna, Prague are discussed. The irregularity taxes his nerves. Would it not have been best to leave the country in peace (May 31, 1933), emigrate legally? (March 16, 1934). "The peaceful dissociation from Germany, the return of what is mine, the transfer of my possessions to the house in Zurich would bolster my ease of mind greatly" February 28, 1934). Would it not be best for him to return to Munich? "In the final analysis one doesn't have to behave like Hauptmann and Strauss but could maintain a serious isolation, refusing any public appearance" (November 20, 1933). But "this is clear to my mind," return is ruled out, impossible, absurd, senseless, and full of dreary dangers for freedom and life (July 20, 1933). Fear is fed by reports of terrors. He has a horror of oppression, prison yards, heavy cotton uniforms, beatings, dirt. "Will my end be miserable?" (September 25, 1933). The idea of falling into the dirty hands of the people who have Theodor Lessing and Erich Mühsam on their consciences awakens his oldest fears, even tears down his consideration for others. "Such a death might apply to a Lessing, but surely not to me" (September 1, 1933). His terror writes that, not he himself.

For a long time he avoids breaking off contact with friends and cutting ties with Germany. "I would consider it a mistake of those in power in Germany, if they forced me into an emigration camp by demanding impossible confessions." He will not acknowledge that he is already in that camp. He gets into an awkward position, inevitably. He would find it somehow good, if the Nazis were to call him back. One would not have to follow that call, after all. "I know that in Berlin there is regret about my being abroad; I want to nourish that & get it talked about, maybe produce a process with the inclination of my return, disavow the Munich louts." Considered in hindsight, that is a fairly crazy idea. The only thing that results is disappointment, even the embitterment of fellow emigrants, to whom Thomas Mann long denies solidarity. I am not like those others abroad, it cries out within him, not a Jew, not a communist, not a writer concerned with rootlessness and decadence. I don't want them to be my neighbors now! I'm no un-German. I am unique, to be confused with no one! My position is exceptional—I must find a path between the hysterical resentment among the emigrants and the collaborators in Germany, must distance myself from the literature of resentment and desperation; I'm not made to consume myself with hate.

The panicked anxiety about his own psychological balance blinds him to the sufferings of his fellow exiles. The deep outrage forces monstrosities out of him. Powerful suffering needs powerful solace. Since he feels himself at least as mortified as Jacob after the boy Eliphas has beaten him black and blue, he also dreams a dream of grandiose major upheaval. Was he not the last survivor of a higher epoch? While the level of the time is sinking and sinking, his own is rising. "Morally and culturally those like me gain something solitarily towering amid increasing leveling (January 31, 1935). He raises himself to a pinnacle. "Feeling of genius" (February 15, 1935).

## THE GREAT DISAPPOINTMENT

The solitarily towering man allows himself to be forced to make a decision in opposition to his own son. "On whom can we count," Klaus Mann wrote to Stefan Zweig on September 15, 1933, "if all those whom we have relied upon the most leave us in the lurch out of consideration for a 'German market'?" Thomas Mann was busy with the publication of his Joseph novel. Klaus exhorts him: "One just doesn't entrust one's fairest ware to a country that one leaves with loathing." He sees no chance for his father's publishing house. "The situation with Fischer is completely hopeless; either he must bring himself more radically in line or he will be entirely destroyed." The matter did turn out somewhat differently; the publishing house was able to leave the country, but Klaus was right in principle—compromises were not possible in the long run.

The first issue of the magazine *Die Sammlung* (The Assembly), edited by Klaus Mann, appeared with Querido in Amsterdam in September 1933. Conceived as a literary magazine, it nevertheless made it clear from the beginning that it ascribed a political mission to literature. A notice in the first issue mentioned the name of Thomas Mann among those who had agreed to contribute. It was all right with him. "I have nothing at all against my figuring in your list (the prospect was really nice)." He even announced a contribution, about the upright theologian Karl Barth ("it is surprising that the man is still at large"). But Gottfried Bermann Fischer was clearly aghast when he set eyes on the first *Sammlung* issue. He demanded and received from Thomas Mann a vaguely disassociating telegram, "in which I do not pardon myself for anything" (diary, September 6, 1933). But that was not enough for Bermann. "Outrageous extortion," Mann notes angrily (September 12, 1933), but then sends a stronger telegram "in which I certainly excuse myself for a lot, and that nevertheless won't be enough." He writes a letter to Klaus in which he defends himself and Bermann. They were far apart. Those inside Germany had totally different standards from those outside, "and those who have burned their bridges behind them will live in a world different from those who could not." Bermann wanted to try the Joseph novel to see what he still might be able to do in Germany. In the Reich there were many defiant and many yearning people. The advance orders were up in the thousands.

I am not indulging in false hope, but the curiosity about how the attempt might turn out is justified and not every consideration about it is senseless and dishonorable. If it is successful, if the public in Germany brings success to a work of an ostracized man, a work already opposed in regard to its subject matter, without those in power daring to prevent it—one has to admit that that would be more just and amusing—for those in power much more vexatious, a more brilliant victory over them than a whole pile of emigrant polemics.

That he files *Die Sammlung* in the category of "emigrant polemics" allows his assessment at the time to be recognized clearly. He hopes for forbearance "by you proud anti-opportunists." Klaus vouchsafed it. But those not yet born at the time wrinkle their brows.

At this time Bermann had not yet made public use of the telegram (and similar declarations by René Schickele, Stefan Zweig, and Afred Döblin). But when on October 10 in the politically regulated *Börsenblatt für den deutschen Buchhandel* (Market Newsletter for the German Book Trade) a warning against the *Sammlung* was printed; to protect his publishing house he saw himself forced to send a communication to the authorities indicating that his authors had been deceived about the character of the magazine and rejected any association with it. As evidence he surrendered the telegrams. All of that was published in the *Börsenblatt* and appeared as the first public comment by Thomas Mann regarding the Hitler state. He knew that it was not salutary. "Klaus telephoned from Amsterdam, where the news from Germany is likewise already being spread. Prepares for the opposition declaration by Querido, which I find natural" (October 14, 1933).

For his part, Klaus reacts discreetly, notwithstanding his disappointment, at any rate avoids a break with his father. "Sadness and confusion" is his first reaction in the diary (September 15); later the word "bitter" is frequent. He is angry much more about Bermann, Döblin, Schickele, and Zweig, but also about Musil—"registered letter from Robert Musil that he was unfortunately *forced* to withdraw his cooperation"—(October 24), than about his father, with whom he has several conversations. Courageously he continues the magazine.

At the beginning of December a heated exchange of words occurs because of another matter. Klaus Mann notes that his father is faced with the question of whether he should become a member of the National German Writers Union, which since had been merged with the National Literature Board. "He is going to do it. Alas" (December 7). He does not expect much more of his father. A day later his having been put to the test seems affirmed. "Ruckus with Magician because I called his attention to the statutes of the German organization. His hear-no-evil, know-no-evil flight into petulance." His father's daily journal entry (December 8) also confirms a vehement exchange of words "because of the required registration with the coercive Berlin organization, which I am considering making," he adds defiantly, "without bothering about the forms and their requirements." He tries to rescue his honor and sends the following high-minded text to Hans Friedrich Blunck, the president of the National Literature Board at the time:

> As an honorary member of the S.D.S. [Protective Association of German Writers] that has merged with the National Association, I may well assume that I and my work are considered now as before to belong to German literature and I hope that in my case no further formalities are required.

Here he was mistaken. The forms arrived on December 22 with the declaration that they had to be signed. The tormented man now writes resolutely in his diary, "I will not do that, and so it's probably the break and the end." The end did not come for a time because the halfway well-meaning Blunck did not insist, but the objections of Klaus, Erika, Golo, and Katia, all of whom were dissatisfied with the head of the family, had after all proved effective and helped his better judgment break through, even though at first only in a nonpublic process.

## A POLITICAL ACT

As far as the public is concerned, he first decided on Don Quixote. For three years he plans again and again to write something against the Nazis and always lets it lie. "Last night I was agitated and in a huff, since K. indicated that Golo, too, as well as his siblings, longed for a statement by me against Hitler's Germany" (September 11, 1933). "I am occupied these days again with the thought of a statement in the form of a calmly serious warning to Germany. . . . But a general paralysis comes to the aid of my natural sluggishness, the whole nature of which is hard to fathom" (November 10, 1933). "Conversation with Reisiger about the crippling inhibitions that oppose a literary dispute with German outrages & among which horror and contempt play a great role. I resist even saying the name of the bogeyman who has been glorified by success and become 'historical.' And how do you grapple with the stony standing coffins of the Oranienburg concentration camp?" (February 11, 1934).

On July 31, 1934, he had again resolved to cleanse his soul and in an open letter to the *Times* to adjure the world and England "to put an end to the ignominious regime in Berlin." Katia, too, had again wanted a liberating statement against the German atrocities so as to put an end to half measures, to dependence, and to the dishonorable practice of being made a fool of (August 5, 1934). But on August 11 he again puts aside the "material for the politicum" and begins with work on a feature, "Ocean Voyage with Don Quixote." But the politicum gives him no peace—from August 17 to 28 he is again fed up with it. Finally, on August 30, the decision is for Don Quixote. But his conscience will not leave him in peace. "I am ashamed of myself at times for fooling around" (September 2, 1934).

But the back-and-forth continues. On April 19, 1935, he plans a "political act," "an open letter or memorandum to the German people in which the feelings of the world toward him were to be commented upon and in a warm, true way they were to be warned against the fate of the *inimicus generis humani* (enemy of the human race). Again it is a matter of rescuing the political soul, whose just and appropriate form I constantly seek."

He would like to have been more courageous, and gradually he did become more courageous. In March 1935 he wrote the speech "Attention, Europe!" for the conference of a committee of the League of Nations. In the manuscript it has the title "Candid Words" and closes with an appeal to will power, to "the courage for a Yes and a No—this courage alone in which a spiritual authority can grow in a world of confusion and aberration." But he himself did not yet have this courage. The concluding passage was omitted from the published speech. The conference was supposed to take place in Nice at the beginning of April 1935. Under pressure from his publisher, who feared encumbrances in relation to the German goverment, Thomas Mann withdrew his participation. Bermann had insisted that just then everything was fine for Mann in Berlin; his assets were to be released within two weeks; there were assurances by the Ministry of Propaganda; the *Frankfurter Zeitung* even wanted to reprint his volume of essays (March 26–28, 1935). Thomas Mann complied again, but the wish grew stronger in those days to break off all contact with him. "It is to be hoped and to be expected that things will be over soon also with Bermann and that the volume of essays (*Sufferings and Greatness of the Masters*) will not appear there" (March 23, 1935). Erika would have been pleased. She was against Bermann from the start and wanted to take her father to Querido.

But Gottfried Bermann Fischer was also in a difficult situation. In the spring of 1935 he did claim to be optimistic, but he too gradually recognized that nothing was to be gained for long from this country for the famous publishing house of the Jew Samuel Fischer. Already, starting in the summer of 1935, he undertook energetic steps toward the emigration of the firm. Finally in April 1936 he achieved the legal transfer to Vienna of the undesirable parts, among them the works of Thomas Mann and Stefan Zweig with the sanctioned parts left behind, among them Hermann Hesse and Gerhart Hauptmann. Through this partition the state of uncertainty that had been unbearable receded. The pressure was also removed from Thomas Mann. Up to this time the destiny of the whole publishing house always depended on his decision. A declaration against the regime in Germany would always have put the publishing house in danger. If one considers all the pressures on Thomas Mann, all the hovering procedures and events of the years from the beginning of 1933 to the beginning of 1936, then his attitude is understandable. He was confined and crippled for many reasons. He had to take too much into consideration. That the "political act," which he greatly desired, would not be successful under these circumstances is clear. He was not free enough for that. It probably would not have been good, if he had forced it prematurely. Only when he was ready to abandon house and money and passport, only when Bermann's emigration was decided, only when he had learned to live without the German market, when he had become an emigrant within himself, could an efficacious and courageous document come into being.

## THE LIBERATION

"She felt that the liberation from the bonds that entangled him and meant to hold him down was vastly difficult, but that the motivation he was able to create was stronger." It was time again for a change. This time it was not Klaus who exhorted his father; this time it was his daughter Erika. It was not easy; it was much more a battle like David's with Goliath, but Erika struck at a more fortunate hour than had Klaus. In January 1936 in the Parisian emigrant magazine *The New Journal* Gottfried Bermann Fischer had been described by Leopold Schwarzschild as the "token Jew of the National Socialist book trade." Thomas Mann protested against that in the *Neue Zürcher Zeitung.* Erika then wrote him an embittered but clever and moving letter:

> As far as I know, Doctor Bermann is the first luminary to whom injustice, in your opinion, has been done since the outbreak of the Third Reich in whose favor you speak out publicly. You have done that for no one before. . . . In summary this remains: The first word "for" comes from your mouth for Doctor Bermann; the first word "against"—your first official "protest" since the beginning of the Third Reich—is directed against Schwarzschild and the "Journal" (in the NZZ!!!). . . .
>
> Your relationship to Doktor Bermann and his house is indestructable—you seem prepared to sacrifice everything to it. In the event that it means a sacrifice for you that I gradually but surely get lost—add that to the others. For me it is sad and terrible,

> > > I am
> > > your child E.

First her mother, Katia Mann, reacts and brings up rectifications, explanations, and considerations from which once again the unprecedented complexity of the whole situation can be recognized. Above all, she opposes the appearance that Bermann's foreign establishment is dependent on Goebbels and could basically be only hostile to emigrants. Added to this are emotional matters. Katia defends her Tommy, the Magician: "Except for me and Medi, you are the only person whom the M. holds close to his heart, and your letter has grieved and hurt him very much." She finds it unacceptable that Erika really threatens to break with her father. "And for me, who am after all an appendage of him, it is also pretty hard."

Her father, too, replies self-confidantly: "Finished writing the 12-page letter to Eri, for her and posterity" (January 24, 1936). Next to what he has to express matter-of-factly in defense of Bermann and in criticism of Schwarzschild, there is again the personal. He does not believe that Erika will be able to withdraw her love from him. "Of that I am fairly confident. A falling-out takes two, as it were, and it seems to me that my feeling for you will not permit such a thing. When I think how you sometimes laughed and had tears in your eyes when I read to all of you . . . You are too very much my child, Eri, even in your anger at me. . . . So basically your anger also comes childlike from me; it is, so to speak, the objectivation of my own scruples and doubt."

That was the truth. The letter already indicates "what I will probably have to do for the sake of my conscience and your anger," namely, a clear avowal of emigration. He mentions that in his case an almost lethal readiness is part of it. Implacable in the matter, in part harsh and mean, Erika writes back. "I do not underestimate the meat-and-potatoes aspect of your position," she scoffs bitingly. Her father would like preferably to publish in what is almost the gutter press of a halfway pseudo-emigrant publishing house that is brought into line politically than sit with Tom, Dick, and Harry in an unequivocal emigrant house.

*This letter is too long; it is three A.M., and I'm afraid I have not found the tones to reach you. Let me beg you again: Think about it. Do not destroy that ungentle Schwarzschild with a terrible reply in the N.Z.Z.—think of the responsibility that will fall to you if, after three years of restraint, you take the credit, as your first asset, of the smashing of emigration and its modest unity—and think about the spectacle that we offer to those "inside." I do beg you very much,*

*a whole lot:*

*E.*

*You're right: basically all of this does not disrupt my association with you, but just that makes the whole thing even more unbearable.*

Did that convince Thomas Mann? "Planned an open letter to Korrodi; K. composed a draft of it during the morning" (January 27). Meanwhile the situation had become critical. Schwarzschild had written that German literature had almost completely emigrated. Eduard Korrodi, the feature editor of the *Neue Zürcher Zeitung*, had replied that Schwarzschild was confusing German with Jewish literature and referred to Thomas Mann, whose works were still being published in Germany. With that, Korrodi had driven a thick wedge between

Thomas Mann and emigration. Now something definitely had to be said in return. When Erika's letter arrives, the open letter to Korrodi is already a closed matter. We actually do not know what was supposed to be in it at that time. If one considers how momentous the consequences of this step were, the diary is unusually restrained. On January 29, Erika comes on a visit. "Loving," the Magician notes. "Conversation with her about things." The content of the open letter seems by no means to be fixed even then. After her visit, Erika writes another letter to her father, concerned, moved, and contrite. How could she have sat opposite him and so passionately contradicted every one of his words? She does not yet know what will happen. "I pray to all our gods that your 'reply' will be good."

It was, exceedingly. Cheerful and relieved, Erika telegraphs from Prague: "thanks, congratulations, bless you." "Strong and resolute words," he had found—on January 31 the writer of the diary has become aware. "I am aware of the significance of the step taken today. After 3 years of hesitation I have let my conscience and my firm conviction speak. My words will not remain without an impression."

On February 3 there were bold and efficacious statements in the *Neue Zürcher Zeitung*:

> The deep conviction, supported and nurtured daily by a thousand human and moral and aesthetic individual observations, that from the present German government nothing good can come, not for Germany and not for the world—this conviction has caused me to flee from the country in whose intellectual traditions I have deeper roots than those who for three years have vacillated about whether they should dare to deny me my Germanness before the whole world. And to the depths of my conscience I am certain that I have done right before my contemporaries and before posterity to stand with those for whom the words of a truly noble German poet apply:

> > But he who does hate evil from his heart,
> > It will expel him from his homeland there,
> > If honored by a folk enthralled apart.
> > Far smarter to renounce the native air
> > Than in a childish generation start
> > The yoke of hate of the blind mob to bear.

The truly noble man is August von Platen. For years Thomas Mann had carried his verses around with him, to make use of them at appropriate moments. Would the new epoch of his life exist under the sign of Platen, the outcast and exiled man, not under the sign of the man on the Frauenplan?

# XV. Joseph and His Brothers

*Around 1939*

The first impulse to talk anew about the biblical tale of Joseph can probably be traced back to April 1924, when the artist Hermann Ebers asked the writer to compose an introduction to a portfolio of paintings about the Joseph legend. Then Thomas Mann reread the story in the old family Bible and felt impelled to amplify it in detail. A journey to the Mediterrannean in March 1925 produces little that is useful, although he came in contact with Cairo, the pyramids, Luxor, Karnak, and the pharaohs' graves in Thebes. Anyway, Thomas Mann believed he had seen Echnaton in person—"Amenophis IV, at whose glass-covered mummy in the porphyry coffin I stood filled with emotion for a long time"; of course, it was Amenophis II, but that does no damage to his emotion. The years 1925 and especially 1926 are filled with extensive preparations. In June 1926 the project continues, still under the definition of "novella"; then from August 1926 on there is talk of a short novel. At this time it is called *Joseph in Egypt*. At the beginning of 1926 the first lines of the prologue are written. The large scope emerges. After more than two years full of interruptions by essays, speeches, and trips, there are around four hundred pages. A second Egyptian inspection from February to April 1930 brings reflection and impetus. Afterward, things progress somewhat more speedily. In June 1932 the first two volumes are finished, *The Story of Jacob* and *Young Joseph*, which then appeared in 1933 and 1934 in Berlin. *Joseph in Egypt*, the third volume, with which the heart of the project was reached, has developed in October 1932 up to the chapter "Joseph at the Pyramids," when first the preparation of the Wagner lecture and then exile interrupt the work for many months.

From 1933 on, the progress can be followed exactly in the diaries. After listless efforts following May 1933, the enterprise gets going again only in August, when Joseph's arrival in the house of Potiphar is taking shape. In spite of constant interruptions, among others the trips to the United States in 1934 and 1935, the third novel is finished in August 1936 and appears in October (with Bermann-Fischer in Vienna). The dimensions had again grown so that a fourth novel, *Joseph the Provider*, became necessary. Before he tackled it, Thomas Mann permitted himself an interlude of recuperation: the Goethe novel *The Beloved Returns*. Originally conceived as a novella (as usual), this project also used up three years, from November 1936 to October 1939 until, after further interim works (again numerous essays and speeches, as well as the Indic tale *The Transposed Heads*), *Joseph* again gets its turn in August 1940. In January 1943, after almost nineteen eventful years, the great work is concluded. "I was excited and sad. But it's done, after a fashion. I see far more a monument of my life than one of art and thought, a monument of *perseverance*" (January 4, 1943). "I got finished with Joseph sooner than the world did with fascism" (January 8,1943). An epilogue follows, the Moses novella, *The Tables of the Law*. In March 1943 the whole mythological-criental material is finally packed up and put away.

## ANTI-BILSE?

HE HAD always merely found, never invented, the *Buddenbrooks* author proclaimed at the time in "Bilse and I"—not invention but inspiration makes the poet. From his midyears on he saw that differently. Beginners write autobiographically, but professionals can do more than that. To complete a virtuoso's piece in empty space is more than talking about yourself. Especially since all too much had already been said about the material of his life. Compared with what had gone before, he planned something entirely foreign. In Lübeck and Munich, in Sanary, Küsnacht, and Princeton useful illustrative material was hard to find to depict the shepherds on the Jordan and the high civilization belonging to the past more than three thousand years ago along the Nile.

Appropriate models for many figures were lacking, and yet they all received an unmistakable physiognomy. Anyone who has read the Joseph novel cannot imagine Jacob other than as brown-eyed with glandular tendernesses, Ruben only as a good-natured giant with a weak voice, Laban as a lump of earth with a drooping eyelid. Many characters who do not occur in the Bible at all, or only very generally, such as the old Minaean, the caretaker Mont-kaw, the dwarfs Dûdu and Gottliebchen or the prison guard Mai-Sachme, did not become disguised allegories but stand before us in the flesh and believable. The chief characters Jacob, Rachel, Lea, Joseph, the brothers (Ruben, Judah, and Benjamin above all), in addition Potiphar, Mut-em-enet, Teje, and Echnaton—all of them, in comparison with the brief biblical story, receive a richly instrumental psychological existence. All of them "fit" in an astonishing way. How did he do that? Thomas Mann confirms, to our astonishment, that *Joseph* was his first work without human models; the characters were all completely invented, in contrast to his earlier dependence on observed reality.

But invented—what does that mean? Inventions can be stimulated and encouraged but not spawned or even compelled. The "sudden idea" is what is decisive. It comes or it does not come. It often does not come during work, but unexpectedly, in a doze, while on a stroll, during physical relaxation. It falls like a shooting star. What and when something occurs to a person still is subject to certain legitimacies. Among them is atmosphere. Whenever Thomas Mann takes a seat at his desk, the world around him must sink away so that a different, magical one can rise. It is pleasing to speak about absolute distances, about what he has not experienced, about the existence of shepherds and sheep breeders, about camels and oases in the desert, about dwarfs, Egyptian chamberlains, and high-browed pharaohs' daughters, and with playful exactitude to show "how it really was." It frees one from the pressure of the present. To plunge in turbulent times from the chaos of the present into the literarily already pre-arranged age of the patriarchs bestowed self-assurance and stability. As his homeland was being lost, the novel was his "rod and staff," as Thomas Mann writes in an allusion to the Twenty-third Psalm. He clung tightly to his novel as Germany sank. While every day stormed his heart and mind with the wildest expectations, Mann wrote "seventy thousand calmly streaming lines." The hate for the present inspired the imagination of a counterworld. The unease of his years of development and the peace of his great work determine one another.

Joseph's world is a counterworld to Germany of the twentieth century. We enter it through Frau Holle's well, into which Goldmarie falls when she tries to get her distaff out. "Down then and don't hesitate," the end of the prologue "Descent into Hell" encourages us. The well is three thousand years deep. Things do not look so strange to us when we arrive below. Mountain and valley, cities, roads, and vine-clad hills, a turbid and swift-flowing river—the fairy tale's meadows around the well show us an already relatively civilized world, one not much different from our own. We will see that (in Thomas Mann) the psychology of these people is almost like our own. Consequently much could be found; not everything had to be invented. A second, closer look then shows us here, too, a world of sources and models.

To limit the sphere of what is invented, let us first count up all the things that are found. Foremost there was the biblical text from the first Book of Moses. The names, the chief figures, the course of action, and a rudimentary psychology were present in it already, unlike in all the novels up to this time.

The nonbiblical sources were the second level. To this belong versions of the Joseph story from other ancient Eastern sources, Jewish sagas, Babylonian myths, Egyptian literature. From this sphere was chosen what conformed to the Old Testament. Here, too, it was a matter of finding, not inventing. A detail found in the literature is fitted into its appropriate place. However, it is a part of the marvel of this great work that motifs and narrative strands are often connected over hundreds of pages, although a subsequent revision of the beginnings was not possible any longer, because the two first novels had already appeared when the third and fourth were written.

The third level of sources is images. The Egyptian parts of the novel make use of innumerable graphic images. The character traits of Potiphar are developed from his figure, that colossal seated statue of Prince Hemon, to whose intelligent and fine head and sturdy limbs Thomas Mann has added the psychology of a eunuch. He had always been a master of the art of deriving what is mental out of the physical. Other crowning achievements are successful with Echnaton, the decadent pharaoh, whose traditional facial characteristics are reminiscent of "a young, elegant Englishman from a somewhat faded lineage."

That explains most of it. Inventing is again revealed after all as finding. What is autobiographical is added as the last level of inspiration. It is the force behind the selection of material, for the story of the "chaste Joseph" was naturally of direct interest to the chaste Thomas. It is found further in the basic intellectual idea, for the gigantic novel has to legitimize his own rejection of sympathy with death. Politics, too, plays a role. Unlike *The Magic Mountain*, which was after all composed in the imperial age, *Joseph* is a republican conception. Joseph should not only resist desire, he should also show the path of an artist from narcissistic arrogance in love with moon and night to current political responsibility—thus, Thomas Mann's own path.

Beyond what is general, there are further numerous footprints from his own life. Most are not fundamental but offer original points that are like icing on the cake. Again and again they partly gave him impish pleasure, partly brought tears to his eyes. In the final analysis the matrix, which guides the idea and decides about putting something read or something experienced into the novel, is after all essentially the same as always, which is why we were able to put a quotation from the Joseph novel in the middle of the section "Primal Odds and Ends." In fact, it is once again "always the same thing," once again the intrusion of drunkenly destructive and devastating powers into a life sworn to composure, once again the song of apparently assured peace and of life laughingly sweeping away the true structure of art.

## ICING ON THE CAKE

Benjamin, the youngest of the twelve, in an obvious way maintains minor connections to Michael, the youngest of the Mann children. The role of pet of the family, the husky short legs, and the helmlike head of hair are part of it.

The old Minaean or Midianite, who buys Joseph from his brothers and takes him to Egypt, can tell what an object is worth from its fiber and grain by rubbing it between his fingers. He is an ancestor of the publisher Samuel Fischer, whose instinct for the literary and business value of a book the whole book trade admired. Egotistically, Joseph believes the Minaean was conveying him, while the latter intends to take him along quite by chance. Thomas Mann, of course, is able to shape the circumstances in his favor. When Joseph is brought to his destination, the merchant is ruthlessly dismissed. "The Ishmaelites of Midian had fulfilled their purpose in life. —they were no longer needed." Ironically, behind this appears the relationship of Thomas Mann to his publisher. Certainly Samuel Fischer made Thomas Mann great—but did not Thomas Mann also make him great? In any event, the writer enjoys the Joseph identification, enjoys feeling like a valuable product that is brought to market by the Minaean and generates a steep price. That is a little game, no more than that, not a fundamental connection. Playfully, Thomas Mann again and again disappears behind his own figures. Teasingly he winks at the reader and challenges him to do the same, to look for figures behind which he can hide his joy and sorrow but also at the same time reveal them insofar as models loosen the obstructed embarrassment, give speech immune to shame, joy, and sorrow, and raise it out of its empty privacy to representative significance.

Dûdu and Gottliebchen, the evil and the good dwarf, one who wants to harass Joseph into misfortune, and the other admiring warner and helper, the phallic, studiedly dignified man and the endearing little old hag: Are these not Lessing and Lublinski, the Jewish critics? Theodor Lessing, the wretched man, who boasts of his ethics and in reality had malicious interest in sin? Samuel Lublinski, the helper, who had praised *Buddenbrooks* so prophetically? Sometimes it seems to Thomas Mann to be so. The one tears him down, the other treats him with great consideration. "Don't buy him," says Dûdu, "the Hebrew, for he is suspicious, although he knows how to babble sweetly." "Buy him, Mont-kaw," whispers the old hag on the other hand. "He is blessed and will be a blessing to your house." Dûdu, who brags about his potency, has a large wife. Did not the dwarf Lessing marry a large woman who is a blond from the German nobility? Who betrayed him soon, however, with a young blond student, for which reason perhaps "Dûdu's" potency was not in the best of order? It serves him right, the evil dwarf! The teasing he made me endure for lacking masculinity! The hate for Lessing also inspires unfavorable things in Thomas Mann, damages his otherwise so incorruptible taste. But let's not take our speculations too far. Dûdu and Gottliebchen, Lessing and Lublinski—that is only one shadowy trace, by no means assured. The large woman can be explained sufficiently from an Egyptian artwork and the antithetic dwarf pair sufficiently from the opposition of intellect and desire. Mann works on "The Dwarfs" chapter on August 10, 1933. At that time he is drastically reminded of Lessing, specifically by his murder, which he comments on heartlessly, still filled with hate. "My old friend Lessing has indeed been murdered. He always was a false martyr." That can be worked into the novel but does not have to be.

Again and again new figures appear; new faces, new characters are used. They do not come out of the void. Mann gave the prison official Mai-Sachme the countenance and the character of the friend of the family, Martin Gumpert, the round eyes and the small mouth and the sedate manner that did not tend to be startled. Further, he lets him dabble in being a doctor and a writer—Martin Gumpert was also an author-physician. "Medical science and writing hide their light from one another to their advantage." Gumpert visited him for a few weeks from August 31, 1940, on. That was just at the right time. He is rather promptly "utilized." From September 20 on, Mann works on the prison chapter.

Mai-Sachme is touching through his constantly unhappy love, first as a boy for a genteel girl, then as a man for the daughter of the early beloved, and presumably a third time in his old age with her granddaughter. In all of that the only thing really autobiographical is being unlucky in love. For Martin Gumpert loved Erika Mann and wanted to marry her, but she hid his Easter breakfast egg, though tenderly, however did hold him off and finally shrugged him loose.

To speak secretively about one's self is satisfying. The story again and again offers opportunities to do so. With Pharaoh's statement, "Whoever has a hard time shall also have an easy time," Mann does himself a good turn, for he counts himself among those who have a hard time. "That we are in a story, an excellent one," Joseph says to Mai-Sachme, but Thomas Mann also wants to say that to his fellow-men, who should be happy to be allowed to be his contemporaries. "But you are also in it because I took you into the story along with me." Charlotte Kestner, née Buff, should be happy that Goethe took her into his story. Katia and Paul should be happy that Thomas Mann took them into his stories. If someone does not understand that, then he is snubbed like Otto Grautoff, the confidant of his boyhood years full of suffering and laughter, who did not seem to know "that he belonged only to my life," but foolishly "wanted to be something himself."

Occasionally, Thomas Mann sits down with the storyteller on the old men's bench. They reflect about matters of love. With nodding heads they assure one another, "We know all that." "To awaken feeling again in us old men," say Jacob the storyteller and Thomas Mann in chorus, "something special must come along." And, prophetically in regard to his later enchantment with Franz Westermeier's handsome eyes, legs, and physique, "You probably think: at seventy-five it can't be quite as bad anymore with your enthrallment and menial desire, but there you're wrong. That goes on till your last breath."

## THAMAR AND AGNES MEYER

"Thamar was fully resolved that, cost what it might, she wanted to intervene in world history with the help of her femininity." Unflinching, ambitious, and striving, she did not want to be part of the crowd like the many but to take the main highway of history. Rooted to the spot by vigilance, she had sat at the feet of Jacob, the man heavy with history, and had been able to make sense out of the prophecy that the Redeemer would come from the tribe of Judah. She therefore desired Judah not for the sake of the flesh but for the sake of the idea, because from him would arise the tribe out of which one day the Messiah should come. But the grizzled Jacob was a little in love with her.

Agnes E. Meyer had fully resolved that with the help of her femininity she would intervene in world history. At least, Thomas Mann saw it like that. She had sat at his feet, the man heavy with stories, and fallen in love with him for his intellect, even if not in the flesh, because the celebrated man wanted none of that. The world-redeeming child that she wanted to have with him was literature. Unflinching, ambitious, and striving she had prepared the way to America for this child, supported it financially, reviewed it helpfully, and deftly translated it into English.

Thamar is a biblical figure and not introduced into the novel for the sake of Agnes Meyer. The only very cautious allusion to his rich American patron again belongs to the top-notch women in love with themselves with whom Thomas Mann incidentally did himself a good turn. The admiration that he pays to Thamar's and Agnes's ambition does no one as much good as himself. For if Thamar's ambition applies to the coming Redeemer, then Agnes Meyer's ambition must apply to a goal at least as important! He is her god. "I love to play with greatness," he had confided to Agnes. On January 16, 1942, she replies when the Thamar episode had just been finished:

> What you say about greatness touched me fantastically—"I love to play with greatness and to live with it on a certain intimate footing." It certainly did not occur to you that that fits my life much more than it does your art.

She plays with greatness, and she takes it a long way. On April 7 of the same year she asks whether something like the alliance of Jacob and God, established for mutual sanctification, could not also be possible in a purely human encounter, if, that is to say, one of them were far superior to the other? She really sees him as God—which does not mean that she is herself small in her own mind. The alliance serves as *mutual* sanctification. She thus also has a task. She wants the bond of souls that a woman ties "to serve the man not as a snare but as liberation." Wisely said. But as free as she was, she was not successful in liberating Thomas Mann, because he did not want to be liberated in the sense that she planned.

From March 29 to April 4, 1942, Agnes stayed near Thomas Mann in Santa Monica, and there were daily meetings. He had read "Thamar" to her, an especially successful chapter. He calls it "a piece, 'with which you did not bother me.'" What an odd statement! Apparently she bothered him with other pieces. Thomas Mann also had to visit her on her last day in Santa Monica—without Katia. "With Meyer in the bungalow. Read 'Thamar' to its end. Eugene at times." (That is her husband.) "Lunch with her. Met artifice with incomprehension." She insists on talking about love, again and again, and she has a very direct manner. Her favorite subject is his inner life. She believes that Thomas Mann has no relationship with people; he writes completely uninfluenced by emotions. He knows better. "Everything serves the explanation of why I do not start a relationship with her. But 'Thamar' proves at least that she 'didn't bother me.'"

No, she did not bother him on the whole; rather, she energetically helped Thomas Mann. She assisted him and his children again and again financially and through her contacts; she got him the well-paid position at Princeton as lecturer in the humanities; through her he became consultant in German literature in Washington, D.C., a sinecure (with an income of five thousand dollars a year); through her, or as the case may be, through her husband, he became acquainted with President Roosevelt. Truly, he could not afford to break with her, even though she occasionally got on his nerves terribly. In his thank-you note after her visit he uses the obliging flowery phrase: "I will not deny that, for my part, it could have lasted a bit longer." That is a bald-faced lie. He was glad that she was gone again. The letter then continues lightheartedly: "But that now lies in the past, and each one must again live on his own and do what he has to do—with the help of the aftereffects of good days." The diary is more truthful. It transmits mostly embarrassments from those days, discussions "about us" (March 30), "painful conversations" (March 31), "much that was awful to keep locked up" (April 3), "captious situations" (April 4). He is glad when the prospect of "this is coming to an end" looms (April 2). In his letters he writes cordially "Dear Agnes," but in the diary he always calls her merely "that Meyer woman."

She had the consciousness of a mission and a pioneer spirit. "I was traveling undiscovered regions of my own mind." She believed that he was like her, a kindred soul, without knowing it. Fearlessly she approached the prudish, the intractable. She believed he was loveless. But of course, he knew: I, too, have lived and loved. But no one should find out about that. She did not know the secret of his restraint. She lacked an understanding of his chastity. Why did he have to defend himself against her? Because she was trying to gain his innermost soul. "You wanted to teach me, dominate me, improve me,

redeem me." Indeed. Her goal—she writes him candidly—was to liberate him from his fear of woman as seducer. He should not be
shocked at this daring feeling. German asceticism was doubtless
something more sublime than the French sinfulness that had destroyed the gifted Rimbaud, but, she continues, "there is a more loving, more sublime discernment where fear disappears entirely and
[that] leads to complete redemption." But he did not want to be delivered of his chastity, above all not by that Meyer woman. What was
said of Thamar, that she was beautiful, even if in a severe and forbid-
ding way, seductive, bewitching, demonic—this Mann says of dear
Agnes nowhere. At the time she was past fifty. She was not his type,
either intellectually or physically. He was not afraid of her. He did not
have to perform some virtuouso trick of virtue to keep her at a distance. He simply did not love her. He considered her a mixture of
Juno and a Valkyrie. Unfortunately, one must assume that mainly
comfort, usefulness, and obligation kept him so long at her side. He
plays a fairly consciously calculated role. "Bravely endured," he compliments himself for the discipline of his role (January 13, 1940). For
generally, it was strenuous. "Shattered by the threshing of empty
straw and by indicating an intellectual presence that is missing"
(March 21, 1951). Only seldom was it entertaining. "An almost unrestrained mendacious New Year's greeting to that Meyer woman" (December 31, 1947). He tried to give her what he was able to give, many
long letters, much respect, much gratitude. But his heart was not in it.
Years later she saw through him. Golo mentions that it says in his
diary, "Statement by the Meyer woman that it is clear from my letters
that I despise her. Since these letters are full of sincerity, admiration,
gratitude, care, even gallantry, that is a very intelligent observation"
(February 14, 1944). "Tonio, you are hard as stone when you want to
hurt," Agnes had written barely a year before, after a quarrel.


## FATHER AND MOTHER, KATIA AND PAUL

We meet more than only decorative characters in the center of the
novel, where in the old Oriental multitude of disguises Thomas
Mann's primal conflicts ply their hidden natures: the decisive battle
between father and mother, the competition between marriage and

homosexuality, the fear of ordeal and subjugation. The reflections of his life cross one another many times in his great works. The chaste Joseph is often the chaste Thomas. But he is also his opposite, a handsome boy whom Thomas loves and whom as a storyteller he keeps before him for years and daily anew with tender sympathy. "Again reread . . . the chapter 'On Beauty' in 'Young Joseph.' Jests about what is most profound in me." What is most profound? His enthusiasm for "the incomparable charm of masculine youth that is surpassed by nothing in the world."

The seductive Mut-em-enet with her sinuous mouth, the wife of Potiphar—she, too, *is* Thomas Mann. Conjuring up demons, he writes into her the trauma of his soul, how it would be if a passion also swept away the artistic structure of his life. Mut, too, had reconciled herself already to an ascetic life as a chaste moon nun when Joseph entered her house and she, devoured by desire, gradually became a witch, the Venus on the Mount, the bearded Ishtar. Surrender to desire, of course, in a certain regard, makes for blissful happiness and liberation, but even more it humiliates and debases in the eyes of one's own reason and in those of a surrounding derisive world.

The narrator, however, does warn against the trusting assumption that for the human being it involves the preservation of a life structure, erected with so much care. "Experiences that one cannot call isolated are evidence that he has aimed much more precisely at his bliss and his ruin and is in no way grateful to anyone who wants to keep him from it." Where does he know that from? His fear revealed it to him. When he has to describe Mut-em-enet's corruption, he does not look only in the ancient Oriental sources. He delves much more into notes that he had made during the time of his love for Paul Ehrenberg. The passion of that time should lend him words for the helpless ordeal of his heroine. He is moved. The passion and melancholy of those long gone days speak to him confidentially and with life's melancholy. Thirty years and more have passed. "Oh well, I have lived and loved; I have in my way 'paid for my humanity.'" It was, in spite of and because of so much renunciation, so much disappointment, his greatest love. For

being overwhelmed, as is expressed by certain tones in the journals from the P.E. time, this "I love you—my God—I love you!"—

an intoxication as is indicated in the poem fragment "O hark, music! —In my ear a shiver of sound wafts blissfully away—" happened—as is probably proper—just one time in my life.

"Muddled, flowering logic of love," the Joseph novel observes in this regard. "We know all that." What does Mut-em-enet whisper? "O hark, music," etc. The narrator adds in this respect, at the time only for his own, today also for our pleasure: "We know that, too." For Thomas Mann experienced and suffered everything himself, also those feverish nights of love "that are only a series of nothing but short dreams in which the other is always there and shows himself cold and full of suspicion, turns away scornfully" in a chain of disastrous meetings. But had he cursed him, the creator of such tormenting nights; had Mut-em-enet cursed him?

> By no means. When morning released her from the torture, what she, exhausted on the edge of her bed, whispered to him from her place to his, was:
> "I thank thee, my salvation! my good fortune! my lucky star!"
> The charitable man shakes his head about such a reply to horrible suffering; in his pity he finds himself disconcerted and made halfway ridiculous by her.

"My salvation! my good fortune! my lucky star!" originates just like the "O hark, music" and the "I love you" from that poem to Paul Ehrenberg that as a secret code meanders again and again through Mann's writings.

Once more the identifications change when years later the time of concessions comes and Joseph can marry. Now wearing the Joseph disguise again, Thomas Mann considers how what was forbidden until now can be allowed in the future, namely, sexuality. What should not have been with Paul had to be with Katia. "He, too," like Joseph, like Adam, "recognized woman only after he had first learned what is good and what is evil: from a snake that would gladly have taught him for her life what is very very good but evil. But he resisted it and had the knack of waiting until it was good and no longer evil."

Like Asnath, Katia was "the virgin of virgins" and the "epitome of girlhood," at first not disposed to surrender her virginity. But "the union of sacredly reserved inaccessibility with an outspoken inclination to let things happen to her and to accept with forbearing her womanly lot" finally made it possible for the mysterious bridegroom to take her, although she raised her arms to heaven "calling for help as though someone were grabbing her around her narrow waist and dragging her into an abduction cart." All of that does not sound exactly like love but much more like that well-considered partnership of two for whom it was to be hoped that love would find them. Asnath and Joseph, Katia and Thomas—they come to a marriage in which first the decision to marry was present and only then did affection follow.

Virginity associates with virginity. Talk on their wedding night is not of blissful melting and the heart-stirring breath of Ishtar but of blood and pain at the difficult "lacerating work."

> And is it not absurd what physical nature, in its customary scheme, thought up for human beings, that they put a seal on love, or in the case of a state marriage, learn to love one another? The ridiculous and the sublime wavered indistinctly in one another in the beam of the hanging lamp even during this wedding night, where virginity met virginity and ripped wreath and veil.

"I read that with pleasure, for it was my case," Thomas Mann wrote in his essay on marriage, admittedly in a somewhat different but not far distant connection.

The menacing Mut-em-enet bears a primal mother's name. She is the Great Mother. Thomas Mann experiences what is homosexual bisexually. Joseph is "handsome as woman and man, handsome from both sides." The motif of bisexuality is mystical and divine to him. It makes him think of a Platen poem that has fascinated him for a long time. "How his spiritualized and supraerotic passion got into my blood when I was in love." He cites it in his diary on February 25, 1934:

> I am to you like woman to man, like man to woman.
> I am to you like body to spirit, like spirit to body.
> Whom can you love else, since from off your lips
> With eternal kisses I drive death away from you?

Bisexuality threatens the world of the father, which must insist on clear-cut separation, but it contains the allurement of the primal one thing, and so the worst is again also the most beautiful. The tree of life must have blossomed bisexually, Joseph explains to Potiphar, male and female at the same time. "Lo, the world is torn in its sex, so we speak of male and female. . . . But the foundation of the world and the tree of life is neither male nor female but both in one."

Mut-em-enet is a cheerless person. Her motherhood is not sheltering but devouring, like that of Ishtar with the beard, the bisexual goddess of fertility, whom Gilgamesh puts to flight because he, like Joseph, "did not want to be reduced to a suffering femaleness through the mannish wooing of a dominating woman, but wanted to be not the target but the arrow of desire." In the arrangement of this novel homosexuality and the world of the mother belong together. Lustful atrocity, incest, homosexuality, and promiscuity belong to the world of the mother.

There are two dreams of happiness. When the one opens to you, the other closes. You can dream about the mother or about the father. The dream of the mother is the dream of merging. It wants to raise the limits of the body, wants you to melt and flow away into a rushing union with everything that lives. Without space and time it lets you float free in the void and without regard and consequences embrace your beloved like Mut-em-enet, "mouth to mouth and with closed eyes," like Hans Castorp, who wants to die in Clawdia/ Pribislav's embrace: "laisse-moi périr, mes lèvres aux tiennes." (Let me perish, my lips on yours.) The motifs remain the same over a long time. In *The Magic Mountain* as in *Joseph*, the mouth is the instrument of the senses and the union of organs (the upper exit of the digestive tract, as Freud emphasizes in an ugly way somewhere), the eye is the instrument of sight and perception.

For the eye belongs to the father. The second dream, that of the father, is the dream of exaltation. It is directed vertically, not horizontally as the dream of the mother is. It wants to get out of the senses to the mind, out of the darkness into the light, out of the multitude to the solitary, out of mergence to individuality. In the decisive moment, when Joseph's flesh rebels against his mind, the features of his father appear to him, gazing worriedly, the brown eyes with pouches underneath. The prematurely dead father has great power over Thomas Mann. The Joseph novel shapes, confirms, and emphasizes the decision for the father, which in *The Magic Mountain* had remained so contestable, since Hans Castorp had after all relapsed again and again into the world of mergence and had ended in sludge and war and death.

The world of the father is represented manifoldly in the novel. First of all, there is Jacob, but there are also the old Minaean, Mont-kaw, and Potiphar. All are fathers for Joseph, all are hostile to the world of mergence, all believe in being loyal; for all of them it is hard. For fathers it is hard. They need the soothing good-night that Joseph says to the Minaean and with which he escorts Mont-kaw to his death. With Mont-kaw Joseph makes a covenant concerning Potiphar that he will never betray the castrato. That is why, when he sums up the reasons for his chastity, not only Jacob's face appears to him but also the benevolent voice of Potiphar.

It is not as though the paternal world were unthreatened. The light is weak and needs protection. In *The Magic Mountain* reason resided only in the head, but death dwelt in the heart. So thought was powerless. Only in *Joseph* does a real victory of the rights of the father occur. Only here is the light successful in inveigling the lower powers into its service. The renunciation of sympathy with death has become for Joseph active application.

> Consciousness of death alone creates rigidity and darkness; consciousness of life alone creates dull commonplace that is also without wit. For wit and sympathy come into being only where solemnity toward death is tinged and warmed through with friendliness toward life; but the latter is deepened and enhanced by the former. Such was Joseph's case; such were his wit and his affability.

## CHURCHILL AND THE BIBLE

Aggressive antireligious thoughts dominated the young Winston Churchill—at least he believed that. Of course, when as a young lieutenant in India he came into deadly peril in the fire of battle, he did not hesitate to beg God for protection and to thank him from his heart when the danger was past.

Thomas Mann begins the small reflection "On the Book of Books and Joseph" (1944) with this experience. That contradictions exist between the scientific worldview and that of the Bible does not bother him. Like Churchill he proceeds from the thought that the heart has reasons that the mind knows not of. His opinion of Bible criticism is

completely passive religiously. His attitude toward this massive con-
glomeration of writing, "which with hundreds of legendary, anonymous, pseudonymous, and more or less historical writers has been
formed into a whole, for which reason there is complete justification
to call God its author," agrees completely with the opinion of the
young British lieutenant in India. It is pragmatic, not dogmatic.
"What is the Bible, considered rationally? It consists of a multitude
of heterogeneous and undeniably also variously significant literary
works of Jewry and early Christianity: myths, sagas, stories, hymns,
and other literary forms, historical chronicles, essays, collections of
proverbs, and codicils of laws, the composition of which, or more
correctly the writing down of which, is spread over a very long period of time, from the fifth century B.C. to the second century A.D. But
many portions reach, according to their origin, far into the past beyond that realm of time: they are vestiges and fragments of gray antiquity that lie around in the Book like colossal orphans." Far from
putting the position of the Book into question, this genesis far more
gives it its value. "Calendar of instructions and comfort, book of
prayers, textbook of recurring celebratory occasions whose great, unmistakable tones we hear at all stages of human life, with baptism,
wedding, funeral, the powerful Book is marked by meditation, pious
confidence, searching devotion, and reverent love of the long pro-
cessions of generations of human beings, a possession of the heart,
unpurloinable, untouchable by any criticism of the intellect."

Mann's theological point is constituted not of demanding from revelation truths that are beyond time, but of being content with the
Bible as a testimonial of condensed historical and cultural experience,
not of deducing from that a debasement of the Bible but to grant it a
high if not absolute rank. The history of its effectiveness has created
the Bible. Therefore he has no qualms about writing further on the
Bible, of correcting it humorously, of modernizing it, and of explaining its imprecisenesses philologically and making them plausible psychologically with playful scholarship. The colorful light refracted in
the dust of history is much more important to him than pure white
light. In opposition to his theological friend and pastor Kuno Friedler,
who once baptized the little child, he objects that the simple tidings
about Jesus are not at all compatible with a church. From the viewpoint of the need for religious comfort by humankind, a church needs
refracted light, needs "a structure of dogma and the primally popular

combination of tradition with religious myth." It does not depend on what Jesus really was but on what was made of Him. Thomas Mann puts himself on the side of Dostoyevski's grand inquisitor, who would ask a returning Christ: Why have you come to bother us?

## GOD, THE FATHER, AND THE ANGELIC CREATURE

"I believe in God, in the United States of America, and in baseball." It was that simple for Babe Ruth, a baseball star of the time. "We talked about God and religion today, and I explained that, with the best of intentions, I could not say whether I believed or not." Thus Thomas Mann in 1941 to Agnes Meyer on the day before Christmas. He continued, alluding to Voltaire's "Ecrasez l'infame!" (but meaning not the Church, but Hitler): "But at times I feel suspicious that I do believe; for without a faith one probably cannot hate 'l'infame,' as I avowedly do."

So faith grows out of hate. He is, first of all, motivated by the ethical and practical. Thomas Mann believes because he needs faith. He can believe only in a useful God. He can do little with the customary God. He does not think much of a Highest Being that would be omnipotent and perfect and would let mankind do nothing real but worship humbly. "Oh, well, the Lord does everything," his narrator mirror image comments sorrowfully on this way of thinking. If God were like that, then He could direct the world according to His pleasure and would not need mankind. Therefore Thomas Mann thinks up a God who is needy. The useful God is a needy God. Thomas Mann opposes the traditional religious humbling of mankind ("What is man, that thou art mindful of him? and the son of man, that thou visitest him?" Ps. 8:5) with great encouragement. What is God, if mankind is not mindful of Him? He trusts that God will not take the frivolity amiss. "I am convinced that He understands a joke."

God and man need one another. They enhance one another mutually. "Purify the godhead and you purify mankind." For mankind the idea of God is an ever-enduring spring that draws his longing upward so that he will not constantly fall back into bestiality. Conversely, man is necessary for God so that He will not be bored. Man is "the product of God's curiosity about Himself." A fascinating entertainment opens up for God—"one needed only to think of the prac-

tice of grace and mercy, of judging and laws, of the emergence of
merit and guilt, of reward and punishment." To a Highest Being that
contemplates only itself and suffices for itself, one less high is to
be preferred that indulges in time and world and the multitude and
even becomes carnate itself when it seems necessary. Because God
can descend and can be found from the purest idea down to the
worldly servant on all the rungs of the ladder, in this way only can
He help man, who for his part can ascend and can get far in his best
specimens. He can get as far as "a little god," like young Joseph when
he dreams his dream of heaven in which he is taken higher and
higher under the protest of the angels, who complain that one born of
a drop of white semen may reach the uppermost heaven. But the
Lord wants to exaggerate for once and makes the boy immeasurably
greater than all other creatures and calls him: "The little God." Only
in a dream, of course.

In reality, it is not so easy to get there. Wearily we climb from rung
to rung, mostly upward but also often far down, and whether at the
end of life we are higher than at the beginning remains to be seen. It
is easier to stick to a rung than to climb up. The gravity of earth pulls
us downward. "I understand better and better what the Christian
means by 'world.' Truly, one must be a man to come 'to God' in spite
of it." He is a man, this Thomas Mann—he likes to pun with his
name.

God is only an anthropomorphic projection, say the critics of religion, the yearning opposite of our imperfection. Thomas Mann agrees
with that, but he leaves out the "only." Projecting is nevertheless a
great thing! He lets Abraham "discover" God and "think Him out"
from clearly recognizable interests, but he does not cry out: "There,
lo, He does not really exist, rather the contrary: Let us all cooperate;
let us discover God and work together on His image." Human beings
need God; "they always imitate only the gods, and they act in accordance with the image that they make of them." God needs human
beings so that He can be invented as great and not low and common.
That God is in need of help gives the religiosity of this novel that
eminently productive, that active and encouraging, trait.

Mann's God is the father par excellence. He bears the facial features
of Jacob, of the father who despises apelike Egypt as the matriarchal
underworld. The face of his father saves Joseph in his hour of temptation. It is the face of God. Doubtless God looks like a human being—

mankind was, after all, created in His image. For Thomas Mann it is the image of the father. God could not appear to him in just any image.

No one has ever seen God. Our talk about Him always is based on images. That is also the case with ecclesiastical theology. What is considered dogmatically true in particulars loses in absolutism because it is never actuality itself. If by "faith" one understands not a system of principles but the factually endowed basis of the fundamentals of life, not a meaning, but a being, then the differences are made relative between those who assume as faithful Christians they are in the right boat and the "unbelievers."

As a Nietzschean, Thomas Mann is first of all a philosophical nihilist. "Believing is a great rapture of the soul. But not believing is almost more blissful than believing"—he lets Echnaton express that jubilantly. He is an unbeliever on the search. He aims to discover how one can live sensibly in spite of an unavoidable lack of belief. He is a pragmatist of faith. He is a nihilist in theory, but in practice he liberates religion from the suffocating clichés of its appointed guardians, whose teachings are like abandoned houses: "They are standing and enduring, but no one lives in them anymore." Their actions bore God. But in reading the Joseph novel God kisses His fingers and cries out, to the secret annoyance of the angels: "It is incredible how thoroughly this clump of clay knows Me! Am I not beginning to make a name for Myself through him?"

To the annoyance of the angels—they consider the "angelic animal" (man) a freak. Why did God have to get involved with flesh and body and time and death? Why this mixture of pure spirit with the bestial? Ironically, Thomas Mann asks, as do the angels, the ancient question about the meaning of creation and the why and wherefor of the suffering in the world. But the direction of his thought is in truth reversed. We find man to be a half-breed of angel and animal. He knows what is most sublime and sometimes does what is basest. How can he be helped? By giving him a God Who draws him upward, Whom he draws upward. By forcing him to "work on the divine."

God, too, knows backsliding. "God has not kept in step," Jacob complains when he believes his beloved son Joseph has been torn to pieces by wild beasts, and even calls the Lord a "fiend." Of course, he is mistaken in this case because being torn apart is only the prerequisite for the resurrection and exaltation of Joseph, and the Lord knows very well what he wants, but what is fiendish already belongs to the essence of this God, who Himself once began as a small desert demon. Abraham and Jacob assist him, of course, to a precipitate career in majesty and purity, but at times the primal rises in him and he has atavistic lapses as do his children. Then he takes the beloved or the son from someone. "Those are remnants of the desert, try to explain it to yourself like that." Thomas Mann's God is not "just" but thoroughly biased; He chooses whomever He will, is also sometimes distracted and unobservant.

"He was not goodness, but wholeness." He is therefore also darkness, evil, and the incalculably terrible—"also the earthquake, the crackling lightning, the swarm of locusts that darkened the sun, the seven evil winds, the dust-Abubu, the hornets and snakes were from God." "Since God is wholeness, He is also the devil," Doctor Riemer points out in the Goethe novel, *The Beloved Returns*. Since He is wholeness, His business is all-encompassing irony.

He does not concern Himself with individuals. He has no sympathy for anyone who stands in the way of a grand plan. He lets the old Minaean move on into the distance as soon as He has no more need of him—although we have become fond of him. It is far worse for Potiphar's steward Mont-kaw—he is removed; God Himself takes care of that because He needs Mont-kaw's position for Joseph. "Joseph was very dismayed, when he realized God's intentions." God can also not be just because what profits one person generally is of damage to someone else in this world. Whether God blesses one person and curses another has nothing to do with moral failings in the one cursed, as though he could have acted differently. Blessing and curse are only affirmations of the one already blessed, the one already cursed. The individual has no choice. He finds himself, and if he understands, it is good. There must be evil for the sake of the good. The role of Cain must be played, just as that of Esau, Ishmael, or the chief baker. Thomas Mann is not fooling us here. His piety knows no cheap comfort. The chief baker will die a gruesome death. His comfort consists only in that his role is equally as necessary as that of the cup-bearer who is pardoned. God is not goodness but wholeness:

But you, master baker, do not despair! For I believe you have given yourself over to evil because you considered it prescribed

as respectable and confused it with goodness, as may well happen. Behold, you are part of God when He is below, and your
companion is of God when He is above. But both of you are of
God, and a raised head is a raised head, whether it be on the
cross or the stake.

God is on the middle rungs of the ladder, as we are. He wants to do
good, but He does not always succeed. He created Eve from Adam's
rib and found that it was good, while the novel comments scornfully:
"And it was well meant." But it did not end well. With love came
suffering also. God, too, is lonely. He wants to be loved. As a result
He is envious. He does not approve of the tender and fastidious emotions with which Jacob chose Rachel to be the most supreme, but
castigates him for it. The unrestrained feeling of one person for another is idolatry. God punishes Jacob for that and teaches Joseph
chastity.

God is father, but on his part He has a father, Abraham, namely,
who beheld Him and thought Him into existence and therefore can
choose to remonstrate Him. That a person can quarrel with God is a
part of the strength of the Old Testament, which Thomas Mann does
not iron out smoothly in a Christian way but emphasizes sharply.
"Hear, Lord," Abraham had objected gruffly at that time, what do
You want, anyway? "If You want to have a world, then You can't ask
for justice; but if it's a matter of justice to You, then You are through
with the world." Cain, too, complains cleverly when God confronts
him because of the murder of Abel. "But who created me the way I
am . . . ? Who put in me the wicked urge for the deed that I undeniably did?"

Nietzsche had written that there is need of the evil God as well as
the good one. He loved the Old Testament. "I find great people in it, a
heroic landscape, and something extremely rare on earth, the incomparable naïvité of a *strong heart*; more than that, I find a people. In the
New Testament, on the other hand, nothing but the petty enterprise
of sects, nothing but a rococo of the soul, nothing but ornamentation,
angularity, eccentricity, nothing but an air of small gatherings of like-
minded people."

Thomas Mann also finds the Old Testament the more straightfor-
ward. A novel about Jesus from his pen is difficult to imagine. He
cannot believe that salvation has already come—what he sees speaks

against it. There is no sign of it; nowhere is our time clearly superior to the time before Christ. The rationale of theologians with their nit-picking "already" and "not-yet" is as pretentious as rationales usually are. I sing the song of him whose bread I eat. Jesus is contemplated unemotionally— He is only one of many who were there before him, such as Tammuz, who is torn to pieces and returns, Osiris, who descends and rises again, such as Adonis and Joseph and the many who will still come and like him will in every death experience resurrection.

When he sees Rachel die, Jacob cries out: "Lord, what are You doing?" In such cases no reply follows. But there an absolute is put on suffering, even the worst kind—being crucified, any kind of torture, the torment of Job, the lamentation of Jacob—beyond which it is transformed into salvation. Even death has its advantages. The non-political observer is of the opinion that life is severe, savage, and wicked at any time, but he also knew that every heart was capable of terror to only a limited extent, beyond which numbness set in, or ecstasy, or even a religious liberation and cheer that meant the conquest of death itself. There is resurrection, there is conquest of death in this novel, but they are not attached exclusively to Jesus. He does appear in various allusions, allusions to the virginal birth, to His teachings in the temple, to the kiss of Judas, to His "I thirst"* on the Cross, and to the road to Emmaus, but Tammuz and Osiris are no less present than He is. But the narrator is hardly interested in the prophesied Messiah of the people of Israel, whom Jacob calls Shiloh.

## ON THE MAGICIAN'S CHASTITY

The degree and type of a person's sexuality extend into his spirituality to the highest degree. Wished for and impossible of being wished for is what Mann calls the deprivation with which he replies to his enthusiasm for the incomparable allurement of virile youths. "The illusionary, cloudlike inconceivable, impalpable that is nevertheless the fullest of suffering enthusiasm"—that unrealizable passion becomes for him the "foundation of the practice of art." Abstinence, to which he saw himself forced by his predisposition, becomes intel-

---

* John 19:28 (Trans.)

lectualized in him to a global principle. He intensifies it already in *Tonio Kröger* to the purity of reality. The artist is chaste. He is only an observer and shaper of life, but does not get involved in it. He is an ironist, therefore not subject to any interest. Irony is the reservation against everything and anything. Translated into the language of religion: The ironist has no part of anything earthly. Spoken in a Paulinian way: He has as though he did not have. (1 Cor. 7:27). In Martin Luther's words: "A Christian human being is a free lord over all things and not subject to anyone. A Christian human being is a subservient menial to all things and subject to everyone." From the standpoint of an ironist, the world is vain, a breath of wind; he ponders on its possible end; as a result he is free, not subject to extortion by anything. He loves it at most in its entirety, but everything individual is equally near or equally far to him. He loves the crowd, but none of those in the crowd. Chastity becomes the fundamental principle of life and perception. It is not merely the masochistic flight of the frustrated. "It is not talk of dark and tedious mortification in the gaunt image of which a modern sense almost inevitably sees chastity." Rather, chastity has humor, superiority, scorn. It is cheerful, wanton, indeed arrogant, for not without reason does it feel superior to others. It is the bright virtue of the father in comparison to the dreary temptation of the mother. But unchasteness is a desecration of the father, incestuous "encroachment of the son into the paternal reserves." It is as though the bisexual sphinx, which has breasts but perhaps also dangling testicles, were to lift its paws from the sand and snatch the curious to its breast. A dream came to Joseph; in which it said to him: "I love you. Betake yourself to me." But he replies: "How can I do such an evil thing and sin against God?"

In chastity there lives a longing for the more sublime that is ashamed of all that is earthly. Therefore it is also the last and most sublime substance of the idea of God. God wants it. He is jealous when a human being is attached to an earthly passion. The meaning of circumcision is the pledge of the sexual organs to God. It is the expression of the bond of fidelity of what is reserved because it is engaged to God. To be chaste even though married, to be free even though manifoldly obliged and bound, fearless because nothing can happen worse than death, because death, however, is not bad for one who sees the starry sky blinking over every grave—to be like that was the wish of Thomas Mann; that was his religion; for that, he needed God. His chastity is love for the purity of God. "The purification of God from dreary perfidy to sacredness retrospectively includes that of mankind in which it is perfected in accorance with God's urgent wish." The graves are present for the sake of resurrection.

## MILITANT CHRISTIANITY

What is impure is dreary perfidy. That Thomas Mann assigns fascism to the antiquated realm of the mother has perhaps little value as a political theory. But it gave him strength for resistance, the power of his chastity. Fascism is what is impure, what is unvirtuous, the babbling foolishness of Baal, irrationality abiding in dark fertility. But the God of the fathers of Joseph is a spiritual God Who has nothing to do with what is below and with death. Thomas Mann opposes fascism with a patriarchal Christianity. The "Conquest of Christianity," as propagated audaciously by National Socialists such as Alfred Rosenberg, calls his resistance into action. "The consciousness of my cultural Christianity that, I confess, hesitates to become 'devout' and to submit to revelation, has been strengthened in recent times" (diary, August 23, 1934).

> Say what you will, Christianity, this flower of Jewry, remains one of the two basic pillars on which Western civilization rests, of which the other is Mediterranean antiquity.

# XVI. Hate for Hitler

*Princeton, 1939*

On November 19, 1936, Thomas Mann had become a Czech. He and Katia Mann became American citizens on June 23, 1944. After his expulsion from Germany, the farewell to Europe became the next great turning point. "Unease and emotion at the conclusion of this five-year epoch in my life" (September 15, 1938).

His acknowledgment of exile opened the way again for a rich international activity as a lecturer. In May 1936, on the occasion of the eightieth birthday of Sigmund Freud, Thomas Mann gives the official addess "Freud and the Future" in Vienna. In June there follows a lecture in Budapest on "Humaniora and Humanism." The loss of his citizenship also caused the withdrawal of the honorary doctorate by Bonn University. To this Mann, already meanwhile honored by the award of an honorary doctorate by Harvard, replied with a sovereign repudiation that, with the title "An Exchange of Letters," was to become the most widespread antifascist position of his entire literary exile. Many copies also reached the German Reich.

While after the conclusion of *Joseph in Egypt*, the Goethe novel *The Beloved Returns* becomes his main literary occupation, other secondary undertakings continue: for example, a speech about "Richard Wagner and the *Ring of the Nibelungen*" (November 1937), an introduction to the work of Arthur Schopenhauer (January to May 1938), an essay "Brother Hitler" (April 1938), and an essay "This Peace," against the Munich Pact (October 1938). Mann founds his own antifascist cultural magazine (*Mass und Wert*, first issue September 1937). In April 1937 he travels to America for the third time, in February 1938 for the fourth time (with the speech "The Coming Victory of Democracy"), and in September 1938 for the fifth and final time. His friend Agnes E. Meyer had effectively assisted in obtaining the immigration papers and had procured for him a position as lecturer in the humanities at Princeton University. Thomas Mann applies himself there with many lectures as an academic teacher from 1938 until 1940.

The summer of 1939 brings an important trip to Europe (Nordwijk, Zurich, London, Stockholm) with a difficult (because of the outbreak of war September 1, 1939) but successful return. The essay "This War" (written November to December 1939) fulfills anew a demand of the day. With the Indic novella *The Transposed Heads* a further literary interlude follows (January to July 1940) until finally in August 1940 the work on the Joseph novel is again taken up. At the same time a steady political journalistic acitivity is constantly in progress—speeches, reading tours, statements of all sorts, prefaces. The bibliography lists over three hundred nonliterary contributions from 1937 to 1945. No German author in exile displayed anywhere near such an extensive journalistic activity. From October 1940 to the end of 1945, Thomas Mann broadcasts a monthly program sent into Germany by the BBC London's "Deutsche Hörer!" (German Listeners!). In January 1940 he makes a lecture tour in Canada (with "The Problem of Freedom"), in February 1940 another one (with the same speech) in ten American cities. In October and November 1941 more than twenty American metropolises are visited (with "The War and the Future," first version). Smaller trips of this sort come in between. Even the president of the United States, Franklin D. Roosevelt, invites him to stop by (January 13–14, 1941). After the Princeton professorship, from 1941 until 1944, he is the consultant in German literature at the Library of Congress in Washington, D.C.

In the spring of 1941 the family moves from Princeton to Pacific Palisades in California, in the Los Angeles area, where there was a large German colony after the emigration wave of 1940. Intensive work on *Joseph* fills the years 1941 and 1942, along with the secondary works. After the conclusion of work on the great novel in January 1943, the Moses novella, *The Tables of the Law*, is completed as a sequel (January to March 1943), a work commissioned for an antifascist book on the Ten Commandments, until—after a short hesitation about whether it would not be better to continue *Felix Krull*, and in an astonishingly short time for reflection and research—the writing of *Doctor Faustus* begins in May 1943. In July 1943 he begins his acquaintanceship with Theodor W. Adorno, who was to become the most important adviser for the Faust novel. In August and October 1943 the speech "Schicksal and Aufgabe" ("The War and the Future," not identical with the 1941 speech with the same title) comes into being, in which Thomas Mann approaches Marxist positions closer than ever before. The most important locations of his speeches are Washington, D.C., Boston, Manchester in Vermont, New York, Montreal, and Chicago (October–November 1943). However, Thomas Mann remains skeptical about attempts at political organization from the Left. Although he takes part in diverse consultations, he still mostly withdraws whenever more than a moral engagement is demanded. In the election campaign of 1944 he supports the reelection of Roosevelt, which then does take place. Roosevelt's death in April 1945 upsets him deeply.

In addition to the continuing work on *Doctor Faustus*, 1945 brings the fundamental speech "Germany and the Germans" in February and March, and in May 1945 as the first text published again in Germany the article

"The Camps" (about the revelation of the German concentration-camp crimes). On May 7, 1945, Germany capitulates. A few days later Klaus Mann is already in Munich as an American soldier and reports to his father from there. The latter does not want to see Germany again for the time being.

## I AM AN AMERICAN

THOMAS MANN is pleased to say that in a radio interview in the year 1940. He likes to acknowledge that he is an American, whereas he never tried to appear as a Czech. He gratefully assumes many of the ways of life of the land. He eats pancakes with maple syrup. America democratically loosens up his somewhat stiff manner. In time he acquires a favorite cigarette (Edgeworth), a favorite popular song ("Don't put your daughter on the stage" by Noel Coward), and a favorite comedian (Jack Benny).

However, he had to wait a long time for a legal naturalization. Not until January 1944 could he take the citizen's test. He was examined for fifty long minutes about the Constitution and the history of the United States—that was no fun, since he, unlike Katia, had not studied anything; the lady who examined him, he thought, had been astonished about the mixture of intelligence and ignorance he represented.

What Thomas Mann did not know: These examinations usually tended to last ten minutes. The employee of the Immigration Bureau did not indicate that she knew exactly whom she had before her. With dry guile she took advantage of the occasion for an extensive conversation with a famous man. Secretly she probably giggled to herself. When she was through, she pulled out a copy of *Buddenbrooks* and had a dedication written in for her. Thomas Mann had suffered a cold sweat for nothing.

He took the actual oath of allegiance on June 23, 1944. The dateline of the diary entry on that day received the solemn addition: "Amer. citizen."

## MORALLY A GOOD TIME

Hitler had the great advantage of producing a simplification of emotions, the No that never for a moment was in doubt, a clear and lethal hatred. The years of battle against him were morally a good time.

A simplification of emotions. The neurasthenic Thomas Mann had from an early age been a man of complex emotions, a dissector of the heart, who longed for simple feelings but did not have them. The resistance against Hitler had an effect similar to that at the outbreak of war in 1914: He simplifies; he liberates from decadence.

A bright and aggressive tone fills the speeches and writings of the simplified man. "It is not nice to hate Hitler," he tells himself (January 28, 1941), but he has the desire to do it, the desire to fight and to curse. "Today I again broadcast to Germany and was unusually on the attack against Schicklgruber [= Hitler]. It does me good." The polemical talent that he earlier sometimes had to spend on unworthy objects now has the authority of an epochal battle behind it. Words hail down vehemently on the German monster. There are hardly any depresssions during these years. The sensitive dreamer has gotten far away from himself; more precisely, the times had gotten his mind off himself. The sublime irony of the early years has given way to a sometimes almost rowdy style, the doubting skepticism of an admirer of Schopenhauer to a pugnacious purposeful optimism. Only seldom does he allow himself something as inopportune as the essay "Brother Hitler." Only quite privately does his old forthrightness sometimes come into play. "During the morning on the Amer. speech. Democratic idealism. Do I believe in that? Don't I just try to understand it as though it were a role?" (November 27, 1937). In a letter the same day to René Schickele one thinks one is hearing the nonpolitical observer, who has read Nietzsche's criticism of Wagner: "Don't you find that these aesthetic problems are basically much more interesting and more natural to us than any politics?" Unfortunately for America, he must now engage in political philosophy and work something up about "the future (very future) victory of democracy."

> Faithfully, I am developing here the intellectual world of democratic idealism—I believe, fairly correctly; I have never studied it, but things do have their own inner logic—, and a kind of political Sunday sermon comes into being, in which it would be better for me if I could have it given by a fictional character instead of giving it on my own in an extemporaneous and dreamlike fashion. Do I believe in it? Largely! But probably not so much that I should give it in my own name. Just between us, it is a role— with which I identify myself as much as a good actor identifies himself with his. And why am I playing it? Out of hate for fascism and for Hitler. But should one let one's thoughts and one's

role be played before such an idiot? Freedom, freedom! It cannot be found in politics as much as there is talk about it.

That is the deeper truth behind everything that is coming. He is still sticking only to the paternal consciousness of duty, not to the mother's heart that wants to ramble freely. Deep inside he does not at all approve of what he is doing. What a senseless sacrifice, to make oneself sick in the battle against fascism! To no longer be roped in. No statements and answers! Why stir up hate? Freedom and serenity! One should finally take one's right to it. He pretends to be convinced of the victory of democracy because that was necessary at the time. "I have been driven into the political arena solely and alone by circumstances very much against my nature and my will." He leans far to the left, not because he was leftist by nature but because the boat threatens to capsize to the right. Not until after the war does he again allow himself to find his role as an itinerant preacher of democracy a bit banal, a bit flat, a bit comical.

The outward battle fills his heart so much that his inner world steps back. There are hardly any secrets during this time. No love affair is known from the American years (except for Cynthia). Also the memories of the past play no great role anymore. Thomas Mann lives in the present. The old homeland is far away. Munich, where he experienced so much, awakens only hate; its destruction served it right, the stupid city. He is not at all sentimental. "Telegram from Klaus in Munich: The house, bombed several times, its skeleton preserved, the inside, already changed before, completely destroyed. — Odd impression. Good to have a new house in friendlier areas" (May 14, 1945). Lübeck fares similarly. The destruction of the Buddenbrook house in a British air raid leaves the man baptized in St. Mary's almost cold. Such rubble could not frighten the man who lives for the future and not for the past. The destruction of Germany must be for the sake of this new future.

The expression of this alienation is the decreasing importance of the daily journals. In 1933 and 1934 up to 350 diary pages are written yearly. In 1935 there are around 230, in 1936, after the Korrodi letter illuminated the political front, still 180. From 1937 on, the annual entries mostly comprise only about 160 pages, reduced for 1944 and 1945 to 140 and 145 pages.

## THANK YOU, MR. HITLER!

Switzerland, his chosen homeland of the years from 1933 to 1938, had required "tact" from the guest without papers. But then came the call to America,

> and all of a sudden, in that giant, free land there was no more talk of "tact," there was nothing but frank, unintimidated, declared willingness to be friends, cheerful, unreserved, under the permanent motto: "Thank you, Mr. Hitler!"

He liked being in America. He praised the American myth, extolled freedom and goodwill, openness and fresh distances in place of the poisoned constriction of weary Europe and rhetorically celebrated "the pioneerlike optimism and hearty belief in mankind of spirited youthfulness, the well-disposed, confident ideas and principles" of his new country. Ever since his reading of Whitman in 1922, America was for him the land of spiritual health. He breathed American air with approbation, especially since for him the country seemed to be the strongest dam against the dark powers that had driven him out of Europe. Later, the eternally blue skies sometimes got on his nerves, but with his first visit (1938 in Beverly Hills), California also pleased him very much.

> A sky of an extraordinarily bright light, under which palm fronds swing, shines in through the jalousies; there is the fragrance of orange trees in bloom and bearing fruit at the same time, and Malayan servants, Filipinos, clear the breakfast table in the adjacent room, to which I have closed the sliding doors. . . . It's like always. A table is there, an easy chair with a lamp for reading, a row of books on the console—and I am alone. What does it matter that I am "far away"? Far away from what? Maybe from myself? Our center is within us. I have experienced the transitoriness of exterior sedentariness. Wherever we are, we are "at home." What is homelessness? My home is in the works that I bring with me. Absorbed in them, I experience all the coziness of being at home. They are language, German language and form of thought, personally developed traditional ware of my country and my people. Wherever I am, Germany is!

## THIS MAN IS MY BROTHER

The "Wherever I am, Germany is" is found in a preliminary draft of the essay "Brother Hitler" of 1938. It is a defiant assertion against the far more patent view at the time that Germany was where Hitler was.

"The fellow is a catastrophe; that is no reason to find him uninteresting as character and destiny." Here the radical aesthete speaks who finds an unusual phenomenon gripping, regardless of what morality says about it. The statement causes an uproar. Gottfried Bermann Fischer wants to have it removed, but Mann replies to him, that he considered "the statement about that fellow"—it should remain. "Politically, after all the rest, it does not matter either, and purely stylistically, it has in its directness a refreshing effect with the otherwise manifold complexity."

The essay was actually supposed to form the widely visible concluding piece of the volume of essays, *Attention, Europe!* Because it does not aim at hating but at understanding, it is more important than the many anti-Nazi polemics and more truthful than many good-natured democratic statements of those years. Anyone who wants to understand must let what is hated into himself. But that sort of thing is always unwanted in politically incited times. Bermann wrote something about the pressure of Swedish authorities; it was feared that the "Brother Hitler" essay would cause intensified persecutions. Publication in the scheduled place had therefore to be canceled. The impudent little work appeared in only two magazines. But the attentive Nazis noticed it anyway. In contrast to the official practice of hushing things up, the SS magazine *Das Schwarze Korps* (The Black Corps) reacted with a scornful article. Thomas Mann, it says there, was still living, "even though in the disreputable world of emigration" and "from the fairly meager printing totals that can be achieved among emigrated Jews." He had desperately attempted to make connections that had nonetheless failed. A good part of "Brother Hitler" is quoted, the "fellow" sentence particularly, and the phrases that followed about "the unfathomable resentment, the deeply festering vindictiveness of this unqualified, impossible man, who was a tenfold failure, this extremely lazy perpetual seeker of asylum not fit for any work, this rejected bohemian artist." Triumphantly, the article answers with the proclamation: "Indeed, what kind of creatures must they be, who let themselves be cornered by a dreary sluggard, perpetual asylum seeker, and total washout!"

The author in *Das schwarze Korps* missed the decisive point. Of course, Thomas Mann was not a sluggard, or a perpetual seeker of asylum, or a washout, and yet he calls Hitler his brother. Why? Because Hitler was an artist like him. "The artist is a brother of the criminal and the madman"—the devil knows! The following applies not only to Hitler:

> In a certain disconcerting way, everything is there: the "difficulty," laziness, and rueful elusiveness of the early days, the "not-to-be-accomodated," the "what do you want, anyway?" the half silly vegetating away in deepest social and intellectual bohemia, the basically arrogant, basically I'm-too-good-for-that rejection of any rational and reputable activity—on the basis of what? On the basis of a dull premonition of being reserved for something entirely indefinable, the mention of which, if it could be mentioned, would make people burst out laughing. In addition, the bad conscience, the guilty feeling, the rage at the world, the revolutionary instinct, the subconscious collection of explosive desires for compensation, the tenaciously active need to justify oneself, to substantiate, the urge for subjugation, submission, the dream of seeing a world lost in fear, love, admiration, shame at the feet of the once-spurned man . . .

Thomas Mann here unmistakably describes his own problems from the time before fame and his own relationship to the public. The will to power gives impetus to the practice of art as it does to politics. The psychology of both has much to do with impetus and little with idealism. Even if success comes, the artist is not satisifed. Mann knows that, too, from his own experience:

> But also the insatiability of the drive for compensation and self-glorification is there, the restlessness, the not-doing-enough, successes forgotten, using them up quickly for self-assurance, the emptiness and the boredom, the feeling of futility as soon as there is nothing to do and nothing to keep the world in suspense, the insomniac force of always having to prove oneself again.

The parallels go much farther. The prior of San Marco from the drama *Fiorenza* (1905) was supposed to be a kind of Hitler, because he proclaimed "the miracle of reborn naturalness," just as Gustav von

Aschenbach in *Death in Venice* because of his rejection of the psychologism of time and his inclination toward the simplification of the soul. Fascism is a return to naïveté—again the motif, which already had to serve as an explanation of 1914, occurs. A diary entry speaks of "the 'National Socialism' anticipated by *D.i.V.* about 20 years before." Even if the tendencies of the time that he shaped then were hardly to be recognized in fascism, they may have had something to do with it and had to a certain extent served for its moral preparation.

Is Thomas Mann therefore a Nazi? He knows hate for the mind. Had not the mind always prevented him from taking part in the life of the fortunate? Why should others receive what was denied him? He recognizes the fascist potential in himself, in the longings for simplification and the anti-intellectual tendencies in his early works, which enter into the *Reflections of a Nonpolitical Man*. If the Nazis today were persecuting popular writers, well, had he not persecuted civilization's literary men at the time? He had undergone everything and thought through everything to free himself from that, as Nietzsche did from Wagner. Nietzsche's alienation from Wagner remained his most important model. "Wagner-like, on the doorstep of ruination, is everything," he states in the "Brother Hitler" essay. "There is a lot of 'Hitler' in Wagner," he writes after the war. But Thomas Mann was also this kind of "Hitler," for both, Wagner and Hitler, are his brothers.

The brother argument is valid only insofar as fascism is actually understood as a simplification of the soul and as an answer to decadence. If this thesis is correct (and it is certainly not totally wrong), what is "fascist" has a gigantic part in the internal life of the twentieth century, for there are answers to decadence that simplify the soul on all sides, from nature and health cults to the most varied brands of fundamentalisms. What is "fascist" in Thomas Mann is in us all. Because decadence is not by any means overcome—just the contrary— fascism also remains an always virulent temptation. Recognizing this temptation is better than denying it. The appropriate antidotes are analysis, irony, reason, and the middle-class ethic.

## THE JEWS WILL ENDURE

Uninterruptedly he battles the persecution, disenfranchisement, and destruction of Jews. Even when Thomas Mann visits Jerusalem, Tel Aviv, and the Jewish settlements in Palestine in the spring of 1930, he is impressed by the accomplishments and by the entrepreneurial spirit of Zionist Jewry. In September 1930 he signs an appeal "Against Anti-Semitism." He continues his involvement with the Jewish cause during the Nazi time with numerous actions. In 1936 he sends the declaration "The Jews Will Endure!" to a Jewish monthly magazine in Prague as a manifesto of support. It shows the old patterns of his thought and for that reason also contains many sentences with vocabulary that sounds questionable today. He had had Jews among his best friends and his worst enemies, from which it followed first of all, in a personal and moderate opinion, that he would prefer to say neither good nor bad "about that race." There were too many kinds of Jews for him to want to call himself a philo-Semite. But anti-Semitism was offensive and contemptible to him in his very soul—the simplest religious feeling had always prevented him from making the slightest concession to this abuse. In a speech before a Jewish association in Zurich a bit later (in March 1937), Thomas Mann expatiates in detail on what we know already from earlier positions: that Jewry was bound to the spirit, that what was Jewish was an indispensable cultural ferment for what was German, that the mission of the Jews was as little achieved in the history of the world as that of the Germans. Anti-Semitism always means that people feel inconvenienced in their evil desires by the Jewish spirit, because they do bad things, play hooky, and want to engage in wartime slaughter. For him the Jews are a tenaciously surviving race that "with dark and intelligent eyes look from a previous world into our world and with ancient racial knowledge, experience in suffering, proven intellectuality, and ironic mind form a furtive correction to our passions." He describes the Jews like he does himself. For they are martyrs, as he himself is. He cites Goethe: "a German author—a German martyr."

He had knowledge about the camps early, already in 1933–34. In 1936 he sent a proclamation "Down with the Concentration Camps" to a Parisian Communist conference. The increase in atrocities strengthened his involvement. He gave an anti-anti-Semitic radio address in New York on March 10, 1940. The intention to systematically exterminate Jews, about which it is so often said that hardly anyone knew anything, was not concealed from him. The Wannsee Conference had taken place on January 20, 1942. At the end of January Thomas Mann, in his "Deutsche Hörer" broadcast, castigated the "trial gassing" of four hundred young Dutch Jews. On September 17, 1942, he notes in his diary: "Report on the Jewish atrocities in Europe. Goebbels: Whether Germany is victorious or is defeated, the Jews will be eliminated." His outrage about this feeds the next radio broadcast statement, which also appears in print under the title "The Jewish Terror." There Thomas Mann publicizes the "maniacal decision for the complete annihilation of European Jewry" and informs the Germans that 700,000 Jews had already been murdered or tortured to death by the Gestapo. "Do you Germans know that? And what do you think about it?" Those in exile in California knew it well in September 1942. There were numerous witnesses to the gassings. The "Deutsche Hörer" broadcast reports about a train locomotive engineer who had fled, who several times had to drive trains loaded with Jews that stopped on open stretches and then were hermetically sealed and filled with gas.

"The Fall of the European Jews" is a speech before an audience of ten thousand in San Francisco on June 17, 1943, which again openly addresses "the maniacal resolution for the total extermination of European Jewry" and does not disregard in silence the millions of victims. In 1944 there follows, with similar intentions, "An Enduring People" and a proclamation on the anniversary of the uprising in the Warsaw ghetto. "Rescue the Jews of Europe!" is already an appeal from the months after the end of the war, which makes the accusation that the poisonous seed of Hitler was deeply planted everywhere in confused minds, so that the Jews at that time had to lead a pariah's life and suffer the most bitter misery. When in 1948 it looked for a time as though the United States would thwart the foundation of the state of Israel, Mann writes a sharp protest, the title of which, "Ghosts of 1938," indicates that a betrayal of Jews would appear to him as despicable as the previous betrayal of Czechoslovakia in the Munich Pact. Those who choose to call Thomas Mann an anti-Semite have all of this to consider.

## SHAMELESS BUT FASCINATING

What gave his anti-anti-Semitism something to worry about occasionally was the paradox that there were Jewish fascists. He hated such Jews, not because they were Jews, but because they were fascists. Theodor Lessing, for example, is for Thomas Mann an intellec-

tual fascist because he wrote a book against the intellect, *Der Un-
tergang der Erde am Geist*, 1924 (The Decline of the World of the Intellect). Why did they have to murder him? When he was of the same
mind as his murderers! At least, that is how it appeared to Thomas
Mann, disregarding necessary differentiations, in a diary entry of
1934. In the same connection there is also mention of Karl Wolfskehl
and Oskar Goldberg:

> Thought of the paradox that the Jews, who in Germany are being
> deprived of their rights and driven out, have a strong share in
> the intellectual matters that are expressed in the political system
> to an extent, naturally very grotesquely, and to a good extent are
> to be considered trailblazers of the antiliberal change: not only as
> members of the George circle, like Wolfskehl, who, if he were
> allowed, would fit in very well in the Germany of today. How
> very much does Goldberg, with his book "The Reality of the
> Hebrews," belong to the prevailing spirit of the age: antihuman-
> istic, anti-universalistic, nationalistic, religio-technical—David
> and Solomon are for him a liberal degeneration. The inner atti-
> tude of this writer, e.g., toward the new state, must [be] fairly
> difficult. He must theoretically approve what he kicks.

Thomas Mann had read *The Reality of the Hebrews* for his Joseph novel
and industriously analyzed it, with permutations of its intellectual
omens. The type of Jewish fascist then appears in *Doctor Faustus* in
the shape of the scholar Dr. Chaim Breisacher, who in the kings David
and Solomon sees "already the degenerate representatives of a faded
late theology" who have no idea any longer about Jehovah, the strong
old god of the people. "In short, for a long time it has not been people
and race and religious reality, but humane gruel."

So much for Breisacher. For the time being Thomas Mann did not
make Goldberg suffer. He did not prevent Ferdinand Lion, the editor
of *Mass und Wert*, from recruiting Goldberg as a contributor to Thomas
Mann's magazine. "Shameless, but fascinating" is how Thomas Mann
found the first contribution of the hated man, an essay "The Gods of
the Greeks," which emphasizes the "volk" as a power susceptible to a
cult against the abstract humanism of the usual reception of antiquity.
The collaboration on the magazine did not last long. The enterprise
stumbled. *Mass und Wert* "stinks with boredom," remarked a good
friend, René Schickele. Planned to be nonpartisan, the magazine also

falls politically into obscurity because it tries to keep an all-too-obvious distance from other exile journalistic enterprises. It also perishes from Lion's lack of convictions. For that reason Klaus Mann ends his collaboration. "I don't want to have anything more to do with 'Mass und Wert,'" he writes to Lion, "as long as you are still the editor of the magazine." Lion finally has to vacate his post in favor of Golo Mann.

In the Faust novel, Thomas Mann lets Dr. Breisacher also bluster about the killing of those unfit to live based on hygiene for volk and race. Oskar Goldberg had actually gone far in a similar way. The removal of Jews from the book of history was imminent, he had written in his book *Maimonides* (Vienna, 1935). "Either the Jews do their duty or they will be eliminated. There is no third choice."

While Thomas Mann on September 11, 1941, had been so good-natured as to write a letter of recommendation for Goldberg, his judgments under the impression of the coming Holocaust become less compromising. On May 1, 1942, he calls *The Reality of the Hebrews* an "explicitly fascist book." For him, Goldberg belongs among the masterminds of the Holocaust because he sees the guilt of the Jews precisely in what always fascinated Thomas Mann, namely, that they are intellect, have intellect. But for Goldberg intellectuality is a betrayal of the ancient, strongly ingrained sense of ethnicity—a betrayal that prompts the just punishment of extermination.

That much inadmissible simplification slips in with everything else is clear. There may have been fascist Jews, but their part in what was happening was small, and books such as those by Goldberg and Lessing remained a concern for the smallest circles of scholars. The supposed fascist Goldberg has nothing to do with real National Socialism. He leaves Gemany already in 1932, and by way of Italy and France, where he is interned for a while, he emigrates to the United States. He does not want to see his "anti-Semitism" confused with that of the German variety. "My anti-Semitism is that of Moses when he smashed the Tablets, and that of the prophets when they called the Jews a filthy people who betrayed his mission and, above all, his power."

Thomas Mann suspected that he himself would be called an anti-Semite because of Breisacher and Fitelberg. He defended himself. His Jews were simply children of their epoch, just as others were, indeed because of their sensibility often its more faithful children. The German residents of the Faust novel were, in the final analysis, not depicted more sympathetically. "It is, after all, as a whole a marvelous aquarium of creatures of the last days."

What he thinks about Jews he puts in the mouth of his Goethe in *The Beloved Returns.* With Goethe he praises the special talents of this remarkable seed, the sense for music, the capacity for medicine, the literary capability. Even average Jews wrote a purer and more exact style than the native Germans. Jews were simply the people of the Book, and there one saw that human characteristics and moral convictions were regarded as a secularized form of religion. The antipathy against them could be compared only with that against the Germans, whose role in destiny featured the most marvelous relationship with the Jews' own. He confesses his fear that one day the hate of the world toward the other salt of the earth, the land of the Germans, might come to an outbreak that would be similar to the destruction of the Jews.

## SELF-LOVE

Today the ego is considered only as the stage upon which various actors present changing dramas. It recognizes "personality," the unmistakable character, the matured result of the Bildungsroman, only as longing. Like Christian Buddenbrook it sometimes wants to be a useful member of society, but it reaches only the tip of the pencil, nothing more goes into the general ledger. Like Thomas Buddenbrook it wants to be vital, but it offers only a pretense. The ego is only a pallid wish.

"Hence everything that has become known about me is only fragments of a great confession, which this little book is a daring attempt to make complete," Goethe confesses in *Truth and Poetry* (II, 7). That was not so self-evident as it sounds today. Until the middle of the eighteenth century, literature had hardly anything to do with confession, with autobiography. The poets did not process their lives but given material, myths, legends, history. The eighteenth century then brings the completely astonishing ascendancy of the middle-class ego with its self-loving psychology, brings in its retinue the aesthetics of originality, the original genius, the unmistakable personality, and with that gradually also the writing of autobiography. With Goethe's *The*

*Sorrows of Young Werther* the literature of what has been experienced begins.

But that does not mean that nothing more was happening now on a broader front. Goethe himself later wrote much that was not auto-biographical—*Iphigenia on Taurus*, for example. One seeks experienced material in vain in the work of Schiller. Also in the work of Heinrich von Kleist the psychoanalysis of literature in spite of many efforts does not discover what fed his formidable creations.

The bridge from religiously motivated to autobiographical writing was the consciousness of mission that the inspired author (breathed upon, touched by the spirit) engaged upon in his writing. That God led every single soul was the basic assumption. From that came modern self-observation. The temperature of the soul was taken daily. From that sprang the middle-class ego-culture. "Confession" is not a religious word for naught. It is a matter of the justification for life, at first before God, but then increasingly before oneself and before society.

Literature becomes narcissistic. It serves the restoration of the ego that has been put into question by contemporaries, the healing of a fragmented ego by the construction of a composed ego, the solacing of a tiny ego by self-grandeur. "The talk is not of all of you, absolutely never, be comforted about that—rather about me, about me." The themes of the writer are: come to terms with traumas (Sigmund Freud), demonstate the good of narcissism (Heinz Kohut), restore an unrestorable lack (Jacques Lacan), assuage an unfulfillable longing.

The stage-ego, as Narcissus, makes use of language to celebrate itself. Goethe's secretary Riemer in *The Beloved Returns* articulates this. Of course, on the one hand poetry is something religious, "a mystery, the incarnation of the divine." On the other hand, it inclines "to self-reflection in a way that lets us associate the old, lovely image of the boy who leans enraptured over the reflection of his own charms. Just as language looks at itself with a smile in poetry, so also do emotion, thought, passion."

## IT IS ALWAYS A LIFE STORY

Charlotte Kestner, nee Buff, the original model for Werther's Lotte, in the year 1816, herself a sixty-three-year-old, visits the aging Goethe, who is sixty-seven. Is a person glad to see a former lover again? Such a thing is generally rather embarrassing. Goethe receives Lotte coolly and stiffly, an official luncheon; only at the very end is there a secret conversation in his carriage that explains why life must be brought as a sacrifice to art.

In Thomas Mann's life there were, of course, diverse later meetings, with Paul Ehrenberg, with Klaus Heuser, but love could in no case be awakened again; embarrassment was paramount; formality remained. No former lover ever cornered him, as Lotte tried to do with Goethe. The novel is an autobiographical fantasy on the theme of how it would be if a former lover were to appear. If "life" were to come and call "art" to account. For Lotte is life, and Goethe is art. It concerns the unavoidable sacrifice of life in favor of art, the artistic structure that must be erected against love. "You see: I am again involved with this theme—the intellect that has become dignified that hides its most idiosyncratic self from the inquisitive world under stiff, cunning masks."

Goethe is a god, like Thomas Mann. Goethe is greatness itself and the desiring ego; Thomas Mann reflects him, as much as ever possible, and is fairly compatible with the sources—his own life and being. Wearing his Goethe mask, he can even defend his vanity and egocentricity. It is fun for him to go around wearing that mask and saying impudent things that would not otherwise be proper. The generations of his ancestors had existed only to propagate the artist as an end product. "Egocentric—! Probably one should not be egocentric who knows natural destiny, summing up, completion, apotheosis, a high and final result that nature has had to pay for most laboriously in order to bring it about."

That Goethe's love affairs involved women bothers the dreamer in love with himself hardly at all. In a letter he approximates Goethe's sexual constitution very closely to his own: "Just between us, I believe that he was admittedly a great amorist but was sexually weak (in spite of all the 'priapism,' that was reported about him at times) and far more dedicated to the kiss than to coitus"—which would relate to his bisexuality. Also, in the novel itself Goethe presents himself as androgynous. There are in general many parallels. Goethe, too, denies himself gratification in most cases, breaks off the relationship before a union and transforms it into art. That applies to Friederike Brion and to Charlotte Buff, and in his old age to Ulrike von Levetzow and to

Marianne von Willemer. Goethe is an aesthete and forsaker like Thomas Mann.

In the diaries of his old age Mann, not seldom, and with pride, makes a note when a morning erection takes place. Right after a few lines, his awakening Goethe also perceives: "What? In a mighty state? In high resplendence? Good, old man!" The catchword "resplendence" was taken over by Thomas Mann from Goethe's famous poem "The Diary," in which a Goethe describes a very similar case, how he, held up on his way home by a carriage indisposition, in an inn meets a pretty and willing waitress who seeks him out at midnight—but, O anguish, "Master Iste" leaves him in the lurch, and the pretty girl falls asleep. He thinks of the nights of love with his wife, where it was all completely different (We were immediately quite undaunted / and served by the good boy many times!"). After this recollection the unexpected happened:

> But Master Iste has a silly notion
> And won't be ordered or dependent,
> Suddenly there, with quiet motion
> He rises up to be resplendent;
> He's at the wanderer's command,
> Not thirsting longer at the well to stay.
> He leans to kiss the sleeping girl at hand,
> But then he stops and then feels pulled away.

For it was not the pretty waitress but the memory of his wife that had awakened Iste. He pulls back. He does not want to trick the sleeping girl.

The Goethe in the novel rhapsodizes about love just as Thomas Mann does. "What is youthful love in comparison to the intellectual power of love in old age? What a skimpy feast is that, the love of youth, in comparison with the giddy flattery that sweet youth receives when greatness of age chooses and uplifts it lovingly." Love in old age is an ordeal, primal odds and ends. The literary work celebrates "always the same thing," as Goethe of the novel knows, "the same thing on unequal levels, escalation, refined repetition of life." But what has been lived must on the other hand remain unique. "I will not see this embodiment again. Wanted to, but was enjoined I should not, which means, abandon it." New work, new love, it is always the same. "The beloved returns for a kiss, ever young—of

course, rather more apprehensive to think that somewhere in her figure subdued by time, old, she is also still living."

"Beloved lips that I kissed—it was there, I had it too, I will be able
to say to myself when I die" (February 20, 1942). A kiss was physically the peak of what same-sex love ever granted Thomas Mann. He
forms a helpful theory for himself about why the kiss is more than
the bed. For coitus is only sensual. But the kiss is spiritual and sensual at the same time, seal of the sacrament, "spiritual because still
individual and highly discriminating—between your hands the most
unique head, inclined backward, under the lashes the smiling earnest
expiring gaze in your own, and your kiss says to him: I love and
fancy you, you, fair particular of God, in all Creation expressly you—
there procreating, anonymously, like all living creatures, fundamentally without choice, and night covers it."

Homosexuality is thought of expressly apropos Winckelmann. "Do
I know your secret?" "Goethe" asks and quotes the fancier of the
statues of antiquity: "To be exact, it can be said that there is only one
moment in which the beautiful human being is beautiful." Winckelmann meant the unrepeatable moment of love, the brief and soaring
flare of passion. "For your aperçu actually really only fits the masculine–primal-masculine, in the moment of youth's beauty contained
only in marble." This Winckelmann also has the subtleties of camouflage from Thomas Mann. "Goethe" sees through them: "What does it
matter, you had the good fortune that 'mankind' is of the masculine
gender, and that you thus would like to masculinize beauty to your
heart's content. It appeared to me in youth—in the shape of a
woman. . . . But not completely, and I do understand your ruses,
think also with the most mellow frankness of the charming blond
waiter lad last summer up on the Geisberg in the restaurant."

By way of suggestion a theory is formed that explains homosexuality by narcissism. What is seduction? The "sweet, shocking touch,
coming from above, when the gods so wish: it is the sin which we
innocently are guilty of. . . . it is the test that no one passes, for it is
sweet. . . . By not performing an act, one escapes the earthly judge,
not the one on high, for you have done it in your heart. . . . Seduction
by your own sex might be looked upon as a phenomenon of vengeance and scornful retribution for your self-inflicted seduction—it is
eternally the infatuation of Narkissos by the reflection of his own self.
Revenge is always connected with seduction, with the test not to be

passed by overcoming." Art takes vengeance on life and kills it: the case in the tale "Tristan." Life takes vengeance on art: the case of Adrian Leverkühn in *Doctor Faustus*. The artist may not love; if he nevertheless does, then he is punished.

Politics, too, offered much opportunity for playful ambiguity. Where I am, Germany is, said Thomas Mann. He has his Goethe say, "You think that *you* are Germany, but *I* am." "Your best ones always lived with you in exile" (whereas Goethe did not live in exile at all). The two ironists scoff at state-persecuted writers: "It is quite indecorous to polish off a writer like a schoolboy. It does not help the state and it damages culture. . . . If he does not continue as before, he resorts to irony, and you all stand completely helpless before it. None of you understand the resources of the mind. Force him with half measures into a refinement that is bearable only to him and not to all of you."

There is also a father present and an untidy mother and life as a work of art. "The older you get, the more prominent the ghostly old man becomes in you, and you recognize him, acknowledge him; consciously and with defiant loyalty you are him again, the father's image that we honor . . . but if there is sufficient madness left in me as a foundation of brilliance, and if I had not inherited the ability of maintenance in good shape, the art of careful management, a whole system of protective artifices—where would I be!" Goethe's house is a "house of art," says Lotte, and that is not meant positively but in the sense of stiff and unnatural.

The novel tapers off in a theory about the victim of life. All the people who surround him are victims of his greatness, Lotte says quite correctly. "They sacrificed to the gods, and finally the sacrifice was the god," Goethe replies. The moth that longingly plunges into the flame becomes the metaphor of this process. Goethe is the flame into which the others plunge, but "also the burning candle that sacrifices its body so that the light can shine." He is at the same time the drunken butterfly that falls victim to the flame—"first and last I am a sacrifice—and am the one who brings it. Once I burned you and will burn you for all time into mind and light . . . death, the final flight into the flame—into the all-in-one, how could it, too, not be only transformation? In my resting heart, dear Images, may you all rest— and what a friendly moment it will be, when we will awaken one day all together again." This final twist quotes the *finis operis* of Goethe's *Elective Affinities*. Finally, the lovers whose fulfillment necessarily remained denied in life can come together in death. Thomas Mann will be united in death with everyone, at the imperishable moment of their highest beauty about which Winckelmann rhapsodized, and every love will be fulfilled.

"It is always a life story," Goethe replies to his son August's question of what he is writing about at the time, whether it was an autobiography or something else. The same with Thomas Mann. "Everything is autobiography."

### OH—REALLY?

Became friends with an Amer. lady and her pretty 16-year-old daughter, who is reading the MM here & who was very excited to sit next to me. Warm feeling . . .

Little Cynthia in a red jacket, lovely . . .

Little Cynthia just from the distance. With her father in the elevator. Ulrike's insinuation . . .

The little girl, with her parents in the distance, saying farewell. Hearty joy. "It was always so pleasant to look at you." — "Oh—really?" Hid at the departure & peeked to see whether I was looking at her. Will not forget her.

1 o'clock. Agnes Meyer downstairs . . . I resolutely kept silent to her about the incomparably favored little Cynthia.

(Diary entries, June 20–25, 1945)

It was nice finally to be able to swagger. He inflated the insignificance in accordance with all the rules of art. He did keep Cynthia secret from Agnes Meyer, but otherwise he did not mince words and went around talking about her on various occasions, more than is found in the diary. He had to record an insinuation of the love affair of Goethe with Ulrike von Levetzow; he strutted in front of Kuno Fiedler to the smiling gratification of his sense for the mythical. And he raves about Cynthia; she was an appealing child, a "lipstick angel with slanted eyes, with incalculable American naïveté and cultural curiosity, a glowing 'devotee,' dreamily happy at being together with me." It had become a flirtation:

I told her: "You like my books and I like you, that's how it is between us." But she insinuated that involuntarily something was left over for the author as well. I said in parting: "Good-bye, Cynthia! I never shall forget you. It was always a pleasure to look at you." — "Oh—really?" Infinite bashfulness—and an enormous pride to take along into the everyday life of college. In short, it was endearing and beautiful. I really will never forget her.

He, who usually could whisper his matters of love only to his diary, boasted about it years later again and even publicly, in *The Story of a Novel: The Genesis of Doctor Faustus*, and again we learn a few new details. Cynthia is said to have found being a college girl "very insignificant." For consolation she read *The Magic Mountain*,

and it was quite lovely to see her walking around with it, especially when she was wearing her bright red jacket, an article of clothing that she preferred, justly and, for all I care, calculatedly, which proved particularly excellent for her slight figure. To encounter here the originator of her difficult but for that very reason uplifting entertainment was probably a surprise, even a youthful adventure, and when on a musical evening her good mother initiated the acquaintanceship, she intimated apologetically that Cynthia was very excited. Really, at the time she had very cold hands, but not later, in friendly conversations in the assembly room or on the decklike balcony that encircled the house. Did she find out that the tender admiration of the difficult, impressive man could be calmed by a reciprocal admiration that carries the eternal charm of sweet youth and that at the last look into her brown eyes does not remain completely silent about her tenderness? "Oh, really?"—

A girl, finally: Of course, that was naturally the first reason for the boasting. A *Magic Mountain* admirer, that may have been the second reason, without which it would never have come to an acquaintanceship. But the third and most important is—Goethe. Almost zealously, Mann recognizes the chance to repeat Goethe's experience with Ulrike von Levetzow. Until now he had always had to transform it into a same-sex relationship, even when he was writing *Death in Venice*, which originally was supposed to have as its subject Goethe's late love, "the debasement of a soaring mind by the passion for an attractive, innocent piece of life." Oh, how much he would like to have

suffered something similar with Cynthia! Yes, little Cynthia is charming and sweet, but his deep passions are only homoerotic ones. The
Ulrike metaphor is therefore too much of a stretch.

For, if you refer to the biographical sketch that Thomas Mann used,
there it tells not about a harmless flirtation but about a deep wound. In
the summer of 1821 Goethe becomes acquainted in Marienbad with
Frau von Levetzow and her daughters, among them the seventeen-
year-old Ulrike. "Old man, can't you stop yet?" he jokes about himself,
comes again in the following summer, and in the one after that, in
1823—"and the fire of love flares up in full power out of the heart of
the grizzled old man." The seventy-four-year-old dances the night
away into his birthday. He wants to marry her—seriously. The grand-
duke himself is his go-between—but Ulrike answers evasively. "There
was a world of difference between snuggling proudly and happily
with the famous, splendid man who showed her his inclinations so
clearly, between allowing caresses and reciprocating them, and—marrying him." The parting is difficult. Goethe is still hopeful when he
writes the happiness and the pain of the vanished weeks into the
"Marienbad Elegy." Not until October 1823 does he know his path:
renunciation.

All of that fit the homoerotic passions of Thomas Mann much better
than they fit the college girl. When it was serious, the novel regularly
ended with renunciation, Thomas Mann writes in "Goethe and Tolstoy." Goethe had "possessed neither Lotte, nor Friederike, nor Lili,
nor Herzlieb, nor Marianne, nor finally Ulrike, nor ever even Frau
von Stein." Thomas Mann has possessed neither Armin, nor Willri,
nor Paul, nor Tadzio, nor Klaus, nor ever even Franzl. What is before
the eyes of the nation today is a work of renunciation.

Renunciation is "the prescription of destiny, the innate, and at the
cost of heavy mental punishment, inviolable imperative of any German intellectual essence. It is the element of responsibility—what is
Christian in Goethe—in Thomas Mann. Their works are works of renunciation, "works of German-taught renunciation of the advantages
of barbarism, in which the thoroughly voluptuous Richard Wagner
indulged himself with such an enormous effect—and with the legit-
imately consequent punishment that his ethnically bacchanal work is
forfeited daily to a rawer popularity.

Could Cynthia have borne such great weight? Correctly, she rightly
had doubts about her significance. "Oh—really?"

## WAR AND PEACE

Thomas Mann was clear-sighted. Already in his "Correspondence with Bonn" he prophesies that it was the sense and purpose of the National Socialist state to whip the German people into shape for the coming war and to make them into an unlimited compliant instrument of war. Unlike Franz Kafka, who took only incidental notice of the First World War, unlike Marguerite Yourcenar, who almost slept through the Second because of nothing but her private life, he followed the political events day by day with anxious attention. He warned the Western powers even before Hitler's march into Austria. "The democracies cannot prevent the war through appeasement and through weakness. They just postpone the catastrophe with such tactics." Of course, he was completely right. "Let the war come!" he notes, tormented by grief and hate, when Austria is then taken. "Écrasez l'infâme! Liberation from this nightmare of disgust! We are suffocating" (March 17, 1938). The news from Vienna was shattering. "Vienna—terrible. Freud. Friedell out the window. Mass arrests among the nobility, atrocities, the most base and cowardly sadism as usual. Arrest of Bruno Walter's daughter. The Anglo-Hitler treaty is thus clearly revealed" (March 22, 1938).

He has a premonition of what will come next: "Seizure of Czechoslovakia by assault" (March 20, 1938). In September 1938 it has happened. Through the Munich pact the Sudeten German territories are surrendered to Germany. "Disgusted, ashamed, and depressed" (September 30, 1938). "It is without doubt one of the greatest infamies in history" (September 20, 1938). After all, his adoptive fatherland is involved; he was a Czech at the time. After the betrayal by England and France he fears the worst. "Very probable that fascism will reach over to America." Before twenty thousand people he speaks at a mass rally for Czechoslovakia in New York's Madison Square Garden. Enraged, he writes the article "This Peace" (in its first printing "The Height of the Moment"), which accuses the European governments of conspiring behind the backs of their people, of having assured an enormous victory for the Gestapo state, of having destroyed the democratic fortification in the East, and of knowingly making it a spiritually broken appendage of National Socialism. "Munich" is his trauma in the time that follows. "The sacrifice of the Czech people by the Munich pact

was the most terrible and humiliating political experience of my life."
The rest of Czechoslovakia is also soon occupied, the German protec-
torates of Bohemia and Moravia formed. "Complete success of Hitler
in the East. The occupation of Prague, the steel region. Romania and
Hungary will follow. On the Black Sea. Oil and grain. Enormous rein-
forcement. England and France without a move. Russia—a sphinx"
(March 14, 1939). But it turned out differently, for this action by Hitler
brought an end to the politics of appeasement.

Poland at the end of August 1939. Thomas Mann fears a new "Munich" and wants war in spite of its incalculable terrors. Daily back
and forth in the diary. On September 1, 1939, Mann comes upon a
happy turn of events at breakfast in a Swedish bath with Bertolt
Brecht and Helene Weigel. England has finally resolved to put an end
to National Socialism. "Now we will talk turkey, Hitler called a madman. Late, late!" (September 2, 1939). He had been right in the end. "I
think a lot of my Bonn letter and its predictions." He was proud of it
and quoted his war prophecy extensively in the battle essay "This
War," which came a bit later. He appealed in it to the German people
to rise up in rebellion. "No people *has* to do anything. A people that
wants to be free is free in that instant." But most Germans saw no
reason for a decisive opposition at the time.

## BERMANN AND LANDSHOFF

When Vienna fell to the Nazis, the S. Fischer Verlag there was also
confiscated. Gottfried Bermann Fischer was able to escape, but the
offices and stock of books were lost. The emigrated part of the publishing house seemed no longer to exist and in the summer of 1939
was legally dissolved. However, Bermann had set up the rights of
copyright and distribution in Chur, Switzerland, in 1936. That turned
out later to be very clever. He would and could, therefore, begin all
over again at once. But it turned out that Thomas Mann, who had
remained with Bermann between 1933 and 1936 only under great
qualms, now recognized his opportunity to desert. In a letter of April
8, 1938, he advises his publisher against starting up in America. Bermann's relationship to Germany had not been as politically clear as
one would expect in America today. He had originally been a sur-
geon—would it not be the best if he would return to that profession

and settle down in the new world as a doctor? In a second, steadfast letter the author personally revoked his loyalty to the publishing house after a more than forty-year business relationship (April 15, 1938). Bermann is hit hard. "Your letter was shattering for me. I had expected anything, just not this, that you in particular would leave me in the lurch at this very moment, which, God knows, is difficult enough" (April 29, 1938). But he is a tough customer. Undeviating, he pursues his plans further. He succeeds in getting his publishng house on its legs again in cooperation with Bonnier in Stockholm. Thomas Mann sends a cable: "At this time cannot consider myself obligated to your new start-up" (May 11, 1938) but notes in his diary "Mixed feelings," and further: "Consultation with Landshoff and Erika about the publisher situation. Recognized that concentration necessary." On May 16 comes a "long, insistent telegram from Bermann with false arguments that do not need to prevent me from cooperation." No, the false arguments did not prevent him. "Later with Landshoff about Bermann's telegram and the answer. Dispatches set up, meeting with L[andshoff] advocated." The meeting brought the desired clarification. In his communication of June 8, 1938, Bermann notifies his author of the agreements struck with Landshoff. The publishers de Lange, Querido, and Bermann-Fischer retain their names but combine their entire operation for Europe. Bermann will cooperate further with Bonnier in Stockholm. In America all three publishers will share in a cooperative enterprise with Longmans Green and arrange a joint inexpensive series. Thomas Mann's production will appear in Europe in Bermann-Fischer Stockholm, in America through Bermann Fischer with Longmans Green. This construction was firm at first, although Bermann in April 1940 was taken into protective custody by the Swedish police because of anti–National Socialist activity and soon after had to leave the country. He directed the publishing house from New York until the end of the war.

Obviously, Fritz H. Landshoff, the competitor, stood behind the attempted withdrawal from Bermann. He was a friend of Erika and Klaus, for a time wanted to marry Elisabeth, and for a long time tried to recruit Thomas Mann as an author for the Querido publishing house, whose German section he directed. Now that the famous author had put himself clearly on the side of exile, there seemed to be a chance for that. But Bermann was sly. He allied himself with his competitor and in the final analysis was one step ahead. Especially because the next blow of fate struck Landshoff, since with the German occupation of Holland in 1940 Querido failed and Landshoff for his part was now dependent on Bermann. Together they founded the L.B. Fischer Publishing Corporation in New York in 1941, which existed until the fall of 1945. Having returned to Holland after the war, Landshoff rebuilt his old firm. But it soon joined the once more newly founded S. Fischer house of the postwar era, at which point the distinguished Querido imprint perished.

## IN THE WHITE HOUSE

The visit took place with cordial insignificance. Thomas Mann had himself made an effort to set it up and also managed it, thanks to influential friends. He loved being near power. Besides, he needed the president of the New Deal—who brought hope for the poor—for Joseph, the provider. The dinner with FDR on June 29, 1935, after the Havard honorary doctorate, lay too far in the past. The diary at that time furnished "Conversational impressions of his energy and autocracy" and "contempt for degenerating democracy"; shortly afterward in a letter to Gottfried Bermann Fischer, he mentions that his government bore dictatorial signs.

But this time he was a guest in the White House for two whole days, January 13 and 14, 1941. On Monday at eight-thirty, breakfast with Mrs. Eleanor Roosevelt, "simple, cordial & nice woman," who took care of him and other guests for almost the whole day. She sends for a doctor, for Thomas Mann has caught cold. Idle morning, then lunch, speech, afternoon nap, concert, tea, dinner, and discussion with students, all arranged by the president's wife. "Characteristic for the keen activity of the woman."

Not until Tuesday is there a conversation with the president, who appears for breakfast. Thomas Mann has his novel in mind. Anything appropriate for Joseph is noted at once: "Naïveté, trustworthiness, cleverness, theatricality, friendliness"—but also things oddly muted: "If you measure his power & significance, it is very interesting to sit at his side." (Otherwise, apparently not.) Then the doctor again, at noon a visit to the Senate, "for a while attended the fairly idle session." Afternoon nap, then press conference with the president, coffee, shaved and packed, then the greatest thing of all: "For a cocktail with the president in his office." Pride: "This cocktail was mixed according to the special instructions of the president." Presentation of copies of his books with dedications. "To Franklin D. Roosevelt President of the United States and of a coming better world as a modest sign of deep admiration." At dinner, with diverse guests, only the president had anything much to say. "He took us up in the elevator and dismisssed us very cordially in the hallway in front of his rooms."

In the following letter to Agnes E. Meyer (of January 24, 1941) the experience is already highly stylized. The tone is two stages more festive, at the same time closer to Joseph. The "dizzying peak of distinction" had been the cocktail in his study,

> —while the other dinner guests were pleased to wait below. And yet we had had breakfast with "him" already! "He" again made a strong impression upon me or even awakened my sympathetic interest anew: This mixture of slyness, sunnyness, fastidiousness, pleasing merriment, and honest faith is difficult to characterize, but something like a blessing is on him, and I am devoted to him as the born opponent to what, it seems to me, must fail. Here is an example of the conductor of the masses in a modern vein who wants what is good or actually what is better and who keeps step with us as perhaps no other man in the world. How could I not side with him? Strengthened, I left him.

That became "an enormous, an unforgettable experience" in an article for Roosevelt in the campaign of 1944 and in an election speech. Roosevelt was a man clever as snakes and guileless as doves, illuminated by intuitive knowledge of the will of the world spirit, the strong man, the tough and sly man, the great politician of the good. It cannot be ignored that Thomas Mann considered what was dictatorial in democracy necessary, at least during those evil days.

## GOLO, KLAUS, AND ERIKA

Thomas Mann was a collective, at least during those years when Katia, Erika, and Golo became active for him, all together in part, partly taking turns, advised and criticized him, copied his manuscripts, shortened them and got them ready for print, wrote texts and letters in his name, administered his business affairs, managed his

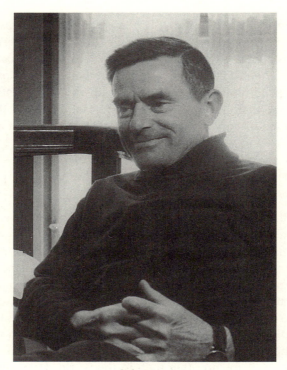

*Golo Mann*

bank accounts, chauffeured him, looked at houses for him, sought out
hotels, organized moves, and much more.

After his emigration Golo Mann had at first been active as a teacher
in France, from where he often visited his parents, and then had
moved to Zurich as the editor of *Mass und Wert*. He was supposed to
take the escape route via Lisbon (May 10, 1940) but he was too spirited. In May 1940 he went to France as a war volunteer to fight
against the Germans. It did not come to that because "the criminal
idiot is borne as though on clouds by the crippled army of millions
right to his goals" (May 22, 1940), that is, because Hitler was in Paris
too quickly. Golo Mann was taken captive in Annecy and interned in
the camp in Les Milles. An escape attempt ended with a new arrest.
His parents were concerned about him (and about Heinrich Mann,
who was likewise still staying in southern France). They expect the

worst, with tortures and concentration camp. "Nazi demands for surrender, with names of militant emigrants. Want at least that these should be shot by the military" (June 25, 1940). They get diplomats involved, endeavor to find possibilities of leaving the country. Golo is freed. Good news from Marseilles reaches them (July 11, 1940) and from Le Lavandou (July 24), bad news from Nîmes (August 5), where Golo is said to have been interned again, which turns out, however, to be a false report. Erika travels to Lisbon, and Agnes Meyer gets the highest authorities involved (August 22). Erika finds a refugee help agent (August 26). On September 20, 1940, Golo and his Uncle Heinrich report from Lisbon after an adventurous flight through France and Spain. On October 13 the red carpet is rolled out for them in New York.

During the following period Golo is a valued coworker with his father. He wrote many comments that appeared under his father's name (for example "Defense Savings Bonds," 1942). In the long run, however, he cannot be kept at home. He becomes an American soldier, active in the intelligence service (March 28, 1944), is promoted to sergeant (February 26, 1945), goes to Luxembourg as a public relations officer (March 14), and also, as one of the first, back to Germany. "Letter from Golo, grieving about the German cities, in general about the extent of the destruction, which is hardly imaginable" (May 17, 1945). While his father was rather decisive in his opinion that the Germans had to be punished, Golo had written Katia that the Germans had been punished enough by the destruction ("if these people have not been punished, I don't know who ever has").

Golo is esteemed but not loved as much as Erika. His presence is useful, but hers is stimulating and uplifting. Whenever she leaves, the heart joins in: "Leave-taking, melancholy, pains" (July 17, 1937). "Parting from Erika, pain and melancholy. Pressed her hand to my cheek and kissed it" (June 30, 1939). "Deeply moved, pain and blessing" (June 17, 1941). And she often departs. Hitler's successes pursue her. At times she writes something poignant, freely in the style of Paul Gerhardt ("O Jesu, Jesu, bury / the torch by me alone / so whatever pleaseth thee / by me is meet and known." —Refrain from the Advent hymn "How shall I receive Thee):

> O Jesu, Jesu, chase me
> Further on my course—

Wherever I may jump,
I pick the wrong horse!

She, too, is incredibly spirited. In the summer of 1940, when the Germans attack England, she goes first to Lisbon and from there to London ("Ache for the child and missing her," August 12), where in the time following she frequently stays. Through her marriage of convenience to the poet W.H. Auden she had become a British citizen in 1935 and therefore had no entry problems. Besides, she had "best papers" because she was active with the British Ministry of Intelligence, later also with the American Intelligence Agency. Further she worked as a war correspondent in London, Cairo, Palestine, and at various other places. Since she had had to give up the Peppermill, the paternal house had become the center of her life, from which she nevertheless deployed a far-reaching anti-fascist activity, with numerous essays, books, lecture tours, organizational endeavors, and mass events of every kind. Her ability to hate exceeded that of her father's considerably. "Don't hate too much," her husband warned her. She defended her father where she could. When she was at home, she helped him. He loved her and worried about her, especially since she had no steady private support, in spite of Martin Gumpert and Annemarie Schwarzenbach, Giehse and other friends of both sexes. "Concerning Erika's somewhat 'frivolous' love life" (November 13, 1940).

Klaus did not take part in office work for his father. He wanted for his part to get him involved with *Decision*, his second exile magazine. "Klaus writes regarding the financing of 'Decision,' whose stipulation they want to make that I sign as editor. Absolutely to be avoided" (April 14, 1941). Despite this resistance, in the following weeks his father endeavors intensively to support the publication, finally gives $1,500 (June 28, 1941), and also wants to help with the liquidation of the enterprise when this seems unavoidable. In addition, Klaus asked him for submissions, partly already finished ones, partly new ones, and received them, too—but the father notes "onerous" (June 16, 1941), "essay for Klaus reluctantly undertaken" and "afternoon, too, on the nuisance" (June 19), specifically, the article "Germany's Path after the Fall of Hitler." "Letter to Klaus concerning a prepublication excerpt from 'Joseph' in 'Decision'—reluctant" (January 26, 1942). In February 1942 the last issue appeared.

In May 1942 Klaus Mann was called up for a physical for military

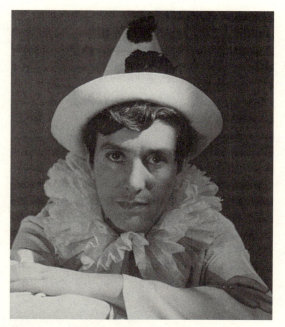

*Erika Mann as Pierrot, from the time of the "Peppermill"*

service and rejected, in September again called up and again rejected, again in December. Now finally they said: "Accepted!" In January 1943 he began his basic training as an American soldier. "Come home when you're unhappy," the father had said at one of the numerous departures. And Klaus came often. He knew where he was at home. "I have been lucky with my family." He had debts, problems as a homosexual, and was addicted to drugs. All of that, taken together, gave his parents great concern. He would not let anything be said to him, particularly on the theme of heroin. "The young man morally and self-critically not quite intact. Can't stand authority, forfeits his right not to put up with it" (June 7, 1937). Klaus was at the time in Budapest, undergoing a withdrawal cure. As far as the "unbourgeois matter" is concerned, as Katia euphemistically calls morphine and whatever else Klaus injected in himself, the parents are resigned. "Took some," Klaus wrote for a time almost daily in his diary. After a collapse of his oldest child, his father notes that Klaus believed he could remain master of the drug. "The fit of crying will probably have

*Klaus Mann*

instructed him about his error" (November 22, 1935). The desire for a total break from the drug seems not to be at hand.

Klaus approached love, death, and addiction differently than his father, who erected his structure of art against them. "Pederasty, intoxication (even with death) always as an enhancement of life, gratefully accepted; never as 'seduction.'" In retrospect, Thomas Mann finds it highly respectable that Klaus becomes a soldier. It appears to him even like a structure of art, praiseworthy. "Neither writing nor love apparently can bother the soundness of your basic substance at all." He quotes his Moses, who has left the bosom of his Moorish woman for the sake of the Ten Commandments. "Now all of you shall see, and all people shall see, whether your brother is unnerved by his black courtship, or whether the courage of God dwells in his heart as in no other."

"Drilling is pretty *hard* for me; foremost, I don't really know what to do with my rifle at all. Nevertheless, I am being treated with a mixture of respect and good-natured irony." In January 1944 Klaus finally arrived in North Africa and takes part, as a member of the "Psychological Warfare Branch," in the conquest of Italy. In May 1945 he is sent from Rome to Germany as a special correspondent of the army newspaper *Stars and Stripes* and from there can report to his father firsthand.

## HEINRICH

Heinrich Mann, in spite of a superficial reconciliation, always remained "civilization's literary man" from the time of the *Reflections of a Non-Political Man*. The highly unjust comment in the diary: "To think, anew, of the glorification at my expense of my brother through the activist literati seething only here" was written not in Munich but in Pacific Palisades. "Resurrection of old torment" (June 24, 1944). The brotherhood in arms during the years in exile produces no significant mutual actions. What they exchange in letters now is not as profound by far as before the First World War. They tell one another about trips, appearances, deadlines, new publications, praise one another, and talk politics a bit. Various manifestos are signed together. But refusals are also not infrequent. Thomas does not want to participate with a Moscow magazine, presumably *International Literature*; he wants to be considerate of his host country and does not want "with all sympathy to be linked too expressly with anything communist." But old Heinrich sticks to his brother in spite of such rebuffs. Legally a Czech citizen, even though living in Nice, it was he who had helped Thomas get Czech citizenship.

In September 1940 Heinrich and his second wife, Nelly, together with Lion and Martha Feuchtwanger, Franz and Alma Werfel, as well as Golo Mann, fled on foot over the Pyrenees to Spain and from there to Lisbon. Now Thomas helped, put his connections to work to get Heinrich money and the necessary papers, picked him up in New York, facilitated his first steps. After the course of the first American year, in which he had a very comfortable contract as a scriptwriter with Warner Brothers, Heinrich became more and more impoverished. Katia and Thomas supported him irregularly at first, then finally with a monthly check. Heinrich became calmer and gentler. "Our natural bond forbids me to be ashamed, and also my—I'd rather say acquiescence to God's will than resignation." He complains quietly and genteelly. He would like to see his brother more often and in a more substantive way. But that does not happen. Thomas is, naturally, very busy—he understands that,

> they leave me alone, which does not matter. Only with you is something missed and not to be recovered anymore, or this might be an untimlely perception. It may be that in the final analysis our personal present time retreats behind the memories. Without premeditation and without my hardly knowing why, I suddenly have begun to read Buddenbrooks.

It is painful to see that Thomas, with all his practical solidarity, does not really allow his brother to take part in his life. He does not open himself up anymore. He keeps him at a distance. He treats him correctly, but not cordially, not equal to equal but like someone to whom he is unfortunately related. The older Heinrich becomes, the bitterer, even sharper become the diary entries. "The problem of Heinrich, with his nurse, whom we can no longer pay, hanging in the balance . . . The sly comedy in the behavior of the old man. He no longer comes to us, since he eats just as well at home" (September 2, 1949).

There was, of course, also the problem of Nelly. Katia and Thomas found their frequently drunk sister-in-law repugnant, ordinary, and foolish, an impertinence, a "terrible trollop" (April 29, 1942). The old quarrel of 1903 came to life again. The cultivated aesthete resists outspoken sexuality and sloppiness. Once he even speaks to Heinrich "about his situation, his intentions, his wife, from whom to separate him was completely futile" (April 29, 1942). To have understanding for an alcoholic slattern would have endangered his own orderliness too much. Here his limits lie. Although he suffered much from Nelly, Heinrich was much more human and sensitive. He loved his wife, even though she had wrecked him economically. She died from sleeping pills on December 17, 1944, at her own hand—"a not only, indeed, almost not at all lamentable event"—as Thomas Mann could not resist remarking in a letter. Heinrich, he noted, owned "not one cent, since his very favorable income had melted away far into the negative through the disastrous goings-on of his wife" (December 20, 1944).

After the war, Heinrich Mann, soon to be eighty, exchanged letters with the East Berlin prostitute Margot Voss. He supported her with money and packages. "My blouse is bursting from the good things." Touching, how she loves him. Without question, the erotic is dominant, but in the sense of a respectful and grateful tenderness, never vulgar. At least from the distance, she wants to let him share her body. She tells him about the color of her hair at the time ("Blond wouldn't be bad either, but then down there, too, you have to learn lessons from an old expert"), about her bosom ("grown by 2 inches," thanks to ham in the package), about her legs ("not as pretty as Nelly's, I think, if they're not bad"), and assures him she is especially sensitive to a variety of things from the navel downward. Heinrich's replies are not preserved, if Margot's heirs or friends are not keeping them as a secret treasure. But he must have had the gift of striking the right tone with her ("since you have such an understanding of my profession"). The old son of a patrician could talk to a woman from the lower classes, not affably, but as equal to equal. Thomas could not have done that.

East Berlin had been wooing the author of *Loyal Subject* for years. He was supposed to become the president of the Academy of Fine Arts. He wanted to accept the honorable invitation, but something in him hesitated. Thomas Mann would gladly have given up the responsibility for his brother; he advised him to accept and got mad when Heinrich did not buy a ship ticket. "Soviet money reaches Heinrich, which he claims is royalties, while it is probably travel money" (September 14, 1949). Resigned, he accepts what cannot be changed. "Heinrich has 'postponed' his departure until spring. Nothing will come of that, it just has to be that way" (October 17, 1949).

Heinrich's death and burial are described briefly in the diary. "Yesterday afternoon with K[atia] with Heinrich. Physically very senile impression" (March 10, 1950). "Brain dead, with only a weakly beating heart. K. there. His passing a matter of hours. Natural shock, without resistance at this event, since it comes not too early and is the most merciful solution. He drew out the evening for a long time listening to music. . . . Tired and moved. The last remaining of five" (March 11). "News in the morning at 7 that at 11:30 at night his heart had stopped. Certification of death and transport. — The most merciful solution . . . K. reports of finding a great many obscene drawings in the desk of the deceased. The nurse knew that he drew every day,

*Heinrich Mann, around 1949*

fat naked women. The sexual in his problems with us siblings, Lulu, Carla, Heinrich, and me. Vikko seems to have been simple, of course, was abundantly unfaithful to his wife" (March 12). "K. to the cemetery in Santa Monica" (March 13). "Meticulous dressing for mourning . . . The participants not very numerous. Wreaths and flowers a beautiful sight. My wreath with 'To my big brother, with love'" (March 14).

## FRIGHTENINGLY LEFTIST GOINGS-ON

"Afterward on the terrace much about Russia, Stalin, etc. The necessity of being distanced. Heinrich's all too positive attitude" (July 8, 1937). In spite of vague sympathies for Communism, he did not let himself be blinded. The much-traveled man never went to Moscow. The future of Germany, he writes to the Soviet Writers Union on the twentieth anniversary of the Soviet Union, was "definitely not the Communist dictatorship." Nevertheless, he was thought here and there to be a Communist writer, that it to say, by the Nazis, and unfortunately also by the American FBI, in whose Thomas Mann dossier there is talk of "Communist background." But certainly not all Communists regarded him as one of their own. Alfred Kurella, in an essay with the title "The Decadence of Thomas Mann," felt compelled to write incredible statements such as that the Joseph novel "was a contribution to the return of the German people to barbarism," and having appeared "in the like-minded S. Fischer publishing company, controlled by an SA leader," served no one other than Herr Goebbels and his propaganda ministry. "That is the spirit of Germany's hangman," the cheeky man adds.

Nevertheless, Thomas Mann remains well disposed toward the land of Dostoyevski. He writes New Year's greetings to the Soviet Union (1942), a contribution to the twenty-fifth anniversary of the October Revolution, congratulations to the Russian Army, and other texts friendly to Russia. Of course, he did not want to be dependent on Russia in any fashion. His greatest fear was that the West, because of fear of Communism, could at one time or another become allied with Hitler. He wants to combat that fear. Under the influence of consultations with representatives of the German Left in exile (diary, August 1 and 2, 1943) he expresses, as a result, "frightening leftist goings-on," but hopes "to guard from scandalous effects by strewing a fair amount of conservative and traditonalistic powdered sugar over them." Poor Agnes Meyer! She had to translate what was politically offensive to her—that the world- threatening alliance of junkers, generals, and heavy industry had to be destroyed, that out of fear of bolshevism all the atrocities of fascism were being consented to, that the fear of the word "Communism" was the basic foolishness of the epoch, and that the future of the world would be hard to imagine without Communist features. The inevitable happened. "Impertinent and deeply upset letter from Meyer about the speech" (September 12, 1943). He replies amicably restrained and quietly ironic. Many things looked worse when written than when they were presented orally, "with my decent middle-class personality."

After the end of the hot war and the beginning of the cold one, the battle against Communist agitation becomes more vehement. "Sometimes the wish that Europe as a whole might be organized communistically and rebuilt based on races. It would be a break for America" (November 22, 1949).

## BRECHT

Bertolt Brecht complained in a letter on December 1, 1943, that Thomas Mann did not distinguish enough between the Hitler regime and the democratic strengths in Germany. That was correct in general, but specifically for the speech "Destiny and Task" it coincidentally did not agree with those leftist goings-on. The decent bourgeois personality had said there that "only a stupid, corrupt upper-class pack of traitors to whom nothing is holy but money and advantage" was working together with the Nazis. But the people were refusing to do so. Seven million had been deported for forced labor, almost two million had been executed and murdered, the hell of the concentration camps contained tens of thousands. An inner emigration numbering in the millions was waiting in Germany for the end of Hitler.

That he had brought that up in public shortly before made it easy for him to reproach Brecht. A thousand people had listened to him when he had given that speech in New York, "but, basically peculiar and probably genuinely German, not a single one of the gentlemen with whom I at the time consulted tentatively about the unification of exiled German opponents to Hitler was among them." Had one been present, doubt about his attitude could not have cropped up. Again (without sweetening) he summarizes what he had said there: "Not Germany or the German people were to be destroyed and sterlized, rather to be destroyed were the guilt-ridden power combination of junkers, the military, and heavy industry, which bore the blame for two world wars. All hope rested on a genuine and purifying revolution that should not be prevented by the victors but promoted and supported by them."

Thomas Mann already knew Brecht and his theater from the Munich days. Even at that time their antipathy was mutual. Occasionally they met in exile, on September 1, 1939, on August 1, 1943, on November 26, 1943, on May 16, 1944, on April 7, 1945, and even more often. Two gentlemen from the FBI came by once (on August 18, 1943) and asked about Brecht and other Communists. Thomas Mann would have taken care to protect himself, although shortly before, there had been a dispute. An extraordinarily hostile depiction of it is found in Brecht's working journal: "when Thomas Mann said last sunday, his hands in his lap, leaning back: 'yes, half a million must be killed in germany,' that sounded completely barbaric. his stiff collar was talking. no battle was mentioned or taken into consideration for this killing; it concerned cold-blooded punishment, and where even cleansing would have been a bestial reason, what is revenge there (for it was the resentment of an animal)."

In July 1943 the politburo of the Russian Communist Party had proposed the foundation of a national committee, "Free Germany." Thirty-eight German Communists in exile, among them Walter Ulbricht, Wilhelm Pieck, and Johannes R. Becher, had concluded a manifesto that, avoiding all Communist slogans, urged the Germans to struggle for freedom against Hitler. Thomas Mann reacted in tortuous agreement. On that August 1, 1943, a group of German emigrants, among them Brecht, Feuchtwanger, Heinrich and Thomas Mann, wanted to formulate a broader declaration. Tormented, Thomas Mann cooperated. "Hours long attempts at a formulation with middling results" (August 1, 1943). But the next morning, uneasiness and the decision for a rejection. Brecht is outraged: "and this morning TH MANN calls up feuchtwanger: he was withdrawing his endorsement, since he had 'qualms of conscience,' this was a 'patriotic declaration' with which the allies were being 'attacked from behind,' and he could not find it unreasonable, if 'the allies punish germany for ten or twenty years.' the resolute wretchedness of these 'bearers of culture' crippled even me again for a moment . . . for a moment even I debated how 'the german people' could justify not only having endured the outrages of the hitler regime but also the novels of herr mann, the latter without 20–30 ss divisions on top of them."

## PRIZE RECIPIENT AND SHADOW PRESIDENT

Similar scenes were repeated. In the fall of 1943, the theologian Paul Tillich, along with other German emigrants, among them Brecht again, once more wanted to found a Free Germany Committee. Among the secret intentions was always that at the time of Hitler's end a kind of shadow government should be ready to take power. The emigrants felt predestined for such a thing. They were in the right morally, but politically in a fantasy world in which at most the question was who would most cleverly misuse their good intentions. This time Thomas Mann first made an inquiry in the State Department and retreated when the American government, as expected, showed no interest. Nevertheless, he had to deny a false report: "The Department of State has not invited me to join or preside over a Free German Committee, nor do I consider the moment opportune for the formation of such a body." He was even supposed to have been the president of this association. He reports to Agnes Meyer about the consultation of November 26: "The meeting with the political lights in New York was, naturally, not pleasant, but I steadfastly carried it out and am glad about my freedom—in spite of the remark of Professor Tillich that I had 'spoken the death sentence for Germany' and in spite of the scornfully embittered face of Bert Brecht, a party-liner, who, if the Russians help to bring him to power in Germany, will do anything mean to me."

Of course, he was flattered that he was to become the president of anything. He comments in an understatement on the report that he had been designated the current president of the intellectual republic with: "Curious" (December 28, 1938). He is the uncrowned king of literary emigration. "Klaus remarks that the emigrants resemble a nation that considers me as its envoy. It seems natural that everyone turns to me" (July 14, 1940). Ludwig Marcuse confirms that: The "kaiser of all the German emigrants was Thomas Mann," "most especially the lord protector of the tribe of writers." The dreams rise even higher. Supposedly it appeared in the newspaper that he had been summoned to Washington and had been appointed president of Germany. "Idealists dream of Th. M. as the president of the second German republic." But he knows what's what. "I would be elected for that sooner by Stalin than by Washington" (February 16, 1943). Still, he likes to note such things. "Meeting with construction contractor X, who asks whether I will be president of Germany . . ." (April 27, 1944). Earlier, a journalist in response to the question "How shall Germany be ruled after Hitler's defeat?" had suggested him as the president of a future German republic. With the exception of a small monarchic minority, he said, and the extreme left, he had the trust of most Germans. Aside from the fact that, at the time, that was certainly a mistake, Thomas Mann answers him declining, and explains it more in detail in a letter to Agnes Meyer:

Only under the strongest pressure would I ever agree to play a political role, knowing full well I would have to make the greatest sacrifice. But I consider the danger very slight that it could be serious. Above all, "Washington" also has to agree, and it doesn't like people of my ilk very much at all. We are "premature anti-fascists"—the expression has amused me very much, but it is used quite officially as an objection against the character, the trustworthiness of a human being.

Yes, it is probably correct that he did not have the trust of the American government. He was not considered quite unreliable by it but was still held in suspicion in a way similar to Bertolt Brecht. Politically, neither had a chance. They should rather have tolerated one another. But the reason for their antipathy probably lay beyond politics. What did this impudently charming, shabbily chic womanizer want but to savor a lust for life that people like us had always kept under control! Brecht's aggressive vitality was aimed at bourgeois habits, at that self-control that Thomas Mann needed so essentially. It was not given to Brecht to see that his opponent was not at all bourgeois inside. He was taken in by the exterior. He cultivated his hate because he needed such an opponent. He wrote gifted but coarse poems about him. "His hands in his scrawny lap," one of them begins, confusing chastity with infertility, "the refugee demands the death of half a million people. / For their victims he demands / a sentence of ten years. The silent sufferers / should be caned." That's how it appeared to him. "To gain a hundred-thousand-dollar name / for the cause of a tortured people / the writer put on his good suit / (with kow-tows) / he approached the proprietor."

He hardly took notice of Mann's literary works. A few scornful opinions come to mind. Thomas Mann, on the other hand, knew Brecht's works very well as a theatergoer in the twenties, but in the thirties also as a reader. He always considered him a "genius in the theater" but adds: "theoretically with a confused doctrine" (July 8, 1950).

Jealousy also played a role. Brecht's productive high point lies in the twenties and thirties. In American exile he lacked stimulation; he had no theater; Hollywood was not an equivalent substitute; Margarete Steffin was no longer alive; new muses were not so easy to find. On the other hand, Thomas Mann carried the prerequisites of his creativity within him. Therefore, too, he could say: Where I am, Germany is. Which Brecht promptly resented. He played Heinrich against him. "Heinrich Mann did not believe, like his talented brother, that German culture was present where he was. . . . When, in his seventies, he climbed the Pyrenees to escape the German and French fascists, *he* did not turn his back on the German people rather on the oppressors of the German people."

If Brecht had found out, it would have had to make him furious— that he had been the second choice for the International Stalin Prize "For the Consolidation of Peace," which he received in Moscow in May 1955. The first choice had been Thomas Mann, and he had refused it. "Query about whether I would accept the Stalin Peace Prize (golden star and 100,000 rubles), which really now, if ever, is completely impossible this year. But what-all one throws away for the sake of the 'free world.' That is, around 300,000 francs" (December 6, 1954). He had previously declined the National Prize of the East German Republic (100,000 East marks) twice, in 1953 and 1954. However, Brecht had received it in 1951.

# XVII. Doctor Faustus

1946

Work on the Faust novel continued almost without interruption. As a rule, two-hundred pages a year came into being, along with all sorts of diversions. From the middle of March to May 1943 he did research and planned. On May 23 the writing began. On May 31 the first chapter was completed, on June 7 the second, on June 24, after essayistic insertions, the third, on July 7 the fourth, on July 13 the fifth, on July 17 the sixth, on August 2 the seventh. A few interim tasks followed, so that the great eighth chapter, containing Wendell Kretschmar's lectures, was not completed until September 22. Revisions took place at a still later time, some of them suggested by Theodor W. Adorno, with whom Thomas Mann had become acquainted at the beginning of July.

October and November for the first time bring long interruptions for lecture tours in the United States and other appearances. Not until December 8, back in Pacific Palisades, does Thomas Mann again revise the eighth chapter before, on December 21, the ninth is taken up. In spite of constant interludes, among them radio news from the "Deutsche Hörer" again and again, every month one or two chapters is finished—on May 9, 1944, the fifteenth, on May 24 the sixteenth, on June 7 the seventeenth, on June 11 the eighteenth. On October 4 the twenty-second chapter is finished, on December 10 the twenty-fourth. The dialogue with the Devil, in chapter 25, fifty-two pages long in manuscript, occupies the author intensely until February 20, 1945.

Afterward there again occur longer pauses, in which the address "Germany and the Germans" takes place. On April 12, 1945, he continues with chapter 26. Work on it is interrupted by the article "The Camps" and a few other texts brought about by the end of the war, work on chapter 27 by a lecture tour and a few days vacation, so that chapter 28 is not begun until August 8. In spite of hindrances of all sorts, by the end of the year chapter 33 is complete.

The year 1946 begins with the chapter 34 and the preliminary work on the speech "Nietzsche's Philosophy in the Light of Contemporary Events," until the months of April and May bring a long interruption because of a serious but successful operation for lung cancer. Then from June to the end of the year, quite speedily, chapters 35–46 are written, in January 1947 also chapter 47, the last one, as well as the epilogue. On February 6 the diary reports "champagne dinner in celebration of the completion of Faustus and the reading of the Echo chapter. Visible emotion. The figure of the child doubtless the best and most poetic in the book. More champagne."

For reasons of copyright, the novel appears first in a printing of fifty copies in New York and immediately afterward with fourteen thousand copies on October 17, 1947, in Stockholm. Its impact spreads at first mainly in Switzerland. Though the work was discussed in the press in Germany, it was obtainable in bookstores only after the Suhrkamp edition in the fall of 1948, possibly (according to a letter to Peter Suhrkamp) not until January 1949.

A statement of accounts, *The Story of a Novel: The Genesis of Doctor Faustus*, written mainly to honor the participation of Theodor W. Adorno, is begun at the end of June 1948 and completed at the end of October. It appears in 1949.

## THOMAS FAUST?

WHEN THE Joseph novel was completed, Hitler had still not been overthrown. What was to be done? Thomas Mann decided to give the war enough time for one more novel. He flirted for a while with taking up the confidence-man novel again. It would astonish people, if a project that had lain idle for decades were to be finished! That would be a grand self-confirmation! "Feeling of magnificence, after 32 years to begin again where I stopped before the 'Death in Venice,' in whose favor I interrupted the Krull." Such patience in such turbulent times, such a large arc, such a proudly asserted unity of life! It would be wonderful to defy the world so visibly, untouchably, imperturbably to reach back for something over which so much emotion and effort had passed, "an example of inner cheerful loyalty to oneself, to show mockingly superior endurance" with the continuation of this frivolous fun from the sunken empire.

But it was to be otherwise. The arc was to become larger, to span not three but four decades. "Morning in the old notebooks. Found the 3-line plan of the Doctor Faustus from the year 1901" (March 17, 1943). It was the seventh notebook in which Thomas Mann leafed at the time. It mentions the plan for Faust in two places, which were, to be sure, written not in 1901 but in 1904:

> For the novel. Driven by longing, the syphilitic artist becomes close to a pure, sweet young girl, carries on an engagement with the unsuspecting girl, and shoots himself just before the wedding.

> Novella or for "Maya." Figure of the syphilitic artist: as Dr. Faust and one who has sold himself to the Devil. The poison works as intoxication, stimulus, inspiration; in ecstatic enthusiasm he can create genial, wonderful works; the Devil directs his hand. But finally the Devil takes him: paralysis. The affair with the pure young girl, with whom he carries on up to the marriage, proceeds.

The plan comes from the time of his engagement, thus from the time of his separation from Paul Ehrenberg. Thomas Mann carried on back then with a pure young girl up to the wedding. Of course, he did not have syphilis, but he felt himself infected in another way, by being an artist and by homoeroticism. When such an artist gets involved with life, vengeful Nemesis will catch up with him. He is afraid that he will either pull his bride down into the abyss or as a husband forfeit his artistic gift. Had not Friedrich Nietzsche scoffed that a married philosopher belonged in a comedy? Would that not apply also to an artist? Inspiration would not come from an innocent, middle-class, happy marriage. It could grow only out of sinful love, only out of homoeroticism.

What was burningly relevant in 1904, of course, had something dependent and almost too routine about it in 1943. Meanwhile, syphilis and paralysis lay far off his path. Thomas Mann is no Faust. Seen biographically, with this material he had bitten off a bit too much. He was not seized by the Devil, not even suggestively. After almost forty years of marriage, he can no longer seriously believe that God would still punish him once more for his middle-class good life. The fear of the invasion of homosexuality into his ordered life had, of course, certainly not dwindled. But after the test with Klaus Heuser, he could be somewhat sure of holding his own in this respect. He has settled down. "During the evening read for a long time in Platen's diaries. Compared and found many reasons for gratitude." He does not have to go to bed with young men, is content with illusion, even considers it more satisfying than reality. "What is illusional of love in homoeroticism is enormously strengthened. All reality leads emotion ad absurdum." Admittedly, even in his forties he still looked around for handsome boys (occasionally also for pretty girls), but one great passion from the Faust epoch is not handed down. All of that could be kept well at a distance. Of course, the Faust novel is full of his own experiences like none other since *Buddenbrooks*, but at the same time it is also the most premeditated, using what is cooled-down autobiography most calculatedly as a means of impact. With the commercially ambitious utilization of remnants, he makes use of all the material from his life that had up to that time not been accommodated. That cannot be called a "reckless biography," although Thomas Mann liked to state that kind of thing. On the one hand the book is closer to him than any other, but on the other hand through its constructed aspect it takes what is private more strictly in hand than any other before.

In 1904 the material had been much too personal, had lain too close to him, had been too compromising, and thus had to remain untouched.

But the writer did not lose sight of it. Already in 1933 he knew that Faust would be his next theme after *Joseph*, at the same time his "last work." In the thirties he places one or another found piece in his folder, obviously already with the intent of linking Faust to fascism. At the time he also rereads the three-line plan (May 6, 1934). He must have kept the idea persisently in the back of his mind, for on the same day that he puts away the Joseph material, he promptly begins the new project, without a pause: "Thoughts of the old novella plan 'Dr. Faust.' Looking around for material to read" (March 14, 1943).

Why Faust? In this material everything came together, what was private as well as public, the routine care of old wounds and the high ethical stance of the battle against Hitler. The primal odds and ends surface again; that is the first reason. Again we have a story in which an artist comes to ruin through love, again Paul Ehrenberg and Katia Pringsheim awaken, as do the "Why am I getting married?" and the shamefully naughty secrets. The second reason is vengeance on Munich. Those who drove him away could now be included in the prehistory of fascism. For reasons of discretion and other considerations, both had not been possible, but now in 1943 were possible, for Munich meanwhile was as far away as Lübeck was when in Rome the first lines of *Buddenbrooks* were put down on paper. Portraits, he wrote later, had not touched his consciousness at all in the time of Faustus. "For that, Europe, Germany and what was alive there—or no longer alive—had become too deeply and distantly separated, sunken, had become too much past and dream."

Third, it was necessary to write a Faust because Goethe had written one, too. Ambition and addiction to fame are at play, the intention of continuing to write a national myth, and in doing that also to caution and instruct his fellow countrymen. He had nothing less in mind than the novel of his epoch, disguised as the story of the life of an artist. That looked great, and it was great, too. And fourth is the thought of the unity of his life. The Faust novel was to be his last work. Even in his youth he had put as his work of old age his "Parzifal." Afterward he would die. Visually for his life that would have been nice, but things happened differently—as a substitute for death, a lung cancer operation, and another quantity of rather great works, beyond every dune new dunes not requiring an absolute end. The theme of life was often varied arbitrarily. "I would not lack for ideas even if I lived to be 120. Too bad about them. . . . For who else can do that?" "Luther's Wedding," too, the work plan taken over from Wagner, over which

Thomas Mann died, would have been primal odds and ends, would have treated the wedding of the monk with the nun. He does not mind seeing himself in the role of Schopenhauer, about whom he said that he offered the rare spectacle of an old man "who up until the last moment, with eerie faithfulness, is concerned with the work of his youth."

America is unable to captivate him in comparison with that. The old perceptions are much stronger. "America is alien to people, provides few cleaving impressions. Somehow must create from the past, from memory, images, intuition" (April 11, 1943).

## RETOUCHINGS

Weeks go by with excerpts, plans, and notes, until on May 23, 1943, a Sunday morning, the diary notes: "Began to write 'Dr. Faust' during the morning." It is the same date on which Serenus Zeitblom sits down in his small study in Freising on the Isar to begin to write the life story of his immortalized friend Adrian Leverkühn. In *The Genesis of Dr. Faustus* it says, concerning this:

> That the high school teacher Zeitblom begins to write on the very day that I myself, in fact, put the first lines on paper is characteristic for the whole book: for the singular actuality that is inherent in it and that, seen from one side, is an artistic device, the playful effort around the realization, proceeding from the exact to the most illusional, of something fictional, the biography and the productions of Leverkühn, but from another side is a ruthlessness never before known, one constantly shattering to me in its fantastic mechanics in the assemblage of factual, historical, personal, even literary realities. . . . This montage technique, which continually alienated me myself, even gave me pause for thought, really belongs to the conception, to the "idea" of the book; it is involved with a curious and licentious intellectual attraction from which it proceeded, with its devolved and then again utter directness, its character as a secret work and life confession that kept the presentation of its public existence completely away from me as long as I was writing it.

Secret work and life confession—anyone who expects to hear confessions now about hidden initimacies will be disappointed; Mann's

statement of accounts divulges only literary and musical sources of
all sorts. An attentive comparison of the report with the diary shows
how consciously the *Genesis* is silent about what is most deeply personal. The *Genesis* says, ostensibly quoting the diary:

> "During the morning in the old notebooks," it says for the 17th.
> "Located the three-line plan of Dr. Faust from the year 1901. Con-
> tact with the Tonio Kröger time, the Munich days, the never real-
> ized novel plans 'The Beloved' and 'Maya.' 'Come up old Love
> and friendship, too.' Shame and emotion at seeing again these
> pains of youth. . . ."

Isn't something missing here? In the original diary (March 17, 1943)
the passage sounds somewhat different:

> During the morning in the old notebooks. Located the 3 line plan
> of Doctor Faust from the year 1901. Emotion at the P.E. and Tonio
> Kr. time. Plans "The Beloved" and "Maya." Shame and emotion
> at seeing again these pains of youth. One cannot experience love
> more strongly. In the end I will be able to say to myself that I
> paid the penalty for everything. The artistic trick was to make it
> qualify as art.

There are small but important differences. P.E. is missing, and that for
which the penalty was paid. In the place of what it really concerned,
in the place of the love for Paul Ehrenberg, Mann makes an allusion
to Goethe: the quotation lacking in the diary "Come up old Love and
friendship, too," from the "Dedication" in *Faust*. One could let oneself
be seen better with that! Once again he camouflages his life behind
great literature.

## THE HERZ WOMAN AT TABLE, UNFORTUNATELY

The Nackedey woman, a shy and hesitant, constantly blushing
creature, dying of shame at every moment, about thirty years
old, who while talking and also while listening blinked her eyes
spasmodically and amicably behind the pince-nez she wore and
at the same time, nodding, wrinkled her nose—so this person
had one day, when Adrian was in the city, turned up at his side
on the forward platform of a streetcar and had, when she discov-

ered it, taken to headlong flight through the full car to the rear, from which, however, after a few moments spent collecting herself, she had returned to talk to him, to call him by name, blushing and turning pale to give him hers, to add something of her circumstances, and to tell him that she considered his music holy, all of which he acknowledged gratefully.

When Thomas Mann still rode on streetcars, the very same thing happened to him in 1924 in Nuremberg, with the book-dealer Ida Herz. Her parents had a shop selling utensils for tripe, spices, and meat, so her characterisics are behind not only Meta Nackedey but also behind Kunigunde Rosenstiel, the coproprietor of a sausage-casings firm, the second of the serving women. The external features of Rosenstiel, however, the woolly hair difficult to manage, and the eyes in whose brownness ancient sorrow seemed to be written, Thomas Mann took from somewhere else, perhaps from Käte Hamburger, who was a friend of Ida Herz. They both wrote well-composed letters, both were Jews and both old-maidish, which in the writer's opinion has its advantages, "for human deprivation is certainly the source of a prophetic intuition that for the sake of such meager origins is by no means less treasured."

Ida Herz—today it is customary either to agree with the master's derision or to complain about the master's uncharitableness. But why take sides when both deserve respect. Herz was a woman of importance and took nothing amiss. She never felt aggrieved or offended. On the contrary, the depiction in *Faustus* made clear her "dramatic place" in his life. She was obviously in perfect agreement with her role as the "serving woman."

She had seen the writer for the first time in 1922, in 1924 spoken to him on the streetcar, in 1925 put his library in order, and from then on—supported by him—collected publications, articles, photographs, and books by and about Thomas Mann and through difficult times preserved them for posterity. That at Carnival in 1927, encouraged by the master, she appeared as the uneducated Frau Stöhr from *The Magic Mountain*—*well*! She went through a lot under Hitler. Incautious as she was and proud of her contact with Thomas Mann, she was arrested in 1934, received amnesty seven weeks later, in 1935 again was accused of an offense against the "malice law" (slander of leading personalities in the state and the Party) and in 1937, after she had already left Germany, was stripped of her German citizenship. In the accusations it stated that she was a Jew by race and by faith, a fanatic opponent of the National Socialist state, had accused district leader Julius Streicher of moral misconduct with children, had described Hitler to her servant girl as a housepainter, had after the national upheaval made no secret of her enthusiastic veneration for Thomas Mann, who had meanwhile been expatriated, and was in a personal exchange of thoughts with him. She avoided the planned renewed incarceration by her flight abroad.

There, Thomas Mann helped variously, and she often visited him. That got on his nerves, however much he liked her. "The Herz woman at table, unfortunately," he notes daily in his diary for a while. Let him cast the first stone who was never bothered by visitors. He needed her at a distance, not nearby, but when it had to be (and in the thirties it had to be), he also tolerated her nearby, played his part, but in his diary he growled maliciousness: "the accursed Herz, who hangs on my every look, unspeakably burdensome and enervating" (April 16, 1935). "Hapless and shameful instrusiveness of the hysterical old maid. My stiffness in response and iciness reminds me of Mama, who acted similarly toward undesirably enamored intrusion. Anyway, I managed at the end a bit of generally cajoling good-naturedness, but resolved not to permit this again" (April 19, 1935). But in September she came again, in flight, and thus not to be turned away. She is taken in as a house guest for more than two weeks. — The Herz woman at table, unfortunately.

She knew what she had in him. When, at eighty-five, she got to read the diaries, she wrote to Klaus W. Jonas that in spite of the mortification that the disclosures had inflicted upon her, she maintained her claim to friendship. Justifiably. For Thomas Mann not only took, he also gave. Several times, and mostly with success, he endeavored to find jobs for her. He wrote 350 letters and cards to her in the course of thirty years, not just heartfelt and fond ones, but among them matter-of-fact, patient, also extensive ones, with never-wearying courtesy. But he turns away what is most intimate. When she tries to divulge the problems in her life, even intimates thoughts of suicide, he points out to her coolly that she lacks the death instinct for that. When she tries to reprimand him for his "Marxism," he puts her gruffly in her place with a "silly." Constantly she worries whether she is not disturbing the master and disturbs him by doing so. "If I had something against you, I would tell you. But I have nothing against you but this."

She sends him books and writing material, cakes and also Easter eggs—*thirteen* Easter eggs, as he remarks with a shudder. "I opened the package and quickly ate one raw with sugar to take the curse on myself. I'll manage to cope with it." He put up with it gladly that he had an archivist during his lifetime—that sort of thing put a smile in his heart. He would not have been opposed if the Yale University Library, where Joseph W. Angell meanwhile was the archivist for the Manniana, had bought her collection from her, but it never came to that, since no one wanted to contribute the money because of the Cold War, and so the collection is today located in Zurich. For her sixtieth birthday he honored Ida Herz with a charming letter which, written in the Leverkühn persona, jokingly recalls the streetcar and the sausage casings:

> How it started, and you, at the time the proprietor of a tripe shop, fled on the streetcar from one platform to the other, and finally spoke to me and we became acquainted: how it then continued, and you always wrote me such well-composed letters, in better German than many a scholar can manage, and from time to time visited me in Pfeiffering; how you were present at the deathbed of poor little Nepomuk Schneidewein, whom we sadly had to turn over to the Devil, and finally when you were again present when I wanted to play from "the Lament of Faust" and in so doing became somewhat devious so that all the guests ran away, except for you and Frau Schweigestill—those are, of course, expansive, significant, moving memories that rise up before the eyes of both of us on this festive day.

That they had been involved with one another for decades now, he continues, one with the the life of the other, she with touching loyalty to his destiny, writing, and activities, he with great respect and sympathy for her condition and mode of life—"for how you marshaled yourself after your expulsion from Germany, how you acted and worked and survived that life, that is so good and honorable that it really deserves every respect and sympathy and friendship."

## SCHWABING AND POLLING,
## PALESTRINA AND PACIFIC PALISADES

There would be no end to the enumeration of all that he treated in
detail regarding his own self. In every case there are traumas. Only
traumas have such a burning sharpness in memory; only they con-
form to a matrix ever the same. We have reported previously about
Ehrenberg, the quarrelsome flirtation, the very daring letter, and the
racist family, in like manner about Polling, his mother, and the suicide
of his sister Carla, and likewise about Katia and Marie Godeau. The
bohemia in Schwabing and the Munich circle of honorees are evoked,
as is demonstrated by Daniel zur Höhe (modeled on Ludwig Der-
leth), Sixtus Kridwiss (Emil Preetorius), Leo Zink (Franz Blei), Chaim
Breisacher (Oskar Goldberg), and many other characters in the novel.
Not only enemies were portrayed, sometimes friends as well. The
Whitman translator Rüdiger Schildknapp is concealed behind Hans
Reisiger, the film agent Saul C. Colin behind Saul Fitelberg, Annette
Kolb behind Jeannette Scheurl. We already know Meta Nackedey and
Kunigunde Rosenstiel. The notorious opera glass was once more
pulled out. After the publication of the novel there were correspond-
ing altercations, with Arnold Schoenberg, with Rüdiger Schildknapp,
with Emil Preetorius and many others. Thomas Mann had to write
Ida Herz soothingly that she should not believe, because of the allusion to the sausage end, that she was Rosenstiel. "That would be
megalomania! It would be the worst kind of hypochondria! And *as-
suming* that the madness contained an electron-sized kernel of truth?
What then? Then we find the desolately sad Rosenstiel—whom you,
posh Londoner, resemble as much as I do Hercules—at the deathbed
of little Nepomuk, and finally she stands like a sentinel straight and
true next to the collapsing Leverkühn."

We learn little from the novel about the childhood of Thomas Mann.
Leverkühn grows up in a village, for which Thomas Mann admittedly
took a bit from his observation of Polling and of the surroundings of
Bad Tölz, but that was not sufficient, for which reason life in the country seems very stylized. Kaisersaschern does have characteristics of
Lübeck. But they do not go far, because what was important for childhood had long since been used literarily from the city of his birth.

The scenes of Palestrina and Rome are inspired by the early Italian

sojourns of Thomas Mann. Memories of the summer of 1897 lie behind the location of the dialogue with the Devil. In Palestrina Thomas
Mann had become certain of his calling to be a writer. There he had
made his pact with literature. The apparition of the Devil has a very
soft echo of the occult. Thomas Mann himself is said to have seen at
the time a similar gentleman on the sofa. He was supposedly frail of
form, with reddish eyelashes, a sallow complexion, repulsively tight
pants, and yellow, run-down shoes. Thomas Mann claims to have
known that it was none other than the Devil himself. Incidentally,
after his lung operation he does his writing in the corner of the sofa,
using a clipboard as a base, no longer at his desk. The sofa stands
today in Zurich. In its right corner one sinks far down and has good
thoughts.

Pfeiffering is Polling near Weilheim on the railway stretch between
Munich and Garmisch, where Mann's mother, after vacation sojourns
from 1899 on, lived with some interruptions from about 1906 until
shortly before her death in 1923. Like Schwabing had been, Polling
was an artists' choice, a secret bohemian tip; many painters were
there and nearby, in Murnau and Kochel. His sister Julia's fiancé,
Josef Löhr, a banker with painter acquaintances, had arranged access.
Polling is idyll and trauma at the same time, a vacation spot but also
the place of meeting with his aging mother, the place of the death of
his sister. His mother appears in the novel as the wife of Senator
Rodde, who after the death of her husband had gone from Bremen to
Munich to enjoy a bit of gusto in life and marry off her daughters.
Mann's sisters Julia and Carla are encountered as Ines and Clarissa
Rodde. Carla had killed herself in Polling in 1910, something the
novel takes over almost undisguised.

The portrait of his mother as the widow of Senator Rodde turns out
to be halfhearted:

Her state of affairs were easy to make out. Dark eyed, her brown,
delicately curled hair only a bit turned gray, with a ladylike composure, ivory-colored complexion and pleasant, still rather well-
preserved facial features, for all her life she had represented a
patriarchal society as a celebrated member, presided over a responsible household with many servants. After the death of her
husband (whose stern portrait, in the regalia of his office, likewise decorated the drawing room), under strongly reduced cir-

cumstances and a position probably not entirely to be preserved in the accustomed milieu, desires had been released in her for a never exhausted and probably never really satisfied ardor for life, which had been intended for a more interesting epilogue of her life in a humanly warmer sphere.

Her daughter Ines is Thomas Mann's mouthpiece, insofar as she "quietly and clearly rejected her mother." Adrian is not assigned the Julia Mann type of mother, rather an unbiographical, wished-for mother. As a contrast to his biological mother, Thomas Mann introduced several other mother figures into the novel: Elsbeth Leverkühn and Frau Schweigestill above all, the "Pietà mother," as she has been called. They fulfill imaginary longings for security in suffering that the real mother probably could not fulfill. When the music teacher Wendell Kretzschmar woos Adrian, it is reported that his mother "in a singular way gathered to herself the head of her son, who was sitting beside her. She twined her arm around him, as it were, but not around his shoulders, rather around his head, her hand on his forehead, and like that, the glance of her black eyes directed on Kretzschmar, and speaking to him with her sonorous voice, she leaned Adrian's head on her breast." Similarly, Frau Schweigestill, at Leverkühn's collapse, raises the head of the unconscious man, "holding his torso in motherly arms." The rescuing gestures indicate wishes for regression, which Thomas Mann also probably had—who wouldn't!

Schwabing had been the place of the rise out of the bohemian into genteel society. The intellectual avant-garde of the imperial age had gathered together here. Experiences of the years around 1900, or at least before 1914, form the kernel of what was narrated. Later Munich, the outbreak of war in 1914, the soviet republic, the fascistoid traits before 1933 leave traces behind mainly on the plane of the figure of the narrator, Serenus Zeitblom. Thomas Mann has him live in Freising, twenty kilometers north of Munich. He may have known the Freising Cathedral Hill and people like Monsignore Hinterpförtner. Yet the Zeitblom sphere lacks a point of view in which there is a Helene Ölhafen and two fascist sons.

Impulses from Pacific Palisades are also incorporated. To them belong the sweet Nepomuk Schneidewein, who in the novel in 1928, five years old, dies horridly from meningitis (in the logic of the novel is taken by the Devil). His model in reality was spared such a fate: the grandson Frido Mann, whose charm the writer enjoyed during the composition of the novel in California. Nepomuk's death is promoted by the structure of the novel and even predetermined in the Faust folksbook, where Doctor Faust has a small son with his paramour Helena.

Frido Mann lives with the fact that his grandfather let him die so effectively and horribly. That will not always be easy. It is said that afterward he was afraid of the undertow of death. Surrounded by overpowering prefigurative models, by the course of lives of his father, his grandfather, his great-uncle Heinrich, his uncles and aunts Klaus, Erika, Golo, Monika, and Elisabeth, he has a difficult time finding his own life course. He followed none of his models. He went back to Germany from California, converted to Catholicism, studied theology, married a daughter of Werner Heisenberg, joined the movement of 1968, took courses again (psychology and humane medicine), and became a teacher and psychotherapist in Münster. He depicted his rich but obviously stressed life, changed by unfulfillable demands, in his autobiographical novel *Professor Parzifal* (1985).

The California exile is also responsible for the meeting with Theodor W. Adorno, who lends the Devil not only many of his thoughts but also in passing his appearance as a bespectacled music intellectual. There is also a self-parody from the time of his exile. The Devil sugggests to Adrian Leverkühn in Palestrina that he say "Where I am, there is Kaisersaschern," imitating the "Where I am, Germany is."

Most of the material from the time of exile is, however, allocated to Zeitblom. His opinions about the Hitler era are variously taken over directly from Mann's essays. That sometimes makes a curious impression, for today we know how different the consciousness of the inner emigrants was from those driven abroad.

## THE ADVISER

Theodor W. Adorno felt that he was as much as slandered from the grave by Thomas Mann. When the third volume of a selection of her father's letters, edited by Erika Mann, appeared in 1965, it also included a communication to Jonas Lesser, from which Adorno had to conclude that he supposedly inflated himself with pride in a not very pleasant way in the light of the spotlight that Thomas Mann had directed at him. It seemed to suggest somewhat that he had actually written the *Faustus*.

Terrible statements. Undoubtedly Thomas Mann had "stolen" from Adorno—with his agreement, to be sure, and that changes the matter decisively; then one cannot really speak about theft. The author of the *Faustus* did, indeed, control broad realms of the musical repertoire, but had no real access to the twentieth century. Basically, his musical taste had not gotten beyond the work of Richard Wagner; the "triad world of the 'Ring'"—he said this himself—was his musical homeland. The way his Faust is presented also comes from Nietzsche's "Case of Wagner." Nietzsche had established that in Wagner everything was a constructed and calculated, artificial and effect-conscious artifact. But should not a great work be conceived and burst forth? How can the modern artist overcome his awareness of his workmanship? The effect of the pact with the Devil is artificial inspiration. Anyone who no longer has natural naïveté is in need of an obfuscation of awareness, in need of a kind of intoxication. The Devil sells this intoxication in the form of an illness. It is the "aphrodisiac of the brain" and bestows the euphoric phases in which the crippling control of the mind is set aside. The Devil promises "a truly happy, enraptured, certain, and credulous inspiration, an inspiration in which there is no choice, no improvement, no tinkering, in which everything is received as blissful obligation; the steps hesitate and stumble, sublime shivers trickle from the head to the toes of the obsessed man, a torrent of tears of delight break forth from his eyes."

But then what should the post-Wagner compositions look like, in general as well as in particular—to begin with, Thomas Mann had no concept of that. The right adviser turned up: Theodor W. Adorno. He knew not only Thomas Mann's problem, he also had ideas about how to solve it, and he knew the most important musical answer of the twentieth century to this problem, namely, the compositional technique of Arnold Schoenberg. Thomas Mann entrusted himself to him as previously to no other adviser. He read his writings, met with him for a number of hours-long conferences, finally turned the entire manuscript over to him (December 5, 1945). Adorno must be regarded as coauthor as far as the musical realization is concerned. It was Adorno who thought out Leverkühn's late compositions, in accordance with very vague specifications by Thomas Mann. If he had demanded it, a financial compensation would have been allowed him, in accord with a middle-class sense of justice. But Adorno had considered it a challenge of the highest order to be permitted to cooperate on *Faustus*, not as an activity by paid help. He emphasizes that in 1957, when an attack forced him to make a sworn deposition:

> During the entire work on the novel "Doctor Faustus" I advised Thomas Mann amicably in all musical questions. The book came into existence under my eyes. The writer never had the intention to awaken the impression that the twelve-tone technique was his invention. . . .
>
> Just as absurd is the imputation that Thomas Mann would have used my "intellectual property" in an illegitimate fashion, specifically because the formation of the musical parts of the novel resulted from complete agreement between the two of us. . . .
>
> Finally, I would like to declare very emphatically that I never received any kind of material remuneration from Thomas Mann.

Far more than Schoenberg, Adorno would have deserved a postscript that assures the intellectual property right, for many formulations by Adrian Leverkühn, Wendell Kretzschmar, and the Devil himself, as any reader of *The Philosophy of New Music* and other writings by the great music theoretician can easily determine, come word for word from Adorno.

He could rely upon it that Thomas Mann's version did not deviate from his own. Not that the two of them heartily liked one another, but high esteem was there from Adorno's side: "I was very attached to him," as well as from Mann's side: "extraordinarily intelligent and well informed," "knows every musical note in the world." Since the assembly of Adorno's thoughts in any event certainly took diligent care, Thomas Mann wanted to clarify things unequivocally for the public. Mainly for that reason did he write *The Genesis of Doctor Faustus*. Adorno's contributions are not only acknowledged but unmistakably celebrated there.

> Repeatedly in the following weeks I was with him with my notebook and pen and, over a good, domestically produced fruit liqueur, hurriedly took down in key words . . . characterizing details that he had put together for the Oratorium. Completely familiar with the intentions of the whole and those of this partic-

ular piece, he aimed precisely at what was most essential with
his propositions and suggestions.

What is said here about Leverkühn's Oratorium, *Apocalipsis cum fig-
uris*, applies to most of the other compositions and musical parts of
the novel also. To this point one can make no reproach of Thomas
Mann. For both, the relationship is fair and harmonious. But it is
threatened by Katia and Erika. A diary observation after a reading
from the *Genesis* is testimony to "Erika's animosity toward Adorno,
whom she would gladly see not so celebrated" (September 12, 1948).
That leads to an abridgment of the *Genesis* in a series of passages
regarding Adorno. The most important of them are related to the
statement quoted above. Completely familiar, it had said there, with
the intentions of the whole and those of this particular piece—and
now the original continuation follows:

> He hit it splendidly with ideas such as about the development
> of the choruses as whispering, split-speaking, and half-singing
> into a very rich vocal polyphony, of that of the orchestra from a
> magical-primitive noise into the most complex music.
>
> Or to the tone exchange of the vocal and the instrumental
> parts, of the "displacement of the border between man and ob-
> ject," of the idea to assign the part of the Babylonian whore to a
> very graceful coloratura soprano and let "its virtuoso runs blend
> with a flutelike effect into the sound of the orchestra," on the
> other hand to lend certain instruments the character of a gro-
> tesque vox humana. The idea that in the despairing piece disso-
> nance should stand for the expression of earnestness and spiritu-
> ality, but harmony and melody for the world of Hell, i.e., of the
> commonplace, is the genuine Schoenberg and even more, Berg's
> school. Out of Adrian's melancholy inclination toward parody he
> developed the demonic merry-go-round of mocking emulation of
> all possible musical styles, out of the motif of the small mermaid
> the word of the "plea for a soul," out of the mixture of "Kais-
> ersaschern" and musical radicalism the formula "exploding
> antiquity."

Anyone familiar with chapter 34 in *Faustus* sees at once how far that
goes into detail. Thomas Mann's pride in authorship got into trouble
at this spot; one notes it in the continuation:

All of that could just as well have been by me; it was by me, as was also the phrase "Last Report from the End of the World," that is applied to the frigid part of the highly tenoralen testis— but my adviser said it before me in the empathy of coauthorship. The most sensible and appropriate tip that he gave me was the substantial identity of the hellish laughter with the cherub chorus, the moving depiction of which I saved for the end of the chapter. It was so that at first I "firmed up" what I had swiftly written down at home: that is, wrote down in precise detail—and then nothing remained for me to do but arrange what was there into a composition, to give it form, as it were, even put it into verse, that is to say: to have good Serenus declaim it with all his might, breathing heavily, with horror and love.

But the family wanted the author's fame to be undivided, even at the cost of the truth. "Strained conversation with K. during the morning about the Adorno revelations, which she finds unbearably disillusioning" (October 27, 1948). Thomas Mann is in a huff but complies, shortens it, and tones it down. He sacrifices Adorno on the altar of family peace against his better judgment. At most, he can be reproached for that. That Adorno was inflated with pride is slander as the result of years of undermining the truth by family gossip and family interest. It is whispered to Jonas Lesser for tactical reasons. Erika Mann spreads the letter to him completely unnecessarily. Had Adorno lived to see the publication of the diaries, he could have been reassured, would not have had to consider that letter to have been Thomas Mann's true opinion.

But Katia, even as a ninety-one-year-old, still wanted to protect her husband and belittle Adorno. It would be a great mistake if Adorno believed that he had written *Faustus* in its substantial points. "He was at times foolish with pretension and a blasé attitude." She did him an injustice.

## THE REAL THING

"Why should it not be found that all the earnings of my book go to the inventor of twelve-tone music?" This angry question is in the diary of December 30, 1948. What had happened? On January 15,

1948, Thomas Mann had written a dedication: "For Arnold Schoenberg, the *real thing*, with sincere greetings," he had inscribed in a copy
of the novel, which had just appeared. That was supposed to be flattering but was awkward. The man so honored replied with a furious
pamphlet, in which a fictive "Hugo Triebsamen" reports from the
third millennium about how he had read in the *Encyclopaedia Ameri-
cana* of 1988 that Thomas Mann was the actual inventor of the twelve-
tone technique, that a thievish composer named Arnold Schoenberg
had appropriated it for himself, which the Faust novel then clarified.
At first, Thomas Mann considers the overwrought document to be the
product of the righteous zeal of the Schoenberg disciples, but the
master had foolishly written it himself. "Today every blackamoor's
child probably knows who the creator of the so-called twelve-tone
technique is," Thomas Mann answered him on February 17. He lets it
be known already at the time that his book would contribute more to
the fame than to the harm of Schoenberg, and that is also what
happened.

Schoenberg felt his entitlement to be especially threatened. Soon
each one would claim to be the originator of his ideas, he writes on
February 25. "My situation is unusual in comparison with other inno-
vators. To the Germans I am a Jew, to the Romanians a German, to the
Communists I am bourgeois and the Jews are for Hindemith and
Stravinsky." Although Thomas Mann was not the right address for
the complaint, he reacted with understanding and took care that all
the following editions of the novel have a postscript to this very day.
"It does not seem superfluous," it begins, "to advise the reader that
the manner of composition depicted in chapter 22, the twelve-tone or
series technique, is in actuality the intellectual property of the contemporary composer and theoretician Arnold *Schoenberg*." With that
the conflict seemed to be put aside. It is hard to explain why Schoenberg struck out again. "Up to now I still have not read the book," he
explains, as though that were commendable. Even without his own
familiarity with the novel, he believes that he can proceed from the
fact "that his Leverkühn personifies me," to have to emphasize that
he never had contracted syphilis and also not become a lunatic. "I
consider that as an insult for which, perhaps, I will have to demand
an accounting." Since Thomas Mann, as an exception in this instance,
has a good conscience, he can reply with firmness: "The thought that
Adrian Leverkühn could be Schoenberg, that the figure was meant as

a portrait of him, is so senseless that I hardly know how to respond."
He also did not suffer from paralysis, although the hero did represent
him in some ways.

> It is painful to see how an important person, because of an exis-
> tence hovering in an all too understandable overexcitation be-
> tween glorification and neglect could become obsessed almost
> deliberately with ideas of being persecuted and robbed and fall
> into venomous altercation. May he rise above bitterness and dis-
> trust and find peace in the secure knowledge of his greatness and
> his fame!

A reconciliation was planned. Schoenberg died before it came into
being. In the realm of music everyone knows his name. But there may
be many among the unmusical who know Schoenberg and his manner of composition only from *Doctor Faustus*.


## RUDI AND PAUL

Most of what he had experienced himself is interlaced with the figure
of the violinist Rudi Schwerdtfeger, who has a relationship with Ines
Rodde, cultivates a tenderly homoerotically tinged connection to Adrian Leverkühn, takes his fiancée Marie Godeau away from him, and
at the end is shot to death by Ines on the streetcar. The model for this
figure—we know long since—is the painter Paul Ehrenberg.

At the same time, Thomas Mann comes into play in several roles.
He is Ines, the suffering lover. "Ines Rodde loved young Schwerdtfeger, and two things came into question concerning this: first,
whether she knew it, and second, at what point her original sisterly,
comradely relationship to the violinist had taken on this ardent and
suffering character." Ines, too, has entered upon a marriage of convenience that lacks a vital foundation, so that what Thomas Mann
could have similarly felt during terrible days applies to her as well:
"Under the cover of middle-class irreproachability, for the protection
of which she had longed so homesick and ailing, Ines Institoris lived
in adultery with one of the boyish darlings of women consonant with
her psychological makeup and even her own behavior . . . in whose
arms her senses, awakened from a loveless marrige, found satisfaction." Inasmuch as Thomas Mann felt debased by his homoerotic in-

clinations, what Ines says will further be right for him, namely, that she wanted to constrain her frivolous, nice "life," in order "finally, finally, not just once but in confirmation and security never often enough to see it in a state that befits its worth, in a state of devotion, of deeply sighing passion!" We are reminded of Blüher, who believed that Eros was the affirmation of a person, without regard to his worth. For once to see the worthless ones on the ground, devotedly, not himself being the one pleading: Ines longs for that; Thomas Mann dreams about it at times. Rudi is reminded of the biblical Joseph: "What will you do when a woman clings to you like a drowning person and wants you completely as her lover? Will you want to leave your outer garment in her hands and flee?" Ines is placed here in the role of the wife of Potiphar, but the story continues differently than in the Bible. What Joseph might have expected in the unchaste case is described here. But Thomas Mann was afraid of such a "success." He could not imagine sexual fulfillment other than as destructive.

Primarily, however, Thomas Mann "is" the shy and chaste Adrian, who is tenaciously courted by Rudi. While Ines depicts fantacized fulfillment, chastity is paramount in the version of Adrian, as in reality, for Adrian goes no farther than clasping hands and using the informal "Du." At least we find out no more than that; nowhere does the text offer suggestive ellipses or other supplementary license. Mann later removed a narrator's reflection about homoeroticism and left standing only a very weak insinuation about it—namely, that the melancholy inclination that Rudi stirred up in Adrian did not disavow the characteristics of erotic irony. Erotic irony had been his code since *Reflections of a Nonpolitical Man* for the love of the lonely spirit for blond life, erotic because of being in love, ironic as a matter of the self-abasement of the spirit in the consciousness of the small worth of the beloved. Thomas Mann did not want to say any more, for he obviously did not want the reader to imagine homosexual practices between Rudi and Adrian.

Platonic love produces works of art. The "child" of this chaste relationship is a violin concert. Rudi wants to perform it so that people will burst into tears. "I wanted to assimilate it so that I could play it in my sleep, and lavish care and attention on it in every note like a mother, for I would be a mother to it, and you would be the father— it would be between us like a child, a platonic child—yes, our concert, that would really be the fulfillment of everything I understand by platonic." Rudi desires from the artist not human, or even sensual, fulfillment, but a work of art. So he reacts to his conquest defensively; he desires the flirtation, not the leaden weight of a lovesick, pessimistic moralist. He would prefer to continue to keep Adrian cold, not hot. That hurts the latter: "That I have nothing to do with humanity, am not allowed to have anything to do with it, is told me by someone who won me with astonishing patience for what is human and converted me into a close friend, someone with whom for the first time in my life I found human warmth." Adrian confesses here what Thomas once said of Paul, that he was a human friend instead of a literary man and a cognitively mute ghost.

Lips are more important than words. Paul had full lips, Rudi too, even in death. "He lifted his head in the attempt to say something, but immediately bloody bubbles appeared from between his lips, whose soft fullness seemed to me suddenly touchingly beautiful." They were lips that lay on one another like cushions, rested full and soft on one another like those of the twins in *The Blood of the Walsungs*, upturned lips full of arrogant sensuality like those of Joseph, who had his smiling double softness from his mother Rachel.

Marie Godeau "is" Katia Pringsheim; her eyes prove it ("black as jet, as tar, as ripe blackberries"), fantasized in the event that the courtship would be a failure and homoeroticism might have drawn a line through his account. That Adrian sends his friend ahead and that the latter courts Marie could be an expression of the anxiety about the ability of being a competitor as a man. In real life Paul sent a congratulatory telegram to Tommy's wedding. He probably did not attempt to dissuade his friend, perhaps even felt freed of a burden.

When Adrian has lost Marie and Rudi, there follows a period of very high productivity, "and it was impossible for one to resist the impression that it meant the pay and balance for the withdrawal of happiness in life and of the permission to love, to which he had been subjected." It remained as in *Tonio Kröger*. Renunciation in life fructifies art.

## NOT SERENUS, BUT ADRIAN

Thomas Mann staged his carefully pressed middle-class image so convincingly that to this day the opinion prevails that the author had

included just as much of himself in Serenus Zeitblom as in Adrian
Leverkühn, the hero and his narrator. He supported this view point-
edly with the allegation of the "secret of their identity." But a closer
look reveals that he gave everything profoundly important to Leverkühn. The primal odds and ends are exclusively Leverkühn's, not
Zeitblom's. Serenus is Catholic, sensual, humanistically cosmopolitan;
he practices antiquated sexual freedom with a cooper's daughter,
marries a Helene Ölhafen, lives in inner emigration, and has two sons
loyal to Hitler. None of that fits Thomas Mann. But Leverkühn is
Protestant, puritanical, medievally alienated from the world, an ascetic homosexual who would gladly find a state of mind but is condemned to be alone. He is the artist with the longing for life cursed to
create, the cold ironist homesick for the puppy-warmth of childhood,
the spirit who yearns for seduction, the one who fears seduction when
touched. On the other hand, what does it matter, if Thomas Mann
provides the narrative figure with a few external details of his life: the
affirmation of war in 1914, his aloofnesss toward the soviet republic
in 1918–19, and some political views from the radio addresses
"Deutsche Hörer" and from the concentration camp article, "The
Camps"? All of that takes place on the level of opinion, not of being.
The narrator is only a mask to hide what is personal. The mask furnishes rhetorical distance to Adrian in order for him to write about
the sufferings of his soul under its protection. But the reader was not
to know that so specifically.

In this regard, too, Thomas Mann retouched his report of Adrian's
genesis. Leonhard Frank had asked him whether he had a model in
mind for Adrian. According to the *Genesis*, he answered:

> Leverkühn was an idealized figure, so to speak, a "hero of our
> time," a man who bears the suffering of the epoch. But I went
> farther and confessed to him that I would never have loved some-
> one imaginary . . . as much as him. I spoke the truth. I literally
> shared the feelings of good Serenus for him, was uneasily in love
> with him from his cavalier school days on, infatuated by his "cold-
> ness," his remoteness from life, *his lack of* "soul" . . . in his "inhu-
> manness" and "desperate heart," his conviction of being damned.

In the diary (July 22, 1944) the corresponding passage is clearly
shorter. The Christ-like phrase of the man who bears the suffering of
the epoch is missing there. Missing there is the identification with

Serenus Zeitblom. Instead of that come personal items: "He is really *my* ideal," yes, narcissistic stuff: "A most admiring and gripping tendernesss for him fills me." In context:

> L. Frank asked yesterday whether I had had a model in mind for Adrian. I said no and called him an idealized figure, a "hero of our time." He is really my ideal, and I never loved an imagined figure so much. . . . A most admiring and gripping tenderness for him fills me.

Nowhere is there talk of a similar tenderness for Zeitblom.

## THE DEVIL

> At times . . . one has the impression that the world is not the exclusive creation of God but a joint enterprise with someone else.

Of course, Thomas Mann did not believe in the Devil in a trite sense. But already in our chapter on the occult we took notice of oddities in regard to the enlightenment of our author. Whether evil spirits exist is a question of definition. If one understands them as allegories, the enlightened soul is half at peace. To individualize the evil of this world by literary figures is not very outlandish for a writer like Thomas Mann. That evil had reality was established as a fact at the latest by Hitler. There would be the Devil to pay, if they could not destroy him and his spawn. "But maybe we are involved with the Devil." The world was not only an aesthetic phenomenon, or if it was really that, seen from a loftier standpoint, then on the great world stage there was also an antagonist. No Faust without a Mephisto. Unlike with Goethe, where the Devil is still very palpably incarnated, Mann's devils can assume various forms. In *Death in Venice* there were diverse leaders of Hades: the stranger in the North Cemetery, the gondolier, the elevator operator, the street singer. Seduction by forbidden love and by death could then appear at that time in varying costumes. In the Joseph novel there was the dog-headed god who proclaimed the way to erotic commingling. The angelic figures who show Joseph the way accompany him in each instance into the underworld, into the abyss, and to Egypt. They, too, are escorts of the dead, even if not exactly devils. They may not exist in everyday real-

ity, but necessity produces them and then indicates approaching figures in real life in a typological schema of this sort.

The Faust novel makes use of the same technique. Pimp and escort
of the dead at the same time are: Wendell Kretzschmar, who leads
Adrian into art; the psychologist of religion Schleppfuss, who instructs him in the theology of evil and sexual seduction; the servant
who drags him to the bordello; the spectacled music intellectual in the
dialogue with the Devil; and the impresario Saul Fitelberg, who, imitating Jesus' temptation in the desert, wants to lay at his feet the
riches of this world. They all signify real temptations of Thomas
Mann: the temptation to sacrifice life and humanity to art, the temptation of sexuality, the temptation of arrogance, and the temptation of
fame and power. The three roles of the Devil in chapter 25 are con-
strued similarly, as pimp, as theologian, and as intellectual, alluding
to three basic fears: the fear of sexuality, the fear of sin impressed
upon him as a young child by his Protestant background, and the fear
of the sterility of a cold intellectuality inimical to life.

Thomas Mann fought fascist Germany passionately and nevertheless identified himself with it deeply. In 1945 he spoke of the Devil's
pact of Hitler's Germany and saw it in the image of Faust, the lonely
thinker in his seclusion, who, out of longing for the pleasures of the
world and dominion over the world, sells his soul to the Devil and
then in 1945 is literally fetched by the Devil. Thomas Mann—he emphasizes it expressly—is bent on suggesting a connection of the German mind with the demonic. He adds that this connection was a matter of his inner experience. And in the same place he defines it:

> Where the arrogance of intellect mates with spiritual antiquated-
> ness and bondage, there the Devil is.

The arrogance of intellect: that is Adrian Leverkühn, that is Thomas
Mann. But likewise spiritual ancientness and bondage are present not
only in Leverkühn but also in Thomas Mann, in his long-held sympathy with death and the regression wish that results. The Devil is there
where highest intellectuality mates with deepest longing for loss of
consciousness. The Devil of Thomas Mann and Germany are one.
"*Brother* Hitler" means that Thomas Mann is looking for fascism in
himself.

Whether he has bestowed too much honor upon the Germans in
doing so remains undecided. "Germany" is Thomas Mann, whose
best comes out as evil through the cunning of the Devil—his subjec-

tivity, his musicality, his romanticism, his art. Evil is the old aestheticism that kills life, that brings it as a sacrifice to art.

Biographically, Thomas Mann could, of course, mean by this only
his early work. As a husband and the father of a family he had certainly made room for life next to art, and politically he had done
everything since his republican conversion to escape the reproach of
life-threatening irresponsibility. In this regard, too, seen biographically, something antiquated, something artificial and overbred ad-
heres to the Faust theme. The pact with the Devil is a temptation long
since overcome by the writer, which he charges the Germans as having succumbed to.

## THE EMOTIONALISM OF IMPURITY

The traditional content of a pact with the Devil is unbounded possibilities in this world at the cost of loss of the soul and eternal damnation in the other. Thomas Mann has secularized that somewhat. The
result of the pact for the artist is the renunciation of life and love. The
result of the pact for the Devil is artistic inspiration, the perfect work
of art, refined taste.

"You may not love," the Devil commands. He is more specific:
"Love is forbidden to you because it warms." So love with heart and
soul, which leads to home and family, is forbidden. Pure sensuality is
permitted; indeed, it is even the means of the conclusion of the pact,
for through carnal union with prostituted courtesan Esmeralda, the
syphilitic infection and with it the pact came about.

"Sensuality (love) can be surfeited not by a human creature but
only through succubi, devil lovers." That is to be found on a page of
notes. There follow oddities that nourish the presumption that homosexual intercourse has to do with the Devil's lovemaking:

> Fury of the Devil because he wants to marry legitimately . . .
> Keeps him blameless through the lovemaking of the Devil. Com-
> mits fornication with the Devil (the Devil is in the female, it is
> homosexual intercourse). — He is forced to use his desire for
> marriage to kill people with whom he has had carnal pleasure.

The Devil is in the female: Thomas Mann read that in the *Witch's
Hammer*, with the help of which the teacher Schleppfuss develops the
view that woman is the representative of all that is carnally minded

on earth—all, thus the homosexual too. For Adrian, Zeitblom's word is valid, "that the proudest spirituality stands opposite the bestial, the naked urge, in its most direct form, and is sacrificed to it most disdainfully." Since Adrian has followed the courtesan Esmeralda and was with her in Pressburg, he is one who is touched. He continues to lead "the life of a saint," as Zeitblom expresses it, but his chastity springs afterward "no longer from the ethos of purity but from the emotionalism of impurity."

Without the thirst for purity there would be no Hell. The narrator of the Joseph novel already reflects on that. "Hell is for the pure, that is the law of the moral world." One can sin only against one's own purity. "If one is a beast, one cannot sin and feels nothing of a Hell. It is arranged in that way, and Hell is very certainly inhabited only by better people, which is not just but is our justice."

Thomas Mann also belongs to the better people. He, too, is an ascetic, but at the same time an initiate. His literary works and the diaries are so full of knowledge and frankness in a sexual regard that one can certainly not speak of "innocence." On the contrary, all his life Mann turns a fascinated attention to that sphere.

That as a husband he experienced sexuality is, of course, undeniable, but it does not suffice as an explanation. The feeling of being touched, of being damaged, of lost innocence must come from the homosexual sphere, at which his deepest longings are directed. Homosexual courtship, so it must appear to him, is from the Devil. We know nothing now about homosexual physical contact. Not a single trace has been preserved. So we remain dependent on psychological evidence, a very unsure terrain. It presents us with the assumption that, probably at an early time, there was some kind of bodily contact that was experienced as degrading, humiliating, and dirtying and left behind a lifelong trauma. It may have been the street hustlers in Naples. In any case, the emotionalism of impurity explains Thomas Mann's work and life better than the ethos of purity could do. Like his Joseph, like his Adrian, he is chaste and affected at the same time. What applies to them applies also to him, that his chastity was not wooden imbecility in matters of love.

But something else is also possible. In an environment of radical taboos, a kiss or some other fleeting caress is the same as a complete sexual peformance under liberal conditions. So an equally deep experience can be had from a forbidden kiss as from a completed coitus.

The shock of the first shy touchings in puberty can be deeper than anything later. A hand, reaching out of a window, a wrist gripped, as though one wished to pull up the other, which of course happens only in the imagination—such a promise can cling as completely as a night of love. Esmeralda brushes Adrian only fleetingly with her arm, but from then on he is no longer free. "The arrogance of the spirit had suffered the trauma of an encounter with soulless desire." The touch burns on his cheek from then on. That was enough, all the rest can be added by the imagination, which makes Adrian then go to Pressburg.

In this connection, an enigmatic dream is worth hearing about: "Notice, response, wander together, not immoderately happy. There remains the memory of arm in arm with wrists clasped." A reflection is added:

> Dream is basically not worse in substance than real experience, which also weakens and vanishes, sinks into the past & is also only dream. Dream can also produce the same kind of "pride of experience" as reality and is completely related in the mixture of happiness and painfulness. The dream figure for whose identity I sought and seek in vain had seen through my inclination (weakness) and forced me in the dream, or from the dream, into reality, whereby that very dream attained the character and the stuff of life.

## KLÖPFGEISSEL

The teacher Schleppfuss represents so much that is not far from the concepts of his inventor. As in the time of *The Magic Mountain*, when he gave more of himself to the world-alienated Jesuit Naphta than to civilization's progressively happy literary man Settembrini, Thomas Mann created in the character of Schleppfuss a megaphone for views that he wanted to know were expressed but which were not held to be correct by public opinion. Then Zeitblom also protests with eagerly humanistic rhetoric, but Leverkühn remains silent.

Even the Joseph novel taught that evil was as necessary as good, and that God was not the good but the whole. Schleppfuss sharpens that to dialectical dependency of good on evil. Evil is an inevitable appurtenance of the holy existence of God. Vice takes its pleasure from the defilement of virtue. The wicked is a correlative of the holy, and the latter an almost irresistible challenge for desecration. Would the good be good at all, if evil did not exist? Augustine—like much else from this chapter, Mann owes the citation to the *Malleus Maleficarum: the Hammer of Witchcraft*—Augustine had even taught that it was the function of the bad to allow the good to appear more clearly, that it was more pleasing when compared with the bad.

The focal point of evil is sex—Adrian Leverkühn even calls it the "natural evil." God has granted to the antagonist more witch's power over sexual intercourse than any other human activity, "not only because of the outward lewdness of this practice but above all because the depravity of the first father was transferred with it as original sin to the whole human race. The act of procreation, characterized by aesthetic beastliness, was the expression and vehicle of original sin— no wonder that the Devil was allowed a particularly free hand in it."

Thomas Mann had once earlier been reminded, in response to the reproach that homosexual practices were unaesthetic, that in that regard common sexual intercourse was no better. As far as the ugliness, demonism, and sinfulness of the sexual is concerned, the view of Schleppfuss may stand close to his own. Of course, it was far removed from the frankness that today dominates public debate about sexuality. What he says about "being touched" sounds at first a bit prudish. But its background is the insatiability of sexual desire. If he seemed to himself to be a sinner, then that was not just some kind of superstitious feeling that the world could be rid of in maturity, but a result of the insight into the general imperfection of mankind whose sensual longing always far exceeds the possibilities of its fulfillment.

He lets two examples from the *Malleus Maleficarum* illustrate his demonology more precisely. They both have to do with his own anxieties about life. A profligate youth (let's call him Thomas) had lived for years with a succubus (let's call him Paul) until "for practical reasons more than true fondness," he entered into marriage with a decent woman. But "he was prevented from having carnal knowledge of her because his demon had constantly lain between them. Therefore his wife, in just disgruntlement, had left him; he for the rest of his life had seen himself limited to his impatient demon." So much for the first example.

"In the city of Merssburg in the diocese of Constance a youth had

also become so bewitched that he could not perform sexual intercourse with women, with one single exception." From these few lines
of the *Malleus Maleficarum*, Thomas Mann develops a great, excel-
lently told story:

> In Merssburg near Constance there lived toward the end of the
> fifteenth century an honest lad named Heinz Klöpfgeissel, a
> cooper by trade, of good stature and health. He had an intimate
> interrelationship with a girl, Bärbel, the only daughter of a wid-
> owed bell ringer, and wanted to marry her, but the wishes of the
> pair met paternal resistance, for Klöpfgeissel was a poor fellow
> and the bell ringer first demanded a goodly position in life from
> him, that he become master in his trade before he would give
> him his daughter. But the affections of the young people were
> stronger than their patience, and the pair had already turned into
> a couple. For at night, when the bell ringer had gone bell ringing,
> Klöpfgeissel climbed in to Bärbel, and their embraces made each
> one seem to the other the most glorious thing on earth.

But one day he and other young companions were feeling their oats,
so they decided to go to women in a sporting house. But there his
otherwise sturdy erection failed, and also a second time, when he
found a landlady willing, his flesh would not rise. Only with his Bärbel, while the bell ringer was bell ringing, did he further have the
most successful hours. That he could do it only with a single person,
left him in no doubt any longer that he was bewitched; he confides to
a priest, who notifies the Inquisition of the case; Bärbel confesses and
is burned at the stake. "Heinz Klöpfgeissel, the bewitched man, stood
with a bare head, murmuring prayers in the mass of spectators."

Like Adrian, like Thomas Mann, Klöpfgeissel is one touched. The
psychological content of the story can be summarized in this sentence: The emotionality of impurity fears affliction. The fear of marriage produces the magic taboo regarding an escapade. It seems certain that any performance elsewhere, above all a homosexual one,
would have to end with a humiliating experience of impotence. One
so touched would also destroy his innocent little Bärbel. In the long
run an escapade would develop a destructive power. For the emotions *have* power. The mere awareness of misconduct, even if the little
Bärbel concerned might know nothing about it, would gradually cor-

rode the unselfconsciousness of both. Love, especially a love as precarious as that for Katia, is sensitive; it requires the most careful protection, if one is touched.

Schleppfuss is not interested in the affects of the healthy mind on the body, only in those of the sick. The body, he lectures, is cooled and heated by virtue of fright and anger; it becomes gaunt with grief, blossoms with joy; mere disgusting thoughts could produce the effect of spoiled food—the sight of a plate of strawberries covers an allergic person's skin with pustules; even illness and death could be the result of psychological effects. Psychosomatics teaches all of that today. If Schleppfuss then deduces, of course, that an alien psyche is able to influence, to bewitch an alien body, if he tries thus to harden the reality of magic, we feel reminded of Count von Schrenck-Notzing and avoid his company.

## SUPERBIA ET GRATIA

Every person brought up a Christian knows the struggle for humility. In puberty, when a human being begins to think, he immediately feels proud. Knowledge is desire, might, superiority, cruelty. In spite of poor performances, Thomas Mann had the feeling, even as a pupil, of being called, chosen, saved for something special. In what way should he be humble? And yet *superbia* is the Christian original sin, wanting to be like God, pride. He who has knowledge stands on a very high mountain, from where the Devil lays the world at his feet (Matt. 4:8–10).

"Get thee hence, Satan!" Jesus had replied on the mountain. But the Devil had not only the riches of the world and its glory to offer but for the very demanding ones in addition his cunning promise up his sleeve: "Eritis sicut Deus scientes bonum et malum"—"For ye shall be as God, knowing good and evil" (Gen. 3:5). That entices Thomas Mann; he eats from the apple and is cursed. Artists are the cursed who, even when shut away from life, penetrate life as though they were God.

Thomas Mann's original sin is *superbia*. The snake's promise is Thomas's greatest temptation. He turns into Faust because his arrogance very early instilled in him the mythical fear of the Fall, of ordeal, and infernal pain. He struggles for humility, but consciousness cannot be suppressed, except in intoxication. It is fate, a curse. It kills. A love that knows itself dies. A human being loves a human being only as long as he does not have the power to judge him. Friedrich Nietzsche says that a religion that can be understood is dead. Achieving naïveté again is impossible. One cannot *want* to forget; limiting oneself artistically is only an aesthetic mummery, nothing genuine or just.

The most subtle temptation is pride in humility. It cannot be suppressed. Bowing to need, self-humiliation then steps into the place of humility. Its primary means are work, mortification, and asceticism. The artist lives as a sacrifice. The sacrificial smoke should rise pleasantly to the nose of God and make Him mild. As sacrificial gifts, the pleasures of life and love lie on the altar. The artist follows Christ insofar as he surrenders his life. Leverkühn is a man who bears the suffering of the epoch. With his inspirited *ecce-homo* face he is at the end no longer Faust but Christ, his farewell meal with his apostles a last supper, and the high G of the cellos the hope for salvation.

Only the hope. The arrogant man can never gain salvation for himself, not even through the surrender of his life. He requires mercy, which at the same time he cannot count on. Mann lets his Faust plead for him by proxy:

Perhaps God beholdeth that I have sought difficulty and have let it turn sour for me, perhaps, perhaps it will be to my credit and my benefit that I concluded everything with such great effort and tenaciousness—I cannot say and have not the courage to hope for that. My sin is greater than that it could be forgiven me, and I pushed it to extremes by speculating in my head that the crushed disbelief in the possibility of mercy and forgiveness may be the most tempting of all for eternal goodness, whereas I do realize that such an impudent calculation makes mercy completely impossible. But based on that, I went farther in my speculation and calculated that this last infamy must be the most extreme stimulus for goodness to prove its infinity. And so on and so on, so that I engaged in a wicked bet with Goodness above, about which was more inexhaustible—it or my speculating—and there you see that I am damned, and there is no mercy for me because I destroyed each thing in advance by speculation.

There is no way out. Thomas Mann does not believe that mankind can help itself. It never exits without guilt. Every life takes the breath from every other life. It is impossible to live right. Thomas Mann perceives his life as "guilt, error, obligation," as "an object of religious disquiet, as something that urgently needs recompense, deliverance, and justification." The older he becomes, the more often does he express the hope that from the most profound wretchedness something like mercy might bud, "the transcendence of desperation—not betrayal of it, but the miracle that comes by way of faith."

# XVIII. Pain and Glory

*1947*

With the article "The German Concentration Camps," which appeared copyrighted in the American press under various titles in May 1945, Thomas Mann's voice was to be heard in Germany again right at the end of the war. There followed "Why I Will Not Return to Germany" (September 1945) and reprints of the speech "Germany and the Germans." The intensive work on *Doctor Faustus*, but also the disappointment about developments after the war, cause a decrease in the political articles. Aside from the weeks of his lung cancer operation (April–May), the year 1946 is filled with work on the Faust novel. The trip to Europe, postponed again and again, does not occur until 1947 (April–September). It leads to readings and lecture tours, among others of "Nietzsche's Philosophy in the Light of Contemporary Events," and recuperative sojourns in London, Switzerland, and Holland. Germany is omitted.

At the beginnning of 1948 Thomas Mann begins to write *The Holy Sinner*. At the end of June, after finishing the eighth chapter, he interrupts it to write the report of accountability, *The Story of a Novel: The Genesis of Doctor Faustus* (until the end of October). The Goethe year of 1949 obliges him to supply numerous lectures and essays, among them above all "Goethe and Democracy." The second postwar trip to Europe lasts from April 25 to August 19 and leads to England, Sweden, Denmark, and Switzerland, also to Germany. On July 25 in Frankfurt's Paulskirche he gives his "Address in the Goethe Year," and in Munich on July 27 the speech "Goethe and Democracy," on August 1 in Weimar once again the "Address in the Goethe Year." That he also visits the Soviet zone of occupation brings him much vexation and leads to the intensification of the political mistrust toward him in America. As a result, in the spring of 1950 the Library of Congress cancels his invitation. He had planned to give his autobiographical speech "My Time" there.

His brother Heinrich had died on March 12, 1950. A third trip to Europe follows from April to the end of August 1950. In the Hotel Dolder in Zurich it brings once more a great experience of the heart, his infatuation with the waiter Franz Westermeier, which deeply arouses the seventy-five-year-old. The essay "Michelangelo's Eroticism" belongs among the direct literary results.

Betweentimes Thomas Mann continues off and on to write on *The Holy Sinner*. At the end of November 1950 the work is concluded and immediately the next is taken up, the continuation of the *Confessions of Felix Krull, Confidence Man*, which had lain untouched for decades and that with many interruptions occupies his time from December 1950 until April 1954. He has no desire to write a further continuation. The Tillinger controversy, in which he is denounced as a "fellow traveler" of Moscow, embitters the first six months of this stay in America. In June 1951 a long lettter to Walter Ulbricht, at the time the deputy minister president of the German Democratic Republic, comes into being, in which Thomas Mann stands up in a committed manner for the political prisoners in the Soviet zone. From July to October he is again drawn to Europe for reading appearances but chiefly for a vacation (Zurich, incognito in Munich, then vacation spots in Austria and Switzerland).

In 1952 the volume of essays *Old and New* appears. The speech "The Artist and Society" comes into being (February–March) and is used many times in the course of the year. *The Black Swan* is begun (May) and is not finished until in March of the following year. Again he is off to Europe, mainly in Switzerland, to Austria, but also many times to Munich, finally also to Frankfurt. The trip begins at the end of June; that it would remain without a return to Pacific Palisades is not originally planned. At Christmas 1952 the family moves into a furnished house in Erlenbach near Zurich.

Pope Pius XII receives the writer for a short audience on April 29, 1953. June brings an honorary doctorate from Cambridge, readings in Hamburg, and a stay in Lübeck and Travemünde. On July 24 Katia turns seventy. The last residence, Kilchberg on Lake Zurich, Alte Landstrasse 39, is acquired in January 1954 and occupied on April 15 after a trip to Italy. Work becomes increasingly more difficult. Yet two great essays, one Eastern and one Western, come into being, and in June–July 1954 the "Essay on Chekhov," after August 1954 the eighty-page "Essay on Schiller," which is finished in several stages by February 1955. A shortened version is read in Stuttgart on May 8, 1955, and in Weimar on May 14 in observance of the hundred-and-fiftieth anniversary of Schiller's death. Research on the Renaissance (after May 1954) takes shape at the beginning of 1955 into a plan to write a drama "Luther's Wedding." A bundle of papers with notes comes into being.

The year 1955 brings many celebrations and honors. On February 11, 1955, the Manns' golden anniversary is celebrated. On May 7 Thomas Mann meets with the West German president, Theodor Heuss. At the end of May there is again a visit in Lübeck and Travemünde. On July 11 Queen Juliana of the Netherlands receives him. Shortly afterward the illness begins that leads to his death on August 12.

# NO, THEY ARE NOT A GREAT PEOPLE

"THE BLOODY dog is dead!" that seemed certain, even though the corpse was not found. Hitler's death, the suicide of other Nazi bigwigs, the end of the war with all its horrors, all of that is commented on extensively in the diary. It almost always offers cause for hate of the Germans. Those who as victors were so incredibly brutal—in defeat they whimper. "No, they are not a great people" (May 4, 1945). Even on the day of capitulation Thomas Mann finds a reversal and confession of guilt missing among the vanquished. "To this moment any renunciation of Nazism is lacking" (May 7, 1945). There is no jubilation for that reason. "What I feel is not exactly elation." This verdict about the Germans had long since been ingrained in the many years of banishment. There was really little to see of changes so deep and poignant that this judgment might have become untenable. A humiliation that might have been equal to the enormity of the crimes in any case exceeds the imagination. But Thomas Mann believed he might expect a modest attitude, conscious of guilt and inclined to make up for it. In the reports of the press he saw only impertinent insolence. The Germans seemed incorrigible, their Nazism ineradicable. "Everything is still the same" (November 8, 1945). Could it be different at all? "What kind of a revolutionized, proleterianized, upended, naked and bare, shattered, faithless, ruined bunch of people will we have to deal with?"—he had wondered that long before the end (January 9, 1944). He ponders on a ghastly thing—around a million Germans would have to be eliminated—but takes it back immediately: "On the other hand it is not possible to execute a million people without imitating the methods of the Nazis" (May 5, 1945). But there must be a stern punishment.

The harshness is not unreasonable. It was the perpetrators finally who now suffered, and it served them right, at least that is how it looked from the distance. In regard to this question, Thomas Mann was not inclined to discriminate. To him, all of Germany seemed to be to blame. He could not see many things more exactly because he himself was so wounded and because he was too far away. There was definitely readiness to atone in Germany, even though pehaps not in the millions and not publicly. But is public atonement not always hypocritical? Those seen atoning are opportunists who adapt to the new relationships of power. Those silent in the land could have escaped the Allied reports.

But would not the psychology of the perpetrators have interested the great psychologist Thomas Mann? This mixture of lust and violence, of blue-eyed faith and neurotic resentment, of boundless idealism and darkest criminality not explained to this day? Is there a greater challenge for the aesthete than to understand the Nazi culprits? Had not the nonpolitical observer once demanded that in a work of literature "each person, and be he the Devil himself, while he stands there and speaks, *is right in the end*; because he *is so objectively perceived* that we are drawn with interest to him and forced to sympathize with him?" As a man, Thomas Mann did not muster this equinamity, not in the least. He hated Hitler. As an artist, however, he said that the fellow had been a catastrophe, but very interesting, and a relative besides ("Brother Hitler"). The great novel *Doctor Faustus*, too, does not look for hate but for insight when it links one's own life and the beloved culture of romantic inwardness expressly with the rise of National Socialism. The artist is wiser, more free, and less partisan than the harsh judgments of the essayist and diarist allow us to suspect.

But he cannot satisfy anyone, neither as an artist nor as an essayist. The Germans did not want to hear about a link between German culture and German crimes, as the Faust novel portrays it. Draconian punitive actions à la Morgenthau, which could still be discussed during the war, were soon no longer in the interest of the Western powers after the end of the war because the Germans were needed as allies against Russia. In spite of the Nuremberg and other trials the Nazis as a whole got off scot-free. What Thomas Mann already noted embitteredly on May 19, 1945, was not entirely mistaken: that the hatred for Russia was exposed with hardly believable impatience, that the litigation of the prisoners of war would never come about, that the air of "Munich" would again blow, and the victory would be gambled away worse than the last time.

He has news from the best source. Klaus Mann was already in Germany in May 1945, visited the house on Poschingerstrasse, and had Hermann Göring interviewed. His daughter Erika saw the chief Nazi a little later, too, and reports Göring's opinion, that if *he* had handled the case of Mann, everything would have happened differently. "A German of T.M.'s stature could certainly have been adapted to the Third Reich." Erika had been accredited as a special correspondent at the great war-crimes trial in Nuremberg. Thomas Mann could obtain an accurate observation from her letters and narratives. He approved the trial as a moral signal, even later, when it became clear how limited its effect was and that many Nazis still or again held their old positions. "Everybody knows that the denazification of Germany has failed completely—if there can be talk of failure where no earnest desire for success ever existed."

## COME AS A GOOD DOCTOR!

It is not true that they had not called him. In July 1945 the Russians call him, but he declines at once, and the newspapers report "that I gently turned down the Berlin invitation." He does not want to step into the service of Moscow. But the *Hannoversche Zeitung* also lures him: "In the depths of our need we still hope for him a little." From a further "Communist-Christian" Berlin newspaper the statements reach him: "We believe you now have a historic work to accomplish in Germany. We need your help. You belong to us." But the best known became the query of the writer Walter von Molo: "With all, but truly all, of the restraint that has been put upon us after the frightful twelve years," he turns to his great colleague:

> Please, do come soon; look into the faces furrowed with grief; see the unspeakable suffering. . . . Come soon like a good doctor who sees not only the symptoms but seeks the cause of the sickness and endeavors primarily to remedy this, who however also knows that surgical interventions are necessary, above all with the many who once placed value on being called intellectual.

That was to be taken more seriously than the Communist invitations. But Thomas Mann had announced numerous times that he wanted to remain in America after the war. He did not think for a moment of complying with Molo's plea. He polished his refusal for a long time in the first weeks of September. It shows how deeply ingrained the shock still was, the "asthmatic heart of exile." The loss of house and land, books, mementos, and property had made it difficult to breathe in 1933, the following debarkations miserable, murderous the radio and press agitation against the Wagner essay, which had cut off his return. Then the vagrant life, the passport worries, the hotel existence, "while my ears rang with the infamous stories that thronged upon me daily from the lost, savaged country that had become totally unknown." He did not understand how one could produce "culture" in the service of Hitler without covering one's face with one's hands and running out of the hall. Besides, he was an American, was bound here and there for honor's sake, had English-speaking grandchildren, and a beautiful house in California. Still, in the courteous closing phrase, he wanted to travel over there sometime, as soon as the hour comes. "But once I am there, I suspect that shyness and alienation, these products of only twelve years, will not be up to a power of attraction that the rather long memories of a thousand years have on their side. Until we meet again then, if God wills it."

## WHY I WILL NOT RETURN TO GERMANY

All of that is understandable, but still not conclusive, at least not morally, and Molo had asked morally. Could Thomas Mann not have returned to Germany? To Munich, cooperating with the cultural reconstruction? His brother Viktor wrote in December 1945 that the Munich municipal council had resolved on the restitution and reconstruction of the house at Poschingerstrasse 1. That was not to be realized, but Thomas Mann did hear something like an invitation in it anyway. It was assumed that he and his family would take up residence there every year for a few months (January 9, 1946). There was, however, no question of that. "Regarding the reconstruction of the Munich house, dictated a warning letter to Vikko" (February 11, 1946). It had to be made clear to those in Munich that he would not think of returning there.

For he was deeply horrified by it. This manifoldly composed horror, which is stronger than anything moral and more fundamental than all the arguments, however politically justified, is the real reason for his refusal. Europe is "a nightmare," as Thomas Mann wrote to Paul Amann,

> and anyone who wishes me well warns of any thought of "homecoming." We must consider that the people there, year after year, slipped slowly into their thoroughly savage and foolhardy, beggarlike and cynical condition and have become accustomed to it.

Suddenly transplanted back, we would play the role of the green-
horn there in a much more ridiculous way than here, and probably be ruined in a year. The difficulties of coming to an understanding are enormous; each contact shows me that because
those over there and in there believe that they have gone through
quite a lot and we shirkers did not, while just the reverse, we
went off and saw the world, and they did not experience those 12
years: for them it is 1933 and they want to continue where they
left off at the time.

But would not that very thing have been the task—to tell the Germans what had really happened during those twelve years? That
must certainly have seemed completely hopeless. "Let self-righteousness be far from me," the one distressed by Molo declares rhetorically.
"Those of us outside had been most virtuous and told Hitler what we
thought." Yes, that's truer. Most virtuously Thomas Mann tells the
Germans what he thinks, all too virtuously. But Molo had asked for a
doctor. The emigrants, too, had been damaged by the twelve years.
They, too, had been made biased and a faction by the situation in the
world. The postwar Mann occasionally displays something of the
dogmatic antifascist, to whom the truth of his theory is more important than life that—as the nonpolitical observer well knew—in its
infinitely manifold form defies any political explanation. He had demanded humanity instead of doctrine from civilization's literary men
at the time. Fascists are people, too. What would have happened, if
Thomas Mann had come? If he had tried to take a hand in the internal reconstruction, to be in solidarity with those destroyed? By any
means to get their ear, touch their heart? "Come like a good doctor."
That would probably have been very dangerous. "In Bavaria American officers have been slain in their sleep by Germans and the house
set on fire" (January 11, 1946). Most writers who tried to reeducate
the Germans failed and, after a shorter or a longer time, left the country again, such as Alfred Döblin or Carl Zuckmayer, and they had not
aroused nearly as much hate as Thomas Mann. Erika, too, warns him
with strong words: "Don't think *even for a minute* of returning to this
forlorn land. It is simply not recognizable as being human." Even
with the finest tact and most intimate knowledge of the situation, she
writes from Zurich on January 10, 1946, again warding off plans for a
visit, "you would not be able to avoid sitting on the fence; you would

be played off by the Russians against the Yanks and by the latter against the Tommies and the French, and in the end bring home only trouble and damage." That is certainly completely right. All in all, Thomas Mann certainly had to act as he did. The situation could not be seen in any better light for him at that time. What is history? Hordes of blind ants move a boulder without knowing where to. Should the writer, too, creep under the stone? Even the bigwigs (Truman, Churchill, Stalin) offer no example. "The chiefs of the 3 world powers produce nothing but nonsense and play the piano" (July 29, 1945).

In any event, at the end of the war Thomas Mann was immediately present journalistically, first with a reprint of his "Correspondence with Bonn" in a new Frankfurt newspaper (diary, April 30, 1945) and then with a moving article about the opening of the concentration camps, which was the occasion for the invitation to Germany by Molo.

Perhaps he would have come anyway, had not Molo's letter been followed by that notorious article "The Inner Emigration." In it the writer Frank Thiess presented the voice of those who had emigrated inwardly. Of course, there really were such people, but Thiess struck the wrong tone. It was his opinion that those inside had suffered more than those outside. About which, he naturally had no idea. Going through conflagration, hunger, and bombs had made him richer in knowledge and experience, he wrote, than if he had watched the German tragedy "from the boxes and orchestra seats of overseas." That he also scorned Thomas Mann's radio broadcasts, the most significant and respected attempt of a German emigrant to be effective inside the Reich, is added—the deaf among the people would not have heard them in any case, "while we in the know felt we were always a few lengths ahead of them." What did people like Thiess— "we in the know"—know, except for their secret entanglement. Thomas Mann suffers. "The attacks, falsehoods, and stupidities work in me through the day and exhaust me like hard labor" (September 19, 1945).

## KÄSTNER

"The most shameful thing that the Germans have done against me, and a classical piece of Saxonian malice": that was Mann's commen-

tary on a further "invitation" to Germany. It came from Erich Kästner.
Subtly envenomed, it speculated about the advantages that the Nazi
era had also cultivated:

> If I ask someone for a hundred marks who has only ten marks on
> him; if I ask him again and ask again, he must in time become
> angry. That's clear. Thomas Mann is a master in the formulation
> of differentiated artistic natures, sicklier, more overrefined char-
> acters; he even prides himself on the significance of the unhealth-
> iness of the heroes of his books, and he goes so far as to consider
> instability, nervousness, cautious deviousness as virtues and
> highly valued. This connoisseurship and predilection always cor-
> responded to the physical frailty of the author himself. Athletes
> and heroes were always a bit suspect to him, and he himself is
> neither one nor the other. Who first got the idea of calling him
> over the ocean amid our rubble?

Kästner, as the editor of the cultural section of the *Neue Zeitung* and
the future president of P.E.N., belongs among the most influential
people in the American zone of occupation. After 1945 he loved char-
acterizing himself as "twelve years verboten." In reality, publishing
partly with Swiss publishing houses, partly under pseudonyms, he
was one of the great suppliers of the entertainment industry in the
Third Reich. He wrote mostly comedies and film scripts; best known
was the UfA big production movie *Münchhausen* (1943). After 1945 he
passed that off as a kind of martyrdom. He could have had it much
better, if he had emigrated, to London, Hollywood, or Zurich, but he
had to remain with his people in bad times. "So, I was a witness for
twelve long years."

Later Thomas Mann nominated Kästner to be a founding member
of the German postwar P.E.N. Club. Kästner also gradually realized
which side his bread was buttered on, and from then on reported
only in an amicable way about Thomas Mann.

## HAUSMANN

As far as I am concerned, the whole "inner emigration" thing can
go hang, to be frank. They all went along, all profited, all believed in the stock of atrocities that they never really felt were

atrocious and never abominated. And now they play heroes and martyrs that stuck with Germany and suffered with her, while we from the comfortable box seats oveseas, etc. It is a considerable piece of impudence.

Among the impertinences of these inner emigrants belonged also an open letter by Manfred Hausmann, in which could be read: "In the year 1933 Thomas Mann, in a long and moving letter to the then Interior Minister Frick, pleaded with urgent words, from Switzerland, where he sojourned at the time with an expired passport, to be allowed to return to National Socialist Germany. He pledged, he wrote, to keep silent and not to get involved in the political agitation. In no case did he want to emigrate. The letter was not answered. And so, against his will, Thomas Mann had to flee from the Third Reich. At the time he would thus gladly have returned to Hitler's Germany. But he was not permitted to do so."

The publication of what Thomas Mann had really written to Frick at the time repudiated the imputations so clearly that the malicious debate quickly suffocated. The attacker wanted to take aim again, but had no success: "Hausmann's reply foolish."


## VIKKO, PREE, AND GODFATHER BERTRAM

Hate, like love, is "a product of insufficient perception." You hate a person only as long as you do not comprehend him. That is more successful from the distance than from up close. When people who had betrayed him and had become Nazis came to him willing to reconcile, Thomas Mann's hate did not last long. He was kind and ungrudging in individual cases, with all his embitterment about the whole.

Letters come from people long lost track of; they are "full of long-silenced attachment" and disturb Thomas Mann at first through the naïve directness of their resumption of contact, as though the twelve years had not existed. From his brother Viktor comes unpleasant news: "arrested for alleged mistreatment of French prisoners." Thomas Mann is supposed to help and does so at once with a letter attesting that brutal behavior is alien to his brother's character. Vikko is grateful, soon afterward writes letters that his brother qualifies as "touching"

*Viktor Mann*

(October 19, 1945) or "sensible" (October 26, 1945) and answers amicably. He has warm underwear and CARE packages sent to him. Devotedly and adeptly Viktor puts himself at the service of his famous
relatives. He admits they are right in all things. His readiness to serve
culminates in the memoir *We Were Five*, which appears in 1949 and
stylistically as well as objectively is adapted as much as possible to
his great brothers. "Always trusting, charming, and good, and meticulous," Thomas comments, when it appears. "Much merry to and fro
about Vikko's book, which in its mendacity, good-natured palliation,
self- and family-glorification and at the same time exhibition of talent
is a very singular case." Viktor Mann does not conceal that he has
been a fellow traveler. But he does not reveal the details. Rather, he
emphasizes his solidarity with Thomas. He says he had written him
two or three letters a year. That is greatly exaggerated. Thomas Mann
kept the letters; the last was dated June 2, 1936. Afterward the contact
basically breaks off completely.

What was suspected: Erika had visited Uncle Viktor in Munich and

confronted him. He had been an active member of the National Socialist Motor Sports Corps, in addition a group leader with the Labor
Front. He had also been considered worthy of joining the party, even
though his service in the Wehrmacht kept him from making use of
this offer. But Erika, too, is not vengeful in the family realm. She ironizes Uncle Vikko ("old sweety," "foolish old Benjamin") but sticks
with him. In the course of denazification proceedings, he lost his job,
and she helped him get it back.

Only Golo Mann is clearer, much later, remarking with sarcastic
unerring aim:

> One would have to be able to enjoy with a clear conscience the
> advantages that were now to be gained. Active in the Bavarian
> Handelsbank as a trained agriculturist, and there not even in a
> managerial position, Uncle Viktor rose quickly to director and
> exchanged his modest apartment in East Munich for an incom-
> parably more elegant one in Schwabing: a rise for which he was
> indebted to the exodus of his Jewish colleagues.

Thomas Mann suspected or knew all of that, but his sense of family
was stronger. A personal reunion came in June 1947 in Zurich. The
diary notes: "Lies, obfuscation, smothering embrace." Viktor had
made use of his chance; it was the caress of the victor. He got hardly
more than that. He died unexpectedly on April 21, 1949.

"Of course, there is a lot of 'Hitler' in Wagner, and you left that
out"—Thomas Mann wrote in an open letter to Emil Preetorius on
December 6, 1949. This book illustrator and art collector, with whom
he had been friends for decades, the scenic director of the Bavarian
Festivals from 1933 unti 1939, had been the object of the rhetorical
question in the Molo letter, whether there had not been honorable
work when Wagner decorations had been sketched for Hitler's Bayreuth or, with Goebbel's permission, cultural propaganda for the
Third Reich had been made abroad in clever lectures.

Pree, as his intimate friends called him, recognizing the signs of the
time, had sought connection at once, and on June 6, 1945, had written
a birthday letter, which reached the sought-after man on July 12: "astonishing letter from Emil Preetorius from a Bavarian village. Clever,
perhaps speculative." Pree speculated indeed, and not at all awkwardly. "Discussion about Preetorius," the diary notes on July 14. Yet
Mann did not hide from the kick in the Molo letter. A second "long

letter of friendship" from the accused man reached him on October
12. The diary compresses it: "Proposals for discussions: Wagner,
Nietzsche, the Germans. The first one to be whitewashed."

For two weeks Thomas Mann polishes a reply, keeps changing it,
then begins all over again, and on October 25 sends off a friendly
letter that almost completely refrains from attacks. Preetorius had
meanwhile composed a reply to the Molo letter, defended himself in a
manner worth listening to, but also allowed himself to be carried
away with the remark: "Your heart has become hard, and your perspective necessarily distorted by the much too great distance." At exactly the right time he received Thomas Mann's obliging letter, so that
he was able to stop the planned printing. A correspondence ensued,
in the course of which Pree later could also not resist passing on the
suppressed letter—at least he claims that on February 23, 1946. A
reaction in the diary is lacking, so the letter probably did not reach
the attacked man, for the exchange of letters continues undisturbed.
A great letter in defense is once more there, dated June 10, 1946, as an
answer to one just as fundamental by Thomas Mann on February 24.
All of that remains moderate, trying for agreement. Only at the end of
1946 does a skeptical remark appear in the diary: "Melancholic letter
from Preetorius, typical for the oversensitive condition of the Germans." The stage designer had meanwhile heard of further skeptical
statements made about him by Thomas Mann and asked contritely
whether, in spite of their correspondence, he had become a nuisance
to the writer. Besides, he had heard that Erika rejected him *en tout*.
But however things were, his admiration and his inner loyalty were
not lessened by that. "Dear Pree," Thomas Mann replies on the same
day, "we outside and you inside, we both probably have a somewhat
pathological sensitivity in things regarding this Third Reich."

The whole thing was glossed over but did not endure. In 1947 *Doctor Faustus* appears, and Thomas Mann has to admit that for the figure of the art collector Sixtus Kridwiss, who speaks in a Darmstadt
dialect, with whom all sorts of prefascist discussions take place in
Munich, he had borrowed some features from Preetorius. Unmistakably:

Kridwiss—graphic artist and book illustrator and collector of
East Asian color woodcuts and ceramics, a field about which he
also, invited by this and that cultural association, in various cities
in the Reich and even abroad, held well-informed and sensible

lectures, was an ageless gentleman with a strong Rhine-Hessen accent and unusual intellectual liveliness who, without a definitive like-minded connection but out of pure curiosity, listened to the movements of the age and to this and that, and called whatever came to his ears "really enormously important."

He himself calls that a murder, in a conversation with Katia: "Bad, bad" (July 18, 1947). But the characterization was probably not completely false, Pree's versatility well on the mark. He is called "Kridwiss" without further ado in the diary (March 4, 1948)—Mann took the name from the *Malleus Maleficarum*—and was probably addressed as that in Germany, too. Mann sends him a copy (May 6, 1948). Preetorius answers uninsulted, praising the writer hymnically and commenting: "The almost already familiar highest tones. 'Magnificent self-enhancement: You belong with that to the blessed artists of the sort of Goethe, Titian, Verdi'" (June 28, 1948).

Pree had meanwhile become the president of the Bavarian Academy of Fine Arts and smoothed the way for Thomas Mann on his visit to Munich in the summer of 1949. Their personal reunion, of course, did not produce a deep trust—on the contrary. Back at home, Thomas Mann writes "Richard Wagner and No End," an open letter to Emil Preetorius. "There is a lot of Hitler in Wagner"—that is his answer to the demand to whitewash Wagner and, by doing so, also Pree. For the latter was not ever quite honest. His Wagner book, which appeared in 1941 and in many passages reads like a polemic against Thomas Mann's Wagner essay of 1933, he shortened in the postwar edition by a few tainted passages and added a bow to Mann's "splendid interpretation." Thomas Mann suspected the dishonesty. "Letter to Preetorius finished," notes the diary on December 7, 1949, and adds: "Doesn't deserve it." The contact afterward becomes weaker. But Pree's niceness was unconquerable. "Call from Preetorius, who on the return from St. Moritz to Munich dined with us. Hearty" (Sepember 25, 1951). Until the writer's death friendly letters are exchanged.

Godfather Bertram, the advisor in the time of the world war, had stood sponsor for little Elisabeth at her baptism in 1918. In "Song of the Child," he is "the affectionate friend, in the well-cut frock coat. / bourgeois elegant, a bit Old Franconian, the German scholar / and poet, full of childlike pleasing cheerfulness." Those were still nice

times! Shortly thereafter, bitterness intervenes. The Old Franconian
could not approve of Mann's republican switch. Little by little he developed into a convinced National Socialist. A long, painfully obsessed letter, "tender, confused, melancholically gripping," arrived on
June 4, 1935. Thomas Mann wrote back, "amicably ironic" (June 16),
from his ship, with a hand moved by the ocean, but received no reply.
The silence lasted fourteen years. The first indirect contact takes place
in 1948. In the denazification process Bertram was classified as impli-
cated; his professorial post was taken away from him, his application
for a pension rejected. A student of Bertram begs Thomas Mann for a
good word. The man addressed is, of course, opposed to Bertram's
reinstatement as an academic teacher, but wishes him a decent retire-
ment sum. Looking back, he characterizes him fairly accurately:

> Ernst Bertram is a dear, fine, and pure, extraordinarily highly in-
> tellectual man and through many years was my and my family's
> best friend. What, to my sorrow, alienated us more and more was
> his enthusiastic belief in the rising "Third Reich," a belief in
> which he was not to be dissuaded by any warning, any evocative
> reference to the trait of evil on the face of its mass movement. . . .
> And selfless and in personal purity he has remained true to this
> belief not only at the time of Hitler's delusional victories,
> the defilement and plunder of Europe but up to the agony of
> the National Socialist state, to the days of its Volkssturm and
> Werewolves.*

You don't abandon something that is sinking; many a faithful de-
luded person thought that. The diary muses: "On Deutschland
Welle** about suicides of 'noble Nazis,' leaving behind 'Better dead
than a slave.' Officers, professors. Bertram? Hardly probable" (May
26, 1945). The meditatively gentle godfather was hardly the type for
suicide. But he still had more pride than Vikko and Pree, unlike them
did not throw himself around the neck of Thomas Mann at once.
Admittedly, he was more involved than they. Even if there were no
personal ignominies known, ideologically Bertram remained loyal to
the Reich. As an essayist and lyric poet he had already celebrated the
Rhine in the twenties. That brought him the German National Joseph

---

* The Volkssturm was the conscripted ranks of older men; the Werewolves were
dissident underground forces. (Trans.)

** As Deutsche Welle it is even today the German overseas shortwave radio broadcast. (Trans.)

von Görres Prize in 1940. The award ceremony at the University of Bonn, the very university that had withdrawn the honorary doctorate for Thomas Mann with aplomb and sensation at the end of 1936, ended with a program highpoint, "Tribute to the Führer and National Songs." On June 28, 1940, the twenty-first anniversary of the "scandal of Versailles," Hitler had marched into the Strasbourg Cathedral. Bertram does not let that escape him in his speech. Before the party and the armed forces, the state and the city, he proclaimed the deep symbolism of that event, the homecoming of Strasbourg, the glorious improbability of the "Arminius feat" of the savior, whom the most profound collapse "shook so deeply, that this shock became the magic of will" and let the vision of the poets of the Rhine become reality.

Thomas Mann learned of similar things in roundabout ways, and he shuddered. "A roundelay of ghosts," he wrote in 1944 about the cultural activities of Bertram and Preetorius. But he liked that beguiled man a lot and would like to have seen him on his trip to Germany in 1949, waited almost longingly for him. But Bertram was ill (or afraid) and sent only a few friendly lines, to which Thomas Mann replied cordially on August 9, 1949. The shame was too great for anything like friendship to have been reestablished. But deep inside, it was at work; what was human rebelled against its desecration by politics. "In the mail yesterday an emotional letter about *Bertram*, who is still involved with me, dreams of me, longs for a talk before his death. Will see him, of course" (August 17, 1954). On August 24 Thomas Mann visited his old friend in Cologne. "Friendly stay in his sensibly attractive apartment, full of personal and artistic souvenirs. His face, aged days of yore. His talkative, sympathetically old-fashioned way unchanged. Cordial relationship, cordial farewell." But a really intellectual exchange about what they had experienced was not possible. The wounds could not be touched. The last word is melancholically amicable. "Dear Godfather," the eighty-year-old writes on a printed thank-you card (June 7, 1955), "we think back often of our visit with you with quiet joy."

## THE GOETHE TRIP AND ITS CONSEQUENCES

Only late was it decided that Thomas Mann would also visit Germany. Originally, he had had only an invitation to Oxford. That Johannes R. Becher asked him whether he would like to come to the

Goethe celebration in Weimar and accept the newly founded Goethe National Prize, he calls in the diary "awkward" (December 27, 1948) and replies dilatorily. In February he still does not want to set foot on German soil. "That the air there already again—in the sign of that 'already again' is everything!—has become unbreathable, one senses even this far away." Invited by Preetorius, he has been considering a visit to Munich since March 1949, but that too is not certain. "If it comes to a visit, then it may easily be improvised." A visit to Frankfurt to accept the Goethe Prize is agreed to on May 3 and then on short notice moved forward from August 28 to July 25. As a result of the shock of the death of his son Klaus at the beginning of June, everything in Germany is to be canceled. Only his Swiss dates are to be kept. Weimar had not been decided on at the time anyway for political reasons—"Reluctance to spoil everything with America" (June 18, 1949). Not until July 9 are the decisions firm, and not until July 25 in Frankfurt are the details settled with East Zone delegates.

Vicious letters had reached him from Germany. He had betrayed Germany and should just stay away. Death threats were among them. The consequences will be sometimes discreet and sometimes intrusive police protection on the whole trip. Even those who invited him gave Thomas Mann the creeps. "What do you think?" he asks his driver and trip coordinator, Georges Motschan, after the Frankfurt reading. "How much blood probably sticks to all those hands that I had to shake today?" With the "feeling as though he were heading for war," Thomas Mann had set off from Zurich on July 23. The trip leads by way of Frankfurt, Stuttgart, Munich, and Nuremberg (where they offer him a tour of the place of execution of the war criminals, which he obligingly turns down in favor of the party premises), and finally to Weimar. "My visit is to Germany, Germany as a whole, not to one occupation zone or another." He is not moved by Munich: "a tattered past, little sympathy for that." He refuses to visit his former house.

"I know that the emigrant does not count for much in Germany," he said in Frankfurt. When he had gone to bed, the guests who had just honored him are said to have bellowed out Nazi songs. In the West German press there was much that was full of hate. That the betrayer of the fatherland who had seen the German tragedy from the boxes and orchestra seats of California now even wanted to visit the Russian zone led to a protest that struck Thomas Mann particularly bitterly, because it did not seem unjustified. The former Nazi concentration camp Buchenwald near Weimar continued to be used by the Russians at the time. According to a demand of a "Society for the Combat against Inhumanity" Thomas Mann should go to see Buchenwald, too, during his visit to the East Zone. That would naturally have been an affront. On the other hand, if he refused, his visit to Weimar would now have to seem like an approval of Russian crimes against humanity. That it came from Eugen Kogon, who during the Hitler era had himself been an inmate of Buchenwald, gave the request moral weight. Thomas Mann had to accept the embarrassment of a refusal of the request. He also had to accept that the East Berlin government would extract propagandistically anything that could be extracted. They prepared an overwhelming reception for him that in its triumphal production put Frankfurt and Munich in the shade. But Thomas Mann was still impressed by it. He allowed himself to be swept away to the point of commenting that the authoritarian people's state indeed had its scary side but still included the benefit that stupidity and impudence had for once to keep their mouths shut.

That saucy statement was "in its complete gratuitousness a really stupid trick." "For I'm not for force and police." The declaration wound up in Thomas Mann's FBI dossier, along with many other seemingly pro-Communist pronouncements. The trip to Weimar and its concomitant appearances made Thomas Mann more and more politically suspect in postwar America. Many erstwhile friends deserted him. Refusals and rejections rained down. Things were not entirely bad for him, thanks to influential friends such as Agnes Meyer; but similar to his daughter Erika, who, after she had been left waiting for an eternity, withdrew her application for citizenship in 1950, she—who as a British citizen had in the service of America battled against Hitler for many years—wrote a deeply embittered letter to the immigration authorities:

I submitted my application almost four years ago. Since that point in time an examination has been going on that unavoidably led to awakening doubt about my character, gradually to ruining my professional career, to robbing me of my livelihood, and—in short—to turning a happy, active, and somewhat useful member of society into a humiliated, suspicious person. Friends of mine have one after another been subjected to two and three hours of interrogation until they have almost collapsed. When it turned out that I was neither a Communist, nor a "fellow traveler," nor the member of a "subversive" registered organization, nor in any

way politically undesirable, the authorities began to poke around
in my private life in a manner that extremely shocked all who
were questioned.

Although this crass form was spared Thomas Mann, the subtle one was
not. It slowly became more lonely around him in America, partly because many Americans turned away from him, partly because more
and more emigrants were returning to Europe. The Goethe trip of 1949
brings another change in his life. It prepares his farewell to the United
States without establishing a new place of residence in Germany. The
writer takes refuge in a kind of rhetorical world citizenship, which
nevertheless had the disadvantage of not having a definite homeland
linked to it. It then terminated in Switzerland. By overlooking a few
things, the world citizen could feel accepted there most easily. Unlike
during the thirties, he was now very welcome there.

Why could he not find a home anymore in Germany? It begins with
the fact that he would have had to decide for the East or the West. He
did not like the Federal Republic, the "American favorite colony" with
its "ridiculous economic boom." But that was not really what it was
all about. Even if the decision had been clearly for the West, as we
must assume, there was something more profound left over. The
abyss between the emigrant and his former home could no longer be
closed, no matter how many honors were involved. There was no
lack of those, but in his heart he did not believe in them. Were they
not the product of a bad conscience? Just overcompensations, not free
and cordial declarations of love? The schism between official glorification and underground hate did not end, at least during his lifetime, in
spite of an undoubted reconciliation with Munich and Lübeck. All too
often he got a glimpse of the fascist grimace under the festive veneer.
When he had signed the guestbook in Bayreuth, he leafed a few pages
back and found what was to be expected. "They are all there, of
course—the whole devil's brood together, Hitler, Himmler, Goebbels,
Göring, all, all!" In the East the festive surface was just as staged.
Mercilessly, they ordered jubilation. "Unprepared as they were," they
used his fame for their purposes, and with their brass bands, their
children's choruses, their streamers and garlands, awakened false associations. That the Free German Youth "from morning to night bellowed their 'Horst Wessel' song of peace" and in between in chorus
yelled "We greet our Thomas Mann," caused Katia Mann to consider
whether it was right "to serve up such extraordinarily fat portions to

the propaganda there." For the West German press that is a welcome cause for orgies of hate. In the *Frankfurter Allgemeine* newspaper, which looks at it today with shame, someone writes on his seventy-fifth birthday that Thomas Mann, dumb with resentment of Germany, had become the advocate of the Eastern oppressors' world, that he was doing everything to prevent the rescue of the West, that he could write but he could not think.

It is particularly tragic that a fruitful conversation could never unfold, not even with the German opposition to Hitler. Why could he not speak with Eugen Kogon who, like him, belonged to the persecuted? Why not with the ex-Luftwaffe officer and later cofounder of the "National Committee of Free Germany," Heinrich, Count von Einsiedel, who had joined the Kogon protest? Why not with the inner emigration? Of course, too many wanted to belong to it subsequently; those who made themselves its spokesmen were not its best. Mention has been made of Thiess, Kästner, and Hausmann. Even the Group 47, gradually being established into the fifties, which had inscribed antifascism onto its founding standards, sought no contact with Thomas Mann, although individual members deviated from this course. Among these exceptions was Alfred Andersch, who was busy with bold plans to bring Thomas Mann, Ernst Jünger, and Bertolt Brecht together at one table. Thomas Mann described the Group 47 ironically as a scurrilous "mischievous bunch." He said he knew the shamelessness of the so-called young generation. The mischievous bunch sought its well-being in poking fun at him, even jeering at him, in any case keeping their distance from him instead of learning from him.

This whole generation would have to die out to restore an unprejudiced relationship to Thomas Mann again, to make respect, admiration, perhaps even love possible, to accept his exemplary nature, and not, as unfortunately constantly happens, to see his small vanities—"Worried about small cracks in the ivory on the knob of the new walking stick"—and to cheaply hold over him his reputed coldness, which was certainly a necessary protection for the man who was becoming ever kinder in his old age.

## RUSSIAN MINK

On an unusually hot May day in the year 1954 a citizen of the German Democratic Republic, a heavy fur coat over his arm, passed through Swiss customs in the Zurich airport. The officials took no umbrage. It was Walter Janka, the head of the East Berlin publishing house Aufbau Verlag, on his way to smuggle Thomas Mann's East mark royalties across the border.

In those long-lost times Walter Ulbricht had allowed the decision that books from the West whose authors and publishers did not enter into contracts with payments in East marks would still be published for the sake of the good of the people. The Aufbau Verlag had upon higher instructions in 1952 issued *The Beloved Returns* and *Buddenbrooks* in its "Library of Progressive German Writers," each in thirty thousand copies. Thomas Mann made a protest against such robbery: "But your idealism and your maxim 'The people's education above all' makes me sick because you combine this good intention with actions through which your publishing house places itself outside of all legal agreements. . . . Do you plan in the future without a contract, to snatch every book that seems to you indispensable for the people's education and to publish it as 'pirated'?"

Since they did not want to affront the celebrated author, a halfway sensible agreement resulted. Bermann Fischer was allowed to publish for the present with the East mark accounts in the GDR and kept the agreement. For Thomas Mann and his family, Janka had an extra treat. He arranged for them the purchase of high-cost consumer products in the GDR. After Katia and Erika had received Eastern furs and had tested and praised them, Thomas Mann had his measurements sent to Fortschritt, an East German national clothing manufacturer, and had a fur coat tailor-made of Russian mink. It was a splendid piece, with an otter collar. He had not had such a one since Munich. Did he remember how at the time, in 1918, he had taken out his fur and how embarrassing it had been for him to be seen in such opulence, "in the 'socialist times'?" And now the first laborers and peasants republic on German soil had delivered him a fur in which he looked like a landowner at the time of the czars.

## THE FIREMAN

But that for this land, to become a citizen of which was for me an honor and a joy, the hysterical, irrational, and blind hatred of Communists presents a danger far more horrible than the native

Communism; yes, that the mania for persecution and the fury of persecution into which they have fallen and which they seem to want to permit completely—that all of this can lead not only to nothing good but will lead to the worst, if one does not quickly come to one's senses, on this occasion became quite clear.

"Alger" was the name of the Manns' new poodle, after Alger Hiss, an American diplomat who, if rumor has it right, was unjustly ruined by the Communist hunt in the McCarthy era. Had the *Fireman* known that, he would have made a poisoned arrow of it. Had he known that the figurehead of German emigration had secretly put much worse down on paper than was collected in his denunciatory file—he would have destroyed him. That Goethe today (in February 1949) would prefer Russia to America, Mann wrote in an unpublished passage (for cautionary reasons) of the speech "Goethe and Democracy." In an essay that then did not appear, there would have been much to read that was urgent about the fascist obfuscation of the American press, about the horrifying moral decline of the country, about its bought-off science that stood fully under the control of the army, about the enthusiasm of those who had collected their wealth under Hitler, about the scandal in broad daylight of German politics, about the hysteria of the Communist persecution. There, if it had not been for the *firemen* watching over published opinion, one could also have read the accusation that America flagellated the human rights infringements of the Soviet Union but silently approved tyranny and the most savage exploitation of slaves in friendly countries such as Iran and Saudi Arabia. "As long as the bourgeois world," it was summarized in the flaming article,

> has nothing more to oppose the Communist promise than the ideal, which has become untenable, of private business, of profit, of competition and the struggle for the best place . . . then our prospects look bad for ridding the world of Communism.

There one might assert ever so often that one was not a Communist and also not a "fellow traveler." In America at the time, much less sufficed to brand a person. *The Fireman* knows the technique. The journalist Eugen Tillinger—he's the one involved—had already described Thomas Mann as "America's fellow traveler No. 1" in December 1949 because of his trip to Weimar. In the magazine *The Freeman*, which was open to him, which Thomas Mann labeled as the "yellow press 'The Fireman'" (March 28, 1951), Tillinger had enumerated a long list of pro-Communist activities by the suspect. A wild back-and-forth of denials, press releases, statements, and letters from lawyers is the result. Thomas Mann even thinks of writing a satire: "The idea of a horribly monotonous confession of guilt in the Russian style occupies me" (April 27, 1951). On the resolution of a member of the House of Representatives, all the articles and documents are officially entered into the Congressional Record. Thomas Mann had to expect a summons by the Committee for Un-American Activities. He had long since been *listed* together with such suspicious contemporaries as Albert Einstein, Lion Feuchtwanger, Marlon Brando, and Norman Mailer. It did not get as far as a summons. Presumably he still had enough influential friends.

The unjust and undignified reproaches and the journalistic attention depress Thomas Mann deeply. "I had to get to be 75 years old and live in a foreign country that has become home to me just to see myself publicly called a liar, by burners of witches who—and that is the astonishing thing—believe no one or listen only to their 'witches.'"

But had he really not lied? At least on one point Tillinger seems to have been right, namely, that Thomas Mann in May 1950 had signed a declaration *pour l'interdiction de l'arme atomique.* Quite independently of the question of whether a movement against atomic weapons could be described as disgraceful, Mann disputes his participation because the action was felt to be guided by Communists. But he did sign; it can be proved today. It may also be that he was deceived. After the writer's lecture at the Sorbonne, a listener got the idea of giving him the petition to sign. Maybe the text was half covered up. The photograph of the document shows, according to Thomas Mann, a "hasty scribble of a signature, which after a lecture—just to get away—one writes left and right on slips of paper thrust out for autographs, but as I never would write as a signature on a document important to me."

## WHY I WILL NOT REMAIN IN AMERICA

All of that affronts him greatly. The wish "Don't die here!" becomes stronger and stronger. So *The Fireman* becomes one of the impulses for his return, even his flight to Europe and for settling in Switzerland, something kept from the American authorities as long as possible. With all his pose as a citizen of the world, he longed somehow for home. "I am drawn by the soil 'from which I came.' " "My irrational desire for the old soil" (June 6, 1952). In spite of occasional attacks of homesickness for the California house under the palm trees, he feels more and more happy as a European. "Fine pastry for tea, provided by Erika. There's nothing like it in America" (Gastein, September 4, 1952). The arc of life is about to close. Munich is sought out many times in the fifties, finally also Lübeck and especially Travemünde, the place he longed for in his childhood—"for the wish is preserved in all of us to return home to what was and to repeat it so that, if it was unhappy, it should now be blessed."

There are things deeper than politics. When the fight against Hitler, which had driven him abroad, was over, the American soil began to quiver under his feet. Palm trees alone were just not enough. The more the political furor died down, old, long-repressed layers of being were driven out of the depths into the light all the more. There were again hours in which all politics seemed a false path and the political moralizing of the artist something insipid and comical, hours in which he still knew only weariness and humanity, saw nothing but comedy and misery, like once his Tonio Kröger, in which he preferred art and religion, morality and inwardness to all democratic babble— like once the nonpolitical observer. Democracy comes from above, the latter had written; but the pessimistic emigrant in postwar America could also have said it. "It should not be pretension, presumption, an impudent demand, but forbearance, modesty, renunciation, humanity . . . democracy—but I keep saying the same thing—ought to be morality, not politics; it ought to be goodness of man to man, goodness on both sides! For the lord needs the goodness of the servant just as much as the latter needs the goodness of the former." That Goethe was not a democrat is only the casually veiled tenor of the speech "Goethe and Democracy" of 1949. "He was against freedom of the press, against the masses having a say, against a constitution and majority rule, was convinced that 'everything sensible was in the minority' and believed openly with the minister who carries out his plans alone against the people and the king."

What is innately his own again appears; that is why he wants to go to Europe. It is not something as much in the foreground as politics by itself that drives him out of America. But let us linger with it for a while because something problematic must still be addressed: the writer's contact with the Federal Bureau of Investigation—that exaggeratedly notorious group of American lawmen that is in reality perhaps comparable to the German Federal Criminal Bureau.

Thomas Mann was always for a strong state, if it were reasonable and humane. That under certain circumstances the citizen had to be under surveillance for the sake of good order did not contest his understanding of democracy. We have heard that in his early years he put himself at the disposal of the Office of Censorship of Theater and Film. Under much more dramatic historical circumstances, those of the Second World War, he occasionally helped the American police, as did his daughter Erika, as did his son Golo. "Fairly long visit by two FBI gentlemen because of the group in Mexico, Katz, B. Brecht" (August 18, 1943). During the time following, there are several notices of the type: "Visit of FBI man, information about E. Deutsch" (January 29, 1944). Often it probably concerns only German emigrants who wished to become citizens and had given Thomas Mann as a reference, but to really judge the matter, one would have to know the other side of events. Presumably the person questioned said mostly helpful things. There is no evidence that he spoke damagingly of Otto Katz and Bertolt Brecht. When Bruno Frank is being investigated by the FBI because of suspicion of being a Communist, Thomas Mann stands up for him with his powerful friend Agnes Meyer. "I vouch absolutely for his faultless patriotism." Only once, in the case of the librarian and literary scholar Curt von Faber du Faur, is there a notation in the diary: "Expressed unfavorable opinion" (October 24, 1944). After 1945 he was apparently no longer questioned.

The dark side of the picture is elaborated more decisively. He suspected certainly that there was also a file on him—as in Germany, as in Switzerland. He was afraid that the FBI could draw the line in regard to his application for citizenship "because of premature antifascism," as the grotesque term reads. Almost all important American artists were under surveillance, as well as all prominent emigrants, thus also daughter Erika and son Klaus. The Thomas Mann dossier contained far more than a thousand items from the years 1937 to 1954, of which until now only a small part, and this with blacked-out names, has been released. A final judgment about this complex affair is consequently not possible.

In the end, being under surveillance meant not only an unpleasant feeling but had consequences. That in the year 1950 he was not allowed to give his annual lecture in the Library of Congress—for that occasion he had written "My Time," with the conviction it was a matter of a historically significant event—that the attacks sharpened so that at first he had to weigh any public word and finally had to remain totally silent politically, and this after his powerful commitment in the antifascist battle, all this stole his feeling of freedom, it choked, suffocated him, infected the air. "Feel myself caught in a world of trouble from which there is no escape" (April 22, 1951). The land that had once seemed to him so generous now showed a brutal face. A "constant further development into a fascist dictatorship" seemed probable to him (March 1, 1952). At the end of June 1952 he traveled to Europe. In a letter to Agnes Meyer of November 7 he still acts as though he wants to return to America.

He goes also because of his daughter "who is simply languishing away because of the removal of any possibility for action." "Staying here for Erika's sake totally impossible, and I myself am unspeakably tired of this country" (March 19, 1952). Thomas Mann was worried about her because of her exaggerated bitterness and irritability. Which was, admittedly, not inexplicable: "Hour and a half interrogation of Erika by the two FBI. A paid agent of Stalin or at least a Party member? Incredible" (October 24, 1951). Katia, too, had to suffer because of Erika (June 6, 1952). Everything, everything drives him to flight.

"Destination reached" (Zurich, July 1, 1952).

## EINSTEIN AND THE BOMB

"Just quite simply next to *him*? It makes me dizzy." That is the dedication on a snapshot that shows Thomas Mann in conversation with Albert Einstein. In the diary there is certainly no talk of dizziness but always of high respect and friendship. Also, they had known one another personally since 1925 at least—being with him had been gripping, it says at the time, "thanks to his gentleness, childlike nature, and modesty!" During Mann's time at Princeton they were neighbors and visited one another often. They were also connected by much else (not only their maladjustment to school)—being driven out of Germany, the common honorary doctorates from Harvard in 1935 and the dinner with Roosevelt that followed, their political solidarity in the United States, petitions signed together; also they were both "listed," denounced as fellow travelers, and finally both were under surveillance by the FBI. Both had been good-hearted world reformers in the Weimar Republic, where Thomas Mann together with Albert Einstein advocated all kinds of things: demanded freedom for the arts, promoted the Red Cross children's homes, fought the filth-and-trash law, stuck up for "Pro Palestine," for Max Holz, were against the military draft and against a pirated publication of Joyce's *Ulysses*, and where he wanted in addition to win the great physicist further for a call against National Socialism and for a "draconian republic," which then did not come to pass.

In 1905 and 1915 Einstein had presented his path-finding theories to his professional public, in 1917 in a book *On the Special and General Theory of Relativity* to a wider public. Thomas Mann was soon interested in regard to the philosophy of time in *The Magic Mountain*, but did not understand very much about it. For him "Einstein" became the synonym for "modern physics," about which he nevertheless understood just as little. For him it overlapped with a "cosmic world-view," from which he hoped it would form "the basis and the fervor of the new humanism, which prepared for the best behind any barbarism."

But first something completely different happened. The formula $E = mc^2$ had postulated that mass and energy were basically the same, and the discovery of nuclear fission had proven this in practice. A single kilogram of coal would, as Thomas Mann was taught, if it were transformed entirely into energy, deliver 25 billion kilowatt hours of electricity. The path to the atomic bomb began with the famous letter that Einstein wrote together with Leo Szilard in 1939 to President Roosevelt. The bomb ought to be built to beat the Germans to it. A gigantic machinery came into being. The man with the "bright and spherical children's eyes," who had innocently offered his hand to the bomb, had long since distanced himself from all that when Hiroshima and Nagasaki were charred.

Thomas Mann comments on the bombs on Japan with Faustian criticism, quoting Goethe against the grain: "Does no created spirit penetrate Nature to the core? The innermost power of the universe is placed at the service of mankind. With that it is in precarious hands." The diary entries are fairly cold in reference to the victims of the bomb, as are Einstein's. Furthermore, Einstein wrote that the invention could eradicate two-thirds of mankind but not mankind itself. One could begin all over again. Then, when the hydrogen bomb is developed, he no longer looks at that so "optimistically." "Television speech by Einstein against the H-bomb. The obliteration of mankind technically possible" (February 13, 1950). Together, in October 1945, they call for the prevention of an atomic war. On November 18, 1946, the diary notes a further proclamation by Einstein. Both call for a United Nations and world government, but belief in this is not great; Thomas Mann is no longer a Settembrini. He is instead convinced "that my avowal will be swallowed up more promptly and soundlessly by the wave surge of doom than the manifesto of great scholars." Still, he will speak out against the rearmament of West Germany, but if one compares earlier political positions, only half-heartedly. A last time, again with Einstein, in 1954 he wants to issue a solemn warning of the threatening atomic war, "deeply, earnestly, and succinctly" (November 19, 1954). On July 4 Erika sets off to London on behalf of her father to carry out probing conversations. Something great is planned, but then came the fatal illness. So Thomas Mann's last word in this matter remained a striking statement in his "Essay on Schiller" (1955):

> Rage and fear, superstitious hate, panicked horror and a wild persecution mania dominate a mankind for whom cosmic space is just right to put strategic bases in and who copies the power of the sun to make weapons of destruction wantonly.

## THE LITTLE PLANET IN A CORNER OF THE UNIVERSE

Very early and then repeatedly, we find characters with split natures in Thomas Mann—the bougeois and the artist in *Tonio Kröger*, the moralist and the aesthete in *Fiorenza*, Lodovico Settembrini and Leo Naphta in *The Magic Mountain*, Serenus Zeitblom and Adrian Leverkühn in *Doctor Faustus*. He himself is also split between an optimistic political essayist and an antipolitical pessimistic writer. The one wants to help the world, the other understood his Schopenhauer and still knew that Being is an unfathomable fiction.

Thomas Mann reacts with the same split in regard to the worldview of astrophysics. As Leverkühn he is not surprised, but as Zeitblom he protests against it. It is a devil, a fictive scholar named Capercailzie, who enlightens Adrian about the enormous dimensions of the galaxies within which somewhere "completely incidental, difficult to detect and hardly worth mentioning," was to be found "the fixed star about which, in addition to larger and smaller satellites, the earth and its little moon played."

But Serenus calls that an infernal attack on human understanding:

> The data of the cosmic creation is nothing but a stupefying bombardment of our intelligence with numbers equipped with a comet's tail of two dozen zeros that pretend they might have something to do with measure and understanding. In this dreadful concoction there is nothing that could appeal to my kind with goodness, beauty, grandeur, and I will never understand the hosanna mood in which certain minds let themselves be displaced by the so-called works of God, inasmuch as they are universal physics. Is there a disposition of God's work that can be addressed at all, to which one can say "So what!" as well as "Hosanna"? The right answer seems to me to be the former rather than the latter to two dozen zeros after a one or even after a seven, which really doesn't matter, and I can see no reason at all to sink in prayer in the dust before the septillion.

So much for the intrepid scholar. He is not completely up to date, for he is up in arms against facts that have been known at least since Galileo. For him as well as for his begetter Thomas Mann, they appear under the code word "Einstein." Thomas Mann, in his "Fragment about Religiosity," had already asked why worship should be given to a God who had created the universe of Einstein. "The universe of Einstein could be even more glorious and more complex than it evidently is, and it would still permit me an attitude completely free of ardor toward its originator." Quite like Zeitblom he writes in 1934: "I cannot help myself: Human cognition, immersion in human life, has a more mature, more adult character than speculation on the Milky Way."

But the worst attack on universal physics was still to come. Capercailzie has at his disposal the Big Bang theory, which was brand new during the time of the genesis of the Faust novel. The cosmos, it presupposes, is in a state of hurtling expansion, about which the red shift of light that reaches us from other galaxies leaves no doubt.

The humanist bridles once again. The horrendousness of physical creation was religiously unproductive. What reverence could be evinced by the idea of an immeasurable disturbance such as an exploding universe? God was in the obligation of mankind for truth, freedom, and justice—"in a hundred billion galaxies I cannot find Him."

His antipode, Adrian Leverkühn, does not go along with closed eyes. However, he is no physicist either but a moralist, even though a negative one. He insists that a physical creation is the prerequisite for a moral one. If it was physically evil (but why ought it be "evil"?), then the good and the moral could be only "the blossom of evil." He derides Zeitblom's geocentric humanism as "Kaisersaschern church-steeple cosmology."

Thomas Mann translated all of that back into his old Schopenhauer. The world is originally "will" and blind instinct, even as an exploding universe. It is actually a stationary Now and Always and Everywhere that assumes the phenomenal form of parts and particles hurtling away through illusionary time and space. Thomas Mann reads Einstein's relativity of place, time, and motion as an affirmation of the Schopenhauerian mystical unity. He makes metaphysics out of physics. General relativity thus creates in him a fairly well-known result: irony. His rescue from the Big Bang is derision. Leverkühn derides the world of astrophysics with his orchestral work *The Miracle of the Universe*. Thomas Mann ironizes its microcosmic opposite between coffee and a soft-boiled egg. "Amused myself at breakfast about the missing link found between energy and matter, the weightless neutrino, which the world is full of because of atomic explosions & in which probably all bodies will dissolve" (October 13, 1948).

Thomas Mann had searched for this missing link since the twenties. "The fact that I know and understand very little about the theory of the famous Mr. Einstein," he explains truthfully in 1923, does not prevent him from observing that in this theory the boundary between physics and metaphysics has become fluid. His Hans Castorp (in *The Magic Mountain*) searches for the origin of life, for primal procreation, thus for that moment in which life issued forth from the lifeless. He sets out on the path to the ever smaller, from the molecule to the atom, which is already so small that it lies on the boundary between the material and the immaterial.

Far from finding an answer, Hans at this point first turns to the presumptive structural similarity of the macrocosmos to the microcosmos. The atom—was it not also an energy-laden cosmic system in which cosmic bodies raced in rotation around a sunlike center and through whose ether-space comets traveled at the speed of light, which forced the central body into its excentric path? Was not, in the innermost part of nature, in its broadest reflection, the macrocosmic universe of stars—whose swarms, heaps, groups, and figures gave the night sky its depth—repeating itself? And, forming the bridge to Leverkühn and Capercailzie: Could there not also in the world of the atom be an "earth"?

> Was it forbidden to think that certain planets of the atomic solar system—these armies and galaxies of solar systems that form matter—that then one or another of these innerworld world bodies was in a state that corresponded to the one that made the earth into a place of habitation for life?

The theme will not let go of the old Thomas Mann. In the diary on December 23, 1951, he reflects how everything is woven together, the human with the animal, the latter with the plant, the organic with the inorganic, Being with Nothingness.

> Everything began and will cease; it will be spaceless and timeless as before. Life on earth an episode; so perhaps all Being an Interval between Nothing and Nothing. How and when in the Nothing did the first vibration of Being appear? This something new. Likewise, the plus for the inorganic that one calls Life, something newly added without anything new in its matter. A third something newly added in the animalistic-organic is that which is human. The transformation is preserved, but something ineffable, as with the turn to "Life" appears.

In the *Confessions of Felix Krull, Confidence Man*, the analogous chapter of which was written in November and December 1951, Professor Kuckuck, in the dining car of the train to Lisbon, spreads out before the Marquis de Venosta, alias Felix Krull, biological and cosmological observations that are friendlier than the cited passage in the diary. Surprisingly, what Zeitblom had called the horrendousness of physics now appears in a reconciled light, in the light of festival. Being is celebrating its tumultuous festival in immeasurable space.

> And he spoke to me about the gigantic arenas of this festival, the universe, this mortal child of eternal Nothing, filled up with material bodies without number, meteors, moons, comets, fogs, untold millions of stars that were linked to one another, arranged with one another through the effectiveness of their fields of gravity into heaps, clouds, galaxies, and suprasystems of galaxies, each of which consists of a vast quantity of flaming suns, rotating and circling planets, masses of thinned gases and cold rubble fields of ice, stone, and cosmic dust.

Professor Kuckkuck, too, knows well about the tiny negligibility of our earth. He gives the most terrible information about it:

> Our Milky Way, I learned, one among billions—encloses almost on its edge, almost as a little wallflower, thirty thousand light years away from its center, our local solar system, with its gigantic, but in no way comparatively important, fiery ball, called "the" sun, although it deserves only the indefinite article, and the planets obeisant to its field of attraction, among them the earth, whose desire and burden it is to whirl at the speed of a thousand miles an hour around its axis and in a second to go twenty miles in order to circle the sun, whereby it forms its days and years— its own, note, for there are others quite different. The planet Mercury, for example, nearest to the sun, completes its course in eighty-eight of our days and also rotates once itself, so that year and day are the same for it. Behold, what happens to time— nothing more than the weight that exudes from any other universal validity. With the white satellite of Sirius, for example, a body only three times the size of the earth, matter is in a state of such density that a cubic inch of it with us would weigh a ton. Earth matter, our rocky moutain ranges, our human bodies would be only the loosest, lightest froth in comparison.

Felix Krull does not react like Serenus Zeitblom with old-fashioned outrage but with enthusiastic excitement. Being, with its immeasurable mighty extension, reminds him of the oceanic primal feeling that he had enjoyed as a baby at the breast of his nursemaid and that is repeated for him with every love affair, reminds him of that which, as still half a child, he "had described with the dream phrase 'The Great Joy,'" an expression that "from early on had been innate in an intoxicating extensive significance." Love explodes the boundaries of bodies. To the Schopenhauerian the ego opens to the universe in it. Sexual boundlessness has religious significance. "I cried out and thought I was going to Heaven," Krull writes about the pleasure that he tried out the first time at the chambermaid Genoveva's white and well-fed breast. An erotic universal sympathy encloses the devilishly senseless whirling of cosmic spaces in *Faustus*. The turmoil of the world, for Schopenhauer inane illusion, in the view of Nietzsche becomes a splendid feast. In a letter Thomas Mann critiques Kuckuck's theories and continues: "Love, understood as a sensual emotion through what is episodic of *Being* . . . And Being then perhaps an evocation of love from Nothing? —Nonsense, you don't understand a word. A small grandson of mine said when he came out of the church: 'When you start thinking about God, you get a *brain impairment*.' A new term and not a bad one." Just as our eyes can see only a narrow portion of the broad spectrum of possible rays, so our entire perception grasps only a tiny fragment of immeasurable Being.

Humanity, too, is substantiated differently in *Krull* than in the Faust novel with Zeitblom's correctly scorned church-tower cosmology. It grows from the consciousness of time. Being is only one episode between Nothing and Nothing, that much is certain, and space and time exists only as long as there is Being. Spacelessness and timelessness is Nothingness; it is incapable of expansion in every sense, "eternity at a standstill." Nevertheless, the concept of time is comforting. What distinguishes Homo sapiens, says Professor Kuckuck, is the knowledge about beginning and end. That life is only an episode does not make it worthless but actually valuable.

> Far from transcience being devalued, it is precisely it that lends value, dignity, and kindness to all existence. Only what is episodic, only what has a beginning and an end, is interesting and arouses sympathy, inspirited as it is by transcience. But everything is like that—the entirety of cosmic Being is inspirited by transcience; and eternal, uninspirited therefore and without the value of sympathy, is only Nothingness, out of which it has been called forth to its joy and burden.
>
> Being is not Well-being; it is joy and burden, and all time-space

Being, all matter participates, even if it is in deepest slumber only, in this joy, this burden, in the feeling, which burdens mankind, the bearer of the most aware feeling, with sympathy for the universe.

"Sympathy for the universe," Kuckuck repeats again and stands up. "Dream of the turmoil of galaxies," he advises Felix Krull. Dream of the plump arm and of the flower. "And don't forget to dream of rocks, of mossy stones that have been lying for thousands and thousands of years in the mountain brook, bathed, cooled, rinsed by froth and flood! Look with sympathy on its Being, the most aware Being at the deepest slumbering, and welcome it to creation!"

Important parts of the Kuckuck dialogue are transferred by Mann into a radio essay that was written at the beginning of 1952 with the title "In Praise of Transcience." At the end of this essay Mann leans again toward church-tower cosmology, but this is newly justified through the praise of transiency that implies the recognition of the smallness of the earth, the little planet in a corner of the universe:

> Astronomy, a great science, has taught us to consider the earth as a rotating little planet in a corner of the universe that is highly insignificant, very peripheral even in its own galaxy in the gigantic turmoil of the cosmos. That is doubtless correct scientifically, and yet I am dubious that truth is exhausted in that correctness. In my heart of hearts I believe—and consider this belief natural for every human soul—that significance in the universal Being befits this earth. In my heart of hearts I keep the presumption that, with that "Let there be . . ." that called the cosmos forth out of Nothingness and with the procreation of life from inorganic Being, this was intended for mankind, and that with it a great attempt is begun, the failure of which through human guilt would be the same as the failure of creation itself, would be its refutation.
>
> Whether that is so or not—it would be good if mankind acted as though it were so.

As long as planets inhabited by intelligent creatures occur only as science fiction, the little planet in a corner of the universe need not have an inferiority complex. If one considers that such a great universe for so few people is actually a grandiose waste of space, one can basically be fairly satisifed.

## SHOWERED WITH THE GOLD OF PRAISE

He would have had cause to leap for joy without pause, for in the last years of his life he was showered with gold like Joseph after his appointment as Pharaoh's supreme spokesman. Like Joseph, Thomas Mann wished that his father, even though with a mixture of concern and pride, in which the pride would have been paramount, could still have seen all of that. For the praise was shared by his paternal heritage. It concerned the enormous accomplishments in his life, his perseverance, and the high quality of his works.

Things were truly happening as though they wanted to overdo it. The rain of honorary chairmanships and honorary presidential positions, the honorary memberships, honorary presentations and honorary citizenships, festschrifts and festive gifts, prizes and medals seemed to have no end. A few handsome slaves to gather the accumulation would have been helpful so that he would not be overwhelmed by the deluge. First he received the Goethe Prize of the City of Weimar in 1949 (20,000 East marks) at the same time as the one from Frankfurt (10,000 West marks), then in 1952 the Feltrinelli Prize (5,000,000 lira), and in 1954 the Stalin Peace Prize (100,000 rubles) that, however, he refused. Then came the honorary doctorates of time-honored Cambridge University (1953), the University of Jena (1955), and the Technical University of the Swiss Federation in Zurich (1955). Altogether, with those he had a total of nine, the one from Harvard together with Albert Einstein, the one from Yale with Walt Disney. The Officer's Cross of the French Legion of Honor (1952) is joined in 1955 by the Commander's Order of Orange-Nassau and the peace class of the order Pour le mérite. A kind fate bestows upon him his golden wedding anniversary, and his eightieth birthday brings congratulations from the entire civilized world. There are personal meetings with the French foreign minister Robert Schuman, the German federal president Theodor Heuss, Queen Juliana of the Netherlands, and with Pope Pius XII. If the implacable law of limited space did not exist, we would have even more to enumerate.

The celebrated man comments: "Strangely festive noisy fading purr of reeling off what is left of my life" (June 13, 1953). He is melancholy. However much he deems the honors as being due him—"It comes to me not entirely unexpected"—he still lacks something. What is official about it does not satisfy a more deeply located inner longing. He cannot be deceived. The honorary citizenship of Lübeck, for example, could be agreed to unanimously only because half of those qualified to vote stayed away from the meeting. He senses also that he is being honored so vociferously because of bad consciences. Because they do not want to hear his messages, they bribe him with glittering praise. Something is supposed to be covered up. Deep within him rumbles and protests what has been repressed for half a hundred years—the heritage of his mother, the free artistic nature, sympathy with death, the romantic licentiousness, the weakness for handsome boys. "Yesterday evening and still before falling asleep: Hadji Murad. That's it! How my eyes are opened! How ashamed I am about the silly 'literature prizes'!" (June 13, 1952). Hadji Murad, the hero of the tale by Tolstoy with the same name, is a half-barbaric Tartar who comes into contact with "civilization" for a while and breaks out of it again—into death. Thomas Mann, so cultivated outwardly, felt like such a half-barbarian. In his innermost heart he was never to be satisfied with what the good society could give. As a citizen he always did his duty and received his reward for that, but what was deepest in him, his mute courtship for sincere love and inner understanding, was not granted.

# XIX. To the Last Breath

*1955*

## INSTEAD OF A CHRONICLE

You probably think: At seventy-five bondage and slavish desire cannot be so bad, but there you are wrong. It continues to the last breath. The spear may have become a bit more blunt, but that the mistress dismisses the servant— that does not happen.

"THE OLDER he became," his child Erika reports, "the more accessible, even softer he seemed. If his difficult youth had feigned 'coolness,' and had the man apparently been distant, often stiff and conventional (out of shyness!), he now pretended to be relaxed, could be very 'close' and tender." One could also chat with him now about Greek love. "Erika, at supper, insists that Frido shows all the signs of homosexuality. I doubt the possibility of deducing the conclusion from childlike grace. . . . For the rest—so what" (January 4, 1949). "Erika on the way home about the archpederasty ('gayness') of the scene. *Soit*" (December 31, 1951).

*Soit:* so what. For all I care. The world knows me. He can tell Katia frankly that he longs for Franzl. With her and Erika a light humorous discussion is convoked on the question of how he can do something good for youth. The works and diaries of his old age are full of erotic themes and sexual allusions. "He still has to—" He describes *Krull* outright as a homosexual novel. After the politically exciting times of the battle against Hitler, the erotic again comes into its own. "To awaken feeling once again in us old people," the narrator of the Joseph novel ponders, "something special has to come along." Of course, the usual came, a handsome waiter in the Zurich Hotel Dolder, but he awakened the feeling quite powerfully.

Wagner's *Tristan*, Thomas Mann writes in the open letter to Emil Preetorius, is something for young people who do not know what to do with their sexuality. So observed, he remained young. "Again could not sleep, since I made Tristan music" (July 12, 1952). He finds no rest. "Very strong sexual potency and need recently. That will never end" (February 27, 1947). "The cross of sex, vexation, suffering, with an element of vanity" (December 14, 1947). "Sexuality—incredible" (November 12, 1950). "Vigorous lasting masculinity showed up at night" (December 31, 1951).

Depressions occur when virility once pauses. Then at once he generalizes it. "My decline, age, is shown in that love seems to avoid me and for a long time I have not seen a human face that I could grieve over" (December 20, 1952). Whereupon he plays the Old Fritz a bit: "My spirit becomes amicably moved now only at the sight of creatures, beautiful dogs, poodles, and setters." In reality all that is a given. "Sight of a youth oiling himself, Greek vase image, image of eternal being" (July 16, 1947). "Aroused night" (October 18, 1947). "At night, after a bit of sleep, masturbated" (August 29, 1954). "Sexual worries at intervals, pain nourished by images along the way, and deep, passionate longing, with the knowledge that reality won't have it" (December 1, 1949).

Not that he would ever have given in to it—but the longing for physical realization is there, stronger than ever. He knows that there is no question of that sort of thing, but he often thinks about it and writes down his thoughts, so that the world will know him. "At evening read Platen's diaries for a long time. Compared and found much cause for gratitude. . . . The illusionary aspect of love in homoeroticism enormously strengthened. All reality leads this emotion ad absurdum. To lie in bed with the captain—how would it have been?" (January 24, 1946). "In these days much suffering desire," reads another of these brooding notes, "and pondering about its being and its goals, about erotic enthusiasm quarreling with the insight into its illusionary nature" (December 4, 1949). "The utmost beauty," it continues, "I would not want to touch it." He wrote about that all his life, but always transformed into a poem, never directly. "To write confessionally about that would destroy me— — —" Then three dashes.

### FRANZL

Munich waiter, handsome. (Zurich, Grand Hotel Dolder, June 25, 1950)

Served by the little "Munich lad." (June 29)

The little lad from Tegernsee greets me beaming, also says "Glorious evening!" and the like. What pretty eyes and teeth! What a charming voice! Didn't know that his body appealed to me. But here is something for the heart, which did not turn up last year. . . .

Asked about his name which, I believe, is Westermaier, or something similar, then about his first name, which is the main thing. What a friendly face and what a pleasant voice! . . . It would be very natural for me to call him Du. (July 3)

See little Westermaier too little. (July 6)

*Franz Westermeier, Zurich, 1950*

Erika plucked at my sleeve while I was still looking into his face and chided me inordinately. Probably should also not have extended the conversation in the hall longer, but was indifferent to looks that possibly observed the heartiness of my parting nod. He notices very well that I like him. Told Erika furthermore that the pleasure at a pretty poodle was nothing very different. This is not much more sexual either. Which she did not entirely believe. (July 7)

Reflection about my feelings for the little lad that really have much of the love for all living creatures. Do not go far in desire. Added to the appeal must be the thought that thousands would enjoy a short conversation as happiness and a distinction—of which something might be in his mind. Injustice of the choice of love. Then the association: "He who has thought most profoundly loves what is most alive." Often quoted. . . . The feeling for the youth is rather deep. Think constantly of him and try to arrange meetings that could easily become offensive. His eyes are much too pretty, his voice much too flattering, and though my desire does not go far, my joy, tenderness, infatuation are enthusiastic and form the background for the whole day. I would gladly do something nice for him, help him go to Geneva or the like. He has certainly long since noticed the pleasure that I have in him—which corresponds naturally to my wishes. . . . Erika meanwhile with K. With both joking about him and my weakness. (July 8)

So this once more, love once more, being deeply stirred by a person, the deep striving for him—for 25 years it was not there and was to happen to me once more. In the evening, for the first time, the young lad served our table. Professional adroitness, courtesy, and "virtuosity" of movements. Glance for what he lacks, his profile not worth singing about while from the front his face is infinitely winning and the discreet, polite voice tinged with the Munich dialect goes straight to my "heart." . . . His neck too fat. His physique virile. Must be about 25 years old, not a boy but a young man. Brown hair, somewhat wavy. The hands finer than I thought. Exchanged a few words with him. . . . Was very moved afterward and glad for the peace of my room. (July 9)

At night, after a short sleep, formidable empowerment and release. Let it be in your honor, fool! A certain pride at the vitality of my years, as at the whole experience, joins in. Banal activity, aggressiveness, the test of how far he might be willing to go does not belong to my life, the secret is in charge. There is also no opportunity and possibility for it. Recoil at a reality very dubious about the possibilities of happiness. . . .

Did not get a glimpse of the arouser the whole day. (July 10)

Everything saturated and overshadowed by sadness of deprivation about the arouser, pain, love, nervous expectation, hourly reverie, distraction, and suffering. Saw his face, what a strong impression it made upon me, fleetingly in the elevator going down. He wanted to have nothing to do with me. His interest in my sympathy seems to me to have died out. World fame is trifling enough for me, but it has no weight at all in comparison with a smile from him, the gaze of his eyes, the softness of his voice! Platen and others, of whom I am not the lowest, experienced that in shame, pain, and despondent feeling that yet has its pride. How slight the energy for reality along with that. Finally, possibilities could exist to give in to the emotion with a purpose, to arrange meetings. If I were to get dressed at once in the mornings and breakfast on the terrace, it could be easy for him to be on duty to serve me. Aside from the dread of powerful emotion and except for the presssure to keep my secret, it is even convenience that holds me back, — antipathy toward activity and enterprise, at so much emotion! —Three more days and I will not see the young man at all anymore, will forget his face. But not the adventure of my heart. He has been added to the gallery about which no "literary history" will report and that reaches back past Klaus H. to those in the realm of the dead, Paul, Willri, and Armin. (July 11)

A friendly dispensation would have it that the young man served us during the main part of the meal. Smiles. I pointed him out to K.: "The one from Tegernsee." Smiles and coquetry. Called him Franzl. Requested another salad. He served with courteous fastidiousness, which befitted him professionally. Asked about his prospects in Geneva. "Still no position." What I had just asked about. Lighted my cigarette. Waiting for the suitable burning of the match in the hollow of his hand. Smile. Deeply charmed again by his face, by his voice. K. found his eyes very flirtatious. Told her he had known for a very long time that I had a weakness for him. Later he disappeared. Was very happy and moved about the friendly and simple exhilaration of the relationship. . . .

When escorting K. from the meal, ran into Him. Greeted him unnecessarily with "Hello," to which he just replied seriously and unintimately with a bow. Obfuscation and new poignancy. If I only had more presence of mind. To have given him 5 francs for a skillful service today at noon would have been right. Afraid that no possibility will come to give him joy. . . . Fell asleep with thoughts of the dear one as I wake up with thoughts of him. "When we still suffered from love." You do it still at 75. Once more, once more! How entirely it is the same old thing with its worry and its enlightenment. (July 12)

At lunch the enchanter was nearby at times. Gave him 5 francs because "yesterday he served so nicely." Indescribable the charm of the smile of his eyes when saying thank you. Too heavy neck. K.'s friendliness to him for my sake. (July 13)

I do not know whether any favorable opportunity will come to say adieu to him, to wish him well. Gone. Perhaps it's already gone, and there probably will be relief—the return to work as a substitute for happiness; so must it be. It is the destiny (and the origin?) of all genius. . . .

Franz served predominantly. Quiet, friendly conversation with him about his Geneva wishes. . . . Told about our departure tomorrow. "Oh!" His incomparably dear face. Was very happy (sic venia verbo) and calmed down afterward. Feeling of consoling harmony. . . .

"He" was in the lobby. As I was escorting K. down the stairs on departing, he stood, obviously waiting, straight and tall near the elevator and wanted to say farewell. We shook hands for a long time. He: "If we don't see one another again." I knew nothing to say but: "Franz, all the best to you! You will find your way!" He was not completely unmoved. That incomparably lovely face. Then hurried to the elevator, when entering said something else about good-bye in his quiet, soft voice, whereupon I was unable to reply. "A sweet lad," to K. who said: "Well, he likes you." Happily mentioned with praise to Erika how charmingly he said adieu. Glad that at last a certain harmony lies over the whole thing. Painfully and gratefully moved. He no doubt felt my affection, secretly also what was tender about it, and was glad. He saw with what deference Beidler took leave of me in the lobby. The conquest he had made of me must be beneficial to his self-confidence, perhaps too much so. Probably nothing like it had ever happened to him. It is as good as certain that I will never see him again, also not ever hear anything about him. Farewell forever, you charming lad; late, painfully stirring dream of love! I will live a little, do a little, and die. And you will mature on your lower path and then fade away. O, incomprehensible life, that affirms itself in love. (July 14)

He was warm-hearted, he felt my love and was proud enough of it to return it to a certain degree and to feel the farewell as a farewell. At the elevator finally, he said: "Maybe we'll see one another again, Herr Mann." (I don't like the way he addressed me.) But how sorry I am that I did not have the calm to reply with something affectionate. "I hope so. I always liked seeing you." One flees. And still the parting was comforting and made me happy.

. . . great unrest and heartbreak. To K., who came over, I said frankly that I "for a time" was after the young man. Afterward took a sleeping pill and slept a bit. . . .

The thought of my "last love" fills me constantly, awakens all the undergrounds and backgrounds of my life. The first object, Armin, became a drunk after the expiration of his enchantment by puberty, and died in Africa. My first poems were about him. He lives in "T.K.," Willri in the "MM," Paul in Faust. All these passions have won a kind of immortality. The introduction to the Amphitryon essay belongs to Klaus H., who bestowed the most upon me. — Plan, with a card, to ask the one left behind for news about the success of his Geneva wishes and to tell him: "I have not forgotten you." (St. Moritz, July 16)

At table slightly humorous discussion with Erika and K. about my intention to offer my recommendation to little Westermeyer. Question of propriety and naturalness. It can be done. . . . Wrote the following to the one left behind: "Herrn Franz Westermayer, Employé du Grand Hotel Dolder, Zurich. Dear Franzl, it would please me to hear from you about whether your friend's letter to the hotel director in Geneva has been sent and whether it has perhaps already been successful. — If I myself can be of help to you with any kind of recommendation, just tell me, please. I will do it very gladly. — With friendly greetings, T.M." — A dry document of sympathy. Will he answer? And how? Of course, writing is difficult for him. And yet, how I long for something to reach me from the hand that sincerely pressed mine. (July 17)

> "Gladly, lady, I would swear
> that I kissed him on the hair,
> and should he express his pleasure
> then on the mouth too in full measure."

Remarkably, the verses from Sibylla's prayer occurred to me again only this morning. Restless sleep, unsteady nerves, emotional heart. (July 18)

If the youth in the white jacket knew how impatient I am to have a few words from him in my hands, he would hurry somewhat more. (July 20)

Why doesn't he write me that he is honored and overjoyed? Beloved dummy! (July 21)

. . . I am waiting for a word from the young lad. (July 24)

With the afternoon mail . . . — dear, simple letter from "Franzl Westermeier." That's what he calls himself, even on the envelope, since I always called him that. Was "really very glad that I thought of him" (thought of him). Has received his position in Geneva, but must stay at the Dolder until the end of the season. Says again cordial thanks for everything. — Opened and read the letter, which has small grammatical mistakes, furtively during the conversation. Was moved and happy because he was "really very glad," which I believe. (July 26)

The words remain with me "I was really very glad that you have thought of me." By the way, I like nothing more than when Erika teases me about those occurrences, conversations with him, the gift of 5 francs, etc. (July 28)

Pain about the youth there. . . .
    Erika recommends . . . a stay at the Dolder. . . . She does it in reference to me and to Franzl there. Shy about the emotional stir and fear that our reunion, if it happens at all, will be halfway or totally unsuccessful. (August 1)

Intention not to go up, and to send greetings to the youth only through Erika. Renunciation. Preferably not again. (August 2)

The last thing I needed would be to see the youth again! The temptation is nevertheless great. (August 4)

On the tennis court below, during a certain morning hour, young Argentine, already an excellent player, perfecting himself with his trainer. Dark hair, face not exactly discernible, slender, admirable build, Hermes legs. The long swing, the playful familiarity with the balls, the walking, running, leaping, occasionally over-enthusiastic prancing. Changes the way he crosses his legs, dangles them, slapping his white-shod feet together, standing up, leaving, returning, gripping the fencing with his hands. White sport togs, shorts, after the practice a sweater over his shoulders. — Deep erotic interest. Getting up from work to look. Pain, desire, worry, aimless longing. His knees. He strokes his leg—what anyone would like to do. — The pain about the one up at the Dolder has during these days . . . deepened and strengthened to a general sadness about my life and his love, all of this for the underlying reason of delusive and yet passionately asserted enthusiasm for the charm of manly youth—incomparable, surpassed by nothing in the world—my happiness and misery long since inexpressible, enthusiastic and mute—not "promesse de bonheur" but only renunciation and indeed one not definable, a wishful impossible wish. — While autographing reread the chapter "On Beauty" in "Young Joseph." Jokes about what is profoundest in me. The illusionary, cloudlike ungraspable, intangible, that is still most miserably full of enthusiasm, nonsense and oath, foundation of the practice of art—— "In your breath let my word be formed."

. . . The distant beauty does not play mornings. After lunch he was there. I could not get enough of looking, compulsive. His swings, running, walking, plunging, bouncing, raising up on his feet is wonderful. I was reading and kept getting up again for him, whose face I cannot distinguish. Pathological enthusiasm for the "divine youth." Deepest pain—because of whom? because of what? Probably I would not even recognize the handsome fellow in the dining room. When he had sat down to rest, his heavenly legs braced against the balustrade (whereby sometimes he seemed to me to lay his head on the shoulder of a female creature whom I could not make out), I closed the blinds and thought: "Dear boy, I have to rest." Closeness of the wish to die because I can no longer bear the longing for the "divine boy" (by which not necessarily this exact one is meant) . . .

The beginnings of this journey lie so far distant that I can hardly consider it one and the same. God knows, I will not forget it. The commanding question is now, whether I shall take part in the visit to the Dolder for tea to see the lovely eyes once more. It would be smarter, but also more cowardly, not to do it. But I have a bit left for the demonstration, to refuse and to send Erika with only a greeting. . . .

In the dining room Erika thought she could point out to me a young man of a fairly indifferent appearance as the tennis god. The glowworm on the palm of the hand. Illusion! Illusion! . . . Substantial shame in all I wrote and did not write. Heated up by the game, the god takes off his white jacket, tosses it casually to the ball boy. To think that I would be happy to catch it! Humility that I notice, and in which I find no pleasure. (August 6)

At lunch we identified the god with certainty as a tall young man wearing a blue sweater and with bare legs. Who slouched while sitting and was disillusion itself. (August 7)

It is time to get away. I'll keep the "images" in my heart. . . . Even a girl with beautiful eyebrows and pleasant features (at the 4-girl table nearby) belongs to them. . . .

I will never really have seen him, and now, since we are leaving, just have to forget what so delighted me in his behavior on the tennis court. Forgetting, getting over it. The last forgetting and getting over everything is death. — Deeply sad. Overfatigued by storms of emotion. (August 8)

The thought often that on this trip I lost myself much too much— in the charm of youth, in sweet faces. That really does rob self-assurance, makes you old and heavy, suffering and envying— where there is nothing to envy. (Zurich, Baur au lac, August 12)

Doubt whether I should join the visit to the Dolder in the afternoon. . . . Explained that I would not participate in the Dolder visit. (August 13)

We drive at noon to the Dolder. Wonder whether I will see the young man again?
        . . . in the dining room. Unfamiliar service. It seems that Erika, using the pretext of telephoning, had asked the young man "to say hello." He busied himself in the foyer of the dining room. . . . My eyes had searched for him the whole time, they hesitated to believe that it was he. "Why, there's Franzl!" He came over. Handshaking, joy. "Well, this is nice that we see one another again!" His charming, pretended and yet also honest facial and bodily movements at the oral repetition of "I was really very glad about your letter!" I had been glad about his good news. It had turned

bad. The position in Geneva had been valid only immediately, and he was obligated until the end of the season in the Dolder. So "he is stuck with nothing." I touched his arm sympathetically. Something else would turn up. Saw his face so precisely, the somewhat slanted brown eyes, the strong teeth, the flattering expression. The robustness of his head and body with a certain childlike tenderness of being, the way he spoke. "As I wrote to you: If I can be of help to you in any way—" Asked him to write me about how he was getting along. Tried to make my address clear to him. He could depend on finding it out at the reception desk—to which I should write it. Could not get enough of looking at him—who soon will probably be a somewhat heavy, Upper Bavarian innkeeper's son. Strong, friendly handshake in parting. — Never more to be met again. He is grateful for my affection—which produces too little practical energy. Could I not have helped him, should I not have spoken to the director, that he release him? Is my gazing, my love, only egotistical pleasure? The difficulty of doing anything for him is my excuse, and he probably does not expect a thing either. But I would write whomever anyway, if he would take my friendship seriously enough and had the adroitness of asking me to do it. — The pressure of his virile hand. His smile, his eyes. Unforgettable in any case. A love, an extreme pleasure, an affection from the bottom of my heart. And yet it is the overjoyed senses, not the "heart." Or is it? I believe little in the word "heart," and yet there exists what it means. (August 15)

Young conductor, handsome, with splendid teeth! . . . My thoughts return a lot, tormented, ashamed, amazed, to the adventures and images of the long journey, my constantly being smitten by all kinds of youths. (New York, August 22)

Aching and sad. Memories smolder of glimpsed and beloved youth. O Dio! O Dio! O Dio! Sore heart. In vostro fiato son le mie parole. I can't get that out of my mind—eyes, Hermes legs, la forza d'un bel viso. . . . May the young man from the Dolder perhaps write me just once! . . . Suffered too much, gaped too much, and was delighted. Let myself be played for a fool too much by the world. Would all better not have been? It was and the handshake, the "I really was very glad" remains a painful treasure. —— Why am I writing all this? Just to destroy it in time before my death? Or do I wish that the world should know me? (Chicago, August 25)

But without doubt, perhaps out of the feeling of a gate closing, my enthusiasm for young masculinity has grown turbulently in recent time, my eye enormously alert and painfully hungry for all of that sort of beauty, my nonsusceptibility for it incomprehensible to the point of contempt. That my capability of admiring the "divine youth" far exceeds that of anything feminine and arouses a longing comparable to nothing in the world is an axiom for me. Hints of the ideal suffice for delight. (On the train to Los Angeles, August 28)

Read in Platen's ghazels and sonnets and found the spectral love verses:

"To you I am like body to mind, like mind to body.
To you like woman to man, like man to woman.
Whom could you else love, since away from your lips
With eternal kisses I drive death away from you?"
Wonderful. (Pacific Palisades, August 31)

Travel bag from Zurich with laundry and papers, among them Franzl Westermeier's letter, which I value exactly as much as the pencil parings of W.T.'s. Nothing has changed in this regard. (Sepember 15)

Come to realize that in all these weeks I have hoped to find with every mail a letter from the youth of the Dolder Hotel. Tenacious silliness. But look how that lasts. (October 28)

Want to note that really until today I look through every new mail to see whether perhaps a missive from little Westermeier is present. Completely or almost completely nonsensical. After all, it has been just three months since I last saw his somewhat insincere eyes. (November 8)

## THE EROTICISM OF MICHELANGELO

"I hope the young man was nice, considerate, and had a concept of the honor that was bestowed upon him by the affection of the mighty one." That is aimed officially at Tommaso Cavalieri, but surreptitiously at "Franzl," who is immediately transformed into an essay. The illusion of love is fundamental to the practice of all art: "In your breath my word takes form" (August 6, 1950). "Nel vostro fiato son le mie parole." Love is an affliction and sweet poison; it is cursed and is yet the foundation and inspiring genius of creativity. Thomas Mann is reflected in Michelangelo. As with the latter, also with him what is sensual has gone astray into the blatantly unworthy and led deeply below his own intellectual and human rank—where cruelly the element of humiliation may goad longing terribly. The "O Dio, O Dio, O Dio!" is the pendant to the incomprehensible "My God!" of the Ehrenberg time. When Thomas Mann asserts that for Michelangelo God was in the lover and not in the beloved, then he puts a formulation from *Death in Venice* coquettishly into the mouth of the Renaissance artist. "But how can it be that I lost myself?"—that is again Michelangelo, though with a side look at his own self. The beguiled man speaks entirely about himself when he calls it "deeply moving,"

> this hopeless slavishness of the mighty man, far past the decent limits of age, to the bewitching human features, whether of the dazzling youth or the resplendent woman—deeply moving the immortal susceptibility for "La forza d'un bel viso," that he praises as the only joy that the world gives him, and that, under curses, under ever-recurring accusations of the love god's cruelty, he calls a grace that carries him alive to the blessed—nothing that would so delight him!

The essay was written in St. Moritz with great devotion at the end of July, right after the stay at the Dolder. Immediately, when chance thrust the writings of Michelangelo into his hands, he recognizes in them his experience with Franz Westermeier again. "There is always talk of the countenance and of the 'Forza d'un bel viso,' to which one surrenders. How completely my emotion came into being from the glimpse of his face" (July 19, 1950). His figure had hardly bothered him. "It must be lovely to sleep with him, but I imagine nothing particular about his limbs and would be tender with them for the sake of his eyes—so, almost because of something 'spiritual.'"

When the "love essay" is finished, he is disappointed, of course. "And yet I carried out the work with so much ardor" (July 31, 1950). Should what already pained Tonio Kröger still be valid, that a warm, deep emotion would be artistically unusable? The essay contains a bit of wit only through camouflage and ambiguity. As a confession alone it would have been decisively too emotional. "What a wealth of passion is here, monument to an enormous and tormented vitality turned into words!" Great words, so grotesquely wrong in dimension as soon as one thinks of the object of this passion, the simple Franzl, whose highest flight of fancy was the dried-up flowery phrase: "I really was *very* pleased." But love is revered even when it is ridiculous. To say the banal so shockingly that mockery dies: Only the very old Thomas Mann had the candor for that. This one time the unfiltered report in the diary is more powerful with its sentimentalities, its incomplete sentences, its dashes than the artistic transformation that followed it.

## MANN AS MADAME

As Rosalie von Tümmler Thomas Mann falls in love with Ken Keaton, as Madame Houpflé with Felix Krull, as Sibylla with Gregorius. The pattern is in the meantime sufficiently well known. The depictions of each particular young man turn out stereotypically.

Not exactly marked by intellect is the harmlessly friendly youthful face of the American Ken Keaton, whom the aging Rosalie has fallen for when she has entered menopause (in the tale *The Black Swan*). Ken's arsenal consists of healthy teeth, long legs, narrow hips, and, since he goes around shockingly wearing sleeveless T-shirts, appealing arms on which Rosalie's eyes linger again and again for self-forgetful seconds "with an expression of deep, sensual sadness." Like the aged Mann and his desirous stare at the tennis player, the good woman was "elated about the enduring ability of her soul to blossom in sweet sorrow." As in his case, also in hers, in the form of her daughter Anna, good sense speaks a different language, wants to avoid the ordeal, demands the removal of the charmer, and mentions that observed in the light he is actually quite ordinary. But the smitten woman keeps on, as Mann each time did, to the extent of decisive kisses and the promise to come to his room the next day. The love ends fatally, like that of Aschenbach, that of Friedemann. Cancer of the uterus, whose symptoms she had read as the return of menstruation and as rejuvenation, brings a quick end to her life.

By hiding behind Madame Houpflé, the author wife of the toilet-bowl manufacturer with the artistic name of Diana Philibert, Thomas Mann found a chance to give freer rein to his desires. No one had

become aware of "the archpederasty ('gayness') of the scene" except
for his clever daughter, who had been initiated into much. He had
written the Houpflé chapter at the end of March, beginning of April,
in 1951 and at the time looked occasionally at his Franzl diary pages.
He goes more out of himself than usual. "We women," he has Diane
rhapsodize, "may say of happiness, that our curvaciousness pleases
you so much. But what is divine, the master work of creation, statue
of beauty, that is all of you, you young, very young men with your
Hermes legs." She knows even more, which actually only he can
know. "C'est un amour tragique, irraisonable, not acknowledged, not
practical, not for life, not for marriage." Madame Mann wants beauty
dumb. "The mind is greedy for rapture that is not mind, the vitality
of beauty dans sa stupidité, in love, oh, he is in love with beauty and
with the divinely dumb to the point of folly and final self-denial and
self-negation; he kneels before it, he worships it in the voluptuousness of self-renunciation, self-abasement, and it intoxicates him to be
debased before it." Nothing is worse therefore than to sleep with a
thinker—"I loathe the complete man with a complete beard, his chest
complete with wool, the mature and now totally grand man—affreux,
horrible! I am grand myself—this very thing I would perceive as per-
verse: de me coucher avec un homme penseur." She falls into poetry,
finishes overblown alexandrines—we write the following in the verse
form that is appropriate, so that what is hymnically churned up is
quite clear. Thomas Mann rhapsodizes. As an aesthete he knows since
the disaster of his schoolboy poems that that cannot go well. He must
resort to a ruse. A trick makes romanticizing possible: He masks himself as the author of light literature Diane Philibert in order, like a
high school boy, to be sentimental with all his heart:

> Le fleur de ta jeunesse
> remplit mon coeur âgé d'une éternelle ivresse.
> Nor does elation end; for with it I will perish,
> but ever will my soul you beauties always cherish.
> You too, bien aimé, you age into the grave
> too soon, but that is comfort and will my heart lave:
> you will forever be, brief beauty's happiness,
> blissful volitility, eternal brief caress!

> After years and years, when—le temps t'a détruit,
> ce coeur te gardera dans ton moment bénit.
> Yes, when the grave us covers, me and thee, too, Armand,

tu vivras dans mes vers et dans mes beaux romans,
that by those lips of yours—betrayed will never be!—
will everyone be kissed. Adieu, adieu, chéri.

What was "unnatural"" was actually something quite natural, Thomas
Mann writes about his incest novel *The Holy Sinner*, "since one should
not be surprised when same loves same." Sibylla is of the opinion
that a girl who has belonged only to her own brother has not become
a woman in the usual sense but is still a virgin and can wear the
maiden's wreath with right. Homoeroticism is similarly pure. Yet
Thomas Mann does not recognize himself so much in the incest of
siblings as in incest with the mother. He "is" Sibylla, in love with
Gregorius. During his Franzl time it was not by chance that a portion
of the prayer occurred to him that Sibylla directs with pleading ardor
to the Holy Virgin and Mother. "Gladly, Lady, it is fair that I kissed
him on the hair, and when he replied, then on the mouth I tried."
That is put in verse in the diary, which is why we will also do likewise in the continuation. Thomas Mann is speaking behind the scene,
while he shows the spectators a Sibylla puppet:

> Still, for the boy too woe is me,
> That him so very young I see,
> and am myself so up in years,
> a woman, skilled with love and fears,
> though, thank God, still in command
> and mistress of the entire land.
> He by my grace may flattered be,
> he does not know of sins by me.
> But will he love me too so kind
> With heart and mind?

He lets the couple be very happy for a while, but the penance follows,
unsparingly; Gregorius spends seventeen years on the bare rock.


## SIN AND GRACE

Thomas Mann felt himself emphatically to be a Protestant Christian.
The playful Gregorius novel, even though it smiled at the legend par-
odistically, preserved "with pure earnestness its religious core, its

Christianity, the idea of sin and grace." Vis-à-vis grace, he wrote to Ida Herz, he knew no irony.

Sinfulness consists in becoming addicted to sex. "Our body is made of sin." Atonement is the work of life. "Saintliness, gained through the origin of sibling intercourse and incest with the mother, atoned for on the rock"—that's how the summary of the novel of the holy sinner reads. Thomas Mann sits with Gregorius on the rock. However, he does not purr himself into a moss-covered marmot there, rather he works. He puts the last chapter of *The Holy Sinner* down on paper shortly after the Franzl trip of 1950. Writing it serves as astonement. "For the production of a life is seldom good—even when it seemed playful, skeptical, artistic, and humoristic—so entire, from beginning to the approaching end, even this frightened need to make amends, sprung from purification and justification, as my personal and so little exemplary attempt to practice art." All courage and every bold enterprise, thus his Gregorius seconds him, "comes from the knowledge of our sin, comes from the ardent longing for the justification of our life, and afterward to settle before God our blame for sin a little."

But that alone could not help. What comes additionally and in Thomas Mann's later days, newly revived, is the thought of grace. It is not repentance that frees from guilt, but God's willing grace alone; a life ready to repent is the result, not the cause, of pardon. The old Thomas Mann hopes as a sinner that he is safe in grace. "It is very possible that love can come out of evil and out of disorder something well ordered." Gregorius, as a priest and a pope, proclaims a charitable absolution: "One is seldom entirely wrong who traces what is sinful to what is good; but God looks upon the good deed mercifully, even if it has its roots in the carnal. Absolve te." Rosalie too is pardoned and dies in agreement with the "deception" that love perpetrated on her. "After all, death is a great remedy for life, and when it took for me the shape of resurrection and love's pleasure, that was not a lie but only goodness and mercy." Mann's Michelangelo calls love with all its torment a grace, which carries him still living to the blessed. With deep emotion he painted handsome youths like the Adam on the ceiling of the Sistine Chapel, whom God the Father, gently concerned, releases from his finger.

But he also painted the damned, voluptuous in flesh, which impressed Thomas Mann in his young years in Rome. "The Last Judg-

ment affected me deeply as the apotheosis of my thoroughly pessimistic, moralistic, and antihedonistic mood." On the right side of the
wall the downward movement, the sinful bodies that descend to Hell,
the rising movement into Heaven on the left: Where would his place
be? Did Thomas Mann fear the Judgment? The "Apocalipsis cum fig-
uris" of his Adrian Leverkühn also paints in musical tones the
damned man who stops the horrible descent "by covering one eye
with his hand and with the other stares horrified into the eternal ca-
lamity"—while not far away from him grace pulls two sinful souls
from the Fall upward to salvation.

Grace—that is said with solace and ease, as though Thomas Mann
had granted a comfortable wishful fantasy. But he did not make it so
easy for himself. He also took damnation into account. His Adrian
Leverkühn tosses his accomplishments onto the scales, everything
that he had tenaciously finished, but he knows that the works do not
redeem, and that makes him despair so that, in the logic of the Faust
novel, he is "fetched by the Devil."

Thomas Mann, too, saw no other way than to atone for his sins
with inexhaustible work. But he knew precisely that theology had
repudiated this path,

> and presumably it was right in doing so. One would probably
> look back on the work done . . . with greater satisfaction. But in
> reality the process of atonement for sin, the—as it seems to me,
> religious—urge for atonement for life through work continues in
> the work itself,

so that every new work must come up to the previous one, the sin
always runs along with the atonement, the stone of Sisyphus always
rolls downhill again, and at the end there would be pure desperation
were it not for grace, "this sovereign power whose nearness sometimes was felt with amazement in life and on which alone it rests to
settle the remnants of guilt of sin as paid off."

One must admit that the work of Sisyphus in atoning for sin was a
bit sweetened for him in this life. The work is not only tooth-gnashing
accomplishment but the imaginary fulfillment of dreams. The writer
may advance to a royal highness or dip into lips, just as he will. Writing is not only penance but also cunning pleasure. The work is
blessed and damned at the same time. Thomas Mann wanted to be
perfect and yet at the same time felt spurned. "For each one seeks to

torso and let himself fall into the water. He did not raise his head again; not even once did he move his legs again, which lay on the shore.

At the splash of the water the crickets were silent for a moment. Now their chirping began again, the park rustled softly, and down through the long avenue muffled laughter sounded.

When his life draws to an end, Thomas Buddenbrook reads Schopenhauer's essay "On Death" and is intoxicated by it:

Death was a happiness, so deep that it could be measured entirely . . . only in blessed moments. It was the return from an unspeakably painful labyrinth, the correction of a grave mistake, liberation from the most hostile bonds and restraints—it made up for a regrettable misadventure.

Dying meant "returning home and freedom," the reader believes. But real death is not at all homelike, but shabby and dirty. Exhausted and tormented, Thomas Buddenbrooks comes from the dentist when a never-known force prostrates him:

It was exactly as though his brain were seized and swung around by an irresistible power with increasing, terribly increasing speed in large, smaller, and ever smaller concentric circles and finally smashed with an immeasurable, brutal, and merciless vehemence against the rock-hard center of those circles. . . . He completed a half turn and slapped forward onto the wet pavement with outstretched arms.

Since the street sloped steeply, his torso was quite a bit lower than his feet. He had fallen onto his face, under which a pool of blood began to spread out immediately. His hat rolled a fair piece down the street. His fur coat was splattered with dirt and melted snow water. His hands, in their white kid gloves, lay stretched out in a puddle.

So he lay and remained lying until a few people had come along and turned him over.

That is not exactly festive. The passage shows that de-individuation does not normally have the form of a gentle dissolution but of shattering vehemence. To death, the expectations of people are a matter of complete indifference. "All his life," his lovely wife complains at the sight of his passing, "no one was allowed to see a speck of dust on him. It is a mockery and an ignominy that the end had to be like this . . . !"

Someone who does not cling to life has a better chance for a more acceptable exit. Hanno Buddenbrook dies at fifteen from typhus. That seems senseless. But for Hanno, death is not the absurd strangler but welcome escape from torment. The feverishly ill boy is on a "strange, hot path" on which he wanders forward to death and which "leads into shade, coolness, and peace."

Cholera, from which Gustav Aschenbach dies, is an ugly disease. But lust is greater than fear. He remains while all the others depart. The death in Venice is at the same time a Liebestod. The metaphor of the one who longs for death is the ocean.

> He loved the ocean for profound reasons: out of the longing for peace of the hard-working artist who desires to find shelter from the demanding multiplicity of phenomena on the breast of what is simple, prodigious; out of a forbidden propensity for the limb-less, the immense, the eternal, for the void, which was diametrically opposed to his task and for that reason seductive.

The eternal, the void, death and love—they are all only one thing; they put an end to multiplicity and with that to the confinement of the individual in the cage of his ego. The narrator continues:

> The longing of the one who endeavors for excellence is to rest on perfection; and is not the void a form of perfection? But now as he dreamed so deeply into the emptiness, suddenly the horizontal feature of the edge of the shore was overlapped by a human form, and when he had recovered his gaze from the limitlessness, and concentrated it; it was the handsome boy who, coming from the left, passed by him on the sand.

Aschenbach will leave this world with his eyes on the handsome boy on the edge of the ocean. The boy is Hermes Psychagogos, the conductor of souls who leads the dead into the underworld. "But to him it was as though the pale and charming Psychagog out there smiled at him, beckoned to him, as though, lifting his hand from his hip, he were pointing beyond, hovering ahead into the promising enormity."

In what relationship do the beauty and the hideousness of death stand? Only art makes the personification of death as a skeleton beautiful. But Thomas Mann has not forgotten the hideousness. In the

gramophone chapter of *The Magic Mountain* Hans Castorp listens to
Verdi's *Aida*. Here, too, a Liebestod is involved. In the dungeon Ra-
dames again finds his beloved Aida, who has come to share his fate
with him in the grave. Was that not terrible? But Hans Castorp nevertheless enjoys

> the vanquishing ideality of music, of art, of the human mind, the
> lofty and irrefutable palliation that allows it to flourish with the
> common hideousness of real things. One had merely to imagine
> what happened here, taken soberly! Two people buried alive,
> their lungs full of marsh gas, would perish with one another, or
> even worse, one after the other, from the pangs of hunger, and
> then decay would begin its unspeakable work on their bodies
> until two skeletons lay under the vault, to each of which it would
> be completely indifferent and unfeeling whether it lay alone or
> two together. That was the real and objective side of things—a
> side and matter apart that was not considered at all in the pres-
> ence of the idealism of the heart, that was most triumphally put
> in the shade by the spirit of beauty and by music. For Radames's
> and Aida's operatic emotions, what they faced objectively, did
> not exist. Their voices swung in unison up to the blessed octave
> hold, assuring that now the heavens would open and from their
> longing would shine the light of eternity.

The passage is epoch-making. That art embellishes is no argument
against it, as though one would in the final analysis have to persuade
it to repress its essence. Embellishment is, rather, its task. It is there to
make what is ghastly bearable. It is civilized to adorn the grimace of
death.

So Thomas Mann knows what he is doing when, in quiet regard at
the horrible that is thus passed by, he presents one of the most comforting deaths that he ever conceived. There is no cheap deception
involved here. We want to cast our gaze at Mont-kaw, Joseph's predecessor in the house of Potiphar, to whom a longed-for death is
granted. The dying of the caretaker is, of course, slow and painful,
but it is accompanied by the words of a handsome boy and is thereby
quite extraordinarily consoling:

> Joseph's right hand lay on the pale hands of the dying man and
> with his left he steadied his thigh. "Peace be with you!" he said.

"Rest blessedly, my father, into night! See, I keep watch and take care of your limbs while you must pass onward to the path of consolation completely without care and need worry about nothing anymore; just think in good cheer of nothing anymore! . . . It's over with toil and trouble and anything onerous. No more misery of body, no urge to retch, no frightening cramps. No disgusting physic, or burning compresses, no bloodsucking leeches on the nape of your neck. The dungeon pit of your infirmity opens up. You wander out and stroll hale and free along the paths of consolation that lead with every step deeper into what is solacing. For at first you pass through grounds that you know already, those that every evening swept you up by the intercession of my blessing, and some heaviness and encumbrance of breath is with you without your really knowing it from your body, which I hold here with my hands. But soon—you will be unaware of the step that takes you across—meadows of perfect ease will receive you, where, not even from the distance and most unconsciously, any distress from here will hang on you and pull you more, and at once you are likewise free of any worry and danger of doubt about how it should be and should seem and what should become of you, and you will be amazed at how you may ever have been plagued with such concerns, for everything is as it is, and behaves in the most natural way, the most correct, and the best, in the most fortunate agreement with itself and with you, who shall be Mont-kaw into all eternity. For what is, is, and what was, will be. . . . So farewell, my father and master. In the light and in ease we will see one another again."

## TIME RUNS OUT

"You do not die until you agree to." Actually, Thomas Mann wanted to die at seventy. He drew up his will in time (June 13, 1944). But eighty, too, is a proper age, after all; this is agreed with by the psalmist, whom the pastor will read at the funeral: "The days of our years are threescore years and ten; and if by reason of strength they be fourscore years . . ." (Ps. 90:10). The writer had always loved round numbers, always measured time, always marked the days and feast days in his diary, Good Friday, Easter, Pentecost, and Christmas, the

Sundays, beginnings of months, the ends of years. "Middle of the month. Time, time!— Feelings about desire and death" (February 15, 1949). Death would come in its time; it would, in any case, be the right one.

He knows it has not yet come that far. "Often I've had enough, but I'm too healthy for death wishes not to be funny." But he is already waiting. "Feeling of dissolution, of helplessness, of decline and of ruin shocks my nervous condition more and more—not of death, unfortunately, since my physical condition endures" (May 17, 1952). He feels he has lived too long. "Approaching 70 Wagner wrote his final work, the Parsifal, and died not long afterward. At about the same age I wrote my work of last significance, the Faustus, a final work in every sense, but kept on living. . . . What I now lead is an afterlife that struggles in vain for sustenance" (July 6, 1953). With curiosity he observes what is approaching him. "Want anyway in these pages to follow the dark development further." He feels neither longing nor panic. "I will live a little longer, do a little more, and die" (July 14, 1950). He is glad when guests leave—"the longing to be alone aims in the end at the quiet in the grave" (July 27, 1953). He expects the end. "When will it catch up with me—still before my birthday? or soon afterward?" (April 25, 1955). His friends die one after the other. "And when will I" (April 22, 1955). He has a presentiment that it is not far away. "Alarming feeling of a solemn dissolution of my life" (June 15, 1955). "The torments of these last weeks were great," he writes on June 20, 1955, alluding to Wallenstein's words on the evening before his death. People were suspiciously nice to him, he remarks in a memorial for Ernst Penzoldt, so there had to be some concern about him.

"One thus lives one's day that already comfortingly begins to redden in the west," he had written to Erich von Kahler a year before his death, "and wishes for those who are to accompany him on the drawn-out passage that it all be tolerable." Then in the hospital he reads Alfred Einstein's Mozart biography and with heavy underlining marks the place where Mozart calls death the "true, best friend of mankind," whose image "does not only not have anything frightening anymore for me, but really something more soothing and comforting."

*Media vita in morte sumus.* He always lived surrounded by death. "Not a day since I have been aware, have I not thought of death and the riddle." He looked into his grave, it says of Hans Castorp, when he saw his bones on his X ray, "and for the first time in his life he understood that he would die." Decay would perform its unspeakable work on him, too. That is sad, but—we have already heard about it—also comforting, since only transitoriness gives life its value, dignity, and interest. "Where there is no transitoriness, no beginning and end, birth and death, there is no time—and timelessness is void at a standstill." Already as Potiphar's wife Thomas Mann had taken the opportunity to defend beauty against Joseph's skeleton argument, that the hair would fall out pitifully, the teeth too, the eyes would be only a jelly made of blood and water, and all the remainder destined to shrink and waste away. "For far from the transitoriness of matter," says the Egyptian beauty, "being one reason less to admire form, it is even one reason more, because it mixes an emotion into our admiration that is lacking in what we devote to the materially constant beauty made of bronze and stone."

With his gaze on death, on the eve of his seventy-seventh birthday, the diaries written up to that time are sealed. "Daily notes from 33–51. Without literary value, but not to be opened by anybody before 20 years after my death" (June 5, 1952). With the sigh "O basically wonderful life!" the next day begins. Katia's sixty-ninth is also the occasion for an accounting. "Talked about the course of life, which was in no way flitting so that you would have had to ask: Where did the years go? Is a long, slow time, rich in experience and also in accomplishment since our marriage and the Tölz days" (July 24, 1952).

He had a small grandson, Frido, who enchanted him. He went into *Faustus* as Nepomuk Schneidewein ("Echo"). When Frido/Echo had enough of something or wanted to be comforted when it was all gone, then he said, "Had it!" Thomas Mann found that excellent. "When I die, I'll also say 'had it!'"

"Curious, curious," said the old Johann Buddenbrook, when it came time to die. Thomas Mann will imitate that, too." "Curious, curious. I said that early on and will say it at the end" (October 9, 1954). "Curious, curious. Something remarkable, this life" (June 30, 1955).


## CONSECRATION AND TRANSFIGURATION

"Death is a great force." In its presence you walk on tiptoe. On the other hand there are people who are so ordinary, "of such an immortal ordinariness and competence that you cannot think they could

ever die, could ever become part of the consecration and transfiguration of death." That is aimed at the blond and blue-eyed ones, at
those unfortunately so seductive. Their punishment is to have to live
eternally in what is banal. It was Paul Ehrenberg who once touched
off these thoughts. "P. is so common that you cannot think he could
ever die. He is not worth the consecration and transfiguration of death."
Hardly that of sleep, a mean parenthesis adds, for sleep and death are
siblings. "You're not dying, after all," Thomas Buddenbrook had
jested, when Christian had complainingly gone into details to him
about his hypochrondria. For not Christian but Thomas had been
worth the consecration and transfiguration. The pastor, a wicked caricature, has no notion of it. The religious signal is set by the idler
brother, Christian, of all people. From his viewpont the death of
Thomas is a victory, a macabre victory over him, a victory in the competition of brothers about who suffered more. Death had taken
Thomas, the one adept in life, and ignored the constantly sick Christian, incapacitated for life. He had "treated Thomas with distinction
and vindicated him, accepted and embraced him, made him dignified
and authoritatively gotten him general, timorous interest," while he
had disdained Christian and would only continue

> to tease him with fifty antics and chicaneries that no one would
> respect. Thomas Buddenbrook had never impressed his brother
> more than at this hour. The success is decisive. Only death brings
> to us the respect of others for our sufferings, and even the most
> piteous sufferings become venerable through it. You were proved
> right, I bow, thought Christian, and with a quick, clumsy move-
> ment he fell to his knees and kissed the cold hand on the quilt.

Without an opponent life has no honor. Anyone who loves life with
care, says Thomas Mann with Heinrich von Kleist, is morally already
dead, "for his greatest mortal strength to be able to sacrifice it decays
because he cherishes it." In a more moderate tone the narrator of the
Joseph novel also expresses his reverence for the end. "Dying means,
of course, losing time and traveling out of it, but in return it means
winning eternity and omnipresence, so life, essentially." Thomas
Mann writes in a letter that we experience death only through the
dying of others. "It is a bitter, enigmatic experience that deeply disturbs all feeling and all spirit—and yet perhaps the experience that
we are actually born to receive."

## ETERNAL LIFE

Nature is obligated, said Goethe to Eckermann, to assign him another form of being when the present one is not able to sustain his spirit any further. "Man should believe in immortality; he has a right to it; it is in accord with his nature." Death and judgment, Heaven and Hell: final things are present in Thomas Mann, even though in a more or less secularized form. Even if they were fictions, what does it matter? They would be cultural concepts of what was otherwise banned from consciousness. "The natural inability to believe in death," ponders the Joseph novel, "is the negation of a negation and deserves an affirming sign. It is defenseless faith, for all faith is defenseless and intense with defenselessness." When somber truth is disconsolate and disconsolate things follow from it, then it is fortifying to cultivate a helpful fiction. Harsh forthrightness that does away with immortality is honorable, but it is helpless after its easy victory and is at loose ends.

Nowhere in Thomas Mann is pronounced atheism to be found. He most certainly had hope for eternal life. By that, he does not mean something obscure. If in the Beyond one could not accomplish something better, he scoffs after a séance, than letting a violin hover and whimper and tying a knot in a handkerchief, then he would gladly forgo a further life after death. He had a different, fairly exact concept about it. Joseph says to Mont-kaw, "We will see one another in light and in ease." In the Beyond, Thomas Mann also wants to see those once loved, his father and his mother, Armin Martens and Willri Timpe, Mary Smith and Cynthia, his brother Heinrich and godfather Bertram, Katia *and* Paul, and indeed without the confines of earth that otherwise spoil any happiness with hurtful things. Reunion after death has the last word in three of Mann's eight novels, in *Buddenbrooks*, in *The Beloved Returns*, and in *The Holy Sinner*, and it is not far away when Gustav von Aschenbach makes himself up into a promising monster to promenade there with the divine boy. Clemens the Mad asks his listeners to include him in their prayer, "so that all of us one day, those of whom I spoke, will see one another in Paradise" (*The Holy Sinner*). "What a friendly moment it will be one day when we awaken together again" (*The Beloved Returns*). "There will be a reunion," says Friederike Buddenbrook. Tony is dubious. "A reunion. . . . If it were only so." Sesemi Weichbrodt has the last word:

"It is so!" she says with all her might and looks at everyone in defiance (*Buddenbrooks*).

Under the protection of literature Thomas Mann could say what enlightened discourse forbade outside of it. Expressed on its own account, what is religious is embarrassing. When Tony Buddenbrook begins to say a loud prayer, all who are there quail with embarrassment. This shame is the mask behind which Thomas Mann hides piety. All religious directives seem to him to be assaults. He wants to trap God in the small chest of language, whereas He is nevertheless beyond all understanding. Every spoken word remains under the constraint of *superbia*. Only he who says nothing can himself hear. One can speak of God as little as of Hell, "because what is intrinsic does not correspond to words." God is an ironist before whom absolutely every statement made by men is eternally ridiculous. Particularly when the highest is concerned, anything edifying must be avoided.

Shame has its reasons. The name of God was much too frequently misused in speech as a cloak for all kinds of interests. The writer cannot use the worn-out religious vocabulary for the time being. His wordlessness is not a sad silence but the opportunity for message. The discreet silence in regard to the eternal is not a blind alley and the suppression of the religious but the fallow gound that the plundered land needs in order to recover. It is taciturnity with an open heart. In it, not in the merely rhetorical excess of what is immanent, is transcendence, which eager Christian critics missed in Thomas Mann.

Only very seldom does Thomas Mann overcome his shame. "We all go thence as hopeless debtors of the infinite," he states "with wet eyes" in an address for the seventieth birthday of his wife.

Then when the shadows fall and I am riddled with angst about all the failures and things not done and actions not taken, then Heaven grant that she is sitting beside me, hand in hand with me, and comforts me as she has comforted me and lifted me up in the crises of life and work, and says to me: "Let it be; you were very good; you did what you could."

The dark angel, who unclasps hands and sends each of us into the solitude of nonexistence—does he really, in each instance, have the commandment and the power to do that? I don't believe it. These very days of her birthday celebration and the gratitude, admiration, respect that is pouring in to her during them, allow me devotedly to doubt the angel's power. What has once been has being still. We will remain together hand in hand, even in the realm of the shades. If any kind of afterlife is granted me, the essence of my life, my work, then she will live with me, at my side.

One doesn't really say something like that. But things go well again. "Even the 'dark angel' did not disturb the mood entirely" (July 25, 1953). At most, as an exception, does one say something like that. Angels require much tact. They can't endure it when they are put on display. What his brother Heinrich surprisingly writes in his old age may also be valid for Thomas: Not the lack of faith but tactfulness made it necessary to leave the existence of God up to others. To assert it or to deny it, both are ironically contradictory, for where is the competency? A human being—about God? "For want of percepti- bility, personal need decides." Must one know whether and how God leads? "But no, conscience, reason, are enough of God. It may always remain unknown where He abides, if not in us." The belief of the skeptic always conceals the same "bold resignation to not knowing, along with the inner certainty in spite of everythng."


## REAL DYING


Best to die like Goethe! "Nature outwitted him lovingly, so to speak. He had suffered, he sank comfortably into the corner of his stuffed chair to rest, to nap, and was gone." Goethe died in an easy chair. For the sake of emulation, that may have been Mann's wish, too. When he was temporarily better in the Zurich Canton Hospital, he could leave his bed for a short time. The very last sentences in his diary, written two weeks before his death, concern the chair. "Leave me in doubt about how long this existence will last. Slowly it will become clear. Shall sit some in the chair today. — Digestive concerns and nuisances" (July 29, 1955).

During the last two weeks he was unable to make diary entries in which there could be things otherwise kept to himself, so that we do not know what Thomas Mann thought beyond the official public statements. His daily awareness probably did not anticipate death. He was fooled somewhat; on the order of Katia they kept silent about the thrombosis in his leg, spoke about phlebitis, and he had readily believed it. That was something that had been treated in 1946. Katia wrote at the time to Klaus Mann that lung cancer was involved, unfortunately. "But the patient absolutely does not *know* it, and if he ever had the suspicion, which I certainly believe, then he has repressed it utterly and accepts completely the version offered him of a harmless lung abscess. We maintain that *inflexibly* as far as the world is concerned, because it would otherwise certainly get back to him, after all, and because it is absolutely unnecessary that he be considered doomed."

He finally knew the power of the mind. He chatted with a congenial lady doctor from Russia on March 14, 1944, about the question of whether one should leave a person sick with cancer in the dark. As a consequence of his honesty, he notes: "Often psychic collapse prematurely." In his Theodor Storm essay he had praised the doctors who beneficently pronounced Storm's stomach cancer a misdiagnosis. It had turned out that the writer reacted to the truth with melancholy, whereas the lie gave him creative euphoria and *The White Horse*.

The sickness unto death began on July 18, 1955, in Dutch Nordwijk with an aching pain in his left leg. It came from a thrombosis. Thomas Mann was flown to Zurich on a stretcher. The attending physicians came to an agreement with Katia on "phlebitis" and announced a six-week period of treatment. But there is a deeper knowledge than that of broad daylight. Consciousness endeavored to believe in the six weeks. But deeper knowledge registered what was not confided at all, those things falling out of the scope of the condition of all previous illnesses (July 22, 1955). The sick man wrote to Erich von Kahler jokingly: "The leg was actually twice as thick as the other; but who gets the idea of comparing the thickness of his legs!" Erika Mann, who was with him during the last days, mentions his noticeable lack of interest in everything that was happening "outside," as though that no longer concerned him. His gaze, "which was suddenly *blue*—a large and blue look from his gray-green eyes," asked about the significance of this illness and whether he would leave the hospital alive. Things seemed to be improving. But "the questioning look from his gray-green eyes seemed always to be larger and bluer."

Death arrived unexpected by the doctors. The treatment of the thrombosis had been successful. The patient seemed to be improving when, after an attack of weakness on August 11, a severe collapse suddenly took place on August 12, for which medical science had no explanation. On the same evening, at eight o'clock, Thomas Mann died with Katia at his side. The expression on his face changed with his passing. "It was his 'music face,'" Erika reported, "that he turned to my mother, the face of one who listens in a simultaneously absorbed and deeply attentive way to the most trusted and beloved."

Only a partial autopsy could clarify the cause of death: An aneurysm in the lower abdominal artery, a sudden massive loss of blood, and a circulatory collapse. Death had outfoxed the physicians. It came from behind, but softly and painlessly, as a compliant star had once augered.

## WHISPERS OF THE DEAD

Jacob did not want to be buried in Egypt, in spite of the highly developed art of mummification. Also he wanted to rest not on the road by Rachel but in a family burial site beside Lea, the mother of the six, and with his forefathers. But Thomas Mann had to give up the family grave. Politics had intervened. Even in death he remained an exile. He had informed his nephew Siegmund Mann in 1937 that he did not want to lie in Lübeck, and his agreement ahead of time declares that any other qualified person could be buried in the family vault at the Burgfriedhof. So today he rests in a comparatively traditionless place, in the beautiful cemetery of his last place of residence, in Kilchberg, with a view of Lake Zurich and blue mountains.

He did not want a cremation. "It may hurt.'" He had wished to have a quiet but distinguished Protestant Christian funeral, and that is what happened. He was spared the interment fate of Schiller, "a completely scandalous story," as he then explains at the beginning of his Schiller essay of 1955: A cheaply carpentered coffin was borne at midnight to the old cemetery in Weimar into the interior of the Kassengewölbe, the mausoleum for prominent indigents, which had a trapdoor. The trapdoor's rusty hinges creaked when it was opened. "The coffin was laid on ropes and lowered into the depths until it hit bottom, any kind of bottom, among other caskets or on top of them. Over the decaying dark into which it had sunk down, the lid closed." Not a word from the mouth of a pastor or a friend, no wreaths, no laurel. Twenty years later the meanwhile awakened piety had great difficulty in picking out the right skull and the pertinent bones out of the tangled mass of destruction.

Still, there were farcical things also in Kilchberg. At night numerous ribbons were cut off of the wreaths, by opponents, ruffians, or collectors. The Cold War pursued Thomas Mann into the grave. The wreaths from the GDR would not fit through the low door of the ancient Kilchberg Cemetery chapel. Stephan Hermlin suggested that the ceremonial wagon wheels be squeezed together a bit to take them through the door diagonally, but the Zurich mentality was not interested in the hammer and compass and anyway preferred to see the wreaths outside in front of the door. Since the delegations of the Federal Republic and the German Democratic Republic both wanted to sit in the first row, a wise cemetery management decided that both should sit in the second row. The Federal Republic as a whole. Its appearance was scant. The federal president Theodor Heuss was sojourning in Lörrach and would not have had to go far. Adenauer—well, Thomas Mann did not like him ("not Adenauer, I rule him out"). But not even a cabinet minister came, only the West German ambassador from Bern. Presumably they shied away from an encounter with the officials from the GDR. The cultural minister Johannes R. Becher had traveled from there with a large contingent. How much propagandistic calculation there was, how much genuine awareness of the greatness of him who had died, is open to question. Not many writer colleagues were present: Max Frisch anyway, Stephan Hermlin, already mentioned, and surprisingly, Werner Bergengruen. Hermann Hesse did not come but wrote a fine obituary. In it he correctly maintained that Thomas Mann grew with the times. "What was behind his irony and his virtuosity in heart, loyalty, responsibility, and the ability to love, for decades not understood by the great German public—all that will keep his work and memory alive far beyond our muddled times."

The grave is very simple, more than modest compared with the stately memorial for Conrad Ferdinand Meyer in the same cemetery. It is hard to find—it lies somewhere among the bourgeois graves. There must be curious discussions when the dead whisper to one another. Finally they are totally free and understand one another completely. There is so much to tell that in life was never expressed or was always misunderstood. If, as at the end of Goethe's *Faust*, the

*Zurich, 1953, on the seventieth birthday of Katia Mann*

eternal Forgiver redeems everyone, then they will study with astonishment the souls of those who in this life were also alien and incomprehensible to them. Nearby rests Ludwig Klages, the philosopher of
irrationalism, whom Thomas Mann did not like. With him the deceased could discuss Bachofen and the symbolism of graves. In a half
circle before the unostentatious square stone for Thomas and Katia,
five grave plots were planned. Only three places are occupied, those
of Erika, Monika, and Michael. Perhaps Elisabeth will join them, if
she is not too firmly rooted in the New World. Klaus lies in Cannes.
Golo did not want to join his father, but he too lies in Kilchberg. He
must now converse with Dora Schrepfer and Hans Redi between
whom he found his narrow grave.

The stone records only the names and dates. We would like to add
here what Thomas Mann himself described as a "grave inscription," a
small dialogue about life as a work of art, namely Goethe's maxim:

"You made it through, quite well at all events.—"
"Just do the same, no breakneck precedents!"

Katia got to be almost ninety-seven years old. No really good times came along anymore. "In spite of children and grandchildren my life has just lost its meaning." She who, otherwise always in control, cried only at her husband's funeral, must have been left pretty much alone after his death with her coolness and impatience, which had always kept her heart hidden, as his had done. Klaus had long since died, and Erika and Michael died before Katia. Monika and Elisabeth were far away. Only Golo later lived with her and did his best. The other visitors came mainly in regard to copyright matters. It was bitter to discover that so little feeling had been left over for her. The Germans did not open their hearts to her either, at least most of them. Thomas Mann had wanted it otherwise. With her quiet service, without the love with which she guarded his being, his life would not have been successful. He wished: "As long as people remember me, she will be remembered."

*Zürich 1955*